154.48

NOVELS
for Students

Advisors

Jayne M. Burton is a teacher of English, a member of the Delta Kappa Gamma International Society for Key Women Educators, and currently a master's degree candidate in the Interdisciplinary Study of Curriculum and Instruction and English at Angelo State University.

Tom Shilts is the youth librarian at the Okemos branch of Capital Area District Library in Okemos, Michigan. He holds an MSLS degree from Clarion University of Pennsylvania and an MA in U.S. History from the University of North Dakota.

Amy Spade Silverman has taught at independent schools in California, Texas, Michigan, and New York. She holds a bachelor of arts degree from the University of Michigan and a master of fine arts degree from the University of Houston. She is a member of the National Council of Teachers of English and Teachers and Writers. She is an exam reader for Advanced Placement Literature and Composition. She is also a poet, published in *North American Review*, *Nimrod*, and *Michigan Quarterly Review*, among others.

NOVELS
for Students

**Presenting Analysis, Context, and Criticism
on Commonly Studied Novels**

VOLUME 50

Sara Constantakis, Project Editor

Foreword by Anne Devereaux Jordan

GALE
CENGAGE Learning·

Farmington Hills, Mich • San Francisco • New York • Waterville, Maine
Meriden, Conn • Mason, Ohio • Chicago

Novels for Students, Volume 50

Project Editor: Sara Constantakis

Rights Acquisition and Management: Moriam Aigoro, Ashley Maynard

Composition: Evi Abou-El-Seoud

Manufacturing: Rhonda Dover

Imaging: John Watkins

For product information and technology assistance, contact us at
Gale Customer Support, 1-800-877-4253.
For permission to use material from this text or product,
submit all requests online at **www.cengage.com/permissions.**
Further permissions questions can be emailed to
permissionrequest@cengage.com

Gale
27500 Drake Rd.
Farmington Hills, MI, 48331-3535

ISBN-13: 978-1-57302-717-5
ISSN 1094-3552

This title is also available as an e-book.
ISBN-13: 978-1-57302-716-8
Contact your Gale, a part of Cengage Learning sales representative for ordering information.

Table of Contents

The Informed Dialogue: Interacting with Literature

When we pick up a book, we usually do so with the anticipation of pleasure. We hope that by entering the time and place of the novel and sharing the thoughts and actions of the characters, we will find enjoyment. Unfortunately, this is often not the case; we are disappointed. But we should ask, has the author failed us, or have we failed the author?

We establish a dialogue with the author, the book, and with ourselves when we read. Consciously and unconsciously, we ask questions: "Why did the author write this book?" "Why did the author choose that time, place, or character?" "How did the author achieve that effect?" "Why did the character act that way?" "Would I act in the same way?" The answers we receive depend upon how much information about literature in general and about that book specifically we ourselves bring to our reading.

Young children have limited life and literary experiences. Being young, children frequently do not know how to go about exploring a book, nor sometimes, even know the questions to ask of a book. The books they read help them answer questions, the author often coming right out and *telling* young readers the things they are learning or are expected to learn. The perennial classic, *The Little Engine That Could, tells* its readers that, among other things, it is good to help others and brings happiness:

"Hurray, hurray," cried the funny little clown and all the dolls and toys. "The good little boys and girls in the city will be happy because you helped us, kind, Little Blue Engine."

In picture books, messages are often blatant and simple, the dialogue between the author and reader one-sided. Young children are concerned with the end result of a book—the enjoyment gained, the lesson learned—rather than with how that result was obtained. As we grow older and read further, however, we question more. We come to expect that the world within the book will closely mirror the concerns of our world, and that the author will *show* these through the events, descriptions, and conversations within the story, rather than *telling* of them. We are now expected to do the interpreting, carry on our share of the dialogue with the book and author, and glean not only the author's message, but comprehend how that message and the overall affect of the book were achieved. Sometimes, however, we need help to do these things. *Novels for Students* provides that help.

A novel is made up of many parts interacting to create a coherent whole. In reading a novel, the more obvious features can be easily spotted—theme, characters, plot—but we may overlook the more subtle elements that greatly influence how the novel is perceived by the reader: viewpoint, mood and tone, symbolism, or the use of humor. By focusing on both the obvious and more subtle literary elements within a novel, *Novels for Students* aids readers in both analyzing for message and in determining how and why that message is communicated. In the discussion on Harper Lee's *To Kill a Mockingbird* (Vol. 2), for example, the mockingbird as a symbol of innocence is dealt with, among other things, as is the importance of Lee's use of humor which "enlivens a serious plot, adds depth to the characterization, and creates a sense of familiarity and universality." The reader comes to understand the internal elements of each novel discussed—as well as the external influences that help shape it.

"The desire to write greatly," Harold Bloom of Yale University says, "is the desire to be elsewhere, in a time and place of one's own, in an originality that must compound with inheritance, with an anxiety of influence." A writer seeks to create a unique world within a story, but although it is unique, it is not disconnected from our own world. It speaks to us *because* of what the writer brings to the writing from our world: how he or she was raised and educated; his or her likes and dislikes; the events occurring in the real world at the time of the writing, and while the author was growing up. When we know what an author has brought to his or her work, we gain a greater insight into both the "originality" (the world of the book), and the things that "compound" it. This insight enables us to question that created world and find answers more readily. By informing ourselves, we are able to establish a more effective dialogue with both book and author.

Novels for Students, in addition to providing a plot summary and descriptive list of characters—to remind readers of what they have read—also explores the external influences that shaped each book. Each entry includes a discussion of the author's background, and the historical context in which the novel was written. It is vital to know, for instance, that when Ray Bradbury was writing *Fahrenheit 451* (Vol. 1), the threat of Nazi domination had recently ended in Europe, and the McCarthy hearings were taking place in Washington, D.C. This information goes far in answering the question, "Why did he write a story of oppressive government control and book burning?" Similarly, it is important to know that Harper Lee, author of *To Kill a Mockingbird*, was born and raised in Monroeville, Alabama, and

that her father was a lawyer. Readers can now see why she chose the south as a setting for her novel—it is the place with which she was most familiar—and start to comprehend her characters and their actions.

Novels for Students helps readers find the answers they seek when they establish a dialogue with a particular novel. It also aids in the posing of questions by providing the opinions and interpretations of various critics and reviewers, broadening that dialogue. Some reviewers of *To Kill A Mockingbird,* for example, "faulted the novel's climax as melodramatic." This statement leads readers to ask, "Is it, indeed, melodramatic?" "If not, why did some reviewers see it as such?" "If it is, why did Lee choose to make it melodramatic?" "Is melodrama ever justified?" By being spurred to ask these questions, readers not only learn more about the book and its writer, but about the nature of writing itself.

The literature included for discussion in *Novels for Students* has been chosen because it has something vital to say to us. *Of Mice and Men, Catch-22, The Joy Luck Club, My Antonia, A Separate Peace* and the other novels here speak of life and modern sensibility. In addition to their individual, specific messages of prejudice, power, love or hate, living and dying, however, they and all great literature also share a common intent. They force us to *think*—about life, literature, and about others, not just about ourselves. They pry us from the narrow confines of our minds and thrust us outward to confront the world of books and the larger, real world we all share. *Novels for Students* helps us in this confrontation by providing the means of enriching our conversation with literature and the world, by creating an *informed* dialogue, one that brings true pleasure to the personal act of reading.

Sources

Harold Bloom, *The Western Canon, The Books and School of the Ages,* Riverhead Books, 1994.

Watty Piper, *The Little Engine That Could,* Platt & Munk, 1930.

Anne Devereaux Jordan
Senior Editor, TALL (Teaching and Learning Literature)

Introduction

Purpose of the Book

The purpose of *Novels for Students* (*NfS*) is to provide readers with a guide to understanding, enjoying, and studying novels by giving them easy access to information about the work. Part of Gale's "For Students" Literature line, *NfS* is specifically designed to meet the curricular needs of high school and undergraduate college students and their teachers, as well as the interests of general readers and researchers considering specific novels. While each volume contains entries on "classic" novels frequently studied in classrooms, there are also entries containing hard-to-find information on contemporary novels, including works by multicultural, international, and women novelists. Entries profiling film versions of novels not only diversify the study of novels but support alternate learning styles, media literacy, and film studies curricula as well.

The information covered in each entry includes an introduction to the novel and the novel's author; a plot summary, to help readers unravel and understand the events in a novel; descriptions of important characters, including explanation of a given character's role in the novel as well as discussion about that character's relationship to other characters in the novel; analysis of important themes in the novel; and an explanation of important literary techniques and movements as they are demonstrated in the novel.

In addition to this material, which helps the readers analyze the novel itself, students are also provided with important information on the literary and historical background informing each work. This includes a historical context essay, a box comparing the time or place the novel was written to modern Western culture, a critical essay, and excerpts from critical essays on the novel. A unique feature of *NfS* is a specially commissioned critical essay on each novel, targeted toward the student reader.

The "literature to film" entries on novels vary slightly in form, providing background on film technique and comparison to the original, literary version of the work. These entries open with an introduction to the film, which leads directly into the plot summary. The summary highlights plot changes from the novel, key cinematic moments, and/or examples of key film techniques. As in standard entries, there are character profiles (noting omissions or additions, and identifying the actors), analysis of themes and how they are illustrated in the film, and an explanation of the cinematic style and structure of the film. A cultural context section notes any time period or setting differences from that of the original work, as well as cultural differences between the time in which the original work was written and the time in which the film adaptation was made. A film entry concludes with a critical overview and critical essays on the film.

To further help today's student in studying and enjoying each novel or film, information on media adaptations is provided (if available), as well as suggestions for works of fiction, nonfiction, or film on similar themes and topics. Classroom aids include ideas for research papers and lists of critical and reference sources that provide additional material on the novel. Film entries also highlight signature film techniques demonstrated, and suggest media literacy activities and prompts to use during or after viewing a film.

Selection Criteria

The titles for each volume of *NfS* are selected by surveying numerous sources on notable literary works and analyzing course curricula for various schools, school districts, and states. Some of the sources surveyed include: high school and undergraduate literature anthologies and textbooks; lists of award-winners, and recommended titles, including the Young Adult Library Services Association (YALSA) list of best books for young adults. Films are selected both for the literary importance of the original work and the merits of the adaptation (including official awards and widespread public recognition).

Input solicited from our expert advisory board—consisting of educators and librarians—guides us to maintain a mix of "classic" and contemporary literary works, a mix of challenging and engaging works (including genre titles that are commonly studied) appropriate for different age levels, and a mix of international, multicultural and women authors. These advisors also consult on each volume's entry list, advising on which titles are most studied, most appropriate, and meet the broadest interests across secondary (grades 7–12) curricula and undergraduate literature studies.

How Each Entry Is Organized

Each entry, or chapter, in *NfS* focuses on one novel. Each entry heading lists the full name of the novel, the author's name, and the date of the novel's publication. The following elements are contained in each entry:

Introduction: a brief overview of the novel which provides information about its first appearance, its literary standing, any controversies surrounding the work, and major conflicts or themes within the work. Film entries identify the original novel and provide understanding of the film's reception and reputation, along with that of the director.

Author Biography: in novel entries, this section includes basic facts about the author's life, and focuses on events and times in the author's life that inspired the novel in question.

Plot Summary: a factual description of the major events in the novel. Lengthy summaries are broken down with subheads. Plot summaries of films are used to uncover plot differences from the original novel, and to note the use of certain film angles or other techniques.

Characters: an alphabetical listing of major characters in the novel. Each character name is followed by a brief to an extensive description of the character's role in the novel, as well as discussion of the character's actions, relationships, and possible motivation. In film entries, omissions or changes to the cast of characters of the film adaptation are mentioned here, and the actors' names—and any awards they may have received—are also included.

Characters are listed alphabetically by last name. If a character is unnamed—for instance, the narrator in *Invisible Man*—the character is listed as "The Narrator" and alphabetized as "Narrator." If a character's first name is the only one given, the name will appear alphabetically by that name.

Variant names are also included for each character. Thus, the full name "Jean Louise Finch" would head the listing for the narrator of *To Kill a Mockingbird*, but listed in a separate cross-reference would be the nickname "Scout Finch."

Themes: a thorough overview of how the major topics, themes, and issues are addressed within the novel. Each theme discussed appears in a separate subhead. While the key themes often remain the same or similar when a novel is adapted into a film, film entries demonstrate how the themes are conveyed cinematically, along with any changes in the portrayal of the themes.

Style: this section addresses important style elements of the novel, such as setting, point of view, and narration; important literary devices used, such as imagery, foreshadowing, symbolism; and, if applicable, genres to which the work might have belonged, such as Gothicism or Romanticism. Literary terms are explained within the entry but can also be found in the Glossary. Film entries cover how the director conveyed the meaning, message, and mood of the work using film in comparison to the author's use of language, literary device, etc., in the original work.

Historical Context: in novel entries, this section outlines the social, political, and cultural climate in which the author lived and the novel was created. This section may include descriptions of related historical events, pertinent aspects of daily life in the culture, and the artistic and literary sensibilities of the time in which the work was written. If the novel is a historical work, information regarding the time in which the novel is set is also included. Each section is broken down with helpful subheads. Film entries contain a similar Cultural Context section because the film adaptation might explore an entirely different time period or culture than the original work, and may also be influenced by the traditions and views of a time period much different than that of the original author.

Critical Overview: this section provides background on the critical reputation of the novel or film, including bannings or any other public controversies surrounding the work. For older works, this section includes a history of how the novel or film was first received and how perceptions of it may have changed over the years; for more recent novels, direct quotes from early reviews may also be included.

Criticism: an essay commissioned by *NfS* which specifically deals with the novel or film and is written specifically for the student audience, as well as excerpts from previously published criticism on the work (if available).

Sources: an alphabetical list of critical material used in compiling the entry, with full bibliographical information.

Further Reading: an alphabetical list of other critical sources which may prove useful for the student. It includes full bibliographical information and a brief annotation.

Suggested Search Terms: a list of search terms and phrases to jumpstart students' further information seeking. Terms include not just titles and author names but also terms and topics related to the historical and literary context of the works.

In addition, each novel entry contains the following highlighted sections, set apart from the main text as sidebars:

Media Adaptations: if available, a list of audiobooks and important film and television adaptations of the novel, including source information. The list also includes stage adaptations, musical adaptations, etc.

Topics for Further Study: a list of potential study questions or research topics dealing with the novel. This section includes questions related to other disciplines the student may be studying, such as American history, world history, science, math, government, business, geography, economics, psychology, etc.

Compare and Contrast: an "at-a-glance" comparison of the cultural and historical differences between the author's time and culture and late twentieth century or early twenty-first century Western culture. This box includes pertinent parallels between the major scientific, political, and cultural movements of the time or place the novel was written, the time or place the novel was set (if a historical work), and modern Western culture. Works written after the mid-1970s may not have this box.

What Do I Read Next?: a list of works that might give a reader points of entry into a classic work (e.g., YA or multicultural titles) and/or complement the featured novel or serve as a contrast to it. This includes works by the same author and others, works from various genres, YA works, and works from various cultures and eras.

The film entries provide sidebars more targeted to the study of film, including:

Film Technique: a listing and explanation of four to six key techniques used in the film, including shot styles, use of transitions, lighting, sound or music, etc.

Read, Watch, Write: media literacy prompts and/or suggestions for viewing log prompts.

What Do I See Next?: a list of films based on the same or similar works or of films similar in directing style, technique, etc.

Other Features

NfS includes "The Informed Dialogue: Interacting with Literature," a foreword by Anne Devereaux Jordan, Senior Editor for *Teaching and Learning Literature* (*TALL*), and a founder of the Children's Literature Association. This essay provides an enlightening look at how readers interact with literature and how *Novels for Students* can help teachers show students how to enrich their own reading experiences.

A Cumulative Author/Title Index lists the authors and titles covered in each volume of the *NfS* series.

A Cumulative Nationality/Ethnicity Index breaks down the authors and titles covered in each volume of the *NfS* series by nationality and ethnicity.

A Subject/Theme Index, specific to each volume, provides easy reference for users who may be studying a particular subject or theme rather than a single work. Significant subjects, from events to broad themes, are included.

Each entry may include illustrations, including photo of the author, stills from film adaptations, maps, and/or photos of key historical events, if available.

Citing Novels for Students

When writing papers, students who quote directly from any volume of *NfS* may use the following general forms. These examples are based on MLA style; teachers may request that students adhere to a different style, so the following examples may be adapted as needed.

When citing text from *NfS* that is not attributed to a particular author (i.e., the Themes, Style, Historical Context sections, etc.), the following format should be used in the bibliography section:

> "*The Monkey Wrench Gang.*" *Novels for Students.* Ed. Sara Constantakis. Vol. 43. Detroit: Gale, Cengage Learning, 2013. 157–193. Print.

When quoting the specially commissioned essay from *NfS* (usually the first piece under the "Criticism" subhead), the following format should be used:

> Holmes, Michael Allen. Critical Essay on "*The Monkey Wrench Gang.*" *Novels for Students.* Ed. Sara Constantakis. Vol. 43. Detroit: Gale, Cengage Learning, 2013. 173–78. Print.

When quoting a journal or newspaper essay that is reprinted in a volume of *NfS,* the following form may be used:

> Bryant, Paul T. "Edward Abbey and Environmental Quixoticism." *Western American Literature* 24.1 (1989): 37–43. Rpt. in *Novels for Students.* Vol. 43. Ed. Sara Constantakis. Detroit: Gale, Cengage Learning, 2013. 189–92. Print.

When quoting material reprinted from a book that appears in a volume of *NfS,* the following form may be used:

> Norwick, Steve. "Nietzschean Themes in the Works of Edward Abbey." *Coyote in the Maze: Tracking Edward Abbey in a World of Words.* Ed. Peter Quigley. Salt Lake City; University of Utah Press, 1998. 184–205. Rpt. in *Novels for Students.* Vol. 43. Ed. Sara Constantakis. Detroit: Gale, Cengage Learning, 2013. 183–85. Print.

We Welcome Your Suggestions

The editorial staff of *Novels for Students* welcomes your comments and ideas. Readers who wish to suggest novels to appear in future volumes, or who have other suggestions, are cordially invited to contact the editor. You may contact the editor via e-mail at: **ForStudentsEditors@cengage.com.** Or write to the editor at:

Editor, *Novels for Students*
Gale
27500 Drake Road
Farmington Hills, MI 48331-3535

Literary Chronology

1898: Lao She is born on February 3 in Bejing, China.

1903: Evelyn Waugh is born on October 28 in London, England.

1906: R. K. Narayan is born on October 10 in Madras, India.

1907: Daphne du Maruier is born on May 13 in London, England.

1910: Paul Frederic Bowles is born on December 30 in New York, New York.

1913: Tillie Olsen is born on January 14 in Omaha, Nebraska.

1923: Nadine Gordimer is born on November 20 in Springs, South Africa.

1925: William Styron is born on June 11 in Newport News, Virginia.

1935: Carol Shields is born on June 2 in Oak Park, Illinois.

1936: Lao She's *Rickshaw Boy* is published in Chinese as *Luotuo Xiangzi* in *Yuzhou Feng*. It is published in English in the United States in 1945.

1938: Daphne du Maurier's novel *Rebecca* is published.

1940: The film *Rebecca* is released.

1941: The film *Rebecca* is awarded the Academy Award for Best Picture.

1948: Evelyn Waugh's *The Loved One* is published in *Horizon*.

1949: Paul Bowles's *The Sheltering Sky* is published.

1951: William Styron's *Lie Down in Darkness* is published.

1958: R.K. Narayan's *The Guide* is published.

1963: Donna Tartt is born on December 23 in Greenwood, Mississippi.

1964: Elizabeth Wein is born on October 2 in New York, New York.

1966: Evelyn Waugh dies of heart failure on April 10 in Combe Florey, Somerset, England.

1966: Lao She dies of suicide on August 24 in Bejing, China.

1968: William Styron is awarded the Pulitzer Prize for Fiction for *The Confessions of Nat Turner*.

1969: Lev Grossman is born on June 26 in Lexington, Massachusetts.

1970: Sarah Dessen is born on June 6 in Evanston, Illinois.

1974: Nadine Gordimer is awarded the Booker Prize for *The Conservationist*.

1974: Tillie Olsen's *Yonnondio* is published.

1979: Nadine Gordimer's *Burger's Daughter* is published.

1989: Daphne du Maurier dies on April 19 in Cornwall, England.

1991: Nadine Gordimer is awarded the Nobel Prize for Literature.

1992: Donna Tartt's *The Secret History* is published.

1995: Carol Shields is awarded the Pulitzer Prize for Fiction for *The Stone Diaries*.

1998: Sarah Dessen's *Someone Like You* is published.

1999: Paul Bowles dies of heart failure on November 18 in Tangier, Morocco.

2000: The film *O Brother, Where Art Thou?* is released.

2001: R. K. Narayan dies of cardio-respiratory failure on May 13, in Chennai, India.

2002: Carol Shields's *Unless* is published.

2003: Carol Shields dies of breast cancer on July 16 in Victoria, British Columbia.

2006: William Styron dies of natural causes on November 1 in Martha's Vineyard, Massachusetts.

2007: Tillie Olsen dies on January 1 in Oakland, California.

2009: Lev Grossman's *The Magicians* is published.

2012: Elizabeth Wein's *Code Name Verity* is published.

2014: Nadine Gordimer dies of pancreatic cancer on July 13 in Johannesburg, South Africa.

2014: Donna Tartt is awarded the Pulitzer Prize for Fiction for *The Goldfinch*.

Acknowledgements

The editors wish to thank the copyright holders of the excerpted criticism included in this volume and the permissions managers of many book and magazine publishing companies for assisting us in securing reproduction rights. We are also grateful to the staffs of the Detroit Public Library, the Library of Congress, the University of Detroit Mercy Library, Wayne State University Purdy/ Kresge Library Complex, and the University of Michigan Libraries for making their resources available to us. Following is a list of the copyright holders who have granted us permission to reproduce material in this volume of *NfS*. Every effort has been made to trace copyright, but if omissions have been made, please let us know.

COPYRIGHTED EXCERPTS IN *NfS*, VOLUME 50, WERE REPRODUCED FROM THE FOLLOWING PERIODICALS:

All Things Considered, 2009. Copyright © 2009 NPR. Reproduced by permission.—*Booklist*, vol. 105, no. 18, May 15, 2009.—*Booklist*, vol. 109, nos. 9-10, January 1, 2013.—*Horn Book*, May/June 2009.—*Horn Book*, May 16, 2014.—*Magazine of Fantasy and Science Fiction*, vol. 117, nos. 1-2, August-September 2009. Copyright © 2009 *Magazine of Fantasy and Science Fiction*. Reproduced by permission.—*Nation*, vol. 255, no. 21, December 21, 1992.—*Publishers Weekly*, vol. 239, no. 29, June 29, 1992.—*Publishers Weekly*, vol. 256, no. 22, June 1, 2009.— *Publishers Weekly*, vol. 259, no. 16, April 16, 2012.—*Publishers Weekly*, vol. 245, no. 20, May 18, 1998.—*Vanity Fair*, September 1992. Copyright © 1992 *Vanity Fair*. Reproduced by permission.—

COPYRIGHTED EXCERPTS IN *NfS*, VOLUME 50, WERE REPRODUCED FROM THE FOLLOWING BOOKS:

Beatina, Mary. From *Narayan: A Study in Transcendence*. Peter Lang Publishers, 1993. Copyright © 1993 Peter Lang Publishers. Reproduced by permission.—Beaty, Frederick L. From *The Ironic World of Evelyn Waugh: A Study of Eight Novels*. Northern Illinois University Press, 1992. Copyright © 1992 Northern Illinois University Press. Reproduced by permission.—Casciato, Arthur D. From *Critical Essays on William Styron*. G.K. Hall, 1982. Copyright © 1982 Cengage Learning.— Coale, Samuel. From *William Styron Revisited*. Twayne Publishers, 1991. Copyright © 1991 Twayne Publishers. Reproduced by permission.— Ditze, Stephan-Alexander. From *America and the Americans in Postwar British Fiction: An Imagolocial Study of Selected Novels*. Universitatsverlag Winter, 2006. Copyright © 2006 Universitatsverlag Winter. Reproduced by permission.—Grant, Joanna. From *Modernism's Middle East: Journeys to Barbary*. Palgrave Macmillan, 2008. Copyright © 2008 Palgrave Macmillan. Reproduced by permission.—Grene, Nicholas. From *R.K. Narayan*. Northcote House, 2011. Copyright

© 2011 Northcote House. Reproduced by permission.—Hare, William. From *Hitchcock and the Methods of Suspense*. McFarland, 2007. Copyright © 2007 McFarland. Reproduced by permission.—Lang, John. From *The Critical Response to William Styron*. Greenwood Press, 1995. Copyright © 1995 Greenwood Press. Reproduced by permission.—Light, Alison. From The Daphne du Maurier Companion. Virago Press, 2007. Copyright © 2007 Alison Light. Reproduced by permission.—McFarland, Douglas. From *The Philosophy of the Coen Brothers*. University Press of Kentucky, 2009. Copyright © 2009 University Press of Kentucky. Reproduced by permission.—McWilliams, Ellen. From *Women Constructing Men: Female Novelists and Their Male Characters, 1750-2000*. Lexington Books, 2010. Copyright © 2010 Lexington Books. Reproduced by permission.—Nogueira, Rui, Nicoletta Zalaffi, and Albert Hitchcock. From *Alfred Hitchcock: Interviews*. University Press of Mississippi, 2003. Copyright © 2003 The Hitchcock Estate. Reproduced by permission.—Orr, Lisa. From *What We Hold in Common: An Introduction to Working-Class Studies*. The Feminist Press at the City University of New York, 2001. Copyright © 2001 The Feminist Press at the City University of New York. Reproduced by permission.—Read, Daphne. From *The Later Fiction of Nadine Gordimer*. Macmillan Press, 1993. Copyright © 1993 Macmillan Press. Reproduced by permission.—Rosenthal, Caroline. From *Reading(s) from a Distance: European Perspectives on Canadian Women's Writing*. Wissner, 2008. Copyright © 2008 Wissner. Reproduced by permission.—Rowell, Erica. From *The Brothers Grim: The Films of Ethan and Joel Coen*. Scarecrow Press, 2007. Copyright © 2007 Scarecrow Press. Reproduced by permission.—Temple-Thurston, Barbara. From *Nadine Gordimer Revisited*. Twayne Publishers, 1999. Copyright © 1999 Twayne Publishers. Reproduced by permission.—Thieme, John. From *R.K. Narayan*. Manchester University Press, 2007. Copyright © 2007 Manchester University Press. Reproduced by permission.—Wang, David Der-wei. From *Fictional Realism in Twentieth-Century China: Mao Dun, Lao She, Shen Congwen*. Columbia University Press, 1992. Copyright © 1992 Columbia University Press. Reproduced by permission.

Contributors

Susan K. Andersen: Andersen is a teacher and writer with a PhD in English. Entry on *Someone Like You*. Original essay on *Someone Like You*.

Bryan Aubrey: Aubrey holds a PhD in English. Entry on *The Guide*. Original essay on *The Guide*.

Rita M. Brown: Brown is an English professor. Entry on *The Secret History*. Original essay on *The Secret History*.

Catherine Dominic: Dominic is a novelist and a freelance writer and editor. Entries on *Code Name Verity* and *Yonnondio: From the Thirties*. Original essays on *Code Name Verity* and *Yonnondio: From the Thirties*.

Klay Dyer: Dyer is a freelance writer and editor who specializes in subjects related to literature, popular culture, and innovation. Entries on *The Sheltering Sky* and *Unless*. Original essays on *The Sheltering Sky* and *Unless*.

Kristen Sarlin Greenberg: Greenberg is a freelance writer and editor with a background in literature and philosophy. Entry on *The Magicians*. Original essay on *The Magicians*.

Michael Allen Holmes: Holmes is a writer with existential interests. Entry on *Lie Down in Darkness*. Original essay on *Lie Down in Darkness*.

David Kelly: Kelly is an instructor of creative writing and literature in Illinois. Entries on *O Brother, Where Art Thou?* and *Rebecca*. Original essays on *O Brother, Where Art Thou?* and *Rebecca*.

Amy L. Miller: Miller is a graduate of the University of Cincinnati, and currently resides in New Orleans, Louisiana. Entry on *Rickshaw Boy*. Original essay on *Rickshaw Boy*.

Michael J. O'Neal: O'Neal holds a PhD in English. Entry on *The Loved One*. Original essay on *The Loved One*.

Bradley A. Skeen: Skeen is a classicist. Entry on *Burger's Daughter*. Original essay on *Burger's Daughter*.

Burger's Daughter

NADINE GORDIMER

1979

Nadine Gordimer was a Nobel Prize–winning South African author who worked tirelessly against the white supremacist policies of the apartheid government of her country. *Burger's Daughter* (1979) is perhaps her most important literary work. Gordimer opposed racism not only as a writer but also as a member of the African National Congress and the friend of prominent antiapartheid leaders. The trial and imprisonment of her friend Abram (Bram) Fischer inspired *Burger's Daughter*. The novel is the story of the daughter of a prominent anti-racism activist of the generation of the 1930s who comes to terms with her past and her identity in the South Africa of the 1970s. The plot also outlines the story of black resistance to the white South African government from the Sharpeville massacre to the Soweto uprising.

AUTHOR BIOGRAPHY

Gordimer was born on November 20, 1923, in Springs, a mining town outside of Johannesburg, South Africa. Her father, Isidore, was a watchmaker who had fled anti-Semitic violence in imperial Russia. Her mother, Hannah, was of English descent and was politically active against the oppression of black South Africans. She organized a day care center for black children. Because of this political activity, the young

Nadine Gordimer *(© Francesco Acerbis | Corbis Entertainment | Corbis)*

Gordimer witnessed a police raid on her household in which papers and documents were confiscated, a scene common in South Africa and played out many times in Gordimer's works, including *Burger's Daughter*. Somewhat irrationally, it seems, Gordimer's mother feared her daughter had a weak heart and so homeschooled her.

Gordimer developed precociously as a writer and published her first story, "The Quest for Seen Gold," in 1937 in the *Children's Sunday Express.* She attended the University of the Witwatersrand, which was racially integrated, but she did not earn a degree. In 1951, she sold her short story "A Watcher of the Dead" to the *New Yorker,* bringing her work to international prominence.

Gordimer married Gerald Gavron in 1949. They had a daughter, Oriane, in 1950 and divorced in 1952. In 1953 Gordimer married the prominent art dealer Reinhold Cassirer, who became her lifelong partner. Their son, Hugo, was born in 1955. Gordimer became

politically active in 1960 with the arrest of her friend Bettie du Toit and the Sharpeville massacre. She became friends with Nelson Mandela's attorneys, including Bram Fischer, and helped to write the defense speech for Mandela's trial in 1966. Gordimer joined the banned African National Congress. Her works took on a political character and were consequently banned in her own country, though they won increasing acclaim in the rest of the world. Her 1974 novel, *The Conservationist*, won the Man Booker Prize.

The British publisher of *Burger's Daughter* imported copies of the book into South Africa in July 1979, within a few weeks of the novel's release. It was immediately banned on the ground that it promoted Communism and created "a psychosis of revolution and rebellion," as quoted by Susan Gardner in "A Story for This Place and Time." While the book was banned, a copy was smuggled into the Robben Island prison for Mandela to read. The following October, the book was unbanned because of pressure from the international literary community and the growing difficulty of justifying the banning of serious literary works to the white South African public. The Publications Appeal Board justified its action by claiming that the book presented no danger because the board doubted it would be widely read owing to its poor literary quality. Gordimer objected to the unbanning because she believed that a black author's work would not have been unbanned, and therefore her unbanning was a product of racism. Gordimer chronicled the events surrounding the censorship of *Burger's Daughter*'s in *What Happened to Burger's Daughter; or, How South African Censorship Works*. This book was published by an underground antiapartheid press in South Africa and is not generally available.

Gordimer was never personally banned (kept under house arrest) or refused permission to travel by the South African government. In 1991, she received the Nobel Prize in Literature. After apartheid ended, Gordimer became active in the cause of preventing HIV and AIDS and was critical of the African National Congress government's handling of the problem. Gordimer cooperated with Ronald Roberts while he was writing her biography, *No Cold Kitchen* (2005) but refused to authorize the work because of its criticism of her stance on the Israeli-Palestinian conflict. Gordimer died of pancreatic cancer on July 13, 2014, at her home in Johannesburg.

PLOT SUMMARY

One

Burger's Daughter is set in 1974, and the title character, Rosa Burger, is an adult. In the brief opening scene, however, the fourteen-year-old Rosa is visiting her mother, who is being held in prison for political crimes, to bring her a blanket. Nine years later, Rosa attends her father's trial, but the narrative description of it is greatly distanced from Rosa's character. There is no doubt about his conviction or his imprisonment for life. The arguments and facts of the matter are completely irrelevant to the political necessities of the government. At the same time, Rosa is having an affair with a young man. Eventually the reader learns he is Conrad, who is on the fringe of the antiapartheid political movement.

Lionel Burger, Rosa's father, dies three years after his trial. Rosa's rootlessness without her father is reflected in her constantly moving from apartment to apartment. Everyone in her circle of friends—her father's friends—seems to be at one or another level of banning (being merely named, for instance, entailed an order from the government not to attend certain public meetings—some friends are even excluded from the funeral). That the police do not raid Rosa's residence to seize her private papers, as commonly happened, shows that the government has little interest in her. They do, however, prevent her from pursuing her work as a physiotherapist in a hospital for blacks in the Transkei. She continues to see Conrad, but not in any serious way, despite moving in with him.

Rosa's memories fill in some of the backstory of her life. Walking by her old house one night with Conrad, she recalls how she passed the night of the Sharpeville massacre, during which the police murdered sixty-nine peaceful black protesters. She also recalls the time years before when she was sent to live with her uncle Coen when both of her parents were arrested at the same time. At the same time, time her black foster brother, Baasie, went to live with black relatives, and the Burger family lost contact with him. Coen worked as a farmer but also owned a hotel, and Rosa has a vivid memory of his black bartender, Daniel (whom Coen beats for stealing alcohol to drink himself, forcing him to drink the dregs from his customers' glasses). She also recalls her father's fellow revolutionary Noel de Witt and her mother.

In the booming South African economy of the 1970s, fueled by mineral extraction, Rosa is able to easily move from job to job. Eventually she goes to work for an investment adviser, but her main duty seems to be being shown off to fashionably liberal clients. One day, she is having lunch in the crowded park outside the office building where she works in Johannesburg and where a white homeless man is discovered to be dead, rather than asleep, on a park bench. The newspapers focus on the story as a demonstration of how heartless South African society has become, a fact of modern urban life. Rosa thinks this hypocritical, since there is no way anyone there could have helped him because he has died overnight and his death is not noticed until noon. Of course the hypocrisy is far larger, since the middle-class white people the papers take to task for not helping the man are, like the paper itself, doing nothing to help the oppression of the majority of their fellow citizens who happen to be poor and black.

Rosa is solicited by several writers who are working on biographies of her father. She consents to talk to a biographer, a legitimate scholar, and their conversation expounds on the basic events of Burger's life, keyed to events in South African history. For example, her parents' wedding (Lionel's second marriage), on August 16, 1946, was delayed two days because of the arrests of antiapartheid activists (including the best man) in connection with the Witwatersrand miners' strike. The historian mentions that Bram Fischer, and several other real-life activists, attended the wedding.

Almost a year after Lionel's death, Rosa runs into Clare Terblanche, the daughter of Lionel's Communist Party comrades, whom Rosa knew as a child. Clare wants Rosa to give her access to her office copy room so she can print copies of a revolutionary pamphlet. An established print shop, the only other option, would not have helped political subversives. Rosa refuses and asks Clare, "Why do you go on with it?" She points out that revolutionary tactics of subversion have done nothing to end apartheid during the last fifty years and she sees no reason why that should change. The only reason they still adhere to revolutionary ideology is that they were brought up with it, not because of any rational calculation of the chances of success.

On the anniversary of Lionel's death, Rosa evades the light police surveillance she is under to visit some of her father's old comrades in a black township outside Johannesburg. She encounters a younger generation of revolutionaries, affected by American black consciousness thinkers like Malcolm X. They view their struggle in racial terms, as black against white, rather than in Marxist terms, as proletariat against bourgeoisie. They resent the fact that in the past decisions about the revolutionary movement were made for them by white men like Lionel Burger rather than by blacks themselves.

Rosa approaches the politically connected and wealthy Boer Brandt Vermeulen to assist her in obtaining a passport (as a named person, she is prohibited from foreign travel). She has a slight connection to Vermeulen because he is her mother's distant cousin (the original Dutch settler population was so small that most Boers are related) and because Lionel Burger offered a second opinion when Vermeulen needed surgery for a rugby injury in high school. Vermeulen is eventually able to get Rosa a passport. To not do so, he suggests, would be an admission that apartheid was wrong: "If he could get a passport for Burger's daughter to travel like anyone else . . . who could say the regime was not showing signs of moving in the direction of change?"

As Rosa is about to board the plane to leave for Europe, she ponders the news that Conrad—whom she is still addressing in her narration—has died in a yachting accident. She also recalls a scene she saw recently while driving near her uncle's farm. She saw a black man driving a donkey cart with his family in it. The donkey had stopped, and the man was savagely and fruitlessly beating it. The intensity of Rosa's reaction verges on the surreal:

> I didn't see the whip. I saw agony. Agony that came from some terrible centre seized within the group of donkey, cart, driver and people behind him. They made a single object that contracted against itself in the desperation of a hideous final energy. Not seeing the whip, I saw the infliction of pain broken away from the will that creates it; broken loose, a force existing of itself, ravishment without the ravisher, torture without the torturer, rampage, pure cruelty gone beyond control of the humans who have spent thousands of years devising it.

This agony stands for South Africa under apartheid. Rosa could easily have reported the man to the police for animal cruelty or just ordered him to stop. As a white person she would have been obeyed without question. But the man is not responsible. If anyone is, Rosa thinks, it is herself, a white South African who has so far been unable to stop what her own people are doing in the country. Also, she cannot bear to become the sort of person who reacts more strongly to animal suffering than to human suffering.

Two

Within a week of obtaining her passport, Rosa flies to Paris and then to Nice, on the French Riviera, to visit her stepmother, Katya. This part of the novel takes on Rosa's narrative voice and is addressed not to Katya but to Rosa's mental image of Katya. Rosa is amazed to actually experience people going about their business and talking freely without fear of political surveillance. She experiences firsthand that whatever national and ethnic problems Europe has, ideological white supremacy (in the form of Nazism, even more destructive and oppressive than apartheid) is a distant memory.

Rosa meets Bernard Chabalier, a professor of French culture, and has an affair with him, largely out of a desire to exercise her own will against the life of political activism imposed on her. When she first meets him, Chabalier asks what she does, meaning what profession she has. She answers in a way that must seem innocuous to him: "I have done nothing." She means that she has neither lived up to her revolutionary heritage nor done anything to escape it. Chabalier begins to make arrangements for her to receive asylum in France, meaning that Rosa would never have to return to South Africa. When Chabalier returns to Paris at the end of the summer, Rosa promises to follow him but decides to first briefly visit England, even though she has been specifically warned not to go there because it is a center for South African political exiles.

In England, Rosa is quickly drawn into the world of antiapartheid activism, where she meets Baasie, her foster brother, who disappeared among his black relatives when the Burgers were arrested. Baasie is embittered over the way Lionel Burger is lionized by the movement and the press. He points out that thousands of blacks suffered far more and died in prison no differently (his own biological father is murdered by the authorities in prison). He considers it a case of white privilege, unseemly in a movement that is meant to liberate blacks.

Three

Rosa has returned to South Africa. The portions
of the text that represent her internal monologue
switch to addressing Lionel Burger. Rosa feels as
if her life has been torn apart by Baasie's rejection. She no longer sees the life she had planned
in France with Bernard as any kind of reality.
Analyzing her reaction, she attributes it to her
immaturity—she had expected Baasie to love her
as when they were children and is infuriated that
he does not—and her lack of political education:
she can think of no response to Baasie's accusations against white liberal paternalism except
those supplied by Communist Party dogma,
which she now sees as inadequate, although
this does not mean accepting his viewpoint.

Rosa resumes work as a physiotherapist in a
Johannesburg hospital. After the Soweto uprising in 1976, her patients include black children
recovering from gunshot wounds inflicted by the
police in retaliation for their throwing stones.
This section includes the text of a pamphlet published by the Soweto Students Representative
Council—a banned work—which was considered a political triumph at the time.

One government response to Soweto is a
mass banning and arrest of resistance leaders on
October 19, 1977. Rosa is among them, although
she has taken no active part in any revolutionary
activity. She is defended by Theo Santorini, her
father's lawyer. As her father treated the guards
in his prison, Rosa works on the back pain of the
prison matron. The only evidence against her—
supplied by informers the South African government has in such circles—is that she met revolutionary activists in London, This is more than
enough to send her to jail for life. As the novel
begins with Rosa bringing a blanket to her
mother in prison, it ends with an unnamed
woman, probably her aunt, bringing fruit to
Rosa. However, Brandt Vermeulen is intervening
on Rosa's behalf to have her released to house
arrest.

CHARACTERS

Biographer

Rosa consents to talk to an unnamed historian
working on a book about her father. He functions in the novel to introduce the research Gordimer conducted into the history of the South
African Communist Party.

Cathy Burger

Cathy is Rosa's mother. Her name is not mentioned until relatively late in the novel, and then
by a historian interviewing Rosa, rather than
Rosa herself. Rosa self-consciously remarks
that she thinks of her father as Lionel but of
her mother as mother and begins to speculate
that it is because her father so obviously
belonged to the revolution and not to her. Yet
the most she can say about her mother is that she
shared her with her dead brother; with her foster
brother, Baasie; with the many other children
sheltered in the Burger household from time to
time; and ultimately with the revolution. Rosa's
most vivid memories of her mother are her desperate attempts to resuscitate her son after he
drowns and that she had a lesbian mistress.
Before her marriage, Cathy had been the general
secretary of an integrated union of mine workers.
But her political sympathies quickly made it
impossible for her to hold any sort of job, and
the government soon outlawed integrated unions.

Colette (Katya) Swan Burger

Colette, called Katya, was Lionel's first wife. She
accompanied him to a Communist Party Congress in Moscow in 1920. She is frequently called
Madam Bagnelli, the surname of her deceased
common-law husband. She is valued by Rosa as
a point of contact with her father's young self.
Marriage of party members was an item of Communist Party discipline, and Lionel had married
Katya without party permission (permission was
given for his second marriage).

Lionel Burger

Lionel Burger is based on a real person, Bram
Fischer, an antiapartheid activist. The name was
changed for the novel, but the choice of pseudonym is interesting: Burger is a common Dutch
name, meaning *citizen*. It reveals that Gordimer
thinks of her character as acting the role of citizen in a republic, standing up to an illegitimate
government, rather than acquiescing as subject
of a tyranny. Part of the postmodern character
of the novel is Burger's relationship with his
daughter, Rosa. As the title indicates, her entire
identity consists in being Burger's daughter,
and all of her interior thoughts and judgments
must be composed with reference to this relationship. But the reader scarcely encounters
Burger, either directly or through his daughter's
perception of him. He appears only as a disem-
bodied voice making the logical and legal case

against apartheid from the witness stand during his trial. Otherwise he is a figure of recollection, either by Rosa or his first wife, Katya.

Rosemarie (Rosa) Burger

Rosa is the main character of the novel and the narrator of approximately half of it. She is the daughter of Lionel and Cathy Burger. She is named after Rosa Luxemburg, a Communist ideologue who was murdered during the political upheavals in Germany that followed World War I, and her paternal grandmother, Marie Burger. She would have liked to have become a lawyer, but given her political background, this would never have been allowed. Neither would she have been permitted to attend medical school, so she became a physiotherapist.

Rosa is conflicted over her political heritage. She never varies from her father's beliefs, but she realizes it is because she is not able to. He thoroughly indoctrinated her as a child and, so to speak, imposed revolutionary ideals on her as a tyrant. She is also aware that he had no hesitation in using her as a tool for advancing his political aims (as in the false engagement to Noel de Witt), just as he eventually gave up his own freedom and life to the same cause. It is unthinkable that she disagree with him—her mind has been trained so that she cannot—but she still resents the limits on her freedom that come with her heritage. Rosa is, in George Orwell's term, unable to commit thoughtcrime against her father's ideals. She is equally resentful of her mother for being something else before being her mother.

Throughout the novel, Rosa is on a quest to understand her own identity. While her father lived, she fulfilled her expected role reflexively, without reflection. After his death, she has to think how to guide her own actions. Her first reaction is to see the struggle against apartheid as hopeless. By exposure to black consciousness ideology and by seeing culture in Europe for herself, she comes to see white participation in the struggle as arising from within the liberal tradition of white culture and therefore as fundamentally different from the life-and-death struggle blacks are engaged in. She finally realizes, however, that she cannot alter her fate. She returns to South Africa and repeats the pattern of her father's imprisonment, though without having committed any revolutionary act other than being Burger's daughter.

Bernard Chabalier

Bernard is a French professor with whom Rosa has an affair. His work concerns the loss of legitimate French identity in the face of internationalizing tendencies that are imposing an Anglophone culture across the world.

Conrad

During her father's trial, Rosa has an affair with a young man whom she knew from his once having visited her father's house on a Sunday when anyone, black or white, opposed to apartheid was welcomed. He lives as a parasite on the wealthy, doing odd jobs like housesitting yachts and country estates; he also works for a bookmaker. At the same time, he is writing a doctoral dissertation on Italian literature.

Daniel

Daniel is a black man who tends bar in Rosa's uncle Coen's hotel. Although Daniel undoubtedly has a family name, it is never mentioned because such details did not interest white South Africans. (As with the omission of family names among black slaves in America, it is a technique of dehumanization.) "Daniel" may well be only a name he is called by whites for their own convenience if his given name is in an African language. His conversations with Rosa reveal the kind of cognitive dissonance that blacks and whites had to live with in apartheid South Africa. When Rosa tells him she is staying with her uncle because both of her parents are in jail, he scolds the girl for making up such a lie. He knows it cannot be true because as far as he understands only blacks go to jail. (In the small rural town where her uncle lives, Rosa sees black chain gangs from the prison performing slave labor for the state every day.) Conversely, when Daniel tries to enlist Rosa's aid in persuading her father to hire his son as a gardener, she asks how old the boy is. When Daniel tells her he is thirteen. Rosa thinks he must be joking, since, as far as she, a white girl, knows, thirteen-year-old boys go to school full-time.

Noel de Witt

Noel is a young Communist activist who is imprisoned while Rosa is in high school. He has no relatives and so would be denied any visitors in prison. Rosa's father contrives a fiction that Rosa is his fiancée. As such she is allowed to visit Noel and exchange information between the activists inside and outside of prison. Rosa actually is in love with him, something no one else knows. Noel is eventually released and immediately leaves the country.

Lily Letsile

Lily is the Burgers' maid. A black woman living under apartheid, she reacts to tragedy and disaster by denying the facts, as she does when she sees Rosa's brother drown and when Lionel Burger is convicted.

Coen Nels

Coen is Rosa's uncle. As a little girl, she has to stay with him once when both of her parents are arrested and tried for treason together. He owns a farm and a hotel in the veld, or countryside. There are a large number of pets at the hotel, all of them maimed, including a parakeet missing a toe on one foot and a three-legged dog. This is meant to suggest the crippled state of South African society.

Theo Santorini

Theo acts as counsel to Lionel Burger during his trial and to Rosa after her arrest. His commitment to the Burger family goes far beyond his legal position, however, being even stronger than that of a family friend, because he shares Lionel's political convictions. This is far from being without risk. Theo is more than once threatened by opposing counsel with being disbarred for Communist sympathies.

Clare Terblanche

Clare is the daughter of two of Lionel Burger's revolutionary comrades and was a playmate of Rosa's when they were children. After Lionel's death she unsuccessfully approaches Rosa to inveigh her to go on with revolutionary activity.

Brandt Vermeulen

Brandt is a Boer aristocrat whom Rosa Burger approaches to assist her in getting a passport. He holds no office but controls great private wealth and has close contacts in the government. He gains support by championing apartheid in the press against its liberal white critics. He is a pretentious pseudo-intellectual who imagines he is a poet and art connoisseur and sexually harasses Rosa. He is meant to symbolize the false intellectual position of apartheid.

Zwelinzima Vulindlela (Baasie)

Bassie's father, Isaac Vulindlela, is a comrade of the Burgers in the Communist Party who is arrested and then murdered in jail by his guards. The Burgers effectively (though not legally) adopt Baasie (as they called him) when his father is arrested. When Lionel and Cathy Burger are arrested together (when Baasie and Rosa are both nine years old), Baasie is taken in by relatives, and Rosa loses track of him. Zwelinzima means "suffering land" in Xhosa, the family's native language. Zwelinzima is embittered by white domination of the black liberation movement. Rather than revering Lionel Burger, Baasie rejects Burger's concern for blacks as merely paternalistic racism. He describes himself during his youth in Burger's house as being "One of Lionel Burger's best tame blacks sent scuttling like a bloody cockroach everywhere, you can always just put your foot on them."

THEMES

Psychoanalysis

Gordimer uses psychoanalysis in a highly original and evocative manner in *Burger's Daughter*. Except in the voice of Lionel Burger with his defense of Communism and racial equality, Gordimer does not rely on sweeping ideological statements, so this theme can be revealed in many small scenes. One of the most interesting of these scenes occurs early in the novel when Rosa and Conrad are walking through Johannesburg at night. They happen to walk by the Burger house (sold after Lionel's imprisonment), and Rosa recalls the events in the house on the night of the Sharpeville massacre. This atrocity is sketched through the information that filtered into the house, which acted as a central headquarters for the opposition to apartheid where the leaders of the South African Communist Party, the African National Congress, and their lawyers gathered.

The massacre is discussed fairly dispassionately, with an emphasis on securing sworn statements from witnesses, although the horrifying detail that the white police refused to clean up the spilled human brains they had shot out because they belonged to blacks is adduced. Lionel, through his contacts in Johannesburg hospitals, is able to determine through autopsy findings that the protesters were shot in the

TOPICS FOR FURTHER STUDY

- The end of apartheid was an uncertain matter for Gordimer in the 1970s and 1980s. In *July's People*, for example, she foresees a violent civil war. In *Burger's Daughter*, however, Gordimer offers a distinct version of the future. She suggests that the white government might have accepted a limited power-sharing arrangement with a black entrepreneurial class and made a show of being more accepting of blacks, for example, by integrating South African national sports teams. The purpose would be to pacify the international community with their burdensome economic sanctions while leaving conditions unchanged for the mass of poor blacks. Write a paper comparing this scenario with what actually happened in South Africa in the early 1990s.

- When, in *Burger's Daughter*, Rosa sees a black man cruelly beat a donkey, she is repulsed by the violence. But she is unable to condemn the man because he has no control over the oppressing forces that have left him a drunken, brutish lout with no more sense than to beat a donkey. This is a metaphor for the condition of South Africa under apartheid. Gordimer makes it clear that both whites and blacks suffer by becoming cruel and degraded enough to carry out the oppression they consider necessary. In the metaphor, then, the pitiable black man doing the beating in some sense stands for the white power structure. She may have been thinking in terms of the violence she and many others feared blacks might use to end apartheid (though violent revolution did not occur). Research the rioting that occurred in Ferguson, Missouri, in the summer of 2014 using the variety of sources available on the Internet. Include contemporary news reports and analytical articles, archived documents (such as the grand jury proceedings against the police officer Darren Wilson), and blog posts and tweets by participants in the protests. Use presentation software for a report to your class in which you analyze the situation in Ferguson in terms of Gordimer's metaphor.

- *Forbidden City* (1990), by William E. Bell, is a young-adult novel about the Tiananmen Square massacre in 1989. Write a paper comparing it with *Burger's Daughter*. Points to consider include the role of political protest in society, state surveillance and oppression, and the role of the Communist Party in the two novels.

- Investigate British treatment of the Boer population in South Africa and write a paper comparing this to the apartheid system the Boers eventually imposed on the black and other nonwhite populations under apartheid. To what degree was apartheid a reaction to the Boers' perception of themselves as an oppressed minority?

---

back. But this narrative does little to excite human emotions of outrage and horror.

Conrad creates another narrative (his attributing the basis of it to Jung rather than Freud is a joke by Gordimer against his ignorant, hippy character). He first reveals that when he was eleven years old he found out his mother was carrying on an adulterous affair. The realization that his mother was not his father's private property caused a flare-up of oedipal desire within him. He then asks Rosa two questions about her own desires, which she denies. He asks first whether she has ever felt the desire to kill something weak and helpless, like a baby, simply for the pleasure of the exercise of power it would entail. The second question is whether she has ever felt an impulse to kill herself. Conrad ends his narrative by saying that the only things that matter to him are sex and death.

Freud theorized that people feel exactly the desires that Conrad discusses but repress them, so that, like Rosa, they are able to deny that they feel anything so horrible. This repression, in Freud's view, is the force that makes civilization possible. Human beings are driven, Freud thought, by the death instinct and the life instinct (death and sex), and only by redirecting those energies to constructive purposes can human beings create civilization.

Conrad's discourse serves two purposes. Because it challenges the reader's own repression, it causes the reader to feel disgust and anxiety, which can be attached to the massacre in Rosa's discourse, making the reader feel more viscerally the appropriate reaction to the atrocity than merely describing it, in terms however dramatic, can do. Conrad's discourse also implies that apartheid was possible only because these repressed desires are available to be redirected to tasks like the police's murdering peaceful protesters. In this way, apartheid was waging war against the very psychological forces that lie at the foundation of civilization and therefore against civilization itself.

Postmodernism

Friedrich Nietzsche, in *The Gay Science*, for example, viewed the modern world of the nineteenth century as something that was coming apart at the seams, something resting on thin ice that was about to be destroyed in a terrible debacle:

> We Homeless Ones . . . We children of the future, how *could* we be at home in the present? We are unfavourable to all ideals which could make us feel at home in this frail, broken-down, transition period; and as regards the "realities" thereof, we do not believe in their *endurance*. The ice which still carries has become very thin; the thawing wind blows; we ourselves, the homeless ones, are an agency that breaks the ice, and the other too thin "realities."

In modernity, identity depends on nationality, class, race, and many other such factors being exploded by critical analysis, revealed as constructs used to exert power and control. The homeless ones of Nietzsche's metaphor are aware of this and therefore have no identity, no home. With the false harbor of modernity left behind, the postmodern writer has the burden of reconstructing the world out of narratives that have no definite meaning, which cannot be

judged as either true or false, but only as stories. Gordimer takes on this problem quite deliberately in the very first pages of *Burger's Daughter*.

The novel begins with five separate descriptions of a particular scene, that of Rosa bringing a blanket to her mother in prison, ranging from a page and a half in length to a single line. Each one presents the scene in a totally different manner, like the shards of a mirror each reflecting the same image from a different angle. The first description is conventional, told by a third-person omniscient narrator focusing on the physical description of things, especially Rosa's appearance. The second analyzes the scene through the reaction of Rosa's classmates to the news of her mother's arrest and establishes the theme of racial politics—between the English and Dutch. The next shard is a quotation from a fictitious document, evidently a journalistic description of the scene in a subversive newspaper. Another shard is a quotation from Rosa's private thoughts questioning the ability of any of the writers of previous documents to understand what really occurred in the scene: "When they saw me outside the prison, what did they see?"

The last fragment of the opening scene seems to come from a document that may be Rosa's memoirs. It is a deeper reflection of her interior thoughts, a passage in which she realizes how utterly different the observations of people witnessing the scene from the outside would be from her own. But she writes no such memoirs; the passage concludes, "My version and theirs. And if this were being written down, both would seem equally concocted when read over. And if I were really telling, instead of talking to you in my mind. . . . " Gordimer is denying the possibility of absolute truth: even the direct experience of one's own life and one's inmost thoughts have meanings contingent upon context and audience. There can be only narratives, never truth.

None of the disparate descriptions can be judged truer, or even more important, than the others; each functions only in its own context. Gordimer feels free to invent documents both real and imagined in the imaginary world of her fiction. The point is that she is writing a history of apartheid, but whatever she writes will not be a true history, only a narrative, no less real or unreal, no more or less important, than other possible or extant narratives.

Soweto is the most populous black urban residential area in South Africa. (© Gil.K | Shutterstock.com)

STYLE

Narration

Burger's Daughter has a complex narrative structure. The narrative voice is constantly changing from section to section and sometimes from sentence to sentence. Perhaps half of the text is narrated in a more or less traditional fashion by an impersonal voice that describes the events in the third person. Equally prominent is the voice of Rosa Burger, the main character of the novel. These sections are presented as an interior monologue in which Rosa pretends to herself that she is talking not to the reader but to another character in the novel. Her pretend interlocutor varies in the three sections of the novel. In the first section, she addresses her lover, Conrad; in the second, her stepmother, Katya; and in the third, her father, Lionel. Other sections of the novel quote from various fictitious and real documents. The fictitious documents include the transcript of Lionel Burger's trial or an article in a Communist Party underground newspaper about Rosa. One real document is a pamphlet published by a student group during the Soweto uprising in 1976. This is significant because the unbanning of *Burger's Daughter* also had the effect of unbanning this antigovernment document.

Allegory

One of the main critical reactions to *Burger's Daughter* has been to read the novel as an allegory. Allegory is a technique by which a narrative corresponds symbolically to some other set of facts that are not actually mentioned in the narrative. Examples of allegory include reading the *Odyssey* of Homer as expounding Neoplatonic philosophy, reading Samson in the Old Testament as a type of Christ, or reading *Nineteen Eighty-Four* in relation to the civilization of the time when it was written. At its most obvious level, Rosa Burger's life corresponds to the history of apartheid in South Africa and to Gordimer's own literary career, which occupies the same time. But, of course, the novel is about the struggle against apartheid, so Gordimer is using allegory only in the broadest sense. Nevertheless, the narrative presents a fictional history, which can at best be said to have a symbolic

COMPARE
&
CONTRAST

- **1970s:** South Africa is dominated by a white supremacist apartheid regime.

   Today: South Africa has political equality among the races and is governed by the multiethnic African National Congress.

- **1970s:** South Africa routinely bans literary works critical of apartheid.

   Today: South Africa enjoys the same press freedoms as other Western countries.

- **1970s:** The South African Communist Party is banned.

   Today: The South African Communist Party is a recognized party and is in the ruling coalition in parliament with the African National Congress.

correspondence to actual history. This is clearest in the case of the character Lionel Burger, who stands as a symbol of Bram Fischer. Fischer himself is mentioned a few times in the novel as if Fischer and Burger are separate entities, but Burger cannot be understood except as a symbol for Fischer. Gordimer's purpose in using this historical allegory, rather than history itself, is to reach the conclusion that historical processes occur within the individual.

Allegory is used in a different way in the larger structure of the novel. The Burger family are Communists, and Communism has a particular dialectical view of history. Events follow one another not at random but as the steps of a logical syllogism. A particular historical economic system, such as serfdom, exists as the thesis. But the thesis has an implicit contradiction that forms an antithesis, in the case of serfdom that economic growth can come about only through the bourgeois merchant class that is excluded from political power. The thesis and antithesis are resolved in a new synthesis, in this case the capitalism of the eighteenth and nineteenth centuries. The synthesis then becomes a new thesis, repeating the process until the final synthesis, Communism with no inherent flaw, comes about. The three parts of the novel can be read after this fashion. The ideological political activism of Lionel Burger that dominates the first part of the novel stands as a thesis. Rosa, however, led by the examples of Conrad and Katya, wishes to lead a different life that aims only at her personal happiness,

exemplified by her departure from South Africa in the second part. In the third part, Rosa realizes a synthesis by pursuing the goal of reform at a personal level.

HISTORICAL CONTEXT

As a South African opposed to apartheid, Gordimer could hardly have chosen any other subject than apartheid as the focus of her literary career under the apartheid regime. To understand apartheid, what the antiapartheid activist Abram (Bram) Fischer (quoted by Gordimer in her article "Why Did Bram Fischer Choose Jail?") called "that hideous system of discrimination" one must understand something of the history of South Africa. The Cape Colony began as a Dutch settlement in the seventeenth century, similar to the American state of New York (originally New Amsterdam). During the Anglo-Dutch wars, South Africa became a British colony, but its white population remained mostly of Dutch origin, speaking the Dutch dialect Afrikaans. There was also a large immigrant population from the Indian subcontinent.

At the end of the nineteenth century, the Dutch revolted against British rule and sought independence. They were suppressed in a conflict known as the Boer War (Dutch South Africans are known as Boers), which ended in 1902. This conflict was similar in scale and character to

Hundreds are killed when the police crush the uprising. (© JPL Designs | Shutterstock.com)

the Vietnam War and saw thousands of Boer civilians rounded up into the world's first concentration camps.

Originally a British dominion, like Canada, South Africa became a republic in 1961. South Africa had, and has, a thriving economy, largely due to the mineral wealth of the country, especially in gold and diamonds. As the Dutch majority took control of the government after World War II, it developed the ideology of apartheid (separateness), at first to exclude nonwhites from voting, which would entail a black-controlled government because three-quarters of the population consisted of nonwhites and hence another loss of Boer freedom.

Apartheid quickly evolved into a form of discrimination even harsher than that in the United States in the Jim Crow South. Blacks were prohibited by law not only from civil rights but also from most professions and business and were required to live in designated black homelands; they could come into the large white cities

only with special work permits. Black ghettos on the outskirts of the cities were walled in. As blacks and even some whites protested against the injustice of this system, the leaders of opposition to apartheid were marginalized as terrorists and Communists and were jailed en masse.

One of the white opposition leaders was Fischer, a prominent corporate lawyer and a descendant of the highest ranks of Dutch political leadership in South Africa. After an outspoken career as an antigovernment Communist activist, Fischer was imprisoned for life in 1966. Because of the dramatic dichotomies of his life and his outspoken and well-reasoned opposition, Gordimer took a special interest in Fischer, first evidenced in her article, "Why Did Bram Fischer Choose Jail?" Fischer's choice was quite deliberate—his trial was recessed so he could work on behalf of the government on an important trade agreement in the Netherlands. No one expected him to return to South Africa, but he did. He must have thought his most important contribution to fighting apartheid was to become a martyr to the injustice of the system. The South African government thought so too and confiscated his ashes after his funeral.

According to Stephen Clingman in *The Novels of Nadine Gordimer*,

> The character of Lionel Burger bears a strong resemblance to the real-life figure of Abram ("Bram") Fischer, one of the most prominent leaders within the SACP [South African Communist Party], upon whose personal history his career has evidently been based.

This resemblance is recognized by students of Gordimer's work. In her article, Gordimer quotes extensively from Fischer's testimony at his trial, particularly as it points out the hypocrisy of the South African government: "The laws under which I am being prosecuted were enacted by a wholly unrepresentative body...in which three-quarters of the people of this country have no voice whatever." As a Western and as an English state, South Africa espoused the same respect for personal political liberty that is enshrined in the US Constitution but ran roughshod over its supposed ideals under the pretense of defending them.

Fischer also played on his own status as a martyr in his testimony:

> If one day it may help to establish a bridge across which white leaders and the real leaders of the non-whites can meet to settle the destinies of all of us by negotiation and not by force of arms, I shall be able to bear with fortitude any sentence which this court may impose on me.

Fischer died in prison in 1975, so he did not live to see it, but that is exactly what happened. In the early 1990s, South Africa repealed apartheid, and in 1994 the country elected its first black president, Nelson Mandela, leader of the African National Congress, a group that had been banned as Communist with Mandela serving a life sentence for sabotage and conspiracy. Fischer had been on the defense team at Mandela's trial in 1962, and Mandela was on the US terrorist watch list until 2008.

CRITICAL OVERVIEW

As world consciousness of the injustice of apartheid increased and because it was the work that followed Gordimer's winning of the Man Booker Prize, *Burger's Daughter* received ample critical attention, especially during the 1980s and 1990s. An important early step in the analysis of *Burger's Daughter*, made by Rowland Smith in his article "Living for the Future: Nadine Gordimer's *Burger's Daughter*" is the observation that the three parts of the novel function as a Marxist dialectical syllogism. Robert Boyers, in his 1984 *Salmagundi* article, grapples with the transformation of Gordimer as a writer represented by *Burger's Daughter*. Gordimer had previously been viewed as a supremely personal author who explored the meaning of individual lives, but in *Burger's Daughter*, she turned more directly than ever before to political, even historical, matters. Boyers concludes,

> She has, in fact, reconceived the very idea of private experience and created a form that can accommodate microscopic details of individual behavior and sentiment without suggesting for a moment that individuals are cut off from the collective consciousness and political situations characteristic of their societies.

In *The Novels of Nadine Gordimer* (1986), Stephen Clingman analyzed *Burger's Daughter* from the historical and other perspectives. He points out that in the novel, "Gordimer is primarily concerned with the predicament facing the inheritor of a revolutionary tradition in the context of South Africa in the mid-1970s." He also pointed out that Freud and Freudian psychoanalysis shape *Burger's Daughter* as much as Marx and dialectical materialism do. Clingman viewed Gordimer as more interested in the moral example of South African Communists, a group in which whites worked directly with blacks,

than in Communism. Moreover, he saw the novel as an application of Gordimer's close observation of life to a new, historical subject matter. He gave details of Gordimer's reliance on historical documents in the novel and even on personal interviews with people who knew Bram Fischer. Lorraine Liscio, in a 1987 article in *Modern Fiction Studies*, analyzed Gordimer as a new kind of African writer not bound by her European roots or by the concerns of the first generations of African postcolonial literature. Dominic Head, in *Nadine Gordimer* (1994), integrated the conclusions of the preceding decade of Gordimer scholarship with his own analysis of her political vision.

After apartheid ended, critics felt freer to treat Gordimer's works on a purely literary level. Brighton J. Uledi Kamanga, in *Cracks in the Wall* (2002), treated irony as the main theme of *Burger's Daughter*, seeing Rosa's every effort to leave her family tradition of activism as forcing her ever more strongly back to the same path. Nobantu L. Rasebotsa, in *Twelve Best Books by African Women* (2009), wrote with more postmodern concern. She theorized that Gordimer was concerned with the transformation of consciousness through the experience of domination and that she related the question of being and existence to existential phenomenology.

CRITICISM

Bradley A. Skeen

Skeen is a classicist. In the following essay, he explores the role of Orwellian doublethink in Gordimer's critique of South African apartheid in her novel Burger's Daughter.

All of Gordimer's writing was ultimately about apartheid. Gordimer saw apartheid as a cancer eating away at the foundations of Western civilization in South Africa. As a master of language, Gordimer was especially concerned about the way that the apartheid regime used language as part of its social control. One of the first thinkers to deal seriously with the way governments manipulate language was George Orwell. Although *Burger's Daughter* is in no sense didactic and does not give Gordimer scope to say, "see, this is how Orwell describes corrupt political language and here is the South African government carrying it out in practice," she makes it clear to a reader familiar with Orwell's writings that the

"

GORDIMER SAW APARTHEID AS A CANCER

EATING AWAY AT THE FOUNDATIONS OF WESTERN

CIVILIZATION IN SOUTH AFRICA."

South African regime was steeped in an Orwellian manipulation of language.

One theme of Gordimer's opposition to apartheid was the exposure of its reliance on doublethink. Orwell coined the term in his dystopian novel *Nineteen Eighty-Four*. In this work, published in 1948, Orwell described the way he perceived politics operating in the actual world, but through an allegory based on a future dystopian society that differs from the real world perhaps only in the extremity of the application of its principles.

In *Nineteen Eighty-Four*, the world is divided into three superstates: Eurasia, Eastasia, and Oceania (including North America and Great Britain, renamed Airstrip One). They are constantly at war but in an ever-shifting configuration. However, history is rewritten so that the current alliances (Oceania and Eastasia fighting against Eurasia, for example) are supposed to have always existed. Orwell based this configuration on the West's change of attitude toward the Soviet Union when the Western democracies suddenly found themselves in alliance with the Soviets against Nazi Germany during World War II. Gordimer commented on this in regard to the South African state's changing attitude toward the Communist Party before, during, and after the war, as recounted by the historian who interviews Rosa Burger about her father.

In *Nineteen Eighty-Four* Oceania is ruled by the Inner Party, with its philosophy of Ingsoc (English socialism), which is used to impose fiction as belief through sophisticated means of controlling the populace's thought and language. One of the most powerful of these means is doublethink. Doublethink is the mental process one uses to support an unsupportable political position. A racist engages in doublethink while denouncing racism as wrong and sincerely believing that while continuing to

endorse and carry out racist policies. Orwell defines doublethink as follows:

> To know and not to know, to be conscious of complete truthfulness while telling carefully constructed lies, to hold simultaneously two opinions which canceled out, knowing them to be contradictory and believing in both of them, to use logic against logic, to repudiate morality while laying claim to it.

Doublethink also requires one

> to forget whatever it was necessary to forget, then to draw it back into memory again at the moment it was needed, and then promptly to forget it again, and above all, to apply the same process to the process itself—that was the ultimate subtlety: consciously to induce unconsciousness, and then, once again, to become unconscious of the act of hypnosis you had just performed.

Although *Nineteen Eighty-Four* is a political fantasy, the concept of doublethink is important because, as Orwell pointed out in his 1946 essay "Politics and the English Language," doublethink (although he had not invented the word yet) is routinely used by politicians in the real world to cover inconvenient truths, not least their own blunders and failings, and by advertisers and anyone else who uses language to manipulate. This pertains not only to totalitarian regimes but also to Western democracies.

Orwell saw doublethink as active in the attempt of supposedly enlightened Western states to cover over their atrocities:

> In our time, political speech and writing are largely the defence of the indefensible. Things like the continuance of British rule in India, the Russian purges and deportation, the dropping of the atom bombs on Japan, can indeed be defended, but only by arguments which are too brutal for most people to face, and which do not square with the professed aims of political parties.

Closely related to doublethink is the use of euphemism to allow citizens to recategorize their state's atrocities as something that at least sounds more acceptable:

> Defenceless villages are bombarded from the air, the inhabitants driven out into the countryside...this is called *pacification*...People are imprisoned for years without trial...this is called *elimination of unreliable elements*.

Doubtless the reader can supply the modern euphemisms meant to cover over the same atrocities that are still going on.

WHAT DO I READ NEXT?

- *Chike and the River*, first published in 1966, is a young-adult novel by the Nigerian author Chinua Achebe. It deals with the effects of the end of colonialism in Africa, in a Biafran cultural context far different from the situation in apartheid South Africa.

- Barbara Temple-Thurston's *Nadine Gordimer Revisited* in Twayne's World Authors Series (1999) is an introductory critical study of Gordimer's work with a chapter on *Burger's Daughter*.

- In *Ideology on a Frontier* (1984), J. Alton Templin shows how the Boer ideological construct of apartheid grew out of Dutch Calvinist theology and the idea that an elect white race was naturally fit to rule over a reprobate black race.

- *July's People* (1981) was Gordimer's next novel after *Burger's Daughter*. It is set in a fictitious future in which the apartheid regime in South Africa is overthrown by a black uprising and a white middle-class family and their servant (called July) find their roles reversed.

- Bruce King's collection *The Later Fiction of Nadine Gordimer* (1993) contains essays on *Burger's Daughter* from a number of critical perspectives.

- *Nadine Gordimer's Burger's Daughter* (2003), edited by Judie Newman, presents material to contextualize Gordimer's novel for students. It includes an interview with Gordimer about the novel, a collection of critical essays, and an assessment of the novel's relationship to the South African political scene in its banning and unbanning.

A modern example is the meaning of *terrorism*. Whatever commonplace definition of the word one is thinking of is probably wrong within the framework of contemporary political discourse, in which it means any military or quasi-military action within or without the laws of war carried out by the enemies of the United States with the corollary that no act carried out by the United States or its allies within or without the laws of war can, by definition, be terrorism.

It is hardly a surprise that a regime as brutal and oppressive as South African apartheid had to use doublethink to reconcile itself with the very whites who perpetrated it and benefited from it. After all, white South Africans were steeped in the Western tradition whose most cherished ideals they betrayed. They had to preserve the illusion that they were an enlightened, Christian culture. Gordimer's characters live in a society in which each individual is required not only to say but also to believe in a fictional representation of reality created by the state, which has little resemblance to reality as it actually exists.

Gordimer began to chronicle the doublethink of apartheid in her essays long before writing *Burger's Daughter*. In her 1963 essay "Censored, Banned, Gagged," Gordimer engaged with the new censorship law, the Publications and Entertainments Act of 1963. Under this law most of Gordimer's works, including *Burger's Daughter*, were eventually banned in her own country. Gordimer pointed out that when politicians were debating the law in parliament, they constantly talked as if it were intended to ban filth, in other words, as if it were directed against pornography. But, as Gordimer, pointed out, every book the law was ever used to ban was censored because of its "nonconformity with the picture of South African life as prescribed and proscribed by apartheid." In this way, literature opposed to apartheid was recategorized as obscene, precisely because of the obscenity of a different kind that apartheid was based on.

Gordimer highlighted a provision of the act, the stipulation that no literature allowed into the country may be such as is judged "harmful to the relations between any sections of the inhabitants" with the specification that this includes "human or social deviation or degeneracy." This apparently refers to racially mixed marriages (a theme that Gordimer made common in her work), which were treated as a form of sexual perversion. But in practice, the law took on an even broader meaning, forbidding any hint that life may be improved by the races in South Africa or elsewhere living together in harmony or equality. Apartheid outlawed the kinship among people—the common hope of the Enlightenment and Christianity celebrated in poetry and song by Schiller and Beethoven, who would have been considered dangerous radicals, in the "Ode to Joy."

In her 1966 essay "Why Did Bram Fischer Choose Jail?"—her first grappling with the career of Fischer, which ultimately inspired *Burger's Daughter*—Gordimer addressed the doublethink in the Suppression of Communism Act. She pointed out that the law had nothing to do with the anti-Communism that gripped the West during the cold war but was used to persecute all "opposition to apartheid, whether inspired by socialism, capitalism, religious principles, a sense of justice or just plain human feeling." Gordimer quotes Fischer himself as pointing out at his trial that the law had nothing to do with Communism, saying,

> These laws were enacted not to prevent the spread of communism, but for the purpose of silencing the opposition of a large majority of our citizens to a Government intent upon depriving them, solely on account of their colour, of the most elementary human rights.

In his fictional defense speech, Lionel Burger explains why he became a Communist. He was disturbed by

> the contradiction that my people—the Afrikaner people—and the white people in general in our country, worship the God of Justice and practise discrimination on grounds of the colour of skin; profess the compassion of the Son of Man, and deny the humanity of the black people they live among. This contradiction that split the very foundations of my life, that was making it impossible for me to see myself as a man among men, with all that implies of consciousness and responsibility.

He found the government's rationale exploded as false in Communist dialectic. In other words, Burger found he could not engage in the doublethink necessary to accept apartheid.

But for Gordimer, the South African government is not the only institution that uses doublethink. Rosa Burger realizes that the younger generation of the Communist Party, represented by herself and Clare Terblanche, has been indoctrinated to use doublethink by its parents. They both know that the party's tactics against apartheid have been used for fifty years without success and therefore are unlikely to have success in the future. Rosa, however, thinks to herself that Clare "would

deal with what was put before her without allowing herself to see it, just as I did." She will think clearly about any immediate problem in its full context but will not allow the facts that this makes her aware of to contradict the mythological narrative of the eventual triumph of the party, which she also believes is true. This is the essence of doublethink.

Gordimer illustrated at length another example of doublethink, which requires further explanation. When Lionel Burger is convicted of subversion and sentenced to life in prison, the family's black maid, Lily, exclaims, "God is going to stay with him in that place [prison]. All the time, all the time. Until he come home." No doubt these are her sincere beliefs, but at the same time she knows that Burger is an atheist and that he is never going to come home. Somehow she is able to hold the mutually contradictory sets of facts in her mind at the same time. The contradiction is so extreme that Rosa (who narrates this episode) offers the reader some explanation: "Here she interceded for us too, mediating our rejection of belief into the acceptable form, for well-off white people, of merely neglecting to go to church." But Lionel Burger would offer a different explanation. In Marxist analysis, religion is merely one means that the ruling class uses to control the oppressed. By offering the false hope that God will somehow help Burger and even arrange his release from unjust punishment, Lily is prevented from even thinking of the practical solution of overthrowing the ruling class. By instilling religion in the oppressed class, the ruling class achieves the thought control that is the purpose of doublethink: revolution becomes unthinkable.

South Africa under apartheid had other similarities to Orwell's Oceania besides its ideological dependence on doublethink. In both states, political power exists on a continuum: in Oceania based on the degree of an individual's political indoctrination (the Proles, the Outer Party, and the Inner Party) and in South Africa on skin color. In South Africa, humanity was divided into four, not simply two, groups: whites, colored (people of mixed black and white ancestry), Indians, and blacks. Political rights, and political oppression, existed along a scale of the four groups. Both ruling regimes tried to use language to bolster their political power. In Oceania, English is being redefined (Newspeak) with the goal of making opposition to the state

Rosa's father, Lionel Burger, died in a prison like this one, where Nelson Mandela was held.
(© Anton_Ivanov / Shutterstock.com)

literally unthinkable because there would be no language capable of describing it. South Africa used the same tactic, redefining the terms used to express opposition. Any idea that racial oppression was unjust was redefined as anti-Western Communism or terrorism, and mixed marriages became a sexual perversion. In *Nineteen Eighty-Four*, Winston Smith believes that change can come only from the Proles because they are not corrupted by indoctrination into Ingsoc. In contrast, in South Africa, the black community was very politically sophisticated, but their efforts had only an indirect effect on the end of apartheid. Only once the black opposition convinced the rest of the world that apartheid had to end and the white power structure became convinced that the inequality on which apartheid was based had to end did change came about.

Source: Bradley Skeen, Critical Essay on *Burger's Daughter* in *Novels for Students*, Gale, Cengage Learning, 2016.

Barbara Temple-Thurston

In the following excerpt, Temple-Thurston discusses the real-world politics that influenced Gordimer when writing Burger's Daughter.

. . . In a mixture of fiction and fact, *Burger's Daughter* is set during the teenage and young adult years of Rosa Burger, born in May 1948, the month and year the National Party came to power in South Africa. In the late 1960s and 1970s the strongest political influence among young black activists in South Africa was the black consciousness movement, a movement that challenged the concept of nonracialism that was so central to the communist party doctrine by which Rosa's parents had lived. Black consciousness was a watershed between generations; it shifted the struggle against the South African regime from one that included all races fighting together for equitable integration to a black-centered struggle that shunned any contact or cooperation with whites whatsoever. This meant that Rosa would experience the movement's repudiation of white activists' efforts in the struggle (something her parents had never had to deal with), and she would face much greater uncertainty about how freedom would ultimately be won.

The radical subject matter of *Burger's Daughter* and its inclusion of quotations and

> THE NOVEL EXAMINES WHETHER THERE IS
> A PLACE IN THE STRUGGLE FOR ROSA AND WHETHER
> SHE CAN CLAIM THE STRUGGLE AS HERS AT ALL."

documents from banned leaders and organizations brought swift reaction from the South African censors. The book was immediately embargoed and banned upon publication, but very shortly afterward, in an unprecedented move, it was unbanned by the director of the very committee that had banned it in the first place. The South African Publication Board's bizarre actions prompted a response from Gordimer. Her pamphlet *What Happened to "Burger's Daughter" or How South African Censorship Works* describes the bureaucratic obstacle course South African censors applied to the book. The furor surrounding these events, as well as the novel's enthusiastic reception abroad, makes it one of Gordimer's most renowned novels.

Rosa Burger's political and personal evolution—though framed by the family and political history of her father, who was leader of the SACP—is most radically shaped in response to rising sentiments of black consciousness, which culminated in the Soweto Revolt of 1976. Rejecting all forms of political participation or affiliation with whites, proponents of the movement argued that no matter how radical their politics, all whites remained complicit in deep and persistent patterns of white supremacy. This challenge to the authenticity of politically active whites brought about a "white consciousness" among white students, an honest and self-searching response that seriously considered the point that black consciousness was making: Only by recognizing the possibility of embedded supremacism could whites work for an authentic alternative. Clingman reports that in the late 1970s Gordimer "showed herself much exercised by the question of 'white consciousness' as a response to Black Consciousness," and that "*Burger's Daughter* can be seen as a fictional way of working out the same problem."

. . . Gordimer recognizes that as historical and political circumstances shift, so the precise understanding and nature of commitment changes; each person must come to his or her commitment anew. The historical circumstance of Rosa's young adulthood was the black consciousness movement, which refocused attention on the divisiveness of race in a new way; for the first time whites had to read themselves as raced, living in bodies defined by color and judged by it. As Rosa notes: "Lionel and my mother did not stand before Duma Dhladlha and [when asked what he would do if he were white] have him say dismissively: I don't think about that" (*BD*). Bishop Desmond Tutu explained the significance of race for the participants of the struggle against apartheid: "However much [whites] want to identify with blacks it is an existential fact . . . that they have not been victims of this baneful oppression and exploitation. . . . It is a divide that can't be crossed and that must give blacks a primacy in determining the course and goal of the struggle. Whites must be willing to follow" (*EG*, 267). Tutu's analysis returns us to the ever-present dilemma of white participation in shaping the future of South Africa. The question becomes what role remains for a white middle-class South African woman and for whom would she be playing such a role. The novel examines whether there is a place in the struggle for Rosa and whether she can claim the struggle as hers at all.

The form and narrative of *Burger's Daughter* are structured in every way to express the quest of the novel. The bildungsroman facilitates Rosa's defection from her father's camp so that she may establish her own identity, an identity that will ultimately lead her back to her own political commitment. Unlike Clare Terblanche, who unquestioningly accepts the politics of her radical parents and enters the same pattern of revolving stays in detention, Rosa rails against the generational conformity of dissident families: "Other people break away. They live completely different lives. Parents and children don't understand each other—there's nothing to say, between them. Some sort of natural insurance against repetition. . . . Not us. We live as they lived" (*BD*). Set free from family restraints after her father's death she pursues a private life, and it is her understanding and experience of the limitations of that life which enable her to rededicate herself to political activism once more. The dialectical pattern of challenge and probation (thesis, antithesis, synthesis) forms the three sections of the novel: Rosa grows up in the Burger heritage; Rosa rejects that heritage for a personal life after her father's death; Rosa finds her personal identity in political commitment and reunites with her heritage. According to Clingman, this pattern is a major part of the way Gordimer tries and tests a "consciousness of history" in all her work.

The novel pursues its resolution through a series of tensional relationships: past and present, South Africa and Europe, private and political, black world and white world, metaphor and history, and first- and third-person narratives. The narrative structure is central to the organization and meaning of the novel, and the alternating first- and third-person narratives provide the lenses through which we view contesting realities. The first-person narrative grants the reader insight into Rosa's internal and private realities, while the third-person narrative— a multivocal text that examines Rosa from every possible point of view—maintains external views of reality, and the contrast exposes the disjunction between inside and out. The function of the multivocal form has been debated, most notably by Clingman, who contests critic Robert Green's view that objectivity is ensured by the variety of external narratives, that there is "no necessary politics of the text *at all* in *Burger's Daughter*." Clingman holds rather that a multivocal text is as manipulable a form as any other and that seeing Rosa from every possible angle (sympathetically, hostilely, neutrally, among others) "has merely led to an apparently necessary outcome: that this is the destiny Rosa was born to, that this is the commitment she must undertake." Hers is a commitment and engagement, however, without any of the glory of her father's position.

Rosa's first-person narrative addresses itself to a different absent consciousness in each part of the novel. She says that "without knowing the reason, at different stages in one's life, one is addressing this person or that all the time, even dreams are performed before an audience" (*BD*). In the first section she addresses the absent Conrad to whom she admits: "If you knew I was talking to you I wouldn't be able to talk. But you know that about me" (*BD*). In the second she speaks to Burger's first wife, now known as Madame Katya Bagnelli, a woman in whom Rosa can find no remaining trace of her connection to Lionel's life. In the last section Rosa speaks to her dead father, explaining her encounter with Zwelinzima and her return to South Africa.

But in addition to the three audiences Rosa addresses, there is a fourth, the reader, who is directly implicated by her use of the second-person *you*. This powerful strategy draws the reader, who begins to identify with the life views of all three addressees, vicariously testing each worldview as the novel progresses. In the last section Rosa takes care to point out the real reason for her return to South Africa, and she asserts the difference between her father's commitment and her own. . . .

Source: Barbara Temple-Thurston, "Living in the Interregnum: *Burger's Daughter* and *July's People*," in *Nadine Gordimer Revisited*, Twayne Publishers, 1999, pp. 79–80, 83–85.

Daphne Read

In the following excerpt, Read examines how Gordimer ties together the ideas of vision and knowledge.

. . . *Burger's Daughter* deconstructs the liberal epistemology of vision, the notion that seeing is the source of knowing, of knowledge. Citing Mongane Serote in 'Living in the Interregnum,' Gordimer has noted the necessity to question the authority of the white 'I am,' the white Eye: 'Blacks must learn to talk; whites must learn to listen.' Seeing privileges the individual who sees; listening forces engagement with the 'other,' suggests the possibility of connection, dialogue, and mutual understanding. The clash between Rosa and Zwelinzima Vulindlela at the end of Part Two of *Burger's Daughter* jolts Rosa from her liberal reveries of another life into a recognition that 'no one can defect.' In her dialogue with her dead father in Part Three, she says, 'I cannot explain to anyone why that telephone call in the middle of the night made everything that was possible, impossible.' The telephone call counterpoints the donkey-scene at the end of Part One, which sent Rosa fleeing to France, in a paroxysm of fear, alienation and white guilt. Though Rosa denies she is a liberal, the phone-call dredges up the language and responses of the liberals Rosa despises. Zwelinzima Vulindlela forces Rosa to 'see' in the dark: 'Put on the light, Rosa. I'm talking to you.' He forces her to 'see' herself as capitalizing on her identity as Lionel Burger's daughter; she defends herself against his criticisms of her behaviour by defending her father. In response to her challenge to prove his political credentials and the implicit taunt that he too has fled the country, he says, 'I don't know who you are.' He challenges her identity, her perceptions, her knowledge, her relationship to the struggle and to her past in which 'Baasie' exists, reified in unexamined assumptions of a shared childhood. In her later private self-criticism, Rosa reflects: 'Repelled by him. Hating him so much! Wanting to be *loved!*—how I disfigured myself. How filthy and ugly, in the bathroom mirror. Debauched. To make defence of you the occasion for trotting out the holier-than-thou accusation—the final craven defence of the kind of people for whom there is going to be no future. If we'd still been children, I might have been throwing stones at him in a tantrum.' This analysis echoes in telling ways her analysis of her decision to leave South Africa: 'the suffering—while I saw it was the sum of suffering to me. I didn't do anything. I let him beat the donkey. The man was a black. So a kind of vanity counted for more than feeling; I couldn't bear to see myself—her—Rosa Burger—as one of those whites who can care more for animals than people.' She is unable to 'read' Zwelinzima when she meets him, seeing only a version of herself reflected in him, but in her self-criticism after the phone call, Rosa makes the shift from the arrogant authority of seeing-and-knowing to the humility of listening and insight.

The focus on how others see her and on how she sees herself reveals another important angle of vision in *Burger's Daughter*. The female subject—Rosa—is constructed in terms of the gaze: the male gaze, both public and private, and the mirror. The subject is divided, constituted from the outside by the public gaze and by state surveillance ('When they saw me outside the prison, what did they see?'), and from the inside by a subject alienated from her self ('I couldn't bear to see myself—her—Rosa Burger—as one of those whites;') 'To be free is to become almost a stranger to oneself; the nearest I'll ever get to seeing what they saw outside the prison.' The divided self is marked as female: it is a woman who asks, what did they see when they saw me? 'I shall never know. It's all concocted. I saw—see—that profile in a hand-held mirror directed towards another mirror.'

The motif of woman-and-mirror is repeated throughout the novel; marking stages in Rosa's growth to autonomy. In France the alienation of the subject under double surveillance—state and self—disappears in the fullness of the love affair: 'In the bar where she had sat seeing others living in the mirror, there was no threshold between her reflection and herself,' and, 'It's possible to live within the ambit of a person not a country....

There's the possibility with Chabalier, my Chabalier.' However, the confrontation with Zwelinzima Vulindlela reorients her self-vision away from this male-centred 'awareness of her own being.' Finally, the narcissism that Rosa has rejected, the distortion of self in the mirror, is reflected in the unicorn tapestry: 'On an azure island of a thousand flowers the Lady is holding a mirror in which the unicorn . . . sees a tiny image of himself. But the oval of the mirror cuts off the image just at the level at which the horn rises from his head.'

Rosa's divided self, the self split by the public and private gaze, is resolved in a double gesture. The first is the conclusion of the internal dialogues that have punctuated the novel; the two 'conversations' with her father in the last part of the novel mark the resolution of their relationship for Rosa and her acceptance of her self. Not surprisingly in a realist novel, she is 'centred' in her 'self' (in the discourse of liberal humanism). The internal dialogue, the silent reading of self and society, is displaced into writing, a more public form of communication; the letter Rosa sends at the end of the novel is written to a 'real person,' another woman. The centred individual moves out of the self-absorption of her scrutiny of the meaning of freedom into political action to expand the meaning of freedom, to make it concrete for others beyond herself. In prison she takes up sketching in an inversion of the observer-image theme throughout the novel. Her still-lifes are 'clumsy' and 'naive' and show problems with perspective and light but, like the patients she helps in the hospital, Rosa puts one foot in front of the other.

The emphasis on the father-daughter relationship, structurally foregrounded in numerous ways throughout the novel and at the end, in particular, by the internal dialogues, obscures the second gesture marking the repositioning of Rosa as subject. Rosa moves out of her orbit around men into self-affirmation in conjunction with other women. She reclaims the Otherness of femininity; that is, though socially positioned as Other in relation to men, she moves beyond that definition. This shift from an immobilizing awareness—and occasional fear—of the defining gaze of male interlocutors (the state, surveillance, journalists, father, 'brothers,' lovers), to autonomous self-defining activity, is not, however, a deliberate feminist strategy rooted in gender-consciousness. It is, rather, one of the multiple deconstructive processes that occur in the novel in response to the pressures of the social and political conditions of South Africa. That is, by pushing at the limits of what she perceives as her fixed identity, Rosa repositions herself in a way that is compatible with, but not informed by, feminism. . . .

Source: Daphne Read, "The Politics of Place in *Burger's Daughter*," in *The Later Fiction of Nadine Gordimer*, edited by Bruce King, Macmillan Press, 1993, pp. 131–34.

SOURCES

Becker, Jillian, "Nadine Gordimer: 'Comrade Madam,'" in *Standpoint*, September 2014, http://standpointmag .co.uk/node/5685/full (accessed November 5, 2014).

Boyers, Robert, "Public and Private: On *Burger's Daughter*," in *Salmagundi*, No. 62, Winter 1984, pp. 62–92.

Clingman, Stephen, *The Novels of Nadine Gordimer: History from the Inside*, 2nd ed., University of Massachusetts Press, 1986, pp. 170–93.

Gardner, Susan, "'A Story for This Place and Time': An Interview with Nadine Gordimer about *Burger's Daughter*," in *Conversations with Nadine Gordimer*, edited by Nancy Topping Bazin and Marilyn Dallman Seymour, University Press of Mississippi, 1990, pp. 161–75.

Gordimer, Nadine, *Burger's Daughter*, Viking, 1979.

———, "Censored, Banned, Gagged" in *The Essential Gesture: Writing, Politics and Places*, edited by Stephen Clingman, Alfred A. Knopf, 1988, pp. 58–67.

———, *What Happened to Burger's Daughter; or, How South African Censorship Works*, Taurus, 1980, pp. 1–74.

———, "Why Did Bram Fischer Choose Jail?," in *The Essential Gesture: Writing, Politics and Places*, edited by Stephen Clingman, Alfred A. Knopf, 1988, pp. 68–78.

Head, Dominic, *Nadine Gordimer*, Cambridge University Press, 1994, pp. 110–12.

Kamanga, Brighton J. Uledi, *Cracks in the Wall: Nadine Gordimer's Fiction and the Irony of Apartheid*, Africa World Press, 2002, pp. 45–84.

Liscio, Lorraine, "*Burger's Daughter*: Lighting a Torch in the Heart of Darkness," in *Modern Fiction Studies*, Vol. 33, No. 2, 1987, pp. 245–61.

Nietzsche, Friedrich, *The Gay Science*, translated by Thomas Common, Dover, 2010, pp. 192–93.

Orwell, George, *Nineteen Eighty-Four*, Harcourt, Brace, 1949, p. 36.

———, "Politics and the English Language," in *The English Language*, Vol. 2, *Essays by Linguists and Men of Letters*, edited by W. F. Bolton and D. Crystal, University of Cambridge Press, 1969, pp. 217–28.

Rasebotsa, Nobantu L. "Nadine Gordimer's *Burger's Daughter*: Consciousness, Identity, and Autonomy," in *Twelve Best Books by African Women*, edited by Chikwenye Okonjo Ogunyemi and Tuzyline Jita Allan, Ohio University Press, 2009, pp. 74–93.

Roberts, Ronald, *No Cold Kitchen*, Real African Publishers, 2005, pp. 588–91.

Smith, Rowland, "Living for the Future: Nadine Gordimer's *Burger's Daughter*," in *World Literature Written in English*, Vol. 19, 1980, pp. 163–72.

FURTHER READING

Cook, John, *The Novels of Nadine Gordimer: Private Lives/Public Landscapes*, Louisiana State University Press, 1984.

Cook gives an unusually integrated treatment of the novels of Gordimer's early and middle period, focusing on their literary and their political content.

Gordimer, Nadine, *The Conservationist*, Jonathan Cape, 1974.

The Conservationist, which immediately preceded *Burger's Daughter*, won the Man Booker Prize. It concerns the growing sense of alienation of a rich white South African businessman from his progressively run factory and its black workers.

Louw-Potgieter, Joha, *Afrikaner Dissidents: A Social Psychological Study of Identity and Dissent*, Multilingual Matters, 1998.

Louw-Potgieter explores the role of personal and social psychology in Boer dissidents. Much of the book is devoted to Bram Fischer, the model for Lionel Burger in *Burger's Daughter*.

Smith, Rowland, ed., *Critical Essays on Nadine Gordimer*, G. K. Hall, 1990.

Smith's volume collects standard critical treatments of Gordimer, including several devoted to *Burger's Daughter*.

SUGGESTED SEARCH TERMS

Nadine Gordimer

Burger's Daughter AND Gordimer

postmodernism

South Africa

apartheid

Communism

terrorism

psychoanalysis

Code Name Verity

ELIZABETH WEIN
2012

Elizabeth Wein's young-adult novel *Code Name Verity* centers on two young women in World War II. As the novel unfolds, one becomes a pilot, the other a British spy. Through the form of a confession to the Nazi secret police, Verity (Julia's code name) recounts the way she and Maddie, the pilot, become friends. Verity allegedly is confessing to her Nazi captors in order to avoid further torture, but by the end of the novel, it becomes clear she is trying to find a way to still complete her mission, which is to obtain the plans to the French hotel where she is being held and which is being used as a Nazi prison, so that the prisoners (British officers and French Resistance fighters) can be freed and the prison can be destroyed. Though Maddie becomes part of a mission to rescue her friend, in the end she must kill Julia so that she is not sent to a secret Nazi concentration camp where she is slated to become a test subject for medical experimentation. Through the course of the novel, Wein explores the notions of friendship and loyalty, as well as the dehumanizing effects of war.

AUTHOR BIOGRAPHY

Wein was born on October 2, 1964, in New York, New York. She moved to England with her family when she was three years old, when her father was sent from the New York City

Maddie and Queenie are stranded when their plane crashes in France. (© Zhukov | Shutterstock.com)

Board of Education to do teacher training in Manchester. At the age of six, Wein traveled with her parents to Jamaica, where her father helped develop a Headstart program, just as he had done in Manchester.

Her father and mother separated in 1973, and Wein and her siblings (a younger brother and sister) returned to the United States with their mother, Carol Flocken. They settled in Harrisburg, Pennsylvania, where Flocken's parents lived. Flocken died in a car accident in 1974, and her parents—Wein's grandparents—raised Wein and her siblings.

Wein attended Yale University and later earned a doctorate in folklore from the University of Pennsylvania in Philadelphia. In 1991, she met Tim Gatland, an Englishman, whom she eventually married. She published her first novel, *The Winter Prince*, in 1993. It was the first in a series of novels about Arthurian legends. In 1995, Wein and her husband moved to England, and in 2000, they moved again to Scotland. Wein, who got her pilot's license in

2003, continues to live and work in Scotland. She published *Code Name Verity* in 2012. She and her husband have two children.

PLOT SUMMARY

Part 1

ORMAIE 8.XI.43–ORMAIE 17.XI.43

Part 1 of the novel is divided into journal-like entries of a confession provided by a British spy, Julia Beaufort-Stuart (whose code name is Verity and who is also known as Queenie) to her Nazi captors. Each section is identified by the city (Ormaie) and the date.

The book opens with Verity's first entry, which explains that she has been captured by the Nazis and is being tortured in a prison situated in an aging French hotel. When she is asked how she can be bribed, she asks for her clothes back. She explains that she has provided pieces of wireless code, one by one, for each piece of

MEDIA ADAPTATIONS

- An unabridged audio version of *Code Name Verity*, published by Audible Audio in 2012, is read by Morven Christie and Lucy Gaskell. Bolinda Audio offers MP3 downloads of the same recording.

clothing. She has made this deal with Captain Hauptstrumführer von Linden, an officer in the Gestapo, the Nazi secret police. As long as Verity writes her story and reveals what she knows about such things as British airfields and the war effort, she will be allowed to remain alive, or so she is promised.

She explains that she was parachuted into German-occupied France, but because of circumstances not yet revealed, she does not have the identification papers that would have allowed her to safely remain in occupied territory. She was captured because she turned the wrong way when looking for traffic (as a British person might, because in England traffic moves in the opposite direction from the rest of Europe). Verity's story includes that of the female pilot who flew the plane that dropped her. Maddie (Margaret Brodatt) becomes an integral part of Verity's story, and the novel as it unfolds is an exploration of their war-forged friendship.

The first part of the story centers on how Maddie became a pilot. In the story, Verity attempts to weave enough legitimate information to buy herself time and to keep von Linden reading. Anna Engel is the civilian woman who serves as von Linden's secretary and who is assigned to make sure Verity keeps writing. She and another officer, Scharführer Etienne Thibaut, supply the intimidation and threats of further torture necessary to compel Verity to continue with her confession.

Maddie, always interested in engines and all things mechanical, helps rescue a female pilot who crashed in a field and subsequently decided

she would like to learn to fly. Verity recounts how Maddie gets her pilot's license and becomes involved in the Women's Auxiliary Air Force. She becomes a radio operator.

Verity recounts the methods she uses to stall when she feels guilty about providing information to the enemy and how torture and pain, or the threat of it, are used to compel her to continue. Though she is supposed to be writing about England's coastal defense program, she uses the opportunity to also convey information about Maddie and her work in range and defense finding. She recounts their first meeting and writes of herself in this encounter in the third person, using her nickname, Queenie. She and Maddie worked together to capture a lost German pilot.

Verity (Queenie) and Maddie become closer friends, admiring each other's strengths. They also, in the middle of an air raid, discuss their fears with each other. Together, they shoot down an enemy plane. In her confession to von Linden, Verity continues to recount her early adventures with Maddie and in doing so attempts to provide the Gestapo captain with information that cannot truly hurt the British but that will seem to him like valuable information. She describes the way she and Maddie were recruited by British intelligence officers. Interspersed into her account of her history with Maddie are pieces of information designed to appease von Linden but also information that appears in the text as underlined. These, as the reader will later find out, are the pieces of information Verity hopes to convey to the British about the layout of the hotel. She also alludes to the torture she endures at the hands of the Gestapo.

Dipping backing into the narrative about Maddie, Verity recounts how Maddie proved herself repeatedly as a pilot and was given increasingly covert and important flights. She works with her former instructor, Dympna Wythenshawe, another female pilot, who helps Maddie secure work as a ferry pilot, moving important personnel in and around England, as part of the civilian-based Air Transport Authority, which Maddie works with in conjunction with her role in the Women's Auxiliary Air Force. At the same time, Queenie, as Verity continues to refer to herself in her narration of the past, becomes part of the Special Operations Executive (SOE)—here her work as a spy begins.

In the present time of Verity's confession writing, she learns what is likely to be her fate. She is to disappear into the "Night and Fog," *Nacht und Nebel*, an expression that means the Germans can do whatever they like with her, as she has endangered security and therefore falls outside of any war crime policies for treatment of enemy combatants and officers. She learns that most likely she will not be executed, but that she will be sent to a concentration camp where she will be the subject of medical experimentation.

In the embedded narrative, Maddie is recommended for special duties flights.

ORMAIE 18.XI.43–ORMAIE 28.XI.43

Having been told that she is to be interviewed by an American radio host, Georgia Penn, for a pro-Nazi propaganda campaign, Verity is being treated slightly better by her captors. She describes Maddie's visit to Scotland, where Maddie spends time in Verity's ancestral home, with Jamie, Verity's brother, who has been wounded in action: he was shot down over the sea and nearly froze to death. He lost all of his toes and some of his fingers to frostbite. At Verity's request, Maddie visited him when he was in the hospital, so seeing him again in Scotland is a reunion for the two. Jamie is caring for some orphaned boys that his mother has taken in.

Verity prepares for her interview and is allowed to put up her hair (with pencil stubs, as she is not allowed to have anything, such as hair pins, that she could use as a weapon). In the interview, Georgia Penn and Verity speak haltingly, because von Linden is also present in the room, and Verity will be tortured if she conveys any information he does not approve of. She is supposed to be representative of the good care the Germans take of their prisoners. When Penn incorporates Verity's code name into the conversation, Verity has an inkling that Penn is not all that she seems—that she in fact is working with the British and attempting to find her. In language designed to convey sensitive information to Penn but not to arouse suspicion in von Linden, Verity communicates as much as she can.

In Verity's confession, she discusses the way Maddie is recruited by a British intelligence officer who originally spoke to both Maddie and Verity and set Verity on her path. Maddie is asked to fly in a special mission, as it turns out, with Verity. Jamie is now flying again as well. The three of them are all at the same airfield. The

same night that Maddie is allowed to tag along on a flight over France, Verity returns to their room covered in bruises and reveals that she is an SOE interrogator. She masquerades as a German double agent and questions captured Germans for the British government. She has been attacked that night and reveals to Maddie that she is known, in this capacity, as Eva Seiler. Despite her bruises, she got the confession from the officer she was interrogating.

When von Linden reads about Eva Seiler, he initially disbelieves Verity. When she encourages a French prisoner, Marie, to lie to avoid torture, he becomes further convinced that this is what Verity has done. Verity gets von Linden to reveal the name of his daughter and tells him that the ease with which she was able to get this information is proof that she is not lying about being Eva Seiler.

When Verity switches back to her narrative, she recounts the events that led her to her current predicament, explaining the way Maddie was to fly her to France. Their plane was shot at, and Verity was forced to parachute to safety. She did not know what happened to Maddie.

Back in the novel's present time of Verity's confession writing, she is taken to witness the beheading of Marie, the French prisoner who lied. She reveals in the confession her real name: Julia Lindsay MacKenzie Wallace Beaufort-Stuart. She alleges that she has told the truth.

Part 2

The narrative switches to Maddie's perspective. Her code name is Kitty Hawk, and she recounts what has happened since the flight into France with Julia. She does not understand why she and Julia have each other's identification papers. Maddie has managed to crash-land the plane. She is greeted by Paul, the SOE operative who was supposed to be Verity's first contact. Maddie explains who she is and is taken into hiding by Paul and members of the French Resistance. A German sentry was killed by the party when they came in search of Verity. The German soldier is subsequently dressed in Maddie's uniform and placed in the plane, which is then incinerated, to make it seem as though the plane has crashed and exploded with its pilot inside.

Maddie is taken to hide in a barn with a family involved in the French Resistance. It is the Thibaut family, and Etienne, who is helping to interrogate Verity, is the brother of Mitraillette, the eldest daughter in the family. Mitraillette explains that Etienne was recruited by the Gestapo and that he knows nothing of their activities. With the French Resistance, Maddie scouts out possible landing sites for British aircraft and learns about bomb making, as she waits for an opportunity to return to England. Etienne unwittingly reveals hints that a British woman is in custody in the hotel the Germans are using for Gestapo headquarters and prison.

Maddie takes on the false identity that would have been Verity's: Katharina Habicht. The Thibaut family explain her presence in their home by telling people she is a distant cousin from Alsace who has come to stay with them. Meanwhile, Jamie turns up as part of the rescue squad sent to retrieve Maddie, but now that they have information regarding Verity's whereabouts, they delay their return to England. They get more information from Georgia Penn, who attempts, through her interviews, to find American, French, and British officers being held by the Germans. The Nazi propaganda radio show is a front for her real mission: finding and aiding in the rescue of Allied officers. Penn shares the information she has gathered about Verity, about her having been tortured, and what Verity managed to convey to her about the hotel. Penn reveals that Julia indicated that Anna Engel, von Linden's secretary, might be close to a "crisis of conscience" and perhaps can be used to their advantage.

Engel does help the French Resistance by bribing von Linden's cleaning lady to steal the manuscript Verity has written. Engel passes it on to Maddie and further provides information about when Verity and other prisoners are being transferred to a concentration camp. Maddie, Paul, Mitraillette, and others in the Resistance attempt a rescue of these prisoners, but the Nazi soldiers transporting them begin to shoot and maim the prisoners. Maddie, hidden with the other Resistance members, begins to weep as their plans go horribly awry, and Julia, hearing her, knows her friend is near. After the soldiers begin shooting other prisoners in the elbows and groin, causing horrific pain but not death, Julia calls out to her friend, and asks Maddie, using the code phrase "Kiss me, Hardy" (a phrase that only they knew the meaning of, as it had come up earlier in their friendship), to kill her so that her suffering could end. Maddie does so.

In the closing of the novel, Maddie and the other Resistance members use the information Julia provided to rescue the remaining prisoners at the hotel and to blow it up. Maddie then returns to England to await her fate. She fears she will be arrested for murder, but upon telling her story, realizes that she will be able to continue to fly.

CHARACTERS

Jamie Beaufort-Stuart

Jamie is Julia's brother. He sustains serious injury after he is shot down over the ocean. Nearly freezing to death, he loses all of his toes and some fingers on each hand. Maddie visits him while he is recovering and sees him again at the family home in Scotland. When he returns to duty, the two are reunited, first at an air base and then in France, when Jamie appears as part of Maddie's rescue team.

Julia Lindsay MacKenzie Wallace Beaufort-Stuart

Julia is known by many names throughout the story. She is the SOE operative known as Verity. In the story she tells about herself, she calls herself Queenie or Scottie. As an interrogator for the SOE, she is known as Eva Seiler. In the beginning of the war, and in the beginning of the narrative she relates, she is a wireless operator. She also knows German and effectively impersonates a German radio operator and helps to capture, along with Maddie's help, an enemy pilot. Her skills do not go unnoticed, and she is recruited for the SOE, working primarily as an interrogator and sometimes as a spy.

In Ormaie, she was to collect architectural plans for the hotel and return with them to England. After she is captured, she deceives her Gestapo captors by pretending to confess her mission to them—concerning wireless codes—but she provides them with false and misleading information. In the end, she accomplishes her mission and is mercifully killed by Maddie before she can be tortured further and experimented on.

Bloody Machiavellian English Intelligence Officer

The SOE officer is never named. He first approaches Julia and Maddie in a pub, when the two, already working in the military, reveal how well they have worked together on and off the air base. Julia is recruited immediately, and Maddie is gradually groomed for future work in the SOE.

Margaret (Maddie) Brodatt

Maddie becomes Julia's best friend. Her code name is Kitty Hawk. Though the two are from entirely different social classes and in peacetime likely would never have met, Maddie and Julia become friends when they work together to successfully talk down and capture a lost German pilot. They admire each other's strengths and complement each other in battle. Once she has crash-landed in France, Maddie takes on the identity of Katharine Habicht, a false identity intended for Julia, because their paperwork is switched. Maddie sees Julia as braver than she is, but in the end, though Julia has endured unspeakable torture, Maddie has to be braver still when she must kill Julia in order to spare her from a fate truly worse than death.

Anna Engel

Anna Engel is a civilian who works as Captain von Linden's secretary. With Thibaut, she is assigned to guard Verity and to compel her to keep writing her confession. Engel also translates the confession into German for von Linden. While Engel is not the primary administer of torture to Verity, she does burn her with cigarettes and hit her. When Verity is interviewed by Georgia Penn, she somehow manages to convey to Penn that Engel's zeal for her job may be waning. Engel is approached by the French Resistance and does in fact attempt to aid them by delivering Verity's manuscript and informing them of the date Verity is to be transported. She later meets with Maddie and conveys her sorrow over Verity's death as well as for what the Germans have done to France.

Katharina Habicht

See Margaret Brodatt

Kitty Hawk

See Margaret Brodatt

Captain Hauptführer Amadeus von Linden

Captain von Linden is the Gestapo officer running the hotel-turned-Nazi-prison in Ormaie, France. He orders the torture of Verity and strikes the deal with her in which she exchanges wireless codes for the return of her clothing. He allows her the time to write down everything she knows about the British war effort in exchange for her continued existence. He displays detachment regarding her torture and completes none of it himself. Verity accuses him of not having the stomach for it.

Von Linden is well read and intrigued by discussing philosophy and literature with Verity, who is well educated herself. He praises her ability to write and comments to his secretary, Anna Engel, about Verity's literary talents. Still, it is von Linden who authorizes Verity's sentencing to a concentration camp dedicated to medical experimentation on live subjects. At the same time, he is warned by his superiors that he should show Verity no leniency, which suggests that perhaps he had advocated on Verity's behalf for a quicker death by execution. It is later reported that he commits suicide, suggesting that he has some remorse for his actions.

Isolde von Linden

Isolde does not appear directly in the novel. She is the school-aged daughter of Captain von Linden and has been sent away to a Swiss school during the war. Verity slyly gets von Linden to reveal his daughter's name and uses this information to prey on his conscience.

Marie

Marie is the French girl whom the Gestapo is torturing in the prison where Julia is being held. Her screams are also torture for Julia, who begs the girl to lie, to do something to end her own suffering. Eventually, she and Julia are tied together and escorted to the courtyard, where Marie is beheaded.

Paul

Paul is an SOE operative working in France and aiding the French Resistance, French civilians attempting to thwart the Nazi security forces and to end the German occupation of France. He is described as lecherous in his advances toward Maddie. He dies after he and his group blow up a bridge and attempt to rescue Julia and other prisoners the Nazis are transporting.

Georgia Penn

Georgia Penn is an American who announces a radio show allegedly for the purposes of pro-Nazi propaganda. However, she uses this position as a front to gather information about

Allied prisoners of war being held by the Nazis. With von Linden, she arranges to interview Verity and during their conversation garners information about Verity, the hotel, von Linden, and his staff. The French Resistance members ultimately use this information to destroy the hotel.

Queenie
See Julia Beaufort-Stuart

Scottie
See Julia Beaufort-Stuart

Eva Seiler
See Julia Beaufort-Stuart

Mitraillette Thibaut
Mitraillette Thibaut, whose real name is Gabrielle-Thérèse (*Mitraillette* means "submachine gun"), is a member of the French Resistance. Maddie lives with the Thibaut family for a time and pretends to be their cousin from Alsace. Mitraillette is part of the group that attempts to rescue Julia, and she leads them after Paul's death.

Etienne Thibaut
Etienne Thibaut is a young Frenchman who has been recruited by the Gestapo. He works as a scharführer, a squad leader, at the prison where Verity is being held, while the rest of his family is involved in the French Resistance movement.

Verity
See Julia Beaufort-Stuart

Dympna Wythenshawe
Dympna is a female pilot who crash-lands in a field and is rescued by Maddie, who is subsequently inspired to learn to fly. Dympna serves as her instructor for a time and also advises her on available positions within the civilian Air Transport Authority. She is both an inspiration to Maddie and pivotal to her career as a pilot.

THEMES

Friendship
In *Code Name Verity*, the friendship between Maddie and Julia forms the heart of the novel. Although the story addresses the strength of these women and their roles in the war effort, Maddie and Julia form a bond rooted in mutual respect. Julia acknowledges that without the war, the two might not have ever met, and even their meeting within the context of the war was a random event. Yet they do meet when they are called upon to work together to help navigate a lost German pilot into their air base.

The two young women spend time later in a bunker, discussing their worst fears and getting to know each other. Not long after, they shoot down an enemy plane together, before taking some time off to go to the pub. Their adventures on the way there, with Maddie trying to teach Julia about finding her way and Julia pretending she is a German spy, inspire an SOE officer to keep an eye on them both and to soon recruit Julia and, later, Maddie.

Though they work well together, they do not actually have very many opportunities to do so. Whenever their paths cross at various airfields, however, they make the most of their time together. By 1943, they are recruited to work together on a mission into France. Their plane is hit, however, and Maddie miraculously is able to land the plane without killing herself in the process, though she makes Julia parachute to safety first.

Before long, Julia is captured for looking the wrong way before crossing the street. She is captured and taken into custody by the Nazis, specifically, their secret police, the Gestapo. She does not have her identification papers and instead has Maddie's. This mix-up in the paperwork is never explained, though it is possible that once Julia realized Maddie was going to have to try to land the plane alone, she switched their papers so that Maddie, a Jewish British pilot crash-landing in Nazi-occupied France, would have a better chance at survival with the identification papers in the name of Katherine Habicht, which is Julia's cover identity. Her friendship and love for Maddie compelled her to give Maddie a chance at survival if she was able to land the plane; Julia compromised her own chances at survival in the process. Even with the mistake of looking the wrong way, she likely would have been able to talk herself out of the situation had she had the proper paperwork. Without it, she found herself in the Nazi prison.

While imprisoned, Julia stays strong, even in the face of the torture she endures, largely because of the memory of her friendship with

TOPICS FOR FURTHER STUDY

- During World War II, Nazi Germany attacked and occupied a number of countries, capturing, imprisoning, and killing most of the Jewish population of those countries in the process. Research the movements of the Nazi army during World War II. Create a map—either as a poster or in an electronic format—in which you describe and trace the advancement of the German army. Provide dates of significant battles and the surrender of various countries.

- Joseph Bruchac's young-adult novel *Code Talker: A Novel about the Navajo Marines of World War Two*, published in 2005, tackles the subject of the war from the perspective of Native Americans recruited to send messages in a code considered unbreakable, as it was derived from their native Navajo language. Read Bruchac's novel and consider the ways in which the government made use of a marginalized group of individuals and in what ways they exploited them. Write an essay in which you provide a summary of the plot, characters, and themes of the novel and discuss the contribution of the Navajo code talkers to the war effort.

- Much has been written about the French Resistance movement during World War II. Carla Jablonski and Leland Purvis's young-adult graphic novel *Resistance: Book 1* focuses on the role in the Resistance of two French children whose father has been captured by the Germans and whose Jewish friend goes into hiding after his parents disappear. With a small group, read *Resistance* and explore the way war and the Resistance movement is treated in this format. Create an online blog you can use as a forum to discuss your ideas about the work and its subject matter.

- *I Have Lived a Thousand Years* is a memoir written by Livia Bitton-Jackson, a survivor of the Nazi death camp at Auschwitz. Originally published in 1997 by Simon and Schuster Books for Young Readers, the memoir details the author's experiences of being captured by the Nazis and taken to the concentration camp. While reading the memoir, consider the ways in which the author and her family attempted to cope with what was happening to them. Write a reader-response essay in which you describe your feelings about what the author conveyed and the means by which she conveyed it (as memoir). Consider what you learned about the war, about Adolf Hitler's agenda, about the Allied forces and their efforts to rescue the Jews from concentration camps. Did your understanding of this aspect of the war shift after reading the memoir? In what ways? How would you characterize your overall reaction to the book? Did reading it inspire you to research this topic further?

Maddie. Julia is sure of her mission, but it is her friendship that gives her comfort, if not hope. She becomes increasingly fearful of the type of death she will likely face at the hands of the Nazis, and it is Maddie who saves her from further torture.

The ultimate test of Maddie and Julia's friendship occurs during the rescue attempt. The Nazi soldiers make it clear that they have no intention of giving in, that for each Nazi life the Resistance members take, the Nazis will kill or maim one of the prisoners, and the Resistance members hesitate. Maddie weeps, and Julia hears her. When Julia shouts, "Kiss me, Hardy," Maddie knows what she must do, and she shoots Julia in order to spare her a fate of horrendous torture. (The "Kiss me, Hardy," line is referred to earlier in the novel, when Maddie and Julia are shooting down the German plane, and Maddie is distraught. Julia quotes the line and explains that those were the last words that

Queenie strives not be noticed in Nazi-occupied France. (© *A_Lesik / Shutterstock.com*)

the British Admiral Lord Nelson said to Sir Thomas Hardy during the Battle of Trafalgar just before his death.) Maddie must summon all of her courage in order to help her friend die a better death, heartbroken that she cannot save her.

While their friendship is inspired by mutual respect and is sustained by an easy companionship, it ultimately is the trust between the two friends that is tested. They spend a great deal of their time together discussing their fears, though Maddie often believes Julia is afraid of nothing. Yet when Julia essentially begs for her life, Maddie knows she is truly terrified of the fate that awaits. Subsequently she has to face her own worst fears, of letting down her friend, of being unable to follow orders, and of being court-martialed, in order to end her friend's suffering.

World War II, 1939–1945

The war is not just the backdrop for the novel. Wein comments on the war and the way it transforms people and their relationships. She does this not only through the drama of the physical torture that Julia endures but also through subtle effects, such as the use of the various types of paper—that confiscated from Jewish prisoners, for example—upon which Julia writes her confession. In this way, she hints at loss, the way so many individuals were taken away and killed, their belongings used or destroyed. In the way the Jews are treated and in the way that Julia sees herself, Wein underscores the way people are dehumanized by war.

The Jews are treated like vermin to be exterminated. They are quite literally viewed by the Nazis as less than people. Julia sees herself similarly, regarding herself as a wireless set, a *thing* that transmits *information* and nothing more. She feels that this is how von Linden sees her, and she remarks that none of the individuals who torture her seem phased by what they are doing. It is a job; she is a lump of flesh to them. Even prior to her capture, in the way that Julia takes on different identities depending on the dictates of her job, because she can become whoever who superiors need her to be, she seems to have difficulty feeling that she is the strong and specific *someone* those close to her, like Maddie, see her as.

Wein emphasizes further that the war takes people apart. She accomplishes this through specific references to gruesome images—for example, Marie's beheading, Jamie's loss of toes and fingers, and the dismemberment of Julia's fellow prisoners during the rescue effort. Wein also clearly intends to convey the way war takes people apart emotionally. After Julia's remains are finally allowed to be buried, Maddie asserts that part of her heart will always be buried back in France with her beloved friend. There is an enduring sense of fracture, of the loss not just of innocence but also of identity and wholeness.

STYLE

Confessional Structure

Code Name Verity is divided into two parts. The first is structured as Verity's confession to the Gestapo officer, von Linden. Within this is embedded a second narrative, the story of Maddie and Julia's friendship, which Julia writes in the third person, using her nickname, Queenie, for herself. This gives the narrative depth and complexity because it incorporates the novel's first-person narrative of Julia's confession with her past third-person recounting of her developing friendship with Maddie.

The confession itself is penned as a journal or diary, with each entry headed by the date, all in November of 1943. The confession is written first on hotel stationery and then, as paper becomes increasingly scarce, on the prescription pad of a Jewish doctor, on pilfered recipe cards from the hotel's kitchen, and on sheet music once owned by a Jewish flautist. These various materials on which Julia writes underscore and symbolize the tragedies of the war—from the French hotel being occupied and transformed into a place of suffering, pain, and imprisonment

to the Jewish doctor and musician whose belongings were confiscated by the Nazis and whose fate was most likely grim. By employing such details as the physical paper upon which Julia pens her confession, Wein tells the story of the war, in addition to the twin narratives Julia is already creating.

The second part of the novel is told in third person from Maddie's perspective. In this way, it serves as her confession, too, especially after she reveals the circumstances that led her to shoot Julia. She fears that she will face murder charges upon her return to England (she does not), and in her detailed and unflinching recounting of events, her portion of the novel, written first in her flight notebook and then on materials she finds in Etienne's room, very much serves the purpose of a confession, mirroring Julia's writings.

Reliability of the Narrator

The primary difference between the two narratives/confessions, however, is in the reliability of the women writing them. Maddie attempts, in her straightforward and guileless fashion, to convey truthfully what occurred during the mission, and her role in the way things transpired. Her audience is herself—she writes to keep herself busy and focused during the time in which she is hidden away in the barn—and for her superiors back in England, for whom she wants to record the events as they happen.

Julia, on the other hand, writes for a different audience and a different purpose. Julia, like Maddie, also writes in part for herself. It calms her and gives her comfort to think of and talk about Maddie. Yet she also seeks to buy time and to provide enough information to von Linden that seems reliable in order to keep herself alive while she attempts to carry out her mission. Simultaneously, she seeks to incorporate enough details within the document so that she can, in fact, carry out the mission and provide the British with the information they need to rescue the prisoners in the hotel-turned-Nazi-prison and then destroy it.

Although she does not live to see the destruction of the place where she suffered so much, Julia does accomplish her goal. Engel becomes increasingly weary of the Nazi tactics and agenda and attempts to aid Julia by telling the French Resistance of her transfer to the concentration camp and, more important, by getting the "confession" into the hands of the

COMPARE
&
CONTRAST

- **1940s:** Women are recruited by the British government for a variety of war-related activities, from piloting transport and military flights, to espionage, to assisting the French Resistance. These war efforts represent a dramatic increase in the types of positions women are allowed since World War I.

  Today: Officially, Great Britain does not allow women to serve in combat roles; an exclusion ban exists, yet British women do serve as fighter pilots and submariners. The official stance prohibits women from serving in close ground combat.

- **1940s:** The French government experiences turmoil, terror, and transition as they face German invasion and occupation, followed by liberation by Allied forces. Control of the country is transferred from Philippe Pétain, the premier of France, who signs an armistice in 1940 with Germany The unoccupied portion of France becomes known as the French State, run by the Vichy government, while the rest of France, the occupation zone, is under German military (Nazi) control. General Charles de Gaulle becomes

president of the provisional government in the aftermath of the war.

Today: France is currently led by Prime Minister Manuel Valls; President François Hollande is the chief of state. As a republic, France is governed by the prime minister and a council of ministers appointed by the president, at the prime minister's suggestion, and by a two-house parliament.

- **1940s:** The British Special Operations Executive is organized in the aftermath of Germany's invasion of France with the mission to sabotage the efforts of the Nazi army in occupied France and later in targets all over the world. The SOE quickly establishes headquarters in London and recruits men and women as agents. After the war, the SOE is absorbed into the British Secret Intelligence Service, or SIS.

  Today: The SOE no longer exists. Its records from the war have been edited for security purposes and released to the United Kingdom National Archive.

Resistance members who use the information contained in it—information to which Engel herself draws attention—to demolish the hotel. At the end of Julia's confession, she affirms repeatedly that she has told the truth—and she has told the truth, about her relationship with Maddie and about the information she needs to convey to the British.

However, from the very beginning, Verity's truthfulness is in question. She opens the novel by stating she is a coward and reveals that she gave up wireless code in order to get her clothes back. Yet the code she provided was false, and in the end she died a hero's death. She intends to mislead the Gestapo, and as she leads von Linden away from the truth of what she is trying to accomplish, so too does she lead the novel's

reader. Like Marie, the French girl being tortured, the reader initially sees Julia as the coward she claims to be. She gives up secrets, while Marie endures unbearable torture. Yet as the novel unfolds, Verity is increasingly likable, despite the fact that the truth about her motives remains hidden for the bulk of her section of the novel.

HISTORICAL CONTEXT

The French Resistance during World War II

Britain and France declared war on Germany in September 1939, after Hitler invaded Poland. The following May, the Nazis began to advance toward France. They were opposed by French and Belgian military, aided by British forces. By early June, however, the Germans invaded Paris, and the government surrendered by late June 1940.

The French Resistance was born then. Those who opposed the German occupation sought to thwart the efforts of the Nazis in whatever ways they could, through both violent and nonviolent means. In 1941, the British SOE began sending agents to France in order to aid Resistance organizations, which were successfully able to sabotage German security force activities and to damage German installations. Captured Resistance members were typically imprisoned, tortured, executed, or sent to concentration camps. Still, the British continued to supply the Resistance members with weapons, and the French continued to fight. The Resistance movement grew stronger and more powerful.

In 1943, as a US-led Allied invasion of France became increasingly likely, the Americans, like their British counterparts, also began to aid the French Resistance. The US Office of Strategic Services (OSS) cooperated with the British SOE to provide weapons and agents on the ground in German-occupied France. French Resistance groups, united under the leadership of Charles de Gaulle, worked with the British and the Americans to set the stage for Resistance support of an Allied invasion in August of 1944. The Allies dropped propaganda leaflets and parachuted supplies to the Resistance fighters. Allied forces approached Paris by mid-August, including US Army forces. Paris was liberated on August 25, 1944. De Gaulle then asked that Resistance groups disband and join the new French army.

British Women in World War II

As Great Britain entered World War II, the government made a move to incorporate women more fully into the war effort than they had been during World War I. Women became part of such groups as the military organization known as the Women's Land Army (in which women were trained for agricultural work in order to free up male farmers for active war service) or civil defense services such as Air Raid Precautions and Women's Voluntary Services.

Although many women began doing mostly clerical work, their roles expanded as the

Commander von Linden holds Queenie in an old hotel and tortures her for information.
(© Matt Gibson / Shutterstock.com)

nation's military needs increased. In 1938, the Auxiliary Territorial Service was formed in order to employ female volunteers for driving and clerical duties, but a year later they were serving in France with British expeditionary forces. They also served in an anti-aircraft capacity as searchlight operators. Women were allowed to join the newly formed Women's Royal Naval Service in 1939; the women on WRNS ships were involved in the plans for the occupation of France.

Also in 1939, the Women's Auxiliary Air Force was created. Some worked with the SOE and parachuted into enemy-occupied territory, such as German-occupied France, to work as radio operators and to help the French Resistance movement. A civil organization known as the Air Transport Auxiliary (ATA) employed American and British women to ferry aircraft and personnel in Britain. Not only did they serve the vital purpose of moving key personnel to where they were needed and transporting aircraft in need of repair to their destinations, they also freed male pilots to serve in combat missions. The ATA included a total of 166 female pilots; twenty were killed in service during the war.

CRITICAL OVERVIEW

Code Name Verity was generally well received by critics. A reviewer for *Kirkus* describes the novel as both "heartbreaking" and "a carefully researched, precisely written tour de force; unforgettable and wrenching." A more in-depth review from Mary Quattlebaum of the *Washington Post* offers a brief overview of the plot and admires Wein's skill with incorporating "intriguing backstories, and allusions to J. M. Barrie's 'Peter Pan.'" Quattlebaum praises the work as a "heart-in-your-mouth adventure" that "has it all: a complex plot, a vivid sense of place and time, and resonant themes of friendship and courage." Marjorie Ingall, reviewing the novel for the *New York Times*, applauds the work as "a fiendishly plotted mind game of a novel." Ingall goes on to discuss the work's themes, noting it "is a rare young adult novel entirely about female power and female friendship, with only the faintest whiff of cute-boy romance." Despite the praise Ingall heaps upon the novel, she does observe that the book will likely be more appealing to adults than its intended teenage/young-adult audience, as the scenes of torture are "fairly graphic, and the period detail is dense." She goes on to note also that, in general, teens will be unlikely to get the more obscure literary and historical references.

CRITICISM

Catherine Dominic

Dominic is a novelist and a freelance writer and editor. In the following essay, she examines the metafictional elements of Code Name Verity *as a means of exploring the significance of the theme of storytelling in the novel.*

Early on in *Code Name Verity*, after Julia has just begin writing about herself in the third person as "Queenie" and after she records how Queenie and Maddie met, Julia pokes fun at Anna Engel's inability to understand her approach to her

> THROUGH THIS SCENE, WEIN ALERTS THE READER TO THE NOVEL'S TENDENCY TOWARD METAFICTION AND CONSEQUENTLY TO THE IDEA AND THE PURPOSE OF STORYTELLING."

"confession." She clarifies this by transcribing the exchange between von Linden and Engel, in which Engel irately insists "she must be commanded to write of the meeting between Brodatt and herself. This description of early Radar operations is irrelevant nonsense." Before explaining that Julia has actually completed this description already, that she is, in fact, Queenie, von Linden chides his assistant, telling Engel, "you are not a student of literature. . . . The English flight officer has studied the craft of the novel. She is making use of suspense and foreshadowing." Engel retorts, "She is not writing a novel. She is making a report." Undeterred, von Linden replies to Engel, "she is employing the literary conceits and techniques of a novel."

This self-reflexive moment is a significant one, because Wein draws attention to the fact that the document Julia is writing, is, in fact (as von Linden points out), a novel—that is, Wein's novel. It is as if, for a moment, a character—von Linden—is referencing the author who created him when he points out that "she is making use of suspense and foreshadowing. . . . She is employing the literary conceits and techniques of a novel." Although obviously it is the character Julia who is writing the document that von Linden refers to, his description of it as a *novel* and her composing the document as a *novel* points to the deliberate decision Wein made to construct her work so that one character's supposedly first-person confession reads like a third-person novel about a wartime friendship between two women.

Arguably, this may be seen as a contrivance that provides great opportunity for reader frustration or distraction. There are times, for example, that Verity is describing, through Maddie's viewpoint, experiences that Maddie had without her, that she could hardly have first-hand knowledge of. She takes the liberties of an omniscient

WHAT DO I READ NEXT?

- Wein's novel *Rose under Fire*, published in 2013, like *Code Name Verity*, explores the experiences of a female pilot during World War II. In this novel, it is an American pilot, Rose Justice, who is captured by the Nazis and sent to a women's concentration camp.

- L. M. Elliot's 2001 novel, *Under a War-Torn Sky*, focuses on the fate of a World War II pilot shot down over France. It is a young-adult novel targeted at a younger audience than Wein's novel. Like *Code Name Verity*, the interaction between the pilot and the French Resistance fighters reveals the spirit and hope and determination of Allied forces and European citizens fighting the oppression of the Nazis.

- Roald Dahl, author of many beloved children's classics, such as *Charlie and the Chocolate Factory* and *James and the Giant Peach*, served as a pilot during World War II. In *Going Solo*, published in 1986, Dahl writes of his adventures during his years of war service.

- *Weedflower*, a young-adult novel published in 2006 by Cynthia Kadohata, examines the experiences of Sumiko, a Japanese American girl whose is forced, along with her family, to live in an internment camp with other Japanese prisoners during World War II. The camp is on a Native American reservation. Both Sumiko and the Mohave boy she meets have the shared experience of being unwanted and restricted by the American government.

- *Code Name Pauline: Memoirs of a World War II Special Agent* (2013), by Pauline Witherington Cornioley, is a memoir written for young adults. In it, the author describes her escape from France in 1940 and her subsequent recruitment and training as a special agent for the British SOE. When the leader of her French Resistance outfit was captured by the Gestapo, the author took command of 3,500 Resistance fighters.

- R. G. Grant's *World War II* is a young-adult resource designed to offer an overview of the war, from the political complexities leading up to the war to the way it unfolded across Europe and beyond. It also provides first-hand accounts from soldiers as well as families left behind. The volume was published in 2008 by DK Children.

---

narrator here, creating thoughts and exchanges that Maddie may have told her about but that she herself was not actually there to witness. Nevertheless, the conceit works effectively enough; it is not criticized by reviewers, who offer high praise for the work.

Because Wein does not maintain the self-reflexivity of the exchange in which von Linden regards Verity's writing as a novel throughout the entire work, it would be inaccurate to describe the novel as a whole as metafiction. Metafiction is fiction that draws attention to itself as fiction, to its own conventions, to its own composition. Certainly, though, the scene described here may be understood as a metafictional moment within a work that has other self-reflexive moments, and by incorporating this scene, Wein draws the reader's attention to the idea of writing, of storytelling. Through this scene, Wein alerts the reader to the novel's tendency toward metafiction and consequently to the idea and the purpose of storytelling.

Why does Julia create a novel—with "suspense and foreshadowing" and "literary conceits and techniques of a novel"—out of her confession? Why does she not simply list code, however dated or faulty, and air base names and locations, however contrived? The answer is complex. The most obvious answer is that Julia is writing for her life. With each day, she buys herself time, time to find a way to complete her mission. She does not expect to escape with her life, but as long as she is alive, there is a shred of hope that she may do so. Additionally, the more complexity she adds to her work, the more believable her web of deceit is likely to be. A list of fabricated facts is less convincing than a human story constructed on the foundation of those "facts." What she writes about herself and Maddie and the way their friendship developed is true, as are the encoded messages for the British about the hotel's layout and design and the habits of the Nazis who run the prison.

Central to the reader's understanding of the novel, however, is the ability to grasp the true reason why Julia writes about her friendship with Maddie in the way that she does. Telling stories, telling *her* story, and Maddie's story, is what enables Julia to survive as long as she does, long enough to get out the information she needs to convey, although ultimately she must leave the document the British will need in the hands of Engel, whom Julia hopes will collaborate. Julia reflects that until von Linden points it out, she had not even realized she was writing about herself in the third person. She maintains, initially, that she is "telling the story from Maddie's point of view, and it would be awkward to introduce another viewpoint character at this point."

However, Julia goes on to say that it is much easier to write about herself in this way than if she attempted to tell her own story from her point of view. "I can avoid all my old thoughts and feelings. It's a superficial way to write about myself," she states. Superficial perhaps, but revealing at the same time. Julia possesses enough self-awareness to realize that there are many thoughts and feelings she'd like to avoid contemplating. She feels as though she is no longer that person she is writing about. "I suppose," she says, "the real answer is that I am not Queenie anymore.... I am someone else now." The fact of her transformation is painful and terrifying. She realizes how much she took for granted in the early days of her friendship with Maddie, how easy it was to be "so earnest and self-righteous and flamboyantly heroic." Julia does not feel that way now. She tells the story of her friendship with Maddie, and she tells it the way she does, in order *to feel better*. Quite simply, stories provide comfort.

Sometimes they comfort through familiarity, as when Julia fondly remembers her early relationship with Maddie, and sometimes they comfort through distance, as when Julia loses herself in her cover story as Eva Seiler when she interrogates German prisoners. She is a storyteller at heart, and when her narrative is interrupted with her current reality, Julia falters. After she is shown the pictures of the burnt cockpit of the plane she and Maddie flew to France in, Julia grows fearful that Maddie has perished. "Oh Maddie," she thinks:

> I am lost. I have lost the thread. I was indulging myself in details as if they were wool blankets or alcohol, escaping wholly back into the fire-and-water-filled early days of our friendship. We made a *sensational* team. I was so sure she'd landed safely.

Here Julia confesses what telling the story of her friendship with Maddie has meant to her; it is escape, it is comfort, and as the novel progresses, it becomes increasingly difficult for Julia to lose herself this way, as the prospect of her own fate—to be sent to a concentration camp—draws near, and as the possibility that Maddie has not survived closes in on her.

Yet she continues to find some relief when she thinks of her friendship with Maddie and tells their story. Coming to the end of a period in which she is allowed to write, Julia pens, "I am out of time again—hell. I was enjoying myself." Wein's incorporation of the *Peter Pan* story into her narrative emphasizes the way Julia views storytelling—as escape. J. M. Barrie's character Peter Pan, a boy who never grew up, appeared in a stage play in 1904 and in the novel *Peter and Wendy* in 1911. Peter Pan lives in Neverland, where he is permanently a youth and has adventures with the group of Lost Boys that he leads. In one adventure, they fight the pirate Captain Hook.

Throughout *Code Name Verity*, Wein makes reference to the story of Peter Pan. Julia compares von Linden to Captain Hook and herself to Peter Pan. She states early in the novel,

> Von Linden resembles Captain Hook in that he is rather an upright sort of gentleman in spite of his being a brute, and I am quite Pan-like in my naïve confidence that he will play by the rules and keep his word.

She likes the idea of escaping not just into her own story but also into the Pan myth, where she can associate herself, with some relief, blithely with a brash yet naïve child. Later in

Queenie's confession tells the story of her friendship with Maddie. *(© djem | Shutterstock.com)*

the novel, Julia describes the night before the flight to France. She recalls Maddie and her brother, Jamie, in front of the fire, perusing maps. The SOE has incorporated the Peter Pan myth as part of their code, broadcasting a message on BBC Radio to tell the "reception committee in France whom to expect that night. It is the first line of *Peter Pan*. 'All children, except one, grow up.'"

The myth has been appropriated by the British government to serve the war effort, and in a way solidifies not just Julia's self-identification with Pan but also her fate. She will be the only one (of the three of them in the room that night) who will not grow up or, at least, not grow any older. The Pan myth here is used by Wein to foreshadow as well as to underscore the idea of storytelling. The British government uses the story of Pan both to convey information and to obfuscate—both to reveal truth and to hide it. Julia uses storytelling in the same way, and Wein repeatedly draws attention to this with her Pan allusions and her nods toward metafiction.

Source: Catherine Dominic, Critical Essay on *Code Name Verity*, in *Novels for Students*, Gale, Cengage Learning, 2016.

Deirdre Baker and Elizabeth Wein

In the following interview, Wein discusses the significance of flight in her novels.

Author Elizabeth Wein is also a pilot, and her two most recent novels, *Code Name Verity* and *Rose Under Fire*, feature young female pilots who ferry aircraft for Britain's Air Transport Auxiliary during World War II. When Elizabeth was in Toronto recently for a book tour, she invited me to join her on a flight in a WWII plane—a Lysander, the same kind Maddie flies in *Code Name Verity* (Rose, in *Rose Under Fire*, flies mainly Tempests and Spitfires). Alas, the flight was cancelled. Instead, we had a conversation about Elizabeth's work.

Deirdre F. Baker: You've made quite a chronological leap in the subject matter of your novels, roaming from The Winter Prince, *inspired by medieval Welsh folklore and The Mabinogion; on to further Arthurian adventures set in sixth-century Ethiopia, or Aksum, in* A Coalition of

YOU CAN COME BACK TO FRIENDSHIP.

YOU CAN LET IT DROP, FOR FIVE YEARS OR

TEN YEARS, AND COME BACK TO IT."

Lions, The Sunbird, *and sequels; and now to books set during World War II. Can you talk a little about the connections between the stories?*

Elizabeth Wein: People sometimes ask me, "Why do you write such different books? Why did you go from settings in sixth-century Britain and Ethiopia to Europe in World War II?" But they're not so different, really. *The Sunbird* is a spy novel about a person who is captured, tortured, and enslaved, and he figures out what's going on and brings down the regime. It's essentially the same plot as *Code Name Verity*, with a heroic character—but set in a different time and place.

DFB: How do you see the protagonists and the nature of heroism developing in your stories?

EW: I think as readers we put ourselves in the protagonist's place because we want to be like that person. That's why sometimes we don't like protagonists who aren't all that nice; we want to relate to the protagonist. But with a heroic character like Telemakos in *The Sunbird*, I feel I want to be able to rise to the occasion; I want to be able to solve the mystery and endure the torture and not give any of my secrets away and maintain my identity throughout it all. I want to be like that. But I don't know whether I'd be able to or not, and that's something *Code Name Verity* and *Rose Under Fire* explore. I've tried to look at different kinds of heroism in these books. My previous heroes are all pretty straightforward: they're strong, heroic characters. So is Verity, but you don't know that at first: you are presented with someone who has collapsed under pressure and appears to be a Nazi collaborator; you don't really know what's going on with her. Maddie's is a different kind of bravery, and then Rose's is another. There are many kinds. My favorite example is in *Little House on the Prairie*, when Ma is sitting in the rocking chair holding baby Carrie, and fireballs—ball lightning—come down the chimney and roll across the cabin, and one of them

rolls under Ma's skirts. "Mary couldn't move, she was so scared. Laura was too scared to think." So Laura runs and pulls the rocking chair away, but it's not like she's consciously being brave; it's just that she has to do something. I think maybe what the difference is between my earlier books and the later ones is that I've started exploring the concept of bravery and the forms it can take.

DFB: Rose Under Fire is set, partially, in the Ravensbrück women's concentration camp, where heinous medical experiments were performed on prisoners dubbed "Rabbits." Can you tell me a little about doing the research for Rose Under Fire?

EW: I do my research the same way for every book I write. I start with books; I do the reading. One of the great things about doing research this way is all the bibliographies you find, which put you on to other stuff. What I started with for *Rose Under Fire* was a big stack of survivor autobiographies. I had a representative sample of several different nations. I had one German woman; a couple of French women; one was a Polish woman who hadn't been one of the "Rabbits" and one was a Polish woman who had; one of them was a countess and an intellectual working for a Catholic university in Poland; one was a student; one was a Resistance worker; one was a Communist. And there was a Dutch woman as well. So there was a real mix there. At first I was very reluctant to read the survivor accounts. I didn't know what I would find, and I was apprehensive about the magnitude of the horror I expected to encounter.

So I was very much surprised by the amount of hope that I found in their stories, how uplifting they were, and how personal; how individual the voices of these survivors were. One of my favorite accounts is by a French woman named Micheline Maurel, who includes a lot of her own poetry in her autobiography. She has such a wonderful sense of self-parody; she's able to step outside and look at herself and be a little bit mocking. She was imprisoned in Neubrandenburg (which is one of Ravensbrück's satellite camps and figures tangentially in *Rose Under Fire*). Maurel says it was worse than Ravensbrück: at Ravensbrück, the guards processed all the stuff they took from the arriving prisoners, so you had a chance to get hold of cigarettes and pencil stubs and bits and pieces of fabric. At Neubrandenburg you had nothing but your prison uniform and the bowl they issued you. It was a very hard life. Maurel worked in a factory making these little bits of springs and wire, and she didn't really know what they were for, but everyone assumed that they were for weapons (just as in *Rose Under Fire*, Rose is assigned to a factory making electrical relays for bomb fuses). On her way out of the factory every day Maurel would reach into the bins where they had been putting all the parts that they had made that day, and she would grab handfuls of them and stuff them in her pockets. She would walk out and then she would scatter them in the woods on her walk back to camp—this was her one act of defiance.

Rose, when she first turns up at Ravensbrück, is more angry than scared. I got that also from Micheline Maurel: she said she used to sit working in the factory feeling rage. She'd been working for the Resistance; she'd been fighting against the enemy; and now she was doing this stupid, pointless factory work. Meanwhile, the war was going on without her. So the accounts gave me lots of different perspectives; it wasn't all fear and terror and horror. There was a lot of other stuff going on. And of course there were friendships and companionships that people were forming that sustained them.

DFB: You bring the Girl Guides into your story. I was very interested to learn that there was a whole company of Girl Guides in Ravensbrück.

EW: That's right. They were Polish Girl Guides who were involved in Resistance work. I knew that the local unit of Girl Guides within the camp helped to save some of the records at Ravensbrück from being destroyed, and I thought, That is really cool; I must bring that into the story. And of course making Rose a Girl Scout created a parallel between her existence in the U.S. as an ordinary American teen and the people she meets who have been involved in the war effort.

DFB: There's a gulf between the naiveté and protectedness of the American Girl Scout Rose and the level of risk involved for the Polish Girl Guides, like Róyczka. It's very effective; you create a powerful sense of the girl Rose living in a bubble.

EW: Recently I have learned about a book called *How the Girl Guides Won the War*. It has a chapter devoted to all the kinds of different activities the Girl Guides and Girl Scouts were doing throughout the world during World War II.

American Girl Scouts were saving tinfoil; British Girl Guides were on patrol looking for flying bombs; and Polish Girl Guides were risking their lives acting as couriers and smuggling explosives for the Resistance.

DFB: I wonder if you could discuss the themes of flight, poetry, and survival, which are all interrelated in Rose Under Fire.

EW: I mentioned Micheline Maurel's poetry; she felt that her ability to write poetry actually saved her life at Neubrandenburg, because she was taken up by a Czech girl who really, really loved poetry. The French were never allowed to get care packages, and a lot of the survival of prisoners depended on receiving such packages. Families sent them bread and sausages and cheese, but the French prisoners weren't allowed to have any, and the Czechs were. It was all based on national borders and on how much at war you were with the Nazis and whether or not they considered you a race to be exterminated, and so on. The Dutch also, I believe, were allowed care packages; the Norwegians were spared having their heads shaved because they were so tall and blonde. So there were variations in the restrictions and treatment. Maurel's Czech friend was getting regular supplies of extra food and shared it with Maurel in exchange for poetry, so I was very much aware going into writing this book that the ability to recite and compose poetry could actually save your life. That's why I wanted Rose to write poetry, but also because I found Maurel's poetry really moving. It was so much a part of the retelling of her experience that I wanted to use it in *Rose Under Fire* as well.

As for the metaphor of flight—Rose's development as a poet is based partly on the fact that she's a devotee of the work of Edna St. Vincent Millay, and some of her poems are quoted throughout the book. The epigraph is a very short Millay poem called "To a Young Poet," and it's about flight, so it seemed appropriate. Poetry, flight—that is what Rose does. And the sky! All the Ravensbrück prisoners say this: that the sky was the one thing that really represented freedom to them, because it was always changing; it was moving and dynamic. And of course there's the end of the book where Rose is describing the principles of flight and she says that you have to have lift in your life; you have to be buoyed up by things; and sometimes you have to be thrust forward into new things . . . so there again you have the metaphor of flight.

DFB: The association of flying and writing evokes the expression "flights of the imagination," which implies relinquishing control and letting the mind soar. That's how some people might think flying and writing are related—however, it seems that for you, a pilot, flying is not a matter of release and freedom but of close attention and intense focus.

EW: Yes, flying is hard for me. It doesn't come naturally. I haven't been doing it since I was twelve, like Rose; I've only been doing it since I was thirty-seven. I have to work at it. When I'm in the air I'm really, really concentrating on flying the plane.

DFB: The kind of poetry Rose writes is very tightly structured and has quite defined rhyme and rhythm patterns. So writing it would be a bit like flying a plane, with all its strict protocols and complicated instruments.

EW: Yes! Rose's poetry—partly it is more tightly structured because she is writing it in 1944, and although some people were writing more unstructured poetry, she was raised on Edna St. Vincent Millay and Rupert Brooke. She quotes some William Carlos Williams, so she's aware that there's other stuff out there, and indeed a couple of her poems are free verse as well; but she's clearly a bit of a traditionalist.

DFB: One of the elements I like in all your stories, and it's especially noticeable in Code Name Verity *and* Rose Under Fire, *is how you don't succumb to romance.*

EW: I quite purposefully try to subvert that. There's a lot of romance out there; we don't have to read it all the time, as a steady diet. There are other aspects to the world. In *Rose Under Fire* in particular there's a subverted romance. That again was driven by Micheline Maurel—she had a sweetheart who was an RAF pilot. She was in prison for two years, and the thought of her pilot helped sustain her. But he went and married someone else: after all, Maurel disappeared for two years, and he must have assumed she was dead. Not every whirlwind wartime romance ended happily; not everybody was committed to waiting. That's what I was playing with there, but also I was playing with the question, Why should it all be about romance?

DFB: It focuses the story much more on female friendship and how it's enduring and fundamental—instead of as a secondary theme to romance and adult life.

EW: You can come back to friendship. You can let it drop, for five years or ten years, and come back to it.

DFB: Another thing I've noticed is that none of your stories have magic in them. You write protagonists who are courageous and heroic in a very realistic world, which is different from the current trend that places child heroes in the realm of fantasy, where a magically endowed protagonist is often saving the world. What draws you to realistic heroism in this way?

EW: It's very conscious. I am a big fan of Alan Garner and have been ever since I was four and my father read me *The Weirdstone of Brisingamen*—we used to live in the shadow of Alderley Edge. I had the art of Alan Garner with me as I was growing up, and of course much of his work was fantasy, but then he stopped writing fantasy and started writing books that just felt like fantasy. *The Stone Book Quartet* was a triumph of this. The four short novels have themes that feel like fantasy and moments that feel like magic happening through them—as when, in *The Aimer Gate*, young Robert Garner climbs up inside the church tower. He gets to the top of the spire and it's dark, and he reaches up to the capping stone and feels letters carved there. He reads them with his fingertips in the pitch dark and realizes that it's his own name. I thought it was so amazing that Alan Garner was able to keep this fantastical feel to his books and at the same time make them realistic. I very consciously set out to do that in my own writing, from the very first book that came out, *The Winter Prince*, to *Code Name Verity* and now *Rose Under Fire*. There's magic in the world, and I want to make people aware of that.

Source: Deirdre Baker and Elizabeth Wein, "An Interview with Elizabeth Wein," in *Horn Book*, May 16, 2014.

Shari Fesko

In the following review of an audio adaptation of Wein's novel, Fesko calls the writing "superb" and the reading "seamless."

The horror of WWII as seen through the eyes of Verity (one of many names the double agent goes by) is believably captured in this superb audio. After Verity is arrested by the Gestapo, she is told to write everything down or face torture or execution. Her writing (in the third person) slowly reveals her past and the circumstances that led to her capture. Like Verity, who often emphatically insists, "I am not English," Christie hails from Scotland, and her accent and tones match Verity's pain and conflict as she wrenchingly recalls her experiences. But that is just the beginning, as Christie is a master of accents, including German, French, American, and English, and she sings a fine rendition of "Auld Lang Syne" and other songs. Gaskell is equally masterful playing Verity's best friend, Maddie (code name Kitty Hawk), a fearless young British pilot. Because Verity changes names (Queenie, Eva, Katharina, Julie) when recounting her double-agent escapades, listeners will have to pay close attention to the intricate plot, which weaves together past and present story lines. But the writing is so superb and both readers so seamless in their deliveries that teens should quickly become engrossed in this amazing historical fiction.

Source: Shari Fesko, Review of *Code Name Verity*, in *Booklist*, Vol. 109, No. 9–10, January 1, 2013, p. 125.

Ginger Clark

In the following review, Clark praises Wein's style and dedication to research.

Wein (*The Empty Kingdom*) serves up a riveting and often brutal tale of WWII action and espionage with a powerful friendship at its core. Captured Scottish spy Queenie has agreed to tell her tale—and reveal any confidential information she knows—in exchange for relief from being tortured by Nazis. Her story, which alternates between her early friendship with a pilot named Maddie and her recent sufferings in prison, works both as a story of cross-class friendship (from an upper-crust family, Queenie realizes that she would likely never have met Maddie under other circumstances) and as a harrowing spy story (Queenie's captor, von Loewe [sic], is humanized without losing his menace).

Queenie's deliberately rambling and unreliable narration keeps the story engaging, and there are enough action sequences and well-delivered twists (including a gut-wrenching climax and late revelations that will have readers returning to reread the first half of the book) to please readers of all stripes. Wein balances the horrors of war against genuine heroics, delivering a well-researched and expertly crafted adventure.

Source: Ginger Clark, Review of *Code Name Verity*, in *Publishers Weekly*, Vol. 259, No. 16, April 16, 2012, p. 66.

SOURCES

"August 25, 1944: Paris Liberated," History.com, http://www.history.com/this-day-in-history/paris-liberated (accessed February 2, 2015).

"Biography," ElizabethWein.com, http://www.elizabethwein.com/biography (accessed February 2, 2015).

"Charles de Gaulle (1890–1970)," BBC, http://www.bbc.co.uk/history/historic_figures/gaulle_charles_de.shtml (accessed February 2, 2015).

Chen, C. Peter, "The French Resistance," *World War II Database*, http://ww2db.com/battle_spec.php?battle_id=153 (accessed February 2, 2015).

"Fall of France," History.co.uk, http://www.history.co.uk/study-topics/history-of-ww2/fall-of-france (accessed February 2, 2015).

"France," in *CIA: World Factbook*, https://www.cia.gov/library/publications/the-world-factbook/geos/fr.html (accessed February 2, 2015).

Harris, Carol, "Women Under Fire in World War Two," BBC, http://www.bbc.co.uk/history/british/britain_wwtwo/women_at_war_01.shtml (accessed February 2, 2015).

Ingall, Marjorie, "The Pilot and the Spy," in *New York Times*, May 11, 2012, http://www.nytimes.com/2012/05/13/books/review/code-name-verity-by-elizabeth-wein.html?_r=1& (accessed February 2, 2015).

MacAskill, Ewen, "Women in Military Combat Is Nothing New, Just Not British," in *Guardian*, December 19, 2014, http://www.theguardian.com/uk-news/2014/dec/19/women-in-military-combat-nothing-new-not-british (accessed February 2, 2015).

Miller, Laura, "'Code Name Verity': The Pilot and the Spy," in *Salon*, August 8, 2013, http://www.salon.com/2013/08/08/code_name_verity_the_pilot_and_the_spy/ (accessed February 2, 2015).

Morris, Nigel, "The Special Operations Executive, 1940–1946," BBC, 2011, http://www.bbc.co.uk/history/worldwars/wwtwo/soe_01.shtml (accessed February 2, 2015).

"Philippe Pétain," BBC, http://www.bbc.co.uk/history/historic_figures/petain_philippe.shtml (accessed February 2, 2015).

Quattlebaum, Mary, "Elizabeth Wein's 'Code Name Verity': Thrilling WWII Spy Drama for Young Adults," in *Washington Post*, July 31, 2012, http://www.washingtonpost.com/entertainment/books/elizabeth-weins-code-name-verity-thrilling-wwii-spy-drama-for-young-adults/

2012/07/31/gJQAzGz2NX_story.html (accessed February 2, 2015).

Review of *Code Name Verity*, in *Kirkus Reviews*, March 1, 2012, https://www.kirkusreviews.com/book-reviews/ elizabeth-wein/code-name-verity/ (accessed February 2, 2015).

"Second World War: Intelligence," National Archives website, http://www.nationalarchives.gov.uk/news/second -world-war-intelligence-may-2013.htm (accessed February 2, 2015).

Singer, E. M., "A Brief History of the Air Transport Auxiliary," British Air Transport Auxiliary website, 2001, http://www.airtransportaux.com/history.html (accessed February 2, 2015).

Wein, Elizabeth, *Code Name Verity*, Hyperion, 2012.

FURTHER READING

Atwood, Kathryn J., *Women Heroes of World War II: 26 Stories of Espionage, Sabotage, Resistance, and Rescue*, Chicago Review Press, 2011.

> Part of a young-adult nonfiction series about women in war, Atwood's volume highlights the war efforts of twenty-six women who were engaged in espionage or combat in World War II, including a female radio operator, an assassin, and a housewife who hid Jews from the Gestapo.

Pelletier, Alain, *High-Flying Women: A World History of Female Pilots*, Haynes Publishing UK, 2012.

> Pelletier's volume presents the careers of female pilots from around the world, including fifty illustrated biographies.

Shapiro, Stephen, and Tina Forrester, *Hoodwinked: Deception and Resistance (Outwitting the Enemy: Stories from World War II)*, Annick Press, 2004.

> This young-adult resource focuses on the means by which the Allied forces used tricks, ruses, and deceptions to gain advantages over the Germans. They discuss such tactics as the use of inflatable tanks and dummy planes to simulate a larger force than was truly present, for example.

Zullo, Allan, *Survivors: True Stories of Children in the Holocaust*, Scholastic Paperbacks, 2005.

> In this resource geared toward young adults, Zullo collects the true stories of nine Jewish children who survived the Holocaust, either through escape or by disguising their identity. Zullo additionally provides introductory comments in which he summarizes the history of the Holocaust.

SUGGESTED SEARCH TERMS

Elizabeth Wein AND Code Name Verity

Elizabeth Wein AND female pilots

World War II AND female pilots

World War II AND Air Transport Authority

World War II AND Women's Auxiliary Air Force

World War II AND Special Operations Executive

World War II AND British female spies

World War II AND French Resistance

World War II AND Nazi-occupied France

World War II AND concentration camps

The Guide

R. K. NARAYAN
1958

The Guide is a novel by R. K. Narayan, who is one of the most well known twentieth-century Indian novelists writing in English. First published in 1958, the novel is set in the fictional town of Malgudi in South India, where most of Narayan's fiction takes place. The story centers on a man named Raju, who is taken by the villagers to be a holy man to whom they turn for advice and wisdom. Raju, who has in fact just been released from prison after being convicted of fraud, has no qualifications to be a holy man, but he goes along with the deception. He has had much experience as a tourist guide and knows how to tell people what they want to hear.

The novel also tells the story of Raju's earlier life from childhood on, including all the events that led up to his prison sentence. To accomplish his twofold purpose, Narayan employs the technique of a double narrative. The story of Raju, the fake holy man, is told in the third person, but the rest of the story of Raju's life is told in the first person.

The Guide is Narayan's most well-known work and is widely considered his best. It not only gives a vivid picture of life in India in that time and place, it also presents a fascinating character study of a man who eases his way through life with a loose regard for the truth but who may by the end of the novel have actually attained the saintliness that his followers see in him. The ambiguous ending leaves readers guessing.

R. K. Narayan (© Dinodia Photos / Alamy)

AUTHOR BIOGRAPHY

R. K. Narayan was born on October 10, 1906, in Madras, India, the son of R. V. Krishnaswami Iyer, a schoolteacher, and Gnana Iyer. Narayan spent much of his childhood living in Madras with his grandmother and a maternal uncle, seeing his parents mainly during vacations. Narayan's grandmother was an oral storyteller, and at an early age he became used to hearing stories from ancient myths and legends. Narayan first went to school in Madras, but in 1922, he was sent to a school in Mysore, where his father was the headmaster.

Narayan was an enthusiastic reader although not, by his own account in his memoir *My Days*, an outstanding student. He did, however, manage to graduate in 1930 with a bachelor's degree from Maharaja's College, part of the University of Mysore. Four years later, he married a local girl named Rajam Iyer; they had a daughter, Hema, in 1936, but Rajam died of typhoid just three years later, in 1939.

In the meantime, Narayan had published his first three novels, *Swami and Friends: A Novel of Malgudi* (1935), *The Bachelor of Arts* (1937), and *The Dark Room* (1938). He had also entered into a correspondence with British novelist Graham Greene that was to last many years. Greene championed Narayan's work, and the two eventually met in London in 1956. By that time, Narayan's work as an Indian writer of novels in English was well established: he had published four novels in the decade between 1945 and 1955.

In 1956, Narayan visited the United States as a result of a Rockefeller Foundation fellowship. While in the United States, he wrote *The Guide*, which was published in 1958. Two years later, the novel won the Sahitay Akademi Award. Over the next three decades, his novels included *The Man-Eater of Malgudi* (1961), *The Vendor of Sweets* (1967), *The Painter of Signs* (1976), *A Tiger for Malgudi* (1983), *Talkative Man* (1986), and *The World of Nagaraj* (1990). He also wrote thirteen collections of short stories, beginning with *Malgudi Days* in 1943 and concluding with *Salt and Sawdust: Stories and Table Talk* in 1993. Among his nonfiction works are *My Days: A Memoir* (1974) and *A Writer's Nightmare: Selected Essays, 1958–1988* (1988).

Beginning in 1985, Narayan served a six-year term as a member of Parliament. In 1990, he moved to Madras with his daughter and son-in-law. By that time, he had received numerous awards, including the National Prize of the Indian Literary Academy (1958); the Padma Bhushan, which is awarded by the government of India to those who have made a distinguished contribution to the nation (1964); and the Benson Medal, awarded by the Royal Society of Literature in the United Kingdom (1980).

Narayan died of cardiorespiratory failure in Chennai (formerly Madras) on May 13, 2001, at the age of ninety-four.

PLOT SUMMARY

Chapter 1

The novel opens in a village somewhere in South India. Raju is seated on a granite slab at the side of a river, next to an ancient temple. A man named Velan, a local villager, comes to him for advice. Only a few days ago, Raju was in prison—his offense as yet unspecified—but now he has

MEDIA ADAPTATIONS

- *The Guide* was adapted for the stage by Harvey Breit and Patricia Rinehart and produced off-Broadway at the Hudson Theatre in 1968.
- *The Guide* was also adapted for a film directed by Vijay Anand in 1965. The film received excellent reviews.

---

suddenly appeared in the locality; he is quite happy to be taken as a holy man by the gullible villagers.

The narrative then switches from the third person to the first person, as Raju recalls his childhood and how he became a tourist guide. His father owned a shop opposite the railway station, well stocked with items that a traveler might want to buy, including fruit and tobacco. Raju would sometimes help in the store. His father taught him reading and arithmetic.

Back at the temple in the present, Velan explains that his half-sister refuses to accept Velan's cousin's son as a husband. He asks Raju what he can do about it. Raju asks to see the girl, and the next morning Velan and the girl bring him gifts of fruit, nuts, and milk. Raju first offers the food to the stone image of a god and then starts telling a story from an ancient religious tradition but cannot remember how it ends.

The story then briefly returns to Raju as a child, recounting how his mother would tell him a story every evening, but often he would fall asleep before it ended.

Back in the present, Raju puts Velan off, saying that he does not want to deal with his problem right now, because there is a time for everything, and he needs time to think about it. Velan accepts this as a very wise response.

Chapter 2

Raju tells more of his childhood. He was sent to school, which was unusual in his village. He learned at the old teacher's own house, on the *pyol*, or front stoop, where about twenty boys would gather. After a year, Raju attended the Board School, which had just opened.

In the present, Velan comes to Raju and is delighted to explain that his sister has accepted the husband who was selected for her. Velan invites Raju to the wedding, but Raju does not attend, not wanting to be in a crowd. However, that does not stop the wedding party from coming to visit him, believing that it was his intervention that made the girl change her mind.

After that, more and more villagers come to visit him in the evenings, convinced he is a wise and holy man. Raju, who knows he is no such thing, is at first uncomfortable at receiving this kind of attention, but he learns to play along with it and even welcome it. One evening, though, he hides from them, but the next day he thinks better of it and waits for them to come. However, no one comes. He sees a shepherd boy, who tells him he was sent by his uncle to see if a man was at the temple. Raju instructs the boy to tell his uncle to come to visit him in the evening.

Chapter 3

Raju narrates more of his youth. Railroad tracks had been constructed, and the first train came to town. As a result, Raju's father became prosperous through his store because of its proximity to the railroad station. He acquired a horse and carriage. Eventually, he opened a shop in the railroad station itself, in addition to his other shop. Raju helped to run the new shop.

Chapter 4

The people return in large numbers to visit Raju at the ancient temple. They regard him as a saint. At Raju's instigation, they set up a school for boys in the hall. A teacher is brought in, and a dozen boys attend.

Briefly, the narrative returns to Raju's childhood. After his father died, he took charge of the shop at the railroad station. He started to sell books, magazines, and newspapers.

Back in the present, at the temple, Raju gives the students talks in the evenings, and soon the parents come to hear him as well. Raju feels like an actor, but he learns to play the part of spiritual teacher well, convincing the gullible villagers that he is offering them great wisdom, even though his words carry little substance or meaning. He leads his audience in holy chants and songs, and they bring in lamps and pictures of the gods. Women come in and decorate the hall. Wanting to look more the part, Raju grows a beard and allows his hair to grow long. The evening meetings are getting bigger, overflowing into the corridors.

Chapter 5

As a young man working at the railway store, Raju became known as Railway Raju. Travelers asked him directions and for information about local places of interest. He became an experienced tourist guide, even though at first he did not know much and relied on his ability to tell a tale. As a tourist guide he met a scholarly, dry man whom he called Marco and his beautiful dancer wife, Rosie.

At Rosie's request, and with the services of Gaffur, the local taxi driver, Raju took the couple to see a cobra dance to the music of a flute. The next day he took them to view some cave paintings, although Rosie came along only because Raju persuaded her, at her husband's request, to do so. Marco and Rosie were clearly not happy together, and Raju became infatuated with her. It took most of the day to get to the cave region, and the three of them stayed overnight at Peak House, a guesthouse at the top of a cliff.

The next day, Raju accompanied Marco to the caves, but Rosie did not care to go with them. Marco was fascinated by the caves and took notes and photographs. Raju returned and befriended Rosie, who admitted that she and her husband had nothing in common and quarreled a lot. She came from a family of temple dancers, an occupation that many considered not very respectable, and she took the opportunity to marry Marco, a wealthy man from a higher class, when it was presented to her.

Marco stayed for several days at the guesthouse, engrossed in the caves. Rosie returned to their hotel at Malgudi, and Raju took the opportunity to show her around town. They began an adulterous affair.

Chapter 6

The narrative returns to Raju in his present role as holy man or sage. Some time, either months or years, has passed, and the villagers still regard him as a saint, bringing him food and gifts. Then one summer there is a drought. Crops suffer. The cattle have no grass to eat and lose the strength to pull the plows. Some of them die. The wells in the village dry up. Fights break out in the village over the price of rice.

Velan's brother comes to tell Raju that Velan has been injured; his group is planning to attack the other group for revenge. Raju is not interested in the quarrel but tells Velan's brother that the villagers should not fight. He adds that he will not eat until they end their quarrel. However, when Velan's brother, who is not very intelligent, delivers the message to his family and their group, he gets it muddled, saying that the Swami (as they call Raju) has instructed them not to bring him any more food until it rains. The men interpret that to mean that Raju's fast will bring rain.

The villagers are so grateful to him that they let their quarrel lapse. They assemble at the temple in great numbers and praise Raju to the skies, regarding him as their savior. Raju is puzzled until Velan explains that they are expecting him to fast for two weeks and stand in knee-deep water for eight hours reciting prayers. Raju is horrified by the prospect, and the following day summons Velan to inform him that he, Raju, is not a saint.

Chapter 7

Marco stayed for a month at Peak House, and Raju spent a lot of time looking after him and especially Rosie. He became very fond of Rosie and lost interest in other aspects of his life. He took an interest in her dancing, which her husband never cared for. She performed for him in her hotel room. Her only desire was to pursue a career as a dancer. Raju agreed to help her, and she said she would approach her husband about it. However, when Raju next saw them, Marco told him his services were no longer needed. Rosie seemed to have turned cold.

For a month, Raju was angry and miserable and bored with his life. Then Rosie turned up at his house, where he lived with his mother, with a trunk. Her husband had left her after refusing to support her desire to become a dancer and also learning about her affair with Raju. Rosie started to practice her dancing, but Raju's mother learned of the situation and did not approve of Rosie's presence in the house. Also, Raju's business declined, and the railway told him to quit the shop.

Chapter 8

Sait, a wholesale merchant, took Raju to court over unpaid debts, also claiming that Raju threatened him with violence. Raju denied this, and his lawyer secured an adjournment in the case. One day Raju's uncle, who advised on family matters, arrived. He spoke aggressively to Raju, and the two men quarreled. The uncle told Rosie she must leave the house. Raju's mother agreed, but Raju said Rosie would not go. His mother threatened to leave the house herself. After she and her brother left, Raju and Rosie lived together as if they were married. Rosie began her dancing career, changing her name to Nalini.

Chapter 9

Helped by Raju's impressive organizational activities and public relations skills, Rosie became extremely successful, winning fame as a dancer. They moved into a bigger house and had many servants, including two gardeners, a driver, and a security guard. Many visitors came, and Raju became a very popular man, a friend of judges, politicians, and other influential men. He and Rosie traveled all over South India for her dance recitals, sometimes being away from Malgudi for nearly two weeks. Raju made a lot of money and spent much of it on servants and the cultivation of an elegant lifestyle. Rosie started to grow weary and wanted to live more simply, but Raju had become accustomed to money, luxury, and influence.

A book arrived in the mail for Raju. It was a work of cultural history by Marco, and in it he thanked Raju for the help he gave him. Raju concealed the book from Rosie, but she found out about it and reproached him for hiding it. Raju then received a letter from a lawyer addressed to Rosie that required her signature in order for a jewelry box that had been left in safe custody at a bank to be sent to her. Marco's signature would also be added. Raju did not show Rosie the letter; instead, he forged her signature and waited for the box to be delivered. After Rosie gave a dance recital at a small town sixty miles away, Raju was arrested on a complaint from Marco and was charged with forgery.

Chapter 10

After two days in jail, Raju was released on bail. Rosie rejected him, and he fell into self-pity. She claimed she would not dance in public again, but she changed her mind and worked hard at her already scheduled engagements so she could hire an expensive lawyer to defend Raju. The lawyer, however, was unable to save Raju from being convicted, and he was sentenced to two years in prison.

In prison, he got on well with the prisoners and guards alike. He told stories and explained philosophies, and the prisoners called him "Teacher." Raju worked hard in the prison garden and generally enjoyed prison life. He also read in the newspaper that Rosie was continuing to dance, and her fame was undiminished. Mani, Raju's servant, visited him and told him that Rosie had moved to Madras. She did not return to her husband.

Chapter 11

The narrative now returns to where it left off at the end of chapter 6. After Raju tells Velan the story of his life, he expects Velan to reject him, but Velan does no such thing. He still reveres him as a swami, a holy man. Raju has no alternative but to embark on the promised fast, although on the first day he cheats, consuming some stale food he has stashed away.

For the next few days he does fast and even stands knee-deep in water reciting the sacred chants. The newspapers report on it, which brings large crowds to the area to observe the great swami in his noble, self-sacrificial act. Raju hates doing it at first, but by the fourth day, he takes it more seriously and even finds satisfaction in trying to do good by his actions. The crowds grow bigger, and the roads get clogged with traffic. An American arrives to shoot film of the swami to show to television audiences back home. Doctors examine Raju and find he is weak.

On the eleventh day of the fast, Raju is advised to discontinue it, but he does not do so. He stands in the water again, and this time he tells Velan that it is raining in the hills. He can feel the water under his feet. His disciples have been holding him up, but now he sinks down, and there the story ends, without further explanation.

CHARACTERS

Gaffur

Gaffur is the taxi driver in Malgudi. He uses junk vehicles that he somehow manages to keep going, and he likes to charge high prices. Raju gives him a lot of business while he is a tourist guide.

Joseph

Joseph is the old caretaker at Peak House. He takes care of all the visitors' needs efficiently and without complaint. Marco is very pleased with his services.

James J. Malone

James J. Malone is a film and television producer from California who travels to India with the support of the Indian government to make a documentary film about Raju's fast.

Mani

Mani is one of Raju's servants after he becomes prosperous. He visits Raju in prison.

Marco

Marco is Rosie's husband. He is a scholarly, taciturn man from an upper-class background who married Rosie after she responded to a newspaper advertisement in which Marco described himself as "a rich bachelor of academic interests." Marco does not get along with his wife and pays little attention to her. He is interested only in his scholarly pursuits, and he spends many hours examining the cave paintings that Raju takes him to see. He has no skill in practical life. When he discovers that his wife is having an affair with Raju and also wants to pursue a career as a dancer, Marco walks out on her. Later he publishes a book on Indian cultural history. He also brings about Raju's downfall by tricking him into forging Rosie's signature.

Raju

Raju lives an eventful life that goes through three main stages. He grows up in the small town of Malgudi, where he helps his father run his store at the railway station. Talkative and ingratiating, Raju becomes known as Railway Raju, and he develops a sideline as a tourist guide. Much of the time, he simply makes up the details he tells the tourists about the local places of interest. As a tourist guide, he meets Marco and Rosie. He conceives a great passion for Rosie and begins an affair with her, which continues after Marco discovers it and leaves his wife. Raju and Rosie then live together, and he encourages her to pursue her love of dancing.

Ravi arranges for her to give performances, and her career is launched, thus beginning the second main stage of his life, when he is Rosie's manager. Through his efforts, as well as her own, she becomes famous, and Raju rises to prominence as a wealthy and influential man through his association with Rosie. He and Rosie move to a bigger house and have many servants. Raju is a good businessman and demands high fees from those who wish to have Rosie perform. He also becomes arrogant, treating people whom he deems of little importance with disdain.

Eventually, his world comes crashing down when he is convicted of forging Rosie's signature authorizing the dispatch of a jewelry box that is being kept in safe custody for her at a bank. Raju serves two years in prison but does not find the experience arduous. Gregarious by nature, he befriends all the prisoners and the prison officials. He is sorry to leave when his sentence is complete.

He then embarks on the third major stage of his life. Only two days out of prison, he is living in an ancient abandoned temple by a river. He is soon mistaken for a holy man by a villager named Velan. Raju, slick with words as ever, goes along with the misperception. He makes empty pronouncements that the villagers take to be expressions of great wisdom. His reputation steadily grows, and large numbers of people come to visit him in the evenings. He even sets up a school in the temple. When a drought comes, there is a miscommunication between Raju and the villagers, as a result of which he finds himself committed to a twelve-day fast to produce rain. He goes through with it, admired by everyone as a saint, even though it makes him very weak and may possibly cost him his life.

Raju's Father

Raju's father built the family house himself, just outside of Malgudi. He also owns a shop. He teaches Raju reading and arithmetic in a stern manner and then insists that the boy attend school. When the railroad is built nearby, Raju's father opens another shop at the railway station and becomes quite prosperous. He dies in his sleep when Raju is still a young man.

Raju's Mother

When Raju is a boy, his mother tells him a story every night from the scriptures or ancient legends. She sometimes disapproves of her husband's attitudes or ideas, but the family home does not seem to be an unhappy one. After her husband's death, she adjusts to life as a widow, but she cannot accept Rosie's presence in the house. She leaves and goes to live near her brother. She and Raju remain on good terms, however, but at a distance. She attends his trial.

Raju's Uncle

Raju's uncle—his mother's elder brother—is a landowner who lives in the village his sister originally came from. He inherited the family house. Raju's uncle is an influential figure in the family and is consulted about all important family matters. When his sister informs him that Rosie is living with her and Raju, he pays them a visit, insisting in a belligerent fashion that Rosie must leave.

Rosie

Rosie is married to Marco. She is a college-educated woman from a family of temple dancers. Her mother, grandmother, and great-grandmother were all temple dancers. Dancers are not considered respectable women, however, so her mother wanted her to pursue some other occupation. Rosie therefore received an education and holds a master's degree in economics.

She marries Marco for his wealth and respectability. However, the marriage is not a happy one, partly because Marco takes no interest in her but also because her real love is for dancing. Her family had agreed that marrying a man of Marco's social standing was desirable, even though it meant that she would have to renounce her dancing, but she cannot adjust to her new life. Soon after she meets Raju she enters into an affair with him, and he encourages her to take up dancing again, which is all she really wants to do. It turns out that Rosie is an excellent dancer and very committed to her art.

After her husband leaves her, Raju arranges for her to give a public performance, and after that she becomes extremely successful and famous as a dancer, taking the name Nalini and traveling far and wide in South India. She grows weary of the intense schedule, however, and she and Raju have their share of disagreements. After Raju is sent to prison, Rosie continues her career and eventually moves to Madras.

Sait

Sait is a wholesale merchant who takes Raju to court over unpaid debts.

Velan

Velan is the villager who first mistakes Raju for a holy man. He asks Raju's advice about his sister, who is refusing to marry the man who has been chosen for her. Velan remains one of Raju's most devoted disciples, even after Raju confesses to him that he is not really a saint after all.

Velan's Brother

Velan's brother is a twenty-one-year-old man of low intelligence. He is responsible for getting the cattle out to the mountainside for grazing. It is also he who is responsible for the miscommunication between Raju and the villagers about Raju's fast. Raju gives him a message to take back, but he gets it all wrong.

THEMES

Deception

Deception is a major theme of the novel, centering on the character of Raju. Raju is an inventive, ingenious, quick-thinking man who knows how to take advantage of any situation that presents itself to him. He has a good imagination, and he knows how to talk convincingly. He seems to lack a firmly grounded moral character, so it is not difficult for him to present himself as something that he is not. He shows this early in his life when he becomes a tourist guide. Although later he does become knowledgeable about the area, at first he knows little about the places he takes people to and just makes up whatever ideas come into his head about them, just so he can keep talking and allow the tourist to believe he is getting his money's worth. Raju explains his methods:

> The age I ascribed to any particular place depended upon my mood at that hour and the type of person I was escorting. If he was the academic type, I was careful to avoid all mention of facts and figures and to confine myself to general descriptions.... On the other hand, if an innocent man happened to be at hand, I let myself go freely. I pointed out to him something as the greatest, the highest, the only one in the world. I gave statistics out of my head. I mentioned a relic as belonging to the thirteenth century before Christ or the thirteenth century after Christ, according to the mood of the hour.

TOPICS FOR FURTHER STUDY

- Using the Internet, research the sadhus (holy men) of India. How does a man become a sadhu? What does a sadhu do? How are sadhus regarded in Indian culture and society? Give a multimedia class presentation on the subject.

- Imagine that *The Guide* is to be made into a movie. Go to the online learning platform glogster.com and create a glog (a digital poster) that advertises the movie.

- Read *Ramayana: Divine Loophole* (2010) by Sanjay Patel, which is a simplified retelling, with over a hundred color illustrations, of the Indian epic about the god Rama. These are some of the stories that inspire Rosie in *The Guide*, and she wants to create new dances based on them. Select one or two stories and present them yourself to your class. If you like to dance, suggest some ideas about how the stories could be presented in that form and even dance them yourself.

- Write a character study of Rosie in *The Guide*. What is her family background? Why does she marry Marco? What kind of woman is she, and what motivates her? Why does she become successful, and does her success make her happy?

———

The deception is harmless enough, and Raju cannot be called a con man or a crook. He does not practice deception when it comes to business matters, but in terms of who he is and what his qualifications are, he will say whatever is necessary to achieve his goals. He has the ability to acquire a little knowledge of something (like dancing, for example) and then discourse on it as if he really knows much more. He always puts on a good performance, as when he persuades a local group to invite Rosie to perform. When he addresses their meeting, he recalls,

I held forth on the revival of art in India so vehemently that they could not easily brush me aside, but had to listen. Heaven knew where I had found all this eloquence. I delivered such a lecture on the importance of our culture and the place of the dance in it that they simply had to accept what I said.... I never knew I could speak so fluently on cultural matters. I had picked up a little terminology from Rosie and put it to the best use.

This habit of allowing people to think something of him that is not really true finds its most dramatic expression in Raju's postprison career as an enlightened sage. Once the villagers make the mistake of thinking that a holy man is in their midst, Raju needs no further prompting. He plays the part to perfection and is quite happy to receive the food they bring him and accept the status they confer on him. For a former tourist guide, business manager, and convicted felon, it is quite a performance.

Martyrdom

For almost the entirety of the novel, the term *martyr* would not be associated with a man like Raju. Raju is a self-promoter—he knows how to advance his own cause. He lives largely for himself. Even when he takes it upon himself to promote Rosie's career as a dancer, he does so not only because he is in love with her but also because he too can make a nice living out of it.

When Raju is first taken for a holy man, after his release from prison, he is a fraud. A holy man in Indian tradition is a man who has obtained spiritual knowledge and wisdom through a denial of the senses and the cultivation of a lack of attachment to material things. This is the opposite of what Raju's life has been, since he has indulged in sensual love and gloried in the accumulation of material possessions.

However, a strange thing happens during the fast that he finds himself engaging upon in an effort to bring about the end of the drought. He did not really intend to get involved in such a thing, because he does not appear to have any genuine religious or spiritual beliefs, and the idea that a holy man could bring rain by fasting and chanting must have struck him as a foolish notion. However, on the fourth day of the fast, a change takes place in him. For the first time in his life, the idea of self-sacrifice—that someone

Rosie leaves her husband to pursue a career in dancing. *(© ostill | Shutterstock.com)*

could do good for others by denying himself—enters his head:

> "If by avoiding food I should help the trees bloom, and the grass grow, why not do it thoroughly?" For the first time in his life he was making an earnest effort; for the first time he was learning the thrill of full application, outside money and love; for the first time he was doing a thing in which he was not personally interested.

When the fast begins to have ill effects on his health, he is urged to abandon it, but Raju is now unrecognizable as the self-centered man he has been most of his life. He insists on continuing the fast and performing the sacred chanting while standing knee-deep in water. He seems oblivious to his own suffering. In his physical weakness, he has gained a different kind of strength, which he had formerly lacked. He has become a genuine martyr, that is, someone who suffers greatly or even dies for a religion or a cause.

The author deliberately leaves the ending open: Raju slumps down, and it is possible that he has indeed given his life to this enterprise, although he may only be extremely weak and in

need of food. In whatever way the ending of the novel is read, there is no doubt that Raju has become a radically different man at the end than he was at the beginning.

STYLE

Point of View

The novel alternates between two different points of view. Raju's postprison life, when he is taken for a holy man, is told by an omniscient third-person narrator, who can describe the thoughts and feelings of all the characters. The story of Raju's life before that point, however, detailing his childhood, his time as a tourist guide, his rise to prominence as Rosie's manager and agent, and his life in prison, is described by Raju himself in a first-person narrative. This is in fact the confessional tale he tells to Velan, which becomes apparent especially in chapters 7–10, which are narrated in the first person, because at the end of chapter 6, the reader is informed through the third-person narrator that Raju wants Velan to listen to the story of his life.

One purpose of the unusual alternating point of view is the need to present in the last phase of Raju's life a more objective view of Raju than he has been able to reach by himself. It also suggests the final shift in his awareness, when he is no longer so concerned about himself and his own situation and is in contrast determined to do some good for others. He is thus presented from a more distant, disinterested perspective than that of his own narrow individual self.

Comedy

Although the book has serious themes, there are many comic elements in it. These are particularly apparent in the first chapter, when the gullible villager Velan mistakes Raju for a great sage. Raju's answers to the man's questions are meaningless platitudes, yet they are cloaked in a kind of aura of profundity. The reader sees this, but Velan does not.

For example, when he cannot be bothered to think much about Velan's problem regarding his sister's marriage, he says, "We cannot force vital solutions. Every question must bide its time." He is putting the man off but making it sound as if he is giving a wise pronouncement. Some of the humor is at Velan's expense, as when Raju starts

COMPARE
&
CONTRAST

- **1950s:** Prohibition of alcohol is common in India following independence in 1947. Madras, Bombay, Maharashtra, Gujarat, and many parts of Andhra Pradesh ban alcohol in the 1950s and 1960s. In the mid-1950s, one-quarter of India's population live in areas where alcohol is banned.

  Today: A few Indian states in the northern part of the country maintain a ban on alcohol. The state of Mizoram in northeast India repeals prohibition in July 2014, after eighteen years of prohibition.

- **1950s:** As the leader of the Indian independence movement in the 1930s and 1940s, Mahatma Gandhi (1869–1948) is revered in the country.

  Today: Gandhi remains revered worldwide for his advocacy of nonviolent protest as a means of social change.

- **1950s:** The atomic age gathers force as the United States and the Soviet Union stockpile nuclear weapons.

  Today: India is one of nine countries in the world that possess nuclear weapons. According to the Federation of American Scientists, India has a stockpile of between 90 and 110 nuclear weapons.

---

to tell a story from one of the ancient texts but cannot remember how it goes and falls silent. Rather than being disappointed, Velan just waits patiently: "He was of the stuff disciples are made of; an unfinished story or an incomplete moral never bothered him; it was all in the scheme of life." Humor also arises from the discrepancy between who Raju is and who he is taken to be, and in the thoughts Raju has as he interacts with Velan, which reveal he is no guru at all and has no interest in being one—although he certainly enjoys the food his disciples bring him.

HISTORICAL CONTEXT

Classical Indian Dance

India has a long history of classical dance, and there are eight different styles of dance, according to *Hindu Online*. The style known as Bharat Natyam is the one that Rosie in the novel practices. Bharat Natyam originated in the temples of South India, where the dances were performed for the gods and goddesses who populate the ancient Indian religious texts. The style takes its name from the ancient sage Bharat, who wrote the *Natya Shastra*, a treatise on the performing arts written around 200 CE, although some regard it as even older, dating back to 400 BCE. In the novel, Rosie is shown studying the *Natya Shastra*.

According to *Hindu Online*, Indian classical dances feature

> the use of the mudra or hand gestures by the artists as a short-hand sign language to narrate a story and to demonstrate certain concepts such as objects, weather, nature and emotion. Many classical dances include facial expressions as an integral part of the dance form.

The dances tell stories from the ancient Sanskrit epics, the Mahabharata and Ramayana. In the novel, Rosie wants to read these texts so she can find stories on which to base new dances.

Under British colonial rule, classical dance lost its popularity in India because the British regarded all Indian art as inferior to Western art, and this resulted in many Indians turning against their own traditions. Temple dancers were regarded as immoral and even associated in the eyes of their detractors with prostitution. Rosie explains how this negative view affected her family of dancers and how, as a result, her mother wanted her to seek some other occupation.

Raju retreats to an abandoned temple after serving his sentence because he does not wish to return home in disgrace. *(© Radiokafka | Shutterstock.com)*

According to "History of Bharatanatyam," "By the first quarter of the 20th century, the classical dance of South India was almost wiped out." However, after this a revival began, which continued after the end of British rule in 1947. In the novel, Rosie is part of this revival of the practice of Bharat Natyam.

Indian Writing in English

India was under British rule for several centuries, so it is perhaps not surprising that eventually it developed a literature written by Indians in English. The first Indian novel in English was *Rajmohan's Wife*, written by Bankim Chandra Chattopadhyay in 1864. In the mid-twentieth century, there were three major Indian novelists who wrote in English. In addition to Narayan, they were Mulk Raj Anand (1905–2004) and Raja Rao (1908–2006). Anand wrote a trilogy, *The Village* (1939), *Across the Black Waters* (1940), and *The Sword and the Sickle* (1943), in which an Indian boy leaves his village and goes to Europe to fight in World War I, after which he returns to India a changed man. Rao, according to William Walsh in *R. K. Narayan: A Critical Appreciation*, did not share Anand's political interests; his work was notable for its "poetic, metaphysical" qualities. His works included the novels *Kanthapura* (1938) and *The Serpent and the Rope* (1960).

In Narayan's essay "English in India," he notes that English is only one of fifteen languages spoken in India but has served a very useful purpose for writers: "English has proved that if a language has flexibility any experience can be communicated through it." He continues, "A few writers in India took to writing in English, and produced a literature that perhaps was not first-rate ... but occasionally it was brilliant. We are still experimentalists." Of his own writing, he says that English has "served my purpose admirably, of conveying unambiguously the thoughts and acts of a set of personalities, who flourish in a small town named Malgudi supposed to be located in a corner of south India."

CRITICAL OVERVIEW

The Guide has long been regarded as one of Narayan's most successful novels, and many regard it as his finest achievement in that genre. William Walsh in *R. K. Narayan: A Critical Appreciation* calls it "a remarkable example of the especially difficult genre to which most of Narayan's work belongs, the serious comedy."

After commenting on the gentleness of the tone in which the novel is narrated, Walsh defines the "organising theme" of the novel as "the complex association of sincerity and self-deception." According to John Thieme in *R. K. Narayan*, many critics see the novel as a demonstration of how a "spiritual *dharma* is imposed on a hitherto worldly man." In answer to the question this raises, of why the majority of the novel deals with Raju's earlier life, Thieme argues that "there are more extensive connections between the two narratives than have generally been noticed." He continues, "Raju's supposed transformation into a 'saint'...can be seen as a logical extension of everything that has preceded it, the final stage in his serial adoption of a range of personae."

K. N. Padmanabhan Nair, in *Irony in the Novels of R. K. Narayan and V. S. Naipaul*, highlights Narayan's use of irony in the novel, for which the author makes use of "the mythico-religious implications of certain deep-rooted and widespread superstitions of the villagers." According to Nair, the principal theme of the novel is "a sort of spiritual transformation."

For Sr. Mary Beatina Rayen, in "The Guide: A Study in Transcendence," the novel also features a transcendence on the part of Raju, understood as "a getting beyond the expected, a spiritual discovery." Rayen notes that Raju is the "most controversial" of Naipaul's fictional characters, and she regards him as "an exceptionally complex human being." Like other critics, Rayen notes Narayan's "comic art and subtle irony" and observes that this is most readily apparent in Raju's interactions with the villagers in the last stage of his life. Rayen also points out a "deeper level" to these episodes, in which Raju is "drawn willy-nilly, by a naïve single-mindedness...into an ambiguously sacred role. He is compelled, by the will of others simpler even than he is, to rise above his limitation."

CRITICISM

Bryan Aubrey

Aubrey holds a PhD in English. In the following essay, he examines the manner in which Raju is transformed from a worldly man into an apparent saint in The Guide.

Narayan got the idea for *The Guide* from a real incident that took place during a severe drought in Mysore. He reports in his memoir *My Days*, as quoted by John Thieme in *R. K. Narayan*:

> As a desperate measure, the municipal council organized a prayer for rains. A group of Brahmins stood knee-deep in water (procured at great cost) on the dry bed of Kaveri, fasted, prayed, and chanted certain mantras continuously for eleven days. One the twelfth day it rained, and brought relief to the countryside.

Out of this, the novelist wove a tale in which an unlikely candidate for sainthood—a worldly former travel guide and business manager for a famous dancer—nonetheless finds it forced upon him by circumstances. The man who earlier in his life was known as Railroad Raju finds himself revered as the savior of his community, and his fame, thanks to the arrival of the American television producer Malone, seems likely to spread worldwide—that is, if Raju lives to see it.

The ending of the story is ambiguous on several levels. At no point does the author say directly that Raju dies as a result of his fast. His ultimate fate is not disclosed. Nor is it certain that rain really is on its way by the last day of the fast. Raju feels that it is and says so, but there is no objective confirmation of it. Of course, even if there were, this does not prove that Raju's fast and ritual chanting brought it about. After all, sometimes it rains.

Having said that, though, there is no doubting the transformation that Raju goes through during the fast. It was not something that he originally wanted to do. The idea comes up in the first place only as a result of a misunderstanding between himself and the villagers, and his attitude to it is plain: "Did they expect him to starve for fifteen days and stand in knee-deep water for eight hours?" He thinks at first that he may be able to survive by keeping a reserve of food and eating it at night, undetected. The arrangement he would actually prefer, he things wryly, is for the villagers to keep him supplied with bonda—a popular snack in South India of

> IT IS AS IF RAJU HAS PASSED BEYOND THE
> SMALLNESS OF THE PERSONAL MIND. HE IS REFERRED
> TO MOSTLY NOT AS RAJU BUT AS 'THE SWAMI'—
> HAVING PASSED BEYOND INDIVIDUALITY, HE IS
> NO LONGER ATTACHED TO A PERSONAL NAME."

potato or other vegetable dipped in batter—for fifteen days, and then he would stand in the river for just two minutes a day, which "should bring down the rain sooner or later."

This is the old, practical Raju speaking, the man who likes to arrange things for his own benefit and likes to enjoy himself and has no particular thoughts about spirituality or the efficacy of any religious ritual. Indeed, he refers not to chanting the required litany but "muttering" it and thinks he will be able to find a way of doing it for less time than the required eight hours a day. Then the rains will come "in their natural course sooner or later."

When he actually begins the fast, he still feels indignant about it. He resents the loss of his privacy and wishes the whole ill-conceived enterprise could quickly be brought to an end. He wants to tell the crowds to just leave him alone; he is not their savior, but he realizes that he cannot back out of it now. The fast has acquired a momentum of its own, and he must continue it.

Raju's saving grace is that he is not entirely a selfish man or a fraud. He wants to at least put on a decent show of going through the required ritual: "He would not like to cheat them altogether about the fast if he could help it." Raju has never been completely without feeling for others; indeed, in a sense, his ability to sense what people wanted and then give it to them was at the heart of his success both as a tourist guide and as Rosie's manager.

What happens now, though, is that the momentum of his actions leads him into new psychic and spiritual territory that he had not planned for. By the fourth day, he actually starts to embrace the fast. He decides to give all he has to it and even becomes enthusiastic about it. For the first time in his life, he is doing something without any thought of personal satisfaction,

love, or financial gain. On that day he chants the litany in a rhythmic manner until the world, as it were, disappears. He has gone beyond the world of the senses and is in some other realm of awareness. He is really becoming a swami, a genuine holy man.

The immediate trigger for this transformation was a feeling of compassion that came over him when he observed the lengths to which Velan, his chief follower, was going to make the penance work. Velan looks after Raju, making him as comfortable as he can, even sitting next to him and waving a fan over him until he falls asleep with the fan still in his hand. This devotion touches Raju's heart. He thinks of someone other than himself and is thus open to his own transformation from selfishness and sensuality to saintliness

Raju's life up to this point had been quite different. While he was with the dancer, Rosie, he was passionately attached not only to her but also to money and luxury. He was an influential, worldly man, but in a trick of fate, he has suddenly entered upon on a spiritual path that found him even when he was not looking for it. Raju had always been naturally gregarious and loquacious. He was a man with the gift of the gab, who knew how to talk in a way that would easily promote his own interests. Now he has moved from speech to silence, from the assertion of self to the negation of self.

This change is mirrored in the narrative structure. The story of Raju's earlier life is told in the first person. Of necessity, it centers entirely on himself, on his own point of view: what he did, how he reacted to events, and what he thought and felt. It is, one might say, ego-bound, quite narrow in its scope. The sections that deal with the present situation, however, when Raju is taken by the villagers for a holy man, are told in the third person. It is as if the narrative camera has been pulled back to reveal a wider, more objective and detached view. At first, the narrator still has insight into what Raju is thinking and feeling. He is at this stage still the same Raju, just viewed through a different lens. However, in the final pages of the novel, Raju's own voice vanishes completely, in terms of his inner thoughts and feelings. The narrator does not present them. It is as if Raju has passed beyond the smallness of the personal mind. He is referred to mostly not as Raju but as "the

WHAT DO I READ NEXT?

- Narayan's *Malgudi Days*, first published in 1943, is a collection of short stories set in the fictional South Indian town that Narayan created.

- *The Bachelor of Arts* (1937) is based in part on Narayan's life during his college years. It follows the growth from adolescence to adulthood of Chandran, an undergraduate student. Chandran falls in love, but his parents refuse to allow him to marry the girl because her social status does not match his. Rebelling against this decision, Chandra tries to become a wandering holy man, but eventually he returns to his parents and is willing to accept their choice of bride.

- *The Illustrated History of South India* (2009) by K. A. Nilakanta Sastri is an adaptation for young readers of a classic work of history first published in 1955.

- Indian writer Arundhati Roy's first novel, *The God of Small Things* (1997), was widely praised and won the prestigious Booker Prize. Set in Kerala, in southwest India, mostly in the late 1960s, it describes the decline of a family, marked by separations, a drowning, a mother's banishment, and other misfortunes.

- *A Passage to India* (1924) by British novelist E. M. Forster, is set in northern India in the 1920s. Whereas Narayan's novels show India as seen by Indians, this novel examines India when it was still under British rule and shows how the British interact with the native population, especially the Muslims, as personified in the figure of Dr. Aziz, who is accused of attacking a British woman.

- Mulk Raj Anand was a contemporary of Narayan's, and both were Indian novelists who published their work in English. Anand's *Private Life of an Indian Prince* (1953) is a story with political and romantic elements set in the early years of Indian independence from Britain.

Swami"—having passed beyond individuality, he is no longer attached to a personal name.

In this light, it is instructive to contrast his earlier loquaciousness with his monosyllabic response to the questions put to him by the American journalist Malone. He is of course weakened by hunger, but the contrast is nonetheless a stark one. The old Raju would have grasped this opportunity for worldwide attention with both hands, but the Swami, the former Raju, is no longer interested in such things. Silence befits him now. There seems to be no reason to detect irony in the events the narrator describes at this point, and many readers will surely be moved by the final paragraph, in which the Swami is entirely focused, at great personal cost, on the completion of his mission. He will see it through, even to the end. The Swami says to Velan

> "Help me to my feet," and clung to his arm and lifted himself. He got up to his feet. He had to be held by Velan and another on each side. In the profoundest silence the crowd followed him down. Everyone followed at a solemn, silent pace.... Raju could not walk, but he insisted on pulling himself along all the same. He panted with the effort. He went down the steps of the river, halting for breath on each step, and finally reached his basin of water. He stepped into it, shut his eyes, and turned toward the mountain, his lips muttering the prayer.

Ambiguity there may be right at the end regarding the rain and the Swami's ultimate fate, but the transformation of the slick-talking Raju into the Swami who responds entirely to the needs of the people is unmistakable.

Source: Bryan Aubrey, Critical Essay on *The Guide*, in *Novels for Students*, Gale, Cengage Learning, 2016.

Nicholas Grene

In the following excerpt, Grene looks at the juxtaposition of the ancient and the modern in The Guide.

...*The Guide* stands at the centre of Narayan's life and work. Written in 1956, on his first visit to the United States, it was published in 1958 as the eighth of his fifteen novels. It won him the award of the Sahitya Akademi, India's National Academy, allowing him to make an impish injoke in *The Man-Eater of Malgudi* where the anti-government journalist accuses the Sahitya Akademi of 'wasting funds giving

A large crowd gathers to watch Raju fast. *(© Naiyyer / Shutterstock.com)*

an award to every Tom, Dick and Harry' (*MM* 189, 138). It has become his most famous single book, if in part because of the 1965 Hindi film adaptation directed by Vijay Anand, with a US version produced by Tad Danielewski, a film which Narayan himself detested; his essay 'Misguided Guide' is a hilarious account of the making of the movie and its—from his point of view—ludicrous misrepresentations of the original (*Nightmare* 206–17). The novel has been much analysed, particularly for its relation to Hindu mythology and belief. Chitaram Sankaram argues that Raju is recognizable as the type of the 'trickster sage,' particularly popular in the traditional religious narratives of Tamil culture. Makarand Panjarape cites as an analogue for the story of Raju a parable of Sri Ramakrishna, in which a thief, on the point of being caught robbing a rich man's orchard, pretends to be a holy man, and is treated as such. He reflects, 'I am not a genuine holy man and still people show such devotion to me. What should I do if I was really a holy man?' and ends up converting. This certainly resembles the situation of Raju, the pretend guru who must face the consequences of his pretence. But, of course, there has been much debate on just how genuine Raju's 'conversion' is at the end of the book, and we only arrive at that point after a long and often satiric account of his career as various sorts of charlatan. Hindu parable in *The Guide* is lodged within a markedly secular setting, a modern world in which traditional myth and religious practice have been abandoned or half forgotten. And the story of Raju is told in a double narrative where it is linked with a second figure almost as ambiguous as himself, Rosie/Nalini the dancer.

Released from prison, at a loss to know what to do, Raju finds himself 'beside an ancient shrine.' It is apparently untenanted, without a priest or worshippers. It is only the presence of Raju there, and the reverential attitude of Velan the villager of Mangala, that revive it as a holy place. Soon we hear of the people of the village refurbishing and decorating its pillared hall, the children coming there for lessons, the adults to hear the pronounce-ments of their newly-created guru. Raju finds it hard initially to sustain his part because of his lack of adequate knowledge:

> He began narrating the story of Devaka, a man of ancient times who begged for alms at the temple gate every day and would not use any of the collections without first putting them at the feet of the god. Half-way through the story he realized that he could not remember either its course or its purport.

This, however, provides a cue for a switch into the first person narrative in which Raju retells the story of his life from his childhood: Narayan has deftly established the convention by which the present action is told in the third person, the intercut autobiography in the first. 'How could I recollect the story heard from my mother so long ago?' (*G* 19, 15). Thus, the account of a religious revival in a jungle village, remote from the town, is matched by the life-story of a contemporary citizen of Malgudi who has to reach back to his earliest memories to fit himself for his part as guru.

Raju can just recall the pre-modern life of his childhood: his father with the wayside shop and bullock-cart, his mother with her devout tales from the Hindu scriptures. And then came the railways. The present-day action of *The Guide* is located in the 1950s, the time of its composition, with talk of atom bombs and air-planes even among the villagers, a film crew on hand to cover the last days of Raju's fast for rain. Narayan may be foreshortening chronology to have the railway only coming to Malgudi within the lifespan of Raju; there was already an exten-sive rail network in India by the beginning of the twentieth century. But the introduction of the railway is made to stand in *The Guide*, as in so many nineteenth-century English novels, for the arrival of modernity. Soon the father's wayside shop is left behind and Raju is installed in the station shop, on his way to becoming Railway Raju, tourist guide to all those who come to visit Malgudi.

Narayan's Malgudi is often thought of as a pre-modern site, the sleepy South Indian town which remains changelessly outside the histori-cal movement of the world outside. The next chapter will deal specifically with this issue of Narayan and modernity. But in *The Guide*, at least, it is a centre of tourism, that most quintes-sentially modern form of movement. Raju caters for tourist consumers who come from all over India, hungry for the sights that Malgudi has to offer. His skill is to be able to adjust his tours, his guide's patter, to the varying tastes of the visitor:

> One thing I learned in my career as a tourist guide was that no two persons were interested in the same thing. Tastes, as in food, differ also in sightseeing. Some people want to be seeing a waterfall, some want a ruin (oh, they grow ecstatic when they see cracked plaster, broken idols, and crumbling bricks), some want a god to worship, some look for a hydro-electric plant, and some want just a nice place, such as the bungalow on top of Mempi with all-glass sides, from where you could see a hun-dred miles and observe wild game prowling around.

Laid out here in eclectic array are the con-sumable sights, ancient and modern, natural and man-made, sacred and profane. Though pilgrim-ages sites are among them—the source of the holy river Sarayu is significantly mentioned more than once—these are secular modern pil-grims rather than actual devotees. The ecstasy over 'cracked plaster, broken idols, and crum-bling bricks' recalls Larkin's ironic 'ruin-bibber, randy for antique' visiting disused Christian churches. But it also gestures towards the inter-ests of one very specialist visitor, the husband of Rosie, whom Raju derisively calls Marco, after Marco Polo the explorer. . . .

Source: Nicholas Grene, "Embedded Myths," in *R.K. Narayan*, Northcote House, 2011, pp. 63–66.

John Thieme
In the following excerpt, Thieme examines the significance of Rosie's dancing.

. . . Rosie's dancing and Marco's archaeo-logical work initially seem to be diametrically opposed. When Raju asks Rosie what interests her, she replies '"Anything except cold, old stone walls"' and both her sexuality and her ambition to be a professional classical dancer in contem-porary South India seem to be at odds with Marco's absorption in what Raju sees as a sterile past: 'Dead and decaying things seemed to unloosen his tongue and fire his imagination, rather than things that lived and moved and swung their limbs.' So they come across as an ill-matched couple who represent a contrast between stasis and kinesis, a dead past and a living present. Raju's narration tips the balance firmly in favour of the latter. Despite his famil-iarity with the ancient cave-paintings that Marco is examining, he is dismissive of the mythic past,

> LIKE NARAYAN'S FICTION, WHICH TRANSPORTS ANCIENT MYTHS AND BELIEFS INTO PARTICULAR CONTEMPORARY SITUATIONS, ROSIE'S PERFORMANCES AS A DANCER OPEN UP THE POSSIBILITY OF A RE-ENACTMENT OF CLASSICAL MODES, WHICH TRANSFORMS 'GROSS AND MUNDANE EXPERIENCES.'"

seeing it as ossified and irrelevant to contemporary living:

> I was bored with his ruin-collecting activities. The wall painting represented episodes from the epics and mythology, and all kinds of patterns and motifs, with men, women, and kings and animals, in a curious perspective and proportion of their own, and ancient like the rocks. I had seen hundreds like them, and I saw no point in seeing more. I had no taste for them, just as he had no taste for other things.

In contrast his fascination for Rosie not only leads him into his affair with her, but also into his becoming the agent who secures her rise to fame as a dancer.

Dance may seem to be a secondary concern of the novel, functioning mainly as a medium for developing Rosie's character, but it is a significant subject in its own right and the details of Rosie's training and career as a dancer afford Narayan with an opportunity to draw on his lifelong interest in Indian classical music, specifically the *karnatic* tradition of South India. Rosie's success is as a practitioner of *Bharat Natyam*, generally considered to be the oldest and most traditional of the six major forms of Indian classical dance and still widely performed in Tamil Nadu, and so, as she trains herself to become proficient in this ancient art, she is undergoing a possible transformation which is analogous to Raju's in the later action. Additionally, dance is a trope for performative identity more generally and Narayan seems to be tracing correspondences between ancient thinking on the nature and significance of *Bharat Natyam* and its manifestations in the present. Raju's possible metamorphosis takes place

after the submerged ancient temple reappears; Rosie becomes a star performer of a classical art form that saw a 'resurgence' at the beginning of the twentieth century and so the novel also deals with the relationship between ancient and modern thinking in the sections that focus on her career. Marco may be the professional archaeologist of the novel, but Raju and Rosie are also involved with excavations of the past.

Rosie is one of a number of Narayan's female characters who confound categories, partly but not exclusively, because of their caste backgrounds. She is, like Shanta Bai in *The Dark Room*, both educated (she has an M.A. in Economics) and a woman who feels she has a stigma attached to her because of her caste background. She comes from a '"family traditionally dedicated to the temples as dancers"' and, she explains to Raju, is consequently viewed as a '"public woman".' His infatuation with her makes him dispute this categorization and he both tells her that she belongs to '"the noblest caste on earth"' and asserts that caste discrimination is a thing of the past. Others, including his mother and his domineering uncle, who later appears on the scene in the role of protector of the family honour, take a different view of a *devadasi*. The novel, which sees her from Raju's unreliable viewpoint, remains ambivalent on the issue of her status, but exhibits little of the attempt to police caste boundaries that informs much of Narayan's early fiction and Rosie's character more generally is presented in a positive light. Unlike the siren figure of Shanta Bai, who serves as a foil to the more orthodox though equally complex Savitri in *The Dark Room*, she is represented as a woman who demonstrates both professional and personal integrity, behaving impeccably towards Raju after he has been dishonest towards her.

Rosie is defined by her dancing and when, with Raju's help, she embarks on her study of *Bharat Natyam*, her absorption in her art seems to distance her from the temple-dancer stereotype, with its lowly associations. In his next novel, *The Man-Eater of Malgudi*, Narayan would include a character, Rangi, who, though not unsympathetic, more straightforwardly embodies the traditional association between temple-dancers and prostitutes. Rosie's training to become a serious exponent of classical dance is, however, built around a study of Sanskrit texts, particularly the methods embodied in the classic work on the subject, Bharat's *Natya Shastra* (or *Science of Drama*), without which she feels it will be 'impossible to keep the purity of the classical forms.' Coupled with this, in a passage which reads as a fictional equivalent of Narayan's decision to enlist a scholar to help him with his own study of Sanskrit texts, she asks Raju to find her a Sanskrit pundit, who can read episodes from the *Ramayana* and the *Mahabharata* to her. Narayan's study of ancient texts led to *retellings* of the epics and other mythic tales and fictional works in which they are transformed in contemporary situations. Rosie's study of the *Natya Shastra* may suggest an attempt to learn the conventions of an ancient form of dance, which if simply copied in a mimetic way would preclude creative reinterpretation. In fact, though, she turn[s] to classic writing on the subject as a source from which she 'can pick up so many ideas for *new* compositions' (my italics) and this is very much in keeping with the spirit of Bharat's treatise. The *Natya Shastra* outlines a theory of *rasas* or tastes, which, though developed primarily in relation to drama and dance, has implications for all artistic genres and stresses the relationship between artistic taste and food consumption. As H.L. Seneviratne observes, the treatise sees the process of aesthetic creation as analogous to the consumption of food:

> Just as the *rasa* of food is an essence derived from cooking the gross material of the ingested food by the action of the digestive fires, the *rasa* of aesthetics is a fine emotion born of the transformation of gross and mundane experience by the multistaged extractive and distillative deliberation involving *anubhava* [extension of the stimulative process by suggestive behavior such as glances and body movement], *vibhava* [refers to external stimulus], and *vyabhicharibhava* [an instance of ancillary or transient emotion: the joy in love].

Narayan would no doubt have baulked at seeing this kind of aesthetic theorizing applied to his work, but *The Guide* is centrally concerned with the performative aspects of identity and an awareness of this helps to pinpoint the particular quality of Rosie's dedication to performance arts. Though she is less of a chameleon than Raju, she too seems to undergo a transformation in her identity—in this case from denigrated 'public woman' to respected classical dancer—because of her devotion to older 'methods' *and* her capacity to restage these in new ways. Like Narayan's fiction, which transports ancient myths and beliefs into particular contemporary situations, Rosie's performances as a dancer open up the possibility of a re-enactment of classical modes, which transforms 'gross and mundane experiences.' Seen like this, then, her career as a dancer provides a loose parallel with Raju's perceived metamorphosis into a *sadhu*, which is the last in the series of roles that he occupies. But at this point the caveat that Narayan might baulk at such a reading should perhaps be remembered, since the episodes dealing with Rosie's rise to fame also contain satirical observations on the contemporary commercialization of *Bharat Natyam* as 'the greatest art business today,' a theme that Narayan also developed in his story, 'Musical Commerce.'

The dance motif also has resonance in relation to the work of the third member of *The Guide*'s eternal triangle, Rosie's husband Marco. The couple seem to be on the edge of a reconciliation when he discovers a fresco of dance notations dating from around the fifth century. At this point, Rosie's enthusiasm for Marco's find suggests a degree of convergence between their interests. However, Marco, resistant to any suggestion that the classical and the contemporary may be related, quickly rejects this, branding Rosie's dancing 'street-acrobatics' and 'not art.' So he remains sceptical about her artistry, whereas the trickster Raju has the vision to see her dancing as 'pure abstraction' and initially evinces a clear preference for her vitality over what he sees as Marco's sterility. Subsequently Raju's estimate of Marco's work is less dismissive. Having initially seen him as a copyist and, it would seem, having had little regard for this particular branch of palaeography, Raju later becomes more sympathetic to Marco's view that his discoveries will 'be responsible for the rewriting of history.' Marco's claim may be inflated, but it is partly endorsed when his work on the cave paintings appears in a beautifully produced monograph entitled *The Cultural History of South India* and is hailed in the press as '"An epoch-making discovery in Indian cultural history".' As with Raju and Rosie, his excavation of an ancient Tamil mode opens up the possibility of transforming present-day experience through performative interaction with the classical past. It is no coincidence that the frescoes he finds contain what Raju calls 'abstract verse about some theories of an ancient musical system,' since this suggests an affinity between his project and Rosie's study of the *Natya Shastra*. Beyond this it is possible to read these passages as relating to Narayan's foray into ancient Sanskrit and Tamil lore, which becomes markedly more evident in this period of his career....

Source: John Thieme, "Middle-Period Novels: *The Guide* to *The Painter of Signs*," in *R.K. Narayan*, Manchester University Press, 2007, pp. 108–13.

Mary Beatina

In the following excerpt, Beatina examines the character of Raju.

... Of all Narayan's characters, Raju is the most controversial. It is comparatively easier to study the mundane-transcendent interactions of other characters in Narayan's fiction than that of Raju, because Raju is an exceptionally complex human being. Moreover, the traditional notions of family and profession are brought to question in Raju.

Balarama Gupta labels Raju as "a selfish swindler, an adroit actor, and a perfidious megalomaniac" in his article, "A Sinner is a Sinner is a Sinner—A Study of Raju" (1981, 135). On the other hand, Narasimhaiah almost canonizes Raju as a saint: "With all his limitations Raju's is a rich and complex life—achieving integration at last. It is worthwhile studying this singular success of the novelist's creation. It is obviously not very easy to make a saint out of a sinner, especially for one with a comic vision of life" (1979, 186). These are two extreme views. It is better to bear constantly two things in mind while discussing the transcendent. First, in Narayan's fiction, there is no absolute integration or liberation; it is therefore misleading to speak of saints and sinners, as though such categories are mutually exclusive. Second, Narayan is not interested in presenting good or bad characters, but in tracing the reactions and vibrations which may affect the inner Self of a person during the process of integration through ordinary events. What counts is the process, not any absolute or final outcome.

Raju's life occurs in three phases: his position as a tourist guide, "Railway Raju"; his adventure with the dancer Rosie and her husband Marco; and finally his life at the village, Mangala. He never settles down with a family life. The remarkable and recurrent features in Raju's life in all three phases are several: his innate tendency to accommodate and please others ("I have to play the part expected of me. There is no escape"; his gregarious nature and his love of public attention ("It is something to become so famous, isn't it, instead of handing out matches and tobacco?"); the complex coexistence of the mundane and the transcendent— "self deception and sincerity" (Walsh 1982, 114); and finally, whatever his pretence and ambiguities may be, his concern for the welfare of those whom he serves, even though this concern is often self-serving.

Raju begins as the son of an ordinary shopkeeper who must occasionally tend his father's shop. He enjoys the position of a salesman in meeting a variety of people. When the railways come to Malgudi, Raju is urbanized, and also with some unique intuition he attains great fame and position in Malgudi and environs as "the guide": "Tourists who recommended him to each other would say at one time, 'If you are lucky enough to be guided by Raju, you will know everything. He will not only show you all the worthwhile places, but also will help you in every way.'" Raju is a helper by nature. His humble beginnings in no way indicate any possibility of his later becoming an "omniscient humanist":

> You may ask me why I became a guide or when. It is for the same reason that someone else is a signaller, porter or guard. It is fated thus. Don't laugh at my railway associations. The railway got into my blood very early in life. Engines with their tremendous clanging and smoke ensnared my senses. I felt at home on the railway platform and considered the station-master and porter the best company for man, and their railway talk the most enlightened. I grew up in their midst. Ours was a small house opposite the Malgudi station. The house had been built by my father with his own hands long before the trains were thought of.

From the time his father handed over the small shop at the station to Raju, Raju has been growing amidst the thrill he derives from the modernity and bustle of the environment. He enjoys company: "I liked to talk to people. I liked to hear people talk." In order to accommodate himself to others and to meet the expectations of others, he equips himself in many ways: "I read stuff that interested me, bored me, baffled me, and dozed off in my seat. I read stuff that picked up a noble thought, a philosophy that appealed, I gazed on pictures ... I learnt much from scrap." He is never left alone: "Although I never looked for acquaintances, they somehow came looking for me." When people come with enquiries or to seek his help, Raju is unable to say "no" to anyone:

> I never said, "I don't know." Not in my nature, I suppose. If I had the inclination to say "I don't know what you are talking about," my life would have taken a different turn. Instead, I said, "Oh, yes, a fascinating place. Haven't you seen it? You must find the time to visit it, otherwise your whole trip here would be a waste." I am sorry I said it, an utter piece of falsehood. It was not because I wanted to utter a falsehood, but only because I wanted to be pleasant.

Without giving serious thought to the enquiries or the subject, Raju furnishes the information in order to please the enquirer, and to accommodate himself to any situation.

Thus, from the beginning of his career, he is an accommodator: "So extreme a degree of accommodation means that Raju's sincerity consists in being false, and his positive existence is being a vacancy filled by others" (Walsh 1982, 122). What Walsh ignores, however, is that Raju's attempts to accommodate, mundane as they are, nonetheless prepare him for the transcendent life he eventually achieves. While Krishna in *The English Teacher* broods over his inability to teach his college students according to his own convictions, here Raju accommodates as a product of others' interests and needs. Raju's personality is shaped as a kind of "selfless detachment," sacrificing self and identity to please others—this is also an essential quality for good business. Such detachment and sacrifice can lead to a loss of genuine identity. It can lead, however, to transcendence. . . .

Source: Mary Beatina, "Mature Transcendence: *The Guide*," in *Narayan: A Study in Transcendence*, Peter Lang, 1993, pp. 93–95.

SOURCES

Alam, Fakrul, "R. K. Narayan," in *Dictionary of Literary Biography*, Vol. 323, *South Asian Writers in English*, edited by Fakrul Alam, Gale, 2006, pp. 252–64.

Halliday, Adam, "Mizoram Lifts 18-Year-Old Ban on Alcohol," in *Indian Express*, July 10, 2014, indianexpress.com/article/india/india-others/mizoram-lifts-18-year-old-ban-on-alcohol/ (accessed December 12, 2014).

"History of Bharatanatyam," Rangshree Dance of India, http://rangashree.org/bharatanatyam-history.html (accessed December 12, 2014).

"Indian Classical Dance," in *Hindu Online*, http://hinduonline.co/HinduCulture/IndianClassicalDance.html (accessed December 7, 2014).

Nair, K. N. Padmanabhan, *Irony in the Novels of R. K. Narayan and V. S. Naipaul*, CBH Publications, 1993, p. 71.

Narayan, R. K., "English in India," in *The Writerly Life: Selected Non-Fiction*, edited by S. Krishnan, Viking, 2001, pp. 467–68.

————, *The Guide*, Viking Press, 1958.

Panjiar, Ronan, "The Tragedy of Prohibition," in *Indian Express*, March 26, 2010, http://archive.indianexpress.com/news/the-tragedy-of-prohibition/490493/0 (accessed December 14, 2014).

Rayen, Sr. Mary Beatina, O. S. M. "The Guide: A Study in Transcendence," in *R. K. Narayan: Contemporary Critical Perspectives*, edited by Geoffrey Kain, Michigan State University Press, 1993, pp. 56–57, 65–66.

"Status of World Nuclear Forces," Federation of American Scientists website, http://fas.org/issues/nuclear-weapons/status-world-nuclear-forces/ (accessed December 14, 2014).

Thieme, John, *R. K. Narayan*, Manchester University Press, 2007, pp. 103, 107–08.

Walsh, William, *R. K. Narayan: A Critical Appreciation*, Heinemann, 1982, pp. 4–5, 114.

FURTHER READING

Hartsuiker, Dolf, *Sadhus: Holy Men of India*, Inner Traditions, 2014.
> Hartsuiker traveled extensively in India as he researched this book about the many holy men, or sadhus, in India, who are popularly regarded as the representatives of the gods. He describes their beliefs and ascetic practices and their dedication to their spiritual calling.

McLeod, A. L., ed., *R. K. Narayan: Critical Perspectives*, Sterling Publishers, 1994.
> This collection of eighteen essays on Narayan's work includes "R. K. Narayan's Dialogic Narrative in *The Guide*," by Sura P. Rath, which discusses Narayan's narrative strategy.

Narayan, R. K., *A Writer's Nightmare: Selected Essays (1958–1988)*, Penguin, 1989.
> This is a collection of short essays by Narayan on a variety of topics, most of them written in an informal, conversational tone.

Srinath, C. N., ed., *R. K. Narayan: An Anthology of Recent Criticism*, Pencraft International, 2005.
> This is a collection of twelve essays on all aspects of Narayan's work. It includes an essay by C. C. Narasimhaiah on *The Guide*.

SUGGESTED SEARCH TERMS

R. K. Narayan

R. K. Narayan AND The Guide

Sadhu

Ramayana

Mahabharata

Indian classical dance

Bharat Natyam

Natya Shastra

Malgudi AND fictional town

India AND holy men

Lie Down in Darkness

WILLIAM STYRON

1951

Lie Down in Darkness (1951) was the debut of the award-winning twentieth-century American novelist William Styron. It immediately made a name for the author owing to its psychologically attuned depiction of a Virginia family fraying at the seams—indeed all through the fabric—because of misunderstandings, antipathies, and unfortunate decisions. At the outset, the novel evocatively settles the reader in August 1945 along the coastline of the Tidewater region of Virginia with the wayward patriarch Milton Loftis facing the darkest day of his life. As the day progresses, the reader slips into the minds of Milton and other characters whose reminiscences open up extended flashbacks depicting life for the Loftises in and around their bayside home in Port Warwick. As the novel portrays a number of pivotal episodes from the Loftises' past, it soon becomes clear that Milton and his wife, Helen, in caring for their daughters—developmentally disabled Maudie and beautiful Peyton—have had trouble maintaining family unity.

It was seen as mostly positive that Styron's novel so adroitly follows in the literary tradition of William Faulkner and other southern and modernist writers. The similarities between Styron's novel and Faulkner's *As I Lay Dying* and, in particular, *The Sound and the Fury*—with regard to character types, narrative structure, themes, even a symbol or two—are prominent, leading some to frame *Lie Down in Darkness* as an

William Styron (© *ZUMA Press, Inc.* / *Alamy*)

apprentice work; after all, Styron was only twenty-six when it was published. Yet most critics are quick to affirm that with its skillful use of poetic language and masterly characterizations, Styron's novel more than merits independent praise and critical appreciation. Readers may wish to consider that although they are conveyed with fifties-era prudence, there are scenes of sexual relations and a great deal of irresponsible drinking. Upon publication, the novel won Styron the Prix de Rome from the American Academy of Arts and Letters.

AUTHOR BIOGRAPHY

Styron was born on June 11, 1925, in Newport News, Virginia, the town where he was raised. His father, William Clark Styron, Sr., was a marine engineer and his mother, Pauline, who had roots in Pennsylvania, was a musician who studied voice and piano in the classical culture center of Vienna, Austria. Pauline died of breast cancer when Styron was thirteen. Having grown up on the banks of the James River, Styron went to Christchurch Preparatory School on the Rappahannock—not the most elite school but a respectable Episcopalian one that Styron found beautiful in its natural setting and came to love. Styron contributed to the school newspaper, though with little career ambition. After Styron entered Davidson College, a Presbyterian school in North Carolina, and then transferred to Duke University, however, Professor William Blackburn recognized his writing talent and gave encouragement that Styron took to heart. His early stories were published in the campus magazine, *Archive*, and later in Blackburn's 1945 anthology *One and Twenty: Duke Narrative and Verse (1924–1945)*.

Styron enrolled in the Marine Corps Reserve, a family tradition, in 1941 while he was at Duke and was called to duty at a South Carolina base in late 1944. He finished officer training, but the end of World War II in the summer of 1945 saved him from being shipped overseas. He was instead temporarily assigned to the Naval Disciplinary Barracks on Hart Island, New York, in Long Island Sound. Styron returned to Duke in the spring of 1946 and graduated in 1947.

After graduation, Styron moved to New York City and briefly worked as a manuscript reader at McGraw-Hill, but aching to write a novel, he was happily fired. He enrolled in a class at the New School for Social Research, learning from a teacher whose other job as an editor allowed him to secure Styron an advance. Drawing on the advance, Styron moved back to Durham, North Carolina, but writer's block set in, and it lingered when he moved back to Brooklyn, New York. He finally found his footing thanks to the graceful hospitality of a peer from the New School, Sigrid de Lima, and her mother in their old house up the Hudson River in Rockland County. By the time Styron was finishing the novel in Manhattan in 1951, the Marines had called him back up because of the Korean War. After enduring with his company not war itself but the trials of a prolonged disciplinary march in the summer heat of North Carolina, he was released, and so was his novel, *Lie Down in Darkness*, establishing his literary career.

Styron went on to live for periods in Rome and Paris, where he was part of the founding of the *Paris Review* as an editor and writer. He wrote essays with regularity, but beyond his youthful efforts, the short-story form appealed to him less, as he realized that his literary strengths lay in the possibilities offered by longer forms. He published a novella, *The Long March*, based on his military experiences, in 1953, but his next novel was not published until 1960. Critics, by this time impatient and overly expectant, were less impressed with this novel, *Set This House on Fire*, the plot of which depicts the declension of the creative spirit in postwar American society, than with his debut. Styron's crowning achievements were his controversial 1967 novel *The Confessions of Nat Turner*, which won the Pulitzer Prize, and the 1979 Brooklyn-set, Holocaust-oriented drama *Sophie's Choice*, which became an award-winning film in 1982. Styron spent most of his life at his home in Roxbury, Connecticut, with his wife, Rose (Burgunder), with whom he had three daughters and a son, and at a summer home on Martha's Vineyard, Massachusetts. He died on Martha's Vineyard on November 1, 2006, at the age of eighty-one.

PLOT SUMMARY

1

The narration opening *Lie Down in Darkness* takes the reader along on a train ride from Richmond to Port Warwick, Virginia. There, in August 1945, Milton Loftis—along with Dolly Bonner, Ella Swan, and two funeral men—is awaiting the delivery of his daughter Peyton's corpse. He recalls first meeting Helen, his estranged wife. Barclay is repairing the broken-down hearse. Mr. Casper sends the increasingly upset Milton to wait in the limousine and recalls the scene at Helen's house the night before. Milton had arrived with the news, desolate, and begged Helen to take him back; she only let him spend the night downstairs. She has declined to accompany Milton to the station but will get a ride with Carey Carr. Helen recalls the day at Uncle Eddie's when four-year-old Peyton was nearly stung by bees, leading Helen to reproach her but Milton to encourage her adventurousness. Helen had turned to Maudie for comfort. Milton talks to Barclay, grows ill, enters a bar

MEDIA ADAPTATIONS

- An audiobook version of *Lie Down in Darkness* on fourteen cassettes, read by Wolfram Kandinsky, was produced by Books on Tape in 1984.

- A reading of *Lie Down in Darkness* by Grover Gardner, produced in 2011, can be downloaded at AudioBook Bay.

- Audiobooks.com has made available a sixteen-minute excerpt of Styron reading the passage about Maudie and Bennie from *Lie Down in Darkness*, available under the title *Great American Authors Read from Their Works*, Vol. 1, *William Styron Reading from* Lie Down in Darkness, published by Calliope Author Readings in 2014.

- As of 2012, a film adaptation of *Lie Down in Darkness* was in the earliest stages of pre-production, to be directed by Scott Cooper. Kristen Stewart was rumored to be undertaking the role of Peyton, but as of 2013, Jennifer Lawrence was professing attachment to the idea of playing the role.

and vomits, and buys some coffee. He reads Peyton's last letter to him.

2

Dolly fetches Milton to rejoin the hearse and limousine, because everything is ready, and they drive off—but soon the hearse breaks down again. Milton, panicking, finds Dolly annoying and remembers his father's long-ignored love advice. He recalls a Sunday when Peyton was nine: they are reading the newspaper out on the lawn. Helen approaches and blames Dolly for leaving a cigarette burn on their rug the night before. As Milton goes inside, Helen reminds him about church. He pours himself whiskey anyway, despite Ella's chiding. Helen becomes angry but can only take the girls to Sunday school.

Later that day, Dolly's family is visiting. Privately with Milton, Helen reveals anger over the visit, a surprise to her, especially because she knows that Milton dislikes Dolly's husband, Pookie. While Milton and Dolly, alone, are exchanging first innuendos, La Ruth screams: Maudie has been tied up and gagged. They free her. After slapping Peyton's face, Helen bears Maudie away. Later Milton brings Peyton to apologize, and Helen dispassionately accepts. Milton also apologizes, for inviting the guests. He drives Peyton out for a father-daughter dinner.

3

The limousine proceeds toward downtown Port Warwick. Dolly realizes that Milton no longer loves her. The night before at the country club, his residence of late, he was talking only of Peyton. After taking a phone call, he returned stricken, hugged a different friend, and drove off alone without telling Dolly anything. Dolly recalls Peyton's sixteenth birthday party at the club in August 1939: Milton dances with Helen until she is too tired, then boldly dances with Dolly. Helen chastises Peyton for drinking; her father had encouraged her. Peyton soon tells Milton that Helen is insisting that she leave the party. Secretly, Milton and Dolly share a first kiss.

Later on, Milton tells a guest that Helen had to take Maudie home. Milton had argued with her and insisted that Peyton could stay. After all the parents have left, Milton and Dolly make love in the golf museum. From the pool, Peyton heads up to the club; Charlie La Farge follows and sees her watching at the museum door. After he scares her on her way out, he consoles her while she cries. In the present, the limousine and hearse drive past Daddy Faith, who is sitting on a Cadillac being admired and praised.

4

Reverend Carey Carr, driving to pick up Helen, recalls the rainy October night when she started seeking his counsel six years ago: she arrives at 10:30, and they have drinks. She tells him of her husband's adultery with "Mrs. X," which she has long (inaccurately) suspected. Helen tells of her strict but beloved military father, her husband's drinking, and the family's happiness back when the girls were five and four.

Helen recalls the day before Peyton left for Sweet Briar school, weeks after the sixteenth-birthday party. From Maudie's window, Helen looks down on the drinking Milton and the already-sensual Peyton as sinners and even hates them. Nonetheless she goes outside and feels congenial, until Peyton rebukes her for repeating a motherly comment. Fuming, Helen tends her garden. When Maudie awakens from her nap, Helen runs over, frantically insisting that Peyton not help her out of bed, but Milton intercepts and soothes her. But then, after loud planes fly overhead, Helen impulsively rushes inside to find that Maudie has fallen down part of the stairs. Maudie is not upset and only bruised, but Helen berates Peyton and says that she (Helen) now has to stay home the next day. Later, she confronts Milton about Dolly. Now officially guilty, Milton can only flee. The next day, after Milton and Peyton leave for Sweet Briar, Helen calls to insist that Dolly join her for tea. After conversing genteelly, Helen confronts Dolly, who first denies anything but then declares that she loves Milton and leaves. Later, Milton returns home, telling Helen that Peyton has missed her.

Driving, Carey recalls Helen's subsequent visits and increasing mental imbalance. Helen is awakened by La Ruth, and Carey is waiting downstairs. La Ruth urges Helen to take Milton back. Indignant, Helen descends.

5

The hearse stalls downtown, then on the highway, and then rolls into a gas station. One night in November 1942, fifty-year-old Milton did two regrettable things. The first was getting drunk, not knowing he would soon be driving to Charlottesville. He had learned to pacify Helen by keeping Dolly in the background, but this pattern was spoiled in December 1941. While the Loftises are hosting a party on Christmas Eve, Dolly, feeling neglected, calls, ruining Helen's mood. Milton goes to her upstairs, and they are momentarily tender together (for the last time). Peyton arrives with Dick Cartwright, intoxicated and planning to go to a party. Upstairs Helen instructs Peyton to stay home, but Peyton leaves anyway. On Christmas day, Milton wakes up with a hangover. He wakes Peyton, who reports that Edward left for military duty when she returned around 3:30 a.m. Upon returning from church with Maudie, Helen starts fixing dinner. She is bitter because Peyton spent no time with Edward. Helen is exceedingly cold during dinner, until Peyton finally gives up and runs outside. She soon packs and leaves for the Cartwrights' house.

Peyton does not come home in the ensuing seasons, though Milton visits her four times that summer (1942). That fall, Helen must take Maudie to the Charlottesville hospital. In Port Warwick, Milton, as an air-raid warden, patrols during alarms. Returning once in November, he finds Dolly at his house with the lights on (against regulations). A taxi driver has refused to take her farther during the blackout. They start drinking, and Milton reluctantly lets her stay while he finishes a letter to Peyton, who will be in Charlottesville the next day. Eventually—the second regrettable thing—he fornicates with Dolly in Helen's bed. That night a woman calls to read a telegram from Helen saying that Maudie is doing poorly, and Milton must come.

While driving to Charlottesville after dropping Dolly off at dawn, Milton drinks. At the hospital, he cannot understand what Helen tells him about Maudie's grave condition. Helen implores him to stick around. After a nurse summons Helen to speak with a doctor, Milton runs into Hubert MacPhail, who invites him to KA, their old fraternity, for a drink; Milton thinks of finding Peyton. At KA, Peyton shows up with Dick but leaves so quickly that Milton cannot get her attention. Hubert, whose son Buzzie refuses to go to the big football game, gives Milton his ticket. Buzzie reports that Peyton went to the Virginian first. Milton arrives there, only for the crowd of youths to abruptly sweep out to the game. As Milton finishes his drink, Pookie and his new girlfriend arrive and oppress Milton with jovial chatter. He offends them, takes their Confederate flag, and departs for the game. There, he does not spot Peyton until the game has ended and again cannot reach her. Peyton returns to KA, where Milton eventually walks in bleeding. He left the game and walked the wrong way, then upon decisively returning fell into a culvert. Peyton bandages him, and he naps. When he wakes up and explains about Maudie, Peyton says he should have just called KA.

Milton and Peyton go to the hospital, where Helen assumes they were deliberately carousing instead of being with Maudie. Helen tells of afternoons at home when the neighboring wartime barracks were being built, and Ella would take the men water. Eventually Maudie accompanied Ella, even sometimes staying when Ella

returned. One day when rain came, Helen went to fetch Maudie and found her sweetly watching Bennie doing magic tricks. Helen believes that Maudie, unlike Loftis and Peyton, knew love. She tells them (perhaps insincerely) they are too late to see Maudie.

Peyton and Dick drink while driving to his house on the Rappahannock. Dick implores her to marry him, but she refuses. They enjoy the peace in the empty house, and, overcoming Peyton's reluctance, Dick makes love to her.

6

Driving Helen to the funeral, Carey must stop for a procession of Daddy Faith's followers. He continues his attempts to persuade Helen to reunite with Milton—but suspects that she has gone crazy. They find the hearse at the gas station. Carey goes into the roadhouse to find Milton drinking beer alone, with Dolly crying nearby. He urges Milton to win back Helen's love. They had reunited after Maudie's death, as Milton stopped drinking. Then in October 1943, Peyton's wedding came around.

On the way to the wedding, Carey marvels at why Milton would even want to stay with Helen. Milton has convinced Peyton that Helen has warmed up and that a home wedding will succeed. At the house, Edward wakes Milton to report that Helen has gone alone to Williamsburg to collect Peyton and her groom-to-be, Harry. Milton gets a beer from the kitchen. He had begged Helen to reconcile with him that November day in Charlottesville. In January 1943, she attempted suicide with pills, but Dr. Holcomb revived her (and suggested psychiatric care). Milton pleaded with her, totally sober, and finally reached and reunited with her. Dolly, abandoned, began sending Milton mementos. Helen and Milton, vacationing in Asheville in April, experienced a moment of marital grace.

On the day of the wedding, Milton finds Peyton upstairs and kisses her. Peyton admits to having lived like a tramp in New York City before meeting Harry. Peyton charmingly suggests a drink, and Milton relents with a stashed bottle. Peyton reports only feigning contentedness with her mother. During the ceremony, Milton feels depressed, but Helen feels exalted. She conceives that Milton rescued her from death after Maudie died and that now she has restored the family; yet she still loathes Peyton.

In the receiving line, Milton is buoyed again by Peyton's warmth and closeness, but he pulses with jealousy when Harry kisses Peyton. Edward orders Milton to drink more. When they all sit down, Milton tries to give Harry a father-in-law's pep talk but seems to make a faux pas. Unsure of what he said wrong, he concludes that Helen's and Peyton's smiles look so fake because they have no real mutual goodwill; they have always been faking it.

La Ruth emerges joyously with the wedding cake while absentmindedly dragging a chain of hot dogs. Ella comes out to yell at her, making La Ruth cry, until Peyton restores good spirits. Overly proud and emotional, Milton assaults Peyton with unfatherly kisses, until she shoves him away and demands he not smother her. Milton realizes that Helen and Harry both have seen. After the cake, the church bells send Milton into reveries of Peyton's childhood. Helen goes outside in a fury to complain to Carey that Peyton's meanness to Milton has ruined the wedding. Carey tries to convince her that she is both misinterpreting and overreacting—and needs mental help—but she dismisses his conspiratorially male perspective. She has been having dreams of a women's apocalypse, with Dolly among the corpses; sometimes, she herself is the enemy. She blurts out to Carey her allegiance to the devil. In the house, Dr. Holcomb, who is basking in Peyton's company and hearing of her troubles, sees across the room both Milton, pouring his heart out to Harry, and Helen, snakelike, entering and seeking out Peyton.

Looking back months later, Milton can hardly remember how things happened next. At the wedding he is telling Harry how much he appreciates Jews when he sees Helen escort Peyton upstairs—signaling doom. Distracted and drunk, he desperately kisses Dora. Seized with determination, he heads upstairs and from the hall hears Helen belittling and insulting Peyton, especially for having revealed her (purported) hatred for her father. Peyton retaliates by clawing at and bloodying Helen's face when Helen makes a derogatory remark about Harry. Peyton then starts sobbing and leaves. Milton steps in to curse Helen. Downstairs, the remaining guests usher the couple off on their honeymoon, and Milton calls Dolly.

Drinking while waiting for the ferry on their honeymoon, Peyton and Harry are questioned by a police officer who turns out to know the Loftises. Peyton's foul mouth offends a woman with a parrot. On the ferry, Peyton and Harry argue over her drinking, her parents, and his talking to a girl while Helen was upstairs with Peyton. She breaks down in tears, and they make up.

At the cemetery, Milton has ordered Dolly to wait in the car. When the family emerges from the chapel, she sees Helen smile at Milton. It starts to rain.

7

Potter's Field, on Hart's Island, is the destination for New York City's unclaimed dead. Prisoners dig the graves. With an undertaker, Harry and Lennie head out to the island to recover Peyton. Harry and Peyton meet in the spring of 1943 at Albert Berger's, when she clings to Harry drunk and sad. Harry brings her home, acting the gentleman, and they soon get together. Lennie has doubts at first but finds her behavior improving with Harry's influence. After the wedding, however, she spurns a psychiatrist and goes off on a weeklong affair. When they find the grave, Lennie tells Harry the death is not his fault.

Peyton (narrating) tells Tony she does not have enough time to make love; also, she is experiencing painful cramps. But he aggressively insists, then leaves. Peyton has visions of her and Harry at peace inside her new alarm clock. The radio relates the recent atomic bombing of Japan. She can hear flightless birds rustling behind walls and following her around. She cleans up the apartment for when she brings Harry back. As Peyton is on her way out, the landlady demands her rent money, and Peyton says Harry will help. She first dreams of birds with Dick Cartwright. She stops in a bar for a drink and feels as if she is drowning. A sailor enters and suggests he knows her: she is Tony's girl. She lies repeatedly. She recalls having her affair with Earl Sanders because she caught Harry feeling another woman's behind. She first daydreams birds with Earl Sanders. She has a second martini and then leaves, and someone directs her north to Cornelia Street.

Abruptly crossing a street, Peyton is nearly hit by a truck. The driver berates her, but a policeman politely ushers her on. At Lennie's, no one is home, and Peyton cries, but she finds a note (to Laura) revealing that Lennie and Harry have gone to Albert's (and directing Laura to tell Peyton that Harry is in Peru). A passing gentleman wipes Peyton's tears. She takes a taxi to Albert's but cannot pay the fifty-cent fare; she tells the driver she will find payment inside. At the door, Cyril reports that Harry has left but ushers Peyton in anyway. Albert waxes philosophic. Lennie at first refuses to admit where Harry has gone. The taxi driver knocks and finally gets his money. Lennie, seeing Peyton's unbalanced desperation, finally says that Harry has gone to an apartment nearby to paint. He instructs her to either come back or go to Laura's if Harry will not see her.

Peyton heads out and at Marshall Freeman's apartment rings the bell but does not respond when Harry calls out. Harry at last opens the door and is angry but lets her in. He is painting a monk among ruins looking up to heaven. She has brought the clock and offers it to him, but he reports that he already knows about it because the check she used to pay for it has bounced, and now he is broke. They argue over her infidelity, and he starts to sympathize, but when she resumes blaming him for failing to try to understand her, he finally rejects her. Outside, she buys a flower, throws her clock down a drain, gives twenty cents to a panhandler, and uses her last nickel to get on the subway. She gets off at 125th Street (in Harlem) among African Americans. She runs from and yells at the birds following her, then enters a loft building and climbs the stairs, to accomplish her last descent. Some floors up, she finds a ladies' room, disrobes, watches the birds fly past her out the window, and follows them.

The rain pours down, and Helen, Milton, and the others reenter the chapel. Milton takes Helen into an anteroom, where he grows hysterical. Helen emerges calmly and rejects Milton finally, so he chokes her for a moment before recoiling. Then he runs out into the rain toward the highway. Helen at last laments being left with nothing.

Later that day, Ella, La Ruth, and Stonewall take a bus to Daddy Faith's baptismal service at the waterfront. La Ruth repeatedly mourns Peyton. Waiting and watching a raft in the shallows, the robed followers grow attentive when a band marches out into the water. A blue-robed man's sonorous proclamations rivet the crowd, and Daddy Faith emerges to give a soothing sermon. Afterward, Ella extols the wonder of the immersion. She rises to praise Jesus ecstatically—as a train, its whistle screeching, heads north into the night.

CHARACTERS

Dora Appleton
Dora Appleton is a wedding guest. Having a grand time, she grants Milton a requested kiss.

Barclay
Barclay is the undertaker's assistant. He is relatively new at the job and knows little about fixing cars.

Bennie
A half-black, half-Indian man working at the military construction site near the Loftises' property, Bennie is not handsome, but he gallantly, silently performs magic tricks for Maudie, and she seems to love him. After a tearful parting one day, he never returns.

Albert Berger
An intellectual with a medical condition that leaves his eyes watering at random, Albert Berger has managed to become host of a highly popular salon, or regular gathering of minds.

Dolly Bonner
Dolly Bonner is the woman with whom Milton has an affair. The intrigue between them first sparks when Peyton is about nine. The two flirt for the next six years (leading Helen to believe an affair has already started), but not until Peyton's sixteenth-birthday party does Dolly succeed in encouraging Milton to seek release from Helen's strictures through adultery. Dolly seems to gravitate to Milton as a step up from the quality and social status of Pookie, her husband, a real-estate broker. Dolly eventually divorces her husband, and the affair continues—minus the year after Maudie's death—to the time at which the novel opens. Dolly's hopes are up because of Milton's impending divorce—October 21, 1945, is his "D-day"—but with Peyton's death, Dolly quickly realizes that Milton is being drawn back to Helen. Her superficial companionship proves meaningless to Milton once his cherished daughter is gone.

Melvin Bonner
Melvin Bonner is Dolly's son and about Peyton's age. He tells on Peyton after she hits him in the face when she is nine. Together, apparently, they tie up Maudie. Peyton calls him Buster.

Sclater (Pookie) Bonner

Mr. Bonner's name is pronounced "slaughter," but everyone calls him Pookie. Dolly considers him an unhandsome clown, explaining her attraction to Milton. Pookie works in real estate and moves to Knoxville, Tennessee, after the Bonners divorce. His ultimate financial success—which may be what attracts Harriet to him—makes Dolly's fate all the more pathetic.

Adrienne Carr

Adrienne mentions rumors of Milton's affair to her husband, Carey. She has a grounded worldview that sometimes makes Carey's religious flightiness seem overwrought.

Reverend Carey Carr

As the novel's white religious figurehead, Carey Carr speaks to the potential ineffectuality of religion in salvaging the souls of the misguided. The problem is that he himself, a failed poet, has obtained only a partial awakening to God—his belief has never been validated—and so while he makes reasonable ethical arguments, his words come from his mind, not his soul. Thus he fails to inspire Helen with redemptive emotions. This is also partly because his perspective sometimes veers into the patriarchal and patronizing, alienating Helen. Ultimately, he fails to achieve his dogmatic goal of reuniting the married couple.

Dick Cartwright

Dick Cartwright is the youth who accompanies Peyton when she returns from school for Christmas 1941 (likely her third year of college). Dick wonders what Peyton sees in him—perhaps a foil to her wildness. By the following year, Dick has given her his fraternity pin, socially sealing their couplehood, and is ready to get married—but Peyton is not exactly interested. After a hormonally frustrating courtship, Dick proves to disappoint Peyton with recurring impotence.

Llewellyn Casper

Mr. Casper, the undertaker, is a steady influence on the mourners but is discombobulated by the repeated failures of his hearse.

Tony Cecchino

Tony Cecchino is the milkman who takes advantage of Peyton's openness after (and perhaps in the midst of) her breakup with Harry. He is selfish, crass, and more enemy than friend.

Cyril

Cyril is a polite friend of Harry's found at Albert Berger's apartment.

Daddy Faith

First appearing in a flashy diamond-studded get-up that seems to undermine his religious authority, Daddy Faith nonetheless draws and properly wows African American crowds when he hosts his annual baptismal ceremony at the waterfront.

Uncle Edward

A coal broker turned army colonel stationed in Pennsylvania, Edward is a bit stiff in social company. He tries to make up for this by being a dedicated—and insistent—drinker, which does Milton no favors.

Marta Epstein

Marta is the woman whose behind Harry touches and whom he kisses (though perhaps just on the cheek). Peyton sees this and enters a weeklong affair with Earl Sanders.

Marshall Freeman

Marshall Freeman, the owner of the apartment where Harry goes to paint, does not appear in the story, but his last name prominently labels his mailbox.

Harriet

Harriet is Pookie's postdivorce partner. She is around forty, beautiful, and a former nurse. Milton crudely insinuates that Harriet only wants Pookie's money.

Dr. Lawrence Holcomb

As the Loftis family doctor, Holcomb assists when Helen attempts suicide. He tells Milton that psychiatric care may be needed and also orders her to stop smoking. A bachelor in his sixties, he takes advantage of the convivial atmosphere at the wedding to enjoy being close to Peyton.

Alice and Chester La Farge

Alice and Chester La Farge, a grocer, chat with Milton at Peyton's birthday party, where they note and later gossip over Milton's scandalous closeness with Dolly.

Charlie La Farge
In their adolescence, Charlie dates and is in love with Peyton. He is Alice and Chester's son.

Laura
Laura, Lennie's girlfriend, is evidently not enough of a friend for the idea of her company to lure Peyton away from suicide.

Lennie
Lennie is Harry's closest friend. Harry stays with him after leaving Peyton. Lennie also proves a good friend to Peyton when she needs it most—and yet she never heeds his instruction to return for support after seeing Harry.

Helen Peyton Loftis
Helen, who married Milton while still in her late teens (he was around thirty), never tries to hide or stifle the sense of propriety she has inherited from her military father. She has perhaps taken to heart the fact that Milton gave up alcohol while courting her. Over time, however, his reestablished drinking and her antipathy to it feed the flames that slowly burn their marriage down. Helen deserves admiration for her devotion to her developmentally disabled daughter—a daughter many people in Helen's circumstances might have passed off to servants for daily care. And yet Maudie's fragility leaves Helen with an overly cautious perspective on parenting, which stifles Peyton and sets up Milton to be the fun parent. That Milton and Peyton can bond and roam free while Helen remains honorably by Maudie's side is at the root of Helen's jealousy and hatred of Peyton. Helen is also greatly affected by Peyton's tying up Maudie and even gagging her. When Peyton allows Maudie to fall down the stairs, Helen is led to conclude that Peyton is the enemy. After Maudie dies, Helen—her mind clouded by a barbiturate and her psychic loops recasting reality—conceives that Peyton has killed Maudie.

In the past, hardly a scene goes by when Helen fails to light up a cigarette; in the present, she has been told by Dr. Holcomb to refrain and is reluctantly succeeding. Through her trials with Milton, ever exacerbated by his drinking and marital betrayal and her inflexibility and ill will, Helen has been reduced to a cold stoicism that no longer allows for the possibility of a mutually loving relationship with her husband. Only when Peyton's funeral service has ended and Milton has fled, rejected by her, does Helen seem to fully realize that she has no one and nothing left.

Maudie Loftis
Maudie is one of the two daughters of Helen and Milton Loftis. With a stunted mental capacity and partial immobility (she must wear a leg brace), Maudie needs constant care even as she matures, most of it coming from her mother. She grows attached to Bennie for both his magic tricks and his kindness. Helen believes that Maudie's tearful goodbye that day as the rain comes signals her preternatural understanding that the two will never see each other again. Maudie's compromised biology eventually leads to her death at about age twenty in a hospital in Charlottesville.

Milton Loftis
Milton Loftis is an antihero, a character who is largely sympathetic but whose flaws—especially his alcoholism—prevent him from bringing about positive outcomes. When he is introduced, Milton is understandably at wit and sentiment's end over the untimely death of his daughter Peyton. As it happens, his effusively despairing, anxious behavior suggests that the significance of the loss of his daughter is more complicated than would be expected. The series of upcoming flashbacks makes clear that over time Milton's family life has become a cauldron of frustration and instability, that he has come to rely too much on Peyton's reassuring youth and beauty—and on whiskey. Milton's alcoholism, fueled by his wife's rigidity (he is already a heavy drinker in college), is the root of most of his problems, including the lack of inhibition he demonstrates in being affectionate toward Peyton beyond the paternal. For example, he gives Peyton his class ring after hearing that Dick has given Peyton his fraternity pin.

Milton meets Helen as a military lawyer—a position, secured by his father, that allows him to evade active duty in World War I and become a captain anyway. He marries her more for her beauty than the compatibility of their personalities. The flaky Dolly suits him better in many respects. The Loftis family situation might have been greatly improved with a straightforward divorce, but Milton remains dependent on Helen's inherited fortune—and after both of their daughters die, he conceives that only with Helen can he regain what happiness his life once contained. Milton is last seen running, angst ridden, from the cemetery toward the highway.

Peyton Loftis

The complex architecture of Peyton's psyche is only hinted at through the first six chapters of the novel. The reader finds that, like many children, she aligns more closely with one parent than the other—Milton over Helen—as first shown in the episode in which she cutely runs, thrilled, from the bees, and Milton is the one to share in the moment. In a more ideal domestic world, Helen's reproaches and Milton's encouragement might have balanced each other out. Instead, Peyton becomes both the substitute object of Milton's affection and the direct object of Helen's jealousy and eventual hatred. With a father whose caring gestures verge on the incestuous (her nickname for Milton sounds like one for a romantic partner, though Bunny is what his grandmother called him) and a mother whose loathing all too often boils over, Peyton proves psychically unstable. Beyond being sexually liberal, she cannot control her drinking, like her father, nor can she control her impulse to fault her romantic partner for any discord between them, like her mother. Thus does she inflate Harry's minor transgressions and take vengeance through rash infidelity—in the process sabotaging her marriage and, ultimately, her sanity and her life. She dies at twenty-two.

Buzzie MacPhail

Buzzie helps Loftis track Peyton before the big game, and it is Buzzie's ticket that gets Milton into the game.

Hubert MacPhail

A member of the same University of Virginia fraternity as Milton, Hubert brings Milton to KA before the big game. He is apparently disappointed by his son Buzzie's lack of virility, which his indifference to football supposedly demonstrates.

Aunt Marion

Marion is Edward's wife and stays mostly behind the scenes.

Mrs. Marsicano

Mrs. Marsicano is the landlady who scoffs when Peyton suggests that Harry will return to pay the rent. The intellectually dampened Charles Marsicano is probably her son.

Harry Miller

Harry Miller is Peyton's lover then fiancé then husband. As an unlikely figure in the Virginia Tidewater, Harry serves as a litmus test for various people's attitudes toward Jews. He is a painter who seems able to absorb people's (especially Milton's) off-key comments with refined equanimity. He truly loves Peyton and has made a noble effort to sustain their relationship, but the weight of her series of unfaithful transgressions is eventually too much for him to bear. When he last sees Peyton, he seems led to the verge of reconciliation—until she shows that she still believes, deep down, that her transgressions are his fault and that he has failed to try to understand her. Seeing that the cycle of reunion and transgression is about to begin again, he gives up hope. He later mournfully collects her body with Lennie.

Earl Sanders

Earl is a mystery writer who manages to sweep Peyton away for a weeklong affair in Darien.

Stonewall

Stonewall is La Ruth's son and has the interests and desires of a healthy child.

Irving Strassman

Dr. Strassman is the Newark psychiatrist Peyton quickly stops seeing. Peyton wryly suggests that she is more intelligent than he is. Rather than probing her more unusual comments for underlying meanings, he simply dismisses them as disconnected.

Ella Swan

Ella Swan is the Loftises' housekeeper. Having come along for Peyton's funeral, Ella remains mostly in the background until the final scene, in which she features prominently, signals her spiritual significance. She draws great strength from her faith. However, she is not always patient with her daughter, La Ruth.

La Ruth Swan

As Ella's daughter, La Ruth also helps around the Loftis household. In less-than-ideal domestic circumstances herself—raising her child with the father absent—La Ruth is perhaps especially sensitive to the implications of Peyton's suicide. Whether because of a lack of faith or not, as her companions in worship suggest, she has great difficulty coming to terms with Peyton's death.

THEMES

Family Relationships

At the center of the web of themes threading through *Lie Down in Darkness* is family relationships. Like many families, the Loftises have their burdens to bear, but in their case, the burdens prove too heavy, the discord runs too deep— stemming from both the behaviors and the personalities of the family members—and the resulting dysfunction cannot be overcome. Helen and Milton both prove to have flaws on which they are unwilling or unable to compromise, and those flaws gradually erode their emotional bonds until nothing but habit and function are left. It is difficult to determine where the fault for the family dysfunction lies. Styron's descriptions of Milton and Helen's relationships with their fathers make clear that, like their own children, they have been profoundly shaped by their familial authority figures. Biology, interpersonal influence, and life circumstance have all contributed to making Helen the judgmental moralist that she is and Milton the amoral drunkard that he is. Above all, perhaps, the tragedy is that the two were drawn to each other in the first place but that their attraction has caused each to overlook the aspects of the other they find repellent, however mildly at first. When two prospective parents enter into a marriage in which they will always be at odds over certain points—especially morality—they may be preordaining irresolvable contradiction in the minds of their children.

Morality

Helen's being "strait-laced in many ways, rather severe" derives largely from her father and his code of ethics, which is molded by Christianity and the military. Helen reports that her father told her, "We must stand fast with the good" and that she has unerringly sought to do so throughout her life. There is nothing wrong with this, of course, being and doing good essentially being the definition of virtuous. The puritanical tilt to Helen's morality is evident in, for example, her total aversion to alcohol; she would break down in tears if Milton plied her with a drink. A pivotal moment thus comes when Peyton has a thrilling yet harmless run-in with some bees— an accomplishment of sorts for a four-year-old—only to have her spirits profoundly dampened by a mother who (partly out of jealousy for the affection that Peyton and Milton share

afterward) can only reproach her for wandering off against orders. This sets in place a pattern of loaded moralizing that has predictable results: the naturally curious daughter explores behavioral possibilities and pushes boundaries—such as when she very misguidedly ties up Maudie— provoking the strict mother to punish her and the lenient-minded father to counter the punishment by fairly dismissing the transgression.

The chasm between Helen's strictures and Milton's utter leniency does not bode well for the daughter. Milton has Peyton's best interests at heart—he wants his daughter to be happy— and yet his failure to establish moral and interpersonal boundaries for her behavior leads to her being unable to adequately distinguish between right and wrong later in life. Between her parents' extremes, she is left to work out a practical sense of morality by trial and error. This is suggested when Milton tells her, regarding men, "I know that any guy you liked would be—," provoking Peyton to interrupt and point out, "No, Bunny, not any guy would be O.K. Just because I liked him." Arguably, Milton, who is ultimately the more powerful influence on Peyton, has been led to his default stance of amorality by his alcoholism.

Alcoholism

Styron reveals the devastating effects of Milton's alcoholism not only by contrasting his actions in sober and inebriated states but also by disclosing the evolutions in his thought processes as he gets drunk, loses whatever moral resolve he may have established, and speciously reasons his way into doing whatever unreasonable behavior occurs to him. This pattern is inaugurated when Milton, inclined to skip church on a Sunday when Peyton is nine, elects to pour himself a drink as a means of both psychic escapism and functional escapism. That he is already intoxicated is what prevents Helen from forcing him to go. In subsequent scenes—including the afternoon with Dolly, at Peyton's sixteenth-birthday party, the day Milton (drinks and) drives to Charlottesville for Maudie, and especially at Peyton's wedding (when Edward earns a share of blame by ignoring Milton's protests about trying to take it easy)—the reader witnesses Milton's habitual drink-inspired descent into selfishness and moral vacuousness. Helen may have her own problems with substance abuse—apparently being dependent on the barbiturate she takes to maintain a deadened emotional stasis—but

TOPICS FOR FURTHER STUDY

- Styron makes substantive use of symbolism in *Lie Down in Darkness*, especially in Peyton's narration in the final chapter, with the birds and the alarm clock. Write an in-depth analysis of these and other symbols and what they signify, using passages from the text to support your contentions. You may find it helpful to consult critical literature on the novel, much of which comments on these symbols.

- Peyton's suicide in *Lie Down in Darkness* leaves several characters grappling with feelings of guilt. Consider the extent to which different characters might be said to have failed to heed warning signals about Peyton's state of mind, including Milton, Helen, and Harry. Imagine that these three have all been advised by psychiatrists to resolve their feelings over Peyton's suicide by writing her a letter. Write such letters from each character's perspective and close each one by having the character state what he or she will do with the letter.

- Read Sharon M. Draper's young-adult novel *Tears of a Tiger* (1994), in which a high-school basketball player, Andy Johnson, must cope with having been the driver in a car accident that killed his best friend and teammate, Robert Washington. They were drinking at the time. Write an essay in which you consider the circumstances of Andy and of Peyton in New York in Styron's novel. In particular, how do their isolation and emotional states compare, what role has alcohol played for each, and what might a reader conclude generally about helping people in suicidal states of mind?

- Search online for photographs that reflect settings and scenes from *Lie Down in Darkness* from the 1940s and earlier, representing everything from transportation to dress styles, natural scenery, and urban environments. Put together a slide show using brief phrases from the novel as captions for the photos, adding era-appropriate music if you like. Post the slide show online or play it for your class.

Milton's alcoholism leads directly to his adultery, his failure to either understand or appreciate Maudie's death, and his failure to intervene when Helen, as he surely knows, is intent on squashing Peyton on her wedding day, among other failures.

Guilt

Milton's alcoholism is just one source of guilt among the characters in the novel. That Milton gives up alcohol to reunite with Helen after Maudie's death and his reluctance to drink heavily at the wedding are evidence that he knows the risks he runs in becoming intoxicated. Yet he does so anyway and eventually regrets it. He also feels remorse over disrupting his family by introducing Dolly into the dynamic. Yet it is only after Peyton's death that he is inundated

with guilt, as he must finally face the fact that he has failed as a father to secure his cherished daughter's well-being.

Peyton, too, engages in patterns of transgression and belated guilt, with more immediate consequences. When she avenges Harry's minor relational transgressions with major transgressions—a series of affairs—she is not unaware of the fault that she assumes for doing so. The wrenching seventh chapter, in which Peyton's thought processes are finally revealed, shows that guilt over her ill-advised actions is psychically tearing her apart.

Helen, it might be said, also deserves a burden of guilt, for her cold, judgmental nature. Yet by the end, Helen's psyche has been hardened to the circumstances, and her conception that Milton and Peyton are the ones at fault in their

The framing story of Lie Down in Darkness *focuses on Peyton's funeral, where few grieve.*
(© Robert Hoetink / Shutterstock.com)

twisted family dynamic is enough to leave her indifferent to Milton's pleas for reconciliation, too proud to relent in her perception of morality.

Isolation

All four of the Loftises end up isolated for one reason or another. Maudie is isolated from birth onward owing to her disabilities, though Helen does what she can to keep her company. The other three, in contrast, create their own isolation through destructive behaviors. Helen allows her resentment of Peyton to flourish to such an extent that she finds it reasonable to insult her in the most unsparing terms, even on her wedding day. As a result, Peyton no longer wants to return home at all. Similarly, Helen's disparagement (however justified) of Milton leads to his vacating her company by seeking solace with Dolly, and thus is Helen left alone. Milton fares little better when he invests all his emotional energy in Peyton and then the frivolous Dolly, at Helen's expense. When Peyton dies, Dolly's cloying manner finally rubs him the wrong way, yet Helen refuses his last pleas for a reunion, and so he, too, is left alone.

The most tragic isolation is easily Peyton's, stemming as it does from her parents' failures, which prefigure her own. Morally uncertain like her father and quick to cast blame like her mother, she tests Harry's patience one too many times and ends up with no one but the likes of Tony to keep her company. In effect, she is alone, without even her far-off beloved father for support. The extremity of Peyton's isolation—romantic, familial, geographic, psychic—allows for the breeding of irrational loops of logic in her mind from which she cannot extricate herself. It also allows for the intrusion of hallucinated birds that help usher her toward her tragic suicidal leap.

STYLE

Flashbacks

The complexity of the structure of *Lie Down in Darkness* places far greater demands on the reader—and potentially elicits greater intellectual rewards—than a straightforward narrative of the same events would have. The broader structure is tangible enough as the present day, the day of Peyton's funeral, is enacted scene by scene over the course of the novel with flashbacks of varying length interspersed throughout. The most significant flashbacks proceed in chronological order—covering the episodes of the bees (Peyton was roughly four), the tying-up of Maudie (nine), the birthday party (sixteen), game day in Charlottesville (eighteen), the disastrous Christmas (nineteen), the wedding (twenty), and finally the day of Peyton's suicide (twenty-two). The structure is complicated further by minor reminiscences being planted within the broader reminiscences, as when Carey recalls Helen's recalling the events around when Peyton turns sixteen.

On the one hand, a straightforward narration of all of these events might have allowed the reader to more steadily absorb the sequencing and logic of the narrative. On the other, Styron's framework of flashbacks itself accomplishes a great deal. To begin with, the novel is explicitly framed as a tragedy by revealing from the beginning the inevitability of Peyton's death. While preempting the suspense ordinarily created by the reader's not knowing what will happen, there remains the suspense of not knowing how and why things will happen, and in shifting this suspense, *Lie Down in Darkness* casts the story onto a more philosophically inquisitive plane. (In terms of the reader's experience, this is analogous to the suspense of a mystery in which the truth behind a crime is gradually re-created, though Styron has more literary intentions.) Also, as the introduction to the novel suggests, the reader, having just arrived at the train station, is first seeing or meeting Milton Loftis and the others on the day of the funeral. And much as in real life, rather than witnessing a years-long story as it plays out, one happens upon a small portion of a story and then learns the rest from remembrances. In terms of understanding the characters—especially Peyton, with her revelatory monologue at the end—this resembles less a picture being drawn in a linear fashion, such that one is aware of the design halfway through, than a picture being drawn in disjointed, haphazard fashion, such that only at the very end is the full image made startlingly clear.

Southern Family Tragedy

The classification of Styron's novel as a tragedy is as unmistakable as the ever-present drink in Milton's hand, Peyton's claw marks on Helen's face, and the color of the black limousine and hearse that bear the characters and novel along from beginning to end. Some critics see Styron stretching back to the roots of Greek tragedy with echoes of the mythical stories recorded by dramatists like Aeschylus and Euripides. In this sense, the robed African American revivalists who appear sporadically in the present-day scenes and at last bring the novel to a close may be recognized as a refigured chorus, commenting implicitly, or explicitly, on the tragic nature of the events unfolding.

A few critics are inclined to specifically consider *Lie Down in Darkness* a southern family tragedy, given that it follows in a tradition of literary works dealing with the downfall of families burdened, as the novel suggests, with a guilt beyond the memory of those enacting the downfall, as instilled by the reproachable history of slavery and rebellion. Thus do elements such as alcoholism, incestuousness, religious withdrawal, denial, and guilt potentially speak to broader cultural issues. Cited as forerunners of *Lie Down in Darkness* are the works of Robert Penn Warren, Thomas Wolfe, and especially William Faulkner. Still, although the story's details are drawn from Styron's native Virginia, he himself has suggested that the drama enacted could have been carried out anywhere at all, framing it as a superficially regional but fundamentally universal story.

HISTORICAL CONTEXT

Virginia in the Early Twentieth Century

In Virginia the era in which *Lie Down in Darkness* takes place is characterized, as Peyton suggests, as the era of the Byrds, especially Harry Byrd. After his father served as Speaker of the Virginia House of Delegates and his uncle as a congressman, Byrd served as state senator (1915–1925) and governor (1926–1929) and then as US senator for more than thirty years (1933–1965). As governor, Byrd gained recognition for a staunch antilynching law that terminated the practice statewide, though he also permitted the state legislature to institute segregation. Byrd was generally progressive in his early years but became highly conservative as a US senator.

Lie Down in Darkness first engages with history around World War I, when Loftis manages

COMPARE
&
CONTRAST

- **1940s:** Approximately nine thousand of the three hundred thousand Virginians fighting in World War II die.

  Today: A total of 72 Virginians die in the Afghanistan War between 2001 and 2012, and 134 die in the Iraq War between 2003 and 2011.

- **1940s:** Laws against driving while intoxicated have been in place in New York since as early as 1910. The nation's first law defining drunk driving by a blood alcohol concentration (BAC) limit is enacted in Indiana in 1939; the precedent BAC limit is 0.15 grams of alcohol per deciliter of blood. Virginia retains its 0.15 limit long after other states reduce the limit to 0.10.

  Today: With a BAC limit of 0.08, as in most other states, Virginia sees fatalities attributable to drunk drivers, including repeat offenders, decrease by 20 percent between 2005 and 2014 owing to the enactment of stricter laws in 2004.

- **1940s:** Before the landmark 1954 Supreme Court case *Brown v. Board of Education* and civil rights legislation passed in the 1960s and beyond, African Americans in the South function in communities that are segregated in terms of everything from school to transportation to public facilities. African Americans in literature are thus often depicted as poorly educated and relegated to supporting roles in the lives of white protagonists. Harlem Renaissance novelists like Zora Neale Hurston shift the focus to the nuclei of African American communities.

  Today: Although some novels reaching back in time, like Kathryn Stockett's *The Help* (2009), make a point of elaborating on points of view within African American supporting casts, novelists like the Nobel Prize winner Toni Morrison take depictions centered in African American communities to the highest literary levels. More generally, novels set in the present-day United States are more likely to feature arrays of ethnicities contributing to the narrative.

---

to avoid active service through his commission as a military lawyer—but one of his closest childhood friend dies in the fighting. Approximately twelve hundred Virginians died in the war, far fewer than the 11,600 who died in the influenza epidemic near the war's end. Generally, the Loftises remain fairly insulated from national and even local history in the course of the novel, perhaps because the scenes that Styron shows are concentrated familial and personal events usually lasting less or little more than a day.

Thus, there is little need for the reader to worry about, for example, Prohibition, which lasted from 1920 to 1933, though one might expect it to have affected Milton's relationship to alcohol. In fact, as Virginius Dabney reports in *Virginia: The New Dominion*, no less than the US assistant attorney general overseeing Prohibition, Mabel Willebrandt, acknowledged that even then, liquor could be secured "at almost any hour of the day or night, either in rural districts, the smaller towns or the cities." Milton Loftis would have been grateful that, as Dabney poetically notes, "it was the era when Virginia's moonshiners were in their heyday, and the burbling of stills smote gently upon the ear in mountain fastnesses and lowland swamps." Loftis would have benefited more, however, from a study on the effects of both moderate and excessive alcohol consumption on the human body conducted by the University of Virginia and Medical College of Virginia, the report of which was produced in 1938 for instruction in schools. Temperance remained the fashion among many, especially the state's Anti-Saloon League, such that the report's suggestions that moderate drinking can help digestion, with no effects on the heart, led to an outcry; despite its "numerous and emphatic warnings against overindulgence," as Dabney notes, the study was sunk by the state legislature and obliterated.

The Great Depression of the 1930s also bears little relevance to the novel, with the Loftises secure less in Milton's legal practice than in Helen's inheritance. World War II, on the other hand, signifies much for Styron. Although in real life he spent much of the war period at college or in the military, the shipyard in his hometown of Newport News was a major producer of aircraft carriers and warships. The town's wartime role is strongly suggested in the name of Styron's fictional town, Warwick, which evokes a lit fuse leading to the conflagration and death of battle. Virginia as a whole was host to some fifty military, especially naval, installations, the most of any US state, Chesapeake Bay being a major launching point for both military and merchant vessels. Also, many damaged ships and survivors of sinkings were brought to Virginia for repair and recovery. In light of the area's importance, there was considerable anxiety over potential German U-boat or air attacks, accounting for the alarms calling local wardens like Milton Loftis into action in the novel.

Of all the proceedings of World War II, the end, with the atomic bombings of Hiroshima and Nagasaki, Japan, in August 1945, has perhaps the greatest significance in *Lie Down in Darkness*. The atmosphere of raw nuclear destruction looms over both the day of Peyton's suicide and her funeral, radio reports being overheard in both scenes. The war is something of a thematic framing device: Peyton's milestone sixteenth birthday party, which is also the first day of Milton's adultery, occurs "the day before the war began," and then the war's end matches the end of Peyton's life and, it appears, of Milton and Dolly's affair. This timing keys in the reader not to the victory achieved by the Allies but to the deaths wrought to attain that victory. Daddy Faith's sermon—by extension the novel as a whole—laments the frightening new age ushered in by the United States' twin acts of civilian massacre.

One section of the story is told from the point of view of Peyton, a beautiful but troubled young woman. (© Photobank gallery / Shutterstock.com)

CRITICAL OVERVIEW

Critics initially responding to *Lie Down in Darkness* vacillated between comments on the derivative qualities of Styron's debut and the undeniably powerful literary quality of the novel. Several early reviews are collected in *Critical Essays on William Styron*. Howard Mumford Jones, in the *New York Herald Tribune Book Review*, representatively remarks that

> despite its echoes of familiar authors, *Lie Down in Darkness* is satisfying work. It is planned with mature intelligence, it is written in a style everywhere competent and sometimes superb, and its slow and powerful stream is fed by insights into human beings beyond the capacity of many better-known novelists.

In his *New Republic* review, Malcolm Cowley remarks that by the 1950s, taking after Faulkner was "among the leading tendencies of the day; but I can't think of any other novel that applies the lessons so faithfully or, for that matter, with so much natural authority and talent." He iterates, "It is a general rule that novels which stay close to their literary models have no great value of their own, but *Lie Down in Darkness* is an exception."

More ambivalently, Harvey Breit, in *Atlantic Monthly*, unconvinced by the plotting, and thus unmoved by the story, but impressed by the style, is led to state that he has "little affection and considerable admiration for" Styron's debut. He nonetheless concludes, "Not least among its virtues, the novel is deeply absorbing. It is a basically mature, substantial, and enviable achievement, powerful enough to stay with you after you have shut it out." Robert Gorham Davis, in *American Scholar*, praises the "marvelous talent" that *Lie Down in Darkness* "constantly and variously displays." He goes on to say, "Styron has dazzling gifts with language, and great observational powers in describing moods, incidents, landscapes and conversations. But it is the moral tension of his best scenes that gives such dramatic interest." Davis concludes, "Styron is remarkably mature already in his novelist's art and in his understanding of human nature."

Keen Butterworth, in a *Dictionary of Literary Biography* essay, points out that Styron's 1951 debut was seen as

> an auspicious first novel, perhaps the best to appear since World War II. Its style, if reminiscent of Faulkner, was distinctly the author's own; its psychological insights, accurate; and its moral vision, mature. It was, in fact, an astonishingly good novel for an author only twenty-six at the time.

Writing for a later *Dictionary of Literary Biography* volume, Regine Rosenthal states, "Styron is a major American novelist who has won wide critical acclaim and stirred controversy by addressing culturally and historically contentious issues." In his Twayne volume *William Styron*, Marc L. Ratner affirms that *Lie Down in Darkness* is historically "one of the important novels of the postwar period.... But the novel's real strength lies in Styron's unique poetic voice." Speaking more broadly, Ratner remarks, "William Styron, because of his poetic imagination and strong moralistic convictions, has assured his place in American letters."

CRITICISM

Michael Allen Holmes

Holmes is a writer with existential interests. In the following essay, he weighs the significance of the concept of free will in Lie Down in Darkness *in both religious and secular terms.*

In what amounts to a minor theme, mentions of the philosophic question of free will can be found scattered throughout *Lie Down in Darkness*. Styron's antihero, Milton Loftis, in particular has concerns about how much control he has over his own actions and destiny, and other characters also weigh their degrees of worldly self-control. The mentions of free will and destiny make clear that the concept is intimately tied with religion, a more prominent theme. A consideration of how the two themes interlock may shed light on the sense of the novel's concluding scene, the African American revivalist baptism.

A long line of philosophers going back at least to ancient Greece have pondered the question of free will and have left a framework of several ontological possibilities given the most credence. From a religious perspective, positing the existence of an omniscient deity suggests that the deity knows not only what has happened but also what will happen throughout time. That throughout time can be already known would suggest predetermination of those events. On the other hand, it may be posited that the deity in question is omnipotent but having created the world refrains from using his power to control worldly events. This leaves room for humankind to exercise free will. Denying the existence of any deity would tend to suggest that individuals are indeed in control of their own actions. Yet again, some are inclined to assign science the effective role of a deity. They conceive that between genetics, brain chemistry, childhood environment, and conditioned responses, free will all but disappears. Others simply believe in predestination.

The structure of Styron's novel creates a sense of a destiny that cannot be avoided in that the opening scene—in which the essential fact of Peyton's death, apparently by suicide, is revealed—is chronologically beyond all of the novel's most critical scenes. There remains some tension with regard to whether Milton and Helen will get back together, although Helen's profound coldness and Milton's profound

> ALL THREE OF THESE LOFTISES, IN THEIR
> PREVAILING WEAKER MOMENTS, LEAN ON THE
> CONCEPT OF FATE, THE IDEA THAT THEY LACK
> CHOICE OR FREE WILL, IN A TOTAL ABSENCE OF
> LEGITIMATE RELIGIOUS SENTIMENT."

emotional distress make them seem far too different, at this point, to be compatible. Furthermore, the marital relationship has a distinct downward trajectory throughout, with only minor peaks of resurgence along the way, such that by the time of the funeral at the novel's end, rationally one expects the worst. What is far more relevant to the tension of the novel is how the dysfunctional domestic environment that Milton and Helen preside over affects Peyton and ultimately leads to her suicide.

The characters also exhibit a sense of fatalism beginning with the opening scene in Port Warwick. As the train bearing Peyton's body approaches, Milton realizes "that he couldn't evade immediacy, and that the train would come . . . , bringing with it final proof of fate and circumstance." This line of thought leads Milton to remark, "Ah, my God," which is spoken weakly, as if Milton, left bereft by Peyton's death, in his pathetic, feeble state, can only attribute the chain of events responsible to God. The question whether he deserves a share of the blame is thus neatly pushed aside, through a psychic reflex that functions as a coping mechanism. Interestingly, in Milton's reminiscence at this point, his father actually calls him willful, reflecting Milton's youthful repudiation of his father's influence over his life. And yet Milton soon thinks with regard to himself, "Not a poet or a thief, I could never exercise free will." This interesting formulation suggests that to strictly follow the functional rules of society, one sacrifices one's free will. Only in disregarding either civilized society's laws or capitalist society's insistence on practical functionality, by being a thief or a poet, can one retain the ability to act with true freedom of body and mind. Coming from Milton, whose underlying sense of remorse already suggests that he has acted untowardly

and bears some responsibility for his daughter's death, this philosophic formulation has the ring of an excuse.

The reader later learns that this formulation, like the italicized text that precedes it, represents the words of Milton's father. The phrasing the elder Loftis actually uses is reproduced later, precisely at the time of Milton's first act of adultery with Dolly. Milton has already permitted his sixteen-year-old daughter to drink whiskey at her birthday party and has even insisted that she do so, provoking the departure of Helen and Maudie. Milton and Dolly have already kissed, and drink in hand, he is rationalizing away any scruples he may yet have about driving a wedge of betrayal and mistrust into his marriage:

> It occurred to him simply and with the heady glow of discovery that in this world there was no way of telling right from wrong and, anyway, to hell with it. What had happened had happened and what might happen *would* happen and so he took a drink and let his knee rest against Dolly's, safe in the all-inclusive logic of determinism.

These thoughts then provoke the remembrance of his father's words: "*My son, most people, whether they know it or not, . . . get on through life by a sophomoric fatalism. Only poets and thieves can exercise free will, and most of them die young.*" With his fatalistic rationalizations, Milton has backed himself into a sophomoric corner. His father's words may have been a warning against joining the mindless masses in blaming fate for one's circumstances, but in formulating that so few people can actually exercise free will, the elder Loftis gives Milton an out: he is certainly neither poet nor thief, and so why should he worry about any consequences of misguided actions he takes simply because he may? "The hell with that, too," Milton thinks, with the specious justification that "he had suffered, he felt."

As the novel progresses, Milton occasionally invokes a fate out of his control when events take a turn for the worse. During the holiday season, when Dolly sets things on edge by calling the Loftis residence (against Milton's wishes) on Christmas Eve, such that Helen is upstairs brooding when Peyton arrives home quite late, Milton experiences a feeling of dread:

> how each minute that clicked past from the time he strode out of Helen's room seemed charged with a violent inevitability, beyond the reach of platitudes: Loftis felt he could have halted the outcome only by dynamiting the house.

WHAT
DO I READ
NEXT?

- Styron won the Pulitzer Prize with *The Confessions of Nat Turner* (1967), controversially taking the perspective of a historic African American slave rebellion leader. His effort was legitimized not only by the award but also by his consultation before publication with a close friend, the prominent African American novelist James Baldwin.

- The novel most directly linked with Styron's debut is *The Sound and the Fury* (1929), by the Nobel Prize winner William Faulkner, the paragon of southern literary stylists. That novel also features circular narration, a drink-addled lawyer, a self-centered and unbalanced mother, a fallen daughter, a suicidal character, and a developmentally disabled person. In turn, Faulkner's *As I Lay Dying* (1930) revolves around a funeral and reminiscences among those present, including the woman who died.

- *All the King's Men* (1946), by the Kentucky native Robert Penn Warren, is a novel Styron cited as marking the turning point in his struggle to become a writer. The novel treats the rise of a politician in the South in the 1930s. In his essay "*Lie Down in Darkness*," Styron praises "its sheer marvelousness of language, it vivid characters, its narrative authority, and the sense of truly felt and realized life."

- Another novel that Styron has cited as highly influential is *Madame Bovary* (1856), the masterpiece of the French author Gustave Flaubert. This novel is recognized as the prototype of modern psychological realism. The title character, like Peyton, finds herself disconnected from conventional morality in such a way that her approach to relationships leads to tragedy.

- Appearing on best-seller lists at the same time as Styron's debut—and being linked to his novel by what resounds as a pessimistic worldview—was J. D. Salinger's classic *The Catcher in the Rye* (1951), which features a teenage protagonist whose disillusionment with the phoniness of modern society has spoken to young adults for generations.

- Although Styron resisted classification as southern of either his novels or himself as an author, *Lie Down in Darkness* is among his works that hearken to the characteristically southern literary tradition. This tradition is explored in *The Companion to Southern Literature: Themes, Genres, Places, People, Movements, and Motifs* (2002), edited by Joseph M. Flora, Lucinda Hardwick MacKethan, and Todd W. Taylor. In it, encyclopedic listings are arranged alphabetically.

It may be true that, as the scene has been set, conflict between the resentful Helen and the free-spirited Peyton is inevitable, but in framing it as such, Milton pushes to the background the fact that his prolonged affair, not Helen's sensitivity, is the culprit behind the domestic trouble. Similarly, when Milton starts wandering around Charlottesville looking for Peyton instead of staying at the hospital with Helen and Maudie—and, as Peyton later suggests, simply

calling for Peyton at KA—he again mourns the supposedly inevitable:

> Peyton, Peyton, where had she gone, and why, and had this day indeed finally become the nightmare which he had dreaded so, and—by instinct, by some vague oppressive mood of fatality—had sensed would be inevitable?

Again, this outlook only obscures the facts that Milton gets excessively drunk the night before (to fornicate in his wife's bed), continues drinking in the morning (as if to ward off the hangover), and makes a poor decision in leaving the hospital in the first place. Subconsciously he must realize his culpability, which lingers when Pookie—the last person he wants to run into—and his girlfriend stroll into the Virginian as Milton finishes yet another drink. Milton wonders, "Was this part of the plan, the nightmare?" It may be a nightmare of sorts, but it is one he has wrought upon himself through amoral decision making.

Milton is not the only character to cast blame for circumstances on some external source or concept. The plump-faced Carey Carr, for example, in considering his lack of masculinity as an adolescent, rather than doing something about it (eat more healthful foods, exercise more), is led to conclude that his condition is "born of a fatal necessity." By later in life and fully acquainted with Christian theology, Reverend Carr has advanced beyond his youthful fatalism to condemn lack of responsibility in others—especially "primitive" religious minds who blame the devil for their misdeeds. Carr conceives of such a sinner: "'The devil *forced* me,' he says, instead of, 'I turned my eyes from Christ's example,' and by this process of negativism is enabled to perform any crime under the sun against humanity and reason." This train of thought attributed to the sinner is not unlike Milton's rationalizing away his adultery through recourse to determinism. But it more specifically speaks to Helen, who does just what Carr discredits when, after taking pleasure in having treated Milton with petty bitterness, she thinks,

> Hadn't this devil, or whoever he was, perhaps disguised himself in order to make her think such a vain mean thought? Although invisible cleverly off-stage, wasn't he prodding her just the same? Nonetheless, she felt most satisfied.

Peyton, meanwhile, shows a fatalism not unlike her father's—inspired by drink. This surfaces when she and Dick are driving to his house after the disastrous Christmas:

> Because of the whisky, which had lulled and deceived their minds, their talk was repetitious and touched with a synthetic exaltation, and its sadness and its mood of fatality gave them a solemn sort of joy.

Like Milton and Helen both, Peyton fairly basks in the sense that she can go on doing whatever she is doing without taking responsibility.

That the Loftises' recourse to fate or the devil to explain away their actions is a negative trait is suggested during the period when Milton and Helen get back together. As R. H. Fossum points out in *William Styron: A Critical Essay*, "Ironically, Milton gives the lie to his own denials of free will in the year following Maudie's death. He stops drinking, breaks off with Dolly, and tries to repair his broken marriage." This is recognized not as a miracle but as "a consequence of a rare act of will on Milton's part." When Carey visits the reunited couple, he is startled to realize that in the Loftises' conversation, there is no mention of "the stern hand of destiny, or anything depressing, for that matter." The idea of destiny is thus specifically framed as a crutch for those whose less-than-ideal lives leave them with wounded sensibilities.

All three of these Loftises, in their prevailing weaker moments, lean on the concept of fate, the idea that they lack choice or free will, in a total absence of legitimate religious sentiment. Helen gives some agency to the devil—and even somewhat comically, if frighteningly, proclaims allegiance to him at Peyton's wedding—but this is not to say that she is a religious person. Despite Carey's efforts to persuade her to lean not on fate but on faith when it comes to making difficult decisions, she never believes strongly enough in God for the idea of faith in him to offer any support. The novel's figurehead for what amounts to pessimistic fatalism proves to be none other than the intellectually pretentious Albert Berger. Faith is the farthest thing from his mind when he speaks with Peyton in her suicidally distraught state. He pities her for having "no real intellectual supports to put your mind at ease." When his social scientist friends despair over the devastating outcome of World War II, he somewhat convolutedly suggests that they are "unwilling to accept the historical determinism, tragic as it is to the spirits of neo-humanists, the historical determinism . . .—they are unable to accept the pure *fact* in all its beauty." While those friends conceive that the wielding of atomic bombs might have been avoided, Albert fairly revels in it, proclaiming, "My view of the universe is harsh and brutal. . . . I do not ask you any more, my pretty, to believe with me that the evil in man is both beautiful and preordained." However much Berger may inadvertently speak to the Loftises' situations, the reader would be hard pressed to argue that his voice is,

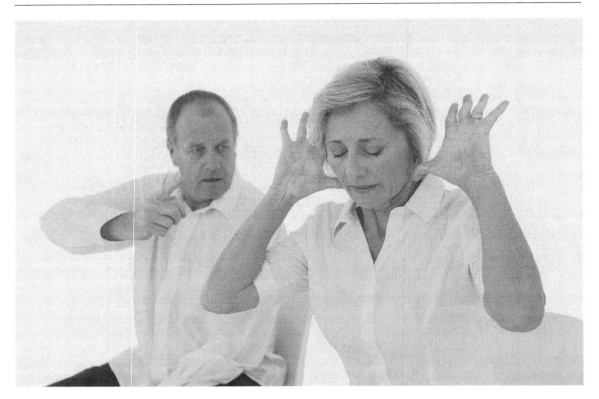

Helen's disgust over Peyton's behavior contributes to her unhappiness with Milton. (© wavebreakmedia / Shutterstock.com)

ultimately, the moral voice of the novel, as dark as both his and the novel's conclusions may be.

The voice that suggests itself as the novel's moral spokesperson is that of Ella Swan. As an African American servant she is largely relegated to a supporting role, left out of the substantial discussions and streams of consciousness of the several Loftises. The reader does not enter Ella's mind through the narration at any point. And yet she makes herself heard on noteworthy occasions, as when Milton skips church and later asks Dolly and her family over. When Milton first pours himself a drink that day, he knows he can expect what he considers "blame and self-righteousness, in impotent reproach" from the African American help. That is, he belittles them to minimize the impact of Ella's reproach on his psyche, but this does not mean she is not morally superior to him.

Ella makes clear that she draws her moral strength—her ability to make moral choices rather than bow to the inevitability of sin— from the divine: "Know who's lookin at you. . . . Good Lawd's lookin down, He say, 'I am de troof and de way and de life,' good Lawd's sayin." When Milton turns blasphemous, she does blame the devil—but to account for someone else's actions, not her own. With his second drink, Milton wryly invites Ella to join him. Scandalized, she makes clear her ability to resist temptation in affirming, "Not me. Not fo' a million dollars. You gwan sin all you want. Ah don't keer." A similar, briefer scene plays out on Peyton's wedding day as Milton is retrieving his first beer of the day, "when Ella, her face wrinkled with reproach, said, 'Now, ain't you ashamed?'" He plaintively responds, "Just one, Ella? The last one before I lose my baby. One won't hurt, Ella." At this relatively sober point in his life, he recognizes a need to make an appeal to Ella, his moral superior, to bless his behavior. But as the day progresses, he drinks far more than just the one, and his associated bad habits—making divisive remarks, smothering Peyton, and failing to act when the situation calls for it—return.

With this background concerning the making of moral choices the reader is eventually led into the novel's final scene. There is some ambiguity to the scene, because Daddy Faith's previous bedazzlingly materialist appearance in a Cadillac has undermined his religious authority. Thus, some critics found his words on this day accordingly vague and empty and judged the scene to be a parody of virtuous religious belief. To the contrary, others found this appearance highly distinguished from Daddy Faith's earlier one. As Lucille M. Schultz noted in "*Lie Down in Darkness*: A Story of Two Processions," his sermon is for the most part drawn directly from biblical language. Thus, his service is legitimate, and so, in turn, is Ella's revelatory experience. Despite all that has gone on that day, she is able to find some inner peace. On her face at one point "was an expression neither grieving nor devout but merely silently, profoundly aware: of time past and passing and time to come, a look both mysterious and peaceful."

After the ceremonial immersion, Ella has a full-on ecstatic experience. She goes through her days making conscious moral choices, relying on God or Jesus to help her make those choices. Moreover the baptism leaves her with "all sins washed away, her warfare accomplished, her iniquity pardoned." Her affirmative cries to Jesus make a powerful counterpoint to the train making a ferocious noise as it passes. Marc L. Ratner, in *William Styron*, points out that "the journey of the railroad train provides an outer movement of inevitability which brackets the novel." Although this symbol of industrialized modern society may accord with the fatalistic worldview shared by the Loftises, and in reality its noise may be louder, Ella's cries signify the ability of the faithful to do good in the world despite all the temptation to be found. Her affirmative cries of "Yeah! Yeah!" likely resonate louder in the reader's soul.

Source: Michael Allen Holmes, Critical Essay on *Lie Down in Darkness*, in *Novels for Students*, Gale, Cengage Learning, 2016.

John Lang

In the following excerpt, Lang explains some of the religious allusions in Peyton's speech in Lie Down in Darkness.

William Styron's first novel, *Lie Down in Darkness* (1951), dissects the moral and spiritual confusion that typifies our "post-Christian" age. By emphasizing his characters' irresolution, their inability to love, and their failure either to

YET WITHIN HER EMOTIONAL AND SPIRITUAL INFERNO, SHE SEEKS A MEANS OF SALVATION."

seek or grant forgiveness, Styron demonstrates both their need of salvation and their refusal of the means which might effect their redemption. *Lie Down in Darkness* might best be termed an etiology of the soul's disorder. Yet although metaphors of disease pervade the book, Styron also indicates the possibility of that disease's remission.

What [recent criticism of *Lie Down in Darkness*] overlooks . . . is Styron's careful use of literary allusions—particularly his use of Biblical passages from the libretto of Handel's *Messiah*—to structure the novel's concluding chapter. That chapter, most of which is devoted to Peyton Loftis' monologue, is fundamental to an understanding of Styron's intentions in the book, intentions that are primarily moral and religious. Peyton's suicide not only confirms the contemporary eclipse of the Messiah but also evinces man's need to recover a relationship with the divine.

Peyton's monologue begins with an epigraph taken from Job 19:23–26, a portion of which likewise opens the triumphal third, and concluding, part of *The Messiah*. The Biblical text is combined with what seem to be Peyton's own reflections.

> Oh that my words were now written oh that they were printed in a book. That they were graven with an iron pen and lead in the rock forever. For I know that my redeemer liveth and that He shall stand at the latter day upon the earth and though worms destroy this body yet in my flesh shall I
> Shall I
> Oh my flesh!
> (Strong is your hold O mortal flesh, strong is your hold O love.)

Whereas Job concludes, "in my flesh shall I see God," Peyton is torn between belief and despair. Yet this passage serves to remind the reader of a redemptive religious tradition and represents the first of several allusions to The Messiah in Peyton's monologue.

Moreover, even before her monologue commences, Styron introduces the figure of Christ, for Chapter 7 opens not with that monologue but with a description of Potter's Field, where Peyton's body is taken immediately after her suicide. Over that desolate area presides a weatherbeaten statue of Christ. Though "it is almost as if this monument were forgotten" (p. 327), its eyes, Styron notes, "still burn like the brightest fires" (p. 327). Upon the statue appears the legend, "He calleth His own by Name" (p. 327), words that ring with irony among the field's "nameless dead," but words that also recall the difference between human and divine perspectives.

The events recorded in Peyton's monologue take the form of a quest. On one level, the monologue depicts her efforts to locate her husband, who has broken with her because of her adultery. But Peyton's search for Harry also becomes a spiritual pilgrimage, a quest for God motivated by her sense of guilt. The monologue's frenetic pace and its tone of almost unbearable anguish powerfully convey the disorder and confusion of Peyton's mind. Yet within her emotional and spiritual inferno, she seeks a means of salvation.

Initially, however, Peyton pursues a spurious redemption, imagining that the jeweled clock she carries will free her from the bondage of time and sin. Like her parents, Milton and Helen, Peyton longs to escape the destructive effects of temporality. In fact, the first words she speaks in her monologue voice this concern: "I don't have enough time" (p. 335). Obsessed with flux, with "the eternal drift" (p. 344), Peyton conceives of the clock as a refuge and envisions herself inside its sanctuary "perfect, complete, perpetual," the timepiece itself "indestructible, shining, my own invention," (p. 335; my italics). Within the clock she and Harry will be safe from the menace of mortality. "Here all our guilt will disappear," she muses (p. 354).

Yet despite such hopes, Peyton occasionally betrays doubts about the clock's efficacy, worrying about Harry's response to it. Will "he understand the miracle of my invention," she wonders, "the soaring dark soul-closet?" (p. 374; my italics). Indeed, Harry does not understand. He rejects not only the clock but Peyton herself.

Stripped of the salvation she has fabricated, Peyton turns to the possibility of divine redemption. Her spiritual quest thus becomes an extension of the search for a father [that] has shaped her life. Moreover, as she contemplates suicide, she associates her marital infidelity with her abandonment of God.

> And I thought: it was not he [Harry] who rejected me, but I him, and I had known all day that that must happen, by that rejection making the first part of my wished-for, yearned-for death-act. . . . oh my God, why have I forsaken You? Have I through some evil inherited in a sad century cut myself off from You forever, and thus only by dying must take the fatal chance: to walk into a dark closet and lie down there and dream away my sins, hoping to wake in another land, in a far, fantastic dawn? It shouldn't be this way—to yearn so for dying: . . . then too I want to be bursting with love, and not with this sorrow, at that moment when my soul glides upward toward You from my dust. What a prayer it was I said; I knew He wasn't listening, marking the sparrow but not me. So to hell. (pp. 382–83)

Despite Peyton's uncertainty and ambivalence in this passage, Styron makes it clear that she possesses more faith than Harry or Milton or Helen or even the minister Carey Carr. Milton has fled the burden of moral responsibility through alcohol, finding in whiskey "a state of palmy beatitude" (p. 55) that displaces any authentic religious consciousness. His will operates almost exclusively, in Eliot's phrase, "among velleities." For Helen Loftis, religion serves as a means of distancing herself from others, of subjecting them to moral judgments while dissociating herself from guilt. Helen uses the concept of sin to bludgeon Milton and Peyton. Carey Carr, though more perceptive than either of Peyton's parents, fails to achieve a vision of the divine. At novel's end, as he witnesses Milton's attempt to strangle Helen, Carr stands impotent, thinking, "my Lord, You shall never reveal Yourself" (p. 388).

Peyton, in contrast, throughout her monologue retains a measure of religious faith. In fact, up until the moment of her suicide, she carries on a mental dialogue between belief and despair. Returning to scraps of conversation she has heard disputing God's existence, she recalls Albert Berger's comment, "there was no God . . . save Him in the spirit of the creatively evolved, in the electrons of a radar screen or in the molecules of DDT" (p. 340). To this creed of scientific pantheism, Harry has replied, with his characteristically amorphous optimism, "God is life-force, love whatever you will, but not death"—whereupon Peyton had silenced both of them by proclaiming, "For now is Christ risen from the dead, the first fruits of them that sleep" (p. 340; I Corinthians 15:20). In this passage Styron has again drawn upon the libretto of Handel's Messiah, for the verse cited appears in the same aria as the lines from Job used in the epigraph to Peyton's monologue. And when Peyton later thinks of her death, she once more considers it in terms employed in *The Messiah*. "Oh God," she declares, "I must die today, but will I not rise again at another time and stand on the earth clean and incorruptible?" (p. 358). Her words here echo the penultimate aria in Handel's composition, which reads: "'The trumpet shall sound, and the dead shall be raised incorruptible, and we shall be changed. For this corruptible must put on incorruption, and this mortal must put on immortality" (I Corinthians 15: 52, 53).

In contrast to Milton and Helen, Peyton actively addresses herself to the problem of personal salvation conceived as a religious quest. The flightless birds that accompany her throughout her monologue symbolize the guilt that thwarts her desire to ascend to God. Altering a line from Dickinson, Peyton remarks, "Guilt is the thing with feathers" (p. 352). Here her substitution of the word "guilt" for Dickinson's "hope" seems initially to move Peyton further into despair. Yet insofar as her recognition of guilt impels her to search for salvation, this consciousness of sin provides renewed grounds for hope. Thus, on more than one occasion, Peyton describes the birds as "peaceful and without menace" (p. 345; cf. pp. 347, 381). By embodying her guilt, they manifest her need of the divine. As Kierkegaard writes, "it is a well-established ceremonial convention that if the finite spirit would see God it must begin by being guilty. In turning towards himself he discovers guilt. The greater the genius, the more profoundly he discovers guilt." Far from being a symptom of psychological disorder, such a sense of guilt is a mark of religious vitality. Peyton's hallucinations indicate the intensity of her spiritual torment. And unlike her parents she accepts responsibility for her guilt and acknowledges its implications. . . .

Source: John Lang, "In Quest of Redemption: The Religious Background of Peyton's Monologue in *Lie Down in Darkness*," in *The Critical Response to William Styron*, edited by Daniel W. Ross, Greenwood Press, 1995, pp. 33–36.

> THAT SENSE OF PEACE AND CONTENTMENT, WHILE OSTENSIBLY THE SUPERFICIAL QUALITIES STYRON'S DARKER IMAGININGS ARE BREAKING THROUGH, ALSO SEEM TO BOLSTER THE WEB OF CONSCIOUSNESS IN THE NOVEL, AS IF 'DOOM' WERE JUST ONE MORE THING TO RELISH 'WITH EQUAL FERVOR.'"

Samuel Coale

In the following excerpt, Coale characterizes Lie Down in Darkness *as a modernist novel.*

TIME AND TECHNIQUES

. . . John Kenny Crane in *The Root of All Evil* ably dissects Styron's four levels of time and his construction of flashbacks, which become more intricately interwoven in the later novels but which first appear in *Lie Down in Darkness*. The transcendent present reveals the narrator telling his tale, more apparent in the upfront analyses of narrators like Cass Kinsolving, Nat Turner, and Stingo; the narrative present provides the occasion when memories are examined, as at Peyton's funeral; major flashbacks include the ceremonial confrontations described earlier; and embedded flashbacks grow out of initial flashbacks as a kind of "unexpected associative memory" (Crane, 135) that pop up during the recapitulated past. All these provide Styron's "architecture" with layers of time crisscrossing one another, creating both density and depth.

Styron applies recognizable modernist techniques to his fiction as well. We discover the stream of consciousness of Peyton's internal monologue, the discontinuities and disruptions implicit in the way minds recall events and characters, and the self-contained, resonant symbols of much modernist fiction—such as birds, clocks, children, and fathers—filled as they are with and refracted through paradoxes, ironies, and ambiguities, the "force field" of the modernist perspective. Styron even provides the appropriate wasteland setting in Potter's Field, in the marshes of Port Warwick, and in consciousness itself, "this land of rocks and shadows, walls sheering off to the depths of a soundless, stormless ocean, while far off on the heights there was a blaze without meaning, twin pyres that warned of a fear blind as dying, twin columns of smoke, a smell, a dreaming blue vapor of defilement." Critics have seized and recognized much of this tradition and x-rayed it accordingly.

Even imagism plays its part in *Lie Down in Darkness*. What Styron accomplishes with ceremonies he also accomplishes with images and objects. Each object is described and set within an ominous backdrop, so that each one seems profound, portentous, weighted down with a sense of doom and futility. An obvious example is a hawk, described as "a wraith, as black as smoke; the pines seemed to shake and tremble but the hawk vanished, sailing up over the roof of a filling station, a dusky shadow, wings outspread like something crucified." And from Milton's perspective, and the book's, "each object surrounding him . . . suggested that it was not *he* who existed at all: he was the inanimate one . . . and these . . . were possessed of thriving, noisy life and the power to drive one witless with anxiety." In effect Styron's palpable universe often seems to contain more ominous life than the characters themselves.

Robert Dale Parker in describing what he calls Faulkner's "novelistic imagination" explores Faulkner's use of repression in his texts, that sequence of withholding information and secrets which creates expectation in the reader and involves him or her in the unveiling of the sequence itself. Such repression, akin to puritanical confessions, simultaneously blocks and demands revelation, making the revelation at once worse and necessary, an experience "in which the intensity of secret sin only increases the urge to pry into and expose it."

This essentially Gothic "architecture" describes Styron's methods as well as it does Faulkner's: "And if modernism . . . heralded the demise of plot in favor of consciousness and technical virtuosity, then Faulkner took the same techniques he learned from modernism and, applying them with melodramatic selectivity, joined them to the new taking for granted of Freud, to the gothic, to romance and to the nineteenth-century American romance-novel tradition. . . . The origin of novels built around momentous mysteries and appalling absences . . . is itself peculiarly modern" (Parker, 12–13). Peyton's

monologue and suicide fit comfortably in such a description.

The effects of this form may be the real triumph of *Lie Down in Darkness*. Time and consciousness appear weighted, thick, coiled, and circuitous. They even share the incestuousness of time's feeding upon itself in the characters' consciousness, a parallel to the incestuous feelings Milton has for his daughter Peyton. In such a way the form dramatizes and makes palpable a significant theme of the novel. Space becomes claustrophobic in such circumstances, for characters feel trapped and imprisoned by memories and one another. In such a realm the Loftis family itself becomes a claustrophobic cell. Richard Gray describes that "powerful sense of reenactment attaching itself to almost every thought and gesture—all this makes us feel that the dark backward and abysm of the old world lies just below the surface of landscape and consciousness, waiting for an appropriate moment to reappear." And thus characters seem like creatures from Poe's tales, "like a somnambulist driven by forces beyond one's personal control, distilling within the blood the inherited obsessions of an entire race" (R. Gray, 287).

"COCOONED" CHARACTERS

All the characters are cocooned in such conscious architecture. They are implicated with one another, caught in the web of one another's failings, feelings, and circumstances. They remain permanently compromised and "doomed." In one way Peyton's suicide seems a triumph, in that she ejects herself from this cocoon. The novel is built on recurrent and resonant motifs and moods, in that kind of weighted consciousness which perpetuates itself and its grief but offers no solution or escape. Sir Thomas Browne's quotation at the beginning of the story declares that "diurnity is a dream and folly of expectation" because of the reality of "the brother of death." In such a context Peyton's suicide in recognizing that dark brotherhood at least takes an almost "positive" stand in choosing to lie down in darkness permanently rather than in the dark, coiling consciousness the other characters haven't the courage to shed.

This web of consciousness undermines any attempt to get to the heart of things, since in this novel such a consciousness *is* the heart of things. When Carey Carr asks himself who was to blame in the self-destruction of the Loftis family, he gets nowhere: "Mad or not, Helen had been beastly. . . . Yet Loftis himself had been no choice soul; and who, finally, lest it be God himself, could know where the circle, composed as it was of such tragic suspicions and misunderstandings, began, and where it ended? Who was the author of the original misdeed?" In many ways Styron's architecture has authored the deed; the formal and intricate web of time and consciousness, as constructed here, has produced the sense of doom and futility. It may be that place where characters exist "only to be drawn back always by some force [they] could never define." The novel's success and power may rest in its form and style.

Conceptually or thematically, the book stands on less certain ground. True, *Lie Down in Darkness* is a study of "a very modern, hedonistic segment of urban rich society living without faith and purpose" (Rubin, 65), and social dissolution dogs its every step. There is a social milieu or veneer presented here in the web and woof of Styron's ceremonies. We get what Albert Berger in the novel refers to as a very southern "*husk* of culture . . . with its cancerous religiosity, its exhausting need to put manners before morals, to negate all ethos." This element is as much implicit in the ceremonial setups with which the novel has been constructed as it is in the theme of social dissolution. There is a decided modern-day. Episcopal Virginia culture, one in which "all real Virginia gentlemen . . . put safely behind [them] tragic thoughts and tragic events," and Episcopalians, "nominally, at least, [are] not inclined by conscience to worry long over abstractions." It is a culture in which Dolly can "[listen] not so much to the substance of what [Milton] said as to the tone of the words, the melodious, really endearing way he said them," and in which wedding guests admire the "soft and sweet, insidiously compelling" voice of Carey Carr, since Episcopalians "are often partial to the home and always partial to the poetic quality of their service."

Styron's melodious South, outside of Port Warwick, is "a land of prim pastoral fences, virgin timber, grazing sheep and Anglo-Saxons. . . . Many were Episcopalians, and all prayed and hunted quail with equal fervor. . . . Destiny had given them a peaceful and unvanquished land to live in, free of railroads and big-city ways . . . and when they died they died, for the most part, in contentment, shriven of their moderate, parochial sins. . . . They lived in harmony with nature and called themselves the last Americans." That sense of peace and contentment, while ostensibly the superficial qualities Styron's darker imaginings are breaking through, also seem to bolster the web of consciousness in the novel, as if "doom" were just one more thing to relish "with equal fervor."

Richard Gray here raises the question, "When the old institutions become irrelevant and the old myths obsolete, *and when our habits of thought and feeling continue nevertheless to be shaped by them*—how then do we change the situation?" Styron, Gray maintains, offers no change but remains caught up in the Loftises's problems, as much as he "depends . . . on the earlier *literary* tradition of the South just as Milton, Helen, and Peyton Loftis all depend on its broader cultural tradition" (R. Gray, 288–89).

This dependence on literary tradition shows up in Styron's characters. The power of his landscape and atmosphere asserts itself almost independently of these more stereotypical characters, as he himself has acknowledged, in "the story's rich possibilities—the weather and the landscape of Tidewater, *against which* the characters began to define themselves: father, mother, sister, and the girl herself, all doomed by fatal hostility and misunderstanding, all *helpless victims* of a domestic tragedy. In writing such a story—like Flaubert in *Madame Bovary*, which I passionately admired—I would also be able to anatomize bourgeois family life of the kind that I knew so well, the WASP world of the modern urban South [italics mine]" (*TQD*, 291). In the novel the characters are described accurately as "this breed of monsters" and as "a family of warriors" (268), but the ultimate accolade may be Styron's own, jotted down in the margin of his manuscript: "These people give me the creeps" (Ruderman, 49).

The Loftises within the architecture of the novel appear one-dimensional and thin. Richard Gray goes so far as to see them as parodies of themselves: Milton as "a comic travesty of the traditional Southern gentleman," Helen as "a parody of the Southern lady, her fragility and gentleness all dissolved into neuroticism," and Peyton as "a brutal parody of the Southern belle" (R. Gray, 288). In this he is fairly close to the mark. Need we rehearse once again Milton's self-indulgent, childish despair and faith, riding on booze and incestuous longings and relying on his "sophomoric fatalism" to get him through; or

Helen's self-righteous Puritan-romantic notions of sin and her sanctimonious inability to forgive; or Peyton's spoiled, explosive rages and sexual misadventures? Carey Carr represents the cultural husk, the minister-as-therapist whose belief in God is as foggy and uncertain as everybody else's. The blacks in their religious murmurings; Harry Miller, the Jewish artist; and Dolly, the fatuous mistress appear almost as stick figures to fill roles rather than as full-blooded souls in their own "rite." . . .

Source: Samuel Coale, "*Lie Down in Darkness*: A Matter of Form," in *William Styron Revisited*, Twayne Publishers, 1991, pp. 41–45.

Arthur D. Casciato

In the following excerpt, Casciato takes a close look at the influence of Styron's editor on the text of Lie Down in Darkness.

A study of the relationship between a writer and his editor can be revealing. Knowledge of the career of Maxwell Perkins, for instance, contributes significantly to our understanding of Wolfe, Fitzgerald, and Hemingway—all three of whom were Perkins' authors. The same is true (though in a less positive sense) of Faulkner and his first editor at Random House, Saxe Commins. Yet this bond between an author and his editor is at best fragile, if only because of the author's sensitive ego. Often an author minimizes his editor's contributions to his work, rationalizing that it is after all his genius that supplies the necessary grist for the editor's mill. Gerald Brace Warner, a novelist himself, has written frankly about this delicate alliance:

> Any writer is lucky to have a hard-headed editor whom he trusts, but even so, and even after repeated experience, most writers are reluctant to admit their faults. After the long hard work, after the intense devotion of mind and imagination, what is done must clearly be done well, and any suggestions for change simply represent the opinion of an outsider with different values and concepts. Writers take pride in being stubborn in their own defense. They assume that men of talent, like themselves, are misunderstood by all who are not writers, by editors and publishers and agents and those who have to do with the commerce of writing. Writers have delusions of their own importance.

William Styron seems not to suffer from such delusions. He has always acknowledged the important role that his Bobbs-Merrill editor Hiram Haydn played in the composition of *Lie*

THE TWO TYPESCRIPTS, 'WORKING' AND 'EDITORIAL,' REVEAL A UNIQUE COMPOSITIONAL PROCESS."

Down in Darkness, the novel which rushed Styron suddenly to prominence on the American literary scene in 1951. Haydn's influence on *Lie Down in Darkness* predates Styron's conception of the novel. In 1947, with only William Blackburn's creative writing classes at Duke University under his belt, Styron enrolled in Haydn's fiction-writing seminar at the New School for Social Research in New York City. Impressed by his new pupil's short-story efforts, Haydn challenged Styron "to cut out the nonsense and start a novel." Styron immediately conceived a story about "a girl who gets in a lot of trouble." When Styron had written only twenty pages, Haydn took out an option on *Lie Down in Darkness* for Crown Publishers, then his employers. But after about thirty more pages, Styron's writing bogged down completely. The young Virginian returned to the South and spent an unproductive year among his familiar haunts at Duke University. Haydn sensed that Styron was foundering and urged him to return to New York. Styron did so, and after a short stay in New York City he took up residence in Nyack, New York, with the family of another novelist named Sigrid de Lima. Later Styron moved to West 88th Street in Manhattan, and approximately a year and eight months after his return he finished *Lie Down in Darkness*. During this period he frequently visited the Haydn home, receiving the encouragement due a "*de facto* member of the family." More importantly, Haydn interceded when the Marine Reserve board recalled Styron to active service before he had finished the concluding section of *Lie Down in Darkness*. As a result of Haydn's efforts, Styron received a three-month deferment and finished his novel. Meanwhile Haydn changed publishing houses; Styron and *Lie Down in Darkness* followed him to his new position as editor-in-chief at Bobbs-Merrill.

Haydn contributed more to *Lie Down in Darkness* than advice, support, and intercession with the military. Many of his suggested emendations and deletions were incorporated into the published version of the novel. Again Styron has indicated candidly, if not quite accurately, the presence of Haydn's hand in *Lie Down in Darkness*:

> And when finally [*Lie Down in Darkness*] was done, I remember how I found truly remarkable [Haydn's] ability then to exercise the editorial prerogative and point out where *he* thought things had gone a little haywire. There were never any major things at all in the book, as I recollect, that he changed; but certainly there were a myriad of little tiny points where he had this marvelous ability ... to detect you at your weakest little moment where your phrase was not felicitous, or accurate, and you thought you could get by with what you put down.... He was not altering the nature of the book, or even much of the prose, but was catching me out in accuracies and grammatical errors, and an occasional badly chosen word. And I think this is beautiful when an editor can do this. It can only improve the book, without compromising the author's intent.

Certainly Styron is correct in stating that many of Haydn's changes involved "little tiny points." But close scrutiny of the holograph manuscript, the "working" typescript, and the "editorial" typescript of *Lie Down in Darkness*— all now housed at the Manuscripts Division of the Library of Congress—reveals that many of Haydn's emendations constitute more than mere editorial tinkering. The two typescripts, "working" and "editorial," reveal a unique compositional process.

Styron remembers sending the novel to Haydn in four or five installments. Haydn, recognizing Styron's native ability and not wishing to dampen his enthusiasm, refrained from suggesting any changes during the initial composition of *Lie Down in Darkness*. A working typescript was prepared from the complete holograph manuscript, and Styron made changes and cuts throughout this typescript. A second typescript was then prepared from the emended one, and this clean "editorial" typescript was given to Haydn who marked his own suggested deletions and emendations on it. Finally, Styron approved each of Haydn's suggestions individually by incorporating them *back* into the first typescript. The end product is two typescripts which have almost identical texts. A third typescript was apparently prepared from Styron's twice revised "working" one and was sent to

Bobbs-Merrill to serve as printer's copy. Though this typescript and the proofs for *Lie Down in Darkness* do not survive, a collation of the "working" typescript and the published novel shows that the usual changes in punctuation, spelling, and other accidental features, as well as some small revisions for style, were made before publication.

Haydn made several kinds of minor emendations: deletion of italics, word changes, trifles of phrasing, and grammatical niceties. His deletion of italics throughout the editorial typescript, in fact, is rather significant. Styron himself has spoken often of having to rewrite the initial third of *Lie Down in Darkness* in order to rid the novel of Faulkner's influence. Obviously, the use of italics to highlight a character's thoughts is pure Faulkner. Haydn's deletion of italics, then, is a good example of his helping Styron to exorcise the "Faulknerian ghosts" from *Lie Down in Darkness*. Haydn suggests twenty-eight of these cuts in the first third of the "editorial" typescript; and Styron incorporates each of these suggestions in the published novel.

Sometimes Haydn's minor changes emphasize an effect. In the first chapter, for example, a middle-aged Helen Loftis dreams of her family's visit to her brother Eddie's farm in the Pennsylvania mountains. At the age of twenty-four she is already neurotically attached to her crippled first-born daughter Maudie. Both the editorial and working typescript versions of this section originally read: "The baby, waking from strange darkness into unfathomable light, began to cry but became quieter, after a while, in her mother's arms." In the editorial typescript Haydn reduces this passage simply and more directly to "Helen crushed the child into her arms." This change more powerfully suggests the cloying and destructive nature of Helen's love, and Styron wisely adopts Haydn's emendation in the published novel.

> ... "Don't hand me that sort of thing," she retorted. "You know exactly what I mean." She ran her hand feverishly over her brow—a theatrical gesture, he thought—raising her eyes skyward. *She's neurotic*, he thought with an oddly pleasant feeling of solicitude. *There is really something wrong with her.*

Here, besides deleting the italics, Haydn changed "neurotic" to "queer." By substituting the suggestive "queer" for the exact, almost clinical "neurotic," Haydn understates Helen's problems appropriately. At this point in *Lie*

Down in Darkness we have had only glimpses of Helen's destructive personality; we have yet to witness her total depravity at Peyton's wedding. Therefore, Haydn's word choice keeps Styron from tipping his hand too early; the reader only becomes curious about this "queerness" of Helen's. Furthermore, the use of the psychologist's term "neurotic" is inconsistent with Loftis' character. A Tidewater Virginia lawyer who thinks of himself as a Southern gentleman is more likely to ameliorate his wife's aberrant behavior by labeling it with a quaint word like "queer." Once again Styron heeds his editor's advice; "queer" appears in the published version of the book.

Another example occurs in the chronology of *Lie Down in Darkness*. In both the holograph manuscript and the working typescript, Styron begins the desolate journey of Llewellyn Casper's hearse and limousine on "a weekday morning in August in the nineteen forties." In the editorial typescript, however, Haydn specifies the date as "1945." Styron's editor again remembered from his reading of the manuscript that Peyton kills herself on the day of the bombing of Hiroshima—6 August 1945. No matter how one views this bit of gratuitous symbolism, the ambiguous dating of the novel at the beginning is inconsistent with its exact dating at the conclusion. Haydn recognized the disparity, and Styron changed the date to "1945."

Haydn again supplies both narrative and rhetorical consistency in the letter from Peyton to Loftis. Although it appears early in the novel, this letter accurately represents Peyton's presuicide mental state. In the working-typescript version of the letter Peyton complains to Loftis about the poignant disorientation which is characteristic of her breakdown:

> Thinking of you helps some, thinking of home—but I don't know, nothing seems to really help for long. I feel adrift, as if I were floating out in dark space somewhere without anything to pull me back to earth again. You'd think that feeling would be nice—floating like that—but it isn't. It's terrible.

In the editorial typescript Haydn emends both occurrences of "floating" to "drowning"—Peyton's most frequently repeated word later in the interior monologue which precedes her suicide at the end of the novel. In the published novel Peyton therefore writes to her father of "drowning" and a connection is established between letter and monologue....

Source: Arthur D. Casciato, "His Editor's Hand: Hiram Haydn's Changes in *Lie Down in Darkness*," in *Critical Essays on William Styron*, G. K. Hall, 1982, pp. 36–40.

SOURCES

Baumbach, Jonathan, "Paradise Lost: Styron's *Lie Down in Darkness*," in *Critical Essays on William Styron*, edited by Arthur D. Casciato and James L. W. West III, G. K. Hall, 1982, pp. 24–35; originally published in *The Landscape of Nightmare: Studies in the American Contemporary Novel*, New York University Press, 1965, pp. 123–33.

Breit, Harvey, "Dissolution of a Family," in *Critical Essays on William Styron*, edited by Arthur D. Casciato and James L. W. West III, G. K. Hall, 1982, pp. 18–19; originally published in *Atlantic Monthly*, October 1951, pp. 78–80.

Butterworth, Keen, "William Styron," in *Dictionary of Literary Biography*, Vol. 2, *American Novelists since World War II, First Series*, edited by Jeffrey Helterman, Gale Research, 1978, pp. 460–75.

Cheuse, Alan, "In Styron, a Literary Landmark Remains," in *All Things Considered*, NPR website, November 2, 2006, http://www.npr.org/templates/story/story.php?storyId=6423964 (accessed January 13, 2015).

Cologne-Brookes, Gavin, "Inheritance of Modernism: *Lie Down in Darkness*," in *The Novels of William Styron: From Harmony to History*, Louisiana State University Press, 1995, pp. 10–44.

Cowley, Malcolm, "The Faulkner Pattern," in *Critical Essays on William Styron*, edited by Arthur D. Casciato and James L. W. West III, G. K. Hall, 1982, pp. 16–17; originally published in *New Republic*, October 8, 1951, pp. 19–20.

Dabney, Virginius, *Virginia: The New Dominion*, Doubleday, 1971, pp. 459–527.

Davis, Robert Gorham, "A Grasp of Moral Realities," in *Critical Essays on William Styron*, edited by Arthur D. Casciato and James L. W. West III, G. K. Hall, 1982, pp. 20–21; originally published in *American Scholar*, No. 21, Winter 1951, pp. 114, 116.

Dibdin, Emma, "Kristen Stewart Not in 'Lie Down in Darkness,' Director Confirms," *Digital Spy*, May 7, 2013, http://www.digitalspy.com/movies/news/a479141/kristen-stewart-not-in-lie-down-in-darkness-director-confirms.html#~p1GXVS5ssRbnyZ (accessed January 17, 2015).

Fossum, R. H., *William Styron: A Critical Essay*, Contemporary Writers in Christian Perspective, William B. Eerdmans, 1968, pp. 8–19.

Hansen, Louis, "Crashes, Deaths Dropped after Tough Va. DUI Laws," in *Virginian-Pilot* (Norfolk, VA), July

15, 2014, http://hamptonroads.com/2014/07/crashes-deaths-dropped-after-tough-va-dui-laws (accessed January 18, 2015).

Janeway, Elizabeth, "Private Emotions, Privately Felt," in *Critical Essays on William Styron*, edited by Arthur D. Casciato and James L. W. West III, G. K. Hall, 1982, pp. 22–23; originally published in *New Leader*, January 21, 1952, p. 25.

Jones, Howard Mumford, "A Rich, Moving Novel Introduces a Young Writer of Great Talent," in *Critical Essays on William Styron*, edited by Arthur D. Casciato and James L. W. West III, G. K. Hall, 1982, pp. 13–15; originally published in *New York Herald Tribune Book Review*, September 9, 1951, p. 3.

Morris, Robert K., "Interviews with William Styron," in *The Achievement of William Styron*, rev. ed., edited by Robert K. Morris and Irving Malin, University of Georgia Press, 1981, pp. 29–69.

Nostrandt, Jeanne R., "William Styron's *Lie Down in Darkness*: A Parable," in *Southern Literary Journal*, Vol. 28, No. 1, Fall 1995, pp. 58–66.

"Operation Enduring Freedom: U.S. Wounded Totals," in *Operation Enduring Freedom, iCasualties*, http://icasualties.org/OEF/USCasualtiesByState.aspx (accessed January 18, 2015).

"Operation Iraqi Freedom; Iraq Coalition Casualties: U.S. Wounded Totals," in *Operation Iraqi Freedom, iCasualties*, http://icasualties.org/Iraq/USCasualtiesByState.aspx (accessed January 18, 2015).

Ratner, Marc L., *William Styron*, Twayne's United States Authors Series, No. 196, Twayne Publishers, 1972, pp. 13–56.

Rosenthal, Regine, "William Styron," in *Dictionary of Literary Biography*, Vol. 299, *Holocaust Novelists*, edited by Efraim Sicher, Thomson Gale, 2004. pp. 331–39.

Schultz, Lucille M., "*Lie Down in Darkness*: A Story of Two Processions," in *Southern Literary Journal*, Vol. 18, No. 2, Spring 1986, pp. 62–75.

"A Short History of Drunk Driving," DrinkingAndDriving.org, http://www.drinkinganddriving.org/Articles/historyof.html (accessed January 18, 2015).

Styron, William, *Lie Down in Darkness*, Vintage International, 1992.

———, "*Lie Down in Darkness*," in *This Quiet Dust and Other Writings*, Vintage International, 1993, pp. 323–28.

FURTHER READING

Cornett, Donna J., *Beat Binge Drinking: A Smart Drinking Guide for Teens, College Students and Young Adults Who Choose to Drink*, People Friendly Books, 2010.

Aiming to influence young adults' drinking habits for the better in lieu of simply refusing to acknowledge them, Cornett offers a guide that speaks directly to youth culture in considering the most responsible ways to appreciate alcohol.

Moss, Elizabeth, *Domestic Novelists in the Old South: Defenders of Southern Culture*, Louisiana State University Press, 1992.

Moss focuses on several lesser-known women novelists from the nineteenth century—Caroline Gilman, Caroline Hentz, Maria McIntosh, Mary Virginia Terhune, and Augusta Jane Evans—to expound upon the underprivileged perspectives of women of the era.

Styron, William, *This Quiet Dust and Other Writings*, Random House, 1982.

A fairly prominent essayist in his day, Styron collected some of his nonfiction in this volume. Sections cover the South, his literary forebears and contemporaries, the military, and his own works, including *Lie Down in Darkness*.

Wallenstein, Peter, *Cradle of America: Four Centuries of Virginia History*, University Press of Kansas, 2007.

Wallenstein's is among the most recent histories of Virginia, home to tobacco, numerous presidents, and societal intersections not far from the Mason-Dixon line.

SUGGESTED SEARCH TERMS

William Styron AND Lie Down in Darkness

William Styron AND southern literature

southern literature AND William Faulkner

William Styron AND William Faulkner

Lie Down in Darkness AND The Sound and the Fury

southern literature AND alcohol

southern literature AND family tragedy

suicide AND tragedy

alcohol AND suicide

The Loved One

EVELYN WAUGH

1948

The Loved One, first published in 1948 in the February issue of *Horizon* magazine, is a novel by British author Evelyn Waugh. Its full title is *The Loved One: An Anglo-American Tragedy*, but despite the word *tragedy* in the subtitle, *The Loved One* is a hilariously satirical novel whose targets include Hollywood, American funerary practices, the snobbery of expatriate Englishmen living in America, and what Waugh regarded as the intellectual sterility of Americans. During the middle decades of the twentieth century, Waugh emerged as perhaps the most celebrated—and sometimes reviled—satirical novelist of the era, and *The Loved One* cemented that reputation.

Waugh wrote *The Loved One* as a result of a trip to Hollywood he took in February and March of 1947. The movie studio MGM was interested in producing a film version of Waugh's 1945 novel *Brideshead Revisited* and in fact offered him $150,000 for the film rights. Waugh was a highly conservative Catholic traditionalist who believed that the modern world was in a state of irremediable decline. He was of the opinion that few Americans truly understood the theological implications of the novel. Because he insisted on having full control over the script to prevent his story from being misinterpreted, the deal fell through. However, during his visit he was given a tour of the famous Forest Lawn Memorial Park (now part of a chain of Forest Lawn cemeteries in the region). He regarded the elaborate funerary practices of

Evelyn Waugh *(© Library of Congress Prints and Photographs Division [LC-USZ62-78969])*

Americans, combined with what he saw as an overall vulgarity and superficiality in American life, as a rich mine that provided him with the raw materials for *The Loved One*.

AUTHOR BIOGRAPHY

Arthur Evelyn (pronounced EVE-uh-lin) St. John (pronounced sin-jin) Waugh was born on October 28, 1903, in London, England, to Arthur Waugh, a publisher and literary critic, and Catherine Charlotte Raban. Waugh had an older brother, Alexander ("Alec"), who would also achieve a measure of fame as a novelist. As a child, Waugh attended Heath Mount preparatory school, where he gained a reputation as something of a bully—a reputation he was never able to shed throughout his life, for he was widely regarded as a cantankerous snob, an apologist for the upper classes, and an anti-Semite who admired such figures as dictators Benito Mussolini and Francisco Franco. At the age of seven he wrote his first story, "The Curse of the Horse Race." He later attended Lancing College in Sussex and Herford College at

Oxford University. His time at Oxford was one principally of dissipation, as he drank heavily, took part in a series of homosexual relationships, feuded openly with his major history tutor, and suffered from severe emotional pressures.

After leaving Oxford (without a degree), Waugh briefly enrolled in art school, but the routine bored him, and he needed an income, so in 1925 he found a teaching job at a boys' preparatory school in Wales. He later held teaching jobs in London, the first of which he was dismissed from for having tried to seduce one of the school's matrons while he was drunk. During the 1920s, he began to write in earnest, and in the late 1920s and 1930s, he wrote and published some of his most famous satires, including *Decline and Fall* (1928), *Vile Bodies* (1930), *Black Mischief* (1932), *A Handful of Dust* (1934), and *Scoop* (1938).

In 1927, Waugh married Evelyn Gardner; the couple's friends jokingly referred to them as "He-Evelyn" and "She-Evelyn." A key event in Waugh's life was his conversion to Catholicism in 1930, and much of his later fiction would attempt to explore the character of man in relation to God and the Catholic Church, which he regarded as a kind of bulwark against a new dark age in the twentieth century. As a Catholic, he was unable to divorce, so, wanting out of his marriage, he obtained an annulment in 1936, allowing him to marry Laura Herbert in 1937.

In the 1930s, Waugh traveled widely, often working as a freelance journalist, and his travels provided him with material for his novels. When World War II broke out, he was trained as an officer, but he was temperamentally unsuited to the discipline of military life. His wartime career as an intelligence officer was largely unsuccessful. In 1945, Waugh published what is generally regarded as his major work, *Brideshead Revisited*, a retrospective novel that explores the unraveling of the traditional English class system and the process of recovering lost religious faith in an increasingly secular world. In 1948, after a visit to Hollywood, Waugh published *The Loved One*. Out of his experiences in World War II, he wrote the Sword of Honor trilogy, consisting of *Men at Arms* (1952), *Officers and Gentlemen* (1955), and *Unconditional Surrender* (1961).

As his health deteriorated during the 1950s, Waugh was dependent on a number of medications that produced hallucinations, an experience he recreated in the semi-autobiographical novel *The Ordeal of Gilbert Pinfold* (1957). These ended when his drug regimen was altered. His health continued to worsen, however, and during the final years of his life, as his popularity as a writer was in decline, he was plagued by a shortage of money and heavy debts. On the morning of April 10, 1966, Easter Sunday, he attended mass with his family; returned to his home in Combe Florey, near Taunton, Somerset; and died of heart failure.

PLOT SUMMARY

Chapter One

The novel opens with two expatriate Englishmen, Dennis Barlow and Sir Francis Hinsley, enjoying drinks as they sit on a veranda on a warm afternoon in Southern California. A third Englishman, Sir Ambrose Abercrombie, joins them. The reader learns that Barlow, the youngest of the three at age twenty-eight, is a poet whose contract with the Megalopolitan Pictures movie studio has not been renewed; that Hinsley was formerly a scriptwriter for the studio but now works in its publicity department; and that Abercrombie, now retired, was formerly a famous Hollywood actor. In the conversation that follows, Hinsley notes that the studio is having trouble rebranding one of its stars: Juanita del Pablo had formerly been made over into an exotic Spanish refugee, but now the studio wants her persona to be that of an Irish colleen. Abercrombie talks about the obligation of British expats to act as ambassadors for their native country.

After dinner, Barlow goes to his job at the Happier Hunting Ground pet cemetery. He receives a call from Theodora Heinkel, whose Sealyham terrier has died. Barlow drives to the Heinkel home, where he and Walter Heinkel load the dog into the cemetery's van. Heinkel agrees to purchase the cemetery's Grade A funeral service for the dog.

Chapter Two

As the weeks pass, Barlow continues to be content with his position at Happier Hunting Ground; the reader learns about his experience as a poet during the Second World War. After his discharge from military service, he went to Hollywood to write a script for a film about the

MEDIA ADAPTATIONS

- A film version of *The Loved One* was produced by MGM in 1965. The film script was written by satirical novelist Terry Southern and British author Christopher Isherwood. The film, directed by Tony Richardson, stars Robert Morse, Jonathan Winters, Anjanette Comer, and Rod Steiger. Smaller roles were filled by John Gielgud, Roddy McDowall, James Coburn, Milton Berle, and Liberace. Running time is 122 minutes.

- In 2007, BBC Radio 4 aired a radio version of *The Loved One*, adapted by Jonathan Holloway.

- In 2012, Hachette Audio/Little, Brown released *The Loved One* as an audiobook. The text is narrated by Simon Prebble. Running time is three hours and twenty-four minutes.

life of Percy Bysshe Shelley, but he never was able to produce the script, leading to his dismissal from the studio.

Hinsley, meanwhile, is failing in his efforts to transform Juanita into an Irishwoman, resulting in *his* dismissal from the studio. In despair, he hangs himself, and it is Barlow who discovers the body the next day. Abercrombie believes that Hinsley was dismissed because he was living with Barlow, who, in Abercrombie's view, has disgraced the British expat community by lowering himself to take a job at a pet cemetery.

Chapter Three

Barlow goes to Whispering Glades to make funeral arrangements for Hinsley. As he passes through the gate, he pauses to read the text carved into an immense wall listing the cliched precepts of the cemetery's founder. He enters the offices, where he meets with a mortuary hostess who explains to him the many options available. Throughout, she distinguishes between the deceased, whom she refers to as a Loved One, and the mourners, whom she calls Waiting Ones. After trying to sell Barlow his own Before Need Provision Arrangements, she turns him over to a cosmetician who will later be identified as Aimée Thanatogenos; Barlow is immediately struck by how unique she is among American women of his experience. She explains to him the nature of the work that she and Mr. Joyboy, her superior, do to make a corpse presentable.

Chapter Four

Barlow obtains a leave of absence from his boss, Mr. Schultz, to attend Hinsley's funeral and to deal with the preliminaries to it. Abercrombie assigns him the task of finding something from Hinsley's writings to read at the funeral and to compose a suitable poem to be read at the grave-side service.

The scene changes to Aimée's cubicle at Whispering Glades, where she and Mr. Joyboy discuss the nuances of their art as it pertains to Hinsley and where Joyboy seems to be flirting with her. Hinsley, whose body was in poor shape because of the manner of his death, is now coiffed, and makeup has been applied. Joyboy arranges his features, and after Hinsley's body becomes rigid, he is posed for viewing.

Chapter Five

Barlow goes to Whispering Glades to ensure all is in order prior to the public viewing. He sees Hinsley's body in the Orchid Slumber Room. Later, Hinsley's acquaintances arrive to pay their respects. Barlow's need to compose a poem for the next day's graveside service is weighing heavily on him. He tours the University Church—a replica of a church in Oxford, England—on the Whispering Glades grounds. He then goes to the Lake Island, also on the grounds, which appears to be a trysting place for couples. He fails to find poetic inspiration.

As he lies in the dense shade, Aimée appears. Barlow recognizes her as the cosmetician he met earlier. Aimée discusses the nature of her art and explains how she got into the mortuary business, making it clear that she has a great love for what she does. Barlow quotes from a poem by John Keats, but Aimée thinks that the lines are Barlow's.

Chapter Six

Joyboy continues to carry on a flirtation with Aimée, principally by sending her corpses with radiant smiles on their faces. Aimée is uncertain whether she loves Joyboy. Earlier, in her perplexity, she wrote a letter to the Guru Brahmin, an advice columnist for the lovelorn in a local newspaper, who wrote in response that Aimée's feelings appear to be those of friendship rather than love. Since then, she has met Barlow and is beginning to suspect that she loves him. Again, she seeks advice from the Guru Brahmin, but in her letter she notes that Barlow is un-American, that he is cynical, and that he lacks religion, citizenship, and a social conscience. Nevertheless, she seems to have feelings for him, in large part because he writes poems for her, although the reader quickly learns that none of the poems are of Barlow's composition but rather are poems he has found in anthologies and presented to Aimée as his own.

Joyboy tells Aimée that the Dreamer (the founder of Whispering Glades) wants to promote her to the position of embalmer. To celebrate, Joyboy asks her on a date, which turns out to be a tawdry affair at his home. The house is shabby, he lives with his mean-spirited mother and her parrot, the food is bland and ordinary, and Joyboy refuses to drive Aimée home because he does not want to leave his mother. Meanwhile, earlier that day, Barlow impulsively proposed marriage to Aimée based on the raise in pay she will presumably get from her promotion. Aimée is enraged by Barlow's lack of sensitivity.

Chapter Seven

The reader learns that the Guru Brahmin is in fact two men and a secretary who answer letters. Mr. Slump is the man who responds to letters that require private answers, such as the letter Aimée has written after her disastrous date with Joyboy. Slump responds with the view that Joyboy is a more reliable choice for her than a glib poet such as Barlow.

Aimée receives a poem from Barlow that was in fact written by British poet Richard Middleton. Barlow asks Schultz for a raise because he wants to marry Aimée. At the Lovers' Nook on the grounds of Whispering Glades, Aimée and Barlow become engaged to marry.

Chapter Eight

Aimée receives another poem from Barlow, this one written by Samuel Taylor Coleridge. She passes the poem along to Joyboy, who asks her about its source and who wants to see more of the poems Barlow has sent her because he wants to show them to a literary friend. Joyboy tells Aimée that Sambo, his mother's parrot, has died. He plans a service for the parrot at Happier Hunting Ground and asks Aimée to attend. Through these developments, Aimée learns of Barlow's deceptions: she had not known where he worked and thought that he had written the poems he recited to her.

Chapter Nine

After Aimée discovers that Barlow has been deceiving her both about his poetry and about his place of employment, Barlow learns that she is now engaged to Joyboy. Barlow confronts her, and once again she is torn between the two men. She again seeks the advice of the Guru Brahmin, learning that in reality he is Mr. Slump, whom she finds by telephone in a bar after he has been fired. He tells her to jump off a building. That night, Aimée commits suicide by injecting herself with cyanide in Joyboy's workroom at Whispering Glades.

Chapter Ten

After Joyboy discovers Aimée's body, he seeks assistance from Barlow. Barlow meets with Abercrombie, who fears that Barlow's plans to become a nonsectarian funeral pastor will further harm the image of the British expatriate community, so he offers to pay Barlow's passage back to England. Unaware of Barlow's impending departure, Joyboy returns, and in exchange for all his savings, Barlow says he will leave town so it will appear that he ran away with Aimée, thus sparing Joyboy embarrassment. After cremating the body at Happier Hunting Ground, Barlow signs Joyboy up for the pet cemetery's annual postcard service so that every year he will receive a card reminding him that Aimée is in heaven wagging her tail for him.

CHARACTERS

Sir Ambrose Abercrombie

Abercrombie was formerly a distinguished British actor in American films. As the leader of the community of British expatriates, he is concerned about maintaining the image of his countrymen in the eyes of Hollywood. He is troubled that Dennis Barlow has taken a job at a pet cemetery, believing that doing so casts the British expats in a negative light. At the end of the novel, Abercrombie offers to pay Barlow's way back to England to get rid of him.

Dennis Barlow

Barlow is the novel's protagonist. He had achieved some measure of fame in his native England as a poet and on that basis was brought to Hollywood to pen a script for a film biography of the British romantic poet Percy Bysshe Shelley. However, his poetic gift appears to have dried up, and he was fired from his job. As the novel opens, he is employed by the Happier Hunting Ground, a funeral home for pets. When he meets Aimée Thanatogenos, he finds himself immediately attracted to her and ultimately asks her to marry him. As he courts her, he frequently quotes lines of classic poetry, allowing her to believe that he is the author of the verses. Like many of Waugh's protagonists, Barlow is rather feckless and a failure—in this case, as a poet, a scriptwriter, and a lover.

Guru Brahmin

Aimée writes to Guru Brahmin for advice. She later discovers that "Guru Brahmin" is a pseudonym, and her letters are answered by Mr. Slump.

The Dreamer

The founder of Whispering Glades cemetery is called "the Dreamer."

Theodora and Walter Heinkel

The Heinkels appear briefly as the owners of a Sealyham terrier that has died. In response to their call to Happier Hunting Ground, Dennis Barlow drives to their home to pick up the dog. He persuades Walter to purchase the cemetery's Grade A funeral service for the dog.

Sir Francis Hinsley

Hinsley is Barlow's Hollywood housemate. In his earlier years, Hinsley wrote the widely acclaimed novel *A Free Man Greets the Dawn*, but he has long since given up writing. Formerly, he was the chief scriptwriter for Megalopolitan Pictures, but as the novel opens he works for their publicity department. He struggles to rebrand an actress named Juanita del Pablo into an Irish starlet. After he is fired from Megalopolitan for his failure to do so, he hangs himself.

Mr. Joyboy

Mr. Joyboy is Aimée's superior at the Whispering Glades cemetery. His claim to be an artist stems from his ability to impose blissful smiles on unsightly corpses. He flirts with Aimée until ultimately he gets her to agree to marry him. Although he presents a debonair image, the image is false, for he lives with his mother, Mrs. Joyboy, and is dominated by her.

Mrs. Joyboy

Mrs. Joyboy is Joyboy's malevolent and mean-spirited mother. She lives with him and her parrot, Sambo, in a tract house in a somewhat rundown neighborhood.

Juanita del Pablo

Juanita never actually appears in the novel. She is a studio actress who previously had been transformed into an exotic Spanish refugee. As the novel opens, Sir Francis Hinsley has been assigned the task of transforming her again—this time into an Irish colleen.

Myra Poski

Myra is Dennis Barlow's coworker at the Happier Hunting Ground pet cemetery

Mr. Schultz

Schultz is Dennis Barlow's cross and irritable boss at the Happier Hunting Ground pet cemetery.

Mr. Slump

Slump works for the newspaper that prints the Guru Brahmin advice column, and in fact he is one of the two men who respond to letters. Slump deals with those letters requiring a private response, putting him in touch with Aimée. He smokes heavily, and his heavy drinking gets him fired from the paper. His last act is to tell Aimée to jump off a bridge.

Aimée Thanatogenos

Aimée is the naïve assistant to the chief cosmetician at Whispering Glades cemetery. Her name is a grotesque combination of words that mean "beloved" and "race (or tribe) of death." She immediately attracts the attention of Dennis Barlow, who woos her principally with lines of classic poetry that Aimée believes he has written. Through much of the novel, she is torn between attraction to Joyboy, who admires her work and who seems to her to be a more solid and dependable person, and Barlow. Ultimately, she agrees to marry Barlow, but when she discovers his deception—she learns that he is not the author of the poetry he quotes to her and that he works at the Happier Hunting Ground—she rejects him. Uncertain what course of action to take, she kills herself with cyanide in Joyboy's workroom.

THEMES

Death

Death is clearly a major theme of *The Loved One*, more specifically, the rituals and practices that surround death and funerals in mid-twentieth century Southern California. Aimée Thanatogenos, whose last name is derived from the Greek and means roughly "tribe of death" or "race of death," works as a cosmetician at the opulent Whispering Glades cemetery, which is modeled after the Forest Lawn cemetery in California. Dennis Barlow works at the Happier Hunting Ground pet cemetery, which ironically mirrors Whispering Glades.

Throughout the novel, the reader is reminded of funerary practices designed to blunt the sting of death by presenting "the loved one"—that is, the deceased—in the most attractive light possible. Aimée and her boss, Joyboy (note the irony of the name), think of themselves as artists, adept at using the tools of their trade and their artistic sensibilities to convert a body—such as the disfigured body of Francis Hinsley—into something that appears blissful and peaceful. Meanwhile, part of Barlow's job is to sell elaborate (and expensive) funeral rites to the owners of dead pets.

Overall, the novel functions as a memento mori, a Latin phrase translated as "Remember that you are mortal" or "Remember that you will die." The concept of the memento mori was foreign in antiquity, but with the spread of Christianity in the Western world, images and symbolism intended to remind people of the transience of life, the hope for salvation in the afterlife, and the vanity of earthly pleasures became widespread; common examples include skeletons, the Grim Reaper with his scythe, hourglasses, skulls, and images of decayed corpses. *The Loved One* provides readers with a satiric memento mori, one that turns the traditional images associated with death on their

TOPICS FOR FURTHER STUDY

- Prepare a time line of key events in post–World War II California, particularly Southern California and Hollywood, in the late 1940s. Post your time line on a social networking site and invite your classmates to comment.

- P. G. Wodehouse was a British humorist who achieved considerable fame during Waugh's lifetime. Wodehouse was the author of seemingly innumerable novels and short stories that satirize the foibles of English upper-crust society. Select a novel or story by Wodehouse. A good possibility would be any of his "Wooster and Jeeves" works about the bumbling Bertie Wooster and his clever manservant Jeeves, such as 1934's *Thank You, Jeeves* (Arrow, 2008). Prepare an essay in which you compare and contrast the tone of Wodehouse's satire with Waugh's.

- Walter Mosley is an African American novelist and the creator of Easy Rawlins, a private investigator who works in the Watts area of Los Angeles. The first novel in the series is *Devil in a Blue Dress*, which takes place in 1948, the year in which *The Loved Ones* was published. Prepare an oral report in which you examine how Mosley and Waugh treat widely differing aspects of postwar culture and society in Southern California.

- Locate Libba Bray's *Beauty Queens*, a young-adult novel that employs dark humor to satirize celebrity culture and beauty pageants. Write a review of the novel as you imagine someone like Waugh would have regarded it. Share your review with your classmates on your website.

- Throughout literary history, satire has been frequently employed to make statements about the absurdity of the human condition. Conduct research on satire online and in print sources. Identify three or four writers from the past to whom you think Waugh owed a debt for his satiric gifts. Prepare a chart that highlights your authors and their works and be prepared to explain to your classmates the connections you see between them and Waugh.

- With a willing classmate, select a scene from *The Loved One* and develop it into a dramatic script. Perform your play for your classmates.

- Conduct research into the mortuary business as it is typically conducted in the twenty-first century. What are some of its practices? Do you think that today's funeral homes and cemeteries try to sanitize death or sentimentalize funeral practices? What might an average funeral home director think of Waugh's satire? Present the results of your research in an oral report for your classmates.

- Pick a modern American business, activity, or institution that you think might be ripe for satire. Possibilities include the fast-food industry, shopping malls, reality television programming, sports, rap music (or any other music genre), animal day-care centers, chain coffee shops, televised singing or dancing competitions, beauty pageants for preschoolers, cheerleading, Wikipedia, and late-night talk shows. Write your own satire exposing the follies and foibles you see in your subject. Share your satire with your classmates, either orally or on your social networking site. (Be sure to avoid offending classmates who might participate in one of these activities.)

- Locate images of the Forest Lawn cemetery (which now consists of a chain of cemeteries in Southern California; the original is in Glendale, California) and prepare a visual presentation for your classmates, emphasizing those features that you believe Waugh satirizes in *The Loved One*.

Setting parts of the story in a funeral parlor and cemetery reinforces the theme of death. (© Marc Bruxelle / Shutterstock.com)

heads by showing tortured, and ultimately futile, efforts to present death in a more benign light.

Culture

During his visit to Hollywood in 1947, Waugh was struck by what he regarded as the vulgarity of American life, although he found similar vulgarity among his fellow Englishmen. Waugh was a staunch traditionalist. Highly conservative in his outlook and committed to Catholicism, he believed that the modern Western world was in a state of decline. He lamented the erosion of the British class system and the weakening of religious conviction. In Hollywood, he felt surrounded by signs of crudeness and boorishness, and these became the object of his satire.

Waugh lamented the superficiality and concern with appearances of Hollywood and the movie industry; a good example in *The Loved One* is the effort to strip Juanita del Pablo of her identity by transforming her first into a Spanish antifascist refugee and then into an Irish colleen. Waugh found the funeral practices of the Forest Lawn cemetery, transformed in his novel into

Whispering Glades, to be vulgar and obsessed with show and performance rather than with the reality of human mortality. The Happier Hunting Ground pet cemetery is an extension of that vulgarity and concern with appearances.

On virtually every page of the novel, Waugh depicts a kind of vulgar excess that he believed marked much of American life. Not willing to let his countrymen off the hook, however, his character Dennis Barlow, who works at the Happier Hunting Ground, is a Briton, and his acquiescence in the vulgarity of the pet cemetery and later desire to become a radio evangelist is part of Waugh's overall indictment of modern life.

Appearance versus Reality

In large measure, *The Loved One* is a novel about appearances, particularly false appearances. Repeatedly, things are not what they seem. The identity of Juanita del Pablo has been transformed by the Hollywood studio system, and Hollywood in general is about the manipulation of appearances and images. Barlow quotes lines of poetry to Aimée that appear (to her) to be of his composition but that in fact he has culled from anthologies. The appearance of bodies brought to Whispering Glades is transformed by the arts of cosmeticians and hair stylists, and bodies are posed for viewing in ways that make them look as though the deceased are enjoying a state of blissful repose. Joyboy appears to be a debonair cosmetic artist but in fact he lives a somewhat dismal life dominated by his abusive mother. The Guru Brahmin is no guru but in fact is a manufactured identity comprising two men—including Mr. Slump, a drunkard Aimée tracks down at a bar—and a secretary who answer letters written to the advice column of the newspaper for which they work. Peaches appear to be juicy and succulent, but they have no stones, and they taste like cotton.

At the center of this focus on appearances is the Whispering Glades cemetery. When Barlow first visits the cemetery after the death of Francis Hinsley, he makes these observations, which Waugh uses to establish a thematic connection between the cemetery and Hollywood:

> When as a newcomer to the Megalopolitan Studios he first toured the lots, it had taxed his imagination to realize that those solid-seeming streets and squares of every period and climate were in fact plaster façades whose backs revealed the structure of bill-boardings.

The reverse is true at the cemetery, where he found it difficult to "believe that the building before him was three-dimensional and permanent; but here, as everywhere in Whispering Glades, failing credulity was fortified by the painted word." He then goes on to read the notice posted on the building, a "perfect replica of an old English Manor," "constructed through of Grade A steel and concrete." Again, appearance substitutes for reality.

STYLE

Satire

The term *satire* refers to any artistic creation, such as a novel or play, whose intent is to use humor, ridicule, and exaggeration to expose the follies, vices, or abuses of a person, a group, or a society. Scholars often distinguish various forms or modes of satire based on how satire was handled by the classical Roman writers Horace, Juvenal, and Menippus. Horatian satire tends to be gentle, relying on wit and lighthearted humor to poke fun at what the author regards as folly. Juvenalian satire, in contrast, is much more bitter, contemptuous, and abrasive. It employs savage ridicule and scorn to attack social evils. Menippian satire is designed to attack mental attitudes or attributes rather than specific individuals or groups.

To specify which satirical mode describes *The Loved One* is difficult. The humor of the novel relies principally on exaggeration; each of the elements of the novel, from its characters to its setting, is exaggerated in a way that exposes what Waugh regarded as a fundamental ridiculousness. At times the humor is lighthearted and witty; at other times, the humor is more biting and savage. However, the targets of the author's satire are readily apparent. Waugh had heard that the Forest Lawn Memorial Park was a place where religion and art were merged to provide mourners with a place of consolation and faith, but he found the place to be macabre, grotesque, and suffused with cuteness and crass sentimentality. Its concern with false fronts and false appearances, mirrored by the false images created by the Hollywood film industry, provided him with a rich source of material for a satiric novel.

Comedy

Closely related to the satirical qualities of *The Loved One* is its reliance on humor. The humor Waugh employs, however, is generally not light or gentle. Rather, he employs a type of humor that is often called *black humor* or *dark humor*. The term *black humor* was coined by the French surrealist André Breton, whose *Anthologie de l'humour noir*, or "Anthology of Black Humor," was published in 1940. The essential feature of this mode of comedy is that it makes light of a subject matter usually seen as taboo for the comic writer: physical or mental disabilities, murder and assassination, disease, atomic warfare, executions (giving rise to the related concept of gallows humor), suicide, death, and funerals. Normally these are subjects that would be approached with respect, if not reverence.

A considerable portion of the comedy of *The Loved One* stems from suicide, death, and funeral practices. A good example occurs at the novel's end. Aimée, left baffled by her inability to sort out her love life, commits suicide by injecting herself with cyanide. She does so at the Whispering Glades cemetery in the workroom of Joyboy, who loves her. He and Dennis Barlow, who also has professed to love her and had asked her to marry him, transport her body to the Happier Hunting Ground pet cemetery, where Barlow cremates her. As the fire roars in the brick oven, he enters the cemetery's office, where he makes a notation in a register to ensure that on every anniversary of Aimée's death, a postcard will be sent to Joyboy: "*Your little Aimée is wagging her tail in heaven tonight, thinking of you.*" This ending puts a macabre, ghoulish period to the novel and provides a pointed example of black humor.

Allusion

Waugh frequently relies on allusion in *The Loved One*. The term *allusion* is inherently somewhat vague. It refers to any reference, whether explicit or implied, to a person, place, or event external to the work at hand. The purpose of an allusion is generally to enrich the reader's understanding and to place the events of the work at hand into a broader context. Writers very often make allusions to earlier literary works, but allusions can be made to essentially anything. In reference to Sir Francis Hinsley and his efforts to transform Juanita del Pablo in conformity with the wishes of the studio, Waugh writes:

> Sir Francis was charged with the metamorphosis. How lightly, ten years before, he had brought her into existence—the dynamite-bearing Maenad of the Bilboa water-front! With what leaden effort did he now search the nomenclature of Celtic mythology and write the new life-story—a romance of the Mountains of the Mourne, of the bare-foot child whom the peasants spoke of as a fairies' changeling, the confidante of leprechauns.

"Metamorphosis" alludes to *Metamorphoses* by the classic Roman poet Ovid. In Greek mythology, the Maenads were the frenzied followers of the god Dionysius. Bilboa is a city in Spain, alluding to Juanita's initial transformation into a fiery Spanish rebel. The Mountains of the Mourne are a romantic mountain range in southeast Northern Ireland. Changelings and leprechauns are fixtures in ancient Celtic mythology. The use of these allusions in this context has a humorous effect, for they treat a trivial subject in an elevated manner.

HISTORICAL CONTEXT

California and the American Dream

Throughout the twentieth century, California was as much an idea as it was a place on the map. California was widely seen as an Eden, a magical land where dreams could come true. In his classic novel *The Grapes of Wrath*, John Steinbeck leads poor Depression-era farmers from the Oklahoma Dust Bowl to California in search of a better life. Al Jolson's song "California, Here I Come" was later covered by numerous artists. "California Dreamin'" is a well-known song recorded by the pop singing group the Mamas and the Papas.

Much of California's growth and development were sparked by World War II. During the war, some fifteen million US civilians moved across state lines. More than two million of those, including large numbers of African Americans, moved to California to work in the state's defense industries. Later, Southern California became the center of the American aerospace industry, and more recently, the state has become the hub of the nation's high-tech industries. Surrounding it all has been the glitz and glamour that have long marked Southern California's cultural and social scene, with high-end automobiles, luxury shopping arcades and avenues, the latest in fashion, opulent mansions that are home to movie stars, the speed and convenience of drive-thru restaurants (which would ultimately replace carhops on roller skates), and the conspicuous consumption suggested by the excess of Waugh's Whispering Glades and Happier Hunting Ground cemeteries. With its relatively benign climate, its miles of beaches, its mountains and forests, California became the fulfillment of the American dream for many people.

Hollywood

Southern California was particularly alluring in the years following World War I, when the dreams of many Americans were writ large in theaters that showed the movies produced in Hollywood, a suburb of Los Angeles, where the film industry located because it could normally count on good weather for outdoor scenes. After the production of the first "talkies"—that is, films with sound, as opposed to silent films—in the late 1920s, Hollywood producers were able to establish a firm grip on the business of producing and distributing films. The result was

COMPARE & CONTRAST

- **1948:** The Hollywood studio system is effectively ended with the decision of the U.S. Supreme Court in the antitrust case *United States v. Paramount Pictures, Inc.*, sometimes referred to as the Hollywood Antitrust Case of 1948.

  Today: The studio system has been replaced by a range of options, including syndication, television rebroadcasts and cable or satellite transmissions, ad hoc combinations of movie production companies and distributors, and movie rentals online and through various retail outlets such as Redbox.

- **1948:** The first In-N-Out Burger is founded by Harry and Esther Snyder in Baldwin Park, California, in Los Angeles County; the restaurant, the first of its kind, is a drive-through hamburger stand where customers can order through a two-way speaker.

  Today: Among numerous fast-food chains, McDonald's alone operates more than 35,000 drive-through stores in more than a hundred countries.

- **1948:** The Los Angeles Pet Cemetery, created in 1928, is the oldest pet cemetery on the West Coast of the United States.

  Today: Now called the Los Angeles Pet Memorial Park and Crematorium, the pet cemetery offers burial services, transportation, cremation, private viewing, and pre-need planning.

- **1948:** Beginning in 1940, to help Americans defray funeral expenses, the Social Security Administration paid a lump-sum death benefit that by 1950 will reach about $148; that figure will rise to about $255 in 1955.

  Today: The median cost of a US funeral as of 2012 is just over $7,000.

---

what was called the studio system—the same studio system for which Sir Francis Hinsley wrote in *The Loved One* and that was able to mold such actresses as Juanita del Pablo to meet the expectations and fantasies of the public.

The studio system that underpins Waugh's novel embodied what economists call vertical integration, meaning that, in the case of films, it linked three activities along the production and distribution chain: the production of movies using contract actors and proprietary sets and film; the distribution of movies, as producers supplied prints to distributors; and exhibition, or showing movies to the final patrons, often in immense movie "palaces" owned by the studios that in some case seated thousands of movie-goers. A significant feature of the studio system was that the producers held such major actors and actresses as Clark Gable, Cary Grant, Bing Crosby, Joan Crawford, and Claudette Colbert under contract. Their contracts generally prevented them from working for competing producers, which in turn meant that their ability to negotiate for higher pay was limited. At the same time, the movie companies labored to create a persona for an actor, changing his or her name and background to turn the person into a star, in much the same way that Sir Francis Hinsley is assigned the task of reinventing Juanita del Pablo.

In 1948, the year in which *The Loved One* was published, Hollywood was dominated by five fully integrated companies: Twentieth Century-Fox, Loew's MGM, Paramount, RKO, and Warner Brothers (the "Big Five"). Three additional companies, Columbia, United Artists, and Universal, were partially integrated. This system of vertical integration, however, was a monopolistic practice that was illegal under the provisions of the 1890 Sherman Antitrust Act, for it stifled any form of competition. The system was thus ended in 1948 by the decision of the US Supreme Court in *United States v. Paramount Pictures, Inc.*, which held that the movie studios

Barlow is fascinated by Aimée from the first time he meets her. *(© Stokkete | Shutterstock.com)*

were engaging in discriminatory and anticompetitive practices. The *Paramount* ruling effectively ended the studio system.

Radio Evangelists

Waugh also satirizes another American "industry" that today would be called televangelism but which in 1948, before television was prevalent, relied on the radio. During the 1940s, evangelists continued a practice that had begun years earlier with the spread of the radio: using radio broadcasts to reach millions of listeners. In the 1940s, the Mutual Broadcasting System sold airtime to radio evangelists, who were able to raise tens of millions of dollars through their broadcasts, even though the network prohibited them from directly soliciting funds; listeners were encouraged to write in for free keepsakes, thus provided an address the evangelist could use to solicit donations. Some of the more popular religious radio broadcasts included *Back to the Bible Hour*, the *Radio Bible Hour*, and the *Lutheran Hour*.

Possibly the most famous of these broadcasts was the *Old Fashioned Revival Hour*, which was launched by Southern California evangelist Charles Fuller in 1937. The broadcast, produced before a live audience, included hymns and animated preaching, and by the mid-1940s it was attracting radio audiences of up to twenty million each week. The broadcasts, which continued until Fuller's death in 1968, have remained popular and many are still streamed on the Internet. Note that Aimée says that she was named after Aimée Semple McPherson, a highly prominent Los Angeles–based radio evangelist in the 1920s and 1930s—who is buried at Glendale's Forest Lawn cemetery. Waugh's depiction of the vulgarity of Dennis Barlow is based in part on the character's later goal of becoming a nonsectarian radio evangelist.

CRITICAL OVERVIEW

The Loved One was widely reviewed when it was first published in 1948, and in general it garnered positive reviews. Cyril Connolly, in a review in *Horizon*, calls the novel a "beautifully constructed, irresistible and haunting affair."

(It should be noted that Connolly was the editor of *Horizon*, the magazine in which *The Loved One* was first published.) A reviewer for *Time* is somewhat less enthusiastic, writing that "the story of the patriotic pretensions and fussy snobbishness of the British film colony is grade A Waugh" but adding, "Less artful is the travelogue of the intricate inanities of Whispering Glades." John Woodburn, however, after calling *The Loved One* a "cold-blooded little novel" in a review for *New Republic*, concludes that "as a piece of writing it is nearly faultless; as satire it is an act of devastation, an angry, important, moral effort that does not fail."

An anonymous reviewer for the *Times Literary Supplement* offers this observation about the novel: "What is shocking in this gruesome little tale is not the preoccupation with corpses but the fact that the live characters are virtually indistinguishable from the dead." The reviewer concluded by calling the novel "witty and macabre, ominous and polished." In a review for the London *Sunday Times*, Desmond MacCarthy writes:

> Beneath satire of any depth there always lies, in addition to a sense of humour and an eye for glaring incongruities, a tragic conception of life. It is that which makes *The Loved One* not only a macabre farce but a significant criticism of life.

In a review for the *New York Times*, Orville Prescott remarks: "Rarely in fiction have such execrably bad taste and such cruel wit been combined in one short satirical novel." Prescott continues: "*The Loved One* is not a book which the squeamish or queasy of stomachs could face with composure. Its humors are ghoulish and its hyena laughter snarls obscenely. Mr. Waugh has never written more brilliantly." He concludes that "*The Loved One* is not only satire at its most ferocious. It is a macabre frolic filled with laughter and ingenious devices. It is devilishly clever, impishly amusing."

Later commentators are in general equally appreciative of the novel. In an article titled "The Pieties of Evelyn Waugh," Donat O'Donnell praises the novel's "calculated outrageousness," which makes it

> one of the most effective stories Mr. Waugh has ever written. Sober and economical in language, neat and coherent in structure, it makes every blow tell, both on the reader's nerves and on the civilization it condemns.

Sean Fitzpatrick, in a review for the *Imaginative Conservative*, agrees with Prescott in emphasizing the savagery of Waugh's humor, calling *The Loved One* "tasteless, irreverent, perverse, and merciless." Fitzpatrick goes on to comment:

> *The Loved One* is, without doubt, a humorous story—but its humor might be considered inappropriate and indecent. Its humor certainly must be considered beyond the pale of the common courtesy and sensitivity we naturally show to those who are grieving a recent death. Mr. Waugh is simply portraying a farce, vulgar though it may be, confident in the belief that it is healthy from time to time to poke fun at serious things.

Fitzpatrick adds that Waugh offered to donate the proceeds from the book to various Catholic charities, but after his archbishop read it, he declined the author's offer.

In an article for *Atlantic* magazine titled "Evelyn Waugh: The Best and the Worst," Charles J. Rolo praises Waugh's work in general, claiming "[t]here are few contemporary writers of the first rank whose imagination runs to such appalling and macabre inventions as Waugh's does." Rolo describes *The Loved One* as "one of Waugh's most savagely amusing books" and remarks that "[a]s a lampoon on the mortuary practices of Southern California, it is a coruscating tour de force." Rolo, however, offers this objection:

> When...the satire reaches out to other aspects of American folkways, it is sometimes either hackneyed or crudely exaggerated.... The éclat of his performance in *The Loved One* is slightly marred by traces of spite, and smudges of acid snob-distaste for all things American.

In an article titled "*The Loved One*: The Artist in a Phony World," Joseph F. Vogel draws attention to the novel's themes. He begins by noting that although the novel was popular with readers, it was in his view "one of the least admired by critics." He goes on to explain:

> Its popularity is easy to explain. It remains topical: the satirized traits—funeral practices, the on-stage phoniness and back-stage venality of Hollywood, the cosmetic homogeneousness of American young women, the cottony tastelessness of assembly-line food, and various others—these are as current and absurd today as when Waugh ridiculed them a generation ago.

Finally, Michelle Cannon, in "Evelyn Waugh's *The Loved One*: A Postmodern Perspective," emphasizes the humor of the novel:

> *The Loved One* is a humorous satire of Southern California lifestyle that makes you laugh and simultaneously feel guilty for laughing at such absurdly morbid situations. While the characters in the text shield themselves from the reality of death with false signs of life, so does Waugh shield his readers from the grotesqueness of these scenarios with humor.

CRITICISM

Michael J. O'Neal

O'Neal holds a PhD in English. In the following essay, he examines the theme of appearance versus reality in The Loved One.

In the first chapter of *The Loved One*, Sir Francis Hinsley, a member of the community of expatriate Britons trying to maintain the appearance of upper-crust gentility and prestige while living in one of the "barbarous regions of the world," is commenting on his earlier efforts to transform Juanita del Pablo into a Hollywood movie star:

> *I* named her. *I* made her an anti-Fascist refugee. *I* said she hated men because of her treatment by Franco's Moors. That was a new angle then. It caught on. And she was really quite good in her way, you know—with a truly horrifying natural scowl. Her legs were never *photogénique* but we kept her in long skirts and used an understudy for the lower half in scenes of violence.

Hinsley continues by commenting on the new image the studio wants for the actress:

> We are only making healthy films this year to please the Catholic League of Decency. So poor Juanita has to start at the beginning again as an Irish colleen. They've bleached her hair and dyed it vermilion. I told them colleens were dark but the technicolor men insisted. She's working ten hours a day learning the brogue and to make it harder for the poor girl they've pulled all her teeth out. She never had to smile before and her own set was good enough for a snarl. Now she'll have to laugh roguishly all the time. That means dentures.

These passages telegraph the themes of the novel. In effect, they encapsulate the themes that much of the rest of *The Loved One* will develop and embellish.

> BARLOW AND AIMÉE SEE LIFE IN ENTIRELY OPPOSITE WAYS. BARLOW SEES SOMETHING APPROACHING REALITY, WHEREAS AIMÉE IS CONSUMED BY THE WORLD OF ILLUSION. IN THIS WAY, THE TWO CHARACTERS REPRESENT THE POLES OF ILLUSION AND TRUTH THAT LIE AT THE HEART OF THE NOVEL."

Juanita is a creation of the Hollywood studio system. In effect, she has no independent existence. Just as she never appears in person to moviegoers, she never appears in person in the novel. She exists only in the form of a persona created by others. In this way, she prefigures the satire associated with the Whispering Glades cemetery, where dead bodies are similarly transformed by the arts of others. In her discussion of her work as a cosmetician for the cemetery, Aimée describes how she and her boss, Joyboy, transform the cadavers that come before them. The reader learns that when she was in college, Aimée studied Beauticraft, learning about permanents, facials, and wax. She is then able to use her education to transform the surfaces of the bodies on which she works into what appear to be living creatures.

Joyboy, too, is depicted as an *artiste* when practicing his craft:

> Next he took a visiting card . . . and a pair of surgical scissors. In one continuous movement he cut an ellipse, then snicked half an inch at either end along the greater axis. He bent over the corpse, tested the jaw and found it firm set; he drew back the lips and laid his card along the teeth and gums. Now was the moment; his assistant watched with never-failing admiration the deft flick of the thumbs with which he turned the upper corners of the card, the caress of the rubber finger-tips with which he drew the dry and colorless lips into place. And, behold, where before had been a grim line of endurance, there was now a smile!

This macabre and comic description of the mortician plying his trade to create a false appearance neatly parallels the Hollywood

WHAT DO I READ NEXT?

- *Brideshead Revisited* is perhaps Waugh's best-known work. Published in 1945, the novel is a nostalgic examination of a British class system that was rapidly disappearing and of the recovery of religious faith.

- A good example of Waugh's earlier satiric comedy is *Scoop* (1938), which satirizes sensational journalism and foreign correspondents and is based on the author's experience as a journalist working for the *Daily Mail* covering Benito Mussolini's looming invasion of Abyssinia in the mid-1930s.

- Waugh's brother, Alec, while less famous, was a prolific author in his own right. His best-known work is *Island in the Sun* (1955), a novel about race relations on a fictional Caribbean island. The novel was made into a successful—and controversial—1957 movie produced by Darryl F. Zanuck and featuring an all-star cast led by James Mason, Harry Belafonte, Joan Fontaine, and Joan Collins.

- Jessica Mitford's *The American Way of Death* (1963) was a celebrated exposé of abuses in the US funeral industry. A revised and updated version of the book was published as *The American Way of Death Revisited* (Knopf, 1998). Mitford argued that funerals had become too sentimentalized, commercialized, and expensive. She further argued that funeral directors exploit the shock and grief of the friends and relatives of the deceased to persuade them to pay far more than necessary for funerals.

- *The Last Tycoon* is the last, unfinished novel by American author F. Scott Fitzgerald. First published in 1941, there is evidence that the author intended finally to call the novel *The Love of the Last Tycoon*, a title used in more recent editions. The novel is an exposé of the studio system in Hollywood during its heyday.

- Readers interested in the history of the Hollywood film industry during the golden years of the 1930s and 1940s will find Douglas Gomery's *The Hollywood Studio System: A History* (2008) a useful introduction to the subject.

- Emma McLaughlin and Nicola Kraus are the co-authors of *The Real Real* (2009), a satirical novel for young adults about the modern entertainment industry, specifically television. As a member of the cast of a "documentary," the protagonist, Jesse O'Rourke, has to contend with phony friendships, staged fights, and product placements. As she and the other cast members become pawns in the network's moneymaking scheme, she struggles to distinguish between what is real and what looks good on television.

- For a social, cultural, and economic history of post–World War II California, a good place to start is Kevin Starr's *Golden Dreams: California in an Age of Abundance, 1950–1963* (2011), part of his Americans and the California Dream series.

- Readers looking for insight into Waugh's perspectives on writing will take interest in "Evelyn Waugh: The Art of Fiction No. 30," an interview by Julian Jebb published by the *Paris Review* and available online at http://www.theparisreview.org/interviews/4537/the-art-of-fiction-no-30-evelyn-waugh.

- *The Loved One* touches on racial discrimination in post–World War II California. A book that examines the African American experience in and around Los Angeles in the postwar years is R. J. Smith's *The Great Black Way: L.A. in the 1940s and the Lost African-American Renaissance* (2006).

studio's efforts—down to the pulling of her teeth—to transform the image of Juanita del Pablo into that which the producers want her to have.

Just as the purpose of the Hollywood studio is to create a performance—to put on a show—so too the purpose of Whispering Glades, and to a lesser extent the Happier Hunting Ground pet cemetery, is to present a show. Throughout the novel, the reader is provided with descriptions of the cemetery and its grounds. There are replicas of English manor houses and medieval churches. The statues resemble those found in famous European museums. The burial areas have such names as Shadowland, Lovers' Nook, and The Lake Isle of Innisfree. The latter, which is also the title of a poem by William Butler Yeats, even features items mentioned in the poem: a wattle cottage, nine bean rows, and the hum of bees, which is simulated electronically. The various "loved ones" mentioned in the novel, such as the elderly woman in the Primrose Room reclining on a sofa, the smiling infant in the Slumber Room as if sleeping, or Hinsley transformed by cosmetics into an aged coquette, underscore the analogy between the studio and the cemetery, where each person, whether living or dead, plays a role in an elaborate theatrical spectacle. In this way, Juanita del Pablo becomes a thematic link, for her transformation from a Spanish senorita into an Irish colleen with red hair and shiny teeth is a reflection of the transformations that are carried out at Whispering Glades.

Another play on the theme of appearance versus reality is achieved through the relationship between Dennis Barlow and Aimée Thanatogenos. Each character represents an opposite perspective on life. Barlow is a realist. He has few illusions. He is coolly capable of putting the body of the woman he professed to love into the crematory at the animal cemetery. He remains cynical and irreverent about Whispering Glades as well as about his own place of employment, about Abercrombie and his British pretensions, and about Joyboy and his artistic pretensions. In this way, Barlow becomes an observer in the book and perhaps a spokesman for the author himself.

Nevertheless, Barlow finds himself attracted to Aimée, who is sincerely and naïvely devoted to the illusions that surround her. She sees Whispering Glades as a sacred place, although she is unable to see that at bottom it is no different

from the Happier Hunting Ground, which she sees as tasteless. She never lapses into the vulgarity of referring to corpses as stiffs. She adheres to her promise to marry Barlow because that promise was made with a kiss at a Whispering Glades shrine. She places great faith in what she sees as the wisdom of the Guru Brahmin, even after she learns that her letters have been answered by the tipsy Mr. Slump. And when Slump tells her to jump out of a window, she actually marches off and kills herself.

Thus, Barlow and Aimée see life in entirely opposite ways. Barlow sees something approaching reality, whereas Aimée is consumed by the world of illusion. In this way, the two characters represent the poles of illusion and truth that lie at the heart of the novel. Barlow, however, runs the risk of being lured away from reality into Aimée's illusory world. The first step in this process is his decision, after his poetic gift withers, to work at the Happier Hunting Ground, where he is forced to take part in its absurd funeral rituals and thus surrender himself in part to the world of make-believe. The next step is falling for Aimée, in this way feeling compelled to pretend to believe in the rituals she adheres to, and by pretending that the poems of others are his own. Finally, he decides to give in to Aimée's demand for a husband of high professional status; to that end, he decides to become a nonsectarian minister and radio evangelist, even though he has no religious convictions. At this point, he has surrendered entirely to the fraudulent world of appearances.

At the end of the novel, Barlow is able to free himself from Waugh's illusory world through Aimée's suicide and by extorting money from Joyboy and Abercrombie as a price for not overturning their images and illusions. Like the hero of a modern allegory, Barlow is able to replace the illusions of youth with experience, which he will carry back to England with him:

> The strand was littered with bones and wreckage. He was adding his bit; something that had long irked him, his young heart. He was carrying back instead a great, shapeless chunk of experience, the artist's load; bearing it home to his ancient and comfortless shore; to work on it hard and long, for God knew how long—it was the moment of vision for which a lifetime is often too short.

Barlow, the expatriate wanderer, the poet who betrayed his art and himself, has found his way back to the world of truth and is now ready to return home.

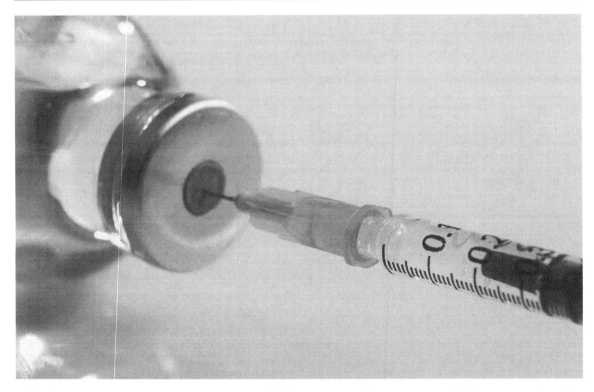

After being goaded by Mr. Slump to jump off a building, Aimée commits suicide by injecting herself with cyanide. (© Luiscar74 | Shutterstock.com)

Source: Michael J. O'Neal, Critical Essay on *The Loved One*, in *Novels for Students*, Gale, Cengage Learning, 2016.

Stephan-Alexander Ditze

In the following excerpt, Ditze examines Waugh's portrayal of characters who work in the entertainment industry in The Loved One.

. . . *Exteriority.* The exteriority of the American characters belonging to the movie and entertainment industries chiefly evokes the impression of artificiality and pretense. Both imagenes are most glaringly represented in Juanita del Pablo's arbitrarily alterable physical appearance. Juanita, whose real identity remains unknown, is an artificial product of the movie industry, having been designed under the auspices of Sir Francis Hinsley. She was previously known as "Baby Aaronson," her original stage-name, before she was "bought" and turned into a Spaniard by the help of plastic surgery. Her new identity matched popular taste and made her "'good for another ten years' work at least'." Due to "a change of policy at the top'," however, Juanita has to sustain yet another change of identity and is scheduled to be turned into "an Irish colleen." This renewed "metamorphosis" entails even harsher encroachments upon her physical integrity, like the replacement of her natural teeth by artificial "'dentures'."

The imagene of (exterior) pretense is also represented by Mr Slump who serves to break down the make-believe facade of physical flawlessness. Mr Slump is the senior member of a team consisting of "two gloomy men and a bright young secretary" who are running the advice column of a Los Angeles newspaper. Under a pseudonymous facade, the column offers its readers pseudo-psychological counsel on a wide range of issues:

> There was a spiritual director, an oracle, in these parts who daily filled a famous column in one of the local newspapers. Once, in days of family piety, it bore the title *Aunt Lydia's Post Bag*; now it was *The Wisdom of the Guru Brahmin*, adorned with the photograph of a bearded and almost naked sage. To this exotic source resorted all who were in doubt or distress.

THE EMOTIVITY OF THE AMERICANS WORKING FOR THE MOVIE AND ENTERTAINMENT INDUSTRIES IS MARKED BY A COMPLETE INSENSITIVITY. NONE OF THEM HAS ANY EMPATHY WITH AND COMPASSION FOR OTHER PEOPLE."

It might be thought that at this extremity of the New World unceremonious manners and frank speech occasioned no doubt; the universal good humour no distress. But it was not so— etiquette, child-psychology, aesthetics, and sex reared their questioning heads in this Eden too and to all readers the Guru Brahmin offered solace and solution.

Above all, the advice column caters for its readers' craving for publicity as well as helping them to overcome their social isolation: "[M]ost of the Guru Brahmin's correspondents liked to have their difficulties exposed to the public. It gave them a sense of greater importance and also on occasions led to correspondence with other readers." Yet, the contrast between the public pretense of the ascetic Guru and the private face of Mr Slump could hardly be more marked. Unlike his neat and clean compatriots, Mr Slump is a shabby and chain-smoking alcoholic shaken by coughing fits that show his deteriorating physical health.

Sociality. The interpersonality of the American members of the movie and entertainment industries is marked by habitual casualness and informality that is symptomatic of the "insensitive friendliness which takes the place of ceremony in that land of waifs and strays."

Yet, similar to their exteriority, the characters' interpersonal behavior is based on pretense to a great deal. Their casualness is just a veneer, a superficial layer of friendliness which conceals a sturdy tendency to ruthless competitiveness. Thus, Mr Baumbein pretends the same deeply false familiarity that the attendants of the story conference show, only to call Sir Francis "just another has-been" behind closed doors. Too much of a coward to break the news of his discharge to Sir Francis, Baumbein pretends to be "'rather busy right now'" and delegates the Englishman to his immediate superior. Behind

Baumbein's faked informality, there lurks a deep-rooted disregard for human concerns as he has no scruples to praise the professional qualities of the very man who actually killed Sir Francis's job in a vulgar and vernacular tone. For Baumbein, an employee's competitiveness as measured by his "'record'" is of far greater importance than long service to the company.

Mr Erikson, Otto Baumbein's Scandinavian-American superior, exposes the ugly face lying behind Baumbein's hoaxed friendliness. Erikson breaks the news of Sir Francis's discharge in "blunt Nordic terms." He handles his "'Termination'" with the cold-blooded routine of a true professional of the system of hire and fire. Instead of searching for words of compassion for the victim of Megalo's staff policy, the little speech Erikson delivers shows the brutality of the American world of business, which equates the value of a human being with its market value and its ability to compete:

The letter is on its way. Things get hung up sometimes, as you know; so many different departments have to give their O.K.—the legal Branch, Finance, Labour Disputes Section. But I don't anticipate any trouble in your case. Luckily you aren't a Union man. Now and then the Big Three make objections about waste of manpower—when we bring someone from Europe or China or somewhere and then fire him in a week. But that doesn't arise in your case. You've had a record run. Just on twenty-five years, isn't it? There's not even any provision on your contract for repatriation. Your Termination ought to whip right through.

Sir Francis's comment that it would have been "'civil'" to notify him of the end of his career serves as an indirect comment on the uncivilized ruthlessness of the whole procedure.

The close link between the imagenes of competitiveness and ruthlessness becomes particularly tangible in the case of Lorenzo Medicy, Sir Francis's successor at the film studios. Medicy does not show the slightest trace of embarrassment when realizing that the "'old Britisher who's just kicked off'" is standing face to face with him. He complains about the state of Sir Francis's former office in a highly vulgar tongue nagging about how "kinda screwy'" it looks and tells his predecessor that all his "'junk'" was "'pushed [...] out into the passage'." His surname has telling qualities. The historical person Lorenzo de Medici was the man to whom Niccoló Machiavelli dedicated his major work *The Prince* (1513), which achieved notoriety as a justification of political brutality legitimized by reasons of state. Medicy's ruthlessness places him as the standard but well-functioning member of an inhumane meritocracy that cares precious little for the soul of the individual and in which only the fittest survive.

Like the members of the movie industry, Slump shows no scrap of interest for, or compassion with, other people either. He is immune to the concerns of readers turning to him for counsel but deals with the letters in an assembly-line fashion (cf. 94). When Aimée calls him to ask for help, he puts the receiver down on the bar to the amusement of his drinking pals and tells Aimée to kill herself (cf. 115).

The diachronic level of the characters' sociality is marked by their foreignness, their predominantly non-Anglo ethnic origins in the field of ancestry and a general uprootedness with regard to their vita. The Heinkels' surname, for instance, clearly echoes their German descent; so does Mr Otto Baumbein's who is probably of Judaeo-German stock.

Lorenzo Medicy is not only eager to comply with the requirements of the American world of business and its emphasis on competitiveness. Medicy also wants to hide his socially unprestigious Italian heritage by having his name pronounced in an anglified fashion: "'[H]e says it "Medissy," like that, how you said kinda sounds like a wop.'" Medicy pretends to be a WASP by negating his background but does not realize that the arbitrary change of his name leaves him disconnected from his own biography and therefore uprooted.

The ultimate consequences of this biographical deracination, which starts with the arbitrary change of one's identity, are illustrated by the character of Juanita del Pablo. Juanita plays the role of a participant as well as a victim of the system of ruthless competition. She was purchased by the studios like an ordinary commodity or lifestock and turned into a marketable good. Hence, her value is synonymous with her market value and measured only by the audience's approval ratings. Juanita patiently endures all measures applied to make her either match the taste of the audience or to comply with the demands of lobbies and public pressure groups like the "'[Catholic] League of Decency'" that is calling for "'healthy films.'" All these measures,

however, only reinforce her loss of identity and feeling of uprootedness.

As a result of Sir Francis's failure to find a new Irish identity for her, she becomes a "nameless actress." She ceases to be an autonomous human being and is treated as mere livestock reduced to her arbitrarily alterable physical appearance. Juanita is increasingly unable to cope with her repeated metamorphoses and her deracination entails the complete disintegration of her personality. Finally, the irretrievable loss of her identity makes the executives of Megalopolitan Pictures even question her physical existence:

> Juanita's agent was pressing the metaphysical point; did his client exist? Could you legally bind her to annihilate herself? Could you come to any agreement with her before she had acquired the ordinary marks of identity?

The elements of her former and her new, though still unsettled, identity clash while she is rehearsing "'The Wearing of the Green'," an IRA war hymn she is ordered to perform at the funeral of the arch-Englishman Sir Francis. Sir Ambrose Abercrombie, who is supervising the funeral preparations, finds it "'[c]urious how flamenco she makes it sound.'"

Like the nameless actress, Mr Slump was forced to undergo a metamorphosis and also suffers from its painful after-effects. Slump "was a survival from the days of Aunt Lydia and retained her style," which proves that he is equally unable to strip off the identity that he is invested with and adopt a new one. He compensates for the resulting strain by resorting to alcohol and nicotine. In the end, however, Slump falls victim to the system of hire and fire with himself being the only person "[u]nconscious of impending doom." In spite of his apparent inhumanity, the reader does feel a certain amount of sympathy for Mr Slump as another victim of the brutal American meritocracy.

The imagene of pretense finds yet another manifestation in the characters' verbality. On the surface, their discourse is marked by a strict observance of the politeness principle. Baumbein, for instance, addresses his interlocutor by a contraction of his first name which is supposed to signal that he as a superior regards his subordinate as his equal. Similarly, Slump demonstrates sympathy with his readers by using a register signalling concern and courtesy. Yet, the linguistic facade breaks down when Slump uses a lexicon that abounds with vulgar expressions in his everyday communication (cf. 94). By the same token, Baumbein's and Erikson's verbal politeness is counteracted by their gross violations of the maxim of tact when explaining to Sir Francis why he was laid off, followed by the vulgar rebuff of Lorenzo Medicy.

Interiority. The cognitivity of the Americans working for the movie and entertainment industries is reduced to professionalism. Only Mr Slump deviates slightly from this intellectual vacuity. Despite his vulgar speech, Slump seems to have enjoyed the blessings of classical education. This is indicated by the fact that he is well aware of the semantic content inherent in Aimée's Greek surname (cf. 115).

The emotivity of the Americans working for the movie and entertainment industries is marked by a complete insensitivity. None of them has any empathy with and compassion for other people. Selfishness and egotism dominate their normativity which is marked by the complete absence of moral and ethical standards. An exclusive commitment toward vested interests is the crucial imagene of the characters' volitionality. Their entire energy and will-power is directed to their survival within the system of competition....

Source: Stephan-Alexander Ditze, "'In the Barbarous Regions of the World': America and the Americans in Evelyn Waugh's Satirical Novel *The Loved One: An Anglo-American Tragedy*," in *America and the Americans in Postwar British Fiction: An Imagolocial Study of Selected Novels*, Universitätsverlag Winter, 2006, pp. 106–10.

Frederick L. Beaty

In the following excerpt, Beaty examines Waugh's treatment of death in The Loved One.

The Loved One, the only extensively ironic novel written after *Brideshead*, appears at first glance so unlike its romantic and overtly religious predecessor as to belie Waugh's declared intention of dealing in "future books" with "man in his relation to God." A parody of the artist's romance, it is a reversion to the approach of the earlier short novels. The personality of its central figure, Dennis Barlow, is an amalgam of traits associated with previous antiheroes and the caddish Basil Seal. The supporting characters are eccentric, the situations are grotesque, and the narrator views all with indifference. In one respect *The Loved One* even outdoes its early counterparts. Whereas in most of the preceding

> EVEN THE MOST MACABRE SITUATIONS ARE TURNED INTO UNFORGETTABLE ABSURDITIES BY THE MATTER-OF-FACT MANNER IN WHICH THE NARRATOR LINGERS OVER DETAILS OF THE UNDERTAKING BUSINESS."

fiction an occasional bizarre death or ghastly murder functions as one element among many in an overall scheme, in *The Loved One* death itself is the ideational matrix from which implications about love, art, society, and religion arise. Partly for that reason the irony is grimmer, with little of the exuberant comedy that sparkles in the earlier works.

Waugh's handling of death in this instance is also distinguished by his altered viewpoint toward it. He is not merely amusing us with the absurdities of civilized or uncivilized barbarism that sometimes result in the extraordinary demise of a character; he is on the attack against practices of which he strongly disapproves. Consequently his writing, undergirded by unqualified conviction, becomes appropriately more satirical. Waugh had passed the point in his creative development where he could approach a subject without seeing it in a religious context; and although he may not have considered *The Loved One* as a religious book in the positive sense that *Helena* and the war trilogy would be, he employs, as a Roman Catholic, a definite set of standards against which to judge. Beneath the superficial façade of his narrator's stance, he unambiguously condemns both the funeral customs and the social climate that pervert the Church's teachings about earthly life, death, and the afterlife. In its basic premises, therefore, *The Loved One* expresses negatively the same perspective on the world as does *Brideshead*, while its irony is better subsumed into both satire and religion. It may look backward for much of its style, but its underlying message is definitely in keeping with Waugh's new resolve.

The impetus for this Januslike volume was Waugh's visit to Los Angeles in February–March 1947 to discuss a proposed filming of *Brideshead* by Metro-Goldwyn-Mayer. Although he was generally disgusted by the falseness and pervasive theatricality of the Hollywood milieu, he became fascinated, as well as appalled, by the beautiful fantasy world of Forest Lawn Memorial Park in Glendale. What he regarded as extreme contradictions in the southern California environment, especially as epitomized by this incredible burial place, apparently stimulated his creative imagination just as scenes of wild disorder in Oxford, London, and Africa had inspired his earliest fiction. But whereas in youth he had delighted in portraying a chaotic world and its incohesive society, the changes that had come over him rendered such an attitude impossible in 1947. Los Angeles appeared to be not merely a Godless city in the simply negative sense but one that had substituted the idolatry of materialism for true Christianity.

Having long been fascinated by the subject of death, Waugh had become interested in what archaeologists, historians, and comparative religionists could deduce about extinct cultures on the basis of their burials. Evidently he believed that the way people respond to death serves as an index to the dominant philosophy with which they confront life. According to Sykes, Waugh often pointed out, in conversations about Forest Lawn, that the ancient Egyptians' obsession "with funerary celebration" provides us with much of our knowledge about their beliefs; and he also wondered what future theoreticians would deduce about modern Western culture from "our burial customs and monuments to the dead." Even before journeying to California, Waugh had toyed with these thoughts in *Brideshead*. Early in the Prologue Charles Ryder imagines the logical but fallacious deductions later archaeologists might make from excavations of a twentieth-century army camp superimposed on the roads and drainage system of a planned suburb. They would likely conclude, Charles surmises, that low-level barbarians had overrun an advanced civilization, since the invaders must have buried their dead far from their primitive settlement and since their women seem to have worn no adornment.

In California Waugh discerned a real-life parallel in the overturning of the old Spanish culture by waves of recent immigrants. In his essay "Half in Love with Easeful Death" (1947), he predicts that fatuous archaeologists of the year 2947 may well come to the wrong conclusions in trying to reconstruct the civilization that gave rise to Forest Lawn, especially since the sepulchral customs of the newcomers, who built that phenomenal necropolis, are difficult to understand even with firsthand knowledge of their mindset. Beneath this tongue-in-cheek humor, however, lies a serious concern, for early in the essay he asserts that historical scholars a thousand years hence may correctly agree "that the great cultural decline of the twentieth century was first evident in the graveyard." Dramatizing this view in *The Loved One*, Waugh turns the obvious excesses and incongruities of the Los Angeles scene into a wild fantasy, which, by indirectly involving readers in the judgmental process, becomes a more effective vehicle for censure than direct denunciation. Crucial to the literary interaction between author and audience is Waugh's return to a detached narrator, who can provoke subjective reactions by being completely objective, prick consciences by being callous toward matters that few can ignore, expose moral problems without being preachy, and encourage readers to draw conclusions because he does not do so.

Some of the choicest comedy arises from the narrator's deadpan humor. By recounting in a sober fashion behavior that characters themselves take seriously but readers regard as essentially funny, he increases the discrepancy and therefore the irony's impact. In the passage describing Aimée's preparations for a romantic evening, he uses such inappropriate and exaggerated diction that her ritual is expanded to ridiculous heights, and his terming of her anticipated fate as "manifest destiny" applies that phrase as it was never meant by American historians.

> With a steady hand Aimée fulfilled the prescribed rites of an American girl preparing to meet her lover—dabbed herself under the arms with a preparation designed to seal the sweat-glands, gargled another to sweeten the breath, and brushed into her hair some odorous drops from a bottle labelled: "Jungle Venom"— [advertised as coming] *"From the depth of the fever-ridden swamp...with the remorseless stealth of the hunting cannibal."*
>
> Thus fully equipped for a domestic evening... she was all set to accept her manifest destiny.

Seen in the context of the novel, this passage reveals additional ironies—that Aimée, while taking pride in being highly "ethical," should employ a battery of drugstore products with the intention of effecting her own seduction, and that in spite of such tactics her hopes are never fulfilled.

Even the most macabre situations are turned into unforgettable absurdities by the matter-of-fact manner in which the narrator lingers over details of the undertaking business. One cannot easily banish visions of Joyboy pinching the thigh of a corpse as merrily as if it were a living friend, or of Dennis firing up the furnace at the pet mortuary to cremate his fiancée as nonchalantly as if she were a dead dog. Nor can one resist a wry smile at the peculiar similarities between Aimee's suitors when in a single chapter the narrator juxtaposes, without comment, descriptions of them at work—the one embalming corpses that convey by their facial expressions his sentiments toward her, the other cremating animals while cribbing poetry to send her.

Among the numerous examples of verbal wrenching in conversation, perhaps most delightful is the complex of misunderstandings, double entendres, and false deductions involving Joyboy, Dennis, and the new apprentice at the pet mortuary. When Joyboy arrives unexpectedly in tears, Dennis, having recently arranged the last rites for Mrs. Joyboy's parrot, asks in jest if there is another parrot to be disposed of. When Joyboy indicates that his distress is about Aimée, Dennis, unaware of her suicide, inquires facetiously—and according to the narrator, "with high irony"—whether he must also take care of *her* funeral. Inadvertently Dennis has hit upon the truth and thereby foreshadowed his own future actions. But Joyboy, taking his rival's repartee seriously, jumps to the wrong conclusion that Dennis must know of their beloved's death and therefore must have killed her. To alleviate the apprentice's embarrassment at the sight of Joyboy's weeping, Dennis ambiguously explains, "We have here a client who has just lost a little pet." Thus with sardonic humor he teases the apprentice into a literal but erroneous interpretation of "little pet" while taunting Joyboy with the epithet's metaphorical insinuations. The reader, however, soon discovers that Joyboy is less perturbed by the loss of his "loved one" than by fears of professional ruin should her poisoned body be found in his refrigerator. . . .

Source: Frederick L. Beaty, "*The Loved One*," in *The Ironic World of Evelyn Waugh: A Study of Eight Novels*, Northern Illinois University Press, 1992, pp. 166–70.

SOURCES

"About Evelyn Waugh," The Evelyn Waugh Society website, http://evelynwaughsociety.org/about-evelyn-waugh/ (accessed November 20, 2014).

Cannon, Michelle, "Evelyn Waugh's *The Loved One*: A Postmodern Perspective," in *Examiner* (West Palm Beach, FL), July 1, 2009, http://www.examiner.com/article/evelen-waugh-s-the-loved-one-a-postmodern-perspective (accessed November 29, 2014).

"Company Profile," McDonald's website, http://www.aboutmcdonalds.com/mcd/investors/company_profile.html (accessed November 13, 2014).

Connolly, Cyril, Review of *The Loved One*, in *Evelyn Waugh: The Critical Heritage*, edited by Martin Stannard, Routledge & Kegan Paul, 1984, pp. 299–300; originally published in *Horizon*, February 1948, pp. 76–77.

DeWitt, Larry, "Research Note #2: The History and Development of the Lump Sum Death Benefit," Social Security Administration website, 1996, http://www.ssa.gov/history/lumpsum.html (accessed November 13, 2014).

"Evelyn Waugh," Hertford College website, http://www.hertford.ox.ac.uk/alumni-development/our-alumni/hertfords-ancestors/evelyn-waugh (accessed November 12, 2014).

Fitzpatrick, Sean, "*The Loved One* by Evelyn Waugh," in *Imaginative Conservative*, December 3, 2013, http://www.theimaginativeconservative.org/2013/12/loved-one-evelyn-waugh.html (accessed December 2, 2014).

Hanssen, F. Andrew, "Vertical Integration during the Hollywood Studio Era," 2009, http://economics.clemson.edu/files/hanssen-studios.pdf (accessed November 17, 2014).

"History," *Old Fashioned Revival Hour* website, http://www.oldfashionedrevivalhour.com/ (accessed November 18, 2014).

"In-N-Out Burger History," In-N-Out Burger website, http://shop.in-n-out.com/history.aspx (accessed November 12, 2014).

"Los Angeles County Economic Development Corporation," Aerospace Industry in Southern California website, August 2012, http://laedc.org/reports/AerospaceinSoCal_0812.pdf (accessed November 17, 2014).

MacCarthy, Desmond, Review of *The Loved One*, in *Evelyn Waugh: The Critical Heritage*, edited by Martin Stannard, Routledge & Kegan Paul, 1984, pp. 308–309; originally published in *Sunday Times*, November 21, 1948, p. 3.

"Menippian Satire," in *Merriam-Webster's Encyclopedia of Literature*, Merriam-Webster, 1995, p. 752.

Mintz, S., and S. McNeil, "Social Changes during the War," Digital History website, 2013, http://www.digitalhistory.uh.edu/disp_textbook.cfm?smtID=2&psid=3493 (accessed November 17, 2014).

O'Donnell, Donat [Conor Cruise O'Brien], "The Pieties of Evelyn Waugh," in *Critical Essays on Evelyn Waugh*, edited by James F. Carens, G. K. Hall, 1987, p. 57; originally published in *Maria Cross: Imaginative Patterns in a Group of Modern Catholic Writers*, Oxford University Press, 1952, pp. 119–34.

O'Neill, Patrick, "The Comedy of Entropy: The Contexts of Black Humor," in *Dark Humor*, edited by Harold Bloom, Infobase Publishing, 2010, pp. 79–81; originally published in *Canadian Review of Comparative Literature*, Vol. 10, No. 2, 1983, pp. 145–66.

Prescott, Orville, Review of *The Loved One*, in *New York Times*, June 23, 1948, http://www.nytimes.com/books/97/05/04/reviews/waugh-loved.html (accessed December 2, 2014).

Review of *The Loved One*, in *Evelyn Waugh: The Critical Heritage*, edited by Martin Stannard, Routledge & Kegan Paul, 1984, pp. 301–02; originally published in *Time*, July 12, 1948, pp. 40–42, 44.

Review of *The Loved One*, in *Evelyn Waugh: The Critical Heritage*, edited by Martin Stannard, Routledge & Kegan Paul, 1984, pp. 304–07; originally published in *Times Literary Supplement*, November 20, 1948, p. 652.

Rolo, Charles J., "Evelyn Waugh: The Best and the Worst," in *Atlantic*, October 1954, https://www.theatlantic.com/past/docs/issues/54oct/rolo.htm (accessed December 2, 2014).

"Satire," in *Merriam-Webster's Encyclopedia of Literature*, Merriam-Webster, 1995, p. 995.

"Statistics: Funeral Costs," National Funeral Directors Association, http://nfda.org/about-funeral-service-/trends-and-statistics.html#fcosts (accessed November 13, 2014).

Sterling, Christopher H., and Cary O'Dell, "Evangelists/Evangelical Radio," in *The Concise Encyclopedia of American Radio*, Routledge, 2011, pp. 279–80.

United States v. Paramount Pictures, Inc., 334 U.S. 131, 1948, Findlaw website, http://caselaw.lp.findlaw.com/scripts/getcase.pl?court=US&vol=334&invol=131 (accessed November 12, 2014).

Vogel, Joseph F., "*The Loved One*: The Artist in a Phony World," in *Evelyn Waugh Newsletter*, Vol. 10, No. 2, Fall 1976, http://www.abbotshill.freeserve.co.uk/EWN10-2.htm (accessed December 2, 2014).

Waugh, Evelyn, *The Loved One*, Dell, 1962.

Woodburn, John, Review of *The Loved One*, in *Evelyn Waugh: The Critical Heritage*, edited by Martin Stannard, Routledge & Kegan Paul, 1984, pp. 303–304; originally published in *New Republic*, July 26, 1948, p. 24.

FURTHER READING

Amory, Mark, *The Letters of Evelyn Waugh*, Ticknor & Fields, 1980.

> Waugh was a prolific correspondent. This collection includes letters from his undergraduate days at Oxford, his literary ambitions and the end of his first marriage, his social life and travels, and his war experiences. It includes numerous letters to the women who inspired him and letters to John Betjeman in which he discusses his deep religious beliefs.

Davie, Michael, *Diaries of Evelyn Waugh*, Phoenix, 2010.

> Davie has produced a one-volume edition of Waugh's diaries, first published in 1976 and reissued in 2010. The volume includes entries beginning in the 1920s up through the end of World War II.

Hastings, Selena, *Evelyn Waugh: A Biography*, Houghton Mifflin, 1995.

> Hastings conducted research for some eight years after having been granted access to Waugh's personal papers by his family. She presents new information about his childhood, his affairs at Oxford, his first marriage, and his later travels.

Hodgart, Matthew, *Satire: Origins and Principles*, Transaction Publishers, 2009.

> This volume constitutes a reference book on satire. It enumerates the themes that have dominated satiric literature over the centuries, such as politics and relations between the sexes. The book examines subgenres of satire, such as lampoons, fables, and travesties. It further explores cross-cultural principles of satiric literature.

Stannard, Martin, *Evelyn Waugh*, Vol. 1, *The Early Years, 1903–1939*, Norton, 1989; Vol. 2, *The Later Years, 1939–1966*, Norton, 1994.

> Readers interested in a comprehensive biography of Waugh will find Stannard's two-volume effort definitive. In comparison with the Hastings biography, Stannard's is more of a literary biography, one that examines the personality behind the writing and the social and historical context in which he wrote.

Waugh, Evelyn, *The Complete Stories of Evelyn Waugh*, Little, Brown, 1999.

> Waugh is best known for his novels, but he also was a master of the short story. This volume contains twenty-six short stories, along with juvenilia and stories he wrote while a student at Oxford. Some of the stories are unused fragments from novels and brief magazine sketches.

SUGGESTED SEARCH TERMS

American funeral practices

black comedy

California history AND post–World War II

Evelyn Waugh

Evelyn Waugh AND The Loved One

Forest Lawn California cemetery

Hollywood AND studio system

Los Angeles Pet Memorial Park and Crematorium

radio evangelism

satire

The Magicians

LEV GROSSMAN

2009

The *Publishers Weekly* review of Lev Grossman's *The Magicians* (2009) describes the book as follows: "Harry Potter discovers Narnia is real." While the statement is a bit unfair—Grossman's story is far more complex than that—it does at least give fantasy fans an idea of what they are in for. After high school student Quentin Coldwater learns that his skills with card tricks actually result from true magical abilities, he enrolls in a college for magicians that is far different from Hogwarts and ends up in the Narnia-like magical world of Fillory.

The Magicians is more appropriate for older students because of references to recreational drug use and alcohol consumption by minors. There are also some sexual situations and violent scenes, though these are not graphic.

AUTHOR BIOGRAPHY

Lev Grossman was born on June 26, 1969, and grew up in Lexington, Massachusetts. Both of his parents were English professors and writers, so he grew up in a household where books, reading, and writing were important. After earning a bachelor's degree in literature at Harvard, Grossman remained at the school for three

Lev Grossman (© *AP Images* | *Brian Ach*)

years studying comparative literature but left before finishing his dissertation.

Moving to New York City, Grossman launched a career as a writer. He wrote on a variety of subjects, from technology to books. His work has appeared in various newspapers, websites, and magazines, including the *Village Voice*, the *Wall Street Journal*, the *New York Times*, *Salon*, *Wired*, and *Entertainment Weekly*. After several years of mostly freelance work, he was hired by *Time* in 2002 and became one of the magazine's top technology writers as well as its book critic. He has won several journalism awards for his work.

In 1997, Grossman published his first novel, *Warp*. His second, *Codex* (2004), was an international best seller. Then Grossman ventured into the fantasy genre. *The Magicians* came out in 2009 and was a *New York Times* best seller. Two sequels to *The Magicians* followed: *The Magician King* in 2011 and *The Magician's Land* in 2014.

As of 2015, Grossman continues to write. He is also busy with speaking engagements at colleges around the country and working as a commentator on National Public Radio. He lives in Brooklyn, a borough of New York City, with his wife and three children.

PLOT SUMMARY

Book I

BROOKLYN

Quentin Coldwater walks through Brooklyn with his friends Julia and James to a college interview. They arrive at their appointment to find the interviewer dead in his house. Quentin speaks with one of the paramedics, and she gives him an envelope that contains a manuscript: it seems to be a previously unknown sixth book in his favorite Fillory series. The wind blows another paper from the envelope into a neglected, wintry garden, and when Quentin follows it, he finds himself transported to a green lawn, seemingly in summer. A young man tells him he is in upstate New York.

BRAKEBILLS

The young man, who introduces himself as Eliot, leads Quentin to meet Dean Fogg, who in turn leads him into a testing room. Quentin catches a glimpse of Julia but then does not see her again. The written exam changes as Quentin works on it and is followed by a series of practical tests, including magic tricks. In the last, Quentin makes a sword materialize out of the desk and demands an explanation about what is going on.

ELIOT

Quentin learns that he is at Brakebills, a college for the teaching of magic. Most of the students have not yet returned after summer break, so Quentin spends time with Eliot, who did not go home for the summer. They go rowing on the river and find the edge of the concealing spells that protect the campus, outside of which it is chilly and dreary.

MAGIC

Quentin attends classes and meets Alice, who is often asked by the professors to demonstrate her considerable magical skills but is painfully shy. Quentin works hard, practicing magical incantations and finger exercises. Now that the other students have returned, Eliot ignores Quentin.

SNOW

Professor March explains to Quentin that he might, with a lot of extra work and study, be able to skip up to second year for the spring semester. Alice and Penny, a boy with a punk hairdo, are also being considered for advancement, so the

MEDIA ADAPTATIONS

- Penguin Audio released an unabridged audiobook of *The Magicians* in 2009. The recording features Mark Bramhall as narrator, and the running time is seventeen hours and twenty-four minutes.

three students work together. On a break from studying, Alice and Quentin take a walk together and discuss the Fillory books. Alice confides that she was not invited to attend the school as most students are but just found her way there herself and was allowed to take the entrance exam. Though Alice and Quentin pass the test and are allowed to skip a year, Penny fails.

THE MISSING BOY

Quentin goes home for Christmas break, but he feels distant from his old life, from James and Julia, and even from his parents. Quentin feels out of place as a new second-year student. Penny starts a fight with Quentin, punching him because he is jealous that Quentin passed the exam.

THE PHYSICAL KIDS

Quentin is tested to determine his Discipline—the specific field of magic with which he has an affinity. The tests are inconclusive. The teachers temporarily group him with Physical Magic, which is Alice's Discipline. After a test to get into the little cottage where the "Physical Kids" hang out, Quentin and Alice are welcomed by Eliot, Josh Hoberman, and Janet Way with a celebratory dinner.

THE BEAST

During a lecture, Quentin plays a prank that distracts Professor March. March mistakes the words of a spell, which allows a strange man into the room: he is small, with too many fingers, and is dressed in a suit. There is a branch hovering in front of his face, hiding it. While the man is there, everyone is frozen, until Amanda Orloff breaks out of his control for a few moments and

tries to cast her own spell. Dean Fogg calls the man "The Beast." Later, Quentin learns that they were frozen in the classroom for hours while several professors tried to enter and that Amanda Orloff was eaten alive by the Beast.

LOVELADY

Throughout the remainder of the semester, everyone is vigilant against other possible attacks. In an effort to improve morale, Dean Fogg decides each Discipline must form a team and compete at welters, a magical game. When Josh fails to appear for one of their welters matches, Quentin looks for him and catches him trying to buy something from Lovelady, who peddles magical trinkets. Josh admits that he does not feel confident when performing magic.

MARIE BYRD LAND

The fourth-year students are transformed into geese and fly to Brakebills South, a branch of the school where they will spend a semester for intense study with Professor Mayakovsky. They learn more about how magic must be altered to fit prevailing circumstances. Mayakovsky transforms the students again, this time into Arctic foxes. Quentin feels joy and playfulness. He finds that, with his fox senses, he cannot resist Alice's scent, and they mate.

Mayakovsky announces the final exam: without supplies and without a map, they must walk to the South Pole. Only Quentin and Alice take the test, which is optional. Just before setting out, Quentin finally speaks to Alice about what happened when they were foxes, and she is not angry. Both students succeed, though Alice beats Quentin by two full days.

ALICE

Quentin visits his parents in a Boston suburb, where they have moved. While he tours the town, Julia finds him. She did not pass her Brakebills test, but the magic used to make her forget failed. She remembers and desperately wants to learn magic.

Back at Brakebills, Quentin and Alice tell the other Physical Kids about their race to the Pole. Alice and Quentin discuss Fillory, and they become a couple. Josh, Janet, and Eliot graduate.

EMILY GREENSTREET

Janet tells the story of Emily Greenstreet. When her affair with a professor turned sour, Emily tried to change her appearance with a spell, which went wrong. She asked for help from a boy who had a crush on her, but he lost control of the magic he attempted and turned into a *niffin*, a kind of dark, magical spirit. Emily left school, and the professor, Mayakovsky, was banished to Brakebills South. Alice is upset by the story because her brother, Charlie, was the boy who tried to help.

FIFTH YEAR

With the older Physical Kids gone and not connecting with the new third years of the Discipline, Alice and Quentin attempt to make friends with others in their year. Quentin goes home with Alice for winter break and meets her parents. Her father, Daniel, has magically created a Roman-style villa and dresses in a toga. Quentin sees Alice's mother only once in a two-week visit. Alice makes Quentin promise they will never become like her parents.

GRADUATION

Alice and Quentin work on their senior projects. The results of Alice's experiment are frustratingly inconclusive, and Quentin fails in his attempted trip to the moon. Dean Fogg takes all of the graduating seniors into a deep underground chamber, where he tattoos each student and traps demons within the tattoos for the students' future protection. Josh, Janet, and Eliot take Alice and Quentin to New York.

Book II

MANHATTAN

Quentin's first few postgraduate months drift by rather aimlessly. A secret fund created by magic for Brakebills alumni means that none of them have to work. Quentin and Eliot experiment with drugs and drink too much. At a dinner party at the apartment Eliot shares with Janet, Josh brings Anaïs, whom they all met at a welters tournament, as his date. Another former Brakebills student named Richard is also there. The group discusses magic and religion. Quentin drinks too much and ends up in bed with both Eliot and Janet. Penny appears the next morning, breathlessly excited.

PENNY'S STORY

Penny explains that he dropped out of Brakebills and has been living in Maine, where he ran into Lovelady, the magic peddler. Lovelady has been feeling hunted and guesses that Penny accidentally acquired a powerful magical object, which Penny believes is one of the magic buttons that the Chatwin children used to transport themselves to Fillory. Penny has been traveling to the Neitherlands, a kind of in-between world, for the past three years and now wants all of them to come with him to Fillory. Using the button, Alice, Quentin, and Penny vanish.

THE NEITHERLANDS

They surface in a fountain in the middle of an open city square. Quentin is excited—if the Neitherlands are real, then Fillory may very well be real. When he turns to Alice, however, she explodes in anger because he cheated on her. Furious, she stalks through the city. Penny catches up, anxious that they might get lost. He is excited to show them around. They return to the Manhattan apartment.

UPSTATE

Everyone takes a turn going to the Neitherlands with Penny. The eight of them—Quentin, Alice, Eliot, Janet, Josh, Penny, Richard, and Anaïs—go to a house upstate to make plans for an excursion to Fillory. They buy supplies like parkas and knives and practice dark spells meant for battle. On the morning they plan to leave, Quentin sees Penny in Alice's bedroom, but even that does not dampen his enthusiasm for the trip.

Book III

FILLORY

They travel to the Neitherlands together, holding hands. Janet has a bad reaction, feeling ill and as if she cannot breathe. Penny scouts ahead through the fountain he thinks will take them to Fillory and reports that it is summertime, but when they return as a group, it is cold. They decide not to risk going back for cold weather gear. They walk through a forest until they come across a stream with a naiad, who gives them a horn to use "when all hope is lost."

They hear a clock ticking, which is the sound of the Watcherwoman, a villainous Fillory figure who tries to slow down time, so Penny fumbles for the button to take them all back to the city. When they return to Fillory, it is warm. A carriage approaches, and a praying mantis–like creature questions them and shoots arrows at them when it does not find their answers satisfactory. They argue about what to do next—continue or go home—until a birch tree creature appears. They follow it.

HUMBLEDRUM

The tree creature leads them to a tavern where they get drinks, talk to a bear named Humbledrum, and try to get information. Humbledrum knows little of importance, however, so they talk with the tree man, Farvel, who tells them the Watcherwoman has been seen in the forest. Penny is eager to take on a quest, and Farvel tells them that they could claim the throne of Fillory by finding a crown in a ruin called Ember's Tomb. The next morning they set off, with Richard staying behind at the inn. They have two local guides, Dint, an expert in battle magic, and Fen, whom Quentin believes is "some kind of martial artist."

EMBER'S TOMB

When they try to enter Ember's Tomb, they are attacked by its guards, a bunny and a ferret. Most of the group from Earth are horrified by the violent fight when Fen and Dint engage the guards, but Anaïs uses a sleeping spell on the bunny and then kills it while it sleeps. They enter the tunnels and walk for hours. They fight another battle against a group of magical creatures, and this time more of the Brakebills group are able to help. Alice looses the demon that Fogg embedded in her back. Janet kills one creature with a gun, though the others are shocked that she brought a firearm into Fillory. Alice and Quentin argue, and she tells him she came along because she wanted to take care of him.

Farther down the passage, they confront a whole host of creatures in a banquet hall. Both Eliot and Josh loose their demons, and Fen goes down under a red-hot iron giant. The group gets separated. Eliot finds Quentin, and Quentin marvels at how strong and practical Eliot is being under these extraordinary circumstances. They travel down an inwardly spiraling corridor.

THE RAM

The group meets up in a central chamber, coming in through separate arched doorways, and share their stories of escaping the battle. There is a ram in the center of the chamber, which Quentin thinks might be a statue until it welcomes them. It is Ember, one of the twin rams who protect Fillory, and Quentin questions him.

Quentin blows the horn given to them by the naiad, but rather than summoning help, the horn

calls forth the Beast. Ember charges, but the Beast flicks him aside as if he weighs nothing. Quentin realizes that the Beast is actually Martin Chatwin, who lost his humanity by doing dark magic so that he could remain in Fillory. Chatwin wants all of the magic buttons because they are the only things that can make him go back to Earth.

Chatwin bites off Penny's hands, stopping him from casting spells. Quentin calls Chatwin "pathetic," and Chatwin attacks him. Alice stops the attack, first with Janet's gun and then with spells. The others join in with battle magic while Quentin recovers. Quentin feels intense pride at Alice's skill. He releases his demon, but Chatwin eats the little creature. Alice uses a difficult spell, letting it spin out of control so that she will become a *niffin*. She looks to Quentin like a sapphire angel. She tears Chatwin's head from his body. Ember speaks, telling them to claim their prize, the crown, but when Eliot picks up the crown he flings it away into the shadows.

Book IV

THE RETREAT

Quentin wakes up in a centaur compound, where he recovers under the magical care of a centaur doctor. His convalescence is long, and he grieves for Alice. He finds a note from Eliot, who apologizes for leaving him. Quentin also finds a copy of *The Magicians*, the sixth Fillory book, which tells the tale of Jane Chatwin's traveling with Ember to visit dwarves. Knowing that Martin would become dangerous, the dwarves give Jane a pocket watch that slows down, speeds up, and reverses time, to help her stop him.

The story is signed on the final page by Jane herself, who is in the room as Quentin finishes reading. He recognizes her as the paramedic from his Princeton interview. With her pocket watch, Jane became known as the Watcherwoman. Quentin wants her to turn back time so that they can save Alice, but Jane refuses because after many tries, turning back time over and over for many challengers, this is the first time Martin was defeated. Quentin tries to grab the watch, but Jane destroys it. After Jane leaves, Quentin sees the Questing Beast, a white stag, from his window and decides to follow it.

THE WHITE STAG

Quentin follows the Questing Beast over land and sea. When he finally catches it and gets his three wishes, he asks for the stag to send him home.

Back in New York, Quentin runs into Anaïs, who tells him a little of what happened in Fillory while he was unconscious. Richard appeared and helped them get out of Ember's Tomb. Even centaur magic could not restore Penny's hands, so when they got back to the Neitherlands, Penny disappeared into one of the city's buildings. Quentin uses a magic key to go back to Brakebills.

KINGS AND QUEENS

Quentin works at a desk job set up for him by Dean Fogg. He has no real responsibilities. He sees Emily Greenstreet in a meeting, and she invites him to lunch. Emily fears magic and blames it for what went wrong with her life.

A month later, Quentin is in his office when the window shatters. Janet, Eliot, and Julia float outside, thirty stories from the ground. Eliot wears the crown they found at Ember's feet. Janet asks him to come with them, because they need another king to rule Fillory. Quentin steps out into the air and flies away with them.

CHARACTERS

Alder Acorn Agnes Allison-fragrant-timber

Alder Acorn Agnes Allison-fragrant-timber is Quentin's centaur doctor. She nurses him back to health after the confrontation with Martin Chatwin.

Alice

Alice is first Quentin's friend and then his girlfriend. She is quiet and shy but one of the most gifted magicians, having more control than most in their first year. Although Quentin hurts and disappoints her by cheating on her, Alice sacrifices herself to save him and destroy the Beast.

Gretchen Alsop

Gretchen is one of the students at Brakebills. She has a limp and walks with a cane. She is the first of the graduating students to get a demon implanted in her back.

Anaïs

Anaïs is first introduced as the leader of the Luxembourg welters team. In New York, she becomes part of the group because she is dating Josh and accompanies them to Fillory. She seems to revel in the violent fighting there.

The Beast

See Martin Chatwin

Bigby

Bigby is "the Physical Kids' unofficial faculty advisor." Quentin is shocked when he learns that Bigby is a pixie.

Professor Brzezinski

Professor Brzezinski teaches potions at Brakebills.

Bunny

The bunny is one of the guards who tries to keep Quentin and his friends from entering Ember's Tomb.

Charlie

Charlie is Alice's brother. He was a Brakebills student who tried to help Emily Greenstreet after she deformed herself with a spell but became a *niffin*, a kind of dark, magical spirit.

Fiona Chatwin

Fiona is one of the Chatwin siblings of the Fillory series. She is "pretty" and "princessy."

Helen Chatwin

Helen is the second oldest of the Chatwin siblings of the Fillory series.

Jane Chatwin

Jane is the youngest of the Chatwin children. Quentin first meets her as the paramedic at his failed Princeton interview, where she hands him the envelope containing the sixth Fillory book, which she wrote rather than Plover. She works as a kind of freelance talent scout for Brakebills, and late in the book Grossman reveals that she is also the feared Watcherwoman of Fillory. She works to stop her brother Martin, who during his time in Fillory has turned into the Beast.

Martin Chatwin

Martin is the oldest of the Chatwin siblings. Quentin notes that "In earlier books he was a changeful character, whose moods swung from cheerful to black without warning." This changefulness allows him to warp into something evil while he hides in Fillory, and he becomes the Beast.

Rupert Chatwin

Rupert is one of the Chatwin children. Quentin thinks of him as "goofy."

Quentin Coldwater

Quentin is the protagonist of the novel. He is a discontented young man, escaping into the seemingly fictional world of Fillory. When he learns that magic is real and finally is able to travel to Fillory, he believes that he will be happy, but the violence and loss he faces there leave him unmoored.

Daniel

Daniel is Alice's father. His presence in the novel provides an example of the aimlessness of some musicians: he uses his magic to create frivolous things, such as the Roman villa Quentin visits with Alice.

Dint

Dint is the male guide who leads the group to Ember's Tomb in Fillory.

Eliot

Eliot is the first person Quentin meets at Brakebills. He is sarcastic and pretends to be bored with just about everything around him. However, he acts as the glue that holds the group together, and he seems to adapt well to Fillory. In the letter Eliot writes at the close of the story, he tells Quentin that he is like family.

Ember

Ember is one of the twin rams who guard Fillory. When the young adventurers find him in the underground tunnels, he is unable, or unwilling, to help them.

Farvel

Farvel is the tree creature Quentin and his friends follow through the woods to the tavern in Fillory. Farvel explains to them that the kings and queens of Fillory must be "sons and daughters of Earth."

Fen

Fen is the female guide who leads the group to Ember's Tomb in Fillory.

Ferret

The ferret is one of the guards who tries to keep Quentin and his friends from entering Ember's Tomb.

Henry Fogg

Fogg is the dean at Brakebills and a powerful magician.

Professor Foxtree

Professor Foxtree, a tall, Native American magician, teaches at Brakebills and officiates at welters games.

Emily Greenstreet

Emily is the "first person to leave Brakebills voluntarily in one hundred fifty years." She abandoned magic after a messy affair with Professor Mayakovsky drove her to try a spell to change her appearance. Alice's brother, Charlie, tried to help her when the spell deformed her facial features and was turned into a *niffin*. Quentin contacts Emily at the end of the story, and she believes that "all this evil, all this sadness, it all *comes* from magic."

Josh Hoberman

Josh is one of the "Physical Kids." He not confident about his abilities with magic, but he is "the group's sharpest observer."

Humbledrum

Humbledrum is the bear that the group meets at the tavern in Fillory. It is difficult to get information from him because of his narrow range of interests and knowledge.

James

James is one of Quentin's high school friends. He is "handsome and smart," but also "kind and good."

Julia

Julia is Quentin's other close high school friend. He believes that he is in love with her, but she is dating James. Julia does not pass the Brakebills exam, but the magic used to erase her memories fails. Because she is able to remember, she drives herself almost mad trying to get into the school. At the end of the story, she is ready to go back to Fillory with Quentin, Janet, and Eliot.

Lovelady

Lovelady is a peddler of magical trinkets who periodically comes to Brakebills.

Professor March

Professor March teaches at Brakebills. He is not popular: "the students called him 'Death' March." It is during one of March's lessons that Quentin plays a prank that allows the Beast into the classroom.

Dean Mayakovsky

Mayakovsky is a former dean of Brakebills, a very powerful magician, and father to Professor Mayakovsky.

Professor Mayakovsky

Professor Mayakovsky teaches at Brakebills South. He is the professor who had an affair with Emily Greenstreet, which resulted in her leaving Brakebills and in Charlie's demise. Because of the tragic scandal, Mayakovsky was banished to the Antarctica branch of the school.

The Naiad

The naiad is the first creature the group meets in Fillory. She gives them the magical horn that they believe will bring help but instead summons the Beast.

Amanda Orloff

Amanda is one of Quentin's classmates and a talented magician, "regularly called on to demonstrate techniques for the class." When she tries to fight the Beast in Professor March's classroom, he consumes her.

Paramedic

See Jane Chatwin

Penny

Penny is one of Quentin's classmates. He wears a mohawk and tries to present a tough punk attitude. He is the first one to find his way to the Neitherlands and leads the others through into Fillory.

Professor Petitpoids

Professor Petitpoids is one of the teachers at Brakebills. She prefers to be addressed as "Witch" and is an expert in "the practical requirements of working magic."

Christopher Plover

Plover is the author of Fillory books. The first clue that the magical land might be real is that "Plover always claimed that the Chatwin children would come over and tell him stories about Fillory, and that he just wrote them down."

Praying Mantis

The praying mantis shoots arrows at the group in Fillory after they engage in a confusing conversation with it. Then its carriage speeds away.

Questing Beast

The Questing Beast is a creature in Fillory, a white stag who grants three wishes to anyone who can catch him. Quentin finds the Questing Beast and wishes to return home.

Richard

Richard is a former Brakebills student who joins the group while they are living in New York. He is an "observant Christian," which is "rare among magicians," and he accompanies them to Fillory.

Ricky

Quentin gets his early magic tricks from a Brooklyn store run by Ricky, who also works as a kind of talent scout for Brakebills.

Professor Sunderland

Professor Sunderland teaches at Brakebills. She becomes Quentin's tutor, trying to help him skip a year at Brakebills. She is young and attractive, and Quentin develops a crush on her.

Surendra

Surendra is Quentin's lab partner at Brakebills.

Umber

Umber is the second of the twin rams who guard Fillory. He does not appear in the story.

Professor Melanie Van der Weghe

Professor Van der Weghe is one of the teachers at Brakebills. She is involved in testing Quentin when he first arrives, and she helps him get settled once he is accepted as a student.

The Watcherwoman

See Jane Chatwin

Janet Way

Janet is one of the Physical Kids. She is clever but self-centered. When Quentin first meets her, he thinks of her as "the loud one: Quentin had seen her holding forth to the others on walks through the Maze and making speeches over dinner in the dining room."

THEMES

Magic

Grossman clearly put a lot of thought into the kind of magic his characters would wield. For example, Quentin learns that there is more than one kind of magic. Professor Sunderland tells him that "Everybody at Brakebills has an aptitude for magic, but there are individual variations—people tend to have an affinity for some specific strain." She explains that what determines a person's discipline is very complicated:

> It has to do with where you were born, and where the moon was, and what the weather was like, and what kind of person you are.... There are two hundred or so other factors which Professor March would be happy to list for you.

Quentin becomes one of the "Physical Kids," and physical magic is one of the rarest disciplines. Other students are illusionists or specialize in natural, knowledge, healing, or psychic magic.

However, even more interesting than these classifications is the way that Grossman's magic behaves. Magic in *The Magicians* is not an easily controllable, completely predictable force. Josh gets angry because he struggles to make his spells work. He yells at Quentin: "Don't you get it?...I do a spell, I don't know if it's going work or not!" Josh is jealous of Quentin's seeming ease with magic, ranting, "You look for the power, and it's just there!...I never know if it's going to be there when I need it. It comes and it goes and I don't even know why!" The uncertainty makes Josh so desperate he considers buying something from the peddler, Lovelady, hoping a charm or amulet might "make it so I could count on it a little more."

Alice, on the other hand, does not let the inconsistencies of magic frustrate her. She seems to feel that its unpredictability is part of what makes it so beautiful and amazing. At the New York dinner party, when the group is discussing

whether magic can be considered a tool, Alice argues that "magic just doesn't *feel* like a tool." She feels it would be "boring" if "casting a spell were like turning on an electric drill." She loves that magic is "irregular and beautiful. It's not an artifact, it's something else, something organic. It feels like a grown thing, not a made thing."

Quentin also seems to appreciate the intricacy of performing magic. When the class begins their studies at Brakebills South, Professor Mayakovsky tells Quentin, "You have been studying magic the way a parrot studies Shakespeare." To truly learn magic, the professor explains, "You cannot study magic. You cannot learn it. You must ingest it. Digest it. You must merge *with* it." Quentin had always wondered why performing magic had seemed so easy. It seemed to him that if one spoke the proper incantation, "Any idiot could do magic." However, he quickly learns at Brakebills South that "magic was like a language. And like a language, textbooks and teachers treated it as an orderly system for the purposes of teaching it, but in reality it was complex and chaotic and organic."

The process of learning about magic becomes a metaphor for learning about life. Although a student can study in books and listen to his teachers, there is only so much preparation that can be done. Practical experience is necessary. Quentin learns that "[e]very spell had to be adjusted and modified in a hundred ways according to the prevailing Circumstances—they adorned the word with a capital letter at Brakebills." Similarly, when one goes out into the real world, one must learn to think on one's feet, make quick decisions, and adapt to the surrounding conditions.

Happiness

Happiness is a major theme of *The Magicians*. Much of the narrative is centered on Quentin and his quest for a self-identity and happiness, though readers also get glimpses into the mindset of other characters in their own search for happiness, such as Alice's coming to Brakebills in spite of her brother's terrible end there and Eliot's lack of regrets about going to Fillory because he was "going to drink myself to death back on Earth."

Throughout Quentin's life, he seems to be looking for a place where he belongs, where he feels happy. He retreats into the fantasy world of

TOPICS FOR FURTHER STUDY

- The various settings in *The Magicians* are important, with each location reflecting what is going on in the story. Find photographs representing the settings of the novel from the everyday reality of Brooklyn, to Brakebills on the Hudson River, to Brakebills South in Antarctica's Marie Byrd Land. Create a PowerPoint presentation using some of these images and share it with your class. Be sure to discuss how each setting illuminates and influences the events of the plot.

- Quentin's obsession with the fictional world of Fillory is central to the story, and Grossman provides hints throughout the novel of the plotlines of the series. Write a short story featuring one of the Chatwin siblings that is part of the Fillory epic. You may elaborate on one of Grossman's ideas. Alternatively, you may develop something completely on your own, but keep the story consistent with Grossman's settings and characters.

- "The Obsidian Trilogy" is a series of fantasy novels by Mercedes Lackey and James Mallory that are suitable for young adults. Read the first novel in the trilogy: *The Outstretched Shadow* (2003). As you are reading, think about the world that Lackey and Mallory have created, a fictional world where magic is commonplace and where forces of good and evil hold sway. Consider how this kind of novel differs from *The Magicians*, in which Grossman places magic in a realistic world where magic is a secret and the difference between good and evil is not always obvious. Write an essay comparing the worlds built by the authors and the uses of magic within those worlds.

- Some of the best-known novels to feature magic in recent years are the Harry Potter series by J. K. Rowling. Grossman includes Rowling's books in a list of his influences and wonders why Harry does not read fantasy novels. "If I had grown up the way Harry did—in an abusive, loveless stepfamily—all I would've done was read fantasy," Grossman said to NPR's Tom Vitale and continues: "I would've been consumed by these...stories about escape and power." So for *The Magicians*, Grossman created Quentin, a hero who is almost obsessed with the fictional (or so he believes) world of Fillory as an escape from a life that does not make him happy. Consider why fantasy and science fiction novels and movies are so popular. The genre is sometimes called "escapist"—do you agree? Prepare a brief presentation of the reasons why people read fantasy literature, including critical consensus about the merits and weaknesses of the genre. Share the presentation with your class and then lead a class discussion so that your classmates can share their viewpoints.

Fillory because the real world does not satisfy him. Once he gets to Brakebills, he has moments where he feels "unexpectedly happy," for example, when Dean Fogg urges everyone to compete at welters or the "amazing outpouring of collective joy" of the class when they are transformed into Arctic foxes, running and playing and yapping at one another.

However, these moments pass quickly and do not bring lasting happiness. With Alice, Quentin does find some real happiness and true companionship. After their interlude as Arctic foxes, Quentin worries that she will be angry with him or that they will not be able to be friends anymore, but "it wasn't awkward at all. It was perfect. His heart clenched with silent

Quentin grows from an awkward high-school student into a talented and daring magician.

(© Jacek Bieniek / Shutterstock.com)

happiness when he saw her." His relationship with Alice is not enough for Quentin, as illustrated by his willingness to risk losing her by cheating on her. Alice sees this in Quentin, telling him, "You just go from one thing to the next, don't you, and you think it's going to make you happy. Brakebills didn't. I didn't. Did you really think Janet would? It's just another fantasy."

In learning that he can perform real magic, Quentin feels that he should be happy and becomes even more frustrated when he finds that not to be true. The narrative explains:

> Who would ever have thought he could do and have and be all those things and still feel nothing at all? What was he missing? Or was it him? If he wasn't happy even here, even now, did the flaw lie in him? As soon as he seized happiness it dispersed and reappeared somewhere else. Like Fillory, like everything good, it never lasted. What a terrible thing to know.

STYLE

Limited Third-Person Narrative

A third-person narrative is one in which the narrator refers to all of the characters as "he" or "she" (rather than "I," as a first-person narrator does). "Limited" refers to the fact that the narration is told from the perspective of a single character. Therefore, the reader is privy to the thoughts of only that character, rather than knowing the thoughts of every character, as is possible with an omniscient narrator.

Limited third-person narration is ideal for *The Magicians* because the protagonist experiences so many things that are new to him. The reader learns about magic being real when Quentin does and sees Brakebills through Quentin's eyes, sharing in his wonder and confusion.

Coming-of-Age Novel

The coming-of-age story is a genre that portrays the path of a character from childhood to adulthood. Throughout *The Magicians*, the reader witnesses the many changes Quentin experiences as he grows from a gawky, uncertain high school student to a thoughtful and skilled, if scarred, magician.

Attending Brakebills for Quentin is like going to college for any teenager. For example, it is the first time he spends a significant time away from his family (though he certainly does not have overprotective or meddling parents). Quentin realizes that he has found his own life—different from his old one before he left for school and separate from his family—when he visits his parents after they have moved away from Brooklyn. He finds he does not miss his old neighborhood and "suppose[s] he must have been shedding his old identity and his old life all along, without noticing it."

Brakebills is a place where he learns to draw on and sharpen his innate magical skills. His classes are formative, but his social experiences with fellow students are equally important, if not more so. Upon graduation, Quentin experiences the lack of direction familiar to many recent graduates:

> But where was he going to go, exactly? It was not considered the thing to look panicked or even especially concerned about graduation, but everything about the world after Brakebills felt dangerously vague and underthought to Quentin.... What was he going to do? What *exactly*? Every ambition he'd ever had in his life

had been realized the day he was admitted to Brakebills, and he was struggling to formulate a new one with any kind of practical specificity.

Quentin finds new purpose once he and his friends find their way to Fillory, but his search for the Questing Beast at the end of the novel shows that he is still searching for his sense of identity. He asks the Questing Beast to send him home, knowing he goes back changed, willing to accept responsibility for his actions, and hoping to tie up loose ends. Though Quentin's growth as a person is not finished, he is no longer a selfish child.

HISTORICAL CONTEXT

The Supernatural in Young-Adult Literature

Elements of the supernatural are everywhere in young-adult literature in the first decades of the twenty-first century. The pages of books targeted at teens are crowded with magicians, vampires, werewolves, and zombies, with series like Stephenie Meyer's *Twilight* (the first of which was published in 2005) and J. K. Rowling's Harry Potter novels (the first of which was published in 1997) selling in record numbers, being adapted to movies, and earning millions with tie-in merchandising. As posited by Liz Rosenberg in her article "Where the Coolest Kids Are, Like, Undead," in the *Boston Globe*: "It's impossible to talk about new trends in young-adult fiction without considering the wildly popular supernatural fiction." Why is the paranormal such a trend in young-adult literature?

Early young-adult books were realistic fiction. The novel *Seventeenth Summer* (1942) by Maureen Daly is considered to be the first book published and marketed specifically to attract a teenage audience, and it is a simple story about a young woman's first love. Other similar romances followed, largely intended for teenage girls, while publishers tried to capture the male teen crowd with novels about sports.

It was not until the 1960s and 1970s that young-adult literature gained critical respect and began to be considered an important part of the sales market by publishers. Authors like Robert Cormier and Judy Blume cemented many of the steadfast themes of the genre: the experiences of high school, such as being misunderstood and feeling like an outcast. The success

of such novels brought lots of imitators, many written by authors less skilled than Cormier and Blume. This resulted in an excess of what Ashley Strickland, in a CNN article, describes as "single-problem novels" because they focus on a single difficult or controversial issue like drug abuse or divorce but fail to round out the novel with a good plot or well-developed characters. Many novels targeted toward teens became formulaic, leading to a decline in the industry of young-adult literature. This low point also happened to occur at a time when the teenage population was at a low (low birth rates in the mid-1970s meant fewer teenagers in the 1990s).

However, a baby boom in the early 1990s meant the beginning of a second golden age of young-adult literature starting around 2000. Teen readers were ready for innovation, not formulaic stories, and novels featuring paranormal events and mythical creatures were immediately popular. Some critics believe it is more than just novelty that attracts teens to supernatural stories; there are many aspects of the paranormal that young readers seem to relate well to. Alexandra Monir, herself an author of supernatural young-adult novels, explains:

> Everything changes so rapidly in our teen years, from our bodies to our emotions, who we thought we were to who we find ourselves becoming. Everything in our world intensifies and looms larger. It can feel more than a little dubious to imagine 9-to-5 adults suddenly stumbling upon magical powers. But a teenager who is still discovering him or herself, who is experiencing so many firsts? Of course they could turn out to be a wizard, or a telekinetic, or a half-Angel, or whatever your fancy.

Jennifer Lynn Barnes, a cognitive science scholar who also writes young-adult books, agrees: "Just like adolescence is between childhood and adulthood, paranormal, or other, is between human and supernatural" (quoted by Strickland). Barnes believes that exploring the supernatural can help young readers to "navigate those two worlds" of adulthood and childhood as well as "dualities of other worlds." Lizzie Skurnick, a publisher and author, explains that young-adult fiction "is always dealing with transformation, whether it be realistic or supernatural.... It's the only genre that can always be both. It shows teen life in full chaos. And that means constant change" (quoted by Strickland).

Until he arrives at Brakebills, Quentin is unaware that his card tricks are aided by real magic.
(© Suslik1983 / Shutterstock.com)

Just as with quality mainstream fiction, good supernatural young-adult literature can do more than just tell an interesting story. Because teens identify with the characters—whose emotions are human even if their bodies are inhuman or infused with magic—it helps them to think about real issues. As Rosenberg explains, "Like all speculative fiction, that of the supernatural allows teenagers to grapple with ideas."

CRITICAL OVERVIEW

Much of the critical attention for *The Magicians* focuses on Grossman's obvious inspirations drawn from other fantasy novels. For example, a review in *Publishers Weekly* labels the book "derivative," pointing out that "Genre fans will easily pick up the many nods to J. K. Rowling and C. S. Lewis, not to mention J. R. R. Tolkien in the climactic battle between the bad guy and a magician." Deirdre Donahue, writing in *USA Today*, compares the novel's allusions to a "a video game featuring scenarios from classic fantasy writers."

Many reviewers, such as Keith Donohue in the *Washington Post*, felt that Grossman used his sources well. Donohue writes

> While this story invariably echoes a whole body of romantic coming-of-age tales, Grossman's American variation is fresh and compelling. Like a jazz musician, he riffs on Potter and Narnia, but makes it his own.

Other critics take a different point of view. Donahue complains that "it becomes a chore to slog through this homage to fantasy filtered through an ironic 21st-century sensibility.... Nifty premise aside, Quentin and company never fully grab our attention." In the *Magazine of Fantasy and Science Fiction*, Elizabeth Hand declares the question moot, asserting that "there's little point complaining that *The Magicians* derives from Harry Potter, *Little, Big*, the Narnia books ... and a zillion other novels—the borrowing is the point."

The *New York Times* reviewer Michael Agger writes that when Grossman strays from borrowed ideas into original material, he falters:

It's the original magic—storytelling—that occasionally trips Grossman up.... [T]he characters have a fixed...quality. There's the punk, the aesthete, the party girl, the fat slacker, the soon-to-be-hot nerd, the shy, angry, yet inexplicably irresistible narrator. Believable characters form the foundation for flights of fantasy.

The Magicians does not quite succeed, Agger concludes, because Grossman relies too much on these character stereotypes. Hand, however, specifically praises Grossman's characterizations in a spot for NPR: "The novel is beautifully written, with well-drawn, believable characters." She says that "one of the coolest aspects of this book is that the students at Brakebills College act like real college students." Indeed, in the *Magazine of Fantasy and Science Fiction*, Hand writes that Grossman is at his best when he branches out rather than sticking to "his original models and their conventions so tightly." As she read the novel, she "kept wondering why...Grossman didn't just write his own damn novel? He's certainly up to the task." Hand clearly states that "when Grossman focuses...on original material...he creates truly spectacular set-pieces."

Perhaps Hand explains it best: though "problematic," *The Magicians* is "a clever, beautifully written fantasy that flickers right on the border of greatness." She clarifies her objections to the book, writing that "my caveats all stem from the fact that this is one of the best fantasies I've read in ages, and I wanted it to be...perfect." *Booklist*'s Ian Chipman also offers a positive view of the novel, writing that "Deep fantasy fans can't afford to miss the darkly comic and unforgettably queasy experience of reading this book."

CRITICISM

Kristen Sarlin Greenberg

Greenberg is a freelance writer and editor with a background in literature and philosophy. In the following essay, she examines the significance of the various worlds in The Magicians.

Anyone who has read the works of C. S. Lewis will note the similarities between his

> QUENTIN THOUGHT THAT STAYING IN FILLORY WOULD BE ENOUGH—HE THOUGHT THAT EACH STEP AWAY FROM HIS DULL, COMMONPLACE LIFE IN BROOKLYN THROUGH THE NOVEL'S VARIOUS OTHERWORLDLY SETTINGS WAS BRINGING HIM A STEP CLOSER TO HAPPINESS."

Narnia and the world of Fillory in Lev Grossman's *The Magicians*. Indeed, Grossman makes no effort to camouflage his interest in and devotion to Lewis's creation. In a list of his cultural influences published in *Vulture*, he describes the first time he read the Narnia series:

When I read *The Lion, the Witch, and the Wardrobe*—I was 8, I'd say—it was the first time I understood what novels were for.... [T]hose books were so important to me—just the very idea that you could pass from this world into a world that was brighter and more magical and more fun and more important. Even at that point—I must've been a sort of gloomy 8-year-old—when I read it I felt like, *yes, this can't be it, this world I'm looking at all around me, there has to be something else.* And when I read *Narnia*, I thought, *yes, of course, there's Narnia.*

Just as Grossman looked to Narnia as a boy, his protagonist, Quentin, looks to mythical Fillory—but Quentin finds that the world he dreams of is real and actually travels there. By contrasting the fantasy world of Fillory with the everyday setting of Brooklyn, the magical school Brakebills, and the other settings of his novel, Grossman drags his hero through a journey of discovery.

The story begins in Brooklyn, but quickly the reader learns that Quentin is never really quite present there. As he walks to his college interview, he does not even seem to feel the cold wind blowing through the fabric of his suit: "He wasn't really there anyway. He was in Fillory." Quentin escapes his dreary everyday reality by thinking of Fillory, the magical fantasy world that filled his boyhood with stories of adventure. Quentin soon finds himself at Brakebills, but he cannot quite bring

WHAT DO I READ NEXT?

- J. K. Rowling's wildly popular Harry Potter novels were an admitted inspiration for Grossman as he wrote *The Magicians*. He includes the series in a list of his cultural influences published by *Vulture*. Grossman explains: "I felt like I was very connected to Harry's story." *Harry Potter and the Sorcerer's Stone* (1997) describes Harry's arrival at his school and his first experiences with wielding magical powers.

- The "GameWorld" trilogy by Indian author Samit Basu consists of *The Simoqin Prophecies* (2004), *The Manticore's Secret* (2005), and *The Unwaba Revelations* (2007). Part spoof and part tribute to the fantasy genre, Basu's series mixes cultural elements of the East and the West with countless allusions.

- Grossman's *The Magician King* (2011) and *The Magician's Land* (2014) are both sequels to *The Magicians*. In *The Magician King*, Grossman broadens the narrative to include the perspective of characters other than Quentin, and Edan Lepucki of the *New York Times* calls *The Magician's Land* "the strongest book in Grossman's series."

- Quentin's first experiences with magic are simple card tricks and other sleights of hand learned at a Brooklyn magic and joke shop. In *Hiding the Elephant: How Magicians Invented the Impossible and Learned to Disappear* (2003), Jim Steinmeyer explains the mechanics behind this kind of magic and provides a fascinating overview of some of its most famous practitioners.

- *Jonathan Strange & Mr. Norrell* (2004) by Susanna Clarke takes place in England in 1806, placing its protagonists right in the middle of the Napoleonic Wars. In *Vulture*, Grossman describes the novel as having a big impact on his thinking: "I read *Jonathan Strange & Mr. Norrell* in May 2004, and...it had an immediate galvanizing effect on me."

- Like *The Magicians*, Ursula Le Guin's novel *A Wizard of Earthsea* (1968; reissued in 2012) features the education of a sorcerer. Grossman explained in *Vulture* that, rather than Harry Potter's Hogwarts, Le Guin's school for magic on the island of Roke was the major inspiration for Brakebills: "You just want to reread those chapters over again so you can stay there." *A Wizard of Earthsea* is the first novel in Le Guin's "Earthsea Cycle."

---

himself to accept what the professors there tell him about magic being real:

> He'd spent too long being disappointed by the world—he'd spent so many years pining for something like this, some proof that the real world wasn't the only world, and coping with the overwhelming evidence that it in fact was. He wasn't going to be suckered in just like that.

Quentin's inability to accept Brakebills as entirely real is highlighted by its physical separation from the rest of the world. The magical charms that protect the campus from prying, nonmagical eyes have caused a kind of rift in time, so that the seasons at Brakebills are skewed from those in the surrounding area. The jarring changes in weather that Quentin notes each time he leaves school reinforce the idea that Brakebills is a world apart—not quite real to him because it is so completely separate.

Quentin goes through his entire first year at school not quite believing. After his first summer break, he follows instructions to a passage that will allow him back to campus. As he waits for the passage to open, he realizes that

> he had never felt so absolutely sure that he was delusional, that Brooklyn was the only reality there was, and that everything which had happened to him last year was just a fan-boy hallucination, proof that the boredom of the real world had finally driven him totally and irreversibly out of his mind.

Grossman presents a whole other world in Brakebills South, where the students are sent for an intense semester of study with the demanding Professor Mayakovsky. The strangeness of the place, a building that "looked like an eighteenth-century English country house planted in the middle of a soaring Antarctic wasteland," sets it apart from the other locations in the story. It also seems otherworldly because "there was no reliable way to measure time at Brakebills South. There were no clocks, and the sun was a dull white fluorescence permanently thumbtacked half an inch above the white horizon." While Quentin is there, he "felt like he was walking on the moon. Giant slow-motion steps, ringing silence, vacuum all around him." The desolation of the place encourages contemplation: Quentin thinks that "he should have been ravenous for human contact, but instead he felt himself falling away from the others, deeper inside himself." Again, Quentin finds himself questioning what is real: he "wondered if the rest of the world, his life before this, had just been a lurid dream."

It is when Quentin first arrives in the Neitherlands that the reader sees how Quentin has been drifting through each setting, always looking ahead to what might come next. Everything always pales in comparison to his imaginings of Fillory. Once he gets to the Neitherlands and realizes that there truly are other worlds, that he might actually be able to travel to Fillory, he is ecstatic. He had not "know[n] he could be this happy."

Fillory is the place Quentin has dreamed of all his life. "I used to envy Martin," he says, "Because I thought he'd finally done it. . . . It was like he broke the bank, beat the system. He got to stay in Fillory forever." He sees all of his problems—his lack of direction in terms of any kind of employment, the way he damaged his relationship with Alice by cheating on her—as "a symptom of the sick, empty world they were all in together. And now they had the medicine. The sick world was about to be healed." Quentin believes that going to Fillory will fix everything.

However, once he achieves his dream of going to Fillory, it does not turn out to be everything he hoped. At first, it does not seem real. The scene outside the tavern has "a dreamlike quality, like a Chagall painting come to life." Quentin tries to dismiss any frustration he feels about Fillory not living up to expectations. Although "Fillory had yet to give Quentin the

surcease from unhappiness he was counting on," he is certain that "relief was out there, he knew it, he just needed to get deeper in." When the group speaks to Farvel and learns that only the "sons and daughters of Earth" can claim the crown and save the land, Penny is pleased that they have a quest. But to Quentin, it still does not seem quite real: "It had a pat, theme-park quality to it, like they were on some fantasy-camp role-playing vacation." During their first experience with real violent fighting using magic, when Bunny and Ferret try to keep them from entering Ember's Tomb, Quentin realizes how unprepared he was for this adventure: "He wasn't ready for this. This wasn't magic. This was the opposite of magic. The world was ripping open."

Quentin had long ago "worked out exactly what he would wish for if anybody ever gave him the chance. He would wish to travel to Fillory and to be allowed to stay there forever." Once he has this wish granted, however, it does not feel like a privilege. He describes himself as being "lost forever in Fillory"—it is difficult to see "lost" as having any kind of positive connotation. Quentin gives himself another quest: finding the Questing Beast. When the creature grants Quentin a wish, he says "Send me home." Is Quentin ready to face "real" life? Or is he giving up his dreams?

After losing Alice and blaming himself, Quentin wishes that he had never learned about magic and never gone to Brakebills, because then "he would never have known the horror of really getting what he thought he wanted." Because the journey to Fillory did not turn out the way Quentin expected, the way it was always portrayed in Plover's novels, with happy, satisfying endings, Quentin takes a strange moral away from "the story of Martin Chatwin": "Sure, you can live out your dreams, but it'll only turn you into a monster. Better to stay home and do card tricks in your bedroom instead."

However, Quentin's true difficulty is that he looks for fulfillment in the wrong places, time and time again. Quentin thought that staying in Fillory would be enough—he thought that each step away from his dull, commonplace life in Brooklyn through the novel's various otherworldly settings was bringing him a step closer to happiness. Quentin's words to Martin Chatwin, who has become the Beast, sum up the nature of Quentin's problem: "There's no getting

Brakebills is in upstate New York, right on the Hudson River. (© *American Spirit | Shutterstock.com*)

away from yourself. Not even in Fillory." Quentin has always looked for happiness to be handed to him. He asks himself, "Wasn't there a spell for making yourself happy?" He seems to think that going to a different place, whether it is Brakebills or Fillory, will be enough to change him, without understanding that he must make an effort to change within himself.

By the end of the book, Quentin's self-perceived failures have driven him to shut down his heart: "It had been a long time since he'd experienced any emotion at all other than sadness and shame and numbness." Therefore, when he sees Eliot, Janet, and Julia outside his office window, "for a moment he didn't understand what was happening inside him. In spite of himself he felt sensation coming back to some part of him that he'd thought was dead forever."

Though the new sensation is painful, "at the same time he wanted more of it." If Grossman offers any hope at the close of *The Magicians*, it is that Quentin is willing to change, to open himself up, and to feel again. It is this willingness, more than the willingness to venture into Fillory once again, that shows that Quentin has learned something from his experiences—that he has changed within himself rather than striving to simply pass into another world, another reality, hoping that it will make him happy.

Source: Kristen Sarlin Greenberg, Critical Essay on *The Magicians*, in *Novels for Students*, Gale, Cengage Learning, 2016.

Elizabeth Hand

In the following excerpt, Hand describes The Magicians *as both "problematic" and "unputdownable."*

I sit at my desk, struggling to write in the endless shadow cast by Hope Mirrlees, J. R. R. Tolkien, T. H. White, C. S. Lewis, Jack Vance, M. John Harrison, Angela Carter, John Crowley, Gene Wolfe, George R.R. Martin, J. K. Rowling [gentle readers, insert your favorite authors here], serenaded by the fitful vespertine squeaks of Stephenie Meyer and her umbrous ilk. Maybe it's the lack of light; maybe global warming has finally starved my brain of oxygen.

> A DEEPER PROBLEM, I THINK, IS THAT IN MANY WAYS *THE MAGICIANS* ASPIRES TO BE BOTH A CRITIQUE OF THE FANTASY GENRE, AS WELL AS A FULLBLOODED FANTASY NOVEL."

But it seems to me an undeniable fact that we live in a post-fantasy world. Can there possibly be a single barren atoll left unpopulated by psammeads or simurghs, a rural corner of Dorimare undevastated by the world-building boom that brought us Gil'ead, Westland, Andor, Tarbean, and the Final Empire? Can there possibly be another golden city, far beyond the dim endragoned dreaming sea? Sisters and brothers, do you really need to read another freaking elf (dragon/ wizard/daemon/shape-shifter/ djinn/ witch etc.) book?

Yeah, well, okay. Me too.

... What would Lewis have made of our tweeting, twittering, endless YouTube-loop of a world, where pleasures (including literary ones) exist solely to be repeated, to the extent that one can feel trapped in a Mobius loop of cultural references, Middle Earth morphing into Narnia morphing into Hogwarts morphing into—

Lev Grossman's provocative, problematic, unput-downable *The Magicians*, a clever, beautifully written fantasy that flickers right on the border of greatness. Grossman's another critic (*Time* magazine) who gets fantasy right by "getting" it—he groks it, we'd say back in the day. His first novel, *Warp*, featured a twenty-something *Star Trek* fan flailing about as he confronts the usual issues of adult life: love, career, meaning, dilithium crystals. His second, *Codex*, ratcheted down the herd factor slightly, by centering on a lost medieval manuscript and a malign computer game. *Codex* was a surprise bestseller, which gave Grossman the freedom to let his geek flag fly with *The Magicians*, a love letter to the fantasy genre that seeks to offer a gentle corrective to its escapist pleasures. Just as the Artemis Fowl books were marketed as "Die Hard with Elves," *The Magicians* will be hyped as one of summer's big books: "Harry Potter for Grownups."

I propose a drinking game—let's all chug a pint of butterbeer every time we hear that catchphrase used to describe *The Magicians*. It's what Grossman's protagonist, Quentin Coldwater, would do. Seventeen as the novel opens, Quentin is dispiritedly facing his college interview with an elderly Princeton alum, desperately wishing the cold streets of Brooklyn were the cobblestone ones of Fillory, the magical kingdom captured in the beloved series penned by Christopher Plover. "Only an American Anglophile could have created a world as definitively English, more English than England, as Fillory." Plover died before completing the fifth novel in his sequence, a book whose dissatisfactions deliberately echo those of Lewis's *The Last Battle*.

But before you can point your wand and shout Expeller adfectatus philologus!, a lost manuscript of *The Magicians: Book Six of Fillory and Further*, is thrust into Quentin's limp grasp. Before you can mutter narratus retexo!, it disappears; and before you can gasp "Rowling v. RDR Books" Quentin has stumbled through a portal and arrived at Brakebills College for Magical Pedagogy.

Brakebills has nothing to do with Fillory: it's a real, live magical place where potential students must pass a demanding entrance exam that makes the SAT look like something out of Quizrocket.com. Googlemaps locates it in upstate New York, somewhere between Bard College, John Crowley's Invisible College, and Donna Tartt's Hampden College. But—there is no other way to put it—this is Hogwarts for grownups, or grownups who fondly recall their lost youth, anyway. The students swear, drink to excess, have sex (occasionally with their instructors) and otherwise misbehave the way we all did betwixt perfecting Fergus's Spectral Armory and Magic Missiles in the duller portions of Practical Applications class.

The novel follows Quentin and his friends through their years at Brakebills to graduation and beyond, when they settle, as one does, into magical slacker life in downtown Manhattan. Turns out that graduating with a degree in magic prepares one for real life about as well as a degree in comparative lit, or cultural anthropology. Though magic solves the problem of earning a living—the Brakebills equivalent of Rowling's Ministry of Magic provides dull-as-wishwater jobs. Or you can just use magic, duh.

But there are still the problems of Meaning, Love, Commitment, even Spiritual Belief—at one point, Grossman trots out a tedious Brakebills grad who's a Christian enchanter. The character and his argument for a Magical Prime Mover were unconvincing, but I appreciated Grossman's effort to present Another View. So Quentin finds that possessing one's heart's desire doesn't make one happy—even going to a magical college and learning to work real magic, having a real magical girlfriend and real magical sex, drinking magical shooters and taking magical drugs—none of it's enough. (Well it damn well would be for me, I thought, but I'm twice Quentin's age and flunked Practical Apps.)

But it's still not Fillory, the fictional Lost Domain that captivated Quentin and all his friends as children. And if for one New York second you didn't think that the Brakebills crew was going to end up there, well, have I got some prime land in the Dead Marshes for you!

Harold Bloom once rather alarmingly described David Lindsay's *A Voyage to Arcturus* as "Through the Looking Glass as it might have been written by Thomas Carlyle." *The Magicians* is Harry Potter as it might have been written by John Crowley. Over and above the Smokey Barnable-esque Quentin Coldwater and his innamorata Alice, whose names form a widdershins anagram of *Little, Big*'s Alice Drinkwater, avid readers will enjoy getting all the Crowleyesque references to other classic fantasy novels—the Hogwartian instructors and spells; the Looking-Glass-World chessboard game that's Brakebill's answer to quidditch; the chapter in which Quentin and his cohort are turned into birds as part of their magical education, a la the Wart in the U.S. edition of *The Once and Future King*. There's little point complaining that *The Magicians* derives from Harry Potter, *Little, Big*, the Narnia books, *The Sword in the Stone*, and a zillion other novels—the borrowing is the point (though not the only one), along with Grossman's prose, which is luminous and will, I suspect, stand up to multiple readings by readers who cut their teeth on J. K. Rowling's books but are now ready for something more sophisticated—Grossman's target audience, I'm sure, and a vast one it is. It's all beautifully done, and it all fits seamlessly into Grossman's meticulously designed, overarching meta-narrative.

Yet I kept wondering why (apart from the marketing angle, which is one huge Because) Grossman didn't just write his own damn novel? He's certainly up to the task. Bloom published an homage to Lindsay's book, a novel titled *The Trip to Lucifer*, which he's since disavowed; *The Magicians* is a far more successful work than that, but it doesn't quite pull off the trick of being an original book composed of other fantasy novels, the way that *Little, Big* is composed of children's books. Part of this is that we've seen this trick before, in books and graphic novels like *The Sandman*, as well as films and TV series such as *The Tenth Kingdom*. Part of it is that Grossman embraces his original models and their conventions so tightly that he can't breathe much new air into them—the faux-Edwardian boarding school feel of Brakebills; the fact that sorcery and modern electronics don't mix (there is little texting at Brakebills); the fact that all the young protagonists are whip-smart, middle-class, educated sorts whose parents would almost certainly have shelled out for the Brakebills College Prep Course, had such a thing been available.

What makes this even more aggravating is that when Grossman focuses his energy and exceptional talent on original material, rather than a pastiche of White or Rowling, he creates truly spectacular set-pieces. The chapter where a Brakebills class is disrupted by the inadvertent summoning of a seemingly benign, even banal entity, is one of the most frightening and unexpected scenes I've read in years. The long sequence that begins as an homage to the avian shapeshifting in *The Sword in the Stone* develops into a glorious, strange, and powerfully moving paean to enchantment that is all Grossman's own. Ditto the exquisite, fractal transitional world that he summons late in the novel, when Quentin and his friends finally journey to Fillory.

A deeper problem, I think, is that in many ways *The Magicians* aspires to be both a critique of the fantasy genre, as well as a fullblooded fantasy novel. Grossman wants to have his potion and drink it too. Other writers have grappled with this, notably M. John Harrison in his *Viriconium* sequence and later short stories, and especially in his 1992 novel *The Course of the Heart*, a book that *The Magicians* sometimes resembles.

Harrison's solution is to deny his readers the solace of seeing what's on the other side of the enchanted wardrobe. He brilliantly constructs fantasy narratives, utilizing all the tricks at his disposal: he's like a master stage magician enticing his audience through the traditional steps in a magic show: the Pledge, or build-up; the Turn, where the trick is actually played; and finally the Prestige, where the disappeared object returns, the woman sawed in half bounds to her feet again, and so on. In fantasy terms, the Prestige is roughly analogous to Tolkien's eucatastrophe, but Harrison is having none of it. In an interview in *Parietal Games: Critical Writings* by and on M. John Harrison, he says

> ...the whole point...is to bring the reader to the point where normally they would go through the portal, they would be allowed to go through the portal, encouraged to go through the portal.... Most of my short stories are kind of portal fantasies but you are not allowed through into the imaginary country, you're not allowed to believe in the fantasy. You're not allowed through, or it's undermined, or it's shown to be just as ordinary as what you left—which is actually the one I favor—mainly because what I'm trying to get the reader to do in that kind of story is this: if you run the reader as quickly as possible through the narrative with plenty of narrative push-through, plenty of speed, you get a crash at the end, you get a real sense of "Whoo! Why aren't I allowed through?" or "I walked through the door and there was no room on the other side" or "I just fell" or "the door was slammed in my face." That is a violent collision.... What happens to the reader in that instant? What happens to the particular fantasy in that instant of coming off the rails?.... To actually see what makes fantasy work, especially how it transfers from our heads to a made narrative. Or at least to make the reader question both the nature of fantasy and the nature of reality.

I quote this lengthy observation because, for much of his wildly ambitious novel, it seems to be exactly what Grossman is about, too. But I think he loses it when the action shifts to Fillory, where, despite his best efforts, *The Magicians* relies on those three cliches against which Le Guin inveighed. The characters are white (though maybe I missed something; they all seemed like pretty bland white young urbanites to me); in Fillory, it's sort of the middle ages; and there's a battle between good and evil. And while Grossman gives lip service to the notion that

Quentin and his friends aren't quite sure whose side they're on in the final showdown, it was pretty clear to me where the lines were drawn.

Finally, I didn't buy the ending, which seemed more a sop to readers' expectations (and the possibility of a sequel) than anything else. Still, my caveats all stem from the fact that this is one of the best fantasies I've read in ages, and I wanted it to be, you know, perfect. I wanted more.

Turkish Delight, anyone?

Source: Elizabeth Hand, Review of *Cheek by Jowl: Essays*, in *Magazine of Fantasy and Science Fiction*, Vol. 117, Nos. 1–2, August–September 2009, pp. 40–49.

Ian Chipman

In the following review, Chipman acknowledges that Grossman drew on numerous sources but praises his take on the fantasy canon as "unique."

This literary fantasy, drawing heavily from the fantasy canon but unique in its reworking of it, can be seen as a sort of darker, modern-day response to the magic-in-the-real-world of Susanna Clark's *Jonathan Strange & Mr. Norrell* (2004). When Quentin, a brooding and insecure teenager gifted with sleight of hand, is invited to enroll in a university for young spellcasters, he is thrilled beyond words. He grew up fervently rereading a series of fantasy books in which a group of children pass from this world to the magical realm of Fillory (read: Narnia), but it turns out the pursuit of magic is just about as boring as studying anything else. At school and in New York City after graduation, Quentin's life seesaws between the mind-numbingly dull application of rote spellcasting and the typical twentysomething pursuit of booze, sex, and repeat. Until, that is, he and his friends figure out that Fillory is real. Grossman sometimes gets bogged down in the minutiae of explaining how practicing magic is tedious, which itself gets awfully tedious. But when the friends endeavor to go on a heroic quest, the matter-of-fact fashion in which their fantastical adventure transforms into a nightmare is as absurdly sobering for the reader as it is for Quentin. Deep fantasy fans can't afford to miss the darkly comic and unforgettably queasy experience of reading this book—and be glad for reality.

Source: Ian Chipman, Review of *The Magicians*, in *Booklist*, Vol. 105, No. 18, May 15, 2009, p. 33.

Publishers Weekly

In the following review, the anonymous reviewer calls The Magicians *"derivative" because of its references to fantasy classics.*

Harry Potter discovers Narnia is real in this derivative fantasy thriller from *Time* book critic Grossman (*Codex*). Quentin Coldwater, a Brooklyn high school student devoted to a children's series set in the Narnia-like world of Fillory, is leading an aimless existence until he's tapped to enter a mysterious portal that leads to Brakebills College, an exclusive academy where he's taught magic. Coldwater, whose special gifts enable him to skip grades, finds his family's world "mundane and domestic" when he returns home for vacation. He loses his innocence after a prank unintentionally allows a powerful evil force known only as the Beast to enter the college and wreak havoc. Eventually, Coldwater's powers are put to the test when he learns that Fillory is a real place and how he can journey there. Genre fans will easily pick up the many nods to J.K. Rowling and C.S. Lewis, not to mention J.R.R. Tolkien in the climactic battle between the bad guy and a magician.

Source: Review of *The Magicians*, in *Publishers Weekly*, Vol. 256, No. 22, June 1, 2009, p. 29.

Melissa Block and Tom Vitale

In the following interview, Vitale discusses some of the sources for Grossman's Fillory.

From NPR News, this is *All Things Considered*. I'm Melissa Block.

MADELEINE BRAND, host:

And I'm Madeleine Brand.

What will Harry Potter do with the rest of his life, that is, after he defeats Voldemort and graduates from Hogwarts? Questions like that drove the thinking behind a new fantasy novel. It's a magical story in itself and it's also a critique of the fantasy genre. Tom Vitale has our story.

TOM VITALE: On first glance, Lev Grossman's *The Magicians* looks very much like a Harry Potter story, only with slightly older characters and an American setting. The hero, Quentin, is a teenager from Brooklyn on his way to a Princeton admissions interview when he's whisked through a portal to an Academy of Magic called Brakebills.

But Quentin differs from Harry Potter in that he reads fantasy novels. And he's enchanted to discover that the magic he's longed for all his life actually exists. Author Lev Grossman.

Mr. LEV GROSSMAN (Author, *The Magicians*): If I had grown up the way Harry did, in an abusive, loveless stepfamily, all I would've done was read fantasy. I would've been consumed by these—just stories about escape and power. And I always wondered why Harry wasn't a fantasy reader.

VITALE: Now 40 years old and the book critic for *Time* magazine, Grossman says when he was young, he was particularly taken with *The Lord of the Rings* by J.R.R. Tolkien and *The Chronicles of Narnia* by C.S. Lewis.

In Grossman's novel, the hero is obsessed with a series of books about a magical land called Fillory, which is much like Narnia. But at Brakebills, Quentin discovers that in real magic, things don't always work out the way they do in fantasy novels. When Quentin casts a prank spell in a magic class, he inadvertently summons a beast who eats one of his classmates.

Mr. GROSSMAN: (Reading) Things like this didn't happen in Fillory. There was conflict and even violence, but it was always heroic and ennobling and anybody really good and important who bought it along the way came back to life at the end of the book. Now there was a rip in the corner of his perfect world, and fear and sadness were pouring in like freezing filthy water through a busted dam.

Ms. ELIZABETH HAND (Book Critic): Really, one of the coolest aspects of this book is that the students at Brakebills College act like real college students.

VITALE: Elizabeth Hand reviewed *The Magicians* in the current issue of *Fantasy & Science Fiction Magazine*. She says the novel is beautifully written, with well-drawn, believable characters.

Ms. HAND: I mean, these are kids or students who are having relationships with each other. Some of them are having, you know, romantic or sexual relationships. There are students who are gay, as well as straight, students occasionally making references to drugs. This is not your mother's Hogwarts.

(Soundbite of movie *Harry Potter and the Half blood Prince*)

Mr. DANIEL RADCLIFFE (Actor): (As Harry Potter) If you could find them all, if you did destroy each Horcrux . . .

Mr. MICHAEL GAMBON (Actor): (As Professor Dumbledore) . . . one destroys Voldemort.

Mr. RADCLIFFE: (As Harry Potter) How would you find them? They could be hidden anywhere, couldn't they?

Mr. GAMBON: (As Professor Dumbledore) True. But magic, especially dark magic . . .

VITALE: In the Harry Potter books and their film adaptations, as in most fantasy stories, there is a powerful malevolent being, a Voldemort or Sauron, who the hero fights in an epic battle. Lev Grossman says he purposely left the villain out of his fantasy novel.

Mr. GROSSMAN: Voldemort and anyone like that in a fantasy novel, any big, bad villain, has a kind of powerful organizing presence on the universe. You know who's good, you know who's evil and you know what magic is for. It's for fighting evil. Well, when you take that away, suddenly the universe gets a whole lot more complicated. Suddenly, it's all shades of gray, and it's not clear who belongs where, and it's not clear what magic is for.

VITALE: In the end, the young magicians in Grossman's novel do use their magic to battle evil, when they discover a portal to the magical realm of Fillory, which they thought only existed in their novels. With Fillory, Grossman says he wanted to reinterpret the Narnia of C.S. Lewis and the role of the lion god Aslan, also depicted in the film adaptation.

(Soundbite of movie *The Chronicles of Narnia*)

Mr. WILLIAM MOSELEY (Actor): (As Peter Pevensie) Aslan, we need your help.

Mr. LIAM NEESON (Actor): (As Aslan) I know. But understand, the future of Narnia rests on your courage.

Mr. GROSSMAN: I remember being very angry as a child and as an adult at Aslan. I always felt that here is a world that had a, you know, a proper god in it, a god who you could see, who would come down and change the course of events, but he didn't do it very much, and he would often let battles go on and events really spin out of control, and people would die before Aslan would step in.

Why would a God not help people in every possible way that he could?

VITALE: So in *The Magicians*, Quentin and his colleagues confront the god of Fillory, a ram named Ember, demanding to know why he let his people suffer.

The Magicians is Lev Grossman's third novel and his first fantasy book. Grossman says he used to care about being a literary novelist, but now all he cares about is telling a good story.

Mr. GROSSMAN: There's a strong tradition in the 20th century that is against storytelling. It is against plot. I wanted to move past that. I wanted to write something that was pure pleasure and pure storytelling. And I felt that in doing so, you didn't have to give up the kind of beautiful, lyrical, self-aware literary language that we associate with literary novels.

VITALE: Lev Grossman says now he's writing a sequel to *The Magicians*. He says magic is a perfect metaphor for the power of language, that words can cast a spell and change the universe.

For NPR News, I'm Tom Vitale in New York.

Source: Melissa Block and Tom Vitale, "Morally Complex 'Magicians' Recasts Potter's World," in *All Things Considered*, August 11, 2009.

SOURCES

"About Lev," Lev Grossman website, http://levgrossman.com/about/ (accessed December 22, 2014).

Agger, Michael, "Abracadabra Angst," in *New York Times*, September 8, 2009, http://www.nytimes.com/2009/09/13/books/review/Agger-t.html?_r=0 (accessed December 22, 2014).

Chipman, Ian, Review of *The Magicians*, in *Booklist*, Vol. 105, No. 18, p. 33.

Dobbins, Amanda, "The Magicians Trilogy Author Lev Grossman Explains His Cultural Influences," in *Vulture*, August 6, 2014, http://www.vulture.com/2014/07/lev-grossman-explains-his-cultural-influences.html (accessed December 22, 2014).

Donahue, Deirdre, "Lev Grossman Doesn't Conjure Up Much in *The Magicians*," in *USA Today*, August 17, 2009, http://usatoday30.usatoday.com/life/books/reviews/2009-08-17-grossman-review_N.htm (accessed December 22, 2014).

Donohue, Keith, Review of *The Magicians*, in *Washington Post*, August 1, 2009, http://www.washingtonpost.com/

wp-dyn/content/article/2009/07/31/AR2009073103670.html (accessed December 22, 2014).

Grossman, Lev, *The Magicians*, Viking, 2009.

Hand, Elizabeth, Review of *Cheek by Jowl: Essays, The Magician's Book: A Skeptic's Adventures in Narnia*, and *The Magicians*, in *Magazine of Fantasy and Science Fiction*, Vol. 117, Nos. 1–2, August–September 2009, pp. 40–49.

Lepucki, Edan, "Enchanted Connections," in *New York Times*, August 1, 2014, http://www.nytimes.com/2014/08/03/books/review/the-magicians-land-by-lev-grossman.html (accessed December 22, 2014).

"Lev Grossman Biography," in *Fantasy Book Review*, http://www.fantasybookreview.co.uk/Lev-Grossman/biography.html (accessed December 22, 2014).

"Lev Grossman–Summary Bibliography," in *Internet Speculative Fiction Database*, http://www.isfdb.org/cgi-bin/ea.cgi?125543 (accessed December 22, 2014).

Monir, Alexandra, "The Phenomenon of Paranormal YA," in *Huffington Post*, March 18, 2013, http://www.huffingtonpost.com/alexandra-monir/paranormal-young-adult-literature_b_2897861.html (accessed December 22, 2014).

Review of *The Magicians*, in *Publishers Weekly*, Vol. 256, No. 22, June 1, 2009, p. 29.

Rosenberg, Liz, "Where the Coolest Kids Are, Like, Undead," in *Boston Globe*, June 28, 2009, http://www.boston.com/ae/books/articles/2009/06/28/young_adults_feel_affinity_with_supernatural_characters_in_books/ (accessed December 22, 2014).

Strickland, Ashley, "A Brief History of Young Adult Literature," CNN, October 17, 2013 http://www.cnn.com/2013/10/15/living/young-adult-fiction-evolution/ (accessed December 22, 2014).

Vitale, Tom, "Morally Complex 'Magicians' Recasts Potter's World," in *All Things Considered, NPR Books*, August 11, 2009, http://www.npr.org/2009/08/11/111751056/morally-complex-magicians-recasts-potters-world (accessed December 22, 2014).

FURTHER READING

Feist, Raymond, *Magician: Apprentice*, Spectra, 1993.
   This is a readily available edition of the first novel in Feist's "Riftwar Saga," which, like *The Magicians*, describes the coming-of-age of a young sorcerer.

Lewis, C. S., "The Chronicles of Narnia," HarperCollins, 2010.
   This boxed set includes all seven of Lewis's novels set in the mythical world of Narnia. This series, which was originally published between 1950 and 1956, was an important source of inspiration for Grossman.

Thomas, Keith, *Religion and the Decline of Magic*, Penguin Global, 2012.
   Thomas follows the history of popular magic through its decline as the Protestant Reformation and scientific advances profoundly altered belief systems around the world.

Wilson, Mark Anthony, *Mark Wilson's Complete Course in Magic*, Running Press, 2003.
   With more than two thousand illustrations, this book offers detailed instructions teaching everything from basic card tricks to levitation tricks worthy of a professional magic show.

SUGGESTED SEARCH TERMS

Lev Grossman AND The Magicians

Lev Grossman AND allusions AND The Magicians

Lev Grossman AND literary critic

Lev Grossman interview

young-adult literature AND supernatural

magic AND coming-of-age stories

images AND Hudson River

O Brother, Where Art Thou?

2000

At the seventy-third Academy Awards, *O Brother, Where Art Thou?* was a nominee for the Best Adapted Screenplay category, having listed its source material as *The Odyssey*, the ancient epic poem by Homer. In reality, the story has only a few incidents and characters similar to ones in *The Odyssey*, though critics agree that the two works share a similar temperament. The film, written by Joel and Ethan Coen, involves three convicts who escape from a chain gang in Mississippi in the 1930s. Ulysses Everett McGill, played by George Clooney, is the Odysseus character, trying to return to his wife before she remarries. The other two convicts, played by John Turturro and Tim Blake Nelson, believe that they are going along to retrieve a fortune that Everett hid before going to jail, racing against time because his hiding place is soon to be flooded by the scheduled demolition of a dam. Along the way, the three meet modern-day equivalents of Homer's Cyclops, Sirens, and the blind prophet Tiresias, along with twentieth-century characters such as a gangster based on Baby Face Nelson, a musician whose story resembles that of bluesman Robert Johnson, a populist southern politician in the style of Huey Long, and members of the Ku Klux Klan. The Coen brothers (Joel directed it, as well as sharing the writing credit) also fill this comedy with sly social references and a hit soundtrack that achieved eight-times-over platinum sales and introduced the twenty-first century to folk music of the 1920s and 1930s.

© Touchstone | Universal | The Kobal Collection | Picture Desk

Released in 2000, *O Brother, Where Art Thou?* was nominated for an additional Academy Award for Best Cinematography by Roger Deakins, and Clooney won the Golden Globe award for Best Actor in a Comedy. The PG-13 film is available on DVD and Blu-ray from Touchstone Pictures.

PLOT SUMMARY

O Brother, Where Art Thou? begins with the sound of pickaxes breaking rock and the words that begin *The Odyssey*: "O Muse! Sing in me, and through me tell the story / Of that man skilled in all ways of contending, / A wanderer, harried for years on end...." After showing a 1930s chain gang of convicts working to pave a road by crushing stones into gravel, the film's three protagonists—Everett, Delmar, and Pete—appear in convict uniforms, chained together, running away through a field.

They steal and cook a chicken, then try to climb into the boxcar of a moving train. When they fail to board the train, they are approached by a man identified in the film's credits as the "Blind Seer," who is driving a railroad handcar along the tracks. He gives them a ride and predicts their future in a vague, cryptic way, much like Tiresias, the prophet who foretells Odysseus's future in *The Odyssey*. They are going to see wonderful things, he says, and find fortune, even though it will not be the fortune they seek. Though his language is mysterious, he does include the specific detail that they will see a cow on the roof of a cotton house, placing his predictions in the time and place of the story.

After they leave him, the three wonder how the Blind Seer could have known about the treasure they seek. Later in the film it will be revealed that they left prison to claim 1.2 million dollars, which Everett says he stole before being arrested. He has told them he hid the money near his home, which is to be flooded in a few days when the nearby dam is destroyed.

They go to the home of Pete's cousin, Wash Hogwallup. As they approach, Wash's son, a tiny boy holding a big rifle, threatens them, saying that he is supposed to shoot anyone who

FILM TECHNIQUE

- Each scene of this film is consistent with a warm golden look that reminds viewers of the sepia tone of older photography. Traditionally, cinematographers have altered the colors of films by adjusting the chemicals in which the film stock was developed. To give *O Brother, Where Art Thou?* its distinctive look, cinematographer Roger Deakins used computer effects to modulate the hue of each scene. Although common today, this digital color correction technology was new and radical in 2000, when the film was released. The outdoor scenes of the film were shot in the summer, in Mississippi, when most of the rural settings were rich with greenery: Deakins had to mute the colors in the computer lab in order to get the golden tinge that is consistent throughout the movie.

- The dolly shot, with a camera mounted on a rolling platform that moves on a stationary track, has been used in film for decades. The original use was to move closer and farther from the action. Many films have placed the actors in the middle of a circular track, so that the camera can move around them, giving viewers the entire range of the scene. At the end of the "sirens" scene in this film, there is a complicated camera movement that moves past the three main characters and the women they are with, seeming to curve behind each couple. This shot was achieved by putting the actors, as well as the camera, on moving platforms: they move toward the camera and rotate as the camera is moving toward and around them, giving the impression that they are floating.

- Throughout this film, the characters' faces are illuminated from off to the side. A strong example of this is the political rally scene, with Everett on the stage talking downward to Penny, seated on the main floor: the light comes up at his face and down at hers, indicating that they are both lit by a single source, giving the scene a sense of continuity. The same lighting technique is used when Big Dan talks to the convicts in the restaurant and when they sit in Cousin Wash's cabin after eating: in short, in any indoor scene. Some films flood actors with light, so that they are the focus of the scene, even though bright and all-pervading light is not realistic. *O Brother, Where Art Thou?* achieves a sense of reality by lighting characters the way that people experience each other in the real world, with light from one specific direction.

- The credits of this film are written in a type style that was popular in the 1930s, when the action takes place. As soon as they are done, the screen is filled with a shot split between cotton field on the bottom and sky above. It is clearly in black and white. The camera pans across the field to the chain gang, and as it does so, more golden brown develops out of the grayscale hue. When the camera shoots upward toward the convicts in their black-and-white uniforms, the sky, which had been gray up to that point, becomes a rich blue, and from then on the film is in color. This technique is similar to the way that one of the most popular films of the 1930s, *The Wizard of Oz*, combined black-and-white filmmaking with color. Viewers first get used to a movie's black-and-white view of the world, but then that older imagery is changed by the introduction of a more realistic look, indicating that an adventure is beginning.

comes from the bank serving papers. Later, as they eat a stew made from a horse that Wash slaughtered a week ago, Wash explains that his wife has run away but that he's keeping it a secret from the boy. On the radio is the "Pass the Biscuits Pappy O'Daniel Flour Hour."

The three fugitives are sleeping in the barn when they hear someone calling through a bullhorn for their surrender—Wash has betrayed them to the authorities for a reward. The police outside set the barn on fire, but when Pete throws a flaming torch back, it hits a police van filled with explosives, setting off fireworks. The little boy, trained to fight authority, drives into the burning barn in his father's car and drives the three convicts out the back door, off to safety. In the morning, they steal the car from the boy and send him home.

The car breaks down, so they go to a general store, where they find that delivery of a replacement part will take two weeks. While there, Everett tries to buy some Dapper Dan, the hair pomade (a styling product) that he likes, but that will take two weeks as well, so he just buys a pack of hairnets.

While sitting around a campfire in the woods, eating roast gopher, Everett, Pete, and Delmar see people in white robes going to the river for a baptism. Delmar races forward, is baptized, and declares that his sins have been washed away. Pete is baptized too. The camera cuts to Sheriff Cooley with hunting dogs finding the convicts' old campfire.

The convicts buy a car with a gold watch Everett stole from Wash. Driving along, they see a hitchhiker with a guitar. The pick up the hitchhiker, who introduces himself as Tommy Johnson. Tommy says that he sold his soul to the devil at midnight at the crossroads. The devil he describes—a white man with empty eyes, led by a dog—fits the image of Cooley, the sheriff in mirrored sunglasses who is pursuing them. Tommy tells them he is going to Tishamingo, a Missouri town, where he has heard a musician can make good money for playing on the radio.

At the radio station in Tishamingo, Everett introduces them as Jordan Rivers and the Soggy Bottom Boys. They sing the traditional song "Man of Constant Sorrow," and the delighted station engineer pays them ten dollars, a respectable sum at the time. As they leave, they pass Pappy O'Daniel, the station's owner and host of the popular "Pass the Biscuits Pappy O'Daniel Flour Hour." He is also the governor of Mississippi, running for reelection.

The fugitives are camping in the woods when they hear the sheriff and his men near their car. They escape down a dirt road by foot and are picked up by George Nelson, looking for the road to Itta Bena, another Mississippi town. He has them jump into the car as the law authorities pull up in the distance. As they speed away, Nelson laughs and fires his machine gun at the police. He takes the convicts and Tommy with him to a small bank in Itta Bena, which he robs with his machine gun. One of the customers recognizes him as Baby Face Nelson, an actual criminal from the Great Depression. Hearing that nickname, Nelson comes close to killing the fragile old woman who said it. Everett calms him, and they leave before the police arrive.

At the campfire that night, Nelson is depressed. He stumbles off into the woods, muttering his goodbyes, leaving the convicts his car and his stolen money.

A man goes to the radio station trying to contact the Soggy Bottom Boys. The recording they made there, he says, is popular all across the state.

Everett is driving down a dirt road when Pete perks up and insists that they stop. He springs from the car and runs to the nearby river, where three women are washing their clothes and singing. Mesmerized, Pete stumbles forward, introducing himself. The women continue to sing and to walk provocatively toward the men, offering them liquor in a jug. The men drink, and the liquor makes them pass out.

Later, Delmar wakes Everett. Pete is nowhere to be found. His clothes are laid out neatly on a rock, as if he has just melted from within them. Suddenly there is a pulsating inside of his shirt. Delmar is afraid until a toad jumps out of the shirt. He is then convinced that the women have turned Pete into a "horny toad" and that they must find a wizard to make him human again.

Delmar and Everett stop at a fine, upscale restaurant, placing the shoebox with the toad in it on the table. When they order, Everett takes out the money they were given by George Nelson, showing the waitress they can pay. A suspicious man with an eye patch, Big Dan Teague, sees them from across the restaurant. He approaches, introduces himself, and says that he has a business proposition for them. He persuades them to have their lunch packed as a picnic and to go with him out into a field. In the meadow, as they finish eating, Big Dan breaks a branch off of a tree. He beats Everett and Delmar with it and robs them. Before losing consciousness, Delmar tells him that Pete is the toad in the box. Big Dan takes the toad and crushes it in his hand, to the horror of Delmar, who believes he is crushing Pete.

The scene cuts to a night setting, where Pete, tied to a tree, is being whipped for information about Everett and Delmar. As Pete begs for mercy, the sheriff's men put a noose over a branch and prepare to hang him.

Everett and Delmar are riding in the back of a truck down a country road. They are discussing Pete's death. They drive past a chain gang of prisoners working on the road and notice Pete among them as they pass.

The scene cuts to Ithaca, Mississippi, where Homer Stokes is campaigning for governor against Pappy O'Daniel. Stokes campaigns with a midget, to illustrate his slogan that he is a "friend of the little man," and with a broom, to show that he is a reform candidate who will clean up politics. He introduces a group of girls to sing on stage, calling them the Wharvey girls.

Walking down the street, Everett hears this and is enraged: the girls are his daughters. He calls them over to them: they were told by Penny, their mother, that Everett was dead, killed by a train. They tell him that Penny is now being courted by Vernon T. Waldrip, whom they call "Uncle Vernon." Penny is at the Woolworth's store.

Everett goes to the store and finds Penny with more of their daughters, including one whom he did not even know about before he went to jail. When Vernon approaches, Everett is upset that he uses Everett's own brand of hair pomade, recognizing it by its distinctive smell. Penny mentions that she and Vernon are to be married the next day. Everett and Vernon fight: even though Vernon's stance is awkward he manages to punch Everett's nose a few times.

Everett and Delmar sit in a theater. The movie is running, and Everett is fuming about his wife's plan to remarry. A line of prisoners, chained together, is brought into the theater. Pete is one. He whispers to Everett that a trap has been set, that he should not go seeking the treasure.

In the prison barracks, Pete lies in his bunk at night. Everett comes to his side to free him. Outside, Pete explains that the women, whom he calls "sireens" (meaning "sirens," creatures of ancient Greek legends that had an irresistible

song), seduced him, tied him up, and then turned him in for a bounty. He tells them that under torture he revealed the secret of the 1.2 million dollar treasure. He feels so guilty that Everett reveals his own secret: there actually is no treasure. He was sent to jail not for stealing a large sum but for practicing law without a license.

Pete, enraged, struggles with Everett for lying to them, but they are interrupted by a group of Ku Klux Klansmen coming through the woods. They are carrying torches and pushing Tommy Johnson, who is black. Following the group is a three-man color guard carrying the Confederate flag. Everett, Pete, and Delmar jump the men and steal their Klan robes, enabling them to sneak into the lynching.

As the Imperial Wizard speaks to the crowd, one of the Klansmen—Big Dan Teague, identifiable by the fact that his hood has only one eye hole—suspects that something is wrong and goes to unmask the three convicts, who are wearing blackface makeup. In the ensuing commotion, the Imperial Wizard takes off his hood to see better: he is the political candidate Homer Stokes.

The three men run, throwing the Confederate flag back at the crowd. Stokes warns that the flag must not be allowed to touch the ground. Big Dan catches it. In the next moment, though, a huge burning cross, cut loose by the convicts, falls on Big Dan and crushes him.

At a Stokes political rally, Pappy and his employees talk about hiring Stokes's campaign manager, Vernon Waldrip, to run their own campaign. The convicts hide in an alley and looking for a way to sneak into the meeting so that Everett can talk Penny into leaving Vernon. They enter backstage with the musicians, disguised in long phony beards. Everett gets close to Penny and is making his case for winning her back when the band breaks into "Man of Constant Sorrow," the song the three recorded in Tishamingo. Everyone in the crowd is excited: the song has been a big hit on the radio. Everett, Pete, and Delmar sing while Tommy accompanies them on guitar, and the crowd realizes that this group is the fabled Soggy Bottom Boys that no one has been able to find.

Stokes shouts racist slurs about the group's being integrated and reveals that they have interfered with a lynch mob he was involved with. The crowd turns against him. Stokes becomes more and more heated, shouting out that the three men are convicted criminals, but the crowd boos him louder and pelts him with fruit until the Soggy Bottom Boys sing, lightening the mood. Seeing how popular they are, Pappy O'Daniel climbs up onstage and dances with them, to cheers from the audience.

Stokes is tied on top of a railroad rail and carried out through the crowd, literally "run out of town on a rail." Pappy, seeing his newfound popularity, uses the power of his office as governor to give the convicts a pardon for their past crimes.

Later, Everett and Penny explain that they are going to remarry. Penny refuses to do so, however, without her original wedding ring, which she believes is in a rolltop desk at the family's old cabin.

Everett, Pete, Delmar, and Tommy go there that night, but Sheriff Cooley and his men are waiting to ambush them. The lawmen have not heard about the pardon, and they have dug three graves for the convicts. At the last minute Everett bows his head and prays to God for mercy, confesses his sins, and promises to mend his ways. A trickle of water quickly turns into a tidal wave ripping through the forest, the results of the destruction of the dam.

The convicts pop up out of the water and grab onto a floating pinewood coffin. Everett, recently contrite, begins to take his usual know-it-all attitude when he looks over and sees a cow on a cotton house roof, as the Blind Seer predicted he would see. This silences him. They find Tommy floating on top of the rolltop desk.

The next day, in the sunshine, Everett and Penny walk down the street, trailed by their seven daughters. Penny looks at the ring Everett has retrieved and determines that it is not hers. She says she will not remarry Everett without her ring, even though it is at the bottom of the lake by now. Everett notes that finding a ring in a lake is a true heroic task. As the youngest of the girls passes the railroad tracks she looks over to see the Blind Seer on his handcar, rolling along, singing.

CHARACTERS

Blind Seer

In ancient Greek literature there is a blind prophet, Tiresias, who foretells the future. Odysseus encounters him in book 11 of *The Odyssey*,

with Tiresias advising him about how to communicate with the spirits of the underworld. In this film, the Blind Seer is an old man who is running a creaky handcar down the railroad tracks. He speaks in riddles to the three convicts at the start of their journey, telling them that they will see many unimaginable things, such as a cow on the roof of a cotton house. He tells them that they will find a fortune, but not the fortune they seek—which comes true in a way, as they do not find the 1.2 million dollars Everett said he had hidden, but they do all end up happy.

At the end of the film, the Blind Seer rides by as Everett and Penny and their daughters walk down the street. He is unnoticed by all except the youngest daughter.

Sheriff Cooley

Cooley is the name of the sheriff who chases the three escaped convicts. Throughout the film he wears mirrored sunglasses, hiding his eyes. Although he is an agent of the law, he appears to be more interested in taking revenge against the three for making him chase them than he is in justice. When they tell him that they have been pardoned, he makes no effort to determine whether there is any truth to the story, but dismisses it with a sadistic smile.

Boy Hogwallup

When the convicts approach Wash Hogwallup's farm, his young son shoots a shotgun at them. They later find out that the boy's mother has run away, but Wash, his father, has been hiding that fact from the boy. Later, when the authorities trap the convicts in a burning barn, the boy rescues them in his father's car, even though he can barely see over the steering wheel. They keep the car and send him back home. Pete, his uncle, angrily tells him to obey his father.

Pete Hogwallup

Pete is the most hotheaded of the three convicts. He loses his temper several times on their journey, such as when he finds out that Everett stole a gold watch from his cousin, even though he could as easily be mad at the cousin who betrayed them all. He can often be seen glaring incredulously at things that Everett or Delmar have said. He is an unintelligent and moody man who was raised in poverty. John Turturro, who plays Pete, is a familiar character actor who has appeared in nearly a hundred films and works frequently with the Coen brothers.

An exchange between Pete and Wash gives viewers a clue to the kind of man Pete is: when he asks Wash how he is, it prompts a response that Pete has "grown chatty." He is as uncomfortable with talking as Everett is comfortable talking.

Despite his temper, Pete is not a dangerous convict. He is genuinely sorry to Everett for having confessed, under pain of torture, and told Sheriff Cooley about their plans. Moments later, when he hears that the treasure they have been hunting never existed, he announces how much this has hurt him: he would have been set free if he had served two more weeks of his sentence, but now he is likely to serve fifty more years. He is enraged, but his anger disappears as quickly as it rose when he sees that their friend Tommy Johnson needs help.

Wash Hogwallup

Soon after escaping from the chain gang, the three convicts go to the home of Pete's cousin Wash to have their shackles removed. Wash lives a life of poverty and bad luck: his wife has left him, and his stories to Pete about relatives include suicide, foreclosure, and diseased cattle. He is eating a stew made from his horse. The convicts go to bed in Pete's barn and wake to find that he has called the authorities so that he can collect the reward on them.

Tommy Johnson

Tommy is a musician the convicts meet and travel with. The story that he explains about himself is part of the legend of Robert Johnson, an American blues musician. Johnson's story is similar to the one Tommy tells about himself in the movie; he was said to have sold his soul to the devil at the crossroads of Highways 49 and 61 in Clarksville, Mississippi, one midnight to gain astounding guitar prowess.

The fact that Tommy is a black man in Mississippi in the 1930s does not bother the convicts, but it does affect how people look at the group. The Ku Klux Klan tries to lynch him at a Klan gathering. Later, when the Soggy Bottom Boys are singing, Homer Stokes (secretly the Klan's Grand Wizard) accuses the group of being "misgenated," or racially mixed. (Stokes intends to say "miscegenated"; his error in misusing this ugly but scientific-sounding term is a signal to the audience of Stokes's own ignorance.) The fact that Tommy can end up with a position in the governor's administration in segregated Mississippi is one element of the film's comic fantasy tone.

The Little Man

The unnamed Little Man does not have any dialog in this film; his only lines are campaign slogans shouted from a moving truck. He is a midget who campaigns for the Stokes campaign, an embodiment of Stokes's campaign promise to stand up for the little man. He carries a broom, to illustrate Stokes's promise to clean up government corruption.

Penny McGill

Penny, Everett's ex-wife, is played by Holly Hunter. The character's name creates another connection to the story of Odysseus, who was struggling to return to his wife Penelope. Like Penelope of Homer's tale, Penny is in danger of being lost to another man. Her engagement to Vernon T. Waldrip is what spurred Everett to break out of jail and return to her.

Penny is angry at Everett for being sent to jail and leaving her. She has told their seven daughters that their father is dead, and she is raising them under her maiden name, Wharvey. At first she refuses to talk to Everett, but she warms to his charm. She is hard-headed, though: before agreeing to marry him again, she insists that he must retrieve her original wedding ring from their old home, situated in the valley that is slated to be flooded. Later, when it proves to have not been there at all, she lightly shrugs off the fact that Everett, Pete, and Delmar risked their lives for it.

Although Everett finds Penny's stubbornness and her arbitrary decisions to be frustrating, he knows better than to disagree with her: when she ends an argument by saying that she has counted to three, he accepts that whatever she has demanded is the way things have to be.

Ulysses Everett McGill

McGill, called "Everett" throughout the movie, is the film's main character, played by first-billed star George Clooney. The character is based on the main character of *The Odyssey* ("Ulysses" is the Roman form of the name "Odysseus").

Everett escapes from prison with Pete and Delmar, to whom he was shackled. He tricked them by telling them that he has hidden over a million dollars that he stole in an armored car theft and that they must get to his home in four days, before the valley is flooded for a rural electrification project. Later, though, he admits that there never was any such treasure. He made up that story in order to reach home because his ex-wife, Penny, was about to remarry. He was not in jail for armored car theft, he confesses, but for practicing law without a license.

Everett claims the right to be the leader of the trio of escapees because of his verbal skills. He is the one who believes he can negotiate with the law officers who surrounded the barn they are hiding in. He sprinkles his speech with words of Latin origin and often takes a patronizing tone with the others, explaining to Delmar and Pete the importance of keeping a positive attitude or his belief in the greatness of the industrial future. His insistence on using a particular kind of hair pomade, Dapper Dan, shows a self-image about his grooming that matches his verbal overreach.

Like Homer's Odysseus, Everett is trying to get home. His wife is being courted by someone else. He is beset by challenges, as Odysseus was, even though, like Odysseus, he has been assured by an oracle (in his case, the Blind Seer) that all will come out all right. Like Odysseus he is a proud man, and his pride is what nearly leads to his downfall until, at the last minute, when the sheriff's men are about to hang him and put him in a grave, Everett begs God for help to see his daughters again.

George Nelson

George Nelson is a stereotypical gangster of the 1920s and 1930s. He is based on the real-life criminal known as Baby Face Nelson and at one point is even called "Baby Face," to which he reacts with dangerous violence. The real Baby Face Nelson, whose name was Lester Joseph Gillis, often used the alias "George Nelson." He was born in 1908 and died in 1934 (three years before this film takes place) in a gunfight with the police in Illinois.

The George Nelson in the film suffers severe mood swings. When he is being chased by the police he is giddy with enthusiasm, shooting at them as he races away. In the quiet around the campfire that night, however, he is so sullen and morose that he stands up and wanders off into the darkness, muttering that the convicts and Tommy can have his money from the bank robbery. Near the end of the film, they see him being led in handcuffs down the street by a mob, and he is once again exuberant, shouting to the three convicts on the sidewalk that his execution will ensure his greatness.

Menelaus "Pappy" O'Daniel

Played by veteran character actor Charles Durning, Pappy O'Daniel is the governor of Mississippi in this film. He is in the middle of a reelection campaign and is losing to the reform candidate, Homer Stokes, until he sees the opportunity to associate himself with the popular music group the Soggy Bottom Boys.

Pappy is a businessman who made his fortune from selling flour. Sacks of flour bearing his face are seen throughout the movie. His company sponsors "Pass the Biscuits Pappy O'Daniel Flour Hour" on the radio, which broadcasts traditional country music. (A comparison can be made to the long-running Public Broadcasting System radio show *A Prairie Home Companion*, which is itself "sponsored" by a made-up product called "Powdermilk Biscuits.") When he is out of the public eye, Pappy is angry and argumentative, frustrated with the slow-wittedness of his campaign staff.

His first name, Menelaus, is mentioned only once in the film. It is the name of the King of Sparta, married to Helen, whose abduction started the Trojan War, from which Ulysses was returning when he underwent his adventures.

Delmar O'Donnell

Delmar, played by Tim Blake Nelson, is the slowest-witted member of the three escaped convicts, but also the kindest. He constantly comments on the action with some understatement, as when George Nelson displays wildly psychotic mood swings and Delmar innocently wonders, "Whaddya suppose is eating George?" After being seduced and drugged by the Sirens and waking up to find a toad inside of Pete's clothes, Delmar is naïve enough to believe that the toad is an incarnation of Pete, transformed through magic.

One time that Delmar takes initiative is when they come across a group baptism in a river: Everett calls him to stay back, but Delmar races forward, eager to be cleansed of his sins. After that he talks of being redeemed and forgiven for crimes that he had previously denied—he admits that his earlier position was a lie and brags that his baptism makes him forgiven of that lie, too.

Delmar wants to use his share of the money to buy back the family farm, on which the bank had foreclosed, a common scenario during the Great Depression.

Homer Stokes

Stokes is running for governor, campaigning as a reform candidate against the incumbent, Pappy O'Daniel. He is winning. His promises are that he will clean up the corrupt government and that he will stand up for the little person. Secretly, Stokes is the Imperial Wizard of the local Ku Klux Klan chapter. He leads a Klan rally that tries, but fails, to lynch Tommy Johnson. When he sees that the three convicts are popular singers aligned with the O'Daniel campaign, Stokes tells the crowd that he has seen them at a Klan lynching, assuming that the crowd views things the way he does: instead, he is run out of town on a rail.

His first name is a reference to the poet behind *The Odyssey*.

Big Dan Teague

John Goodman plays Big Dan Teague, a Bible salesman with an eye patch. His large stature and his single eye make him reminiscent of the Cyclops, a fierce creature in *The Odyssey* who attacks Odysseus's men and crushes them until they manage to blind him. In this story, he sees Everett and Delmar eating in a restaurant, in possession of a bundle of money. With them is a shoebox holding the toad that Delmar believes is Pete, transformed, but that Big Dan assumes must hold something valuable. Big Dan invites them out to a secluded area, promising them a business deal. Once they are away from everyone else he beats them with a club he has pulled off of the tree and robs them. His final act in this scene, squeezing the frog to death in his hand, echoes the way the giant Cyclops killed the men who were with Odysseus.

Later, at the Ku Klux Klan meeting, Big Dan recognizes the three convicts. He chases them, but a gigantic burning cross—the symbol of the Klan—teeters over and crushes him.

Vernon T. Waldrip

Waldrip is engaged to marry Everett's ex-wife, Penny. Penny sees him as a good, stable influence for their girls. When Everett returns to town, the two men fight. Though they both have ridiculous fighting stances, Waldrip is able to punch Everett in the nose a few times.

He is also the manager for Homer Stokes's gubernatorial campaign. Since Stokes is winning, his opponent, Pappy O'Daniel, goes to a Stokes rally to hire Waldrip away from him. He is outraged when Waldrip says that it would not be moral to change sides, Soon after, Everett and his friends, performing as the Soggy Bottom Boys, shift popular sentiment toward the O'Daniel campaign, and Waldrip is no longer needed by either side.

THEMES

American Culture

O Brother, Where Art Thou? centers on the basic American belief in equal opportunity. In older cultures with rigid social classes, the chance for a person to rise from poverty to wealth, from rags to riches, may exist, but such a rise is very unlikely. Shifting from one social class is simply not expected in most established societies, while the belief that a person can be born poor and end up rich is a defining trait of America's national identity. This film is filled with images of the downtrodden, of people in the agricultural South during the Great Depression, from convicts being used as slave laborers on a chain gang to the list of troubles that have beset Pete's cousin Wash. The adventure is driven, though, by the promise that each of the three convicts will be able to walk away with his share of the stolen armored car money that Everett says he has hidden. It is their "fortune": the promise that they will no longer suffer in poverty.

Over the years there have been countless mechanisms promising to raise the impoverished up to wealth overnight, from lotteries and other forms of gambling to the widespread recognition to be gained from winning reality competitions. All are based on the American democratic principle that the only thing that separates the rich from the poor is money, not any inborn social worth.

Greek Mythology

This film is only loosely based on the story of *The Odyssey*—the facts of Ulysses Everett McGill's journey home do not align with Homer's story of Odysseus, but the stories are similar in tone. Everett is not a king returning from war but a convict

TOPICS FOR FURTHER STUDY

- The Coen brothers used the basic form of *The Odyssey* to tell a story that takes place in the Great Depression. Decide on a time in history that interests you, read about it, and write your own story using different aspects taken from Homer's tale. Present it to your class with an explanation of the Homeric elements you used.

- John Ford's movie *The Grapes of Wrath*, released in 1940, is considered a significant artwork about life in the Depression. Watch Ford's movie, based on the classic novel by John Steinbeck, and choose the one scene you think most looks like a scene the Coen brothers would have done. Read about some other movies of theirs and consider their characteristic style. Present the scene from *The Grapes of Wrath* to your teacher and classmates, and explain what you think defines a Coen brothers scene.

- Some movies of the early 1930s showed gangsters as folk heroes and sympathetic losers struggling against the corrupt social structure that had caused the economic collapse. By the end of the decade, though, the Hayes Production Code, followed voluntarily by the Hollywood studios, allowed gangsters to be shown only as ruthless thugs who were mentally and morally unstable. Read about the Hayes Production Code online. Although such a restrictive code could not be applied across the board to movies today, choose which elements of the code you think studios should adopt today and write an essay explaining why you think these standards would be more useful than harmful.

- T Bone Burnett, the musician who compiled the best-selling soundtrack for this film, recorded the songs featured in it with traditional folk musicians before the film was even shot. Put together a collection of ten or fifteen songs you think are the best in any given musical style and then write a script treatment or outline for a script that would incorporate those songs into its story.

- Irene Latham's young-adult novel *Leaving Gee's Bend* has been praised for its realistic presentation of the rural South during the Great Depression. Its story concerns a ten-year-old girl, Ludelphia Bennett, who needs to travel across the county for medicine for her mother. The circumstances and the tone could not be more different from those of this film, but Latham shows the same fascination with the culture of the time that the Coen brothers had. Read this book and keep track of the ways that Ludelphia, who is black, is treated similarly to the white adult criminals in *O Brother, Where Art Thou?* Write an explanation about which of these two views you think is more realistic and why.

- One of the greatest movies ever made adapting a Greek myth to modern circumstances is Marcel Camus's 1959 film *Black Orpheus*, which presents the ancient Greek story of the lovers Orpheus and Eurydice as if it took place during Carnival in modern Rio de Janeiro. Read the myth before watching the movie and then make a list of aspects that had to be changed to make the story work in the more modern setting. Put together a montage of scenes that you think violate the feeling of the myth and present them with an explanation of how you think it could have been handled better.

---

returning from prison, where he was sent for practicing law without a license: still, his desperation to regain his family, if not his homeland, is the same. He is not a leader who is responsible for a ship full of subordinates but instead is in the company of two peers—still, his slight intellectual advantage makes Everett responsible for them the way Odysseus was responsible for his men.

Penny McGill, unlike Penelope of *The Odyssey*, is not in the position of being forced to choose from a group of eligible suitors, pressured to marry one. She does not live in doubt about her husband's fate because she knows that he is alive, although she does not know that he is out of prison. The economics of the time urge her toward remarrying for the sake of her seven daughters in much the same way that Penelope was pressured to remarry to bring a king to Ithaca.

The Sirens of the epic poem lure men to their death, while the "Sireens" of the film capture Pete for reward money. The Cyclops of the poem is a giant monster who kills men in a senseless rage, but the Cyclops of the film, Big Dan Teague, is a dishonest Bible salesman who robs them, though he does smash the toad that Delmar thinks is Pete with just as much monstrous rage as his mythological counterpart.

Overall, the film adopts the mood of Homer's epic more than the story of it, using images of the Great Depression in the South to show modern audiences what makes the Greek myths believable at heart.

Rebirth

Rebirth is one of the most abstract themes carried throughout *O Brother, Where Art Thou?* In Christian religions, baptism is traditionally used to represent rebirth, with a person being doused in water that represents the amniotic fluid that surrounds a baby in the womb. Early in this film, baptism is played for comic effect: Pete and Delmar race enthusiastically to participate in an outdoor group baptism at a river, with Delmar later claiming that his crimes—including the sin of lying about just how many crimes he has—have been washed away from his soul.

Everett's baptism is less literal. Just as he is about to be killed by Sheriff Cooley's men, he absolves himself of his sins, renouncing his biggest sin, pride. In what he believes is his last moment of life, he puts himself in the hands of God, admitting that there is a higher authority that has the power to forgive him. By coincidence, a torrent of water races through at that very moment, saving his life and giving him the chance to be with his daughters that he prayed for. It happens to be water like the symbolic cleansing water of baptism, and it washes away his crimes, his criminal thoughts, and the men

who would not forgive him, allowing Everett to be reborn to a clean, new start.

Populism

Populism is a strain in American politics in which politicians appeal to the majority of voters, ordinary people in the lower and middle classes, by identifying themselves as belonging to their ranks. A politician might come from a wealthy family, but as long as that person can convincingly present himself or herself as someone the voters would like to sit down and drink a beer with, as someone who feels the pain of those economically suffering, then that politician has a great chance of connecting with voters on an emotional level. Populism was understandably a strong political strategy during the Great Depression, when poverty was widespread and those who had managed to maintain their wealth were distrusted.

In this film, Homer Stokes is ahead in the race for governor of Mississippi because of his populist campaign. His gimmick of traveling around with an actual little person serves to make the point that he supports "the little man," a common expression for the poor, the downtrodden, those with no political power. Americans have traditionally seen themselves as being scrappy underdogs who must fight hard to be victorious, and Stokes does a good job of framing himself in this role until Pappy O'Daniel, the incumbent governor, shows that he is like the common people in an instant, when he dances and sings with the popular Soggy Bottom Boys.

Racism

This film provides an unrealistic, stylized view of the Ku Klux Klan, a white supremacist group at the height of its popularity in the American South in the late 1800s and early 1900s, dedicated to keeping white Protestants in power and often using force, including murder, to attain its goal. The formality of the Klan meeting in the group, with chanting and group choreography and the centuries-old symbol of the cross set aflame, reflects the mindset of such a group: following such crowd behaviors allows the members to believe that they are in touch with ancient traditions. While they used the tactic of bullying and intimidation, Klansmen believed that there was something noble and intellectually elevated about their racism. The power of music and group motion almost obscures the idea that they are there to kill a man, Tommy Johnson, because of the color of his skin.

American racism is idealized near the end of the film when Homer Stokes—up to then the leader in the governor's race—reveals that he is affiliated with the Klan (though he does not say the group's name, there is little doubt that anyone in the South in the 1930s would know what "secret society" he is referring to). Once his racism is revealed, the crowd turns against Stokes, hauling him off like a criminal the way that bank robber George Nelson is later hauled off down the street. In actuality, membership in the Ku Klux Klan would not be a political disadvantage at that time and place. By showing the crowd turn on Stokes, the Coen brothers are viewing that world from a modern perspective.

STYLE

Nature

Much of *O Brother, Where Art Thou?* takes place outdoors, in woods and by rivers and on dirt roads. It makes sense for a story about escaped convicts who are trying to avoid being caught, but it also serves to give the story a universal feel, linking it closer to its source, *The Odyssey*. A story that takes place in indoor settings would be more closely linked to the specific society where it is set, reflecting the architecture and therefore the tastes and style of its time. While the outdoor settings tap into the universal feel of nature, they also allow viewers to indulge in a little nostalgia for a time before interstate highways and malls and housing tracts paved over many of the settings presented in the film.

The biggest event in the film is, of course, the torrent that roars through at the film's climax. This flood serves as a reminder of the awesome power of nature: the dam that is destroyed is freeing the water to power electricity turbines, which would eventually bring electricity to the rural areas presented here, giving them the chance and reason to civilize nature.

The Power of Music

The music chosen for the soundtrack of this film is an important element in setting the film's tone. The songs were specifically chosen to evoke a particular time and place—the American South during the Great Depression—and the film uses them to give the story a deeper meaning than the

Coen brothers can do with their comic script. Songs like "O Death" or "In the Jailhouse Now" or "I Am a Man of Constant Sorrow" serve to remind viewers that the Depression was not as silly as it is depicted in this comedy, that in fact people wrote heartfelt songs at the time to give a voice to their fears, their hopes, and their unhappiness.

When they can, the Coen brothers work the music into the script. Some of the songs are heard on the radio and even sung by the convicts themselves on broadcasts. Some are heard in passing—at a political rally or at a revival meeting. Even when an occasion would not call for music, though, the film bends reality to include it. The Klansmen at their meeting in the woods and the Sirens washing clothes in a stream each move and sing with much more coordination than anyone could realistically expect under such circumstances. In these scenes, the Coen brothers are evoking the standards of movie musicals, which often follow their own unique logic, weaving music and dance into the characters' actions without any attempt at realism.

CULTURAL CONTEXT

The Ku Klux Klan in the 1930s

The Ku Klux Klan is a significant presence in this film. It poses a threat to Tommy Johnson, who is adopted by the central group as one of their own, and later, when Homer Stokes makes his membership in the group known (he is actually the local chapter's leader, its Imperial Wizard), it is the cause of his downfall. For many Americans, the Ku Klux Klan has represented a lethal threat, the embodiment of racial and religious intolerance, though it is easy to see how, by the start of the twenty-first century, it had been diminished in relevance enough to be represented as just another joke.

The group began during Reconstruction, the period after the end of the Civil War. In the southern states, this period marked a significant increase in white citizens' fear of black citizens. For one thing, the blacks who had been slaves suddenly had unprecedented political recognition, and there was always the suspicion that they would use their gains against the people who had held them in slavery. At the same time, white southerners had just lost a long, costly war and felt vulnerable. In this environment, the

© *Touchstone | Universal | The Kobal Collection | Picture Desk*

Klan, a group of masked vigilantes who were willing to intimidate blacks with violence and death, were supported by many. As laws fell into place to suppress the social equality of blacks—the infamous "Jim Crow" laws that restricted black citizens' rights to vote, to buy property, to use the same businesses or even the same hospitals as whites—the Klan's popularity dimmed.

The second era of the Klan began in the 1920s. The group's familiar cry for racial "purity" was expanded to resistance against immigration and especially Catholics and Jews. During this time, the group was estimated to have reached about four million members, giving it its historic height of popularity soon before this film takes place. In the 1930s, however, membership was diminishing because of media attention. The more people knew about the Ku Klux Klan, the more limited this secret society became.

In the 1960s, the civil rights era, the Klan had one more resurgence. Again, violent tactics drew national attention to their message of divisiveness, making the Ku Klux Klan known throughout the land as a group promoting hatred. As racial equality took root in the last quarter of the twentieth century, the Klan's relevance receded. According to the Anti-Defamation League, an organization founded in 1913 to fight religious injustice, the Klan may be experiencing another wave of popularity in the years after *O Brother, Where Art Thou?* was produced,

using such politically hot issues such as immigration, gay marriage, and crime and merging their message with other white supremacist groups such as the neo-Nazis.

Message Films

This film is associated with *Sullivan's Travels*, by director Preston Sturges, because its title is taken from a serious film that a character in that movie wants to make. He feels that it is better to make an important statement about the world through film than to make a comedy. During the 1930s, many filmmakers used their craft to tell uplifting or insightful stories.

The Depression is usually counted as beginning with the global stock market crash that began on October 29, 1929, a day often referred to as Black Thursday. Through the course of that day, the stock market lost 11 percent of its value, but by the end of the day much of that had been regained, so the net loss was only 2 percent. It had been falling significantly through September and October, though, and analysts saw Black Thursday as a sign of a loss of investor confidence. By the following Tuesday the market was indeed down 11 percent from where it had been the week before; it continued to lose value for the next three years, eventually reaching its low point on July 3, 1932, when the Dow Jones Industrial Average (a representative selection of stocks) was down 90% from its high on September 2, 1929. The losses in the stock market meant losses throughout the economy. By

1932, thirteen to fifteen million Americans were unemployed—roughly 20 percent of the country's population.

The economic troubles affected almost all Americans. The film industry suffered, even though sixty to eighty million people still went to the movies every week. Movies were a source of entertainment that people on limited incomes could still afford, with ticket prices around thirty-five cents. Many of the movies that Hollywood put out at the time offered escapist fantasies for downtrodden audiences, such as screwball comedies and extravagant musicals—things that could help people forget their woes. But there were also serious movies that were more direct about offering their viewers hope in troubled times. Films like Charlie Chaplin's *Modern Times* or Frank Capra's *Mr. Deeds Goes to Town* (both from 1936) were comedies, but comedies that made a point about the unfairness of the political system that had made life difficult for good, honest, poor people. Directors like Capra, Sturges, and King Vidor knew that with so many poor people going to the movies, films about poor people would be popular, and so messages about economic injustice were a natural fit with the entertaining movies the studios made.

CRITICAL OVERVIEW

When it was released in 2000, most film critics found *O Brother, Where Art Thou?* to be a pleasing, if inconsequential, movie. There were critics who found it to be less accomplished than its immediate predecessor in the Coen brothers' catalog, *The Big Lebowski*, a detective film parody that has become a cult classic over the years due to a strong central performance by Jeff Bridges. Some critics compared *O Brother, Where Art Thou?* unfavorably to that film, and some simply did not feel that it was an honest effort by the filmmakers, but the majority were impressed with it as a fun-filled triumph of style over content.

One of the most extreme examples of a supporter is Peter Bradshaw, who reviewed the film for the *Guardian*, a British newspaper. Bradshaw was impressed with the film's humor and wit: "Simply," he summarizes in his introductory paragraph, "this is a film which is impossible to dislike, and moves with an easy, approachable

swing. . . . It's a film to tap your feet to, in every sense." Bradshaw's review ends with high praise, saying the movie "is made with marvellous clarity and fluency, and Joel and Ethan Coen attain a comic simplicity that other film-makers can only dream of." A review at the *Time Out* website lists, among the film's strong points, its Cinescope filming and the plot twist of the flood at the end. The author writes, "Great dialog, superb 'Scope camerawork from Roger Deakins, and a genuinely wondrous deus ex machina are among the delights."

In *New York*, Peter Rainer expresses admiration for the movie's sincerity. "In most of the Coens' movies, it seems as if the brothers are up in the clouds taking potshots at their people," he writes, "but here they seem more indulgent and affectionate." He adds at the end of his review, "This is the Coen brothers' most emotionally felt movie, and that's not meant as faint praise."

One reviewer who sees the film quite differently is Jonathan Rosenbaum, of the *Chicago Reader*. Rosenbaum praises the filmmakers' previous two movies, but he calls *O Brother, Where Art Thou?* "their worst." Characterizing it as "a piece of pop nihilism," he accuses the Coens of being "so contemptuous they can't even come up with characters."

Roger Ebert, another reviewer from Chicago, also found himself underimpressed by this film, though, unlike Rosenbaum, he acknowledges its better qualities. "All of [the scenes he examines in his review] are wonderful in their different ways," he writes in summary, "and yet I left the movie uncertain and unsatisfied. I saw it a second time, admired the same parts, left with the same feeling." He goes on to explain his mixed emotions: "I had the sense of invention set adrift; of a series of bright ideas wondering why they had all been invited to the same film." Even the reviewers who found the film to be unsuccessful found elements to like, while those who were fans sometimes threw themselves into praising it with unbridled enthusiasm.

CRITICISM

David Kelly

David Kelly is an instructor of creative writing and literature in Illinois. In the following essay, he dismisses the idea of O Brother, Where Art Thou? *as*

WHAT DO I SEE NEXT?

- A serious look at a similar situation, and possibly an inspiration for this film as it was for many others like it, can be found in director Mervyn LeRoy's 1932 classic *I Am a Fugitive from a Chain Gang*, starring Paul Muni. The situation of being wrongly convicted and escaping is distinctly not played for laughs, while the film typifies the sort of message of social justice that was common in Warner Brothers films during the Great Depression. It is available on DVD and Blu-ray from Warner Home Video and is not rated.

- The Coen brothers took the title *O Brother, Where Art Thou?* from the title of a film that the character John L. Sullivan wants to make in Preston Sturges's social satire *Sullivan's Travels*, released in 1941 by Universal. In that film, Sullivan is a profitable comedy director who longs to make films with social meaning. Like this film, *Sullivan's Travels* is a road picture: Sullivan takes off to travel the country to get in touch with the poor people that his Hollywood lifestyle has blocked him from. Joel McCrea stars as Sullivan, and Veronica Lake stars as an actress who longs to be in one of his films. This classic comedy, unrated, was released as one of the prestigious Criterion Collection series of DVDs in 2001.

- Many of the Coen brothers' films are praised by critics for their varying levels of comic inventiveness. The 2013 film *Inside Llewyn Davis* shares a special bond with this film because of the significance of the music on its soundtrack. The story follows a musician in the 1960s folk music revival in New York's Greenwich Village through a few days of struggling to work, pursue his art, and stay ahead of creditors. Like all of their films, it was written by Joel and Ethan Coen and directed by Joel. This film, rated R for offensive language, was released on Blu-ray and DVD by Sony Pictures.

- Meredith Salinger and John Cusack star in Walt Disney Pictures' 1985 PG-rated road trip movie *The Journey of Natty Gann*, a story about a teen girl who travels across the country during the Depression to reunite with her father, riding freight trains and sleeping in barns, with the companionship of a wolf. Salinger won the Best Actress Award and the film was nominated for Best Picture, both from Young Artist Award.

- The political situation in this film has echoes of the story of the famous Huey Long, populist governor of Louisiana in the 1920s and 1930s. Long's story was the basis for Robert Penn Warren's novel *All the King's Men*, which was adapted to two acclaimed films. The unrated 1950 version, directed by Robert Rossen, won Academy Awards for star Broderick Crawford and several costars and the Golden Globe for Best Picture, while Steve Zaillian's PG-13 2006 remake, starring Sean Penn, Jude Law, and Kate Winslet, brings the story alive for modern audiences.

- The story of blues musician Robert Johnson, who claimed to have sold his soul to the devil for musical skill, is the basis of *Crossroads*, a 1986 film. The film tells of a road trip, with Ralph Macchio (then famous for his *Karate Kid* movies) playing a music student obsessed with the Johnson legend: he goes from New York to Mississippi with a bluesman played by Joe Seneca who claims to know Johnson's secrets. Although Macchio was the top-billed star, the focus of the film is on African American culture in the South in the early twentieth century. This film is rated R for implied teen sexuality and drinking and is available on DVD from Sony.

"THE 1930S INTRODUCED SYNCHRONIZED
SIGHT AND SOUND IN 'TALKING' MOTION
PICTURES, YIELDING A NEW SENSE OF CINEMATIC
REALISM. THE NEW TECHNOLOGY DREW
FILMMAKERS THE SAME WAY THAT MODERN
TECHNICAL ADVANCES SUCH AS 3D HAVE
LURED TODAY'S DIRECTORS, WHO HAVE SEEN
OPPORTUNITIES FOR STORYTELLING OPEN
BEFORE THEIR EYES."

an adaptation of The Odyssey, *focusing instead on the joy with which the Coen brothers fill their comedy with time-honored clichés from Depression-era Hollywood.*

The credits of the Coen brothers' 2000 film *O Brother, Where Art Thou?* are preceded by the opening lines of *The Odyssey* and are followed by a declaration that the film was based on Homer's epic poem. Because of this, viewers tend to look for *The Odyssey* in the film, and they often end up disappointed. This film is no more an adaptation of Homer than *The King's Speech* (about a British king who overcomes stuttering to be an inspiration to his people in World War II) is an adaptation of Shakespeare's *Richard III* (about a man who overcomes his physical deformity to take the British throne through treachery and deceit). Even by Hollywood's low standards, famous for transforming soul-searching and thought-provoking material with the crowd-pleasing "happy ending" and for making more movies about writers such as Ernest Hemingway and Truman Capote than about the works those writers wrote, the idea of calling *O Brother* a film "based on" *The Odyssey* is quite a stretch.

If the connection between the two works strains credulity, though, the claim about their relationship does its job perfectly. This *is* a comedy, after all. It is actually a comedy of broad range, one that finds humor in subjects large and small, from its social satire of the Ku Klux Klan aping the ritualistic march of the Wicked Witch of the West's minions to the shtick of veteran

character actor Stephen Root twitching his way through a performance as a blind radio producer to the fall-down slapstick of George Clooney, chained to two other men, yanked backwards off of a moving boxcar while he's in the middle of smooth talking some rough-looking hobos. By these meager standards, the inappropriateness of saying this film is "based on" an enduring work of literature cannot fail. The more the film is unlike its supposed source material, the funnier the overstatement of that claim becomes.

There are echoes of *The Odyssey* throughout *O Brother, Where Art Thou?*, but they are just slight reminders of Homer's work. On its own, the film could never explain the epic poem. The film does, for instance, have a man struggling to return to his home, a wife (actually, and significantly, an ex-wife) being courted, a one-eyed big man, and a group of attractive women who lure men. The lead character's unused first name is Ulysses, and another character is named Homer, though there is nothing poetic about him. Rather than focusing on the Homeric references that might just be jokes sprung from inflated pomposity, it is more satisfying and worthwhile to examine the film's true inspiration: the Great Depression, as seen through the lens of Hollywood motion pictures.

The Depression itself, as the subject of a comedy, would be—well, just as depressing as the idea sounds. It would count on audiences to have an extended bout of mean-spiritedness, to laugh time and again at the misery of others. The film indulges audiences in this style of humor briefly, when Cousin Wash helps Pete catch up with how his life has been going of late: his wife has left him, and a cousin lost his home to foreclosure and committed suicide; Uncle Ratliff's livestock were killed or rendered unproductive by anthrax, and he lost a son to mumps; and Wash himself is eating a horse that he slaughtered last week. It is funnier on-screen than it is in print, but no amount of ignorant hick accent could keep such abject misery entertaining for long. This film is not laughing at the Depression, though: it is laughing at the clichés that have been handed down since the Depression, that persisted for generations of film audiences but by the time of the film were beginning to fade from our cultural consciousness.

The film is rich with signifiers about the Depression, the kinds of things you can reliably expect to see in almost any movie about that era, and the Coen brothers display them with the kind of delight that can only come from someone who knows and delights in movies. The first category of these is the objects and characters that no movie about the Depression can do without. Hobos, for instance. There were unattached travelers before and after the ruined economy gave so many people no place to go home to, from the refugees of the Civil War to the communal youth culture of the 1960s, but the Depression yielded a hobo mystique that has, if anything, grown in stature since its day. Any mention of the hobo will lead inevitably, of course, to the art of hopping on and off of trains and climbing into open boxcars, as that is remembered by movies as the definitive method of hobo transportation. Entire films, from *Emperor of the North* to *The Journey of Natty Gann*, have been centered on boxcar riding. It is surprising, then, that it appears only in *O Brother* in the scene mentioned earlier, when the one convict who cannot make it onto the moving train pulls the others to whom he is shackled off into the embankment. Despite the fact that they do not travel by rail—probably because the story remains somewhat localized in backwoods Mississippi—and they do not carry bindle sticks (those sticks with round bundles wrapped in bandanas) over their shoulders, these three are certainly hobos. They travel the back roads, catch rides when they can, share what they have with others in their condition, and eat whatever they can.

It is in the category of food that the film draws off of Depression clichés with the most enthusiasm. Did anyone ever actually steal a pie that was cooling on a windowsill? For that matter, did anyone ever actually leave a pie on an unwatched windowsill to cool? It doesn't matter if it was done once, a thousand times, or never: the image is familiar from thousands of movies and cartoons, and a turn-of-the-century Coen brothers movie about the Depression would never leave it out. Similarly, the scene of the convicts scrambling around after a live chicken was fairly common, most closely echoing a similar scene in *Gone with the Wind* (1939), in which the great comic Eddie "Rochester" Anderson, as Uncle Peter, stalks a scrawny rooster to serve the starving household a Christmas dinner after the war. A later scene in *O Brother, Where Art Thou?* shows the three men eating their catch over an open campfire, a common scene in Depression movies. Not as common is when they later feast

on a gopher: gopher meat was not really a comic device of Depression comedies, but "gopher" is certainly a funny word, especially the way Tim Blake Nelson, as Delmar, presents his offer to Clooney's Everett.

There are other elements of the film that recall the 1930s with fondness. The railroad handcar, for instance, may be lost from memory because we simply are not a culture as dependent on trains and train tracks, but that only serves to make them relics that mark their time, like a mosquito frozen in amber or a mastodon sunk into a tar pit. Placing the Blind Seer on a handcar is as much a nod to Laurel and Hardy short features as it is to the actual times, a sign that the Coens were looking more at movie history than at either reality or *The Odyssey* when they put this story together. Also, a film from the times would not be complete without a folk legend bank robber, so the story draws a real person, George Nelson, into its mix in improbable circumstances, giving him a manic-depressive personality that is not even meant to resemble anything real. The film's Baby Face Nelson is more fascinated by his own reputation than anyone around him seems to be, but it is a fact that there was indeed a cult of gangsters in the early part of the Depression that grew out of the general resentment toward a legal system that had left many, many people hopeless.

The 1930s introduced synchronized sight and sound in "talking" motion pictures, yielding a new sense of cinematic realism. The new technology drew filmmakers the same way that modern technical advances such as 3D have lured today's directors, who have seen opportunities for storytelling open before their eyes. At the same time, the Depression put a financial check on Hollywood's advances and pushed that storytelling toward verbal, not visual, techniques. With restraints on their budgets but with both sound and visuals together at their disposal, a new generation came to the fore. They understood film in a different way than silent movie directors had, and they told stories that reflected the wishes and dreams of those turbulent times. The language of Depression-era films, from trains to gangsters to hobos to political rallies, came to define the era, even as those symbols became increasingly clichéd from one generation to the next.

O Brother, Where Art Thou? does not tell the story of *The Odyssey*. Nor does it tell the story of

© *Touchstone | Universal | The Kobal Collection | Picture Desk*

the Great Depression. It does tell the story of what film-literate people at the end of the century—specifically, Joel and Ethan Coen— think of the legacy of the Depression, as it was crafted by the Hollywood studios. It is as artificial as any adaptation from a classical source is bound to be, though maybe just a little more reverent in spirit.

Source: David Kelly, Critical Essay on *O Brother, Where Art Thou?*, in *Novels for Students*, Gale, Cengage Learning, 2016.

Douglas McFarland

In the following excerpt, McFarland examines the use of allusion in O Brother, Where Art Thou.

. . . Although the climax of *O Brother* occurs with the Tennessee Valley Authority flooding the McGill ancestral "homeland," the picaresque set of adventures turns toward its conclusion at the Klan rally that McGill and his fellow escapees have infiltrated in order to rescue Tommy (Chris Thomas King), the African American blues musician they had met and befriended earlier in the film. But more importantly, through its rich collection of allusions to other texts, the scene provides its audience with the most striking and most unsettling set of comic incongruities in the film. These incongruities not only satirize the hooded Klansmen but also challenge the audience to move beyond the aesthetic pleasure of the film's postmodern wit. What has been called the "engaged reinvention" of popular mythologies that the Coen brothers demonstrate in *The Hudsucker Proxy* (1994) here takes on the form of a set of radical and disturbing contradictions.

Allusions to *The Odyssey*, Busby Berkeley, Leni Riefenstahl, the Three Stooges, Robert Johnson, and *The Wizard of Oz* (Victor Fleming, 1939) all appear in the episode. Although these references play off one another in both obvious and subtle ways, the scene is grounded in a particular moment in American history: the activities of the Ku Klux Klan in the South in the 1930s. This is, of course, a particularly dark episode in the history of the republic and one that taken in isolation would generate some combination of outrage and guilt in the typically liberal audiences that the films of the Coen brothers might attract. The rich array of allusions, in short, cannot be separated from a historical context that elicits moral condemnation.

> THE COENS ARE MISCHIEVOUS BOYS; IN
> THIS INSTANCE, THEIR MISCHIEF CHALLENGES
> THE COMPLACENCIES OF THE POSTMODERNIST
> AESTHETIC."

It is this historical grounding that undermines a postmodern reading of the episode. The assemblage of popular mythologies, pop culture references, and classical allusions does not, in this case, constitute what Fredric Jameson and others term "pastiche." Unlike parody and satire, pastiche, according to Jameson, is "the cannibalization of all styles of the past, the play of random stylistic allusion[,]" and thus constitutes a "neutral practice," an artistic and cultural form that has been emptied of any ethical perspective and "amputated of satiric impulse." The postmodern pleasure of pastiche is the pleasure of recognizing references, so that engaging a text becomes a game of identification. Moreover, through this consumption of cultural signs, there emerges in the audience a sense of belonging to an "exclusive community," one detached from both traditional socioeconomic classifications and conventional ethical codes. Membership in this sophisticated coterie group, which many in the audience of a Coen brothers film might expect, is sabotaged, I think intentionally, by the context of a Klan lynching of an African American. There is quite simply no possibility of avoiding the historical setting of the episode and the ethical response that that setting demands. Although the scene in question does expose the audience to a heterogeneous grouping of aesthetic styles and allusions, these do not occupy a neutral space devoid of normative values and of what Jameson refers to in this context as "real history."

The most obvious consequence of this grounding is that the engaged and directed point of view of satire replaces the neutrality of postmodern wit. The scene opens with McGill and his two fellow travelers looking down from under cover at a Klan ceremony, which they soon learn is a lynching. The members of the Klan are marching in synchronized patterns that immediately call to mind a Busby Berkeley set piece. The Klansmen are, therefore, being mocked as silly men, in silly outfits, and in silly dance formations. Like Satan's band of devils in *Paradise Lost* who are compared to a swarm of insects, the self-importance of the Klansmen is deflated through a visual simile. The satire is reinforced through a Homeric parallel. The charlatan Bible salesman (John Goodman) who has robbed and beaten McGill and Delmar (Tim Blake Nelson) now shows up at the rally. His role as the uncultured and violent Cyclops of *The Odyssey* mocks the office of Grand Cyclops of the Klan.

The set of allusions taken together suggests, however, something more sophisticated than satire, something that relies on irreconcilable comic incongruities within that set of allusions. Perhaps the most outrageous and resonant reference in the set piece is to *The Wizard of Oz*. The rescue of Tommy from the hands of the Klan visually evokes the rescue of Dorothy from the Wicked Witch of the West. The three escapees take the parts of the Scarecrow, the Tin Man, and the Cowardly Lion. The Klan becomes the army of the Wicked Witch. This creates a jarring incongruity, one that is intensified by the contextualization of the allusion outside its original historical setting. Although *The Wizard of Oz* was made in the final years of the Depression and is in some sense a typical thirties "road" picture, its presence in the film will resonate with most of the audience in the context of the fifties, sixties, and seventies. For many years before the advent of home video technology, the film was annually shown on television and became an anticipated event, an almost ritualized staging in the living rooms of American families. An allusion to the film generates not simply a memory but nostalgia for "a privileged lost object of desire." In an impish and insidious manner, the Coens have uprooted this warm memory and relocated it to a 1930s Klan rally and execution.

The effect of the allusion on the audience is threefold. First, there is the pleasure in simply identifying the allusion, the sense of belonging to the sophisticated coterie group I mention above. Secondly, there is the pleasure in witnessing a childhood fantasy defeat evil. It is the Scarecrow, the Tin Man, and the Cowardly Lion who rescue Tommy from the clutches of the Klan and flatten its Cyclops. The innocence of a childhood fantasy proves stronger than racism.

But thirdly, the allusion creates a disturbing and ironic incongruity: that between the dark recess of Mississippi in the 1930s and the living rooms of postwar baby boomers and their children.

Kierkegaard is instructive in understanding the effect if not the purpose of this irony. He asserts in the *Concluding Unscientific Postscript* that "irony is the *confinium* [boundary] between the aesthetic and the ethical." The relationship between these two stages and the role that irony plays in the advancement from the former to the latter is treated extensively by Kierkegaard in *Either/Or*. In part I, a young man argues for the aesthetic point of view in a series of heterogeneous papers on topics as diverse as music, drama, crop rotation, and eroticism. In discussing these subjects, he asserts that one must distance oneself from commitment to any one particular form of artistic expression or to one exclusive human relationship. The aesthete is dimly aware of the existential contradictions of life, but he would avoid them by continually seeking out new experiences, preoccupying himself with the surfaces of life, and generally playing "shuttlecock with all existence." "Everything in life," says the aesthete, "is regarded as a wager. The more consistently a person knows how to sustain his arbitrariness, the more amusing the combinations become." The aesthete must constantly be changing his orientation to the world.

Part II of *Either/Or* consists of two letters written to the young man by a judge who represents the so-called ethical point of view. He challenges the self-styled aesthete not necessarily to adopt a specific ethical perspective but to act in the world, to overcome his indifference. "It is not," he explains, "a matter of choosing between willing good or willing evil as of choosing to will." The aesthete should, in short, cease to be the "plaything for the play of his arbitrariness." The task of the ethicist is to make the young man confront the comic contradictions of the human condition, the ironic incongruities between the body and the soul, the finite and the infinite, the necessary and the free, which inform the human condition.

Jameson's understanding of the postmodern world and the individual enmeshed within its plethora of signs is uncanny in its similarity to Kierkegaard's understanding of the young aesthete and his need for new and changing experiences. Jameson asserts, "What has happened is that aesthetic production today has become

EVERETT DISCOVERS MUSIC CAN FREE SOCIETY FROM UNJUST SHACKLES, THANKS IN LARGE PART TO RECORDS AND RADIO."

integrated into commodity production generally: the frantic urgency of producing fresh waves of ever more novel-seeming goods...at ever greater rates of turnover." It is precisely this consumer of aesthetic commodities whom the Coen brothers confront in their staging of the Klan rally. They do it by fashioning a disturbing comic contradiction that defies the consumptive pleasures of their audience. The filmmakers' role is that of the judge in *Either/Or* who demands that the young, sophisticated aesthete confront the ironies of the human condition. Unlike *The Hudsucker Proxy*, whose comic perspective interrogates socioeconomic conditions of a specific era, the ironic incongruities of *O Brother* act against its own audience. The Coens are mischievous boys; in this instance, their mischief challenges the complacencies of the postmodernist aesthete....

Source: Douglas McFarland, "Philosophies of Comedy in *O Brother, Where Art Thou?*," in *The Philosophy of the Coen Brothers*, edited by Mark T. Conrad, University Press of Kentucky, 2009, pp. 47–50.

Erica Rowell

In the following excerpt, Rowell discusses the significance of music in O Brother, Where Art Thou?.

... While the movie allusions tend to focus on the law and its unjust chokeholds, *O Brother*'s in-story songs often hook into other main themes—such as religion, faith, poverty, and especially freedom. Soulful music courses through nearly every scene, becoming another primary chain and a freeing agent. The result is a newfangled musical, where characters sing and occasionally dance. It's not Rogers and Hammerstein. It's Coen and Coen...and T-Bone Burnett.

Joel Coen calls the movie "a valentine to the music" in the soundtrack's liner notes. "Music became a very prominent feature very early on in the [script]writing, and it became even more so as we went along," he explained. Avoiding clichés, the selections from America's diverse songbook directly play on the film's main themes. The weave of tunes spanning several decades gives *O Brother* charm and staying power while defining the setting's strife and joys. But then, ever since *Blood Simple*'s upbeat murder cleanup accompaniment helped add the neo to the noir, the Coens' exceptional musical choices have been a stylistic hallmark.

Thematic relevance and an organic plot fit are prime factors for the Coens' music tracks. In *Raising Arizona* Ed's choice of the murder ballad "Down in the Willow Garden" to soothe her son after a nightmare subtly—and riotously— impugns her maternal instincts. *Barton Fink* uses Stephen Foster's "Old Black Joe," about a slave seeking release, as a centerpiece for Hollywood slave Bill Mayhew. *The Hudsucker Proxy*'s "Memories Are Made of This" underscores its panoply of old movie references. *Fargo* introduces the perpetually trapped Jerry Lundegaard with Merle Haggard's lyrics about big city freedom. And before *The Big Lebowski* cranks up its rock-and-roll fantasy, the cowboy-inflected "Tumbling Tumbleweeds" sets in place nostalgic underpinnings with a wink to L.A.'s frontier days. With the notable exception of "Danny Boy" in *Miller's Crossing*, the Coens' music avoids the obvious while amplifying themes spot-on.

Music is so embedded in *O Brother*'s story line that song titles filter into dialogue. Big Dan's pun of "Dough, Re, Me" references Woody Guthrie's song about money's undue power as well as *The Sound of Music*. Homer Stokes, who wants to preserve white culture and heritage, ironically alludes to Louis Jordan's jivey "Is You Is or Is You Ain't My Baby?" British rock and roll great Led Zeppelin, a group steeped in American blues, gets an obvious plug with Sheriff Cooley's "stairway to heaven." In the next breath, he quotes a famous funeral hymn from about a hundred years earlier: "We Shall All Meet By and By." The casual, at-times ironic, song-dropping demonstrates the staggering effect music has on culture—it crosses geographic boundaries, crisscrosses time periods, infuses everyday life, and reflects the zeitgeist.

Song is *O Brother*'s ultimate connector, as the opening work song and the "O muse, sing in me" line suggest. From there, Everett's journey

examines American mores through the interplay of music and society. As he and his band of brothers find common ground among their fellow man, mixed musical styles emerge that alternately poke fun of, reflect on, and offer hope for society. Ultimately, song, like comedy in *Sullivan's Travels*, helps produce racial healing and proves more generally to be a powerful, vital antidote for society's ills. It lifts people's burdens, bridges racial and other divides, and reflects the life force of culture.

The opening uneven playing field between haves (the law) and have-nots (the laboring cons) is divided by race and class. Its rhythms are too. The ballad's brutal authoritative vendetta—a story line imitated in the plot—communicates that the deplorable system in place would make anyone, in the words of Marvin Gaye, want to holler. Archivist Lomax elaborates:

> In most societies the individual can look to organized authority as in some sense beneficent or protective, . . . But increasingly, the laborers of the Deep South, floating from camp to camp, often from prison to prison, came to feel that they had nowhere to turn. There was, as usual in black tradition, a musical response. It came in the sudden emergence of the lonesome holler, and later the blues, notable among all human works of art for their profound despair.

The blues come a bit later in *O Brother*, too, first with the black handcar driver and then more full on with Tommy. His "Hard-Time Killing Floor Blues" (performed by actor Chris Thomas King) sketches the contours of the conditions he and his fellow drifters face: "Times is harder than ever been before/And the people are driftin' from door to door/Can't find no heaven." As with "Po' Lazarus," *O Brother*'s blues set the stage for racial and class issues and provide comfort and escape until the divide is bridged.

The division of labor depicted in the emblematic chain gangs sets in place the key struggle between Capital and Labor, which informs so much of Everett's adventures—and the authorities' abuse of power. Sturges invokes the political battle in over-the-top strokes at the start of *Sullivan's Travels*, but as both his film and *O Brother* make clear the grotesque abuse of Capital over Labor in the name of capitalism needs fixing. Satire is the main method of attack, and *O Brother*'s buoyant title sequence announces that mordant modus operandi.

The whimsical "Big Rock Candy Mountain" paints *O Brother*'s hobo Neverland in utopian hues that belie widespread privation: "In the Big Rock Candy Mountain, all the cops have wooden legs/And the bulldogs all have rubber teeth and the hens lay soft-boiled eggs." By sugarcoating the hobo life's hardships with tantalizing lies, Harry McClintock's 1928 song offers up in substance and feel a sneak preview of Everett's manipulations. The stolen money awaiting the cons is just as fantastic. Their gullibility paints them—especially the goofy, innocent, neophyte Delmar (who confesses in the movie theatre he's a virgin)—as "punks."

> Many of the old-time hoboes took along with them everywhere a "punk"—a younger tramp who, according to the rules of the road, had to wait on his master hand and foot, to die for him if required. Many of these boys were lured away from their farms and small towns by tales as fanciful as that told in this favorite hobo chantey. "The Big Rock Candy Mountain."

The song also points to money woes, a main source of *O Brother*'s conflict.

Economic issues are humorously echoed at the campaign rally. As Everett tries to impress an unimpressed Penny with his latest employment scheme—posing as a dentist—the Soggy Bottom Boys perform "In the Jailhouse Now." The backdrop is perfect. In the vein of "The Big Rock Candy Mountain," Jimmie Rodgers's song about "Ramblin' Bob who used to steal gamble and rob" drolly describes a rogue like Everett, who, short on money and willpower, has fun but ends up behind bars. Penny's whole reason for the divorce is that she doesn't need a jailbird husband; she needs a reliable provider. Everett's musical skills solve this problem.

As the trio's quest gains speed, music develops the plot, elaborates the themes, and charts societal change. Where the first two songs illustrate largely divergent musical styles, many subsequent selections illustrate a cross-pollination of influences. The blend of blues, bluegrass, "old-time," and Appalachian mountain music—all sounds of the American South—underscores both racial and social harmony in a diverse culture. Even in the days of segregation "white and black traditions certainly interacted, both in musical styles, as well as instruments—whites borrowed blues and banjos from blacks; blacks borrowed ballads and fiddles from whites."

Ultimately, equal rights and job opportunities are antidotes to the hard times codified in the movie's songs. When Everett sings his theme song, the exuberant reception to "A Man of Constant Sorrow" represents the tipping point on racial attitudes and the opportunity for decent employment. Like Sully noting the importance of comedy through the cartoon. Everett discovers music can free society from unjust shackles, thanks in large part to records and radio....

Source: Erica Rowell, "*O Brother, Where Art Thou?*: A Song," in *The Brothers Grim: The Films of Ethan and Joel Coen*, Scarecrow Press, 2007, pp. 164–67.

SOURCES

"Baby Face Nelson Biography," Biography.com, http://www.biography.com/people/baby-face-nelson-9542636 (accessed December 10, 2014).

Bowen, Jerry, "What Movies Mean to Us in Hard Times," CBS News, February 22, 2009, http://www.cbsnews.com/news/what-movies-mean-to-us-in-hard-times/ (accessed December 18, 2014).

Bradshaw, Peter, Review of *O Brother, Where Art Thou?*, in *Guardian*, September 14, 2000, http://www.theguardian.com/film/2000/sep/15/culture.reviews (accessed December 16, 2014).

Buchanan, Kyle, "From Shawshank to Skyfall, How Master Cinematographer Roger Deakins Got These Ten Shots," Vulture.com, February 21, 2013, http://www.vulture.com/2013/02/how-master-dp-roger-deakins-got-these-10-shots.html (accessed December 19, 2014).

Ebert, Roger, Review of *O Brother, Where Art Thou?*, RogerEbert.com, December 29, 2000, http://www.rogerebert.com/reviews/o-brother-where-art-thou-2000 (accessed December 16, 2014).

"The Great Depression," History Channel website, http://www.history.com/topics/great-depression (accessed December 18, 2014).

"Ku Klux Klan," Southern Poverty Law Center website, http://www.splcenter.org/get-informed/intelligence-files/ideology/ku-klux-klan (accessed December 18, 2014).

"The Ku Klux Klan Rebounds," Extremism in America, Anti-Defamation League website, http://archive.adl.org/learn/ext_us/kkk/intro.html (accessed December 18, 2014).

Love, Patrick, "October 24th 1929: Stock Market Crash Hits Banks, Firms, Economists," in *OECD Insights*, Organisation for Economic Co-operation and Development, http://oecdinsights.org/2011/10/24/october-24th-1929-stock-market-crash-hits-banks-firms-economists/ (accessed January 5, 2015).

O Brother, Where Art Thou?, directed by Joel Coen, Touchstone Pictures, 2000, DVD.

Rainer, Peter, "Primal Screens," in *New York*, http://nymag .com/nymetro/movies/reviews/4187/ (accessed December 16, 2014).

Review of *O Brother, Where Art Thou?*, in *Time Out London*, http://www.timeout.com/london/film/o-brother-where-art-thou (accessed December 16, 2014).

"Robert Johnson Biography," Biography.com, http://www .biography.com/people/robert-johnson-9356324 (accessed December 10, 2014).

Rosenbaum, Jonathan, Review of *O Brother, Where Art Thou?*, in *Chicago Reader*, http://www.chicagoreader .com/chicago/o-brother-where-art-thou/Film?oid = 1050960 (accessed December 16, 2014).

FURTHER READING

Leiter, Andrew, "'That Old-Timey Music': Nostalgia and the Southern Tradition in *O Brother, Where Art Thou?*," in *Southerners on Film: Essays on Hollywood Portrayals since the 1970s*, edited by Andrew B. Leiter, McFarland, 2011, pp. 62–74.

> In this essay, Leiter looks at ways in which this film, though it takes place in the South, fights against the traditions of the "Southern" film. Instead of reflecting the time in which it takes place or the traditions from which it draws, it instead reflects the new, modern South that has grown to be homogenized.

McFarland, Douglas, "Philosophies of Comedy in *O Brother, Where Art Thou?*," in *The Philosophy of the Coen Brothers*, edited by Mark T. Conard, University of Kentucky Press, 2012, pp. 41–54.

> Unlike reviews in magazines, which take a superficial look at a film's structure and sometimes give a little background behind its social significance, McFarland digs deeply into the cultural underpinnings that can be found in

the film. This essay is not easy reading, but it is rich with references and allusions.

McKenna, Christine, "Joel and Ethan Coen," in *The Coen Brothers: Interviews*, edited by William Rodney Allen, University Press of Mississippi, 2006, pp. 163–87.

> This interview was conducted for *Playboy* magazine in 2001. Because of the timing, the brothers talk much about *O Brother, Where Art Thou?*, as well as many of their earlier movies. As can be expected from two writers, the Coens are witty, insightful, and open in discussing their works, and any interview with them is worth reading in order to appreciate their view of the world.

Mottram, James, *The Coen Brothers: The Life of the Mind*, Brassy's, 2000.

> This book serves as a good biography of the writing/directing team in their formative years in Minnesota, significant to the sense of nostalgia permeating their films. It is limited by being published in mid-career, in 2000; *O Brother, Where Art Thou?* is the last film Mottram examines in the book.

SUGGESTED SEARCH TERMS

O Brother, Where Art Thou? AND The Odyssey

Coen brothers AND Great Depression

Coen brothers AND Clooney

O Brother, Where Art Thou? AND 2000 film

O Brother, Where Art Thou? AND folk music

Great Depression AND modern cinema

Great Depression AND comic views

The Odyssey AND film adaptation

Coen brothers AND southern politics

Coen brothers AND religious salvation

Rebecca

1940 When Daphne du Maurier's novel *Rebecca* was published in 1938, it was an instant best seller. Almost immediately, studios wanted to make a movie of it. Alfred Hitchcock, a middle-aged British film director at the time, read the book before it was published and wanted to film it, but he could not afford to buy the rights. The rights instead went to David O. Selznick, a powerful Hollywood director, who brought Hitchcock to America for the first time to film this novel. Hitchcock went on to direct some of the best-known films ever made, including *North by Northwest*, *Rear Window*, *Psycho* and *The Birds* (also adapted from a du Maurier story). While *Rebecca* was shooting, Selznick was putting the finishing touches on one of the greatest block-busters in Hollywood history, *Gone with the Wind*.

Rebecca has touched generations of audiences because of its near-perfect blend of romance and mystery. The story involves a poor girl working in Monte Carlo, where she meets a wealthy, handsome man and falls in love with him. They marry, and she returns with him to his home, Manderley, one of the great English estates. As she struggles to understand her new social role, she finds that she understands even less about her new husband and suspects that he has never gotten over the death of his first wife, Rebecca. Questions about Rebecca's death arise, leading to questions about who she really was and who is trying to bury the past.

Maxim de Winter was played by Laurence Olivier, fresh from his turn as Heathcliff in *Wuthering Heights*. His new wife is played by Joan Fontaine in an Oscar-nominated performance. Nobody plays *Rebecca* in the film: her presence is only that of a memory.

PLOT SUMMARY

After the opening credits, *Rebecca* begins with a shot of the moon, with clouds crossing it. The camera goes through the gates of Manderley, a huge estate that the narrator mentions dreaming about at the start of the film as well as the start of the novel. The camera moves up a long driveway, overgrown with vegetation, until it shows the big mansion in shadows. The narrator admits that she can never go back to Manderley again, which leads to the start of the story.

The story begins with Maxim de Winter, a man in his mid-forties, shown standing on a cliff near Monte Carlo, in the south of France, looking down into a churning, hostile sea far below. The narrator, a girl of about twenty, thinking that he is about to jump, calls out to him to stop. He sends her away, but the spell that drew him to the edge is broken, and he walks away from the cliff.

The narrator sits in the lobby of the Princess Hotel with Mrs. Van Hopper, the woman she works for. Mrs. Van Hopper recognizes Maxim de Winter as an internationally known socialite, and she calls him over. De Winter is obviously interested in the narrator, so he joins them for coffee and tries to bring the girl into the conversation Mrs. Van Hopper is monopolizing. After he leaves, Mrs. Van Hopper complains that the narrator was trying too hard to work herself into the discussion, making the young woman self-conscious. As they enter the elevator Mrs. Van Hopper mentions the death of de Winter's wife.

Later, while Mrs. Van Hopper is ill with a cold, the narrator has lunch in the hotel dining room alone. She knocks over a vase, dousing her table with water. De Winter, also dining alone at the same restaurant, insists that she leave her wet

FILM TECHNIQUE

- Most of this story is told from the perspective of the second Mrs. de Winter, with the camera showing her in almost every scene. When de Winter is describing the night Rebecca died, however, the film director faces a difficult situation: it is a scene that the second wife did not witness, but it could not be shown in flashback, because that would entail having an actress play Rebecca, ruining her ghostly mystique. Director Alfred Hitchcock solved this problem by showing the scene from Rebecca's point of view: as de Winter narrates the event, the camera pans around the room, starting with the cigarette-filled ashtray he mentions. It shows the things Rebecca would have seen. Although the camera does not show Rebecca, de Winter moves as if she is there, and at the moment when he describes her falling to the ground and fatally striking her head he backs against a door, slamming it, creating a loud sound to match the sound of her head hitting the floor.

- This film begins as the novel does, with the narrator announcing that she dreamed of Manderley. This little bit of exposition from some unspecified time in the future helps establish the dreamy mood of the story. The only other time the film uses voice-over is during the dream sequence, about thirteen minutes from the start: the protagonist tosses fitfully in her bed as Mrs. Van Hopper's explanation of Rebecca's life and death rings in her ears. This dream shows just how much the character feels threatened by the memory of Rebecca. Visually, the scene consists of nothing but Fontaine's face, with ominous shadows thrown across it, but Hitchcock uses the slightly distorted, echoing words spoken by Mrs. Van Hopper to show how deeply Rebecca's death haunts her, even though at this point in the story there is no hint of foul play.

- Most viewers would agree that Mrs. Danvers is a frightening character, even though she usually speaks as if she wants to help the new Mrs. de Winter. One way that Hitchcock made her menacing was by limiting her motions. Judith Anderson, the actress who plays Mrs. Danvers, is very seldom seen walking in this film. She does not enter a room, she is just there, at the protagonist's side, without warning. Hitchcock is not implying that she has any supernatural powers, at least not on any logical level, but omitting basic motion from what viewers experience of the character makes the audience feel that there is something about her that defies logic, making her more menacing than she otherwise would be.

- Franz Waxman's soundtrack for this film is generally melodramatic, with violins establishing the gothic mood of each scene. This mood is usually in the range of melancholy or fear. The music stays in the background, unnoticed. Once in a while, though, the music will swell up and make itself prominent. The most conspicuous example occurs when Maxim de Winter tells his wife that she is wrong for thinking he still loved Rebecca when actually he *hated* her: the music punctuates "hated" with a loud blare of horns and strings. Another example of the stinger is the way the music swells up when the girl comes to nervously say goodbye to de Winter and he asks if she wants to go to Manderley: when she finally realizes that he is proposing to her, she stumbles backward, and there is a blast of violin music. By today's refined tastes, even a film that uses soundtrack music liberally would be over-explaining if it used a musical stinger to draw attention to a dramatically important moment.

table and join him at his. When she explains that she does some painting and that there is a place she likes to paint by the sea, he offers to drive her there in his car. At the sea they talk freely, delighting in each other's company. She tells him she once bought a postcard of a beautiful house she later found out was Manderley, the home he says he lived in all his life. When she mentions someone who drowned nearby, he becomes nervous and insists on taking her home.

They start dating each other while Mrs. Van Hopper is ill, without telling her. At one point the narrator overhears Mrs. Van Hopper telling her nurse about the first Mrs. de Winter, Rebecca, who drowned tragically.

Mrs. Van Hopper receives news that her daughter is to marry and she makes plans for herself and her companion to leave for New York immediately. The companion searches around the hotel for de Winter, to say goodbye. Eventually, she finds him in his room. He gives her a choice: leave with Mrs. Van Hopper or marry him. Then he phones for Mrs. Van Hopper to come to his room and he tells her of their wedding plans. When he leaves, Mrs. Van Hopper accuses the narrator of being tricky and underhanded.

After a happy marriage and honeymoon in Venice, de Winter and the narrator, now Mrs. de Winter, go to Manderley. She is apprehensive, intimidated by living in such a grand place, especially when she sees the entire staff assembled to meet her. Mrs. Danvers, the head of the housekeeping staff, is particularly cold and frightening. She later finds out that Mrs. Danvers arrived at Manderley with the first Mrs. de Winter—Rebecca. She shows her the door of Rebecca's room and tells her that it is the most beautiful room in the house, with the best view.

Frank Crawley, who manages the estate for de Winter, arrives while Mrs. de Winter is having breakfast alone on her first morning at Manderley. He is friendly and open. When de Winter and Crawley leave, Mrs. de Winter is awkward and uncomfortable with the servants. She feels herself being pressed into doing everything just as Rebecca would have. When she enters the room Rebecca used after breakfast for writing letters, Rebecca's dog, Jasper, gets up and walks out. Someone phones asking for Mrs. de Winter, but the narrator does not imagine that this is about herself: she says that Mrs. de Winter is dead. When she drops a porcelain figure of

Cupid from the desk, she is so self-conscious that she hides the pieces: later, Mrs. Danvers accuses Robert, a butler, of having stolen or broken this figure, so she has to admit that she did it, causing her great embarrassment.

De Winter's sister Beatrice and her husband, Giles Lacy, come to visit. At lunch, Giles slips by saying that it is a good thing Mrs. de Winter does not sail, realizing almost immediately that he has inadvertently made a reference to Rebecca's death by drowning.

Beatrice turns out to be quite friendly, telling Mrs. de Winter in private that de Winter is particular about clothes and hair, which makes her feel diminished because he never paid any attention to hers. Beatrice also warns her about de Winter's terrible temper, which Mrs. de Winter has not seen either.

Mr. and Mrs. de Winter take a walk down to the beach. When Jasper runs away Mrs. de Winter follows him, to de Winter's annoyance, and finds a furnished cottage. At the cottage is Ben, a slow-witted local fisherman who makes cryptic references to someone who has gone into the sea. When Mrs. de Winter returns to de Winter, he is furious. He shouts at her for going to the cottage and makes her cry. She takes a handkerchief from the pocket of the raincoat she is wearing, only to find it is Rebecca's.

Mrs. de Winter has a chance to talk about Rebecca with Crawley. She finds out that she drowned, that her body was not found for a few months, and that de Winter was the one who traveled to a town up the coast to identify her corpse. When she asks what Rebecca was really like, he answers that she was the most beautiful creature he ever knew.

Some time later, Mrs. de Winter comes to de Winter wearing a new, fashionable dress and a different hairdo, thinking that he might be more interested in her. They watch movies of their honeymoon together but are interrupted with news of the broken Cupid figure. She ends up apologizing to the staff, and de Winter is angered by her, saying that she is acting more like a maid than like the mistress of the house. He becomes enraged when she suggests that he married her because she is simple and plain and there would be no gossip about her—the word "gossip" sets him off. She says that she will go away if he is unhappy with their marriage, but he says that he cannot answer that question. The home movie is still rolling in the projector, showing them happy and natural on their honeymoon in Italy.

One day when de Winter is out of town, Mrs. de Winter sees someone in the window of Rebecca's room. She hears Mrs. Danvers coming down the stairs with someone and hides in the library, but the man, after leaving through the door, comes to the library window and talks to her. He is Jack Favell. It is clear that Jasper the dog knows him, and he is familiar enough with Mrs. Danvers to call her "Danny." He is charming but menacing. When he leaves he asks Mrs. de Winter to not mention his visit to her husband.

With great hesitancy Mrs. de Winter goes to the room they just left, Rebecca's room. As she is looking around, Mrs. Danvers comes in. She shows Mrs. de Winter Rebecca's personal items, handling them with such adoration, bordering on obsession, that it frightens the younger woman.

After returning to her study, Mrs. de Winter sits at her desk and has a revelation. She rings for Mrs. Danvers and tells her to take all of Rebecca's things out of the study. When Mrs. Danvers objects, saying that these are Mrs. de Winters's things, she stands up for herself and boldly asserts that now *she* is Mrs. de Winter, not Rebecca. She promises to keep quiet about Jack Favell's visit.

Mrs. de Winter asks to have a costume ball, the way they used to at Manderley when Rebecca was there. While she is sketching possible designs for her costume, Mrs. Danvers suggests that she go as one of the people in the portraits that line the hall. She even directs her to one, saying that it is Mr. de Winter's favorite painting. On the night of the ball, she dresses in private and comes downstairs feeling a delight of anticipation, but as soon as he sees her de Winter flies into a rage. He chases her away, telling her to go and change clothes. Upstairs she finds Mrs. Danvers, who admits that she told her to dress that way because it was the costume Rebecca wore to her last costume ball. As Mrs. de Winter is crying, Mrs. Danvers opens the window and calls her to it. She says de Winter does not love her, that he loves only the memory of Rebecca, and whispers in her ear that Mrs. de Winter might as well jump. Fireworks announcing a shipwreck break the spell, as everyone from the costume party runs toward the shore to help.

When she reaches the shore, looking for de Winter, Frank Crawley tells her that the diver who went looking for the wrecked ship found another boat—the one Rebecca was sailing when she drowned. She finds de Winter in the cottage and apologizes for her costume. De Winter is distracted, feeling fatalistic. Rebecca's body was found in the boat, he tells her. The woman he identified as Rebecca was not her at all. He knew that when he identified the body, because he put Rebecca's body in the boat the night of her death. Although she believes him to be a murderer, Mrs. de Winter promises to stay with him, because she loves him. She admits that she always felt that she could not measure up to his love for Rebecca, and de Winter explains that he hated her. When Mrs. de Winter first met him on the cliff in Monte Carlo (the story's first scene) he was there remembering how, on their honeymoon, four days after they were married, Rebecca had admitted to him that she was not faithful to him and never would be. She had offered to pretend to be a good wife to him, but she was hateful and conniving. She seduced Crawley, and she had an affair with Jack Favell.

The biggest difference between Daphne du Maurier's novel and the film is the way the death of Rebecca is explained. In the novel, de Winter admits to killing her. Films made by the Hollywood studio system, however, had to follow the moral code, and it was considered too immoral to show the hero of the story living a happy life after committing murder, so the screenplay alters the events. One night, de Winter explains, he came to her in the cottage on the shore, where she often met her lovers. She talked about having a baby, taunting de Winter that it would not be his child but he would have to raise it anyway. As they argued he hit her, but she stood up. Then she tripped and hit her head and died. He put her into the boat, took it out to sea, and drove holes through the hull with a spike. Mrs. de Winter tells him to keep quiet about these events and not admit what he has done.

Crawley phones the cottage to say that the constable, Colonel Julyan, wants de Winter to examine the body they have found. At the morgue de Winter admits that this is Rebecca and that he was wrong about his earlier identification. A new inquest is called to find out how Rebecca died.

Before the inquest, Mrs. de Winter worries that de Winter will lose his temper. The inquest is held in a school. It favors de Winter. Ben speaks cryptically, denying that he saw anything, afraid to be sent to the asylum. Things take a change, however, when Taft, the man who used to take care of the boat, testifies that the valves for draining it were left open and that some of the holes seem to have been made from the inside. These facts imply that Rebecca's death would have to have been suicide. As de Winter is being questioned about his relationship with Rebecca, his anger rises, but before he can blurt out anything incriminating, Mrs. de Winter, in the audience, faints, creating a diversion.

They go to their car, where they are met by Favell. He shows them a note Rebecca sent him the day she died, implying that it has evidence that will implicate de Winter in her death. They move from the car into the nearby tavern, to a private room, but de Winter has arranged for Colonel Julyan to be there. Favell speaks openly about being Rebecca's lover. They read her note: it says she has seen the doctor and must see Favell at the cottage that night. The unspoken assumption is that she is pregnant and that she would not call the child's father, her lover, to meet her and then kill herself before they talked. When they are discussing a motive for de Winter's possibly murdering Rebecca, Favell calls Mrs. Danvers into the room. From her they extract the name and address of Rebecca's doctor in London. Favell tells them that this doctor will confirm that she was going to have a child and that it was not de Winter's child, which would provide him the motive for her murder.

They drive to London and talk with Dr. Baker. He does not recognize Rebecca's name, but he knows her description as a "Mrs. Danvers." According to his records, that woman was not pregnant but had terminal cancer. As opposed to Favell's assumption, this diagnosis actually does support the theory that she would commit suicide.

De Winter and Crawley leave to drive back to Manderley. Favell phones Mrs. Danvers to tell her that Rebecca committed suicide and that de Winter's name is clear. As they drive through the woods toward the house, de Winter sees light in the sky ahead. Mrs. Danvers has set the house on fire. Mrs. de Winter has escaped and is wandering around outside, looking for de Winter when he arrives. Together, they turn toward the building, where they can see Mrs. Danvers in the window of Rebecca's room just before Manderley collapses into a flaming heap.

CHARACTERS

Dr. Baker

When there is some question about whether Rebecca was pregnant with Favell's child or not, Mrs. Danvers directs the inquest to Dr. Baker, in London. Baker does not recognize Rebecca's name because he treated her under an alias. He does, however, remember the woman quite well, even remembering, a year later, how she took the news that she had terminal cancer.

Ben

Ben is a mentally challenged fisherman who is seen several times on the beach at Manderley. He talks in riddles about a woman who went away into the water and his fear of being put into the asylum, which is why he insists that he will not say anything about what he has witnessed. His half-truths seem to imply trouble for Maxim de Winter. At the inquest into Rebecca's death, it is explained that Ben once saw Rebecca and Favell together and Rebecca threatened to have him put in an asylum.

Frank Crawley

Crawley, played by Reginald Denney, is the manager of Manderley, taking care of the complex task of running a huge estate while the owner, Maxim de Winter, has been away to Monte Carlo and then on his honeymoon. Crawley is a kind man who forms an immediate alliance with Mrs. de Winter. Though being at Manderley is overwhelming and intimidating, she finds in Crawley a sympathetic man who will be straight with her. After the trial, when de Winter tells Crawley that he had felt guilty for Rebecca's death all that time, Crawley is supportive and nonjudgmental.

Mrs. Danvers

Mrs. Danvers is the housemaid at Manderley. Mrs. de Winter is intimidated by her, always suspecting that she has some sinister intent. Even though Mrs. Danvers says that she wants to help Mrs. de Winter adjust to life at the estate, her manner is threatening.

After she has been around Manderley for a while, Mrs. de Winter finds out that Mrs. Danvers is not one of the estate's original servants. She came there with Rebecca. This helps to explain her fanatical dedication to Rebecca's memory. When she is showing Mrs. de Winter the things in Rebecca's room, including the pillowcase that she embroidered herself for her former mistress, she has a crazed gleam in her eye. It is clear that she is more than just sentimental about someone she loved, that she is unhinged.

Her love for Rebecca translates to a hatred of the new Mrs. de Winter, whom Mrs. Danvers will not allow to replace her mistress. She does what she can to humiliate the new wife and then nearly talks her into jumping out a window to her death.

In the end, when she is unable to see de Winter convicted for Rebecca's death and is goaded by Favell with the thought that he might live happily with his new wife, Mrs. Danvers burns Manderley down. She stays faithfully in Rebecca's room, though, dying there in the fire.

George Fortescue Maximilian de Winter
See Maxim de Winter

Maxim de Winter
De Winter is known throughout the film as Max, though in the novel the narrator specifically notes, with jealousy, that only Rebecca called him Max and everyone else called him Maxim. He is played by Laurence Olivier, who is frequently cited as one of the best film actors of all time.

He was raised as a wealthy aristocrat and has the sense of entitlement that is natural for a man used to being in charge. He also has a powerful temper. Both of these personality traits make him the opposite of the shy, poor girl he marries in the film, which in some way accounts for why life at Manderley is so mystifying to her. He barks orders at the servants and is openly sarcastic to Mrs. Van Hopper's face—things his wife would never dream of doing. In addition, he behaves oddly about things related to Rebecca, such as the cottage by the shore and the costume she once wore to a ball. His wife interprets his odd behavior as evidence that he still loves Rebecca, until de Winter blurts out that he hated her.

Once his secret is revealed, de Winter and his wife have to worry that he might become angry during the inquest into Rebecca's death and make it look as if he killed her. He almost does incriminate himself, but she distracts the court by falling over in a faint. Later, when he finds out that Rebecca had cancer, de Winter forgives himself for his part in her death. As he tells

Frank Crawley, she used his temper to goad him, hoping that he might kill her.

Mrs. de Winter
Actress Joan Fontaine was nominated for an Academy Award for her role as the film's central character, based on the narrator in du Maurier's novel. Her name is never given in either version. She starts the story as a poor girl, working in Monte Carlo as a paid companion to the overbearing Mrs. Van Hopper. When the sophisticated, wealthy, and tormented Maxim de Winter showers her with attention, she cannot believe that he is actually interested in her romantically, a suspicion that will continue well into their marriage. She is too self-conscious to confront Mrs. Van Hopper, who berates and insults her. Her low social situation has left her few options but to do what is asked of her.

When they marry she becomes Mrs. de Winter, the mistress of Manderley, a famous fictitious British estate. She is intimidated by having servants, unsure of how to treat them. This is shown in the way that she hides a small porcelain figure that she has broken, and her humiliation when de Winter mocks her for being afraid of what the staff will think of her. In the novel, she points out to him that she only feels comfortable with Clarice, who was hired to be her maid, because Clarice has not been a maid before and therefore is as new to the manor house life as she is.

Her self-effacing shyness reaches its breaking point one night, after Mrs. Danvers, who is still devoted to the memory of the first Mrs. de Winter, intimidates her with the fine things Rebecca had. After thinking it over she calls Mrs. Danvers to her study and insists that Rebecca's things be taken out of there, asserting that she, not Rebecca, is Mrs. de Winter now.

The night Mrs. Danvers tricks her into dressing up for a costume party in a dress that upsets de Winter, she contemplates suicide, at Danvers's suggestion. She is stopped from jumping out a window by the coincidental commotion of a shipwreck.

When she learns that de Winter hid Rebecca's body after she died accidentally, she is not horrified, as he expects her to be. She is relieved: all this time she thought that the husband she loved was uninterested in her because he was still in love with his dead wife. When she finds out that he hated Rebecca, she sets about helping him fight against possible criminal charges, so they can start their life together without the specter of the dead woman hanging over them.

Rebecca de Winter

Rebecca does not appear in the film or the novel, even though she is the focus of both. She was Maxim de Winter's first wife. She is remembered for being the perfect socialite. She ran the estate, Manderley, and threw magnificent parties. She was an accomplished hunter, rider, and sailor. She was beautiful. In short, she was everything that the film's protagonist, the second Mrs. de Winter, feels that she herself is not, an impression that is only magnified by the obsessive, protective devotion that Rebecca's old servant, Mrs. Danvers, still has for Rebecca.

It is not until late in the film that the new Mrs. de Winter finds out that Rebecca was far from perfect. She was promiscuous and admitted as much to her husband on her honeymoon, daring him to divorce her. She frequently brought her lover, Jack Favell, to the cottage by the beach on the Manderley property. As described in the novel, she seduced Crawley, the estate manager, and then dumped him. When she knew she was going to die of cancer, she picked a fight with de Winter and then tripped and hit her head while they were fighting, leaving him with a guilty conscience, thinking that he had killed her.

Jack Favell

Favell, Rebecca's cousin, is played by famed character actor and sometimes leading man George Sanders. He comes into the story as an oily, mysterious presence. He is the sort of cheerful person who always calls the dark Mrs. Danvers "Danny," but under his cheer is a sinister undertone. He visits Manderley when he knows de Winter is not there because he knows that de Winter does not approve of him, and rightfully so: Favell was Rebecca's lover.

When Rebecca's body is found, Favell shows up outside of the trial, trying to blackmail de Winter with a letter that he says will prove that Rebecca would never have committed suicide. De Winter is not intimidated by his insinuations, though, and turns Favell and the letter over to the police immediately. In the end Favell loses, and his accusations against de Winter prove useless, but, still smiling, Favell keeps trying: he is a car salesman, and even as Colonel Julyan, the magistrate, is warning him about the possible punishment for blackmail, Favell offers to sell him a car.

Frith

Frith is the head butler at Manderley and the head of the household staff. Unlike his counterpart, Mrs. Danvers, Frith is loyal to Mr. and Mrs. de Winter: while the inquest about Rebecca's death is going on, he takes a moment to offer the young mistress of the house his support.

Colonel Julyan

Colonel Julyan is the magistrate in charge of investigating Rebecca's death. He has a friendly relationship with de Winter, the prime suspect in a possible murder, as Favell notes.

Beatrice Lacy

Maxim de Winter's sister is friendly to his new wife but also intimidating. She gives the younger woman tips about how to get along in her new social position, including hairstyles and clothes and ways to cope with neighbors who expect a certain behavior from the people running Manderley. Though her advice can help Mrs. de Winter fit in, Beatrice's strong, confident personality serves to make her feel even more self-conscious.

Giles Lacy

Giles is played by Nigel Bruce, famous for his role as Dr. Watson in more than a dozen Sherlock Holmes films. As in those films, he plays this role as comic relief: Giles often says the wrong thing, like being overheard speculating that de Winter's new wife must be a chorus girl because he had heard that she was young and pretty. At the costume party Giles foolishly wears a weight lifter costume that draws attention to his out-of-shape physique.

Robert

Robert is the younger butler at Manderley. At one point he is accused by Mrs. Danvers of breaking the Cupid figurine that Mrs. de Winter actually broke. Her hiding this mistake has made Robert suspect, a situation that grows until his job is on the line. In the film, de Winter explains after the truth comes out that Robert can now dry his tears, a reference to a longer discussion in the novel about what a sensitive man he is.

Taft

Taft is the man from the boatyard who used to take care of Rebecca's boat. During the inquest into her death, his testimony that the valves were opened before the boat sank and holes were drilled into it is what makes the police start suspecting that Rebecca did not die in an accidental boating accident but was in fact murdered.

Mrs. Edythe Van Hopper

When the film begins, the main character is working as a paid companion for Mrs. Van Hopper, a loud, opinionated, somewhat dimwitted American. She is blinded by her own self-image. She does not notice that Maxim de Winter is not at all interested in her when he sits down with her and his companion or that the younger woman has been going out to meet de Winter while Mrs. Van Hopper has been bedridden with a cold.

When she hears that de Winter is taking her companion away to marry her, Mrs. Van Hopper is as upset about the loss of her imagined friendship with him as she is about the loss of her employee. Privately, she scolds the younger woman, accusing her of seducing de Winter and trapping her with sexuality.

Mrs. Van Hopper's Companion

See Mrs. de Winter

THEMES

Self-Consciousness

Joan Fontaine's performance in this film captures the tone that Daphne du Maurier's novel gave to the voice of her unnamed narrator. She is skittish, fearful, and always feeling the sting of social pressure. She avoids eye contact. She twitches, stutters, and frowns slightly, although not quite enough for anyone else to notice.

The character is understandably self-conscious. She is a poor girl with no family, living in a world where wealth and family connections are all-important. It does not help that she works for Mrs. Van Hopper, who is overbearing and rude: her employment with this woman at the beginning of the film does nothing to help her self-esteem. Almost as bad as the way she lets Mrs. Van Hopper push her around is the fact that the man she falls in love with, Maxim de

Winter, has been raised from childhood to be masterful and assertive.

The way de Winter views the world is the opposite of her perspective, and it is natural that the more forceful personality would dominate. This is brought out in both the novel and the film by the broken Cupid figurine incident. When it breaks, Mrs. de Winter is embarrassed, and she hopes to hide her clumsiness, but the incident has many unforeseen consequences. She thinks that putting the pieces away and saying nothing about them will make the figurine forgotten, but Mrs. Danvers blames the loss on Robert, forcing Mrs. de Winter to speak up to protect an innocent man's job. Her confession is made worse when de Winter pressures her to explain why she lied about it, and worse still when he gently mocks her self-consciousness to Mrs. Danvers, and even worse when he tells his wife that she has behaved about this as if she were a maid, not the mistress of the house.

When Mrs. Danvers pushes her too hard, taunting her with Rebecca's clothes and style, she asserts herself, declaring out loud that she is Mrs. de Winter, not Rebecca. Later, de Winter's confession that he covered up Rebecca's death and that he will likely go to jail for it elevates her to equal footing with him, as she tries to build his confidence.

Social Class

For this story to work, it is very significant that the protagonist should come from a different social class than her surroundings. For one thing, this provides audiences with an entry point into life at Manderley. The average American viewer would be just as confused about the workings of an English manor house as she is, so they sympathize with her. Most viewers would not know which halls lead to which parts of a mansion like this or what to wear to a formal costume ball or how to deal with a visitor like Favell, who has come to visit the housekeeper when the master of the house is away. Most viewers, finding themselves in any similar situations, would worry about the trouble a wrong decision might cause.

The class difference also helps to show what de Winter finds attractive about his second wife. Throughout the film he is charmed by her innocence, even as he shows himself to be burdened by the responsibilities that come with his social position. He cannot even walk through a hotel in

TOPICS FOR FURTHER STUDY

- The lives of the characters in this film have been continued in several novels, none of them ever reaching the level of success that du Maurier achieved in voice and characterization. Read the most recent one, *Rebecca's Tale*, written by Sally Beauman and published with authorization from the du Maurier estate in 2007. As you read it, form opinions about how Beauman worked with another author's characters. In an essay, identify one scene that you think does not sound realistic, given the characters you know from the film, and one scene that you think Beauman captured perfectly for the characters, and explain what makes you feel that way.

- In 1945, director Alfred Hitchcock and producer David O. Selznick worked together again to create *Spellbound*, a film about an insomniac psychiatrist (played by Gregory Peck) who thinks that he has killed the man who held that job before him. One of the outstanding features of the film is a flamboyant, extravagant dream sequence inspired by the surreal art of painter Salvador Dali. Watch *Spellbound* and, following its inspiration, choose another painter you think could be used to illustrate Mrs. de Winter's dreams about Rebecca. Put together a visual sequence, either animated or as a slide show, that you think might use that painter's vision to bring her ideas to life. Present your sequence along with an explanation about what the images show.

- Oliver Stone's 1993 film *Heaven & Earth* shows what might have happened if this story had taken place in a different culture. It focuses on the experiences of Le Ly (Hiep Thi Le), a young girl who is abused by South Vietnamese and North Vietnamese soldiers in Vietnam during the war, goes to work for a family in Saigon, and eventually marries a U.S. Marine (Tommy Lee Jones) who brings her to the United States with him, though he still suffers guilt about his part in the war. Watch this R-rated film and identify the aspects you think Le Ly's relationship with Steve Butler has in common with Maxim and Mrs. de Winter's relationship. Chart the similarities between the two cinematic cultures that most people would think have nothing in common, then write a scene in which Le Ly and Mrs. de Winter meet to compare their experiences.

- In the movie, Rebecca is described as being fashionable and beautiful but also immoral and cruel. Generally, a person who is that disconnected from his or her outward appearance would likely be suffering from a severe personality disorder. Research the psychology of charming but cruel people and present your theory to your class about whether you can categorize Rebecca as a sociopath, a psychopath, a narcissist, or some other designation.

- Neither du Maurier's novel nor Hitchcock's film describes how the second Mrs. de Winter came to be working for Mrs. Van Hooper—where her home is and why she can't go there again. Following the style of your favorite young-adult author, write a short story that accounts for her life in the years before she goes to Monte Carlo. At the end of your story include a page that explains which specific elements of the author's style you mimicked in your work.

France without someone like Mrs. Van Hopper calling out for his attention. Like a king, he is called upon to judge disputes among those under him. For a man who needs to watch his social position, who is also burdened with the guilt of his first wife's death, the innocence of a young woman with no social ties seems as much of an ideal as his life of wealth and fame seems to her.

Death

One reason the second Mrs. de Winter is so intimidated by Rebecca is that Rebecca is dead. She is not a person one can compete with; she is just a memory. The more the protagonist learns about Rebecca, the more she assumes that everyone who knew her, who speaks so fondly of her, suffers for her loss. Mrs. Danvers makes her infatuation with Rebecca clear, and it is obvious that she feels cheated by her death. It is then reasonable to assume that de Winter himself never talks about Rebecca because her death pains him, as well. She is misled throughout most of the film into confusing his guilt for grief.

When de Winter finally does talk about Rebecca, he describes her as if she has supernatural power to reach out beyond the grave, to harm him from the afterlife. He says that she has won when her body is found a year after her death, as if her spirit is still pursuing him. De Winter is suffering because Rebecca's death has taken her out of reach forever, which would let her take revenge on him every day of his life.

Marriage

De Winter's marriage to Rebecca seems like the perfect marriage to most people. In contrast, the marriage between de Winter and his second wife does not seem very strong to the people who know them. Although he has elements of a romantic hero, de Winter is too practical and world-weary to pay much attention to traditional courtship rituals. He loses his temper with his young companion, calling her foolish; he takes for granted that she can see his love for her, and seldom expresses it; he proposes to her by shouting from the next room. When they return to Manderley after their honeymoon, he falls immediately into his role as master of the estate, leaving her to flounder with her social role and to wonder what he thinks.

This is why the scene of them watching home movies about their honeymoon in Venice is important. In Venice, the social anxiety of Monte Carlo was relieved. She did not have the judgmental stare of Mrs. Van Hopper to contend with, and he did not have his memories of his horrible Monte Carlo honeymoon with Rebecca. The pressures of running the great estate of Manderley on unequal social footing were yet to emerge. The honeymoon films lack sound, but they clearly show the de Winters to be a happy couple, enthralled with each other and

having something that is rare in their lives: fun. Presumably, that is the way their marriage will be after the end of the movie, with the burden of Rebecca and Mrs. Danvers and Manderley having been lifted from them.

STYLE

Light and Shadow

As with any black-and-white movie, the cinematographer of *Rebecca*, George Barnes (the only individual to win an Academy Award for this picture) uses the interplay of light and darkness to enhance the visual texture. Each scene is cluttered with objects of varying degree of darkness, from the mist passing in front of the moon in the very first shot to the rich complexity of the ocean seen from a high cliff at Monte Carlo to even the street outside of the school where the inquest is held, visually busy with bicycles and shadows. This is especially true with the interior shots of Manderley, each of them filled with objects that make the scene feel cramped. Where there are not old relics or large furniture in the background there are shadows from outside draped across the wall. This enhances the claustrophobia that Mrs. de Winter feels, trapped in her life there. The only room at Manderley that is bright and open is Rebecca's, which is ironic because this is the room in the house that holds the most evil.

Faithful Adaptation

Alfred Hitchcock was said to have favored making significant changes to the story that had already been read by millions of people who had bought and borrowed Daphne du Maurier's novel. Once he was hired to direct the film, he and Philip MacDonald produced a lengthy treatment that outlined plans for a horror film steeped in violence. While he would be able to fulfill his vision in other pictures (such as his adaptation of du Maurier's *Jamaica Inn*, made in England in 1939), the producer, David O. Selznick, had different plans. Selznick had paid a fortune for a best-selling novel, and he did not intend to alienate the novel's many fans by putting an entirely different story on screen.

As a result of Selznick's efforts, most of the scenes in the movie correspond with scenes from the novel. Some of them are shifted in order—for instance, the young woman does watch de Winter looking over the cliff at Monte Carlo in the book, but that is not where they meet—but such changes are done for compression, in order both to retain a memorable scene from the du Maurier version and also to tell the story quickly. Some changes show Hitchcock's particular style, such as the implied sexual threat of the Jack Favell character (who is just a drunken boor in the book) or the sensual way Mrs. Danvers handles Rebecca's clothes. The biggest change—that de Winter has not actually murdered Rebecca in the film—is just a matter of detail. He recounts a fight, during which she died, and hiding her corpse, so even though he is technically not guilty of murder, most of du Maurier's original scenario is retained.

CULTURAL CONTEXT

The Film and World War II

According to Frank Miller, writing at the esteemed Turner Classic Movies website, *Rebecca* began filming on September 8, 1939. Five days earlier, on September 3rd, Great Britain and France had declared war against Germany, in response to the German invasion of Poland. The beginning of World War II had significant emotional effects on the British actors and director of this film and ultimately had some effect on how people viewed the final product.

On August 23, 1939, German chancellor Adolf Hitler and Joseph Stalin, leader of the Soviet Union, reached a nonaggression agreement. The German-Soviet Nonaggression Pact prohibited the two countries from taking military action against each other for the following ten years. Germany had already broken a similar pact that it had made with Great Britain by invading Czechoslovakia a few months before. As a result of that aggression, Great Britain and France had sworn on March 31 to defend Poland against any similar aggression. Both countries hoped to persuade the Soviet Union to join them in their stand against Germany's expansion, and there was good reason to do so: annexing Poland would take German power right up to the Soviet border. So Hitler sent a representative to Stalin, suggesting a pact against aggression that would last one hundred years, coming back with a much more modest ten-year agreement. A week after the Soviet-German pact was signed, Germany invaded Poland, and in a few days France and Great Britain declared war on Germany. America supported the Allied powers against Germany and its allies but was not directly involved in the war until Pearl Harbor was bombed two years later.

The start of the war made it impossible for the film's director, Alfred Hitchcock, to film in England. But having lived in England all his life, Hitchcock was familiar with the sort of ancient mansion that Manderley, which is so central to the plot and mood of the film, would have been. He sent scouts to photograph some of the great mansions of England, as well as similar ones in Canada, to provide sources of inspiration for the construction crew at MGM studios to create their version of Manderley. The end result, though, is more gothic than a real mansion of its size and stature would be, more a product of Hollywood imagination than a place that might actually exist.

Great Manor Houses

The traditional manor houses of England, of which Manderley in this film is just one example, descend from a long tradition that grew out of the social and political structures of the medieval period. As the center of a political district in the fourteenth and fifteenth centuries, such places were built with defense in mind, with strong walls and towers suited for battle. They housed the lord of the manor, who had political power over the people in the district, collected taxes from them, and held court to settle their disputes. This formal arrangement changed over the centuries as England grew away from the feudal system of government toward a representational one, and the significance of those living in the manor became, as depicted in *Rebecca*, more symbolic than formal. Still, the families that had lived in the manors for centuries, like the de Winter family, were usually the richest in their rural surroundings and therefore had more economic influence than anyone else nearby.

Starting in the late nineteenth century, the estates that provided incomes for the manor houses began to dwindle. The Industrial Revolution shifted the economy toward manufacturing, while at the same time tax laws provided fewer and fewer shelters for the aristocracy. In the early twentieth century, particularly between the two world wars, many estates were cut up, and the large old manor houses, too big to justify their existence, were sometimes demolished.

© *Selznick / United Artists / The Kobal Collection / Picture Desk*

About that time came a renewed interest in their preservation as significant parts of the nation's history, and several laws were passed, particularly the Town and Country Planning Acts of 1932 and 1944, which gave local governments more power to stop demolition in the name of development in order to preserve local culture.

There are different theories about the particular house that inspired Manderley. Many attribute it to Menabilly, an estate dating back to the time of King Henry VII (reigned 1485–1509) that Daphne du Maurier's family lived in from the 1940s through the 1960s, after the novel and film had made her a literary success. The author herself, though, attributed some of her ideas about Manderley to Minton Hall, in Cambridgeshire, which she remembered visiting as a child. Today, television viewers are most likely familiar with the manor house tradition from the way it is depicted in *Downton Abbey*, the popular BBC television program shown around the world.

CRITICAL OVERVIEW

Rebecca was released to almost universal acclaim in 1940. David O. Selznick, the producer, put a budget into the filming that the story deserved,

allowing it to go almost half a million dollars over its initial budget. Alfred Hitchcock, directing his first Hollywood movie, used the advanced cameras and sets and costumes that being at MGM put at his disposal to their greatest advantage. Critics and audiences recognized the quality of their combined effort. As Mae Tinee of the *Chicago Tribune* exclaims in her review on April 6, 1940, "I didn't think they could do it! Capture the suspense, the horror, the beauty and the strange eeriness of 'Rebecca,' the book. But they have!" Tinee goes on to call Joan Fontaine "the surprise sensation of the year" and Judith Anderson's portrayal of Mrs. Danvers "bitingly impressive." She notes that the scenery, "gorgeous or weird, was photographed with marvelous cunning and the settings and costumes are THE LAST WORD." Though not all reviewers were this enthusiastic, they still found the film impressive in style and presentation. An unsigned review in *Variety* at the time of its release calls it "one of the finest productional efforts of the past year," while predicting, inaccurately:

> It will receive attention from critics and class patronage as an example of the power in narrative drama of vivid screen portraiture, but general audiences will tab it as a long-drawn out drama that could have been told better in less footage.

In the years since it was released, popular enthusiasm for the film has remained steady. Many critics count it among Hitchcock's best films, even though it was made between his lower-budget period of working in British cinema in the 1920s and 1930s and the period in which the Hitchcock name came to represent a particular kind of suspense and horror with such films as *Vertigo* (1958), *North by Northwest* (1959), and perhaps his best-remembered film, *Psycho* (1960). Jeffrey M. Anderson of the website Combustible Celluloid calls it "an extraordinary film...one of Hitchcock's sturdiest and most enchanting works." As Peter Bradshaw explains in the *Guardian*, a British newspaper,

> The sheer, swooning pleasure that this film affords—its melodrama, its romance, its extravagant menace—makes it a must-see. Quite rightly, it was included in this paper's recent list of the best cinematic adaptations, and it really is a masterclass in craftsmanship.

The film was nominated for eleven Academy Awards, including Best Actor for Laurence Olivier, Best Actress for Joan Fontaine, Best Supporting Actress for Judith Anderson as

Mrs. Danvers and Best Director for Alfred Hitchcock. It did win Best Picture that year, but the only individual recognized was George Barnes for his black-and-white cinematography.

CRITICISM

David Kelly

Kelly is an instructor of creative writing and literature in Illinois. In the following essay, he looks at how the supporting roles in Rebecca, *particularly Mrs. Van Hopper and Jack Favell, are crucial to making the lead characters interesting.*

The most memorable character in Alfred Hitchcock's 1940 version of *Rebecca* is the young heroine. She grows in the course of the story from a stammering young servant who cannot even allow herself eye contact with a grown man to the wife who rules palatial Manderley, who consoles her husband over the fact that he had to murder his mocking, promiscuous wife (though in the film it is not an actual murder, just a crazy string of implausible events designed to avoid calling it that). She is the first-person narrator of Daphne du Maurier's novel and the protagonist who is in just about every scene of the film, and Joan Fontaine renders her with an amazing performance.

The position of second most memorable character in the film is a tie. On the one hand, there is the brilliantly cruel, casually focused man the young woman falls in love with, Maxim de Winter. He is played by Laurence Olivier, often cited as one of the most brilliant actors of his generation. It is easy for readers of the book to see why she would fall for de Winter, a man who never actually courts her but who behaves from the start as if their love and subsequent marriage are simply a foregone conclusion. He is absolutely self-confident, a man in control of past, present, and future. Their relationship, though, serves as a classic example of the expression "it works on paper"—as acted out on the screen, de Winter's casual control of her life is a lot less charming. Maybe it's Olivier's forced staginess, undermining de Winter's lack of self-awareness, or maybe there is just no way a man who shouts "I'm asking you to marry me, you little fool" from the next room could ever be an entirely engaging person.

What de Winter loses in the translation from book to film is picked up by the character of

> FLORENCE BATES RENDERS MRS. VAN HOPPER ALMOST EXACTLY AS SHE IS IN THE NOVEL, WHILE GEORGE SANDERS, A LEADING AND ALSO SUPPORTING ACTOR IN MANY FILMS, BRINGS AN OLD PRO'S COMFORTABLE ASSURANCE TO A ROLE THAT COULD EASILY HAVE BEEN PLAYED TOO MENACING OR TOO NASTY OR TOO DESPERATE."

Mrs. Danvers. In the book, Mrs. Danvers is unpleasant and creepy, but in the film Hitchcock makes her a supernatural presence, less of an old dog like Jasper who has lost his master and more like a vengeful devil. Judith Anderson deserved her Oscar nomination for rendering the character that people talk about years after they have seen the film. If a film could have three lead characters, Mrs. Danvers would count as a lead.

In movie vernacular there are the male and female leads and then, under them, all of the supporting actors. Sometimes a supporting role by a great actor will stand out, as Anderson's Mrs. Danvers does. Sometimes, though, the supporting actors are the place to look if one wants to gauge the quality of a film: supporting characters can be the most fun, and it is evident that the actors are having the most fun playing them. Precisely because the supporting roles are meant to stay in the background, existing only in their relationship to the leads, a look at how they operate in a film always helps viewers understand the main characters better.

In *Rebecca*, there are two supporting characters who add a little fresh air into an otherwise stodgy, terse situation: Mrs. Van Hopper, the vulgar rich American dowager the protagonist works for in the opening scenes, and Jack Favell, who shows up in the middle and then at the end of the story. Florence Bates renders Mrs. Van Hopper almost exactly as she is in the novel, while George Sanders, a leading and also supporting actor in many films, brings an old pro's comfortable assurance to a role that could easily have been played too menacing or too nasty or too desperate.

WHAT DO I SEE NEXT?

- Humphrey Bogart, Barbara Stanwyck, and Alexis Smith star in the 1947 film *The Two Mrs Carrolls*, about a woman who marries a painter and then begins to suspect that he murdered his first wife. This film, based on a Broadway play that was itself based on a London play, was released on DVD and Blu-ray by Warner Brothers in 2011. It is not rated.

- The opening shot of the camera approaching the gate of Manderley, passing through the gate, and approaching the house in the fog and the closing shot of the embroidered pillowcase engulfed in flames are echoed in the opening and closing of *Citizen Kane*, Orson Welles's groundbreaking masterpiece of 1941 that broke the rules of visual storytelling. Welles's story is a purely American tale of the rise from poverty and fall into obscurity of a great man, the fictional Charles Foster Kane. While *Rebecca* is considered a fine example of a film romance, *Citizen Kane* is known for innovations that still seem fresh today. It is unrated and available from Warner Home Video.

- The 2011 film of Emily Brontë's classic novel *Jane Eyre*, which practically set the standard for gothic romances, is aimed at modern teenage audiences. For once, the actress playing Jane is near twenty, the age Jane is in the novel. The film stars Mia Wasikowska as Jane, a poor girl who comes to be a governess at the huge, gloomy estate Thornfield Hall and ends up falling in love with the enigmatic, haunted master of the manor, Rochester, played by Michael Fassbender. It was directed by Cary Joji Fukunaga. This PG-13 film is available on Blu-ray and DVD from Focus Features.

- Critics considered Joan Fontaine's performance in *Rebecca* to be superior to her performance in Alfred Hitchcock's *Notorious* the following year, but it was the second film that won Fontaine the Oscar. The story is familiar: Fontaine is a shy woman who marries a charming man, played by Cary Grant, whom she soon suspects has plans to kill her. Released in 1941, it is available today from Warner Brothers.

- The 1993 film *Remains of the Day*, from a novel by Kazuo Ishiguro, concerns the emotional entanglement of the behind-the-scenes staff at a British manor house in the years leading up to World War II. Anthony Hopkins and Emma Thompson were nominated for Oscars for their performances as a head butler and head maid who put duty over emotion as they run a house during the last great era of British power, roughly the time that *Rebecca* was released. Director James Ivory was also nominated, as was the picture. This film is rated PG and is available on Blu-ray and DVD from Columbia Pictures.

- In 1997, Masterpiece Theater remade *Rebecca* as a miniseries. While the actors in the newer version (Charles Dance as de Winter, Emilia Fox as Mrs. de Winter, Diana Rigg as Mrs. Danvers) cannot compete with the actors in the classic version, the longer miniseries format and the sweeping scenery make up for it for contemporary audiences. PBS released it on disc in 2003; because it was made for television, it has no MPAA rating.

Anyone who has seen a society comedy from the 1930s has seen a matron like Mrs. Van Hopper. She is cut from the same cloth as Margaret Dumont, the comic foil for the Marx Brothers in many of their films, and Marie Dressler, who played Carlotta in George Cukor's star-studded production of *Dinner at Eight*. She delights in social ranking, swoons (or, as a woman of her set would probably put it, "gets the vapors") when someone violates social convention, and is catty with younger women and flirty with younger men. Mrs. Van Hopper is in no way an original character, but her presence in *Rebecca* is crucial.

She appears only in the first half hour of the film and then is out of the story forever, but that half hour is key. It is easy to accept the tension between Mr. and Mrs. de Winter when they set up their home in Manderley together, but viewers have to be convinced first that these two people—the timid poor girl and the steely aristocrat—would fall in love and get married to begin with. They have good looks, but it would be a shame if that were all they had to attract each other: audiences do not want to root for superficiality. They have the old notion that "opposites attract and complement each other's shortcomings" going for them, but without a good catalyst, opposites *don't* really attract; they repel.

The greatest bond the leads have at the start of this film is that neither of them is Mrs. Van Hopper. Maxim de Winter is a serious man, so tortured by guilt that he has returned to the cliff where his dead wife told him, four days into their marriage, that she would never be faithful to him. Would he even notice a quiet, stammering girl half his age? Probably not, if Mrs. Van Hopper had not deliberately attracted his attention across the hotel lobby. And how could a girl like her learn to loosen up and talk to a man of wealth and social prominence like Maxim de Winter? Well, Mrs. Van Hopper has wealth and social prominence, and de Winter is certainly easier to talk to than she is.

Romance is in the air around Mrs. Van Hopper because her crudeness simply makes everything around her seem more attractive, and her hypochondria makes everything seem more honest. De Winter's terse mood swings are refreshingly authentic compared to her forced cheeriness, and the girl's insecurity is certainly easier to take than someone who is rude without even knowing it. In the novel, du Maurier mentions Mrs. Van Hopper's cigarette butts scattered all over her bedroom, including her cold cream jar: Hitchcock boils this down to one memorable close-up of her cramming a lit cigarette into a full jar of cold cream. If the two leads sometimes seem too fragile, the alternative offered here is certainly much worse.

While Mrs. Van Hopper is functional, moving the plot along by making audiences appreciate the romance that blossoms so quickly between de Winter and the girl, Jack Favell has a trickier function in the film. His character exists in part to serve the plot, but another part of his function is less easily defined. He is there to stir up the air of menace and mystery that is suffocating young Mrs. de Winter at Manderley.

When Favell appears at the end of the story, he serves a specific function. Hitchcock is boxed into a corner, as was du Maurier before him. Late in the tale, Maxim de Winter has gotten away with murder or pseudo-murder, being too well respected by the local authorities to be suspected. The story could end there, with the de Winters happy that the secret has been removed from between them. It could end, or it could move on to Mrs. Danvers burning down Manderley. Not yet, though. There needs to be a bit more time between de Winter's confession to his wife and Danvers's revenge.

As a plot device to while away fifteen or twenty minutes on-screen, Favell's blackmail scheme serves admirably. The story has gotten pretty somber by this point—the hero has confessed to murder (or murderous thoughts)! There is a possibility that this could make de Winter seem like a cad who is getting by on his social standing. It is a good time to contrast him with Favell, a car salesman who talks as if he should be a romantic hero, who says things about justice for his dead cousin and lover but is willing to forget justice for a cash payout. After confessing to murder (or murderous intent) and making it clear that the beautiful love story at the center of *Rebecca* is marred by the fact that de Winter married with this huge, personality-defining secret he planned to keep from his wife forever, Favell comes in to show what a real scoundrel looks like.

His function at the end is clear: he attempts blackmail and ends up under police scrutiny. His first appearance in the story, though, is just one line of dialog after another of oily menace for its own sake. Young Mrs. de Winter, uncomfortable at Manderley as she is, hears him in the house and she hides. A servant who finds her cowering in the corner would do her best to put her at ease, but Favell calls her out on it. Like de Winter himself, who earlier called her out for hiding a broken Cupid figurine, Favell is so comfortable in his own skin that her discomfort amuses him. Unlike de Winter, though, he focuses on Mrs. de Winter with a predatory, sexual stare.

© *Selznick | United Artists | The Kobal Collection | Picture Desk*

If the biggest mystery in *Rebecca* is why Maxim de Winter is so alternately absentminded and prone to anger, the second-biggest mystery is why in the world Favell would be "visiting" Mrs. Danvers that day. Viewers are invited at first to think that there may have been a happy time in the past, when Rebecca was young and her cousin visited and "Danny," as he calls her, was a trusted and beloved servant. If that were the case, then the fact that he is now a con man and she is a vengeful depressive could be a little moving—a testament to sentimental attraction. How likely is that, though? What could the two of them have talked about during that visit, once they had exhausted "Wasn't Rebecca something?" and "Remember the time she...?" There is no sign that they were conspiring to destroy de Winter that early in the story—some sort of conspiracy is clearly hinted at when Mrs. de Winter catches Favell having sneaked in through the back door, but no conspiracy emerges. It does not make sense, but it works. This is a film about a young woman who feels overwhelmed by the world she has plunged into, and it would be just too convenient, too cinematic, to tie up all of its mysteries in the end.

There is no denying that the male and female leads are important in making Daphne du Maurier's popular novel work on-screen and that Mrs. Danvers, as malice incarnate, nearly steals the show from them. But the whole thing might have collapsed if the supporting characters had been handled badly. Joan Fontaine and Laurence Olivier and Judith Anderson do wonderful acting, and they are capably held up by Gladys Cooper as Beatrice, Nigel Bruce as Giles, C. Aubrey Smith as Colonel Julyan and especially Reginald Denny in the thankless supporting role of the amiable, dedicated supporting man, Frank. Sometimes, though, the best support comes from giving the leads opposition. Romance is fine, but *Rebecca* is a story of menace and mystery, and in these, Florence Bates's Mrs. Van Hopper and George Sanders's Favell really delivered.

Source: David Kelly, Critical Essay on *Rebecca*, in *Novels for Students*, Gale, Cengage Learning, 2016.

William Hare

In the following excerpt, Hare discusses the casting of Joan Fontaine in Rebecca.

FONTAINE AND THE PROCESS OF SELECTION

...Hitchcock demonstrated his casting astuteness, an important instinct in the repertoire of any genius director—or filmmaker, as he preferred—in selecting Joan Fontaine. The choice occurred following a long process he did not need. Selznick's flamboyance surfaced during the selection process. The publicity-conscious producer had received significant attention with his earlier quest to find the perfect Scarlett O'Hara for *Gone with the Wind*. While Vivien Leigh was ultimately cast, the list of those who also tested embodied a who's who of the screen's present and future leading ladies, including Katharine Hepburn, Bette Davis, Joan Crawford, Susan Hayward, Lana Turner and Paulette Goddard. Selznick sent a score of actresses before the camera to test for the role of Mrs. de Winter. Hitchcock not only argued with Selznick over possibilities, he was only one of three directors involved in analyzing the actresses, as the producer brought in consultants. George Cukor and John Cromwell, two directors whose judgments were valued by Selznick, were also included.

By August 19 the choice had been narrowed to Anne Baxter, Margaret Sullavan, and two talented sisters who would eventually both receive Best Actress Oscars, Olivia de Havilland and Joan Fontaine. Vivien Leigh, Loretta Young, Susan Hayward, Lana Turner, Virginia

> THE WAY IN WHICH FONTAINE WAS INITIALLY INTRODUCED TO THE ROLE IN THE FILM THAT WOULD PROVE HER STARRING BREAKTHROUGH WAS NOTHING SHORT OF STORYBOOK OPPORTUNITY."

Mayo and Geraldine Fitzgerald had also been tested. Olivia de Havilland was reluctant to compete with her sister for the role. She had just completed *Gone with the Wind* under Selznick and recognized that her own opportunities had thus far been more significant than those of her sister. Baxter, at 16, was eliminated due to her youth.

The two persons whose creativity Hitchcock would rely upon most during his life, wife Alma Reville Hitchcock and Joan Harrison, reached a casting conclusion with which neither the director, the producer, nor the two directorial consultants, Cukor and Cromwell, agreed. Alma and Harrison preferred Baxter, even at 16, to Fontaine, whom they found "too coy and simpering to a degree that is intolerable." Hitchcock's female brain trust found Margaret Sullavan "far ahead of either."

Selznick rejected Sullavan, believing that the actress, known for onscreen fire, lacked credibility in a role calling for extreme passivity. By the end of August Selznick and the three directors considered Fontaine to be the best candidate, and asked her to do another test. She politely responded that, while honored to accept the role, she would not comply with the request. Fontaine was slated to marry actor Brian Aherne on August 19, then leave on her honeymoon. With filming time drawing near, Selznick wired Fontaine the day after her wedding, requesting that she return on Labor Day for final wardrobe fittings and the start of principal photography.

Hitchcock and the entire production received a damaging shock when, on September 1, Germany invaded Poland. Two days later England declared war on Germany. Filming began September 8 amid concerns on the part of Hitchcock and the largely British cast that London would be bombed. Hitchcock fear [sic] for his family in England, and concerned about the inexperience of his leading lady. With all the problems and distractions, filming progress was uncharacteristically slow for the first few weeks.

LIFE IMITATES ART

. . . Joan Fontaine, a young actress in her early twenties, received the opportunity of a lifetime when she starred in a film adapted by a dual Pulitzer winner from a novel by England's premier gothic author of the time. It was produced by the celebrated young man in a hurry who had just delivered *Gone with the Wind* to audiences. The film was directed by his newest contract acquisition, a British legend in his own time making his American debut, while her male starring counterpart was one of the most exciting talents to cross the Atlantic from London to Hollywood in years, fresh from his role as the haunted Heathcliff in the 1939 William Wyler triumph produced by Samuel Goldwyn, *Wuthering Heights*. All the same, her account of filming *Rebecca* could be summarized in the title of her 1978 autobiography, *No Bed of Roses*.

The way in which Fontaine was initially introduced to the role in the film that would prove her starring breakthrough was nothing short of storybook opportunity. "I had met Paulette Goddard one night at Charlie Chaplin's the year before," Fontaine related, "a night that was to change the course of my career. At dinner, where Paulette presided, though it remained a mystery whether she was Mrs. Chaplin or not, I found myself seated next to a heavyset, bespectacled gentleman who seemed particularly knowledgeable and pleasant. Soon we were chattering about the current best sellers. I mentioned that I had just read *Rebecca* by Daphne de [sic] Maurier and thought it would make an excellent movie. My dinner partner gazed at me through his lenses. 'I just bought the novel today. My name is David Selznick.' Who was I and would I like to test for the part of 'I' de Winter? Would I!"

Alfred Hitchcock occupied a special place in Fontaine's estimation for his ability to work with actors. "Before George Cukor, I'd never worked with an 'actor's director' and have worked with few since," the star candidly asserted. "Most of them, like George Stevens, knew the camera well, but once George said, 'Action,' the actor was supposed to know his lines and make the best of them on his own. On the other hand, Hitch had a good ear. He had patience, authority. He had taste. Most of all, he had imagination. We liked each other and

I knew he was rooting for me. He had a strange way of going about it, as actors who have worked with him have verified. His technique was 'Divide and conquer.' He wanted total loyalty, but only to him."

While the young actress felt good that director Hitchcock was on her side, trouble loomed in the form of her male lead, the dynamic Olivier. Hitchcock confided to Fontaine during the first week of filming that Olivier was disappointed that his fiancée, Vivien Leigh, had been bypassed for the role. He later related that Olivier had spoken to him again about Fontaine, this time stating bluntly that she was "awful" and that "Vivien was the only one who should play opposite him." Reports from the Goldwyn Studios set of *Wuthering Heights* revealed that Olivier had lobbied director William Wyler to cast Vivien Leigh in place of his leading lady, Merle Oberon.

Fontaine conceded that she could hardly be friends with Olivier after learning about his conspiratorial action, but the friction extended beyond his complaints to Hitchcock. One morning, less than six weeks following Fontaine's marriage to Brian Aherne, Olivier blew a take and erupted with a four-letter word. While conceding that she had seen the word scrawled a few times on walls, Fontaine had never heard it spoken aloud, and registered an expression of shock. Hitchcock observed it, and sought to caution his male star.

"I say, Larry old boy, do be careful," Hitchcock said. "Joan is just a new bride."

Turning toward his leading lady, Olivier asked, "Who's the chap you married?"

"Brian Aherne," the young bride proudly boasted.

"Couldn't you do better than that?" Olivier snapped as he strode off.

Joan Fontaine conceded that Olivier's nasty retort shattered her. As to Olivier's claim that his fiancée should have played the female lead in *Rebecca*, the demure, sensitive Fontaine proved a better choice for the unique role of a tender-hearted, frequently hurt young woman experiencing the pangs of adjusting to a new life which appears well beyond her. Leigh was fresh from her celebrated triumph which would win her a Best Actress Oscar for *Gone with the Wind*, in which she played a mercurial firebrand. Even by exercising the most disciplined performing technique it is difficult to envision the charismatic Leigh displaying the level of unique, submissive

> PART OF THE STRUGGLE OVER THE FILM WAS BETWEEN SELZNICK'S LOVE OF THE LAVISH, OF EXPENSIVE COSTUMES AND BIG HOUSES, AND HITCHCOCK'S DESIRE FOR SURFACE REALISM AND THE CAREFULLY OBSERVED DETAIL OF THE EVERYDAY."

vulnerability and overall sensitivity realized by Fontaine. Also, with the image of Leigh as Scarlett O'Hara fresh in mind, the film audience would find it difficult empathizing with her in such a totally different role, so strong was her performance as the never-say-die, "tomorrow is another day" heroine of Selznick's spectacle. . . .

Source: William Hare, "America, Selznick and a Gothic Challenge: *Rebecca*," in *Hitchcock and the Methods of Suspense*, McFarland, 2007, pp. 41–42, 56–58.

Alison Light

In the following excerpt, Light examines the faithfulness of Hitchcock's film as an adaptation of du Maurier's novel.

It's not just that Hitchcock's *Rebecca* wasn't exactly Daphne du Maurier's; it wasn't entirely Hitchcock's either. Arriving in Hollywood in 1939, Hitchcock's first American feature was overshadowed by David O. Selznick, the producer who had bought him and who liked to run things his way. 'Selznick's *Rebecca*' (as the publicity had it, relegating the director to the position of a 'mentor' who had 'collaborated' with Selznick) was to be 'the most glamorous picture ever made'. Made in 1940, it was heralded as the successor to *Gone With the Wind*, the film which in fact absorbed nearly all Selznick's energies during the actual shooting of *Rebecca*, though he reserved the last edit to himself and laid in the corny Franz Waxman score.

But it was the feminine angle of *Rebecca* that caused ructions. Or rather which Selznick defended in injured tones, rejecting as 'distorted and vulgarised' Hitchcock's first treatment of the novel, and insisting that the picture respect 'the little feminine things which are so recognisable and which make every woman say, "I know just how she feels. I know just what she's going through."' And this meant sticking to the story.

Selznick was renowned for his filming of literary classics (*Little Lord Fauntleroy, The Prisoner of Zenda*). He revered the capacity of film to bring books and their characters to life. The promotion of *Rebecca* concentrated on book tie-ins. From lending-library stands in cinema foyers to illustrated bookmarks, advance screening for 'book experts' and 'thorough school coverage', the literariness, and thereby the borrowed cultural cachet, of the film was enhanced. Tributes to 'the importance of the du Maurier family in English letters and the stage' mingled with shameless exhortations to the English distributors to 'cash in on the appeal of Your Famous Bestseller'. A letter competition invited local girls to discuss such nervous topics as 'Should A Girl Marry Outside Her Social Class?' or 'Would Yon Marry A Man You Knew Little About?' (though not, it should be noted, 'Why Marry A Man Old Enough To Be Your Father?').

There was every kind of tension between Selznick and Hitchcock. Hitchcock was impatient with the idea of movie-making as 'picturisation'. But he also in later years disowned the film as catering too much for the female audience Selznick clearly had in mind. 'It's not a Hitchcock picture,' he told François Truffaut. 'It's a novelette really. The story is old-fashioned; there was a whole school of feminine literature at the period, and though I'm not against it, the fact is that the story is lacking in humour.' (Two of the scenes which Selznick had cut from the script were of vomiting: hearty male jokes, presumably.) The taint of the novelettish lingered: 'Boots library in its level of appeal,' sneered Lindsay Anderson in 1972, with public-school hauteur and far more cultural snobbery than 'Hitch', who wanted to make films that could be both experimental and popular.

Slavishness to the literary and, even worse, to the woman's novel of the 1930s, was compounded by the kind of romantic glamorisation of settings and of actors that offended Hitchcock's more democratic sensibilities and documentary leanings. Where Selznick was drawn to the past, the gorgeous and the patrician, Hitchcock wrote articles in the thirties championing 'the only genuine life and drama' in Britain, that of 'ordinary everyday citizens'. He proclaimed himself a believer in the 'little man', loathing 'dress shirts, cocktails, and Oxford accents', the bottled-up stiff breeding of the English upper classes and the stagey actors who mimicked them. Like Laurence Olivier playing Maxim de Winter, du Maurier's suave but tormented hero.

It is easy to see *Rebecca* as a transitional, settling-in kind of film: Hitchcock's debut in Hollywood, his compromise with the producer-director system, his trial run of the superior resources that the American film industry had to offer. In the *auteur* theory, which charts the director's progress as the inevitable development of his genius (followed usually by the sad decline of the old man: enter his young disciples), *Rebecca* is an 'immature' film which nevertheless shows 'the Master' emerging from his apprenticeship. In their now classic account of Hitchcock, Eric Rohmer and Claude Chabrol did their best to blame du Maurier for any of the film's faults, curiously arguing that while Hitchcock absolutely faithfully adapted the 'gossipy and somewhat affected novel', he turned it into something quite different—a 'modern and disquieting' thriller.

Did they read the book? Fans of du Maurier's original might well argue that far from Hitchcock saving her novel, *Rebecca* provided him with the kind of material that brought out his strengths. *Rebecca* was in fact a long way from the Edwardian novelette or the standard fare of interwar romance, which is why it survived when so many titles faded into oblivion. (Who now reads Berta Ruck?) Transporting the gauche heroine to the aristocratic Manderley, the novel kicks off where most romances end, with life after marriage. None of du Maurier's novels close to the sound of wedding bells: rueful, violent, frequently gloomy, *Rebecca* is the most introspective of the lot. A post-romantic novel, it suggested that at the heart of every marriage is a crime.

More about hate than love, du Maurier insisted, *Rebecca* is above all a study in jealousy. The girl's first-person narration, her incessant imaginings about the dead Rebecca and her projections of her (and Rebecca's) life back and forth into past and future, crosses precisely that unstable psychological territory of fantasy and obsession, of guilty memory and fearful innocence, which were to become Hitchcock's hallmark. Herself a shy and lonely young wife, du Maurier wrote as the second Mrs de Winter. Her own romance with Frederick Browning, the strong, silent man who had swept her off her feet, was rapidly wearing thin. 'Tommy' or

'Boy' Browning, a war hero of the First World War, still suffered from nightmares and depressions: the family nickname for him became 'Moper' (though he became better known as one of the generals in the disastrous command of Arnhem through Dirk Bogarde's portrayal of him in Attenborough's *A Bridge Too Far*). Billeted abroad, Daphne dreaded regimental functions and found herself haunted by fears of her husband's passion for his ex-fiancée, Jan Ricardo, dark-haired, beautiful and exotic.

Part of the struggle over the film was between Selznick's love of the lavish, of expensive costumes and big houses, and Hitchcock's desire for surface realism and the carefully observed detail of the everyday. *Rebecca* begins as a love story and advances as a thriller. Manderley (like Tara in *Gone With the Wind*), with its loyal retainers and sumptuous breakfasts, represents a conservative longing; it bespeaks another kind of England (the sort that went down very well in Hollywood), frozen in the aspic of tradition. Manderley is the England Hitchcock must have felt well shot of, inhabited by stuffed shirts with cut-glass accents, as closed to him as to the nameless, and thereby average, girl. The film works hard to deglamorise it.

The first prospect of Manderley is not a view at all. Obscured in the pouring rain, it is reflected like a miniature paperweight model in the misty windscreen of the car (one of the many shots that seem to prefigure *Citizen Kane*, which came out the following year). We are never asked to marvel at sweeping shots of the grounds. Very little is made of the romance of Cornwall. The retinue of servants, who might be expected to stir up the viewers' envy and admiration, merely underline the girl's nervousness. Mrs Danvers, in particular, Rebecca's sinister housekeeper, appears suddenly and soundlessly, reminding us that servants make intimacy and ease impossible. In the film, as in the novel, Manderley, as Rebecca's home, is ultimately repudiated as excessive (like a good bourgeois, the girl is shocked by the leftovers), false and corrupt. It must be—and is—destroyed in the cleansing fire at the closure of both.

Hitchcock enjoys gently debunking the upper classes, making mild fun of the barmy upper-class relatives, using George Sanders, in a wonderfully camp performance (as Jack Favell), to expose their snobbery and complacency. The orphaned heroine may be Cinderella but she is also, in her shabby cardigans and sensible skirts, clutching her handbag, Miss Ordinary of 1938 (the kind of 'thoroughly nice girl' Hitchcock wrote so warmly of). Hitchcock brings the romance down to earth by means of contemporary idiom: 'toodle-oo,' 'right you are,' or the pipe-smoking Maxim, a brusque father-figure, telling his schoolgirl wife to stop biting her nails and eat up her breakfast: '"There's a good child."'

The topography of the Gothic—both its literal and emotional geography—is where Hitchcock really meets du Maurier. Combining the extravagant with psychological realism, it had room for Selznick too. The crenellated towers of remote Manderley, the long corridors down which the child-bride is compulsively drawn toward the secret atrocities of the hero-villain's past, the hint of deviant sexuality and the eroticism of death, *Rebecca* recasts many of those elements of the Gothic which had for centuries provided a pre-Freudian vocabulary for what we would call repressed desires. Hitchcock's camera works constantly to capture the vulnerability and insignificance of the girl dwarfed and isolated in draughty baronial halls or shrinking on oversize plush sofas alongside cabinets of treasures (Susan in Kane's Xanadu comes to mind again). As curiosity impels her—'What was Rebecca really like?'—we watch her framed against vast oaken doors, reaching up like a prying child to turn the handle and enter the forbidden chamber, drawing back the curtains and veils in which Rebecca, and all she stands for, is shrouded. Alice in Wonderland (Joan Fontaine wears a velvet Alice band and Olivier calls her 'Alice', to reinforce the point) wandering in Bluebeard's Castle.

A home-movies scene, in which the anxious and insecure girl silently watches images of her own past happiness ('only four months ago,' so quickly does romance wither), is one of many brilliant improvisations for visualising the breakdown of her identity as she disappears into her fantasies of Rebecca. But unlike du Maurier. Hitchcock and Selznick, whatever their intentions, cannot really identify with the girl's point of view. The hindsight of the voice-over in the first five minutes is never resumed. They only give us half of the story of female identification and projection.

Joan Fontaine's tremulous expression in close-up always emphasises passive dissolution: what the film cannot show is her pleasure in imagining Rebecca, the active component of longing which could take the girl beyond her dullness, her orthodox femininity. The famous scene in Rebecca's bedroom, where Mrs Danvers seductively invites the girl to take Rebecca's place, shows Joan Fontaine's humiliation, disgust and nausea at being situated as voyeur. It conveys little of the voyeur's satisfactions. The novel, on the other hand, is as much *attracted* to Rebecca, her thrilling independence and sexual assertiveness, as repulsed by her: 'She had all the courage and spirit of a boy [...] She did what she liked, she lived as she liked. She had the strength of a little lion too.' Hitchcock and Selznick's script tries to limit this kind of damage: they don't want their female viewers believing that being Rebecca, and acting like a man, might be a great deal more fun than marriage to boring old Max....

Source: Alison Light, "Hitchcock's *Rebecca*: A Woman's Film?," in *The Daphne du Maurier Companion*, edited by Helen Taylor, Virago Press, 2007, pp. 295–300.

Rui Nogueira

In the following interview excerpt, Hitchcock compares artists and filmmakers, noting that each has his own style.

ECRAN: What to do when one has only an hour to interview one of the pillars of cinema history and several hundred questions to ask him? Where to begin? What to choose? The answer to this dilemma is implicit in the interview that follows.

HITCHCOCK: I never think of the films I make as being *my* films. I'm not that vain or egotistical. If I were to make films for my own satisfaction they would certainly be very different from those you see. They would be much more dramatic, more realistic, possibly without humor. The reason why I have specialized, so to speak, in suspense is strictly commercial. The public expects a certain type of story from me and I don't want to disappoint them.

The "director-author" instinctively takes up a certain type of subject. For me this constant is my specialty. I know very well that when the public goes to see a Hitchcock film, they will be very disappointed if they don't find one or more crimes in it. That is a rule that even critics can't escape. Some years ago, in 1949, I agreed to make a film that was a vehicle for Ingrid Bergman, *Under Capricorn*. Well, it didn't work. When it first came out a Hollywood critic wrote, "We had to wait 104 minutes for the first shiver." I didn't want it to be a "shivers" film. For reasons of the story there was in fact at a certain point a scene with a shrunken head on a bed, but that was all. If that remark has remained engraved in my memory, that is because it shows how the public and critics think about my work. One day Fellini made this comment about *The Birds*: "I would never have had the courage to make people wait so long before showing them the first bird!" Even people in my field of work can be disappointed at not immediately finding my trademarks: knives, slit throats, "shivers."

ECRAN: One may find your theory on "auteurs" in the mouth of Joan Fontaine in Rebecca: *"My father always painted the same flower because he thought that when an artist had found his subject he had only one desire—to paint nothing else."*

HITCHCOCK: Yes, that is very evident with painters. We can see it clearly when we visit a museum. Looking at paintings by different masters, we notice that each of them has his own style. We recognize at one glance a Rousseau, a Van Gogh, a Klee. So I ask myself why one should not always recognize the mark of a director or a filmmaker (I do not like the word "director" because I find this term incorrect and prefer the label "filmmaker"). I believe that one of the main reasons for this difficulty in identifying the stamp of a director is that most of them do not have a particular style. The quality of the film they are making generally depends on the quality and importance of the subject matter. As for me, the content of a story, the plot, does not interest me at all. It's the manner of recounting that fascinates me. What attracts me is to discover what will provoke a strong emotion in the viewer and how to make the viewer feel it.

Moreover, I think that in all artistic domains we attempt to create an emotion. The importance of a work of art, no matter what sort, is to evoke a reaction. It doesn't matter what sort of reflex is stimulated. As soon as one says "I like" or "I hate" that signifies that one is no longer indifferent. I very much like the story of the young couple in a museum of modern art. They stop, perplexed, in front of an abstract painting. Suddenly a hand with a finger pointing at them emerges from the frame and says, "I don't understand you either."

A filmmaker can repeat himself just like a painter. If you were to ask me. "Why did Boudin always paint the seashore and never the zoo?" I would answer "Simply because he never had any more desire to paint a zoo than I have to make a musical comedy."

When a critic is not very deep—which is the case less rarely than one might think—he limits himself to retelling the story of the film that he sees. He considers relating the events as equivalent to doing "criticism." That strikes me as a very lazy attitude, unless it is a way of hiding profound ignorance. Why should it be different for a film critic than for an art critic? It is accepted that an art critic must know his subject, right? He must know, for example, that Cézanne is one of the precursors of the modern movement in art and that the most important thing for him was to translate visual sensations. Similarly for me, when I take on a screenplay I feel the same needs.

Often when I have just finished a film, I ask myself why I did it and wish I hadn't made it. Perhaps that's because I don't like being obliged to go to the studio every morning to say that it's not the right color and we have to have another and to correct everything that is wrong. For me the entire construction of a film has already been done during the elaboration of the screenplay. One often says, concerning the theater, that a play does not exist when it is not being presented before an audience, that it's at the moment when the public and the creator come together that the play becomes a whole. But I am too deep this morning, don't you think? Ask me another question.

ECRAN: What I like about your films is the precision of your mise-en-scéne *[sic]. Even in minor films like* Dial M for Murder *(1954) and* To Catch a Thief *(1955) you succeed in a few seconds with the opening shots in plunging us fully into the subject matter.*

HITCHCOCK: Certainly. Just look at *Frenzy:* in the first scene one sees a body floating on the Thames and one understands immediately that this is not a drawing room comedy.

ECRAN: A genre that you tried only once, in 1941, with Mr. and Mrs. Smith.

HITCHCOCK: Yes, that's true. But you must understand that it was not really a film for myself. I had just finished, in rapid succession, *Rebecca* and *Foreign Correspondent* when Carole Lombard, who had become my friend, said to me, "Why don't you direct me in a film?" I accepted her suggestion. The script had been written by someone other than me, but since my profession was filmmaking, I took it, I went on the set, I yelled "Roll it" and "Cut," and I made it. As simple as that. You find it a sad comedy? Perhaps. That must be reflected on the face of the owner of the little restaurant where Robert Montgomery and Carole Lombard go....

Source: Rui Nogueira, Nicoletta Zalaffi, and Alfred Hitchcock, "Hitch, Hitch, Hitch, Hurrah!," in *Alfred Hitchcock: Interviews*, edited by Sidney Gottlieb, University Press of Mississippi, 2003, pp. 119–21.

SOURCES

Anderson, Jeffrey M., Review of *Rebecca*, Combustible Celluloid website, http://www.combustiblecelluloid.com/classic/rebecca.shtml (accessed December 26, 2014).

Bradshaw, Peter, Review of *Rebecca*, in *Guardian*, June 29, 2006, http://www.theguardian.com/film/2006/jun/30/alfredhitchcock.thriller (accessed December 26, 2014).

Gaitonde, Vishwas R., "A Tale of Three Houses: Menabilly, Milton Hall and Manderley," in *Prague Review*, October 17, 2013, http://praguerevue.com/ViewArticle?articleId=2197 (accessed December 26, 2014).

"German-Soviet Nonaggression Pact," History.com, 2014, http://www.history.com/topics/world-war-ii/german-soviet-nonaggression-pact (accessed December 26, 2014).

Miller, Frank, "Behind the Camera on *Rebecca*," Turner Classic Movies website, http://www.tcm.com/this-month/article/191138%7C0/Behind-the-Camera-Rebecca.html (accessed December 26, 2014).

Review of *Rebecca*, in *Variety*, March 26, 1940, http://variety.com/1940/film/reviews/rebecca-1200413156/ (accessed December 26, 2014).

Swift, Dean, "The British Manor House & the Manorial System," General-History website, http://general-history.com/the-british-manor-house-the-manorial-system/ (accessed December 26, 2014).

Rebecca, directed by Alfred Hitchcock, 20th Century Fox, 2008, DVD.

Tinee, Mae, "Intelligence and Imagination in Film *Rebecca*," in *Chicago Tribune*, April 6, 1940, p. 17.

"World War II: Timeline," United States Holocaust Memorial Museum website, June 20, 2014, http://www.ushmm.org/wlc/en/article.php?ModuleId=10007306 (accessed December 26, 2014).

FURTHER READING

Armstrong, Richard, "The Wandering Woman in Rebecca," in *Screen Education*, Fall 2008, pp. 131–36.
Rather than viewing the film as a horror or romance picture, Armstrong explains it in the context of the "woman's picture," a unique subgenre during the 1940s.

Brill, Lesley, *The Hitchcock Romance: Love and Irony in Hitchcock's Films*, Princeton University Press, 1991.
Much has been written and said about Hitchcock's views of male/female relationships and his own relationships with the actresses that he used in his films. This book does not talk much about *Rebecca* because the director was limited in what he could do expressively with the character, but it gives a context in Hitchcock's work to show how he approached du Maurier's material.

Coffin, Lesley L., "Chapter One: Rebecca," in *Hitchcock's Stars: Alfred Hitchcock and the Hollywood Studio System*, Rowman & Littlefield, 2014, pp. 1–12.
Hitchcock's growth as a power wielder in Hollywood is laid out in great detail in this book, but the chapter about *Rebecca*, his first Hollywood movie, is particularly interesting. Decisions about casting and budget that were made while making this film give insight into the final product that emerged.

Leff, Leonard, *Hitchcock and Selznick: The Rich and Strange Collaboration of Alfred Hitchcock and David O. Selznick in Hollywood*, University of California Press, 1999.
The making of *Rebecca* was the first time the famed director and producer worked together, and it was followed by a string of collaborative films that included *Spellbound* and *Notorious*. While relationships between directors and producers are not always that significant, in the case of this film, the way the two personalities combined had much to do with how the final product came out.

SUGGESTED SEARCH TERMS

Hitchcock AND du Maurier

Hitchcock AND Rebecca

Hitchcock AND du Maurier AND Selznick

Hitchcock AND Hollywood

Rebecca AND du Maurier AND film

du Maurier AND screen adaptation

Joan Fontaine AND Laurence Olivier

Rebecca AND screen romance

David O. Selznick AND du Maurier

Rebecca AND Mrs. Danvers AND film

Rickshaw Boy

LAO SHE

1936

Lao She's *Rickshaw Boy*, first published in 1936, is considered a masterpiece of modern Chinese literature. Set in the 1930s in the bustling city of Beijing, *Rickshaw Boy* depicts the lower classes, the poverty stricken, and the hopeless with unblinking accuracy and unmasked outrage. Xiangzi, a comically straightforward man who wants only to own his own rickshaw, is thwarted at every turn by the blind apathy of the society in which he lives. This society cannot bring itself to care for others. The only concern is for the self. In this, Lao's first novel to feature a member of the working class as its protagonist, the author spares no detail in his illustration of Xiangzi's pursuit of his one, simple dream: hardship without reward, vices tempting the senses, isolation, loneliness, and the dehumanizing daily scrabble for money. The novel altered the course of modern Chinese literature with its depiction of the poor. *Rickshaw Boy* was a best seller in the United States and has been translated into more than a dozen languages.

AUTHOR BIOGRAPHY

Lao was born Shu Qingchun in Beijing on February 3, 1899. His father, an imperial palace guard, was killed in the Boxer Rebellion of 1900. As the Qing Empire that his father served crumbled, Lao's family was poverty stricken and witness to terrible acts of cruelty. Lao attended Beijing Normal University, graduating in 1918, after which he became a schoolteacher. Traveling to England in 1924 alongside a Christian missionary, Lao taught Chinese at the University of London School of Oriental Studies.

In London, Lao began to have his first three novels serialized in China's premier literary publication, *Short Story Magazine*. The novels were *The Philosophy of Lao Zhang* (1926), *Zhao Ziyue* (1927), and *The Two Mas* (1929). Lao returned to China in 1931, accepting a teaching job at Shandong University. In 1931, he was married to the painter Hu Xieqing, with whom he would have four children. He decided to quit teaching in order to concentrate his attention on writing. Soon after making this decision, Lao published *Rickshaw Boy*. The novel, serialized in the literary magazine *Yuzhou Feng* (or *Cosmic Wind)* from September 1926 to May 1937, was Lao's first to focus on a member of the lower class. The novel proved popular throughout China and the surrounding areas. Shortly after its publication, the Second Sino-Japanese War broke out, and Lao directed his attention toward producing patriotic and anti-Japanese works to aid the war effort. In 1946, Lao accepted an invitation from the U.S. State Department to travel to the United States because of the popularity of the first English translation of *Rickshaw Boy*. He stayed in the United States until 1949, after the formation of the People's Republic of China.

His later work is made up almost entirely of dramas, the most praised of which is *Teahouse* (1957), a history of China's social upheaval that has a cast of more than sixty characters. During the first days of the Cultural Revolution in 1966, a transcript of Lao's ambivalent opinions toward Marxism and Communist Party Chairman Mao Zedong himself was made public. As a result, Red Guards roughly interrogated Lao regarding his loyalty and looted his home. On August 24, 1966, Lao drowned himself in Taiping Lake in Beijing.

PLOT SUMMARY

Chapter One

Rickshaw Boy begins with the introduction of a man named Xiangzi, whose nickname is Camel. Xiangzi is a rickshaw puller in Beijing. A poor man with no family, his dream is to own his own

MEDIA ADAPTATIONS

- *Rickshaw Boy*, adapted as a film by Ling Zifeng and starring Siqin Gaowa, was produced and distributed by the Beijing Film Studio in 1982.
- *Rickshaw Boy* was adapted as an opera, composed by Guo Wenjing. It premiered at the National Centre for Performing Arts in China in 2014.

rickshaw so as to not pay daily fees on a rented one. By working very hard and not indulging in vices like other rickshaw men, Xiangzi saves enough money to buy his own rickshaw. Because he cannot remember his birthday, he decides he will celebrate the day he purchases his rickshaw as the day of his birth. With his own rickshaw, every penny he earns is his own.

Chapter Two

Xiangzi and his rickshaw are one entity in his mind. He runs tirelessly to honor his machine. Rumors of war reach his ears, but he ignores the news that soldiers are confiscating vehicles outside the city. He takes a risky fare that brings him outside Beijing, where soldiers stop him. They take his rickshaw away before forcing him to join their march. During an enemy attack, Xiangzi uses the distraction to escape on foot.

Chapter Three

Xiangzi decides he cannot abandon the soldier's camels, which most likely will be forgotten by the panicking, retreating soldiers. Seeing the trapped animals as kindred spirits, he returns to camp to lead the quiet animals away by their tether. He walks all night without rest, at first chastising himself for bringing the animals along with him. Happily, he realizes with an epiphany that he can sell the camels and use the money to buy a new rickshaw. Coming to a village, Xiangzi negotiates the sale of the three camels, though he does not get enough money from the deal to buy a new rickshaw immediately.

Chapter Four

Xiangzi continues his journey home to Beijing. He talks of camels in his sleep, earning him his nickname. He heads to Harmony Shed—the closest place to a permanent home he has in the world, where Xiangzi had previously rented rickshaws and slept. The owner of Harmony Shed is Fourth Master Liu, a shrewd man in his late sixties. His daughter, Huniu, is romantically interested in Xiangzi, but he does not return her feelings. The small family welcomes Xiangzi back with some surprise and listens to his story over dinner. Fourth Master Liu agrees to keep the money Xiangzi earned from the camels safe, but Xiangzi refuses his offer of a loan.

Chapter Five

Xiangzi pushes himself very hard to earn enough money for a new rickshaw, alienating the other pullers who live at Harmony Shed and Fourth Master Liu in the process. Huniu continues to flirt unsuccessfully. Fourth Master Liu knows his daughter likes Xiangzi but does not want her to be married. Xiangzi remains oblivious to her and her father's feelings. Xiangzi finds a private client and briefly moves out of Harmony Shed, only to quit the job after he is mistreated.

Chapter Six

Returning to Harmony Shed depressed, Xiangzi is seduced by Huniu. The next morning, he is worried that his actions might ruin his working relationship with Fourth Master Liu. Despite his fears, he returns to Huniu again that night.

Chapter Seven

Xiangzi accepts a position at the house of Mr. and Mrs. Cao. Mr. Cao is a good-hearted man who treats his servants with respect. Xiangzi is proud to be employed by such a fair-minded man, though he feels a nagging guilt over the events leading up to his departure from Harmony Shed. One day, he gets into a wreck, throwing Mr. Cao from the rickshaw. While he expects to be fired for this mistake, Mr. Cao blames the accident on the stray stones lying in the street and forgives Xiangzi. Gao Ma, the family's outspoken maid, assures Xiangzi that his worries are unnecessary.

Chapter Eight

Xiangzi recovers from his embarrassment after the wreck. He discusses his finances with Gao Ma, who has a natural talent for money management, but he decides to go it alone rather than invest with a group. He purchases a bank made from a gourd to store his money. The days grow colder with the approach of the New Year. Unexpectedly, Huniu comes to visit him.

Chapter Nine

Huniu makes a scene, accusing Xiangzi of being no good. She reveals that she is pregnant with his child, and Xiangzi is devastated. She tells him to come to her father's birthday party to win his favor so that he will consent to their marriage. As a gesture of good faith, she gives Xiangzi the money he had left at Harmony Shed for safekeeping. Xiangzi is happy to take the money back, but he is wary that she is trying to trap him.

Chapter Ten

Xiangzi regrets not making more friends, as he could use some advice. He cannot find a way out of the situation. Waiting for Mr. Cao outside of the movie theater, Xiangzi meets an old man and his grandson, Xiao Ma, who are struggling to make ends meet, pulling their own rickshaw. Xiangzi sees his past in the young boy and his future in the worn-down old man. He realizes his hopes of success are futile and decides not to put up a fight against Huniu.

Chapter Eleven

Xiangzi resists the urge to give up hope, thinking that as long as he has the gourd full of money, he has nothing to fear. One day, pulling Mr. Cao, he realizes he is being followed. Mr. Cao tells him not to panic and asks to be dropped off at the house of his friend Mr. Zuo instead of at home. Mr. Cao gives Xiangzi instructions to go to his house and have everyone leave with their things. He warns Xiangzi that he might be taken up by the police but that Mr. Cao will help him if something goes wrong. When Xiangzi arrives at the Cao residence, he is stopped by Platoon Leader Sun, the leader of the soldiers who took Xiangzi on their march. He is now a detective. He tells Xiangzi that Mr. Cao is in trouble because he is a member of an underground political party. He warns Xiangzi to flee or else get into trouble with the rest of the household, and then he steals his savings from the gourd bank.

Chapter Twelve

Xiangzi struggles with the events of the day, unsure as to where he should go. He wanders the city briefly before returning to Mr. Cao's house. He finds Gao Ma waiting in his room. She tells him the family escaped successfully. Xiangzi tells her he is going to sleep at their neighbor's house and look for new work in the morning. He asks her to tell this to Mr. Cao and to warn him that Mr. Zou's house is not safe either. Xiangzi climbs over the wall to the neighbor's house and finds Old Cheng, another rickshaw puller. Old Cheng lets Xiangzi sleep in his quarters for the night. Mr. Cao had been betrayed by one of his students at the university, an activist named Ruan Ming. Because Mr. Cao did not give Ruan Ming a passing grade, Ruan Ming reported him to the National Party as a political radical. Xiangzi considers sneaking back into the Caos' house to steal some valuables but decides against it.

Chapter Thirteen
Old Cheng tells Xiangzi to go see Mr. Cao. When he arrives at Mr. Zuo's house he finds that Mr. and Mrs. Cao left the city. Xiangzi, upset, realizes he must return to Harmony Shed. He has nowhere else to go. Huniu and Fourth Master Liu welcome him back. He helps them prepare for Fourth Master Liu's birthday party. Huniu tries to drop hints to her father that Xiangzi would be a suitable husband. The other rickshaw pullers living in Harmony Shed become alienated both from Xiangzi, for his preferential treatment, and from Fourth Master Liu, who does not offer them an invitation to his birthday party.

Chapter Fourteen
Fourth Master Liu is delighted by the success of his birthday party. Toward the end of the party, when few guests remain, Huniu and her father begin to argue. He reveals that he knows Huniu has her eye on Xiangzi, but he will not give his consent for them to marry. She tells him she will leave if he does not approve. He kicks Xiangzi out of Harmony Shed, accusing him of conspiring to take his daughter away. Huniu reveals she is pregnant with Xiangzi's child and will leave along with him.

Chapter Fifteen
Xiangzi and Huniu are married. They move in together in a housing project, living on Huniu's modest savings. On their wedding night, Huniu reveals that she is not pregnant. Showing no remorse, she tells Xiangzi that he should be grateful to have her as his wife, despite her trick.

Xiangzi, already miserable, suffers more when Huniu demands that he not pull a rickshaw.

Chapter Sixteen
The tenement housing where Huniu and Xiangzi live provides little comfort to the impoverished residents. Only Huniu enjoys herself, feeling superior to those struggling to make ends meet. Xiangzi, hating his idle life, begins to pull rented rickshaws again. Huniu feels betrayed when she learns what he has done. Xiangzi fights back, telling her he will always pull a rickshaw, no matter what his circumstances are. Out of curiosity, Xiangzi passes by Harmony Shed to find it has been sold and the name changed. He does not tell Huniu, but they reach a compromise so that Xiangzi may continue pulling a rickshaw. He feels a spike of happiness.

Chapter Seventeen
Xiangzi investigates the sale of Harmony Shed but cannot discover where Fourth Master Liu lives now. He tells Huniu what he knows. Spring reaches the tenements, increasing Huniu's discomfort in her new situation without her father's safety net. She gives Xiangzi the money to buy a rickshaw. Although an alcoholic and violent neighbor, Er Qiangzi, has a rickshaw for sale, Xiangzi does not want it. Huniu buys it over his objections. Er Qiangzi had sold his daughter, Fuzi, into marriage and beaten his wife to death. Because of this, Xiangzi associates the rickshaw with a coffin. He begins to pull again, leaving Huniu home alone. She is terribly bored until Fuzi unexpectedly arrives back in the tenements, abandoned by her husband. The two women become close friends. Er Qiangzi sees her return home as a financial burden on the family, as her husband left her nothing. He suggests she sell her body to make ends meet for the family. Huniu, rather than share Fuzi's sadness at this prospect, eagerly offers to help her get started—lending her money for new clothes and renting out a room in the apartment she shares with Xiangzi for Fuzi to use with her clients. Xiangzi does not know of these developments.

Chapter Eighteen
Huniu becomes pregnant. Both Fuzi and Er Qiangzi are ashamed of Fuzi's employment. Xiangzi finds the brutal heat of summer is too much for his body to take, but the violent summer storms prove even worse. Caught in

a terrible storm with a client who will not let him stop to take cover, Xiangzi falls ill.

Chapter Nineteen

Xiangzi is forced to stay at home healing for almost a month. Though he is careful when he returns to pulling, he is much weaker than he was before the sickness and prone to relapses. Huniu grows huge with child, refusing to exercise out of superstition that she may lose the baby. The closer she comes to delivery, the more evident it is that the labor will be very hard. Unable to afford a hospital visit, Huniu demands that Xiangzi bring a medium to talk to the spirits. As Huniu struggles to deliver, the medium and her assistant, recognizing the dire situation, sneak out when the couple is not watching. The midwife informs Xiangzi that Huniu will not survive, and in fact both the baby and Huniu die during childbirth.

Chapter Twenty

Xiangzi sells his rickshaw to pay for the cost of the funeral. Fuzi helps him with simple chores while he sits, stunned. He realizes with a shock that Fuzi is in fact his ideal wife. When Er Qiangzi comes to the apartment accusing Xiangzi of taking advantage of Fuzi, Xiangzi throws him out of the house. However, he realizes he cannot support himself, Fuzi, Er Qiangzi and Fuzi's two little brothers. He moves out, telling Fuzi he will return for her. Leaving the tenement, he finds he cannot pull a rickshaw with the same fire of the old days. He begins to smoke cigarettes and gamble. For the first time, he befriends the other rickshaw pullers. He finds a private client named Mr. Xia, a wealthy man who has taken a concubine as a second wife. He hires Xiangzi as a rickshaw puller for her.

Chapter Twenty-one

Mrs. Xia seduces Xiangzi, after which he quits the job and returns to live at the rickshaw shed. He begins to drink, to fight, to tell others that although he tried to make something of himself, the effort was a waste. He treats his passengers poorly and ignores traffic laws. One day, he picks up Fourth Master Liu. The two men fight, and Xiangzi reveals that Huniu has died. He refuses to tell her father where she is buried.

Chapter Twenty-two

Having told off Fourth Master Liu, Xiangzi feels a rush of positive energy. He wants to try to start

again. He decides that the only two people he can trust are Fuzi and Mr. Cao. He visits Mr. Cao first, finding him back in his old home. Gao Ma, the maid, greets Xiangzi with delight. Mr. Cao listens as Xiangzi tells him of his troubles; he tells him about Huniu, Fuzi, and all the trials he has faced. Mr. Cao agrees to hire him back as well as provide housing and simple maid work for Fuzi. Mood soaring, Xiangzi races to the tenements to find Fuzi, but he discovers she no longer lives there. He is devastated, and he returns to smoking and drinking.

Chapter Twenty-three

Xiangzi runs into Xiao Ma's grandfather, who tells him his grandson has died. He tells him that Fuzi is most likely at the White Manor, a notorious brothel. When Xiangzi arrives there, he is informed that Fuzi hanged herself shortly after arrival. Xiangzi cannot cope with this news. He stops bathing, starts drinking heavily, and driving his rickshaw dangerously. He goes to visit Gao Ma, who asks why he never came back to Mr. Cao's. He tells her he was sick and asks for money for medicine, which Mrs. Cao gives him, but he spends the money on his vices. He takes jobs marching in rallies and parades.

Chapter Twenty-four

With the arrival of an early, pleasant summer comes the announcement that Ruan Ming, now a political prisoner, will be publicly put to death. Excitement grows in the city over this event. While the crowd swells on the day of the execution, Xiangzi sits by the bank of the lake, counting his money. He has sold out Ruan Ming, who had become a corrupt rickshaw union organizer and had met Xiangzi at the many protests and rallies he held. Seeing Ruan Ming as a man who sold ideas for money, Xiangzi decided to do the same, selling out Ruan Ming for the equivalent of sixty dollars. When no one would rent rickshaws to Xiangzi anymore, he turned to parading for money, lazily carrying his banner down the street for protests, wedding procession, and funerals. He does not care what fate waits for him at the end of each day: "Xiangzi took part in untold numbers of burial processions but could not predict when he would bury himself."

CHARACTERS

Camel

See Xiangzi

Mr. Cao

Mr. Cao is the generous and kind professor who hires Xiangzi as his private rickshaw puller. Xiangzi greatly enjoys his time working for Mr. Cao and his wife. A disgruntled student, Ruan Ming, turns Mr. Cao in for his allegedly radical beliefs. Mr. Cao is forced to leave the city temporarily as a result. After his return, Xiangzi comes to him in desperation, and Mr. Cao agrees to hire him back, and even provide work for Fuzi, after hearing his life story. However, Fuzi has died, and Xiangzi is too heartbroken to accept Mr. Cao's offer of work.

Mrs. Cao

Mrs. Cao is Mr. Cao's wife. She is well mannered and caring toward the household servants.

Old Cheng

Old Cheng is the rickshaw puller for the next-door neighbors of the Cao family. He lets Xiangzi stay the night with him after the family flees to Mr. Zuo's house. He and Xiangzi are not close friends, but he treats Xiangzi very well while he is a guest.

Er Qiangzi

Er Qiangzi is Fuzi's alcoholic father. He sold Fuzi into marriage, and then he destroyed himself with drink, mourning his decision. He beats his wife to death in a drunken rage. When Fuzi unexpectedly returns home, abandoned by her husband and penniless, he encourages her to become a prostitute so that the family can make ends meet. He sells Xiangzi a used rickshaw.

Fuzi

Fuzi is the unlucky daughter of Er Qiangzi. Her name means "little lucky one," but she suffers terribly. She is sold into marriage by her father, abandoned by her husband, and forced to return to her shattered family with nothing to show for her time away but a pair of silver earrings and a calico dress. She becomes friends with Huniu. At her father's insistence, she becomes a prostitute in order to provide for her family, but she is ashamed of her fate. After Huniu's death, she realizes her love for Xiangzi. He leaves her to try to find stable work so that he may support her family. After waiting, she finds work at the White Manor brothel, but she is so disgusted by herself that she commits suicide.

Fuzi's Little Brothers

Fuzi's two little brothers are too young to help the family financially. They were witness to their father's terrible actions against their mother.

Fuzi's Mother

Fuzi's mother was beaten to death by her husband, Er Qiangzi, while Fuzi was away.

Gao Ma

Gao Ma is Mr. and Mrs. Cao's direct and opinionated maid, who provides a voice of reason to counter Xiangzi's often backward ideas. After Xiangzi and Mr. Cao are in an accident, Gao Ma insists that Xiangzi stop blaming himself. She has a natural talent for investing, but Xiangzi does not take up her offers to help him with his money. Gao Ma is always happy to see Xiangzi when their paths cross.

Huniu

Huniu is the daughter of Fourth Master Liu. She tricks Xiangzi into marriage by pretending she is pregnant. After her father disowns her, she and Xiangzi are wed. They move into a rundown apartment complex and live off of Huniu's savings, as she would rather spend time with her new husband than have him work. Huniu is temperamental and hard to satisfy. She looks down on rickshaw men but allows Xiangzi to return to work after she discovers she is pregnant. Huniu befriends Fuzi, a neighbor from their building. She dies during childbirth, along with the baby.

Fourth Master Liu

Fourth Master Liu owns Harmony Shed, the closest place Xiangzi has to a home. He rents rickshaws to rickshaw pullers, providing the men room and board as well. He is a keen businessman with strict rule over his domain. He is disappointed that he has no male heirs, but he does not consider Xiangzi a worthy partner for his daughter, Huniu, despite observing her attraction to him. After an argument at his birthday feast, Fourth Master Liu disowns his daughter. He sells Harmony Shed and retires. When Xiangzi picks him up as a customer later, he tells Fourth Master Liu of his daughter's death but does not reveal where she is buried.

Old Man Liu

See Fourth Master Liu

Ruan Ming

Ruan Ming is an activist university student. When he fails Mr. Cao's class, he decides to bring down his professor, destroying his good name by accusing him of radical politics. Later, as a rickshaw union organizer, he becomes close to Xiangzi. Xiangzi turns him in to the government as a radical, and he is arrested. In the novel's final scenes, he is paraded through the streets on his way to be publicly executed.

Platoon Leader Sun

Platoon Leader Sun is the leader of the soldiers that march Xiangzi from the city. He appears later in the novel as a detective who investigates Mr. Cao. He warns Xiangzi that he may be implicated in Mr. Cao's guilt. He breaks Xiangzi's gourd bank and steals his savings.

Mr. Xia

Mr. Xia is a wealthy man who has recently taken a concubine (a mistress) as his second wife. He hires Xiangzi as a rickshaw puller for Mrs. Xia, his new bride.

Mrs. Xia

Mrs. Xia is Mr. Xia's new wife. She seduces Xiangzi secretly.

Xiangzi

Xiangzi aspires to own his own rickshaw. Though his name means "well omened" or "lucky," terrible misfortune befalls him. He is physically strong and excels at his trade. He is uneducated but full of lofty morals. He does not indulge in vices and does not associate with other rickshaw pullers. After his rickshaw is stolen, he tries to get back on his feet, but as soon as he is stable again Huniu tricks him into marriage by pretending she is pregnant with his child. After Huniu dies in childbirth and Xiangzi loses much of his strength to a long-term illness, he takes up smoking and drinking. He becomes less careful in his work, and his morals begin to crumble. Just when he is given a chance to redeem himself and provide a home for Fuzi at Mr. Cao's, Xiangzi discovers that Fuzi has committed suicide. After that blow, he no longer cares for anything. He becomes a careless, apathetic man, looking to get ahead in whatever way is easiest. He stops pulling rickshaws because no

sheds will trust him with rentals. He begins marching in processions for money. There he meets Ruan Ming, whom he sells out for a small sum. Left without hope, Xiangzi does not care whether he lives or dies.

Xiao Ma

Xiao Ma is a young boy who pulls a rickshaw alongside his grandfather. Xiangzi sees his past in the boy. Later, Xiao Ma's grandfather tells Xiangzi that the boy has died.

Xiao Ma's Grandfather

Xiao Ma's grandfather is in very poor health. Xiangzi takes pity on him and buys him some food after he faints. He and his grandson own their own rickshaw but still struggle to make ends meet. Xiangzi realizes that Xiao Ma's grandfather is a vision of his own future. The thought that owning his own rickshaw might not bring him success and happiness makes Xiangzi upset. Xiao Ma's grandfather later helps Xiangzi find where Fuzi has gone when she moved from the tenements. He tells Xiangzi that poor people, like a swarm of grasshoppers, are powerless alone but unstoppable when they unite.

Mr. Zuo

Mr. Zuo is a friend of the Cao family. They flee to his house after Ruan Ming exposes Mr. Cao's political beliefs.

THEMES

Apathy

Living in a corrupt society, the lower class in this novel does not band together to bring about change; instead, they are too focused on their own small lives to care about their neighbors. The apathetic mood poisoning Beijing's poor keeps them from seeing their potential power as a large, unhappy group suffering under similar circumstances. Rather than pull each other up, they push each other down in order to help their own cause. Ruan Ming's execution provides a perfect example of the apathy of the other characters. Rather than see the execution of a political activist and union organizer as a threat to their own safety, to their rights as workers, to their humanity, they see the execution as a moment's entertainment, a brief diversion from the struggles in their own lives. They are not

TOPICS FOR FURTHER STUDY

- Read the young-adult novel *Rickshaw Girl* by Mitali Perkins. How does the experience of a rickshaw puller in an Indian village compare with the life of a puller in Beijing as described in *Rickshaw Boy*? Compare and contrast the two depictions of rickshaw pullers in a paper, using examples from both texts.

- Create a blog in which you explore the history of Beijing. Post interesting facts and photos you find about the ancient city, citing all your sources. At least one entry should focus on Beijing in the 1930s, about an aspect of life in the city during the time in which *Rickshaw Boy* is set. Free blog space is available at http://www.blogger.com.

- The first two chapters of *Rickshaw Boy* center exclusively on Xiangzi and do not introduce any other major characters. Write a short story that similarly focuses on only one character as he or she goes about an ordinary day. Explore that person's hopes and dreams, fears and hardships.

- How does Lao define and show individualism in *Rickshaw Boy*? Is individualism depicted as a positive or negative trait of Xiangzi's character? How does Lao's definition differ from your own concept of individualism? With a small group of students, explore Lao's definition of this concept as well as your own. Take notes in preparation for a class discussion on the definition of individualism across cultures.

thinking deeply because they are so beset with problems they cannot afford to consider the larger picture.

Xiangzi, too, gives in to apathy. After his hopes of happiness and stability are dashed, he forgets his pride in his own strength of body and mind and instead wastes away pursuing vices. "Fight poison with poison," he thinks. This sentiment is nonsensical unless one has been so beaten down by life that self-destruction seems the only option, and that is the option Xiangzi chooses. The once proud, strong, healthy, and honest man has caught the sickness of apathy that spreads throughout the poverty-stricken quarters of the city. The hope that the poor will recognize the strength in their numbers is never realized in the novel. The only mobilization of the masses in *Rickshaw Boy* is to watch a political prisoner—one who could have helped them—be put to death. Selfishly sold out by Xiangzi, Ruan Ming, who himself once selfishly sold out Mr. Cao, is executed, and no one can shake off the apathetic fog long enough to question why.

Individualism

For Lao, individualism is the root of the problems facing the poverty-stricken working class of Beijing society. Individualism in Lao's perspective translates to selfishness, a willingness to isolate oneself from society for one's own good rather than help others rise out of their struggles for the good of the many. Xiangzi's individualism alienates him from those around him. He is blinded by his desire for independence, resulting in the fragmentation of his relationships. For example, he does not respond to overtures of friendship from other rickshaw pullers, choosing to isolate himself so that he may work harder and earn more. By doing this, he loses the opportunity to lean on his brothers of the trade when he is down. When Huniu ensnares him, he realizes that friends could have given him advice, possibly helped him escape from her marriage plot, but because he has no one he is trapped: "A man alone cannot hold up the sky!"

In *Rickshaw Boy*, an individual by himself cannot change even his own circumstances, let alone right wrongs in the larger society. Xiangzi believes he can exist in a vacuum, guided by his personal moral code, but no such vacuum exists. The outside world constantly interrupts his desire for individuality, in the form of soldiers confiscating his rickshaw, Huniu's deceiving him into marriage, and even nature's punishing summer storms leaving him sick and unable to work. Xiangzi's idealized concept of independence is gradually eroded until it is a misshapen impulse to step on the back of another for his own gain. His once mighty principles fall one by one, until he becomes a ghost of the man he once was: "Someone who strives only for himself knows how to destroy himself—the two extremes of individualism." Xiangzi destroys

The novel is set in Beijing in the 1930s. *(© TonyV3112 | Shutterstock.com)*

himself, giving in to the vices he once rejected, no longer caring for his health or appearance, looking only for the next coin. Because he did not care for others when he was healthy, morally fit, and successful, no one cares for him when he sinks low. Individualism destroys Xiangzi's life.

STYLE

Symbol of Individualism

A symbol is an object that represents something else, often a complex concept. In *Rickshaw Boy*, the rickshaw is a symbol of individualism. Xiangzi's pursuit a rickshaw of his own is a symbolic quest to attain individuality, a quest that is doomed from the start. Soldiers steal Xiangzi's first rickshaw from him. Thus, despite successfully achieving his goal of independence, society interferes, stripping Xiangzi of his individualism and livelihood in one sweep. Xiangzi's next rickshaw does not live up to the first. He buys it out of desperation to support himself and Huniu during her pregnancy, and it has a violent past. Xiangzi's ideal rickshaw, the rickshaw that represents

individualism, fades further into the distance the more he falls away from his moral center, until the dream is forgotten entirely. Instead of the pure individualism that the rickshaw represents, the independence and self-sufficiency Xiangzi once craved, Xiangzi chooses an apathetic, even nihilistic (despairing) individualism, betraying Ruan Ming for a small sum of money.

Detached Mood

The mood of a work of literature is the ambiance that surrounds the narrative, or how the work makes a reader feel. The mood of *Rickshaw Boy* is remarkable in that, despite the tragicomic missteps and injustices that mark Xiangzi's gradual decline, the novel avoids melodrama. Instead the reader watches Xiangzi's life unfold with a sense of detached observation, not overwhelming sympathy. The mood is one of resignation and complacency (smug satisfaction, the opposite of the restlessness that could produce change), as the narration acknowledges the cruelties of the world but offers few suggestions for how to break up the apathy of the citizens of Beijing toward each other's struggles.

COMPARE & CONTRAST

- **1936:** Rickshaws are a common sight in major cities such as Beijing, before the advent of motor vehicles.

  Today: While human-powered rickshaws are rare, bicycle rickshaws and motorized rickshaws are widely in use.

- **1936:** China is on the brink of the Second Sino-Japanese War, a war that will lead to both Chinese and Japanese involvement in World War II.

  Today: Chinese-Japanese relations remain volatile, with points of contention ranging from the seizure of land to military exercises in the East China Sea.

- **1936:** The city of Beijing is called Beiping, which means "Northern Peace" for a period between 1928 and 1949, when the capital of China is Nanjing.

  Today: Beijing, meaning "Northern Capital," is the capital of the People's Republic of China, with a population of more than twenty million people.

HISTORICAL CONTEXT

Beijing, 1930s

Rickshaw Boy acts as a time capsule, providing modern readers with many details about life in Beijing in the 1930s. From the dangerous political climate that leads to Mr. Cao's troubles and Ruan Ming's execution to the daily operations of Harmony Shed, Lao paints a vivid picture of the bustling city. Fear of war is so commonplace that it comes and goes with the seasons: "War and rumors arrived like clockwork every year during planting season." Poverty is so widespread that escape seems impossible. Jean M. James writes in the introduction to the 1979 translation, *Rickshaw*, "The terrible life of the poor depicted in *Rickshaw* is hard to believe, but sociological studies conducted in Peking [Beijing] in the twenties describe the same conditions and worse." The growing pains of a country modernizing unevenly, set upon by constant war both from outside (Japan) and from within (civil war and the activity of warlords in the countryside), and suffering a climate of political fear as Communism gradually spread had left behind a vast multitude of uneducated and impoverished citizens who are downtrodden and hopeless to change their circumstances in a society so eroded. *Rickshaw Boy*'s Xiangzi, a pure man with a clear, attainable dream, is used by Lao to exemplify the sheer madness of the city's corrupting influence. Xiangzi is beaten down morally, physically, and economically, until he is rendered unrecognizable. Xiangzi's stubborn individualism is to blame for his downfall, a symptom of life in Beijing in the 1930s, in which war and poverty fragment relationships and drive simple people to desperate acts. The setting of *Rickshaw Boy* acts as a character, exerting a force that is felt on all the characters, from the richest private rickshaw client to the lowliest tenement dweller.

May Fourth Movement

On May 4, 1919, student activists took to the streets of Beijing in protest of the Treaty of Versailles, which ended World War I and awarded Chinese land to the Japanese. At the root of the protest was the notion that the world saw China as an isolated, feudal land, as yet untouched by the modernity of the larger world. The May Fourth Movement that grew from the initial protests sought to change that impression through embracing modernity, especially in the arts. Lao remained politically ambivalent throughout his life and did not identify himself as a May Fourth activist. However, he was influenced by European and American arts while living in London, developing a particular

The protagonist is nicknamed "Camel" after a plan to make money by selling several of the animals does not go well. *(© Andrea Izzotti / Shutterstock.com)*

fondness for the works of the nineteenth-century English novelist Charles Dickens. Anne Witchard writes in *Lao She in London*: "Lao She's refusal to jettison all aspects of traditional Chinese culture would distinguish him from his May Fourth peers. His modernism would be formulated in its own Chinese terms." As shown in the themes of *Rickshaw Boy*, Lao shared the concern of the May Fourth Movement toward the quality of the Chinese national character. Witchard writes: "Activists of the May Fourth Movement embraced literary fiction as a key solution to perceived national degeneracy." Lao's distress over the apathy of the people and their selfishness resonates through every action and word of Xiangzi and his fellow characters as they struggle alone against insurmountable poverty.

CRITICAL OVERVIEW

Rickshaw Boy was a sensation not only in China but also, quite unexpectedly, in the United States, where it became a best seller after the first English translation of the novel was published in 1945. The novel's popularity led the U.S. Department of State to invite Lao She to visit, an offer that he happily accepted. The novel has been translated into German, French, Spanish, Japanese, Korean, Russian, Italian, and Czech, among others.

Critics almost unanimously consider *Rickshaw Boy* to be Lao's finest work. Witchard praises the novel in *Lao She in London* as: "his *magnum opus*, [an] acclaimed proletarian classic." In the introduction to the 1979 version, James writes: "In *Rickshaw* we have what is, in fact, a proletarian novel of the most realistic reportorial sort, written in the language of the people." To many critics, Xiangzi exemplifies the dangerous nature of consumerism, capitalism, and self-interest. Xiangzi is not a proletarian hero who rises up against an unjust system. He is a proletarian sacrifice, trampled beneath the uncaring heel of society.

In *Lao She: China's Master Storyteller*, Britt Towery considers the novel's originality and its impact on Chinese readers of the time: "Such a story of the disenfranchised of Chinese society had never been so dramatically presented to the Chinese public.... Lao She was reaching new heights in modern Chinese fiction." Previously, literature focused on high society. In fact, *Rickshaw Boy* is the first of the author's work to feature a working-class protagonist. Ranbir Vohra writes of the novel's legacy in *Lao She and the Chinese Revolution*: "This novel is Lao She's masterpiece and, perhaps, the best work of its kind in modern Chinese literature."

Of Lao's lasting reputation in China and around the world, Howard Goldblatt writes in his introduction to *Rickshaw Boy*: "Lao She ... remains one of the most widely read Chinese novelists of the first half of the twentieth century, and probably its most beloved."

CRITICISM

Amy M. Miller

Miller is a graduate of the University of Cincinnati and currently resides in New Orleans, Louisiana. In the following essay, she examines the combination of individualism in Xiangzi and apathy in Beijing that causes the rickshaw puller's moral collapse in Rickshaw Boy.

In *Rickshaw Boy*, a corrupt society gradually wears down the lofty morality of Xiangzi, who wrongly believes that he can succeed on his own. Because he fails to make lasting connections with his fellow rickshaw pullers when he is well, he has no one trustworthy to turn to when his luck turns. As a result, the company he falls into when at last his strict standards crumble is of the basest type. Xiangzi, an orphaned country boy with no real home, is a creation of Beijing. Pure and proud at the novel's beginning, he ends up broken and shameless, plucking used cigarette butts from the ground, a "degenerate, selfish, hapless product of a sick society, this miserable ghost of individualism." Xiangzi's downfall is a result of his steadfast desire for independence coupled with the apathetic atmosphere of the city he calls home.

Xiangzi is introduced to the reader as an honest if unintelligent man. He knows what he wants—a rickshaw of his own—and has a concrete plan to succeed. This plan relies heavily on his individualism: he is naturally a loner, preferring a spiritual union with the machine over being distracted by friendly camaraderie. James

> XIANGZI'S DOWNFALL IS A RESULT OF HIS STEADFAST DESIRE FOR INDEPENDENCE COUPLED WITH THE APATHETIC ATMOSPHERE OF THE CITY HE CALLS HOME."

writes: "*Rickshaw* is the first important study of a laborer in modern Chinese fiction. [Xiangzi] is not mocked, not blamed, not praised, but analyzed and despaired of."

Xiangzi's concept of labor combines mysticism with mechanics. To make money he must run fast, and to run fast he must be healthy; being a fast, healthy runner honors his rickshaw. If he lived in a vacuum, this rational philosophy of labor would naturally pay off quickly. But Xiangzi works in a war-plagued, crime-ridden, politically unstable city overrun with poverty and corruption. To be a success in Beijing, one must navigate slippery social circles; one must be willing to bend here and there and circumvent the rules of civilized society. Fourth Master Liu, for example, has mastered this; his stints in prison have taught him distrust, slyness, and cruelty. Huniu takes after her father: she is a masterful manipulator of simple Xiangzi. Ruan Ming, a member of the educated class, is a perfect example of the inherent corruption of the city. He reacts to bad grades not by studying harder but by betraying his kind professor to the authorities. He betrays the only sterling character in all of *Rickshaw Boy*, Mr. Cao, who could act as Xiangzi's savior twice in the novel if the city's poisonous environment and Xiangzi's back luck did not prevent it. First, when Xiangzi is at his most content, Mr. Cao is forced to flee his home due to the scheming of Ruan Ming, who acts with the apathy one expects from the citizens of the city as he turns on his mentor. Later, when Xiangzi is on the brink of doom, Mr. Cao offers again to help him. Unfortunately, when Xiangzi returns to the tenement to collect Fuzi and begin their new life together at Mr. Cao's, Xiangzi discovers Fuzi's tragic death. If he had not left her behind, perhaps she would not have been driven to such desperation. After observing the tragic consequences of his own actions toward Fuzi, Xiangzi loses the will to live.

WHAT DO I READ NEXT?

- *Teahouse* (1957), considered Lao's greatest play, spans fifty years and includes more than sixty characters. Told in three acts, the play illustrates both the steady social change and the sudden, shocking shifts in community values throughout generations of Beijing's citizens as China leaves behind its imperial past and enters the modern world.

- *Rickshaw Beijing: City People and Politics of the 1920s* (1993) by David Strand is a thorough examination of city life in Beijing, focusing on the daily struggles of the city's working class, with detailed chapters on rickshaws and their pullers.

- Lu Xun's *The Real Story of Ah-Q and Other Tales of China* (2010) features the collected short stories of one of China's greatest modern authors and a forerunner to Lao She, who wrestled Chinese literature from the ostentatious influence of the elite, reinventing it in the ordinary language of the working classes.

- Laurence Yep's young-adult novel *The Magic Paintbrush* (2003) tells the story of Steve, an orphaned boy who lives with his uncle and grandfather in San Francisco's Chinatown. With the aid of a magical paintbrush, young Steve overcomes his culture shock and learns the history of his distant homeland.

- Aldous Huxley's *Brave New World* (1932) is set in a futuristic society in which genetic engineering, a rigid caste system, and enforced communal standards dictate every moment of a citizen's life in order to create an unending sense of happiness and contentment. When John, a savage with no knowledge of these complex rules, is brought from the village where he lives to the World State, he is first frightened by and then corrupted by what he observes. As in *Rickshaw Boy,* a wicked society is responsible for the downfall of a genuine and honest person.

- Shen Congwen's *Border Town* (1934) follows Cuicui, a girl from rural China who is raised by her loving grandfather. The novel presents peasant life in pre-Communist China, as Cuicui must choose between two suitors while worrying over her grandfather's failing health. The book was banned in China under Communist leader Mao Zedong.

- Eileen Chang's short-story collection *Love in a Fallen City* (2006) explores relationships in China: the rules governing love and courtship, the consequences of breaking these rules, and the gaping divide between ancient tradition and modern influence in the arena of romance.

James asks: "Is there a hero in this novel? [Xiangzi] is but a pawn. Is there a villain? When people are struggling to survive they do so by climbing higher on the bodies of others." In the case of Xiangzi, that statement is nearly literal. After all is lost, he finds employment marching in funeral parades for low wages. Xiangzi may have been mistreated by fate and chance, but he has done himself no favors by adopting an attitude that rejects the help of others. Watching old rickshaw men struggle in the cold winter months, he feels happiness at his own youth and strength, not recognition of himself in their situation. When this revelation does come while watching young Xiao and his grandfather, he nearly loses all hope. He refuses financial help, he refuses emotional support, he refuses to express himself until, too late, he reveals everything to Mr. Cao. Vohra praises Xiangzi's resilience in the face of evil, writing that he "is a colossal figure; he is a symbol of China's hungry, patient millions, and if he has not possessed the

The protagonist works hard pulling a rickshaw, but his seemingly simple life is filled with difficult decisions. *(© Pigprox | Shutterstock.com)*

moral strength he did, he would not have survived the pressures." When Xiangzi can no longer stand up against society's crushing pressure, he collapses magnificently, becoming not just lecherous, deceitful, and vile but the most lecherous, the most deceitful, and the most vile, vice-ridden creature haunting the streets of Beijing, selling out a rickshaw union organizer—a man fighting for better conditions for Xiangzi's own beloved trade—for what amounts to sixty dollars.

Ironically, Xiangzi, who desires nothing more than his own rickshaw, nothing less than complete independence, is brought down by the society from which he so desperately wants to stand apart. Goldblatt writes: "The bankruptcy of individualism in the face of a corrupting and dehumanizing social system is both the political and moral message." Xiangzi, though bull-headed and strong, cannot resist the ever-downward pull of the society around him. Because he attempts to stand up against it alone, he cannot win. However, because of the apathy and poverty washing over the populace, they cannot find in themselves the

will to stand up and fight together. Thus, while the solution to the depraved condition of Beijing is for its citizens to stand together under a moral code as strict as Xiangzi's, Xiangzi instead joins the crowd, abandoning the belief in what is pure and good in favor of apathy. Vohra writes: "The accusing finger points not at [Xiangzi] but at the nature of society as a whole, a society that has failed to protect its poor." Crushed under the wheels of change, forgotten by those whom fortune has favored, the poor cannot cope even with the challenges that nature brings. Hot summers and cold winters conspire against them, and when the simplest needs of shelter and food are not met, higher thinking and problem solving become impossible tasks. The poor drown their sorrows with their vices instead, like the alcoholic terror Er Qiangzi, because they do not have the energy left to fight back against their circumstances, nor the power to observe each other's pain and realize it is a reflection of their own suffering.

Xiangzi's stubborn adherence to individualism leads to his anguish, certainly, but, as Vohra points out, "the society in which he lives is an immoral one, in which the poor and the weak are exploited and made to suffer every kind of injustice and wrong." Ultimately and unfortunately, a thoroughly beaten Xiangzi decides to join those who exploit by selling out Ruan Ming. This does not mean Xiangzi is not a victim of society himself, nor does it mean Ruan Ming has not done his share of exploiting in the past. Lao's Beijing would not be itself without the moral degradation of all its inhabitants, exemplified in the great gathering of the populace to watch Ruan Ming be put to death, "a pleasant diversion during the long, refreshingly sunny days." This event that brings the city together, engineered by Xiangzi, is a photographic negative of what could save the city's soul: the poor masses gathering to demand their rights, their happiness, a chance in the world. Instead Ruan Ming is paraded down the road and shot while Xiangzi counts his money by the lake, the sickening result of the corruption of a once pure man.

Misguided by his desire for independence, brought down by the immorality of the city's inhabitants, Xiangzi loses his long, proud fight against vice, greed, and apathy. An unsympathetic victim, he is consumed by the sins he strove against when he was a stronger, more hopeful man. The difference between the Xiangzi who dreams of a rickshaw of his own and the Xiangzi who sways drunkenly down the road picking up cigarette butts is immeasurable, but the course of his downward spiral is devastatingly simple to understand. Xiangzi's stubborn individualism leads him down an ever-narrowing street while the scheming citizens of Beijing lie in wait for him like upturned stones.

Source: Amy Miller, Critical Essay on *Rickshaw Boy*, in *Novels for Students*, Gale, Cengage Learning, 2016.

David Der-wei Wang

In the following excerpt, Wang examines the juxtaposition of farce and melodrama in Lao She's work.

One of the most important novelists of the 1930's, Lao She (pseudonym of Shu Qingchun, 1899–1966) presents us with a double image. Few readers will be left unstirred by the hilarious plots, dangling narratorial postures, and paraded clowns that enliven his early works. But when engaged in a critical survey of his merits, readers have been more apt to praise his

> BECAUSE OF ITS POLARIZATION OF GOOD AND EVIL, INDULGENCE IN HYPERBOLIC RHETORIC, AND REFUSAL TO CAST CHARACTERS AND THEIR ACTIONS IN THE ORDINARY WAY, MELODRAMA HAS ALWAYS BEEN CONSIDERED AS THE OPPOSITE OF REALIST/NATURALIST WRITING."

vivid portrayal of ordinary life, his compassion for the underdog, or the warmth of his humor. While his *Luotuo Xiangzi* (Camel Xiangzi, 1938) has been acclaimed as one of the best works of modern Chinese fiction written before the eve of the second Sino-Japanese war, novels such as *Lao Zhang de zhexue* (The philosophy of Lao Zhang, 1928) and *Lihun* (Divorce, 1933) have received much less attention. To regard Lao She as a humanitarian realist or good-hearted humorist is certainly justified, but in so doing one overlooks his comic talents and makes him merely a good practitioner of the kind of orthodox realism initiated by writers such as Lu Xun. In fact, what truly distinguishes Lao She from other May Fourth writers is not so much his mimetic exposure of social abuses as his exaggeration of them in terms of both farcical and melodramatic discourses. These discourses derive their powers from excessive displays of laughter or tears, the dramatic reversal or parade of moral/intellectual values, and, most important, the compulsion to defy the sanctioned mode of representation.

Lao She was born to a Manchu family of limited means in 1899, a time when the Manchu name ensured neither social privilege nor a secure future. His father, a guard of the Imperial Palace, died protecting the forbidden city in the Boxer Rebellion, while the Emperor and the Imperial Dowager had fled to the west. Lao She and his mother survived the bayonets of looting soldiers only by miraculous luck. But these infantile traumas bring not so much sadness as muffled laughter to Lao She's recollections. One discerns a sense of absurdity when he relates his father's sacrifice for an empty cause, or his own survival under most unlikely conditions. He "remembers" how, as a baby, he survived the "foreign devils": "I was sleeping soundly when they entered our house. If I had awakened, they would have sliced me up with their swords, since they were angry not to find anything valuable in our home."

This sense of absurdity provides the basic tone of Lao She's laughter, laughter directed not only at a world full of irrationalities but also at Lao She himself trapped in such a world; not only at amusing subjects but also at subjects which could elicit indignation or tears. This ambiguous laughter can be heard when Lao She describes, in a self-mocking tone, his marginal identity as a Manchu growing up in the Republican period, his poor family situation, his lonely overseas experiences as a language teacher, and his untimely absence from two of the most important scenes in modern Chinese history—the post-May Fourth days and the Chinese Communist takeover of the mainland—due respectively to his teaching commission in England and to his tour in the United States.

But Lao She might have burst out with his most outrageous laughter in the Great Cultural Revolution, a historical event he would have hoped to miss. Years after being designated as a "People's Artist" by the government, Lao She found himself the "enemy of the people" in the heyday of the revolution. When things are suddenly deprived of the meanings they should have, nothing is left but infinite chaos punctuated by a peal of demonic laughter. It should be no surprise that Lao She chose to end his own life by drowning himself. For a king of laughter, suicide may well painfully recapitulate the ironic telos of his philosophy of laughter, in that it carries out to the extreme the auto-destructive tendency always embedded in his mockery and self-mockery, while indicating a final scorn at the absurdities he had been through all his life.

Laughter is the means by which Lao She questions the cultural/moral codes that sanction the concept of the real in his society. This profane laughter cannot be fully appreciated till we pay equal attention to Lao She's pursuit of melodramatic tears: "Although I am not opposed to tearjerkers, I wish I could write something that will bring down the house, and make people really feel exhilarated. To tell the truth, laughter and tears are actually two sides of one coin." In this chapter, I will attempt to analyze the laughter in Lao She's fiction in two ways. First, I will reassess Lao She's comical/satirical fiction in

terms of the modes of farce and melodrama, drawing out the carnivalesque impulse in his discourse of laughter and tears, and describing its nihilist undercurrent. Second, I will point out the link between the two seemingly contradictory images (or styles) of Lao She, the compassionate humanist and the cynical joker, by showing how his most flamboyant and hilarious narratives contain a poignant inquiry into the absurdities of life in modern China, while his "hard-core" revelations of human suffering can evoke a dubious mood of festivity.

FARCE AND MELODRAMA: TRANSGRESSIONS OF THE REAL

Lao She's comic/farcical discourse is drawn from two major sources: the kind of grotesque realism perfected by Dickens and the rhetoric of buffoonery of Late Qing exposé fiction. Lao She taught Chinese at the University of London School of Oriental Studies from 1924 to 1929, and finished his first three novels in London. As his critical essays indicate, he is quite familiar with eighteenth and nineteenth-century English writers ranging from Fielding to James and Conrad; among these writers, Charles Dickens stands as his major model. Lao She admits that his first novel, *The Philosophy of Lao Zhang*, is an imitation of Dickens' *Nicholas Nickleby*. Lao She's indebtedness to Dickens' novels is best manifested in his exuberant language, melodramatic plotting, and huge gallery of grotesques. Both writers tend to consider social evils and irrational institutions not only monstrous but absurd as well. Yet this parallel should not keep one from noticing that Lao She was a diligent student of classical Chinese fiction and folk performing arts such as story telling and *xiangsheng* (a Chinese form of comic talk show). As Jaroslav Průšek observed a long time ago, to give his comic fiction a special ironic effect, Lao She revived the story telling technique of classical Chinese vernacular fiction. It is equally clear that he drew upon late Qing exposé fiction as a source for the modes of buffoonery and burlesque.

Lao She's first novel, *The Philosophy of Lao Zhang*, can be read as a good example of the author's farcical/melodramatic discourse. In the novel, Lao She ridicules the chaotic situation of modern Chinese society, caught in a drastic transformation from the old to the new. The novel's dominant character is Lao Zhang, a villainous rural schoolmaster and a cunning moneylender.

The "philosophy of Lao Zhang" is to grab money by whatever means possible—a "threefold way of pilgrimage for cash." Lao Zhang's businesses include a tiny school with only one class, a grocery store selling things "ranging from green onions to opium," geomancy, and a position in local government. Lao Zhang converts from one religion to another freely, depending on the fluctuations of the meat market. With Volpone-like energy and ingenuity, Lao Zhang's desire for money is amplified to lust for power and women; the novel is a record of the way in which he fulfills all his goals. The novel also has several subplots, including the account of a squire's attempt to marry an educated concubine, a Chinese Salvation Army officer's thriving career as a preacher, and two idealistic students' aborted love affairs. All related to Lao Zhang's businesses of money lending and teaching.

In characterizing Lao Zhang as a moneylender and a vicious school master, Lao She may have in mind the images of both Ralph Nickleby and Mr. Squeers of Dickens' *Nicholas Nickleby*. Lao Zhang also reminds the reader of Quilp of *The Old Curiosity Shop* (which was translated into Chinese as early as in the late Qing period), in that both enjoy harassing youngsters and enslaving their own wives. Whereas Dickensian grotesques are portrayed as egoists who fabricate a self-centered world in the form of ostentatious routine, or practice strange mannerisms as an (unconscious) defence mechanism, Lao She's clownish characters like Lao Zhang act with an aggressive force that knows no restraints. Unlike Dickens, who tends to reveal the psychological motivations of his characters' grotesque behavior, Lao She creates Lao Zhang as an invulnerable robot. Neither social norms nor moral criteria are barriers to Lao Zhang's lust and ambition; instead, he makes use of those norms to develop his own system of values. Thus we have the doubtfully pleasurable expectation of seeing Lao Zhang continuously step beyond the limits he sets for himself to work out something more outrageous. In fact, the novel is organized like a series of spectacles presided over by Lao Zhang, with each one more hilarious (abusive) than the last.

Satirical comedy is too general and benign a term to describe Lao She's vision of the real as conceived in *The Philosophy of Lao Zhang*. With all the gratuitous violence and ambivalent laughter, what he really tries to create is something like a farce. Celebrating in an ironic manner a world turned upside down, *The Philosophy of Lao Zhang* may well be the first modern Chinese novel written deliberately in the farcical mode; Lao Zhang is the lord of misrule and his "philosophy" is the norm of chaos.

When treated as a narrative mode, *farce* refers to a type of writing that uses outrageous comedy to defy formalistic and thematic conventions, attack preestablished values, and test audience sensibilities. It often highlights a series of carnivallike episodes in which physical actions (collision, abuse, mockery, disfigurement, and so on) temporarily overpower intellectual and emotional control. The agents of farcical action are clowns who present themselves either as laughable victims or comic assailants, or as a combination of the two. Through the clowns' radical behavior, farce also implies a mentality or even an ideology which, in Bakhtinian terms, "disintegrates" the existing order in terms of imaginative "degradation." But at the core of farce is its ambiguous view of chaos: its characters' irreverent, comically violent attacks on each other and the surrounding society generate a certain new order, the audience's pleasure derives both from distancing the embarrassing or uncomfortable circumstances and from imaginative involvement in them.

A definition of farce such as this does not, of course, apply to all of Lao She's comic fiction. In the case of *The Philosophy of Lao Zhang*, I shall argue that Lao She tends to add a dimension of sentimental melodrama to his farcical discourse, so as to salvage his fiction from the total denial of meaning. In some of Lao She's short stories, nevertheless, one finds a full-fledged expression of the farcical mode. "Kaishi daji" (The grand opening, 1933), for example, deals with four quacks running an expensive charity hospital like a three-ring circus. Almost without any medical knowledge and facilities, they nevertheless manage to attract many dupes looking for magical cures. They encourage an old lady with ulcers to eat as much Beijing duck as she wants, and prescribe a shot of jasmine tea as a new medicine for an officer with venereal disease. At one time, they almost mistake a fat man for a pregnant woman; at another, they bully a patient with hemorrhoids to pay more for anaesthetic treatment—right in the middle of his surgery. The story contains a relentlessly festive atmosphere hitherto unseen in modern Chinese fiction, celebrating the quacks' undeserved prosperity and laughing at their patients' pain. Similar examples can be found in other short stories: "Baosun" (Grandson, 1933) in which a grandmother feeds her pregnant daughter-in-law so well that she is the focus of a hilarious horror when she delivers a thirteen pound baby; or "Liucun de" (A woman from the Liu village, 1934) in which a monstrous shrew persecutes her husband, family, and even the whole village, in the name of God, since she is a converted Christian.

On the other hand, Lao She's concept of farcical norms may well be traced back to late Qing exposé fiction such as, say, Wu Woyao's *Strange Things Seen in the Past Twenty Years*, a novel deriving its vitality from the absurd events and characters it openly denounces. Just like Wu Woyao, Lao She feels indignation over the stories he himself is recounting, but he assumes a so called extroverted attitude, collecting, studying, and classifying the stories as if he were enjoying the lavish display of his own social knowledge. Even more noticeable is the fact that Lao She projects in his novel an order highly reminiscent of that conceived by the late Qing exposé fiction, one where, as Doleželová-Velingerová has described it, "evil always defeats good," and "the great evil defeats the minor one."

In *The Philosophy of Lao Zhang*, we find that, with stylized gestures reminiscent of the clowns in traditional Chinese theater, Lao Zhang appears to the reader as dangerous *but* funny. Though he personifies an emancipated energy that transgresses all social and moral norms, we are so attracted by his seemingly inexhaustible imagination and protean mannerisms that we tend to neglect the offensiveness and radicalism embedded in his absurd actions. The new values forged by Lao Zhang and other minor villains in the novel are the opposite of those endorsed by a sober society. The label, "modern education," ensures nothing but higher enrollments and richer administrators; a "democratic election" is a new euphemism for winning a governmental job by bribery; "freedom of the press" allows journalists to slander and blackmail at will; "liberalism" inspires rich men to marry as many women as they want—girls with a modern education being especially welcome. Thus, Lao Zhang "is indeed an important figure in the town of Erlang! If Lao Zhang were unfortunately to die, it would be a disaster even bigger than losing a saint, because, after all, what saint could be like him, mastering both the pen and the sword, and communicating with both the living and the dead." The plot develops through a procession of slapstick interludes all starred in by Lao Zhang. He and his friends thrive in the novel all the way to the end. It is the good or sensible characters who are expelled from the scene.

Though the laughter Lao She aims to arouse remains as ambivalent in essence as ever, his comic/farcical scheme is more elaborate in terms of caricature and mockery than his late Qing predecessors. In *The Philosophy of Lao Zhang*, he creates a plural narrator "we," referring to a group of spectators who observe the ongoing chaos from a safe position. In no danger of finding themselves persecuted, they can make condescending jokes at the expense of those who are suffering. This plural narrator sounds most like the classical story-teller when he adopts colloquialisms and clichés to establish the linguistic illusion of intimate, direct communication with readers, and when he takes a detached middle distance to judge the story narrated. Lao She also adds to his voice a pompous style by practicing Dickensian formality of syntax and figures of speech. The oily, ostentatious rhetoric runs in such a way as to blur social values, dissolve the pain the characters should feel into a miming of it, and turn an otherwise sad story into a hilarious extravaganza. As if speaking for the public, the "we"-narrators invite readers to join "them" and relish the comic villains' performances. And as readers, the most embarrassing moment is when we find ourselves not only laughing *at* Lao Zhang and his friends but *with* them.

Lao She is clearly uneasy about the subversive undertone suggested by this kind of laughter. He continuously interjects into the second part of the novel voices of sober-minded characters or his own as implied author. With the remarkable increase of narrated monologues, authorial interruptions, and sententious descriptions, all punctuated by heavy sighs and/or tearful gestures, one cannot help noticing that the young and innocent characters are fighting a losing battle against Lao Zhang and his cohorts. Amid the outrageous laughter, there arise cries, however muffled by the comic villains, which attempt to spell the name of the evil, to articulate the pain and sadness the good has undergone, and to solicit the full range of emotional responses from the reader. These interpolations deflate the coherence of the novel's farcical effect, and point to the narrative mode of melodrama, the mode highlighting excessive expression and moral hyperbole.

This melodramatic tendency can especially be seen on the level of plot. As the novel progresses, Lao Zhang falls in love with his student's beloved and wants to take her as his concubine. He plans to have a magnificent wedding in Western style, and will invite only those friends who have concubines as his guests. Lao Zhang's dark force is now looming ever larger, threatening to break the ethical relation between teacher and student, to violate the virginity of the heroine, and to disintegrate social order completely.

By *melodrama*, I refer to a narrative mode that espouses an exaggerated presentation of moral and emotional conflicts, in such a way as to intensify the values of life in a theatrical form. Aiming at inflated and extravagant expression, a melodrama features extreme situations or states of action. Among its major characteristics are the indulgence of strong emotionalism, moral polarization, and artificial plotting. It often begins with the persecution of the good and ends with the reward of virtue, via such actions as dark conspiracy, suspense, and breathtaking adventure. However frivolous it may appear, at the core of melodramatic writing lies a deep concern with the moral consequences behind our everyday life and actions; its aim is to restore the lost social order and ethical imperatives. This pursuit of what Peter Brooks calls the "moral occult," the quint-essential meaning of life, foregrounds conflicting values otherwise relativized or even naturalized in the continuum of our daily existence. Seen in this light, an effective melodrama acts out both our anxiety in the search for the hidden moral configuration of lived experiences, and our fantasy of carrying out such a configuration in a moment of wish fulfillment.

Because of its polarization of good and evil, indulgence in hyperbolic rhetoric, and refusal to cast characters and their actions in the ordinary way, melodrama has always been considered as the opposite of realist/naturalist writing. But insofar as any representation of the real needs a narratorial pattern or dramatic arrangement, the difference between realist and melodramatic writings, as some critics have pointed out, is a matter of degree rather than of kind. Nineteenth-century European fiction by Balzac, Dickens, and even Flaubert and Zola has provided numerous examples along this continuum. In the case of Lao She, therefore, the question I would like to raise is not whether his melodramatic imagination has transgressed the boundary of the authentic discourse of realism, but whether this transgression has brought any new perspective on the Chinese reality under discussion.

The question becomes even more intriguing, when one places melodrama next to farce, and asks how Lao She mixes the two modes in telling his realist stories, and what moral and psychic results he brings forth. Both farce and melodrama are used by Lao She as a heightened literary response to a reality immersed in contingency and chaos. In a world where values have been thrown into question, one can rely only on extreme rhetorical measures to define the blurred image of the real. By means either of radical laughter or of polarized sentiments and overt moral schematization, Lao She tries to bring to the fore facts that can no longer be mediated in ordinary language. He thus sees the meaning of the real not in the reflection but the refraction of the objects he encounters. Compared with his peers, Lao She's realist strategy partakes of a strong skepticism concerning its own function, while his pessimism about the possibility of representing the real as it is, and his play with rhetoric forms give his writings a modernist touch.

Beneath the two modes' formal recourse to the rule of excess and theatricality, however, there is a fundamental difference between their epistemological assumptions. Whereas melodrama aims at the nomination of the manichaean struggle of good and evil behind chaotic reality, thereby projecting a longing for the return of a certain order, farce ventures to laugh away any such efforts. If melodrama celebrates the search for the moral occult, farce defies that search as one of the world's dirty jokes. Throughout Lao She's career, the effect of farce may seem less and less visible, as melodrama remains the persistent force of his narrative. But a sophisticated reader will find that Lao She's melodrama is made possible only because it is subsumed by a farcical impulse. Even his sad works contain a titillating element, ready to turn sentimental expressions into hysterical giggling. Beyond the level of plot, therefore, one must notice a battle between the two forms which is just as melodramatic.

This tension can be seen in the ending of *The Philosophy of Lao Zhang*. Whenever Lao She tries to speak in clear language about the menace of evil and the eventual triumph of morality, he ends up doing so amid chuckles. Lao Zhang's wedding does take place as promised, and to nobody's surprise, it turns out to be a circus of follies. But the wedding is never completed, because of the last minute intervention of a member of the local gentry, Regional Commander Sun, and a rickshaw puller with a chivalric spirit, Zhao Si. The two rescuing figures appear to be stereotypes from classical Chinese vernacular fiction: Regional Commander Sun enacts the traditional role of the impartial judge, while Zhao Si revives the chivalric spirit of a knight-errant. Both, however, undergo a certain degradation in Lao She's world. Sun must buy Lao Zhang off in order to stop the wedding, and Zhao Si is simply ignored by everyone. The lofty ideals of justice and chivalry are jokes in Lao She's world. His moral scheme is articulated only at the expense of immediate laughter.

In the epilogue, we are told that Lao Zhang was never thwarted by the aborted marriage. He eventually fulfills his ambition of not only becoming a provincial commissioner of education but also buying two concubines at the price of one, "and the bargain has become one of the memorable achievements of his life." The young lovers, however, are never reunited. Lao Zhang's student is forced by his parents to marry a country girl, and his girl friend wastes away and dies.

Lao She thus mixes two possible endings together, a farcical one that acknowledges a society turned upside down by the prosperity of villainous clowns and buffoons, and a melodramatic one that asserts the horror and pain that results from the persecution of the good by the wicked. At issue here is not which ending leans more closely toward reality, since both farce and melodrama are derived from a systematic distortion or exaggeration of the real. What is noteworthy is that the two modes undercut each other's aesthetic and moral premises, thereby forming a phantasmal vision which indicates a critical mockery, rather than a mimesis, of the real. Whereas Lao She's melodramatic wish brackets the chaotic world with a plenitude of meaning, his farcical impulse reinscribes such a wish in terms of parody, portraying not an order restored but an ordered chaos....

Source: David Der-wei Wang, "Melancholy Laughter: Farce and Melodrama in Lao She's Fiction," in *Fictional Realism in Twentieth-Century China: Mao Dun, Lao She, Shen Congwen*, Columbia University Press, 1992, pp. 111–20.

SOURCES

Goldblatt, Howard, Introduction to *Rickshaw Boy*, Harper Perennial, 2010, pp. v–xv.

James, Jean M., Translator's introduction to *Rickshaw: The Novel Lo-t'o Hsiang Tzu*, University of Hawaii Press, 1979, pp. vii–xi.

She, Lao, *Rickshaw: The Novel Lo-t'o Hsiang Tzu*, translated by Jean M. James, University of Hawaii Press, 1979.

———, *Rickshaw Boy*, translated by Howard Goldblatt, Harper Perennial, 2010.

Towery, Britt, *Lao She: China's Master Storyteller*, Tao Foundation, 1999.

Vohra, Ranbir, *Lao She and the Chinese Revolution*, Harvard University Press, 1974, pp. 1–18, 98–115.

Witchard, Anne, *Lao She in London*, Hong Kong University Press, 2012.

FURTHER READING

Fei, Loo Pin, *It Is Dark Underground: Student Resistance to the 1930s Japanese Occupation of China*, edited by Steve Chadde, Uncommon Valor Press, 2014.

This witness account of the sweeping student protests against the occupation of China by Japanese forces in the 1930s during the Second Sino-Japanese War begins where *Rickshaw Boy* concludes, illustrating the growing political tensions between classes and ideologies in China on the brink of war.

Fung, Chi, *Reluctant Heroes: Rickshaw Pullers in Hong Kong and Canton, 1874–1954*, Hong Kong University Press, 2005.

Fung's study of rickshaw pullers in Hong Kong and Canton examines the physical, economical, and political experience of rickshaw pullers throughout eighty years of Chinese history.

Lao She, *Blades of Grass: The Stories of Lao She*, translated by William A. Lyell, Sarah Wei-Ming Chen, and Howard Goldblatt, University of Hawaii, 2000.

This collection of fourteen short stories and a portion of an autobiographical novel focuses on interpersonal relationships and the tension between generations in 1930s Beijing. The selections offer a variety of styles and genres.

Link, Perry, Richard P. Madsen, and Paul G. Pickowicz, *Restless China*, Rowman & Littlefield Publishers, 2013.

This study of modern China considers the great speed with which the country has risen to become of the world's most powerful economies. Particular attention is paid to how the citizens of China are coping with the rapidly changing nation as old ideologies are swept away to make way for modernization and globalization.

SUGGESTED SEARCH TERMS

Lao She

Rickshaw Boy

Lao She AND Rickshaw Boy

Luotuo Xiangzi

Lao She AND Luotuo Xiangzi

Luotuo Xiangzi AND Cosmic Wind

Camel Xiangzi

Lao She AND Camel Xiangzi

Rickshaw Boy AND Howard Goldblatt

Rickshaw Boy AND 1936

Rickshaw Boy AND 1945

The Secret History

DONNA TARTT

1992

Donna Tartt's *The Secret History* created a small sensation when it was first published in 1992. It made the *New York Times* best-seller list and has enjoyed a loyal cult following in the decades since. It is a novel about classicists (students of Greek and Latin) and, like its characters, has little contact with the literary world after the 1920s, forgoing the forms of modern literature. Often dismissed by critics as a melodrama, the novel takes the form of a Greek tragedy, the story of a hero destroyed by his own flawed character. Tartt uses the older literary world she inhabits to indict the faults of a modern America she views as doomed by its lack of intellectual sophistication. The central event of the novel is a murder, and that act is revealed in its first pages. It is not a murder mystery, however, but investigates the mystery of why the murder happened. The answer is the evocation into reality of the Greek god Dionysus, who is just as violent, just as likely to induce insanity, as he is in Euripides's play *The Bacchae*.

AUTHOR BIOGRAPHY

Donna Tartt was born in Greenwood, Mississippi, on December 23, 1963. She grew up in Grenada, which is also in the Mississippi Delta. For a writer of her prominence, she is remarkably successful at maintaining her privacy, so

Donna Tartt (© *Ulf Andersen / Hulton Archive / Getty Images*)

relatively little is known about her life. This is compounded by the fact that little serious scholarship has been produced about her writing as yet. She spent the year 1981–1982 at the University of Mississippi, where she pledged a sorority. Tartt's creative writing professor at Mississippi, Barry Hannah, recognized her as a genius and was instrumental in her transfer to the writing program at Bennington College. According to Hannah, she was unusually well read for an undergraduate, having taken on authors like John Keats and the French romantic poets on her own. She also studied classics at Bennington, with Claude Fredericks. Tartt began working on *The Secret History* as part of her class work. Her classmates included Bret Easton Ellis, Jill Eienstadt, and Jonathan Lethem, all of whom also became successful novelists. She briefly dated Ellis.

After ten years of work on *The Secret History*, she published it in 1992. She had some difficulty finding a publisher, and at least one editor told her she had to rewrite it, since no woman had ever written a novel told by a first-person male narrator. According to Ellis, the same editor said she would be better off selling shoes. Once in bookstores, *The Secret History* was well received and became an immediate best seller. Tartt affirms that her aristocratic southern background, with its pastimes of hunting, heavy drinking, and secret societies informed the novel.

Tartt has published only a few short stories and took eight years to finish her second novel, *The Little Friend* (2002). Her third novel, *The Goldfinch*, was published in 2013 and won the Pulitzer Prize for Fiction in the following year. Tartt has revealed to interviewers that she works assiduously at writing, eight hours a day or more, and sometimes goes without sleep in her compulsion to write. This obsessiveness is reflected in *The Secret History*. When Richard is upset and, "didn't work for the rest of the night," this is viewed as an exceptional if not fantastic state of affairs. Tartt still writes everything in longhand. She periodically has her manuscripts typed and then writes all over the typescript with colored pencils and staples note cards (Post-It notes are too modern) onto the pages to add more revisions. She avoids the modern practice of speaking tours that are usual for a writer of her prominence and considers even the brief lectures and interviews that come with each new book a burden that she is happy comes only once every ten years. As of 2015, Tartt is reportedly working on a project inspired by the myth of Daedalus and Icarus for the prestigious Canongate Myth Series.

PLOT SUMMARY

Prologue
In the prologue, the novel's narrator, Richard Papen, describes the murder of Bunny, committed by Richard and his fellow classics students from Hampden College. They surprised Bunny while hiking in the mountains and threw him down a cliff. They supposed that the body would be quickly found and the death ruled accidental with hardly any police involvement. However, no one found the body for weeks because it became covered by a spring snowstorm, and Bunny was declared missing and became the object of a police search, which proved unsuccessful.

Book I

CHAPTER 1

Richard Papen grew up in the small town of Plano, California. His father ran a gas station and had no ambition for his son except that he should work at the station with him and eventually take it over. With difficulty, Richard persuades his father to send him to a local college, where he wins an award for his study of ancient Greek. Richard parleys this into a full-ride scholarship at the fictional Hampden College in Vermont. Although he wants to major in economics as preparation for a career, he wishes also to continue his study of Greek. (Unusual for a classics student, he has no Latin.) He finds out that the classics department has only a single professor, the highly eccentric Julian Morrow. Morrow initially rejects Richard on the ground he is not eccentric enough, and Richard finds that Morrow has only a small coterie of students: the twins Charles and Camilla, Francis, Henry, and Bunny. Richard contrives to meet them and impresses them with his knowledge of Greek. They advise him to approach Julian again and make a better impression by wearing more formal clothes (supplied to him by Julie Poovey, his dormmate and the wardrobe mistress of Hampden's drama department) and giving him a bouquet of flowers. This time Julian accepts him. In their discussion, Julian makes it clear that he studies the classics because he feels alienated from the modern world, an attitude he encourages in his students. He also forces Richard to drop all of his other classes (except French) and commit to studying exclusively with him for the rest of his college career. Richard accepts because he feels attracted to the otherworldliness of Julian and his students. On the first day of his new classes, he is met on the way to class by Francis, who sexually propositions him in very unidiomatic Latin; Francis lets it go when he realizes Richard does not understand. In class, they briefly discuss the local town, which seems to be inhabited only by fundamentalist Christians. Bunny suggests that they are so fallen away from the Greek ideal the six of them would have no trouble attacking and massacring the town by themselves. The more formal class discussion focuses on the Greek idea of divine possession.

CHAPTER 2

Bunny invites Richard to lunch at a French restaurant in the town that caters to faculty and the local upper class. Bunny makes himself obnoxious by taunting the waiter as gay. Trying to fit in with the aristocratic atmosphere of his classmates, Richard presents Bunny with an entirely fictional account of his life, suggesting that he comes from a wealthy family that has a number of orange groves. They follow dinner with several bottles of champagne and one of brandy, running up an enormous bill. Bunny reveals he cannot pay because he has forgotten his wallet; Richard confesses he has no way to pay either. Bunny calls Henry, who comes and pays the bill and drives them home. After dropping Bunny off, he apologizes to Richard for Bunny's unconscionable behavior. Despite appearances, Henry and Bunny are old and best friends. Richard is quickly integrated into the group of classics students, who spend all of their free time together too. He is invited to the weekly dinner party hosted by Francis at a mansion in the countryside outside the town that belongs to his aunt. The house is described in overtly gothic terms. Richard says, "I saw, in sharp, in black silhouette against the sky, turrets and pikes, a widow's walk."

Among his new friends, Richard is happy for the first time in his life. However, he notices that he is still excluded to some degree. The other five will sometimes vanish for hours at night and when he next sees them, they have small injuries and a pat but obviously fabricated explanation for their absence. He notices incidents that are beyond his understanding, such as when Bunny terrifies the others by singing "The Farmer in the Dell."

The one thing they have in common with ordinary college students is their constant heavy drinking, though their tastes run to champagne and dry martinis rather than cheap beer. One morning when they are badly hung over, the group goes wading in the lake by the mansion, and Camilla steps on a piece of glass and cuts her foot quite badly.

CHAPTER 3

The end of the fall term brings a crisis for Richard. Henry and Bunny are going on a tour of Italy, and the rest of their circle are going to spend the break with their families. Richard, however, looks upon the prospect of returning even for a few weeks to Plano as an expulsion from paradise; nor is he certain that his father would pay for the trip. He cannot stay in his room, since the dorms are closed over the break to save the cost of heating them during the severe

Vermont winters. He finds out from a secretary in the student housing office that there is a hippie who runs a mandolin factory in the bad part of Hampden who lets students spend the break living in his warehouse in exchange for minimal labor in mandolin production. Richard arranges to take advantage of this. However, the warehouse proves also to be unheated and even to have a hole in the roof. During the day he works in a college office, but at night Richard sleeps in the bitterest cold. He claims to the reader that, coming from California, he has no idea of what a space heater or electric blanket might be. He eventually develops pneumonia, which results in his increasing mental disorientation. He realizes he needs help and phones his family but, on hearing his father's voice, decides he would rather die than rely on them. Before it is too late, Henry, returned early from Italy, rescues Richard and takes him to the hospital. He finishes his recovery in Henry's apartment until the new semester begins. Although he cannot discover the details, Richard becomes aware that there was some crisis between Henry and Bunny.

CHAPTER 4

As the semester begins, it becomes obvious that whatever happened in Italy is known to the others and is affecting all their behavior. Richard can soon see that the idyll of the previous semester cannot be repeated. In fact, on the weekend before classes start, Henry, Francis, and the twins disappear. Bunny is still around but seems terribly distracted. Richard goes to Henry's apartment to retrieve his Liddell & Scott Greek dictionary and finds it has been cleaned out: the only things remaining are two heavy suitcases. He snoops around and finds out Henry has bought four one way-tickets to Argentina for the following Monday. However, on Monday morning the other students are all in Julian's class as usual. That afternoon Henry explains to Richard what has been going on. They had indeed planned to flee to Argentina and ultimately to Uruguay, but to do so they needed money. Francis volunteered to draw money from his trust, only to discover that his mother had already withdrawn the annual limit. So they had no choice but to return to college and think of some other plan. Richard guesses from their desperation and many odd aspects of Bunny's behavior that they are fleeing because Bunny is blackmailing them with knowledge that the others had committed a murder. This

is nearly correct, as Henry explains. Henry and the others had begun the previous fall to attempt to replicate the Bacchic rites of the Greek God Dionysus, which they had studied in class. Richard was excluded because Henry felt they did not yet know him well enough, and Bunny was eventually excluded because he simply did not take the matter sufficiently seriously. Richard believes they are the first people to attempt this for two thousand years (though in fact Rudolf Bultmann and some of his fellow classics students at the university of Tübingen did precisely the same thing in the years before World War I, and, for example, similar ecstatic rituals were common among European peasants throughout the medieval and early modern periods, usually being classed as witchcraft if they came to the attention of the authorities). To do this, they meet in the woods outside Francis's house in the middle of the night and fulfill the basic requirements of Greek ritual, for example, purifying themselves by washing their hands with spring water. They try several techniques that are often used to induce ecstasy—what is often called an altered state of consciousness— such as fasting, using natural intoxicants (they seem to believe Robert Graves's claim that laurel leaves contain a hallucinogenic drug), and dancing. Finally, Henry decides that what they need is belief. This is the point at which Bunny is excluded. Somehow achieving that belief, they succeed and are able to see Dionysus and obtain a state of mystical union with him. Henry explains to Richard that he now understands Greek artistic depictions of Dionysus. They are not inaccurate but bear the same relationship to the reality that a drawing of wavy blue lines does to the ocean. During the experience they run for miles through the countryside and, as Greek Bacchantes, are reported to have killed and dismembered animals during their ecstasy; also, they kill and dismember a local farmer. When they come back to their senses and realize what they have done, they decide the best thing they can do is simply leave and find their way back to Francis's apartment. There is nothing to connect them to the dead farmer, and the incompetent local police are unlikely to ever suspect them.

CHAPTER 5

Bunny is waiting for them at Francis's apartment. He sees them covered in mud and blood. They tell him the blood came from a deer they hit (though their car is undamaged). He may suspect they dismembered a deer in a Dionysian frenzy. A few days later, however, he reads in the newspaper about a farmer who was killed the same night, and he starts joking in the school cafeteria, in his loud obnoxious voice, that maybe it was no deer but the farmer they killed. He will not leave the topic alone. Although Bunny is not really blackmailing his fellow students, they are constantly terrified that someone, like a campus police officer, will overhear him and believe him. The only way they can think of to shut him up is by spending more and more money on his meals. This leads to Henry's taking him to Italy, where Bunny finds Henry's diary and reads confirmation that the other students indeed killed the farmer. They do not think that Bunny will purposefully turn them in but that his ineptitude will eventually reveal their secret. With Henry's money running out and no further way to mollify Bunny with expensive dinners, they came up with the plan to flee to Uruguay. That having failed, they have no idea what to do. Bunny's increasing instability exerts increasing pressure on the others, and Charles in particular starts to drink even more heavily than usual. Francis makes another pass at Richard. Bunny eventually figures out that Richard is in fact poor and torments him with the prospect of exposure. His knack of ferreting out everyone's weak points finally leads him to expose Charles and Camilla's incest. Eventually, Henry decides he has to kill Bunny. He comes up with a plan to serve him a meal with poisonous mushrooms, protecting himself with an antidote he found in a medieval Persian poisoner's handbook. (He had to teach himself classical Arabic to read it.) Richard, who had actually studied chemistry, assures him the plan is quite mad. One night Bunny goes to Richard's dorm room, becomes violently ill, and tells him about the murder. Henry concedes his poisoning plan is too esoteric to work but becomes more anxious to kill Bunny quickly, before he tells someone else. He devises the plan of committing the murder while they are hiking, which is the scene described in the prologue.

Book II

CHAPTER 6

Bunny was the only classics student to have friends at Hampden outside of their closed circle, and they are quick to report his disappearance. The school offers a reward to find him, and the search becomes a large manhunt. Students join with the police and FBI in searching the mountains above the school. The classicists join in; otherwise, it would have seemed suspicious. They carefully avoid the place where they know his body is. The whole affair seems grimly comic to Richard and the others. The fundamentalist Christians who run the car repair shop in town go on the local television station and blame their competitors, who happen to be Arabs, making them out as terrorist agents of OPEC (the Organization of the Petroleum Exporting Countries). (This recalls the circumstances of economic competition in which most accusations were made against Christians in the Roman Empire.)

CHAPTER 7

Bunny's body is found only some weeks later, and he is given a lavish funeral by his family. They invite Henry and the other classicists and put them up in their house. The guests spend the time in an intoxicated and drugged stupor. Henry smears dirt from the grave on his shirt, a typically Greek practice.

CHAPTER 8

Back at Hampden, the students discover that Bunny had sent Julian a letter, describing the first murder. Most likely Julian figured out the circumstances of the second. In any case, he suddenly retires from the school. He does not turn his students in, but he does refuse to see them again. He had encouraged Henry and the others in their Bacchic experiment and probably considered himself at fault.

Charles's alcoholism becomes worse and he is arrested for drunk driving and forced into a rehabilitation program. Henry and Camilla had been having an affair for some time and now start living together. Finally, when the others are having dinner together, Charles, having escaped from the hospital, confronts them. He is drunk and intends to kill Henry, whom he blames for driving him to this point. When Henry and Charles struggle over the gun, Richard is shot, but not fatally. Henry kills himself.

Epilogue

With Henry dead, the ties that held the others together are cut. Richard eventually finishes a degree in English and becomes a professor. Charles and Camilla retire to their grandmother's house in Virginia. Camilla eventually becomes a caretaker for her aging relatives.

Years later, Francis sends Richard a suicide note. Richard flies out to Boston and finds him in the hospital; he has slashed his wrists. His family discovered he was gay and forced him into a marriage under the threat of cutting him off financially. They found an empty-headed socialite for him, but he preferred to die. Having failed in his attempt, he has no choice but to go on. He has written Camilla, too, and when she arrives the three of them go to Ash Wednesday mass. She reveals that Charles had been in rehab again but ran off with a woman from the program. Richard proposes to Camilla but she refuses him. The one they both really loved was Henry.

CHARACTERS

Francis Abernathy

Francis, like all the classics students except Richard, comes from a wealthy background. In his case, his mother ran away from home as a rock-band groupie. When she returned pregnant she was shuffled off to grandparents who raised Francis as well. He was educated at a prep school in France.

Tartt has a highly unusual approach to characterization. Rather than letting the development of her characters unfold through their actions, she uses the device of Richard's supplying an explanation to his readers, drawing character sketches in two tightly constructed sections of her novel, achieving an effect like a summary in an encyclopedia article. Francis, for instance, is described as

> Angular and elegant... precariously thin with nervous hands and a shrewd albino face and a short, fiery mop of the reddest hair I had ever seen. I thought (erroneously) that he dressed like Alfred Douglas... beautiful starchy shirts with French cuffs; magnificent neckties; a black generous greatcoat that billowed behind him as he walked and made him look like a cross between a student prince and Jack the Ripper.

Alfred Douglas was Oscar Wilde's lover, and this is one of many hints Tartt drops throughout the novel of Francis's sexuality.

Edmund (Bunny) Corcoran

Bunny stands out from his classmates as crude and obnoxious, with low literary tastes. His father was a Clemson football star who became a banker. Unlike the families of the others, Bunny's family keeps up the conspicuous display of wealth, although it has nothing but debt. Bunny is

> a sloppy blond boy, rosy-cheeked and gum-chewing with a relentlessly cheery demeanor and his fists thrust deep in the pockets of his knee-sprung trousers. He wore the same jacket every day, a shapeless brown tweed that was frayed at the elbows and short in the sleeves.... His voice was loud and honking, and carried in the dining halls.

Bunny is dyslexic and completely unprepared for college work. He exhibits every kind of racial and ethnic prejudice, as well as contempt for anyone he thinks might be gay, but it is not clear just how much this reflects his unsophisticated manner of speech or if he is in fact a hardened bigot. Bunny eventually discovers that the others are practicing Bacchic religious rites in secret and that in the process they have murdered a local farmer. He becomes more and more unstable, and the others fear that he will eventually expose them. This causes them to plan his murder, which supplies the plot of the novel.

Camilla Macaulay

Camilla is named after the female warrior in Virgil's *Aeneid*. She and her brother, Charles, are tinged with the gothic. They are lovers as well as twins and are the most mysterious of Julian's students. Tartt foreshadows the revelation of their relationship in her initial description of them: "I saw them together a great deal, and at first I thought they were boyfriend and girlfriend, until one day I saw them up close and realized they had to be siblings." Incest is a common theme of gothic literature. The twins are also orphans, a condition Richard looks on with envy. They come from a background of great wealth, having been raised among horse farms in Virginia.

Charles Macaulay

Charles is perhaps the least developed character of the classics students and is often lumped in with his sister as a pair, as in their initial description: "And perhaps most unusual in the context of Hampden—where pseudo-intellects and teenage decadents abounded, and where black clothing was *de rigueur*—they like to wear pale clothes, particularly white." White, like a bloodless corpse, is symbolic of death, and their color choice relates to the unhealthiness of their relationship. Tartt's description of the twins, as "like figures from an allegory, or long-dead celebrants from some forgotten garden party" relates to the nature of Tartt's novel as an allegory and its theme of the Dionysian mysteries.

Julian Morrow

Julian is the only classics professor at Hampden. His faculty colleagues concede that he is a distinguished scholar but consider him hopelessly eccentric and criticize him for accepting only students who accept his own views. The justification given for the toleration of this behavior is that he is independently wealthy and donates his salary back to the school. Julian espouses traditionalism, a political ideology, and his five students seem to accept his views and look upon him as a sort of savior. Julian's surname, Morrow, suggests that he represents the future for his students, an ideal that they aspire to. He is a contrast to the other faculty at Hampden, who are presented as senile, impotent, and addled by postmodernism. Typically, there is "a course called 'Invariant Subspaces' which was noted for its monotony and virtually absolute unintelligibility." Julian's background remains mysterious, but some hint is provided by old photos from *Life* magazine and newspapers discovered by Henry. They show a much younger Julian with famous actresses like Vivien Leigh and Marilyn Monroe.

Richard Papen

Richard is the main character and narrator of *The Secret History*. He is ashamed of and dissatisfied with his lower-class identity and sees his embrace by Julian and his classmates as a chance to create a new and more palatable identity for himself. He fabricates an entirely false version of himself as coming from a family of wealthy orange growers, but his assumed identity is no less artificial than Julian's or that of his fellow students; it is just not as well constructed. An episode from his dismal childhood is one of many foreshadowings of the novel's larger theme of ecstasy. Comparing his home town of Plano to the hellish city of Pandaemonium in John Milton's *Paradise Lost*, Richard says,

> In high school I developed a habit of wandering through shopping malls after school, swaying through the bright, chill mezzanines until I was so dazed with consumer goods and product

codes, with promenades and escalators, with mirrors and Muzak and noise and light, that a fuse would blow in my brain and all at once everything would become unintelligible: color without form, a babble of detached molecules.

Julie Poovey

Julie represents the modern world that the other characters of the novel find so distasteful. She has her own constructed identity as a hippie (something from a previous generation) devoted to the hedonistic pleasures of sex and drug use. She is a drama major, a professional in constructing false identities. Julie is part of the modern world represented by the campus life of Hampden. Naturally this is much taken up with drunken parties with loud rock music that makes meaningful discussion impossible. To the classics students and to Richard, once he identifies himself with them, they seem to be the irruption of hell on earth. A girl Richard meets at one of these parties seems to be "A Cheerleader of the Dammed." According to Richard's new perspective, "The music was insanely loud and people were dancing and there was...a Dantesque mass of bodies on the dance floor and a cloud of smoke hovering near the ceiling." Richard is grateful when he is rescued by Camilla, who, once they are outside of the party, comments, "Those things are hellish."

Henry Winter

Henry comes from a wealthy family in St. Louis. He is not forthcoming about this past, but he evidently suffered some sort of injury as a child, which left him bedridden for years. As a result, he was homeschooled during that time by private tutors. He finished his secondary education at prep schools in Europe. Unlike his fellow students, Henry has a gift for languages and is highly proficient in Latin and Greek. In fact, Henry, "had published a translation of Anacreon, with commentary, when he was only eighteen." (Anacreon was a Greek poet.) He also knows many more esoteric languages, such as Coptic and Sanskrit. On at least one occasion, he publicly exposed the bad French of the French teacher at Hampden. During the course of the novel, Henry teaches himself Arabic. Tartt's initial description of Henry throws the traditionalism of the classics students into contrast with the corrupt modern world symbolized by Hampden:

> He wore dark English suits and carried an umbrella (a bizarre sight in Hampden) and he walked stiffly through the throngs of hippies and beatniks and preppies and punks with the self-conscious formality of an old ballerina.

THEMES

Classicism

Classicism is the study of the Greek and Latin languages. These had been the official languages of the Roman Empire and had been in use in the Mediterranean world in the first millennium BCE. Many of the greatest works of Western literature were produced in these languages, especially Greek, by authors including Homer, Sophocles, Plato, and the writers of the New Testament. The reacquisition of knowledge of Greek, which had been lost in Western Europe, was also a foundational factor in the Renaissance. Up until World War I, education meant education in Greek and Latin. While other subjects such as mathematics and science might be studied in high school or university, any educated person would be highly proficient in the classical languages. Classicism has declined in modern times and has become a rarity.

A superficial reading of *The Secret History* suggests that Tartt's student characters are highly proficient in Greek, but Tartt reveals, through what may be considered an in-joke to her readers who understand Greek, that this is not the case. Richard, initially an outsider to the group has, at the beginning of the novel, completed two years of study of Greek at a university. The standard course in beginning Greek consists of a year-long grammar survey in which students simply learn the structure of the language, a third semester devoted to a grammar review and short, simple readings, and a fourth semester in which actual Greek texts are read. In Richard's case this was the New Testament, which is the simplest commonly read Greek book. His classmates at Hampden may have studied for longer, since they are likely to have attended elite private high schools. But at the beginning of the novel, all of the students' knowledge of Greek is revealed to be rather simplistic. Richard first meets the others by eavesdropping on them as they work on a Greek

composition assignment in the library. They are arguing over whether to translate the phrase *to Carthage* using the Greek proposition *epi* with

The story is set at fictional Hampden College, which was likely inspired by Tartt's alma mater, Bennington College in Vermont. *(© Danny Xu | Shutterstock.com)*

either the dative or accusative grammatical case. Charles, a proponent of the dative, actually provides the accusative by mistake: "*Epi tō karchidona.*" Bunny suggests the ablative case, and when it is pointed out to him that this is a Latin, not a Greek, case, he meaninglessly responds, "Aorist, ablative, all the same thing, really . . .". At this point, Richard introduces himself to the group by proposing a solution to their dilemma that seems to them a stroke of genius. Rather than simply explaining to them that *epi* with the accusative is correct, he thinks they should dispense with prepositions and cases altogether and turn the city name Carthage into a locative adverb: "Just add *zde* to *karchido.*" This is rather desperate Greek that actually defeats the purpose of the assignment. The passage, then, reveals a secret to Tartt's initiated readers but keeps it from others.

Greek Drama

The Secret History is far too sprawling to be formally compared to the highly concise form of Greek drama, but drama nevertheless forms the background of the novel. The drama that Tartt has most in mind is Euripides's *The Bacchae.* Richard mentions it by name once, but it plays a very important role in what the reader is presented of Julian's lectures. His reference to "Springs of honey bubbling from the ground" is an allusion to one of the many miracles that occur in the play. He seems to take its nightmarish vision of divine vengeance as a sort of ideal that he and his students should aspire to. In the play, the god Dionysus returns to Thebes and takes vengeance on its citizens and its king, Pentheus (his nephew), for their assertion that he is no god and that his mother, Semele, bore a son out of wedlock to a mortal, rather than to Zeus. He drives the women of the town mad and causes them to wander in the mountains above the city dismembering small animals in a frenzy. He possesses Pentheus, too, and drives him to spy on the women disguised in feminine clothes and a long-haired wig (a point that the play presents as humiliating for a Greek man). In their frenzy, Pentheus's own mother and aunts mistake him for a lion and tear him apart too.

In a less limited sense, Tartt's presentation of her characters is highly dramatic. They are all playing parts that they have written for themselves. They look like college students in a film made in the 1920s, not one in which college is presented as the most up-to-date and modern thing, like Harold Lloyd's *The Freshman*, but one where the costumes superficially suggest the film is set in the nineteenth century, like Ernst Lubitsch's *The Student Prince in Old Heidelberg*. (Richard even compares Francis to the lead character of this film.) Their highly artificial appearance is carefully cultivated to set them apart not just from their fellow students but also from the modern world. Unlike other Hampden students, who wear a uniform of denim pants and T-shirts, they wear suits, carry umbrellas, and even sport pince-nez glasses (but of the stage prop variety, with clear glass instead of lenses). Richard tries to fit in, buying an old Harris tweed jacket from Goodwill. As Richard himself says,

> I envied them, and found them attractive; moreover this strange quality, far from being natural, gave every indication of having been intensely cultivated. (It was the same, I would come to find, with Julian: though he gave quite the opposite impression, of freshness and candor, it was not spontaneity, but superior art which made it seems unstudied.) Studied or not, I wanted to be like them.

STYLE

Literary Allusion

The title *The Secret History* tells the casual reader that he is going to encounter something private and hidden, but read in the context of Greek literature, it takes on some further meanings. The title is borrowed from a book by the sixth-century CE Greek historian Procopius. Procopius was the court historian to the Roman emperor Justinian and in that capacity wrote a laudatory chronicle of his reign in two works: *The Wars of Justinian* and *The Buildings of Justinian*. He also wrote a third book, titled *The Secret History*, which was not published in his lifetime. This work covered roughly the same period and subject matter as *The Wars of Justinian* but also reported court gossip (for example that Justinian's wife, Theodora, was a witch and committed adultery on a grand scale) and also attempted to explain the sources of Justinian's

public actions in his private ambitions and vices, which were not revealed as part of imperial propaganda. This suggests already that Tartt's novel will also be an exploration of the personal and the hidden. It is not coincidental to her purpose either that Procopius is the last author in the classical canon; later authors are categorized as medieval. This suggests that Tartt's work will concern something belonging to a past utterly cut off from modernity, despite the novel's modern setting and character. The word *secret* itself is also interesting. In terms of the ancient Greek world, a secret is something revealed to the initiates of a Greek mystery cult but of which all knowledge is kept from the general public. To Tartt, as an initiate into the mysteries of classicism, this will suggest the novel's connection to the theme of the Greek mysteries.

Mystery

The murder mystery is a modern literary genre, and to a degree *The Secret History* participates in that genre. Buy *mystery* is a Greek word and originally meant secret religious rites, like those of Dionysus, and Tartt's novel is much more concerned with that sort of mystery. Not all Greek mysteries involved ecstasy, but those of Dionysus did. Early in the novel, Julian lectures about ecstasy. He begins by saying, "We have been accustomed to thinking of religious ecstasy as a thing found only in primitive societies." He expands: "Yet they [the Greeks] were frequently swept away *en masse* by the wildest enthusiasms—dancing, frenzies, slaughter, visions—which for us, I suppose, would seem clinical madness, irreversible. Yet the Greeks—some of them, anyway—could go in and out of it as they pleased." This is not quite correct. Modern psychology describes religious ecstasy as a natural phenomenon. *Ecstasy* is a Greek word that means "existing outside." The ancient Greeks thought of the soul's leaving the body and therefore perceiving things that the physical senses are blind to. (Christian mystics adopted the same language.) A psychologist today, however, might say that during such an experience, perception is detached from the senses and perceives the internal psychological world, in a process similar to dreaming.

Ecstasy is a well-documented phenomenon in the scientific literature of psychology and the history of religion. Julian's detailed explanation straddles the traditional and modern explanations of the phenomenon: "The revelers were apparently hurled back into a non-rational, pre-intellectual state, where the personality was replaced by something completely different—and by 'different' I mean something to all appearances not mortal. Inhuman." In fact, despite his expressed distaste for Freud, Julian expresses a highly Freudian understanding (which owes more to Plato than Freud would have cared to admit) of ecstasy: "All truly civilized people—the ancients no less than us—have civilized themselves through the willful repression of the old, animal self." He continues: "The more cultivated a person is, the more intelligent, the more repressed, then the more he needs some method of channeling the primitive impulses he's worked so hard to subdue." Julian uses Platonic, or rather Neoplatonic, language, to describe the part of the human being that experiences ecstasy when he calls it the "primitive, emotive, appetitive self." But that is not quite correct. In Neoplatonic psychology, the appetitive self is what is most directly connected to the body and therefore cannot step outside to experience a divine vision.

Despite the well-developed psychological and anthropological understanding of ecstasy as a natural phenomenon, Tartt presents the students' encounter with Dionysus as something fantastic, approaching the material of a fantasy novel. When Henry finally reveals to Richard that he and the others had been engaged in the mysteries of Dionysus, this exchange follows:

> "What happened?" . . .
> " . . . it worked."
> "It *worked*?"
> "Absolutely."
> "But how could—?"

For modern, educated Westerners with an entirely secular outlook, mystical ecstasy is something supernatural and cannot be real. Having a vision of Dionysus is something that has to be accepted even in a work of fiction by the willing suspension of disbelief. If one were present at the conjuration of an angel by a ceremonial magician or of a ghost by a spiritualist, a modern person would expect that nothing would happen, that no angel or ghost would appear, for example, on a video recording of the event, because angels and ghosts are supernatural and therefore not real. But if one accepts that ecstasy is a natural part of human psychology, there is absolutely nothing surprising about *it's working*.

In the novel, Henry eventually provides a description of what he experienced:

> It was heart-shaking. Glorious. Torches, dizziness, singing. Wolves howling around us and a bull bellowing in the dark. The river ran white. It was like a film in fast motion, the moon waxing and waning, clouds rushing across the sky. Vines grew from the ground so fast they twined up the trees like snakes.

Camilla later gives a supplementary account. "I remember a pack of dogs. Snakes twining around my arms. Trees on fire, pines bursting into flame like enormous torches." These descriptions are based on ancients texts such as Euripides's *The Bacchae*, Ovid's *Metamorphoses*, and Homer's *Iliad*. In the latter, the final duel between Achilles and Hector is described as taking place with infinite slowness, as in a dream, and a modern reader of the passage may be reminded of slow-motion film editing, just as the description by Henry suggests modern time-lapse editing. Henry and Camilla saw the same things not because they saw objective realities that some neutral observer would have seen, but because they had been prepared for the experience by reading the same books: mystics see what their tradition has indoctrinated them to see.

Tartt harvests another detail from *The Bacchae* when Richard asks, "But these are fundamentally *sex* rituals, aren't they?" Henry does not want to answer, but eventually says, "Of course . . . You know that as well as I do." In the play, Pentheus accuses the Bacchae (female worshippers of Dionysus) of using their rites as a cover for sexual promiscuity. But it is revealed that nothing of the kind is going on and that his accusation is the result of prejudice. And, indeed, sexual deviance was a common charge made against one's cultural opponents in antiquity. The Romans, for example, represented the Christian mass as an orgy in which the Christians had sex indiscriminately, including with blood relatives. Tartt's acceptance of the charge of sexual deviance is a gothic element, similar to the relationship between Charles and Camilla.

HISTORICAL CONTEXT

The Reconstruction of Ancient Religion
The main action of the novel concerns the revival of ancient Greek religion. It seems strange to present it in those terms, however, since the

COMPARE & CONTRAST

- **1980s:** Although personal computers are growing in popularity and affordability, the Internet does not yet exist for the general public. College students rely on their college library for their books and research.

  Today: At any American college, every student will have his or her own laptop and be connected to the Internet, where the totality of Greek literature is available together with the Liddell & Scott dictionaries used by the characters in *The Secret History*.

- **1980s:** The characters in *The Secret History* are completely dependent on landline telephones; Richard in particular, living in a dormitory, does not have a private phone and must rely on pay phones. The students have to establish elaborate codes of calling, ringing and then hanging up and calling again to make sure they catch each other's calls.

  Today: Practically everyone carries a cell phone, especially college students.

- **1980s:** On American college campuses, gay people generally remain closeted out of fear of persecution or abuse; open bigotry is not generally considered shameful.

  Today: Gay people are closer than ever to political and social equality. In 2015, same-sex marriage was made legal nationwide, and open bigotry is generally stigmatized.

---

characters hardly seem to consider their actions in religious terms at all. They never, for example, call themselves pagans or take any other interest in religious ritual except for their ecstatic experience of Dionysus. Although, with the exception of Richard, they are nominally Roman Catholic, they are remorselessly hostile to Christianity, mocking the evangelical Christians who inhabit the town of Hampden and fantasizing about waging war against them. Their teacher Julian tells them:

> Easy to see why the Romans, usually so tolerant of foreign religions, persecuted the Christians mercilessly—how absurd to think a common criminal had risen from the dead, how appalling that his followers celebrated him by drinking his blood. The illogic of it frightened them and they did everything they could to crush it.

In fact, the Romans did very little to persecute Christians until the time of the Emperor Diocletian at the end of the third century. While Christianity was illegal, it was prosecuted only sporadically, in response to public complaints. Roman judges were often puzzled over exactly why Christianity was outlawed in the first place, and even more so as to why accused Christians preferred to die rather to burn a pinch of incense on an altar for the sake of the community. That fact is significant. In the ancient world, religion was a communal activity: the entire community, whether of the city or the Roman Empire, worshipped the gods together for the sake of all. Religion, by its very etymology, means the forces that bind a community together. Christians were suspect because they set themselves off from the community, which made it look as if they were plotting against it. The same fact also reveals why the students in *The Secret History* have no interest in conventional Greek religion; their whole identity is built around separating themselves from their community as absolutely as possible.

Tartt's fictional classics students are not alone, however, in their interest in reviving Greek religion. There are organized groups in both the United States and Greece that are attempting to reconstruct ancient Greek religion. The relations between pagans and Christians in antiquity reveals a difficulty faced by any such attempt. Greek religion was shared by the entire community: its cults were by and large the

The group confronts Bunny while he is hiking, and Henry pushes him into a ravine. *(© mrfiza / Shutterstock.com)*

cults of cities, not of individuals. But in the modern Christian world, anyone practicing ancient Greek religion will necessarily belong to a tiny esoteric minority. In Greece, in particular, where Christianity is sanctioned as the state religion, the effort faces opposition and even persecution. In the United States, the main group reconstructing ancient Greek religion emerged from the larger Wicca movement in the late 1990s as isolated individuals sharing the same interests began to make contact on the Internet. Today, the main group that formed is called Hellenismos and is based on a website (http://www.hellenismos.us/). A small proportion of the group's members actually perform rituals together, but most remain solitary practitioners. This is standard in every form of American neo-paganism, so members usually do not acknowledge the important differences between what they practice and the communal religion in ancient Greece they are trying to resurrect. While activities that produced the kind of ecstatic state the characters in *The Secret History* experience were very rare in ancient Greece, Sabina Magliocco, in her book *Witching*

Culture: Folklore and Neo-Paganism in America, points out that it is precisely that kind of experience that is especially sought out by neo-pagans, specifically because it is individual:

> Pagans often experience powerful visions and trances during rituals. These can range from very personal images that resemble vivid waking dreams, to experiences of actually embodying deities . . . But the experience of altered or alternate consciousness that reveals a previously hidden, spiritual reality is the core of the Neo-Pagan movement, uniting Pagans and Witches even beyond shared practice.

There are also several neo-pagan groups in Greece that are more focused on communal ritual, even if it must be limited to the members of their own small communities. These include the Supreme Council of the Ethnic Hellenes and the Dodekatheon (whose name refers to the twelve Olympian gods). Their main goal is to gain legal recognition for their own existence. In 2006, they succeeded in having the worship of the traditional gods decriminalized, and they next want to be recognized by the state as a religion. Their ultimate goal is be able to worship in actual ancient temples.

CRITICAL OVERVIEW

The *Secret History* is too recent to have attracted very much in the way of critical analysis. This is not unusual, but in particular classicists have written nothing of note about the work, perhaps because it is so detached from the life of an ordinary American university classics department. (Nonetheless, the phone lines of classics departments were kept busy in 1992 and 1993, with readers asking for translations of its Greek and Latin quotations.) The initial reviews of *The Secret History* were mixed. Barbara Melvin, in "Failures in Classical and Modern Morality: Echoes of Euripides in *The Secret History*," one of the few scholarly articles to assess the novel, suggests that the book suffered from reviewers' bias in that its central subject matter of classics is elitist and politically incorrect. In contrast, she finds Tartt's juxtaposition of Greek morality with contemporary society to be a powerful and important theme of the work.

Turning to the reviews themselves, Richard Eder, writing in the *Los Angeles Times*, like many reviewers, first notes the overwhelming publicity campaign for the novel conducted by its publisher Alfred A. Knopf. He finds Tartt's characterizations to be weak. Accordingly, he judges the second half of the novel, after the murder plot has played out, inferior, since the section must be about the unraveling of character, and there is, in his view, precious little character to begin with. For Eder, the novel is about Richard's infatuation with the world conjured up by the impossibly romantic and elitist group of classicists, a theme Eder finds could easily be mistaken for satire. Like many commentators, he mistakenly believes that Bunny is actually blackmailing his classmates. Michiko Kakutani, writing in the *New York Times*, has a more positive opinion of the work. She recognizes it as a bricolage of styles and intertextual references (from sources ranging from *The Bacchae* to Evelyn Waugh's *Brideshead Revisited*) but finds it well constructed rather than ramshackle. She, too, asserts that Bunny is a blackmailer. She does not fault Tartt for the Dickensian melodrama of her plot but complains that the monolithic, calculating coldness of the characters prevents the concomitantly necessary Dickensian moral resonance: there is no guilt, no fall from grace, and no redemption. As the title, "Hype" of Gary Krist's *Hudson Review* notice of *The Secret History*, implies, he, too, is bothered by the massive publicity employed to promote the novel. However, he finds the book "is actually good. Granted, it's not flawless, and it too descends ultimately into melodrama and bathos." He notes the unreality of its characters as one of the book's flaws. Like Kakutani, he finds the book atmospherically similar to *Brideshead Revisited* and cites Tartt's fascination with the "highly affected tone of sophistication [of her characters], as well as a naked fascination with wealth and its trappings." François Pauw, in his two-part article in *Akroterion*, gives a sophisticated analysis of *The Secret History*. He provides an intertextual reading of the novel against its source material in Euripides and finds that it is a Greek tragedy in novel form. Henry is a tragic hero destroyed by his classical flaw of pride.

CRITICISM

Rita M. Brown

Brown is an English professor. In the following essay, she analyzes The Secret History *in connection with the philosophy of traditionalism.*

Although used more loosely today, in the strictest sense humanism is the philosophy of the Renaissance. In the fourteenth century, it was university student slang for the study of the secular works of antiquity, such as Ovid or Livy, as opposed to theological texts, which made up the core curriculum. To the early humanists like Plutarch, humanism meant the recovery and republication of lost works by non-Christian Roman authors and their use as a foundation for transforming society. Although the late medieval world was in many ways more advanced than the Roman Empire had been, for example in technology or in the wealth and material condition of Western Europe, the humanism of the Renaissance was founded on the belief that the Roman Empire had represented the pinnacle of human achievement and the only way forward was to understand and imitate its culture as closely as possible.

In the early twentieth century, although the Latin, and by then the Greek, classics were still the centerpiece of elite education, humanism was a historical concern. No one doubted that the modern world, thanks to the Enlightenment and the scientific revolution, had far surpassed the achievements of antiquity, not only in the scientific understanding of the universe but also in the wealth and freedom of every individual and above all in the wisdom and sophistication of civilization. The disaster of World War I shattered this confident illusion. It showed that the modern achievement had not been a pathway to utopia but had resulted instead in destruction and bloodshed on a scale that the ancient world could not have imagined. Primitive forces like nationalism and imperialism, which were also part of the ancient inheritance, had used modern science and technology to kill millions of young men for no apparent reason. The main reaction among intellectuals was a desire to abandon the past altogether and start working on an entirely new model of civilization. The result is easiest to see in the modernist art, music, and literature that came into being then, which bear almost no resemblance to traditional forms.

But the disaster of modernity led to another reaction, one that is known as traditionalism. The term *traditionalism*, even in a political sense, has an even wider range of meaning than humanism, but in a narrower sense, traditionalism is a philosophical and political movement that began in Western Europe in the 1920s. It was and remains a fringe movement, almost completely unknown outside of its own circles, but its history has been written by Mark Sedgwick in his *Against the Modern World: Traditionalism and the Secret Intellectual History of the Twentieth Century*. Traditionalism is a radicalized return to Renaissance humanism. It holds that during some golden age in the past, human life existed as an integrated whole full of wisdom and purpose. At some point, human life was struck by a disaster traditionalists refer to as modernity. This does not mean World War I but refers to the first break with received cultural tradition. Depending on the particular version of traditionalism, this can be as late as the Enlightenment or as early as the birth of Christianity or even the Iron Age. Cut off from tradition, human life became a sordid affair stripped of all meaning

and significance. Traditionalists accept the apocalyptic concepts of Indo-European and Semitic cultures as a pledge that what was lost will eventually be restored. Unlike other ideologies, such as Marxism, with a similar dialectical view of history, traditionalism pointedly offers no solution to the problem it poses, except to patiently wait for the cycles of history to restore the significance that had been lost. Human actions are too feeble to change things; traditionalists can only wait for the ultimate restoration of the past.

Traditionalism began in the 1920s in France, with the work of René Guénon, who saw a greater continuity with the traditional world in Islam than in Christian Europe and eventually moved to Egypt and converted to Sufi Islam. In Italy, traditionalism was represented by Julius Evola, whose private spirituality centered on the practice of ceremonial magic. Despite its lack of faith in human action, traditionalism has a history of political action. The Nazi Party was founded by the traditionalist Rudolf von Sebottendorf, but when Adolf Hitler seized control of the party, he completely transformed its nature, and Sebottendorf ended up in a concentration camp. Evola tried to exert influence over Italian fascism, but his opposition to Christianity caused his writings to be censored by Benito Mussolini's regime. Although traditionalism shares many features with fascism's self-presentation, its insistence on medieval and Roman-style aristocracy was ultimately incompatible with the actual plutocratic character of fascism; traditionalism is radically anticapitalist. Traditionalist groups were responsible for a number of terrorist attacks in Italy throughout the 1960s. The Romanian historian of religion Mircea Eliade was perhaps the best-known traditionalist because of the prominence of his scholarly work. Today, traditionalist parties are able to elect members of parliament in Greece and Russia; while some traditionalists like Evola rejected Christianity, in both these cases the medieval church, rather than the pagan Roman world, is taken as the lost ideal.

It is very unlikely that Tartt, particularly at the time she wrote *The Secret History*, had ever heard of traditionalism; it is completely outside of the mainstream intellectual tradition of which she is a part. Before the publication of Sedgewick's monograph and the migration of traditionalist groups to the Internet, traditionalism

WHAT DO I READ NEXT?

- If Julian Morrow has an inspiration in the real world, it might be the British classicist Robert Graves. He became famous as a war poet after World War I and in the 1930s as a novelist (*I Claudius* is his best-known work). He spent time in Hollywood and, like Julian, had his picture taken with various starlets. His study *The White Goddess* is a foundational document of Wicca and the New Age movement generally. His survey of Greek mythology, *The Greek Myths*, is still often used as a college textbook, but his *Greek Gods and Heroes* (1965) treats the same material, retelling the myths for a young-adult audience.

- Tracy Hargreaves has written *Donna Tartt's "The Secret History": A Reader's Guide* (2001) as a companion to Tartt's novel. She surveys the reviews and other critical notices of the book and gives a biography of Tartt based on her infrequent interviews.

- The four novels that make up the *Sea of Fertility* tetralogy (*Spring Snow*, 1969; *Runaway Horses*, 1969; *The Temple of Dawn*, 1970; and *The Decay of the Angel*, 1971)

are the political testament of Yukio Mishima, an author who, like the European traditionalists, was at war with the modern world. The novel embraces the romanticization of violence in Japanese culture and its heritage in the traditional Shinto religion, as well as in Buddhism, which was an avocation of Henry's in *The Secret History*.

- *The Little Friend* (2002) is Tartt's second novel. It is a southern gothic work, exploring the effect of a child's death on an aristocratic southern family.

- *Nothing to Do with Dionysos?*, a collection of essays edited by John J. Winkler and Froma I. Zeitlin in 1990, examines Greek drama and its patron god Dionysus (the variation in spelling in the book's title should be noted) in his social role within Athenian culture.

- Neil Gaiman's *American Gods* is a novel that shows the old gods waning in America in the face of new deities called into being by the modern world. The novel was first published in 2001; an expanded edition was released in 2011.

---

was very hard to even encounter, let alone seriously study. Nevertheless, it is clear that the philosophy that Julian and his students espouse is substantially identical to traditionalism. Insofar as traditionalism is a sort of hyper-humanism, it seems more likely that Tartt independently recreated traditionalism as an exaggerated form of her characters' proper study of classics. Nevertheless, her characters clearly embrace many specifically traditionalist doctrines.

A pervasive theme of *The Secret History* is that the modern world is a kind of hell. Tartt's depictions of the modern world range from her comparing a shopping mall to Milton's pandaemonium, the capital of hell in his epic poem *Paradise Lost* (1667), to a college party as a descent into Dante's *Inferno*. The literary

sophistication of her references stands in sharp contrast to the vulgar realities she condemns. The characterization is reciprocal: according to the rumors on campus about the classicists, "they worship the . . . Devil." Modernity is represented in the novel by two microcosmic images. The first is Hampden College itself. It is a vision of hell filled with useless, senile professors and drunken, drugged students pretending to be hippies, from which the classicists are completely and irrevocably cut off. The other is the warehouse where Richard spends the Christmas break. It is ruled by an old hippie, and simply existing there is a life-threatening experience. Traditionalism, particularly the British traditionalist sect of Aristasia, sees the 1960s counterculture as its mortal enemy. The counterculture is viewed as the most acute form of modernity and rejection of tradition and is referred to as *the Pit* (although, in fact, the actual origins of the counterculture share many intellectual roots with traditionalism and fascism). The college students are ignorant criminals (the individuals shift between campus life and biker gangs) obsessed with sex and intoxication. The hippie who owns the warehouse pretends to have a connection with tradition (manufacturing instruments like mandolins and dulcimers) but is completely indifferent to human suffering. When the classics students contemplate the possibility of being arrested for murder, one of the factors they repeatedly bring up is the inevitability that the press would misidentify them as hippies; it seems as dreadful to them as the prospect of jail itself.

The classicists, on the other hand, are set apart by their aristocratic character and above all by their special connection to antiquity. When Julian tells his students, "The Greeks, you know, really weren't very different from us," he does not mean not very different from modern people; he means not very different from them in particular because they are in revolt from the modern world. As he elaborates, "Are we, in this room, really very different from the Greeks or the Romans? Obsessed with duty, piety, loyalty, sacrifice? All those things which are to modern tastes so chilling." He defines the modern world as a place without duty, piety, loyalty or sacrifice. What distinguishes the classicists from modernity is an innate quality that is part of their aristocratic essence. During his second, successful interview with Julian, Richard analyzes the professor's conversation:

> Despite its illusion of being rather modern and digressive (to me, the hallmark of the modern mind is that it loves to wander from its subject) I now see that he was leading me by circumlocution to the same points again and again. For if the modern mind is whimsical and discursive, the classical mind is narrow, unhesitating, relentless. It is not a quality of intelligence that one encounters frequently these days. But though I can digress with the best of them, I am nothing in my soul if not obsessive.

The very way that they think is different from and superior to modern people. As Richard describes them, they

> were imposing enough, and different as they all were they shared a certain coolness, a cruel, mannered charm which was not modern in the least but had a strange cold breath of the ancient world: they were magnificent creatures.

When Julian begins his lecture, he says, "I hope we're all ready to leave the phenomenal world, and enter into the sublime?" The modern world is as inferior to the ancient in Julian's metaphysics as the physical world is to the divine.

It naturally follows that the classicists have no interest in the modern world. Richard scandalized the others

> by the fact that I read papers and watched news on television from time to time (a habit which seemed to them an outrageous eccentricity, peculiar to me alone; none of them were the least bit interested in anything that was going on in the world, and their ignorance of current events and even recent history was rather astounding. Once, over dinner, Henry was quite startled to learn from me that men had walked on the moon. "No," he said, putting down his fork.

The greatest achievements of modern science are irrelevant because they are by definition inferior to antiquity.

The classicists perceive everything in a different way from modern people. When Henry is discussing Bunny, he concludes, "He certainly has no gift for scholarship. They [i.e., his parents] should've apprenticed him to a painter when he was young instead of sending him to all those expensive schools for learning disabilities." The modern response, the special education, is an attempt to make Bunny over so that he fits into the modern world. The traditional response is to cultivate whatever special qualities the child has. Where in the modern world, though, is there an atelier where a teenager can apprentice for a career as an artist without a standard education? A similar example is Henry's uncanny rapport with poor people. He is generally able to win them over because he does not condescend to them as do modern rich people but instead has a paternalistic attitude, as a Roman landlord had for his peasants. It would never occur to him to consider them his equals (a revelation that goes a long way toward Richard's never explaining his true situation). In the novel, anyway, the poor enthusiastically respond to a true aristocrat.

It would be a mistake to conclude that Tartt embraces the beliefs she supplies her characters. While those characters may condemn the hippie warehouse owner for his lack of concern for Richard's life, Henry and the others show an appalling lack of remorse for having killed the

Charles, jealous and drunk, brings a gun to Henry and Camilla's hotel room. *(© MyImages - Micha / Shutterstock.com)*

farmer. The fact that their lives end in suicide and misery is Tartt's judgment against them. In the frontispiece to the second book of *The Secret History*, Tartt quotes the prominent classicist E. R. Dodds' Sather lectures, *The Greeks and the Irrational*: "Dionysus [is] the Master of Illusions, who could make a vine grow out of a ship's plank, and in general enable his votaries to see the world as the world's not." In her view, their traditionalism has blinded her characters from accepting the world as it is. They are mistaken for not embracing the same mainstream intellectualism she does and are punished as dissidents.

Source: Rita M. Brown, Critical Essay on *The Secret History*, in *Novels for Students*, Gale, Cengage Learning, 2016.

Roane Carey

In the following review, Carey calls The Secret History *"an excellent first novel."*

I hadn't planned to read Donna Tartt's *The Secret History* (Knopf). I was irritated by the publicity steamroller, and I had been disappointed once before by breathless proclamations that Bennington College had produced a literary genius. I quickly changed my mind after glancing at the first dozen or so pages. I was hooked by Tartt's elegant prose, sharp wit and deft characterization: My interest was also piqued because I felt a more than passing kinship with the. book's protagonist, who is desperate to. escape the torpor of Middle America, and who believes he finds the promised land of the life of the mind at a small liberal arts college in the Northeast.

One might think the excesses of a clique of college snobs is unfertile ground for a superb novel, but this little band of miscreants is not engaged in the usual mindless debauchery; they're devoted to an idea, planted by their beloved professor, which they pursue tragically too far. Tartt skillfully implicates the reader in the actions of her heroes, thus heightening the tension. The details of the book's central crisis may seem farfetched to some, but Tartt's storytelling abilities overcome any such complaints. It would not be inappropriate to recall *The Possessed*, or perhaps to imagine Leopold and Loeb reappearing in our own time.

The Secret History is an excellent first novel.

Source: Roane Carey, Review of *The Secret History*, in *Nation*, Vol. 255, No. 21, December 21, 1992, p. 775.

Publishers Weekly

In the following review, an anonymous reviewer describes The Secret History *as "sometimes ponderous" but "highly entertaining."*

Tartt's much bruited first novel is a huge (592 pages) rambling story that is sometimes ponderous, sometimes highly entertaining. Part psychological thriller, part chronicle of debauched, wasted youth, it suffers from a basically improbable plot, a fault Tartt often redeems through the bravado of her execution. Narrator Richard Papen comes from a lower-class family and a loveless California home to the "hermetic, overheated atmosphere" of Vermont's Hampden College. Almost too easily, he is accepted into a clique of five socially sophisticated students who study Classics with an idiosyncratic, morally fraudulent professor. Despite their demanding curriculum (they quote Greek classics to each other at every opportunity) the friends spend most of their time drinking and taking pills. Finally they reveal to Richard that they accidentally killed a man during a bacchanalian frenzy; when one of their number seems ready to spill the secret, the group—now including Richard—must kill him, too. The best parts

> FOR *THE SECRET HISTORY* IS, AMID ITS VAST ENTERTAININGNESS, AN EXTREMELY SERIOUS BOOK: A BOOK WHOSE VERY ESSENCE IS THE SURVIVAL OF FORMALITY IN A FORMALITY-STARVED ERA."

of the book occur after the second murder, when Tartt describes the effect of the death on a small community, the behavior of the victim's family and the conspirators' emotional disintegration. Here her gifts for social satire and character analysis are shown to good advantage and her writing is powerful and evocative. On the other hands, the plot's many inconsistencies, the self-indulgent, high-flown references to classic literature and the reliance on melodrama make one wish this had been a tauter, more focused novel. In the final analysis, however, readers may enjoy the pull of a mysterious, richly detailed story told by a talented writer.

Source: Review of *The Secret History*, in *Publishers Weekly*, Vol. 239, No. 29, June 29, 1992, p. 50.

James Kaplan

In the following excerpt, Kaplan looks at possible sources of inspiration for The Secret History.

Donna Tartt, who is going to be very famous very soon—conceivably the moment you read this—also happens to be exceedingly small. Teeny, even. "I'm the exact same size as Lolita," she says. "Do you remember that poem from the novel?" She recites,

> *Wanted, wanted: Dolores Haze*
> *Her dream-gray gaze never flinches.*
> *Ninety pounds is all she weighs*
> *With a height of sixty inches.*

We're sitting over a country breakfast in Smitty's, a homey café in Oxford, Mississippi—site of the university, Ole Miss, and hometown of another Mississippi writer, name of Faulkner. Who may have won a Nobel, but whose books never, in his lifetime, made anything like the commercial splash Donna Tartt has already made with her first novel, *The Secret History*, published this month by Knopf.

Tartt taps her Marlboro Gold on the ashtray. She is a kind of girl-boy-woman in her lineaments, with lunar-pale skin, spooky light-green eyes, a good-size triangular nose, a high, pixieish voice. With her Norma Desmond sunglasses propped on her dark bobbed hair, her striped boy's shirt and shorts from Gap Kids (the only store whose ready-to-wear fits her), and her ever-present cigarette, she is, somehow, a character of her own fictive creation: a precocious sprite from a Cunard Line cruise ship, circa 1920-something. A Wise Child out of Salinger.

"I know a *ton* of poetry by heart," Tartt says, when I comment on her recital of the Nabokov rhyme. It's true. She has an alarming ability to simply break into passages, short or long, from her favorite writing. She quotes, freely and naturally, from Thomas Aquinas, Cardinal Newman, Buddha, and Plato—as well as David Byrne of Talking Heads and Jonathan Richman of the Modern Lovers. And many others.

"When I was a little kid, first thing I memorized were really long poems by A. A. Milne," she says. "Then I went through a Kipling phase. I could say 'Gunga Din' for you. Then I went into sort of a Shakespeare phase, when I was about in sixth grade. In high school, I loved loved *loved* Edgar Allan Poe. Still love him. I could say 'Annabel Lee' for you now. I used to know even some of the shorter *stories* by heart. 'The Tell-Tale Heart'—I used to be able to *say* that.

"I *still* memorize poems," she says. "I know 'The Waste Land' by heart. 'Prufrock.' Yeats is good. I know a lot of poems in French by heart. A lot of Dante. That's just something that has always come easily to me. I also know all these things that I was *made* to learn. I'm sort of this *horrible repository* of doggerel verse."

Donna Tartt seems, in many ways, a figure from another decade: a small, hard-drinking, southern writer, a Catholic convert, witheringly smart, with an occluded past, sadness among the magnolias. Wasn't that Flannery? Or Carson? Or Truman, or Tennessee? Surely not a figure from the post-MTV generation. Yet here she is, not yet thirty, coming out of obscurity in Greenwich Village—where she lives with a cockatiel, Horace, and a pug, Pongo (and no television)—into supernova-hood, weighing in among the serious contenders. For *The Secret History* is, amid its vast entertainingness, an extremely serious book: a book whose very essence is the survival of formality in a formality-starved era.

It's commercially serious, too. In early 1989, Tartt's Bennington classmate and friend Bret

Easton Ellis introduced her and her project (it was three-quarters done; she had an outline for the rest) to his agent, ICM honcho Amanda Urban. This was more than a favor: Ellis had been reading the novel, as it progressed, for six years, since he and Tartt were in their second year at college. He thought she had the goods. So did Urban. "She said, 'My God, it's incredibly well written—I can't stop turning the pages,'" Ellis recalls.

Urban accepted Tartt as an unsigned client; two years later, with the completed (866-page) manuscript in hand, Urban was able to whip up a bidding frenzy among several publishing houses. The winner, Knopf, paid $450,000 for the book (which it made back almost immediately, and then again, in foreign sales). Shortly thereafter, Alan Pakula's Pakula Productions paid another large sum for the privilege of attempting to turn the book into a motion picture. This is a book that was on boil long before it even hit the stores: so great was the demand for five-hundred-page advance reader's editions of *The Secret History* that Knopf had to print an unprecedented second run.

What's all the fuss? This: *The Secret History* is about a small, singular cadre of classics students at Vermont's Hampden College (a tiny ultra-liberal, ultra-artistic school not unlike Bennington) who, for the strangest of possible reasons, slay a stranger, and then one of their own. It is a huge, mesmerizing, galloping read, pleasurably devoured in a few evenings: a book which, unlike the vast preponderance of page-turners—or, for that matter, the vast preponderance of first novels—is gorgeously written, relentlessly erudite, and persistently (and quite anachronistically) high-minded. It is (the strangeness compounds) a murder mystery in which the two killings (and all sex scenes) take place offstage, and in which the only mystery is *why*—the who, what, when, where, and how all being known virtually from the word go. *"The snow in the mountains was melting and Bunny had been dead for several weeks before we came to understand the gravity of our situation."* Thus—deadpan, chockablock with beauty and portent—one of the classic first sentences of our vehemently anti-classical time.

But then, Donna Tartt is more than mildly fixated on things classical. As good a place to begin as any is the fact that she has a largish obsession, bordering on the cultic, with T. S. Eliot. The ringleader and chief malefactor in *The Secret History,* an eerily grave polymath called Henry Winter, comes from Eliot's hometown, St. Louis, has the same first name as Old Tom's brother, wears tiny, old-fashioned steel-rimmed glasses and "dark English suits and carrie[s] an umbrella (a bizarre sight in Hampden) and . . . walk[s] stiffly through the throngs of hippies and beatniks and preppies and punks with the self-conscious formality of an old ballerina."

Tartt's answering-machine message is the Man Himself, reading, solemnly, from "The Waste Land": "I see crowds of people, walking round in a ring. / Thank you. If you see dear Mrs. Equitone, / Tell her I bring the horoscope myself: / One must be so careful these days."

Indeed. Like Eliot, and like another idol, J. D. Salinger, Tartt is not at all averse to interest in her work. Period. When it comes to the perky, personal, prying tone of our time, her reservations are grave. The title of her book is not without autobiographical meaning. Her skittishness about being interviewed is formidable. But as Bret Easton Ellis (the co-dedicatee of *The Secret History*) will later tell me, with the rueful tone of One Who Knows, "You can't be Salinger and be represented by ICM."

One can do one's best, however.

. . . Tartt began writing the novel that would become *The Secret History* in her second year at Bennington. She began showing it to Ellis almost at once. "I don't know if any of this would've happened without Bret," she says now. "I started seeing it around 1983," Ellis says. "It wasn't much different at all from the way it is today."

Then, as now, the story centered on a small group of overrefined classics students; only then no one had any doubts about the book's sources. Early on at Bennington, Tartt had fallen in with a small clique of literature students that clustered around Claude Fredericks, a brilliant but odd teacher who admitted few people to his classes. "I wanted to take Greek from him, but he turned me down," Jill Eisenstadt says, raising an eerie echo of *The Secret History*. "I always thought if you *wanted* to take Greek, why should anyone turn you down? I don't think he liked women."

Like Fredericks, the group was exceedingly well-tailored—a startling eccentricity at Bennington, where even the children of the super-rich wore the rattiest jeans and T-shirts. Tartt was the only female in the group. Soon her friends noticed she'd exchanged skirts and dresses for trousers, and begun getting her hair

cut boy-style. She also developed an intense friendship with Paul McGloin—a tall, thin, pale upperclassman with a dry, sarcastic wit, a dazzling facility for languages, and a partiality for dark suits, who reminded one classmate of a quieter William S. Burroughs.

The group kept very much to themselves. An encyclopedia entry about Bennington notes, "A close relationship between students and faculty is encouraged." Some would say this understates the case. The school has always had a hothouse atmosphere, and tutorials are the rule. "Cliques grow up around certain teachers, and the mentor relationships get very intense," an alumnus says. "*Very* intense. There was definitely an air of Svengali about Fredericks—it seemed to go beyond even what was normal for Bennington."

No one is suggesting human sacrifices took place. But friends noticed the changes in Tartt—who was a wonderful storyteller, but famously closemouthed when it came to her own life—and wondered whether the novel was somehow a key.

"The only really tense moment she and I ever had was in this writing tutorial where she'd brought the novel," Bret Ellis says. "It was just me and Donna and one other girl. At that point I'd read the first eighty to ninety pages of *The Secret History*. I thought it was beautifully written; I only had one criticism. I said, 'Here's this guy, the narrator, a freshman at college, and he has no sort of sexual feeling, no desire at all. It just doesn't seem realistic.' She gave me the stoniest look I ever got. I almost wilted into my chair.

"And you couldn't say anything about Claude Fredericks in front of her," Ellis adds. "It'd be the end of the evening."

Ellis, who took one course with Fredericks and failed, paid an esoteric tribute both to the strange coterie and Tartt's nascent novel in *The Rules of Attraction*, referring, en passant, to "that weird group of Classics majors stand[ing] by [at a party], looking like undertakers," and "that weird Classics group . . . probably roaming the countryside sacrificing farmers and performing pagan rituals." How far was his tongue in cheek? It's always hard to tell with Ellis.

As for Tartt's relationship with McGloin, "I never did get a handle on it—it didn't seem right to ask," says a friend. "They were very, very private people. The kind of people who would invite you into the drawing room, but never upstairs. . . . "

Source: James Kaplan, "Smart Tartt," in *Vanity Fair*, September 1992.

SOURCES

Coffey, Edel, "The Very, Very Private Life of Ms Donna Tartt," in *Independent*, November 26, 2013, http://www.independent.ie/lifestyle/interview-the-very-very-private-life-of-ms-donna-tartt-29780543.html (accessed December 16, 2014).

Dodds, E. R., *The Greeks and the Irrational*, Sather Lectures 25, University of California Press, 1951, pp. 270–82.

Eder, Richard, "Corrupting the Classics," in *Los Angeles Times*, September 13, 1992, http://articles.latimes.com/1992-09-13/books/bk-1143_1_secret-history (accessed December 16, 2014).

Eisenstadt, Jill, "Donna Tartt," in *Bomb*, Vol. 41, 1992, pp. 56–59.

Euripides, *The Bacchae*, translated by William Arrowsmith, in *Greek Tragedies*, Vol. 3, edited by David Grene and Richmond Lattimore, University of Chicago Press, pp. 189–260.

Galbraith, Lacey, "The Art of Fiction No, 184: Barry Hannah," in *Paris Review*, Vol. 172, 2004, http://www.theparisreview.org/interviews/5438/the-art-of-fiction-no-184-barry-hannah (accessed December 12, 2014).

Johnston, Sarah Iles, "Whose Gods Are These? A Classicist Looks at Neopaganism," in *Dans le laboratoire de l'historien des religions: Mélanges offerts à Philippe Borgeaud*, edited by Francesca Prescendi and Youri Volokhine, Editions Labor et Fides, 2001, pp. 123–33.

Kakutani, Michiko, "Students Indulging in Course of Destruction," in *New York Times*, September 4, 1992, http://www.nytimes.com/1992/09/04/books/books-of-the-times-students-indulging-in-course-of-destruction.html (accessed December 16, 2014).

Krist, Gary, "Hype," in *Hudson Review*, Vol. 46, No, 1, 1993, pp. 239–46.

Magliocco, Sabina, *Witching Culture: Folklore and Neo-Paganism in America*, University of Pennsylvania Press, 2004, pp. 152–84.

Melvin, Barbara, "Failures in Classical and Modern Morality: Echoes of Euripides in *The Secret History*," in *Journal of Evolutionary Psychology*, Vol. 17, 1996, pp. 1–2, 53–63.

Pauw, François, "If on a Winter's Night a Reveler: The Classical Intertext in Donna Tartt's *The Secret History*," in *Akroterion*, Vol. 39, No. 3, 1994, pp. 141–63; Vol 40, No. 4, 1995, pp. 2–29.

Sedgwick, Mark, *Against the Modern World: Traditionalism and the Secret Intellectual History of the Twentieth Century*, Oxford University Press, 2004, pp. 95–117.

Tartt, Donna, *The Secret History*, Random House, 1992.

FURTHER READING

Carpenter, Thomas A., and Christopher A. Faraone, eds., *Masks of Dionysus*, Cornell University Press, 1993.
　　The essays in this important collection treat Dionysus in Greek myth and cult, noting his role as patron of drama. The methodologically modern articles are an important supplement to older works like Dodd's *The Greeks and the Irrational* from which Tartt drew her inspiration.

Evola, Julius, *Ride the Tiger: A Survival Manual for the Aristocrats of the Soul*, translated by Joscelyn Godwin and Constance Fontana, Inner Traditions, 2003.
　　Originally published in 1961, Evola's *Ride the Tiger* is probably the single most important work by a traditionalist author. It defines how, in the author's view, aristocratic tradition alone makes the realization of the individual possible and criticizes in great detail the circumstances of the modern world that work against such self-realization.

Tartt, Donna, *The Goldfinch*, Little, Brown, 2013.
　　In *The Goldfinch*, Tartt's Pulitzer Prize–winning novel, a thirteen-year-old boy is in a New York Museum viewing Carel Fabritius's seventeenth-century painting, *The Goldfinch*, when a terrorist's bomb kills his mother and dozens of other people. During the resulting confusion, he steals the painting. The novel chronicles the boy's life as he grows up in a world of wealth and privilege.

Waugh, Evelyn, *Brideshead Revisited*, Chapman and Hall, 1945.
　　Commentators have often pointed out that Tartt's seeming worship of aristocratic culture in *The Secret History* is modeled on Waugh's nostalgia in this novel for an aristocratic world in England that was already disappearing.

SUGGESTED SEARCH TERMS

Donna Tartt

The Secret History AND Tartt

modernism

classicism

mysticism

Dionysus/Dionysos

neo-paganism

traditionalism

The Sheltering Sky

PAUL BOWLES

1949

Published originally in 1949, Paul Bowles's *The Sheltering Sky* was voted one of one hundred best English-language novels from 1923 to 2005 by *Time* magazine. The story centers on Port Moresby and his wife, Kit, a married couple originally from New York who travel to the North African desert, in part in an attempt to resolve some deep and lingering marital difficulties. Accompanied by their friend, Tunner, the couple are tragically unprepared for the challenges they will confront, physically, spiritually, and emotionally. In the end, only one of the three survives the journey unscathed. One lies dead in a Saharan hospital, while another is left wandering the streets of Oran in a state of madness and despair. This novel involves mature themes and scenes of sexual violence that are not suitable for younger students.

AUTHOR BIOGRAPHY

Paul Frederic Bowles was born on December 30, 1910, in Jamaica, Queens, New York City, the only child of Rena (nee Winnewisser) and Claude Dietz Bowles, a dentist who was, according to all reports, a cold and domineering parent. Inspired by his mother, who would spend hours reading to her son, Bowles was a voracious reader. Writing followed soon after,

Paul Bowles *(© Everett Collection Inc | Alamy)*

and by age seventeen, he had a poem accepted for publication.

Bowles entered the University of Virginia in 1928 but dropped out in the spring of 1929, bought a one-way ticket to Paris, and sailed to Europe. He spent the next few months working for the *Paris Herald Tribune* before returning to New York City in July, where he took a job at Duttons Bookshop in Manhattan and began studying musical composition with Aaron Copland. His parents insisted he return to the university, which he did, only to drop out a second time one year later. Bowles then returned to Paris, this time accompanied by Copland, and almost immediately began work on his first musical composition. His "Sonata for Oboe and Clarinet" debuted at New York's Aeolian Hall on December 16, 1931, and was lambasted by critics.

While in Paris, Bowles became part of Gertrude Stein's famous circle of writers and artists. On Stein's advice, Bowles and Copland traveled to Tangier in the summer of 1931, before making a brief sojourn to Berlin (where he met Stephen Spender and Christopher Isherwood) and then returning to Africa in 1932, traveling through Morocco, the Sahara, Algeria, and Tunisia. He returned to New York in 1937, where he worked for a number of years as a stage and orchestral composer.

In 1938, he married writer Jane Auer in what is best described as an unconventional union; both were homosexual and often took lovers outside the marriage, but Bowles and Auer reportedly remained emotionally close. Bowles continued his success as a composer. His light opera *The Wind Remains* (1943) was conducted by Leonard Bernstein, and his translation of Jean-Paul Sartre's play *Huis Clos* (*No Exit*) was not only directed by the great John Huston but also was awarded a Drama Critics Award in 1943.

Having picked up his pen to write fiction again, Bowles was awarded a generous advance from Doubleday in 1947. With the money he moved himself and Jane to Tangier, where he made his permanent home. He traveled alone into the Algerian Sahara to work on a novel, which he completed in nine months. The book eventually became *The Sheltering Sky*, and it was published by John Lehmann in England after Doubleday turned it down. Bowles would go on to publish a collection of stories titled *A Little Stone* (1950) as well as a series of novels (*Let It Come Down* in 1952 and *The Spider's House* in 1955), while continuing to compose music and building an impressive archive of recordings of music from various ethnic groups in the region. Bowles also became a familiar figure (along with Jane) in Tangier social circles, hosting such visitors as Truman Capote, Tennessee Williams, and Gore Vidal.

When Jane suffered a mild stroke in 1957, Bowles focused his life on caring for her as her health deteriorated until her death in Malaga, Spain, in 1973. Following Jane's death, Bowles continued to live in Tangier, writing and hosting the occasional workshop under the auspices of the American School of Tangier. He returned to New York once more in his life, to attend the Paul Bowles Festival at Lincoln Center.

Bowles died of heart failure on November 18, 1999, at the Italian Hospital in Tangier. He was eighty-eight years old.

PLOT SUMMARY

Book One: Tea in the Sahara

Book One is framed by an epigraph from Argentine essayist and culture critic Eduardo Mallea: "Each man's destiny is personal only

MEDIA ADAPTATIONS

- *The Sheltering Sky*, adapted as a film by Bernardo Bertolucci and starring Debra Winger (Kit), John Malkovich (Port), and Campbell Scott (Tunner), was produced and distributed by Warner Bros. in 1990.
- Audible Studios released an unabridged audio book of *The Sheltering Sky* in 2012. The recording is read by actress Jennifer Connelly and runs 10 hours and 30 minutes.

insofar as it may happen to resemble what is already in his memory."

CHAPTER ONE

Port Moresby awakens from a dream, unsure of the time of day or where he is. He hears his wife, Kit, moving in another room. He struggles to recall his dream.

CHAPTER TWO

Port, Kit, and their friend, George Tunner, sit in a café in an unnamed North African city poring over maps, although Port is far more engaged in the process than the others. He is explaining to the others the difference between tourists (which he does not see himself as) and travelers (which he believes they are). They booked passage to North Africa from New York based on Port's earlier experiences in the region, but even he has some reservations now that they are actually in the country. That said, they do agree they are excited to be in a country that is far removed from the monotony and boredom of postwar America.

CHAPTER THREE

Port and Kit are in a hotel room, where Kit expresses her concern about Gunner's propensity for gossip, especially since the trio will be back in New York one day and will have to be part of the same social circles. There is tension in Port and Kit's marriage, evident as he kisses her before leaving the room.

CHAPTER FOUR

Port walks through the streets of the city, slightly nervous and somewhat indifferent in his curiosity. He witnesses a stone-throwing battle between two groups, before meeting an Arab man, Smail, who takes him to a café for tea, conversation, and the offer of a prostitute. Port spontaneously accepts the offer, and the men leave the café.

CHAPTER FIVE

Port and Smail travel to the edge of town and then down into the valley to a tent village. Port enters a dirty and disorderly tent, where he is joined by Marhnia. She makes the men tea before preceding to recount the legend of three beautiful young women and their metaphoric taking of tea in the Sahara. Port has sex with Marhnia, imagining Kit as a silent onlooker. Overcome with guilt, he tries to dress and leave, but Marhnia, under the pretense of affection, tries to steal his wallet. He pushes her aside and rushes from the tent.

CHAPTER SIX

Kit awakens in the hotel room, taking some time to reflect on her marital problems with Port and contemplating using Tunner, whom she finds annoying, as a source of excitement in her life and perhaps a catalyst to force Port to spend more time attending to their relationship. Tunner arrives to wake her up. As she scrambles to get dressed, she realizes that Port has not yet returned. Tunner realizes the same thing very quickly and after a quick breakfast persuades Kit to join him for a walk. Port arrives and is angry to discover Tunner present.

CHAPTER SEVEN

After sleeping the entire day, Port ventures down to the hotel bar, where he meets Kit before going to the restaurant for dinner. They watch Eric Lyle, a revolting young man, argue with his mother, a travel writer touring Africa. Port and Kit also argue about Port's whereabouts the night before and the fact that he discovered Tunner in their hotel room upon his return. Kit retires to their room, while Port and Eric talk more about traveling and the complexities of North Africa.

CHAPTER EIGHT

Kit is waiting up for Port when he arrives, and their argument continues. In the morning, Port crosses paths with Eric, who offers them a ride to Boussif, which is five hours by car compared to eleven hours on the local trains. The one condition is that they do not have room for Tunner, which means that he will have to take the train and meet up with them later in the day. Kit refuses to leave Tunner behind, prompting another argument with Port. In the end, Port goes with the Lyles by car, leaving Kit and Tunner to make the journey together by train. Meeting Kit in the dining room following Port's departure, Tunner celebrates with an expensive bottle of champagne.

CHAPTER NINE

Port arrives in Boussif with the Lyles and begins to explore the city amidst the bickering of the mother and son.

CHAPTER TEN

Riding the old train, Kit and Tunner share a compartment for the journey, into which Tunner has brought another six bottles of champagne. The two get drunk and flirt, until the train makes one of its many stops and Kits takes a moment to step off the train. Reboarding, she mistakenly enters a fourth-class carriage car. She panics, seeing danger everywhere. Rushing through the train's outdoor passageways, she returns to her compartment soaked by the rain and shaken. Tunner's seduction is consummated before the train reaches Boussif.

CHAPTER ELEVEN

Over breakfast the next morning, Port listens as Mrs. Lyle wonders aloud about how her son contracted his infection, which she suspects comes from his carousing with prostitutes. Port is somewhat taken back at the condition of the hotel, but Mrs. Lyle assures him it is quite luxurious when compared with others in the region. Port sets off to explore Boussif while Kit sleeps.

CHAPTER TWELVE

Kit awakes in her own room in Boussif, only to find Tunner in her bed. Frantic, she sends him to the room reserved for him. Finally reconnecting over lunch, the three discuss the war's impact on civilization and North Africa specifically before Tunner retires to his room for a much-needed rest. Kit and Port follow, talking briefly on Port's bed before drifting off.

CHAPTER THIRTEEN

Port and Kit ride rented bicycles toward a local cliff, relaxed and comfortable in each other's company. Finding themselves high above the desert, they stop to reflect. Kit sadly recognizes that although they both appreciate the view, their philosophies about life and their understandings of the future are vastly different. Kit is wracked with guilt about having slept with Tunner, while Port reflects on his life and marriage.

CHAPTER FOURTEEN

Two days later the trio departs by bus for Ain Krorfa, accompanied by clouds of dust and seemingly thousands of flies. In the days leading up to departure, Port had been increasingly frustrated by what he saw as Tunner's efforts to intrude upon any private time the married couple has. Port decides that he will get rid of Tunner at the end of the bus ride and make the rest of the journey with Kit alone.

CHAPTER FIFTEEN

As the bus approaches Ain Krorfa, the nuisance of the flies intensifies, as do the complaints of Kit and Tunner over everything from the dust to the garbage in the streets to the absence of anything of interest to the displaced New Yorkers. Tunner vows to escape the town at his first chance, a declaration that Port seizes upon as an opportunity to rid himself of his companion. He arranges with Tunner to travel to Messad with the Lyles under the pretense of reconnecting in Bou Noura.

CHAPTER SIXTEEN

Tunner heads off for Messad, leaving Kit and Port in Ain Krorfa. Kit is miserably hot and dirty and stays in the hotel room while Port explores what there is of the town.

CHAPTER SEVENTEEN

The eve of the departure for Bou Noura, Port ventures out into the night with Mohammad, a waiter in the hotel restaurant. Mohammad takes him to a local brothel, where Port is transfixed by a young blind woman dancing to the music in the room. He tries to buy time with her but is frustrated in his attempts and leaves the brothel angry.

Book Two: The Earth's Sharp Edge

Book Two is framed by an epigraph from French essayist and philosopher Paul Valéry: "'Good-bye,' says the dying man to the mirror they hold in front of him. 'We won't be seeing each other any more.'"

CHAPTER EIGHTEEN

This chapter begins with the brief history of Lieutenant d'Armagnac, commander of the military post at Bou Noura, whose notoriety stems from his treatment of a young woman, Yamina ben Rhaissa, who might or might not have committed the crime of which she was accused. D'Armagnac is also the authority who deals with Port, whose passport has been stolen.

CHAPTER NINETEEN

Port is ushered into d'Armagnac's office, dressed in layers of clothing inappropriate for the heat. D'Armagnac senses that Port's health is bad, though Port denies it. Port is certain that Eric Lyle stole his passport as revenge for Port's refusal to lend him money. Port grows more emotionally distant and increasingly incoherent as the aggressive illness begins to set in. He is determined to head to El Ga'a, where he believes the desert warmth will help him recover his health.

CHAPTER TWENTY

Port spends two days trying to gather information about his intended destination, when he is called to d'Armagnac's office. He is informed that his passport has been found (it had been sold on the black market) and was being brought to Bou Noura by another American traveler: Tunner. Port is horrified that Tunner is returning into his life and, after making the officer a promise that he will not leave town for three days, rushes to the bus station to book immediate passage to El Ga'a. Kit is unaware what has transpired and is bewildered by Port's sudden rush to catch the bus. Port comes down with a serious chill as the bus moves through the desert night.

CHAPTER TWENTY-ONE

Port sleeps deeply on the overnight bus trip, his illness worsening. El Ga'a is filthy, and Port finds it difficult to even move, let alone walk through its streets. Kit begins to panic when no hotels will allow her to book a room, and her anxiety increases when she discovers why: the city is infected with an epidemic of meningitis, an acute inflammation of the protective membranes covering the brain and spinal cord. With Port lying in the street and no hotel available, Kit is left to the mercy of some locals, who carry Port outside the city limits (for a substantial fee) to a waiting truck to take them to a nearby town.

CHAPTER TWENTY-TWO

Arriving at the city of Sba, Kit is met by some soldiers who identify Port's illness as typhoid. They tell her that the best treatment is rest, give Kit some medicine for Port, and arrange for a bed for him in the local hospital. Kit spends the night and the next day caring for Port with water, soup, and the fever pills. As his fever deepens, Port begins to ramble incoherently and angrily. His condition worsens, and Kit finds herself feeling a solitude she has never imagined possible.

CHAPTER TWENTY-THREE

Tunner arrives in Bou Noura with Port's passport and meets with d'Armagnac. Making matters worse in Sba, Kit angers the local authorities when she cannot produce a passport for her husband. Port falls deeper into the grip of typhoid and begins to scream loudly in the room. As Kit paces on the roof of the hospital, trying to get a grip on her emotions and form some type of plan about what to do with Port, she sees a familiar figure arrive in town. Tunner arrives with the passport, and he and Kit are reunited, albeit with guilt on both sides, given Port's condition.

CHAPTER TWENTY-FOUR

Returning to the hospital room, Kit finds Port dead. Pacing the room, she is shocked when Tunner knocks on the door and stands quietly until she tells him quietly that Port is fine and that she will meet him later that evening in the garden. With Tunner dispatched, Kit locks the door to Port's room and climbs from the small window. She escapes the city.

CHAPTER TWENTY-FIVE

D'Armagnac and Tunner reflect on the disappearance of Kit, with the latter remaining focused on finding her and returning her to New York. Tunner works diligently through the day to find some clues as to her location. Heading to his hotel room to rest, he discovers Eric Lyle stealing from Port's suitcase. A fight ensues, and Tunner knocks Eric to the ground.

Book Three: The Sky

Book Three is framed by an epigraph from German novelist Franz Kafka: "From a certain point onward there is no longer any turning back. That is the point that must be reached."

CHAPTER TWENTY-SIX

Having slept in the desert beyond the city, Kit awakens. She brazenly joins a camel caravan guided by two men, one younger and the other older. She travels with the men and is raped repeatedly by both men. She quickly becomes emotionally attached to the younger of the two, Belqassim. When they approach Belqassim's village, Kit disguises herself as a man so that he can smuggle her into his household of numerous wives.

CHAPTER TWENTY-SEVEN

Kit falls into a routine as a hidden woman, but inevitably the wives discover the deception and attack Kit, tearing off her clothes. Belqassim arrives, shouting to drive the women away. Kit turns to him for solace, crying. Her tears anger Belqassim, who confines her to her room. As Belqassim's visits become less and less frequent, Kit becomes increasingly agitated to the point that she plans to escape the household at the first opportunity. She accomplishes her escape by bribing the wives so they will allow her out the door of the house onto the street.

CHAPTER TWENTY-EIGHT

Wandering in the village in near madness, Kit attempts to buy food with a thousand-franc note, which draws an enthusiastic crowd. Led away by one of the men, Kit is robbed of everything except her passport.

CHAPTER TWENTY-NINE

Found and brought to a local convent, Kit has slid into madness. She refuses to eat or talk and is violent to the point that she is chained to a bed until transport to the American consulate in Oran can be arranged.

CHAPTER THIRTY

Back in Oran, Kit is guided to a local hotel by a representative of the consulate, who informs her that Tunner has been in constant contact, hoping to find her. He has, in fact, come to Oran to take her back to New York. Kit appears terrified at the prospect of going back, and when the cab stops in front of the hotel, she escapes yet again into the crowds and winding streets of the city. The novel ends with a passage describing the sights and sounds of the city.

CHARACTERS

Lieutenant d'Armagnac

Lieutenant d'Armagnac is the commander at the military post in Bou Noura who assists Port in finding his stolen passport and later works with Tunner to reunite the trio in Sba. The story of Yamina, which is a key part of d'Armagnac's history, underscores the potentially destructive powers of the Sahara in terms of both physical threats and cultural misunderstandings.

Belqassim

Belqassim is the younger of the two caravan drivers that Kit joins after leaving Sba and the one for whom she develops a deep emotional attachment despite his ongoing sexual abuse. Disguising her as a man in order to sneak Kit by his many wives, Belqassim spends part of every day with her until he sees her cry one day. His interest wanes, prompting Kit to make a daring escape.

Captain Broussard

Captain Broussard is the military authority in Sba and deals with Kit once Port is placed in the local hospital suffering from typhoid. Broussard is naturally and aggressively suspicious of Kit's presence in the Sahara with a sick husband and no passport for him but allows her some lenience, given Port's illness. He is angered when he discovers Port has died and Kit has disappeared into the night.

Eric Lyle

Eric Lyle is a sleazy young Englishman traveling with his mother, a travel writer. Although he is generous in offering the group transport in the family car, he tries to borrow money often, steals Port's passport, and is caught pilfering from Port's luggage following his death. He is the symbol of corrupted civility in the novel, a man with the pretence of culture but whose core values are degraded and destructive.

Mrs. Lyle

Mrs. Lyle is the mother of Eric and a travel writer touring North Africa. She talks incessantly and is generally an irritant to Port and Kit.

Marhnia

Marhnia is the dancer and prostitute that Port visits in the tent village on the outskirts of the town. She is described as "slim, wild-looking...

with great dark eyes." She is dressed in "spotless white, with a white turbanlike headdress that pulled her hair tightly backward, accentuating the indigo designs tattooed on her forehead."

Mohammad

Mohammad is Port's guide in Bou Noura. He is a source of much frustration when he cannot deliver the blind dancer to Port as requested.

Katherine (Kit) Moresby

Kit Moresby is described as "small, with blonde hair and an olive complexion" and "saved from prettiness by the intensity of her gaze." Superstitious, she is haunted throughout the first part of the novel by an acute consciousness of a pending sense of doom but lacks the strength of will to chart a path separate from that of her husband. Vulnerable to the charms and attentions of the more engaging Tunner, she gives in to her desires during an overnight train ride. Wracked with guilt over her infidelity, she follows Port into the Sahara and tends to him when he is overcome with typhoid fever.

The death of Port cracks Kit's already frail psyche, and she rushes into the Sahara rather than turning to the authorities for help. Picked up by two men in a caravan, she is raped repeatedly and taken into the home of the younger man as an addition to his collection of wives. Eventually escaping, she finds brief respite in a local convent before being taken back to the American consulate in Oran, where she is informed that Tunner is en route to take her back to New York. Panicking at the thought of being forced to reenter the civilized world, Kit waits for her moment and bolts from the cab transporting her to a local hotel. The novel ends with her disappearing into the maze of streets and noise that is Oran. As Tennessee Williams notes of the character of Kit, she "wanders on like a body in which the rational mechanism is gradually upset and destroyed."

Porter (Port) Moresby

Port Moresby is a member of the New York intelligentsia who becomes weary of a life lived in ideas only. He sets out to escape, preferably to remote places. He manipulates Kit and Tunner to choose North Africa over Europe and once there indulges his own desires for sex and adventure without any regard for the needs of his wife and his friend. Growing jealous and frustrated with Tunner, he arranges for him to travel in one

direction while Port and Kit set off in another. He is unaware, however, that he has contracted typhoid fever, which grows intensely and progressively worse until he finds himself facing death in a land he will never understand and that resists his every step forward.

Yamina ben Rhaissa

Yamina ben Rhaissa is part of Lieutenant d'Armagnac's history. A young woman arrested by d'Armagnac for a crime she might or might not have committed, she dies from a scorpion's sting while in prison.

Smail

Smail is an Arab man who meets Port during an evening walk in Oran and takes him to a restaurant for tea and conversation and then offers him a visit to a prostitute in a tent village outside the city limits.

George Tunner

George Tunner is the third member of the party of traveling Americans, invited into the adventure by Port. Tunner is "a few years younger" than Port, "of sturdier build, and astonishingly handsome." He often appears overly casual, almost aimless, with "features [that] were formed in such a manner that in repose they suggested a general bland contentment." More of a cipher (a character of zero psychological or moral depth) than a fully formed character, Tunner moves through the various challenges more effectively than either Kit or Port, in part because he rarely engages emotionally or spiritually. Accordingly, he avoids any of the pitfalls that affect his friends so dramatically and returns to New York relatively unscathed. Even his seduction of Kit aboard the train is lifted out of an American cultural context: sweet talk and champagne.

THEMES

Colonialism

Deborah Root gives this definition of the term *Orientalism* as brought to prominence by the cultural theorist Edward Said: "Within the colonialist construct that has come to be called Orientalism, the Orient," which is reconfigured in Bowles's novel as North Africa, "exists as the terrain where a particular kind of experience is available to the Western subject, an experience

TOPICS FOR FURTHER STUDY

- *The Sheltering Sky* has a long history of inspiring musicians to attempt interpretations of the whole or parts of the novel (the band the Police took on the story told to Port in Chapter 5, for instance, as the inspiration for the song "Tea in the Sahara"). Take up the challenge and develop (and present to your class) a musical interpretation of a specific chapter or scene in the novel. As part of this exercise, you will also produce a set of performance notes, in which you explain what appealed to you about the novel and what you are hoping to convey in the musical interlude.

- Bowles had a particular interest in T. S. Eliot's poem "The Waste Land" (1922), which is often considered one of the most important and influential poems of the twentieth century. Read Eliot's poem and write a considered and thoughtful essay in which you discuss the influences of Eliot's work as you find them in Bowles's novel.

- Bowles is very specific about the towns and cities that Port and Kit travel to throughout their journey. Create a poster or digital "map" in which you trace their travels, with each stop represented visually (pictures), textually (quotations from the novel), and in as many other ways as you think relevant. Be prepared to present your finished map to your class.

- Critic Jay McInerney and others suggest that *The Sheltering Sky* is about exploring "the chaos that underlies the civilized mind . . . concerned not so much with the meeting of cultures as with the peeling away of layers of acculturation, the stripping of character and humanity to essential elements." Read William Golding's novel about young adults, *Lord of the Flies* (1954), and write a well-structured, thoughtful essay in which you compare or contrast the two novels in relation to McInerney's statement.

at once mysterious, dangerous, and compelling." This definition works perfectly for understanding the motivation of Port, Kit, and Tunner as they set out as travelers in a strange and dangerous land only to confront directly many of the assumptions and preconceptions informing colonial thinking about other places and cultures. Leaving behind an American culture that is safe in its monotonous familiarity, the trio find themselves freed from cultural guidelines and rules and thrust into a place in which such guidelines have never applied and never will apply. More specifically, colonialism refers to the establishment and maintenance of powers that allow one territory (France, in the case of *The Sheltering Sky*) to impose political control over another territory.

In this sense, *The Sheltering Sky* aligns with such novels as Joseph Conrad's *Heart of Darkness* (1899) and William Golding's *Lord of the*

Flies (1954), which set out to illuminate a number of potentially fatal flaws in any colonial project. Specifically, these novels emphasize that a military presence (as symbolic of imposed order) has little impact on the real culture of a place. As the story of Yamina indicates, the complexities of culture are very often lost on colonial authorities, rendering them to varying degrees misguided or wholly ineffective (prostitution, theft, and bribery are rampant despite the colonial presence in North Africa).

Second, and more troubling, is the common sense among these writers that civilization (one of the keywords validating any colonial initiative) is merely a facade and that even the most intelligent and cultured of people, given the right circumstances, will return to behavior that would be considered anything but civilized in their home countries. Conrad's Kurtz loses his sanity as he devolves into an unrestrained extermination machine. Golding's schoolboys return to a tribal mentality that ends with the murder of one of their schoolmates. Port dies a spiritually vacant man, while Kit finds her deepest emotional connection with a man who rapes her repeatedly.

Nihilism

Generally, nihilism is the belief that all values and moral codes guiding individual behavior are baseless. True nihilism would be nearly impossible to achieve, so the term is often associated with extreme pessimism and even a radical skepticism. Bowles's *The Sheltering Sky* aligns loosely with the nihilism associated with German philosopher and cultural critic Friedrich Nietzsche, who argued that modern society is on a downward spiral that would end with such a corrosive effect that all moral, religious, and spiritual foundations on which civilization was founded would be worn away to nothing. Such an absence, or void, would leave humankind in the greatest crisis in history. In this sense, the crisis faced by Port and Kit can be read as an expression of a nihilist perspective.

By the middle of the twentieth century, when Bowles was writing, nihilism had become a common set of ideas for existentialists writers and thinkers. Softening the destructive edges of classic nihilism somewhat, the existentialists focused more on the emotional turmoil arising from an individual's coming face to face with his own understanding of nothingness, or that life is meaningless and that emotions and ideas are empty of any communal or relational value. This thread of nihilism gave way to a kind of hyperintellectualized indifference to the world.

In this sense, Port is a stereotypical existential nihilist, seeing his emotional detachment as a kind of protective shield and using his sense of intellectual superiority as a rationalization for decisions that lead, inevitably, to his own slippage into the absolute night (his greatest fear) and his wife's decline into total madness. Nihilism provides little defense, in the end, against the very real powers of the Sahara or against the physical, emotional, and spiritual dangers that threaten individuals in such environments

It is interesting that the only member of the trio to survive the journey relatively unscathed is Tunner, the one character whose casualness and avoidance of moral imperatives and expectations

The story is set in the north African desert.
(© Denis Burdin / Shutterstock.com)

seem to let him almost skip across the surface of the Sahara without ever feeling the fullness of its powers on his own soul or psyche.

STYLE

Setting

Setting is broadly defined as the overall placement of a work in terms of geographic place (North Africa and more specifically the Sahara), historical time (postwar, late 1940s), and social circumstances (a colonial territory with various languages and cultures). In *The Sheltering Sky*, setting plays a far more prominent and powerful role than just an intricately described backdrop. North African cultures and the Sahara itself are almost like characters, interacting with Kit and Port, in particular, in more significant ways than their friend, Tunner, or the caricatures of Eric and Mrs. Lyle. Arguably, it is the setting of this novel (in all its vivid complexities) that is the most compelling element of the book, posing challenges and threats at every turn through its multitude of languages, physical heat, swarms of insects, plethora of diseases, and wholly unyielding resistance to control. It also presents vistas so beautiful as to be beyond belief to the North American imagination.

COMPARE & CONTRAST

- **1949:** When Bowles first visited North Africa, and specifically Tangier, in the 1930s, it was a country destined for political turmoil, having been recognized as an international zone in 1923 under the joint administration of France, Spain, and Britain and remaining so until June 1940, when Spanish troops occupied the country in what was described as a temporary wartime measure. Diplomatic negotiations between Britain and Spain led to a strengthened guarantee of British rights regarding Tangier as an international zone. The territory reverted to its prewar status in October 1945 before joining with Morocco following the restoration of sovereignty in 1956.

  Today: Tangier is Morocco's second most important city, behind only Casablanca. Still heavily reliant on tourism, it has replaced its reputation as a mecca for speculators, gamblers, and literary and artistic expatriates with one more aligned with cruise ships and well-heeled visitors from Spain and other parts of Europe.

- **1949:** Americans visiting North Africa usually travel by ship, which is the most cost-effective way.

  Today: Following World War II, commercial air travel expands rapidly, reducing both the time and the cost of such a trip dramatically. In 2015, a flight from New York to North Africa costs well under $1000.

- **1949:** Typhoid fever is still common in many parts of the world, especially in underdeveloped regions.

  Today: Typhoid fever has been in rapid decline since the mid-twentieth century due to the development of vaccinations and improvements in public sanitation, with current rates sitting at around five cases per million people per year. However, the disease remains a very real threat in underdeveloped countries. An outbreak in the Democratic Republic of Congo in 2004–2005, for instance, claims 214 lives and sees 42,000 reported cases.

Third-Person Omniscient Narration

The Sheltering Sky is told in a common form of third-person narration in which the teller of the tale (not to be mistaken for the author of the story) assumes an omniscient (all-knowing) perspective. This position allows the narrator to dive into private thoughts (of Kit, for instance, as she tends to Port on his deathbed), to narrate otherwise secret events (Port's visit to Marhnia), or to jump effortlessly through space and time to reorder the recounting of events (as in chapters nine and ten). The third-person omniscient narrator brings depth to Bowles's novel, allowing readers to "see" the psychological fraying and eventual breaks as both Port and Kit slide away from civility and sanity.

HISTORICAL CONTEXT

The Effects of World War II

The 1940s was a decade that saw most of Europe, Asia, and Africa impacted profoundly by World War II. Of particular relevance to this novel was the North African Campaign, which took place from June 1940 through May 1943 and included campaigns fought across Libya, the Egyptian deserts (known as the Western Desert Campaign), and Morocco and Algeria (known as Operation Torch). Countries from both sides had colonial interests in the region since the nineteenth century, further intensifying the conflict.

Operation Torch was a brief but important engagement that began officially on November 8,

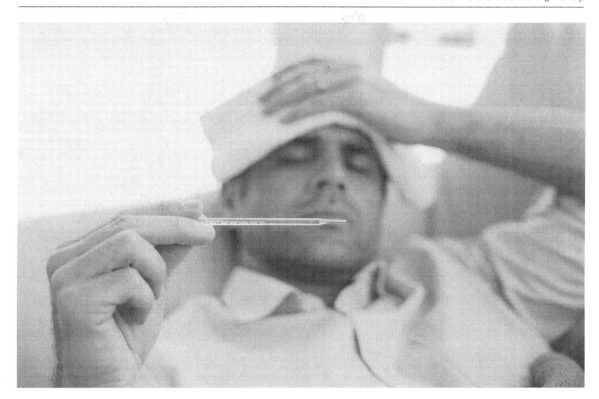

Although Port gets medicine for his fever, he dies while Kit leaves his bedside to meet Tunner.
(© wavebreakmedia | Shutterstock.com)

1942, and culminated on November 11. In an attempt to create a pincer formation around German and Italian forces, American and British troops landed in French North Africa. They expected little or no resistance but faced fierce battles in Oran and Morocco. In Algiers, by contrast, a coup d'état (resistance fighters' overthrow of the reigning government) provided unimpeded landings and capture of the entire local command. After three days of talks (and threats), an order came from France to cease armed resistance at both cities.

The postwar culture that Port, Kit, and Tunner react against as members of New York's intelligentsia was one of rapid economic expansion, rising consumerism, and unprecedented challenges to the American dream. The latter feeling was captured most compellingly in such works as Arthur Miller's play *Death of a Salesman* (opening in February 1949), George Orwell's dystopian novel *1984*, and Shirley Jackson's *The Lottery and Other Stories*.

At the same time, the chilling effect of McCarthyism, empowered by the investigations launched under the auspices of the House Committee on Un-American Activities, continued to constrain many of the generation's most creative directors and writers. Arts and culture seemed doomed to variations of the banal and compliant as blacklists gathered among such creative forces (and Bowles's friends) as composers Leonard Bernstein and Aaron Copland and writer Allen Ginsberg. Other significant names affected by the oppressive politics of the day included Charlie Chaplin, Albert Einstein, Langston Hughes, Arthur Miller, and iconic folksinger Pete Seeger.

Internationally, the decade ended with signs that the future might be defined by technological advances in warfare that appeared ominous even in 1949. In August, the Soviet Union tested "Joe 1," its first atomic bomb, based on the design of the bomb dropped on Nagasaki, Japan, in 1945. Closer to home, World War II veteran Howard Unruh tragically raised awareness of the potential social and human costs of the residual effects of war when he killed thirteen people (including three children) during a twelve-minute walk through his Camden, New Jersey, neighborhood. At age twenty-eight, he became America's first official single-episode spree killer.

CRITICAL OVERVIEW

The famed playwright Tennessee Williams, reviewing the *The Sheltering Sky* for the *New York Times*, describes his engagement with the novel as "thrilling" given that

> it brings the reader into sudden, startling communion with a talent of true maturity and sophistication of the sort that [he] had begun to fear was to be found nowadays only among the insurgent novelists of France.

Williams goes on to suggest that Bowles "appears to bear the spiritual imprint of recent history in the western world" due to what Williams calls the "philosophical aura" of the novel. He concludes that

> a good many people will read this book and be enthralled by it without once suspecting that it contains a mirror of what is most terrifying and cryptic within the Sahara of moral nihilism, into which the race of man now seems to be wandering blindly.

Reflecting on his lifelong relationship with the novel, critic Joe Stretch describes Kit and Port's journey as "delirium, a fever [that] grips the novel and its characters." Despite the darkness overwhelming the novel, Stretch praises its impact on readers' lives: "In showing us the horror of life," he suggests, "Bowles also guides us back. Not with cheap consolation or a happy ending. Truth, in all its frightening, ungraspable beauty, is shelter." Mark Webster, in *Tech*, continues this theme, noting that

> Bowles uses the symbolic overtones of the story to good effect, developing a parable of Western civilization meeting wilderness and an alien culture....Each brushstroke seems not so much to be adding layers but stripping away the façade to reveal the decadence and corruption underneath.

As Mel Gussow summarizes in his 1999 obituary in the *New York Times*, Bowles remained throughout his life "an artist whose name evoked an atmosphere of dark, lonely Moroccan streets and endless scorching deserts, a haze of hashish and drug-induced visions."

The Sheltering Sky was adapted into film by Bernardo Bertolucci in 1990, with Debra Winger and John Malkovich cast as Kit and Port

Moresby. In reviewing the film adaptation, Roger Ebert laments the fact that he has read the book, which

> is so complete, so deep and so self-contained that it shuts the movie out. Bertolucci shows us the outsides and surfaces, and a person seeing this movie without having read the book might ask what it is about.

What it is about, Ebert goes on to write, is "a tone of mental voice, about the way this new reality is filtered through the sensibilities of the characters," who experience

> a new, cold, unforgiving reality—a land where people do die, where independent American wives do suddenly become sexual chattel, where an ancient land and its ancient society are majestically indifferent to the veneer of truths that these Americans naively believe are self-evident.

Peter Travers of *Rolling Stone* concurs, noting that the "thirst for meaning in all [the] angst" of the film "can only be quenched by Bowles book; Bertolucci's two-hour-plus opus leaves the mind and heart parched."

As Webster notes, the novel "served as inspiration for the Beat generation of poets and writers" for whom "its existential themes and exotic locales would influence many of the figures of that time as well as the later '60s generation."

CRITICISM

Klay Dyer

Dyer is a freelance writer and editor who specializes in subjects related to literature, popular culture, and innovation. In the following essay, he explores one of the central tensions of The Sheltering Sky: *the conflict that occurs when an idealized imagining of a place and culture collides with the realities of that place.*

The relationship between individuals, the natural world, and other cultures is often captured in a variety of complex and often contradictory terms, including but by no means limited to tourist, traveler, adventurer, explorer, and expatriate. Imbued in advertisements and popular culture with an air of excitement and the allure of discovery, these activities are often portrayed as predominantly positive, life-transforming experiences that elevate levels of social consciousness and awareness. In

WHAT DO I READ NEXT?

- Bowles's autobiography, *Without Stopping: An Autobiography* (1972), is a compelling look inside the life of a man once called a romantic savage.

- *Heart of Darkness* (1899) by Polish writer Joseph Conrad is a haunting novella (adapted by Francis Ford Coppola into *Apocalypse Now* in 1979) that covers many of the same themes as Bowles's *The Sheltering Sky*: the facade of civility and the human tendency to devolve into violence, the breakdown of social mores in strange and distant lands, and the power of a foreign landscape (in Conrad's case, a jungle) to impact individuals in powerful and often tragic ways.

- English novelist E. M. Forster's *A Passage to India* (1924) explores the misinterpretations and misguided judgments that shape colonial-era engagements, in this case between British settlers in India.

- Robert Kirkman's comic-book series *The Walking Dead* (2003 onward) explores many of the themes established in Bowles's novel against the backdrop of a zombie apocalypse. Rick Grimes's struggle to adapt and protect his family in a dangerous new world is not too far removed from Port's attempts to bring himself and Kit safely through the Sahara in postwar North Africa.

- Suzanne Collins's *The Hunger Games* trilogy (2008–2010) for young adults explores the social systems and cultural traditions that might emerge if the basic structures and values of civilization move too dramatically. Just as Kit and Port find themselves in a society with unfamiliar rules, Katniss Everdeen finds herself forced to either kill other children or be killed, all in the name of a national spectacle.

- Daniel Young's 2012 documentary *Paul Bowles: The Cage Door Is Always Open* is a wholly engaging story about Paul and Jane Bowles, from their unique marriage in New York through their journey (creative and spiritual) to Tangier.

- Afghan American writer Khaled Hosseini's debut novel *The Kite Runner* (2003) recounts a young man's struggle toward identity and autonomy against the backdrop of the collapse of Afghanistan's monarchy, the exodus of refugees to the United States, and the rise of an oppressive Taliban regime.

---

this sense, the diversity of the world has been reimagined in terms of relatively simple paired oppositions: here-there, familiar-new, ordinary-exotic, and so on. The otherness of place and culture is something that is simply "out there" to be experienced, drawn from, and managed via a guide book or tour company. Bowles's *The Sheltering Sky* offers a corrective to such representations, exploring the potentially dangerous consequences of approaching a place or culture that has only been imagined from a safe distance.

Of the three Americans that Bowles spills into the Sahara, only Port has been to North Africa before. However, even he is unable to comprehend the desert (and by extension the geographies through which he travels) beyond the imagined and symbolic meaning that preoccupies his imagination. Whenever he even sees a map, he begins "studying it passionately, and then, often as not, he would begin to plan some new, impossible trip which sometimes eventually became a reality." Port is obsessed with the idea of movement, specifically with movement that will take him as far away as possible from what he sees as the consumer-based, postwar American way of life that he has come to despise.

> DESPITE PORT'S CONVICTION THAT A TRAVELER IS AN INDIVIDUAL OF MULTIPLE ATTACHMENTS, FEELING AT HOME EVERYWHERE, READERS BEGIN TO REALIZE THAT HE IS A MAN WHO HAS YET TO FEEL AT HOME ANYWHERE AND THEREFORE FEELS PERPETUALLY OUT OF PLACE AND DISLOCATED."

Significantly, Port defines himself as a traveler, not a tourist. To Port, the distinction is particularly important:

> The difference is partly one of time, he would explain. Whereas the tourist generally hurries back home at the end of a few weeks or months, the traveler, belonging no more to one place than to the next, moves slowly, over periods of years, from one part of earth to another.

Port's definitions are important, for his own sense of "traveler" cuts him off from the emotions often associated with journeys and exploration, notably excitement mingled variously with uncertainty and even hesitation in the face of the unknown. Despite Port's conviction that a traveler is an individual of multiple attachments, feeling at home everywhere, readers begin to realize that he is a man who has yet to feel at home anywhere and therefore feels perpetually out of place and dislocated. Port is drawn to North Africa because he has romanticized the idea of securing distance from postwar America, so the remoteness and isolation of the region and its inhabitants are particularly appealing to him.

Despite the distance traveled, however, Port approaches the challenging and vast landscape with a North American lens firmly in place. He compares himself to his great grandparents and their successful (and nation-forming) engagement with the American wilderness many generations earlier and sees his journey with Kit as part of a similar narrative of resistance and trailblazing. Like his ancestors, he perceives the vast, empty, and silent space of the Sahara as a tabula rasa (blank slate) onto which he can inscribe a narrative that runs as a counterpoint to the one that he left in New York City.

Ironically, he also sees the Sahara as a vastness that takes the form of "a solid thing up there" that can shelter him, somehow, from what he calls the "absolute night" that threatens him at all turns. Initially, his journey provides him with two things that comfort him deeply: light and silence. Port is too dislocated from his place in the world and his emotions to understand that the absolute night is not an external, environmental threat but an internal, psychological one that is distorting his view of the Sahara as well as of himself, both physically and emotionally.

Kit does not feel her husband's urge to be in perpetual movement and definitely does not share his fascination with the Sahara. For most of the novel, in fact, she lives in fear of an environment that she was led to believe by Port's judicious selection of photographs was rich with attractive vistas, exotic gardens, and postcard-like markets: "While he was making his campaign speeches for Africa as against Europe," he had

> shown her...a carefully chosen collection of photographs he had brought from previous trips: views of oases and markets, as well as attractive vistas of the lobbies and gardens of hotels which no longer operated.

The North Africa that Kit expected, in other words, was one that was constructed by her husband prior to their departure from America. It is not surprising, then, that Kit does not share Port's enthusiasm for the locale or the journey he has planned for them.

Whereas her husband turns outward to attempt to cure his malaise, increasingly to escalating levels of risk taking (culminating in his contracting the fatal typhoid fever), Kit turns away from the landscape and into the bed of Tunner, the most typical of American characters in the novel. Sadly, even adultery (arguably a civilized kind of risk taking) gives Kit no reassurance or sense of emotional comfort. She does find some distraction, at least, in her familiar consumer goods brought with her in her luggage. Surrounding herself with her things from home, Kit feels sheltered and protected from the otherness that surrounds and frightens her. Ultimately, the futility of her efforts is one of the major tragedies of the novel, given that the deeper into the Sahara she travels with Port, the more difficult she finds it to connect emotionally with her things from home.

Kit's reaction to the vastness of the Sahara is far stronger than that of her husband, who dies

After Port's death, Kit is taken in by a camel driver and later becomes his fourth wife. *(© posztos / Shutterstock.com)*

as disconnected and disengaged as he lived. Whereas Port fears a manifestation of his own detachment (the absolute night), Kit fears something much more familiar to readers of exploration or even Gothic writings: she fears the void, the emptiness, and the unknownness of what surrounds her. She feels trapped in the openness, regardless of the fact that there are no physical barriers impinging on her freedom of movement. She is imprisoned by heat, thirst, and the always-present danger that she sees everywhere.

One of the most troubling questions of the novel, especially considering Kit's fate, is why she stays with Port, given her growing anxiety. The answer, again, is disconnection. Kit, like Port, is disconnected from her own feelings to such an extent that they do not prove an effective catalyst to action. Evolutionary theorists talk about the fight-or-flee response as being part of our genetic coding as human beings, which suggests Kit should either fight (pointlessly) against the overwhelming presence of the Sahara or flee it for safer havens elsewhere (the more constructive reaction, in this case). Yet she does neither,

opting instead to ignore her emotions and remain passive in the face of her anxiety. Port does very little by way of responding to his wife's feelings, tending instead to suggest that they are connected through their responses, fearing the same thing despite the fact that his reactions are really projections of his own emotional detachment.

Although Port mocks the image of the tourist, his reaction to the different world that is North Africa and to his wife's obvious (and growing) anxiety turns him into almost a caricature of that which he despises. He comes to the Sahara full of preconceptions and considers himself somehow distanced from the physical and cultural realities into which he has immersed himself and Kit.

It is when his passport is stolen that Port begins to lose grip of his identity. Without the one piece from home that allows him to mark himself as distinct from (that is, not part of) the culture around him, he is no longer able to declare himself as not of that place. Kit's fear of being trapped becomes Port's reality, and suddenly North Africa and the Sahara shift in his mind from any other place a true traveler ventures to into a real threat. Typhoid finishes what this collapsing vision of self begins, and Port dies, a victim of the place that he once thought of as his sheltering escape from the mundane and the routine.

Without Port, Kit realizes that her fear of the void has been realized and she is now alone, trying to survive as a stranger in a strange land. She tosses aside her once precious artifacts from home and wanders into the desert, where she becomes dependent on and is abused by a series of indigenous groups. When she does make her way back to the American consulate in Oran, she presents an American passport but not a semblance of an identity or sanity that would be recognized by any Westerner. She wanders back into the streets, disappearing forever into the void she once feared so deeply.

Bowles selects a powerful quotation by Franz Kafka to open book three of *The Sheltering Sky*: "From a certain point onward there is no longer any turning back. That is the point that must be reached." Both Port and Kit reach this point of no turning back, one through death and the other through madness. Bowles, in other words, presents readers with two extremes: Port, who lives his entire life alienated from the world and himself, and Kit, who is essentially absorbed in the natural world around her and stops being American, lucid, and self-determining in one dramatic step.

Source: Klay Dyer, Critical Essay on *The Sheltering Sky*, in *Novels for Students*, Gale, Cengage Learning, 2016.

Joanna Grant

In the following excerpt, Grant examines the effect of the Middle East and the desert on Western travelers in The Sheltering Sky.

...Bowles's vision of the desert is one of terrifying blankness. His ear is attuned to a more ghastly, hysterical frequency of laughter, one marking the complete annihilation of the Western subject, not just its salutary gerrymandering. Between the two of them, Durrell and Bowles map the terrain of contemporary Anglo-American orientalism, an imaginative construct consisting more than ever of bizarre extremes of glamour, kitsch, and horror.

In a way, Bowles's celebrity as an eccentric genius presiding over a diverse array of friends and lovers in the interzone of Tangier was the

> IN THEIR OWN WAYS, THE BRITISH LYLES AND THE FRENCH OFFICERS HAVE MANAGED TO FIND FICTIONS THAT GUARD THEM FROM WHAT LIES BEYOND THE SHELTERING SKY OF THE NOVEL'S TITLE—THE AWFUL, INDIFFERENT ROAR OF A MEANINGLESS UNIVERSE."

creation of Gertrude Stein, who first ordered him to visit the port city in 1931. Bowles's debt to the primitivism and magical thinking characteristic of modernist conceptions of the exotic Other may be seen in his autobiography, *Without Stopping,* in his description of his first sight of Morocco:

> Straightaway I felt a great excitement; much excited; it was as if some interior mechanism had been set in motion by the sight of the approaching land.... I had based my sense of being in the world partly on an unreasoned conviction that certain areas of the earth's surface contained more magic than others. Had anyone asked me what I meant by magic, I should probably have defined the word by calling it a secret connection between the world of nature and the consciousness of man... which bypassed the mind.... Like any Romantic, I had always been vaguely certain that sometime during my life I should come into a magic place which in disclosing its secrets would give me wisdom and ecstasy—perhaps even death.

Bowles's magic would work to strip away the accumulated encrustations of the Western ego, rationality, convention, and chauvinism that often went under the name of "consciousness" in primitivist discourses and are here lumped together under the term of "mind." His course of treatment for the novel, and for the Western subject, would prove to be more radical than Durrell's, for example. Bowles was convinced that the epoch in which he lived was one of decline and fall. Writing in 1953 to Harvey Breit of the *New York Times,* he said that "he had no great objection to being called decadent, if the word is used in such a way that it is clear the user considers my work to be a reflection of the period in which it was written, a period which by every possible cultural standard is assuredly a decadent one" (qtd. in Carr 224). Bowles here creates his own definition of decadence. True decadence, in his opinion, lies in "incompetence and commercialism," two of the classic bugbears of modernism (qtd. in Carr 224). Literary representations of the kinds of maimings and other deviant acts often finding their ways into Bowles's dryly sinister tales, on the other hand, could serve as a kind of literary shock treatment. "I believe unhappiness should be studied very carefully," Bowles wrote; "[y]ou must watch your universe as it cracks above your head" (qtd. in Carr 225). Like the Decadents of the previous century, Bowles sought to embrace and chronicle the long, often lovely suicide of Western culture.

Indeed, Bowles took a great deal of gleeful pleasure in the thought of what his magic city of Tangier could do to Western complacency. Forget past comfortable relations between Western subject and Near Eastern object, relations in which the Anglo-American looked lovingly at representations of the noble Arab or Moor, seeing themselves reflected at twice their natural size. In Bowles's world, the vast energies contained in the battery of the desert city corrode and dissolve the Western ego instead of polishing it:

> In defense of [Tangier] I can say that so far it has been touched by fewer of the negative aspects of contemporary civilization than most cities of its size. More important than that, I relish the idea that in the night, all around me in my sleep, sorcery is burrowing its invisible tunnels in every direction, from thousands of senders to thousands of unsuspecting recipients. Spells are being cast, poison is running its course, souls are being dispossessed of parasitic pseudo-consciousnesses that lurk in the unguarded recesses of the mind.

(WS)

Bowles's most famous work, the novel *The Sheltering Sky,* represents just such a magical spell. The work tells the story of Port and Kit Moresby, a modern, cultured, sophisticated, wealthy American couple seeking to escape Western civilization and themselves—a parallel quest—by means of a journey into the Sahara. The sophisticates get more than they bargained for, as the impersonal forces contained in the arid zone combine to penetrate the porous surfaces of their minds and bodies, dissolving all boundaries between the subjectivities of the Westerners and the abject beings and substances flooding their sensoriums with disease, disgust, horror, and desire.

Ironically enough, the callow pseudo-sophisticates of *The Sheltering Sky* believe they are escaping the decadence of a burnt-out Western civilization when they land in North Africa. In the Sahara, Port, Kit, and Tunner hope to find and commune with the primitive. Port begins the novel as the dominant personality of the three, and his wife parrots her husband's strictures concerning the unfortunate leveling effect of the late war:

> [Kit says] "The people of each country get more like the people of every other country. They have no character, no beauty, no ideals, no culture—nothing, nothing."

> Her husband reached over and patted her hand. "You're right. You're right," he said smiling. "Everything's getting gray, and it'll be grayer. But some places'll withstand the malady longer than you think. You'll see, in the Sahara here . . ."

For all of Port's confidence in his own knowledge concerning North Africa—"He did not think of himself as a tourist; he was a traveler"—the marks of war have been left on Morocco, Algeria, and the Sudan, the countries through which they journey. The corpses of military vehicles are simply the latest burned-out, used-up souvenirs of a colonialism that has left squalid, unsettling, and occasionally sinister traces on the cities and on the bodies of the populace. The forces of colonial exploitation and mute rebellion on the parts of the colonized have settled into a quiet yet lethal battle of wills.

The greatest weapon the natives and their landscape share in this conflict seems to be the ability to shatter the primitivist, nostalgic illusions of the Western traveler. Port, Kit, and Tunner are immediately confronted with a less than appetizing prospect:

> [The Arabs'] European clothes were worn and gray; it would have been hard to tell what the cut of any garment had been originally. The nearly naked shoeshine boys squatted on their boxes looking down at the pavement, without the energy to wave away the flies that crawled over their faces. Inside the café the air was cooler but without movement, and it smelled of stale wine and urine.

So much for the glamorous East. Tatty Western clothing worn incongruously by natives and the swarming of flies—these two symbols emerge as metonymies of the Middle East as abject zone. Brown bodies wearing "white" clothes that have seen better days or have been assembled "incorrectly" trigger a sense of the uncanny in the white observer. Flies carry filth and trigger our feelings of disgust and a desire for avoidance. Beginning the novel with this description of encroaching dirt and excrement foreshadows the steady incursion of abjection that will eventually claim the bodies and minds of our travelers.

A good deal of the very dark humor of this text derives from the inexorable closing of the supposed gap between the cultural attainments of Western civilization and the so-called savagery of the natives. Of course, Port, Kit, and Tunner *think* they want to close this gap, but the way they finally do so forms no part of their original itinerary. Before they meet their respective fates, the young Americans encounter the representatives of two older colonial powers, Britain and France. The waning British Empire has its representatives in the persons of the Lyles, a mother and son who write and illustrate travel narratives for a living. The "ludicrous," "horrible," "caricature[d]" descendants of a long line of more distinguished explorers, these two grotesques still believe themselves to be the superiors of the French and the natives. The mother spouts degenerationist clichés: "The stupidity of the French! It's unbelievable! They're all mental defectives. Madame Gautier herself told me they have the lowest national intelligence quotient in the world. Of course, their blood is thin; they've gone to seed. They're all part Jewish or Negro. Look at them!"

Fears of miscegenation are often figured as a kind of reverse colonization in degenerationist discourse, as a form of contamination. Such fears read acts of intercourse between natives and colonists or travelers as avenues of transmission of both literal and figurative degeneration. Such is the case with Mrs. Lyle, who treats the Arabs with disgust and rancor, claiming "'They're all contaminated,'" and that "'Some filthy swine of an Arab woman'" has given her son "'An infection, an infection'.". Mrs. Lyle's shrill rants against the degeneracy of the French and the Arabs rebound upon her when it is revealed that she and her son Eric are engaged in an incestuous relationship. Ironically enough, a native catches them in the act, revealing the abject pleasure they take in the violation of the incest taboo.

In contrast to the perverse, incestuous, deceptive Lyles, the provincial French administrators who represent their mother country manage to negotiate a harsh country by psychically disconnecting from as much of it as possible. Lieutenant d'Armagnac, who becomes very put out at having to deal with the drama of Port's missing passport, begins his posting in the Sahara full of primitivist fantasy; his "true enthusiasm for the natives had lasted three years." After that, the "period of his great devotion to the Arabs," he abandons "his half-dozen or so Ouled Naïl mistresses," gets himself a proper French wife, and contents himself building a pleasant house and garden for his bride. His countryman, who assists Kit after Port falls ill, attempts to head off Kit's hysteria by sharing his philosophy of contracted horizons and phlegmatic realism: "What we have in our hands is always enough.... You must be realistic, madame. If you stray outside that, you do harm to everyone." This pragmatism echoes that of the bourgeois parvenus caricatured by Wyndham Lewis in *Filibusters in Barbary* in the person of the obese groceress (see Chapter 3). In their own ways, the British Lyles and the French officers have managed to find fictions that guard them from what lies beyond the sheltering sky of the novel's title—the awful, indifferent roar of a meaningless universe. Tellingly, fantasies of becoming one with the Noble Savage have been passed over by both the racist Lyles and the determinedly pragmatic Frenchmen. Only the Americans prove themselves romantic—or foolish—enough to blunder into an alien environment that is literally inhospitable to them....

Source: Joanna Grant, "What Lies Beyond the Sheltering Sky?," in *Modernism's Middle East: Journeys to Barbary*, Palgrave Macmillan, 2008, pp. 161–66.

SOURCES

Bowles, Paul, *The Sheltering Sky*, Ecco, 2014.

Ebert, Roger, Review of *The Sheltering Sky*, RogerEbert.com, January 11, 1991, http://www.rogerebert.com/reviews/the-sheltering-sky-1991 (accessed December 7, 2014).

Gussow, Mel, "Writer Paul Bowles Dies at 88," in *New York Times*, November 19, 1999, http://www.nytimes.com/library/books/111999obit-p-bowles.html (accessed December 7, 2014).

McInerney, Jay, "Paul Bowles in Exile," in *Vanity Fair*, September 1985, http://www.maryellenmark.com/text/magazines/vanity%20fair/925E-000-005.html (accessed December 7, 2014).

Root, Deborah, "Misadventures in the Desert: *The Sheltering Sky* as Colonialist Nightmare," in *Orientalism and Cultural Differences*, Vol. 6, 1992, http://culturalstudies.ucsc.edu/PUBS/Inscriptions/vol_6/Root.html (accessed December 7, 2014).

Stretch, Joe, "Book of a Lifetime: *The Sheltering Sky*, by Paul Bowles," in *Independent*, August 18, 2012, http://www.independent.co.uk/arts-entertainment/books/reviews/book-of-a-lifetime-the-sheltering-sky-by-paul-bowles-8053566.html (accessed December 7, 2014).

Travers, Peter, Review of *The Sheltering Sky*, in *Rolling Stone*, December 12, 1990, http://www.rollingstone.com/movies/reviews/the-sheltering-sky-19901212 (accessed December 7, 2014).

Webster, Mark, "*The Sheltering Sky* Remains Topical Lesson in Culture Clash," in *Tech*, Vol. 110, No. 27, May 15, 1990, http://tech.mit.edu/V110/N27/sky.27a.html (accessed December 7, 2014).

Williams, Tennessee, "An Allegory of Man and His Sahara," in *New York Times*, December 4, 1949, http://www.nytimes.com/books/98/05/17/specials/bowles-sheltering.html (accessed December 7, 2014).

FURTHER READING

Bowles, Paul, *Travels: Collected Writings, 1950–1993*, HarperCollins, 2011.
More than forty essays and articles set in locales that range from Paris to Ceylon and all parts of North Africa make this collection a tale of Bowles's life and history set against a backdrop of travel and reflection. Rich with photographs, this edition comes with an introduction by one of the twentieth century's preeminent travel writers, Paul Theroux.

Caponi-Tabery, Gena Dagel, *Paul Bowles: Romantic Savage*, Southern Illinois University Press, 1994.
An engaging interpretive biography, this book posits Bowles's aesthetic and political motivations for both his literary and musical compositions. It reveals both his relationship with the key influences of his generation as well as his penchant for idiosyncrasy and challenge.

Carr, Virginia Spencer, *Paul Bowles: A Life*, Northwestern University Press, 2009.
A noted biographer of such literary figures as Carson McCullers and John Dos Passos, Carr has written a book that is as much cultural history as biography. Entertaining and detailed, it neatly captures the intellect, politics, and complexities of a man who would become an icon of his generation.

Green, Michelle, *The Dream at the End of the World: Paul Bowles and the Literary Renegades in Tangier*, HarperCollins, 1991.
In this eminently entertaining book, Green looks at a generation of artists, musicians, and writers from the 1950s and 1960s who were drawn to Tangier for its promise of abundant sex and drugs, exotic attractions, and general bohemian seediness.

SUGGESTED SEARCH TERMS

Paul Bowles

The Sheltering Sky AND Bowles

postwar culture

Sahara AND literature

nihilism AND literature

exile AND literature

North Africa AND literature

colonialism AND literature

Someone Like You

SARAH DESSEN

1998

In *Someone Like You* (1998), Sarah Dessen's second novel, the first-person narrator, Halley, and her best friend, Scarlett, learn to be strong as they go through an unusual junior year of high school. Scarlett has to decide what to do about an unwanted pregnancy, and Halley has to overcome pressure from her boyfriend to have sex. Though the adults try to be caring, the friends find that they are each other's best support through the crises. Dessen creates strong female characters, like Scarlett, who is named for the protagonist of *Gone with the Wind* (1936), by Margaret Mitchell. She is noted for her positive treatment of teen life without being didactic or sentimental. Her stories make clear that adolescence is a time of both trial and triumph, tests and setbacks that propel the characters to grow up. Though middle class, the characters face the same challenges as most teens, including drugs, parental conflict, abuse, disability, neglect, death, low self-esteem, and sex.

AUTHOR BIOGRAPHY

Dessen was born on June 6, 1970, in Evanston, Illinois, to parents who both became professors at the University of North Carolina at Chapel Hill, Alan C. Dessen, an English professor, and, Cynthia Dessen, a classicist. She has one brother. Dessen attended Greensboro College in North Carolina but eventually enrolled at the University of North Carolina at Chapel Hill and graduated in 1993 with highest honors in creative writing. She supported herself as a restaurant server during college and after graduation as she focused on writing. Her first book, *That Summer*, a young-adult novel, was published in 1996 and received good reviews. She continued writing young-adult fiction about teen issues of growing up in contemporary America. Dressen takes many stories from the high-school experience she had in privileged middle-class Chapel Hill. She puts Chapel Hill scenes and fictionalized versions of her high-school friends in the books. Her main characters are girls becoming women. *Someone Like You* was her second novel, published in 1998.

Dressen has been a lecturer at the University of North Carolina at Chapel Hill, where she lives. She is married and has one daughter. Her other books include *Keeping the Moon* (1999), *Dreamland* (2000), *This Lullaby* (2002), *The Truth about Forever* (2004), *Just Listen* (2006), *Lock and Key* (2008), *Along for the Ride* (2009), *What Happened to Goodbye* (2011), *The Moon and More* (2013), and *Saint Anything* (2015).

With a dozen novels to her credit, Dressen is popular with both teens and teachers who assign her books in classes. She has won national recognition and numerous awards for each of her books. *Someone Like You* was an American Library Association Best Books for Young Adults selection and a Quick Picks selection. It was a Best Book of the Year Selection by *School Library Journal* and won the South Carolina Young Adult Book Award, 2000–2001. Dressen's other novels have also been cited and given awards by the American Library Association and *School Library Journal* and have been named New York Library Book for the Teen Age Selection and International Reading Association Young Adult Choice. Dessen was a *Los Angeles Times* Book Prize finalist for *This Lullaby* (2003).

PLOT SUMMARY

Part One: The Grand Canyon

CHAPTER ONE

The first-person narrator, fifteen-year-old Halley Cooke, is telling the story of her best friend, Scarlett Thomas, and their unusual junior year of high school. Halley is at Sisterhood

MEDIA ADAPTATIONS

- *How to Deal* (2003) is a film based on Dessen's first two novels, *That Summer* (1996) and *Someone Like You* (1998). It was directed by Clare Kilner and starred Mandy Moore, Allison Janney, and Trent Ford. It was distributed by New Line Cinema and Focus Features.

Camp—a camp for young women her mother has enrolled her in against her will—during the summer before junior year and receives an emergency phone call from Scarlett, who is at home. Scarlett is in shock telling of the death of her sixteen-year-old boyfriend, Michael Sherwood, in a motorcycle accident. Halley is also shaken, because they grew up with Michael in their suburban neighborhood of Lakeview. Halley remembers when Scarlett and her mother, Marion, moved there when she was eleven. Scarlett had red hair and was generous, competent, and responsible. She immediately bonded with Halley as her best friend, and their lives became intertwined.

Halley calls her mother, Julie, from camp and says she has to come home immediately to support Scarlett in her need. Halley's controlling mother is a therapist specializing in adolescent behavior and believes she knows how to handle Halley and other teens. She wants Halley to stay at camp. Halley insists on coming home, and her mother gives in. Halley and her mother have always been close, but now they are drifting apart, and neither seems to know what to do about it. When Halley arrives home, she runs across the street to enfold Scarlett in her arms. Scarlett is weeping, and Halley is moved, because Scarlett has always been the strong and brave one. She has always taken care of the house and of her thirty-five-year-old childish mother. Now Halley has to hold Scarlett up, and she knows their lives are changing.

CHAPTER TWO

The two friends live parallel lives but envy each other. Scarlett is beautiful and plucky, and Halley is pretty but lacks confidence. Halley has a conventional family with two parents, and Scarlett has a dysfunctional mother.

The boy who dies, Michael Sherwood, was handsome and popular but did not fit in with others. His best friend, Macon Faulkner, attends the same high school as the girls do and Michael did. Michael dated the wild and rich cheerleader Ginny Tabor for a while and then the head cheerleader, Elizabeth Gunderson. Halley calls Michael an equalizer because he is accepted by all the students. The summer before his death, Michael and Scarlett had an intense and secret romance. Marion tells Scarlett she will try to come to the funeral, but she has to work at the mall doing make-overs for glamour photography.

Halley goes to Scarlett's room to dress her for the funeral and discovers Macon Faulkner in Scarlett's bed. He has a hangover and has come to Scarlett to share their grief over Michael's death. Scarlett says she has taken him in because Macon is really messed up with problems and was Michael's best friend. Scarlett has a bad time at the funeral because no one knows of her relationship with Michael. The cheerleaders, Ginny and Elizabeth, are acting hysterical with grief, but it is Scarlett whom Michael really loved. After the funeral, as Scarlett and Halley drive home in a rainstorm, they offer a ride to Macon, who is walking around soaking wet. He refuses; Halley thinks he is mysterious as he disappears into an alley.

CHAPTER THREE

Michael worked at Milton's Market in Lakeview, and that is how he met Scarlett. Scarlett and Halley are cashiers, and Michael worked in produce. One day he offers Scarlett a kiwi fruit on their break, and they fall in love. Halley feels left out of their union, but Scarlett is so happy. Halley has taken a picture of the couple at the beach, and it is the only one of them together. Two weeks before his death, Michael tells Scarlett he loves her. Since the funeral, Scarlett has withdrawn into herself and does not want to go to her junior year in high school.

When Halley's class schedule is messed up, she runs into Macon Faulkner, who as the school's bad boy gives her hints about how to get around in the system. He tells her about his

Jedi mind trick, whereby he gets his way with teachers and officials by telling them what he wants them to think. They discover they are in the same physical education class, and that class becomes the happiest time of the day for Halley. She likes his boldness and begins to change her behavior to share his pranks and way of thinking. She loves his rebellious and funny nature.

Halley's father, Brian, is completely wrapped up in the popularity of his radio show, *Brian in the Morning*. He embarrasses Halley by making her a character he talks about on his show. Her mother has made her the subject of her books on adolescent behavior. Both of them want her to play roles, and that is why she is attracted to Macon, the rebel who does what he wants.

CHAPTER FOUR

Macon finally asks Halley out. She has been wanting this but feels she is not attractive. Meanwhile, Halley goes to Scarlett's house, where Marion is getting ready for her first date with an accountant, Steve Michaelson. Both Scarlett and Halley think he is a loser. He dresses like a conservative accountant by day but has a hobby of dressing up as Vlad the Warrior for medieval enactments on weekends. Halley's mother keeps trying to make her take back her old boyfriend, Noah Vaughn and invites the Vaughn family for pizza on Friday nights. Halley finds Noah boring and constantly tries to avoid him. Halley decides she has to keep her relationship with Macon secret because her mother insists on controlling her life.

Scarlett and Halley go to Ginny Tabor's party so that Halley can meet Macon. Ginny is drunk and gossips about who is in which bedroom with whom. Her parents are out of town, and half the high school is there. After someone spills wine on the carpet, she orders everyone out. They do not see Macon, and Halley assumes she has been stood up. She tells Scarlett he would not want to date someone like her. Scarlett becomes angry and says anyone would be fortunate to get a beautiful and smart girl like Halley.

Macon makes excuses about why he missed Halley at the party. She begins telling lies to her parents to sneak out with him. Macon, however, has mysterious friends whom he does not explain to her. He butters up her father, who accepts

Macon, but her mother disapproves and tries to break off the romance.

Part Two: Someone Like You

CHAPTER FIVE

At work at the supermarket, Scarlett tells Halley she has discovered she is pregnant. Suddenly Halley realizes again that she has to be the strong one to get her friend through this. She is there when Scarlett tells her mother. Scarlett and Marion have an argument about whether Scarlett should have an abortion. Marion is in favor of the abortion so that Scarlett will not ruin her life by being a teen mother like she was. She makes an appointment for Scarlett, who is against the abortion. Scarlett tells Halley that keeping her was probably the only unselfish thing Marion has ever done.

Halley runs into Macon at school, and he tells her to save the next night for him. It is Halley's sixteenth birthday. Halley agrees, though her mother has already planned a party for her. At school, Halley gets a call from Scarlett asking her to pick her up at the abortion clinic. Marion has dropped her off there, but Scarlett cannot go through with the procedure. Halley persuades Macon to skip school and go with her to pick up Scarlett. Scarlett says that she has decided to keep the baby and understands that her whole life will change. Halley says she will stand by her. Halley's mother confronts her about lying and skipping school. Halley is punished and grounded.

CHAPTER SIX

Halley's parents assume she has skipped school because of Macon. Marion telephones Halley's mother and asks her to come across the street, where they have a long conference. Marion tries to persuade Julie to counsel Scarlett about the abortion. When Julie returns home, she tells Halley that Scarlett and her mother have reached a compromise. Scarlett can give birth to the baby if she puts it up for adoption. Julie believes Scarlett is making a mistake, but Halley supports her decision.

CHAPTER SEVEN

At the supermarket, Macon wishes Halley a happy birthday, and she explains she is grounded. She has a party with her parents at a restaurant. Later that night she hears a car rumbling in the street and sees its lights blink as a signal. She leaves the house and gets in Macon's

car in her pajamas and jacket. Macon drives to a secret place he and Michael had found at Topper Lake near the dam, and he kisses her.

CHAPTER EIGHT

Scarlett and Halley chart the progress of the pregnancy with a book that details the symptoms of morning sickness and other changes Scarlett will go through. Halley is getting closer to Macon, but Elizabeth Gunderson, the cheerleader and homecoming queen, warns her that Macon is sweet but treats girls badly. At school Scarlett has to go to the bathroom with morning sickness, and Ginny Tabor overhears her conversation with Halley about the baby. Soon, the gossip is all over school that Scarlett is pregnant with Michael's baby.

CHAPTER NINE

Grandma Halley, for whom Halley is named, has dementia, and Halley prepares for her death, remembering the close times with her grandmother. She understands that her mother is also a daughter and watches her concern over losing her mother.

Halley and Scarlett watch Steve's alter ego Vlad the Warrior emerge as he starts wearing leather and odd clothing. Although Scarlett is the one who needs attention, she has always played mother to Marion and tries to warn her about the weirdness of the boyfriend.

Cameron Newton, a new boy in the school, is considered strange, but he is a gifted artist who has lived in France. Cameron becomes Scarlett's friend and supporter, along with Halley, against the other students, who eventually accept Scarlett's condition. Macon continues to drive by Halley's house at night to squeal his tires and wake up the neighbors, trying to get Halley's attention. Once, he takes her to his own bedroom in his mother's penthouse. Halley arrives home past curfew, and her mother confronts her about the lies she tells to be with Macon. Halley realizes she has become someone else with this boyfriend, a girl who can break her mother's heart and not look back.

CHAPTER TEN

In a visit to the doctor, Halley and Scarlett ask whether childbirth is painful. The doctor says it is to some degree but that women get through it. She recommends childbirth classes. Julie takes Halley out to dinner so the two of them can have a private talk. She tells Halley that because of the changes in Halley's behavior since she began spending time with Macon, she feels that she does not even recognize her anymore. She says Macon is not good for Halley and insists that she break off the relationship. Halley rebels and distances herself from her mother. Her mother suddenly has to leave town to take care of her own mother, who is dying.

CHAPTER ELEVEN

Halley feels the freedom of her mother's departure. Her father is more lenient with her and does not ask questions. Scarlett is working extra shifts at the grocery store to buy baby things. She begins to hang out with Cameron and joins a teen mother support group. Halley starts skipping school with Macon and having fun. Macon begins putting pressure on her to have sex with him, and Halley has a hard time pushing him away. She feels she will lose him if she does not give in. She asks advice from Scarlett, who tries to warn her that she needs to make her own decisions. She admits sleeping with Michael was a mistake, that one has to be ready for such a step because it always changes things.

CHAPTER TWELVE

For Thanksgiving, Halley and her family spend time with Grandma Halley, who is in a hospital. They stay at her house, and Halley discovers her grandmother's letters and photographs. In a moment of closeness, she shares them with her mother and announces that according to the letters, Grandma Halley fell in love with an Indian boy when she was nineteen.

CHAPTER THIRTEEN

As Scarlett's pregnancy is beginning to show, her boss at the supermarket tries to talk her into quitting. She refuses, and he gives in. Halley is proud of Scarlett's courage and responsibility toward her child, but she herself feels on slippery ground because she has not decided how to handle Macon.

Halley hears from Elizabeth Gunderson that Macon is hanging out at Rhetta's. Halley realizes there is a lot of Macon's life she knows nothing about. She does not know Rhetta and has not been invited there. She asks him about it, but Macon is elusive. Their relationship becomes difficult, like a battle. She does not see him often and knows she is losing him. She asks to go to one of his friend's parties on New Year's Eve and decides she will give in to him then.

CHAPTER FOURTEEN

On New Year's Eve, Scarlett hands Halley some condoms to take with her as she tries to talk her out of her decision to give in to Macon. Macon and Halley arrive at a house on the edge of town where there are alcohol and drugs and people sleeping with each other in various bedrooms. Halley is surprised to see Elizabeth Gunderson there and in bed with the host. Halley gets stoned. Elizabeth casually mentions that she was dating Michael at the same time Scarlett was. As Macon returns and tries to make love to Halley, she realizes she does not want this as it dawns on her that Michael was with two girls at the same time. He did not really love Scarlett. She hates herself for almost making the same mistake and rushes out into the night to throw up in the woods at the stroke of midnight.

CHAPTER FIFTEEN

Macon is angry as he drives the sick and anguished Halley home. They argue. Suddenly there are bright lights and shattering glass.

CHAPTER SIXTEEN

As they wait for the ambulance, Macon holds Halley's hand and tells her he loves her. Though Halley has minor injuries from the car accident, the hospital holds her overnight because of the concussion. Scarlett comes to the hospital to see her and says that Macon has not even waited to see how she is. Halley's parents come for her and stay by her bedside.

CHAPTER SEVENTEEN

Halley lets her mother take control of her life. Her mother does not ask questions but just takes care of her. Macon keeps trying to see her but cannot get to her. She realizes he was not what she thought he was, but it is hard for her because she cared for him. One night he throws a rock at her window, and she comes out to tell him she cannot see him anymore. She knows she deserves better.

Part Three: Grace

CHAPTER EIGHTEEN

Halley's parents take photos of her in her junior prom dress. She is going with her old boyfriend, Noah Vaughn, and Scarlett is going with Cameron in a maternity prom dress his mother has made for her. Things have changed with Halley and her mother. Both are trying harder to get along. Macon is now dating Elizabeth Gunderson. Halley has taken Lamaze classes with Scarlett as they prepare for the big event in the ninth month. Marion has finally come around and is looking forward to the birth of her grandchild.

At the prom, Noah gets drunk and tears Halley's dress. He leaves, and when Halley sees Macon with Elizabeth, she feels attracted to Macon again. Elizabeth tells Halley that Macon still loves her. Halley replies that she does not care for Macon anymore. Suddenly, the news goes around the dance that Scarlett has gone into labor. Scarlett, Cameron, and Halley leave for the hospital, driven by Macon and Elizabeth.

Halley is frightened at being Scarlett's support. She calls Marion, who is not home, and then her own mother. Halley feels the whole thing is over their heads as Scarlett becomes frightened and asks for drugs. Halley tries to run away from giving Scarlett the breathing instructions they learned, but Julie tells her it is her duty to be Scarlett's partner and pushes her through the door. Halley admires her mother's wisdom and realizes that her mother is part of her.

CHAPTER NINETEEN

The baby is a girl, Grace Halley, and there in the emergency room are many of the students in their prom clothes. They all cheer at the news.

CHARACTERS

Brian Cooke

Brian Cooke is the father of the first-person narrator, Halley. A nice man, he is intimidated by his wife and gives in to her ideas about how to raise their daughter. He has a corny sense of humor and is wrapped up in his popular local radio show, *Brian in the Morning*, on which he embarrasses his daughter by using stories about her.

Halley Cooke

Halley Cooke is the first-person narrator and main character. She is named for her Grandmother Halley and Halley's comet. She tells the story of her trials in junior year of high school. Her best friend is pregnant, and Halley is trying to decide whether to have sex with her boyfriend. Halley has been a perfect daughter, the subject of her mother's counseling books on teenagers. She

suddenly finds she has a rebellious streak as she strives to be herself and out of her mother's control. The widening gap and fight with her mother sadden her but seem necessary as she has to sort out what in her is unique and what is her mother's agenda for her.

Halley has a problem with self-esteem, though her friend Scarlett points out she is pretty and smart. Her mother has probably enrolled her in the camp for young women to find her strengths in the summer before junior year. Halley is bored with her safe and dull boyfriend, Noah, chosen by her parents. She is attracted to the bad boy, Macon Faulkner, because he is witty and rebellious and finds her attractive. She begins to adopt his behavior and views and to reject warnings about him. When he pressures her to have sex, she wants to believe they are in love but hears rumors about his other girls.

What helps Halley to find herself is her friendship with Scarlett, who has given in to sex with her boyfriend and exemplifies the consequences of an unwanted pregnancy. Scarlett is the example of a young girl finding her own way and braving censure to do what she feels is right for her, to keep and support her baby. In helping her friend through her pregnancy and birth, Halley finds her own courage to accept who she is and not what others want her to be.

Julie Cooke

Julie Cooke is a psychologist and therapist specializing in adolescents. She is confident that she knows all about raising a teenager and that in the books she has written she can tell other parents what to do. Her daughter, Halley, has always been perfect and in tune with Julie's ideas, until she turns sixteen. Suddenly, there is an inexplicable gap between mother and daughter as Halley rebels, lies, skips school, sneaks out with a boy she is forbidden to see, and contemplates sex and drugs. Julie's reaction is to become stern and bossy, issuing orders that her daughter ignores. Though Halley sees her as the heavy, Julie is not a bad mother. She counsels Scarlett on her pregnancy and makes peace between Scarlett and Marion. Her strict guidelines are seen in a different light once Halley gets into trouble and in the car accident with Macon. Julie tries to soften and become more understanding and trusting of Halley at the end. Their relationship matures and survives.

Macon Faulkner

Macon Faulkner is the best friend of Michael Sherwood, the boy who dies in a motorcycle crash. After Michael's death, Macon hangs out with Michael's girlfriend, Scarlett, and her friend, Halley. He makes the stiff and conventional Halley laugh at his witty and rebellious ways and tempts her to go on pranks. She is attracted to him, yet Macon is mysterious with his numerous and different cars, strange friends, other girls, and parties he does not explain. He is the son of a single rich mother who does not pay attention to him. He may be mixed up in drugs or criminal activities. Macon is a con man who charms Halley's father but not her mother. He keeps pressuring Halley to go to bed with him, and she decides to give in to keep from losing him. When she understands that he has been lying and that he has unsavory friends and selfish motives toward her, she backs out and gives him up. The crash resulting from his drunken carelessness is the final proof she needs.

Elizabeth Gunderson

Elizabeth Gunderson is the head cheerleader at the high school. She dates Michael Sherwood the same summer Scarlett does. Scarlett supposes that Michael dated Elizabeth before her, but Halley discovers he was dating them both secretly at the same time. He has given them the same earrings. Halley hates Elizabeth for her snooty ways and sarcasm, yet she finds that Elizabeth tries to warn her about Macon and to show some sympathy for her predicament. Because she could have been in the same situation herself, Elizabeth does not understand why Scarlett would ruin her life to have Michael's baby. Elizabeth is a respected leader in high school, but she runs around with a wild crowd and knows Macon better than Halley does. She becomes Macon's girlfriend after Halley but confesses to Halley that Macon still loves Halley.

Grandma Halley

Grandma Halley is Halley's grandmother on her mother's side, and Halley has been named for her. Halley was close to her growing up and remembers the time in 1986 when she and her grandmother saw Halley's comet together. Halley feels her grandmother is more understanding than her mother. When she reads letters her grandmother received as a young woman, Halley discovers that she had an Indian boyfriend with whom she corresponded for two years, unknown to her family. Halley feels justified in her feelings and greater self-worth in identifying with her grandmother.

Steve Michaelson

Steve Michaelson is Marion's weird boyfriend, who is a conservative accountant by day but part of a medieval enactment group on weekends. His alter ego is Vlad the Warrior.

Cameron Newton

Cameron Newton is a new boy at the high school. He is unusual, and Scarlett takes him under her wing. He becomes a best friend and supporter in her pregnancy, taking her to junior prom when she is nine months' pregnant. A talented artist, Cameron has spent five years in France, is a good cook, and has a more liberal point of view than the other students.

Rhetta

Rhetta is a mysterious girlfriend or friend of Macon's at whose drug parties on the outskirts of town he spends time, keeping it secret from Halley.

Michael Sherwood

Michael Sherwood is the boy with whom Scarlett Thomas is having a summer romance. He dies in a motorcycle accident the day after the sexual encounter by which Scarlett becomes pregnant. He and Scarlett met at Milton's Market, where they both worked. He is described as a magical boy who makes people laugh and has friends in every group at the high school. He is an equalizer or peacemaker, yet a loner and individual. He claims to have broken up with Elizabeth but was also secretly dating her the summer he dated Scarlett.

Ginny Tabor

Ginny Tabor is the shallow, self-centered cheerleader who briefly dates Michael Sherwood. She likes to spread gossip and give Scarlett and Halley a hard time. She lives in a richer suburb and has wild parties when her parents are out of town.

Marion Thomas

Marion Thomas is the mother of Scarlett, Halley's best friend. Marion and Scarlett live across the street from Halley and her parents. Marion is a thirty-five-year-old single mother and is presented as childish and somewhat self-centered.

She is a makeup artist at the mall and dresses provocatively. Halley finds her fascinating. In a role reversal, Scarlett is the responsible one, keeping the household together. She mothers Marion, who shows poor judgment in boyfriends and is a chain smoker. Marion wants Scarlett to have an abortion because she was a teen mother and does not want to see Scarlett ruin her life. In the end, she accepts her grandchild.

Scarlett Thomas

Scarlett Thomas is the best friend of Halley Cooke, the narrator. She is a major influence on Halley's life, like a twin sister. Halley admires Scarlett for her beauty, confidence, independence, bold way of taking control of her own life, and not caring what others say about her. Scarlett refuses to have an abortion, keeps the baby, continues high school, refuses to resign from her job, and counsels her mother and Halley with wisdom and compassion. She befriends the new boy, Cameron, the way she has always protected Halley. Halley sees Scarlett as a role model for becoming a responsible and authentic person. Scarlett knows who she is and what she wants and is not discouraged by the opinions of others.

Noah Vaughn

Noah Vaughn is Halley's first boyfriend. She has broken up with him but has to keep seeing him because their parents are friends. Halley dislikes Noah and tries to escape from him whenever she can because she finds him dull and boring. He is tall and skinny and has acne. As a prom date, he ignores Halley, gets drunk, and tears her dress.

THEMES

Family

Someone Like You gives several portraits of teens and their family interactions. Ginny Tabor and Elizabeth Gunderson are popular cheerleaders but lead privately wild lives of which their families are unaware. Ginny has a party when her parents are out of town. Elizabeth is shown to be a responsible big sister but is also running around with many boys. Scarlett and Macon come from dysfunctional single-parent homes. Scarlett has to be the adult in her family because her mother Marion acts as if she never left

adolescence. Marion depends on Scarlett to take care of the house and organize her life. When Scarlett is in trouble, her mother is not able to respond to her needs. Macon comes from a wealthy background but has no parental supervision or love. He is spinning out of control with wild friends and shadowy business partners. Halley, on the other hand, has a more traditional family, with a mother and father who work and care about her. In her mind, they are overly strict and controlling, but after she sees what other teens face who are basically on their own, she begins to find security in her family situation. She surrenders to her psychologist mother after Macon gets her into a car accident while drunk. The mother-daughter relationships between Scarlett and Marion and Halley and Julie are realistically depicted as evolving over time and through difficult circumstances. In the end, both of these relationships survive and become stronger. The author shows adolescence as a time when family relationships are tested as the teen changes and grows toward adulthood and more independence. Both Halley and Scarlett learn how to negotiate with their mothers yet make their own important decisions.

Peer Pressure

Dessen shows that becoming an adult in contemporary society is difficult because of peer pressure. A young person like Halley has been happy identifying with her parents until she begins to mature. Suddenly, the opinions of parents hold no weight because they represent childhood and the past. Halley's father seems corny and embarrasses her. Her mother becomes the enemy who does not understand or let her go where she wants to or even choose her own friends. Halley seeks other role models and wants the acceptance of peers. She feels she is unattractive to boys and other girls her age. She lacks confidence, so when Macon gives her attention, she tries to adapt to his thinking and behavior, feeling she is competent to make her own life without parental interference. Macon is the rebel and shows Halley it is fun to be a rebel, to get around the rules. He makes her feel free, and she assumes she is becoming more grown up, as she smokes, drinks, and lies. Macon pressures her to have sex, implying she is childish and prudish or does not love him. She joins the secret lives of the other teens, like Elizabeth Gunderson, who is respected for her grades and being head

TOPICS FOR FURTHER STUDY

- Do a presentation on the life and work of Father Flanagan (1886–1948), who founded Boys Town, a refuge for delinquent boys. Father Flanagan believed there were no bad boys, only a bad environment. Use slides and clips from the 1938 film *Boys Town* starring Spencer Tracy and Mickey Rooney. In your discussion of Flanagan's work include the example of Macon Faulkner from the novel. He is a bad boy, perhaps involved with a gang and crime. How bad do you think he is? Are the lines less clear today than in Father Flanagan's time? Include information on gangs, teen crime, and rehabilitation methods.

- Read *The Moves Make the Man* (1984), a young-adult novel by Bruce Brooks. This sports novel features the friendship between an African American boy, Jerome Foxworthy, and a white boy, Braxton Rivers III, around 1961, the time of the civil rights movement, in North Carolina. Brooks, like Dessen, is a graduate of the University of North Carolina at Chapel Hill but writes about the same location almost forty years earlier. The novel covers the problems of racism, domestic violence, abuse, and death. The book won awards from *School Library Journal* and the *New York Times*, the *Boston Globe*–Horn Book award, and a Newbery Honor award. In class discussion contrast the high-school challenges of boys versus girls, white versus black, and the 1960s versus the 1990s presented by Brooks

and Dessen in their novels. What issues have not changed and are still relevant to all teens? Write a short summary of the points that come out in class and turn it in with your own comments at the end.

- Read about the coming-of-age experience of another American ethnic group in Judith Ortiz Cofer's *Call Me Maria* (2004), about a Puerto Rican girl. In class, discuss the unique challenges of teens from different races and cultures, citing this book as a primary example. On a class blog or webpage, include photos and stories, both literary and actual, of teens from various cultures in America, highlighting both differences and similarities for teens growing up today.

- Develop a group presentation on teen sex in which small groups are responsible for different topics, such as peer pressure, sexual abuse, protected versus unprotected sex, teen pregnancy, abortion, being a single mother or a teen father, teen marriage, sexually transmitted disease, and social services available for teens with sexual issues. Each small group can conduct research and turn in a short paper citing sources on the assigned topic. One presenter from each small group can show the larger group the conclusions with a media-rich presentation on each topic.

- In an imaginative role reversal, write a short story from the perspective of a parent dealing with a difficult teen.

---

cheerleader but is becoming promiscuous and using drugs. Michael Sherwood, Scarlett's boyfriend who dies in the motorcycle accident, is popular, funny, and independent minded. Everyone likes him, yet even he is found to be lying and leading a secret life with two girlfriends, Elizabeth and Scarlett. Halley gets drawn into this world of peer pressure though

she has been raised with different values. Her mother has enrolled her in a camp during the summer to help her avoid this kind of pressure. Halley wants to leave family but has not yet made a complete transition to adulthood. Choosing the right companions and role models is important for a smooth path toward maturation.

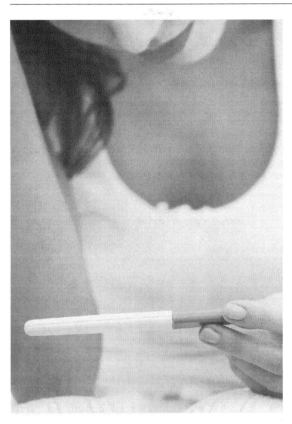

Scarlett finds herself pregnant, and though her mother pushes her, she decides not to have an abortion. (© Piotr Marcinski | Shutterstock.com)

Friendship

The friendship between Halley and Scarlett is the focus of the novel. Both girls have other people in their lives trying to bring them down or tell them the wrong path to follow. Scarlett believed Michael was the one who loved her and trusted him, and she gave in to him. She warns Halley not to do the same with Macon unless she is very sure, because she realizes through her pregnancy that she made a mistake. The author tries to show the difference between social friends and true friends. Ginny and Elizabeth have a crowd they run around with. Michael and Macon were best friends. But they do not always bring out the best in each another. These are social connections. Halley and Scarlett, however, are shown to be true friends, because they are good for each other. They try to stand by each other in rough times and bring out the best in the other. When Halley is letting Macon lead her astray because she wants to see herself as attractive, Scarlett

tells her she can do better because she is beautiful in herself. When Scarlett is ostracized in high school for her pregnancy, Halley stands by her and becomes her labor partner. Scarlett's mother, Marion, does not take into account Scarlett's own feelings when she tries to force the abortion. She thinks only of her personal point of view. Halley becomes strong enough to support her friend's choice. She eventually sees Scarlett as her worthy role model, for though Scarlett can make a mistake, she becomes stronger as she takes responsibility for it.

STYLE

Young-Adult Novel

Traditionally, there was no separate category of young-adult fiction; teenagers read adult classics. Early examples of popular books read by teens and adults alike are *The Adventures of Tom Sawyer* by Mark Twain (1876) and *Little Women* by Louisa May Alcott (1868). These stories featured teens or young adults as characters. Greater awareness of adolescence and its special trials came in the late 1950s and 1960s. In addition to being literary classics, *The Catcher in the Rye* by J. D. Salinger (1951) and *To Kill a Mockingbird* (1960) by Harper Lee are classic coming-of-age novels.

Young-adult fiction helps teens make the transition to adulthood. It is a genre that has grown with awareness of the importance of this period of life. In the youth culture of the 1960s, teen novels made a breakthrough in realistic depictions of problems such as drugs, pregnancy, and suicide (*A Girl like Me* by Jeanette Eyerly, 1966; *A Blues I Can Whistle* by A. E. Johnson, 1969). In the 1970s, young-adult fiction took off with what became known as the fab five novels about adolescence: *I Know Why the Caged Bird Sings* by Maya Angelou (1970), *The Friends* by Rosa Guy (1973), *The Bell Jar* by Sylvia Plath (1971), *Bless the Beasts and Children* by Glendon Swarthout (1970), and *Deathwatch* by Robb White (1972). Young people identified with the problems and protagonists.

In the 1970s through 1990s, a young-adult market grew that featured authors for readers twelve to eighteen years old. The plots typically involve a main teen character encountering problems in society, family, or just growing up. Examples are Judy Blume's *Are You There God?*

It's Me, Margaret (1970) and S. E. Hinton's *The Outsiders* (1967). The novels dealt with issues and discussed information that teens were not getting at school or from parents. Teens have always enjoyed literary classics, but young-adult fiction became a separate field with authors appealing particularly to modern teen lifestyles and issues.

In the 1980s, young-adult fiction swung back from realism to escape romance with such series as Sweet Valley High, created in 1983 by Francine Pascal. The late 1980s and 1990s saw the rise of ethnic young-adult novels, such as Sandra Cisneros's *The House on Mango Street* (1984), about Chicana life in Chicago, and Jacqueline Woodson's *If You Come Softly* (1998), about interracial love in New York. In the early twenty-first century, young-adult fiction embraces genres from realistic problem novels to fantasy and science fiction and crosses over to the best-seller list for general readers with works such as *The Book Thief* by Markus Zusak (2005). It encompasses ethnic groups, such as Joseph Bruchac's *Code Talker* (2005), about a Navajo teen in the Marines, and sexual orientations, such as growing up gay in Nancy Garden's *Good Moon Rising* (1996). Young-adult literature tries to affirm the value of individual integrity over social expectations and helps teens identify with their culture.

Problem Novel

A problem novel is one genre of the novel that has been used extensively in young-adult fiction. A problem novel addresses a specific social issue, such as poverty. In teen fiction, this genre is considered helpful for teens to consider problems they may have but do not feel they can discuss or problems that other teens are having and they should know about. The topics are those that were taboo at one time, especially in literature for the young, but have come to be treated openly and realistically, such as rape, drug addiction, divorce, abortion, gang warfare, death, mental illness, depression, racial prejudice, and domestic violence. *Someone Like You* treats the problems of teen pregnancy in a realistic manner. In previous times, an illegitimate pregnancy ruined a young woman's reputation and chances for a normal life. Even today, with more options for pregnant teens, Dessen shows the difficulties to be faced. Scarlett is from a suburban background, surrounded by support systems, and yet she still has to muster courage

to face her trial and decisions. The obstacles are addressed stage by stage: discovery of pregnancy, telling family and friends, decision to keep the baby, earning money, continuing school, Lamaze classes, the trials of pregnancy, and the birth. Problem novels, unlike romances, go into realistic and lengthy detail on the subject, and the outcome is not always happy or ideal.

Coming-of-Age Novel

The coming-of-age novel, or bildungsroman, has been a popular genre of novel since the nineteenth century. *Great Expectations* (1860) and *David Copperfield* (1850) by Charles Dickens and *Jane Eyre* (1847) by Charlotte Brontë show the transformation of a child into a young adult. Transformation and growth were topics interesting to readers in the romantic and Victorian periods. These topics continue to be timely as growing children encounter obstacles in the social world and learn how to negotiate as they acquire skills and wisdom. The maturation process comes with a problem to be solved. In *Someone Like You*, both Scarlett and Halley come of age in their junior year of high school and overcome great pressures. Scarlett faces disgrace and hardship as an unmarried teen mother. Halley faces the temptation of sex and drugs with a wild crowd. They both have to sort out the kind of person they want to be. Scarlett decides to accept the responsibility of being a mother. Halley decides she is not ready to hand her life over to an irresponsible boy who does not love her. By standing up for themselves, they learn their limits and strengths and come out knowing who they are. This is effectively portrayed through Halley's first-person point of view, which presents an authentic teen voice.

HISTORICAL CONTEXT

Suburban Life

Suburbs are residential areas outside the central or inner-city area. Generally middle- or upper-class neighborhoods, suburbs resulted from migrations of wealthier people away from the poorer ethnic neighborhoods of the inner city, and this trend escalated after World War II. Suburbs gave rise to a culture of secure neighborhoods, academically excellent schools, shops and malls, and a homogeneous racial identity. The suburb of Lakeview outside a nameless city

COMPARE
&
CONTRAST

- **1998:** Teen pregnancy and nonmarital birth have social stigma attached, but young women like Scarlett are accepted and helped by the community.

  Today: The rate of nonmarital births continues to increase, especially among the young, the poor, and certain ethnic groups. Social programs for intervention and support are in place, such as the President's Teen Pregnancy Prevention Initiative through the US Office of Adolescent Health, and shelters for pregnant teens are sponsored by the Department of Housing and Urban Development.

- **1998:** Suburban high schools are places where middle-class students pursue academic

  excellence in preparation for college but are also experimenting with sex and drugs.

  Today: Suburban and inner-city high schools are known for violent incidents in which students carry guns to school.

- **1998:** The generation gap is depicted as a lack of understanding and communication between old and young.

  Today: The generation gap is often spoken of in terms of technology and earning power. Young people are more up to date with technology skills than adults are but are falling behind their parents in earning power because of the slower US economy.

---

is where Halley and Scarlett are neighbors. They compare themselves to the richer students in their high school, who come from the posher suburb where the cheerleader Ginny Tabor lives. The students from the wealthier suburb, however, are a wilder bunch who experiment with sex and drugs because their parents are largely absent.

Many young-adult novels explore problems of the inner city and minority cultures. *Someone Like You*, however, is set in a white neighborhood like the one Dessen grew up in. It seems safe, and Halley and her best friend live right across the street from each other. The girls work as cashiers at the local grocery. Marion, Scarlett's mother, works at the mall doing makeovers on middle-class women. The story remains centered on home and school, the poles of teen life, except for the nighttime cruising in cars with dates. In her rebellion, Halley ventures outside the safe suburb for a party in a run-down house on the outskirts of town where more dangerous activities are taking place. She survives that scare to return to her safe suburban life, watched over by her parents.

Chapel Hill, North Carolina

Chapel Hill, North Carolina, is Dessen's hometown, where both her parents and later, she, taught at the University of North Carolina. Chapel Hill, like other university towns, has a liberal and tolerant atmosphere, evidenced by environmental ideals, art fairs, and intellectual openness. Chapel Hill was the first white town in the South to elect an African American mayor. The Morehead Planetarium, built in 1949, was the first planetarium on a college campus. Astronomy becomes a symbol for a larger view or longer memory in the novel. Halley's comet is both an event and the source of Halley and her grandmother's name. The comet was discovered by the English astronomer Edmond Halley in 1705. Halley's memory of watching its periodic return in the sky with her grandmother in 1986 is a sustaining part of her identity.

Though a university town with a large population, Chapel Hill has a small-town feel, an important influence on the kinds of scenes Dessen depicts in *Someone Like You*, according to interviews with the author. Her readers recognize locations in Chapel Hill in her novels, such

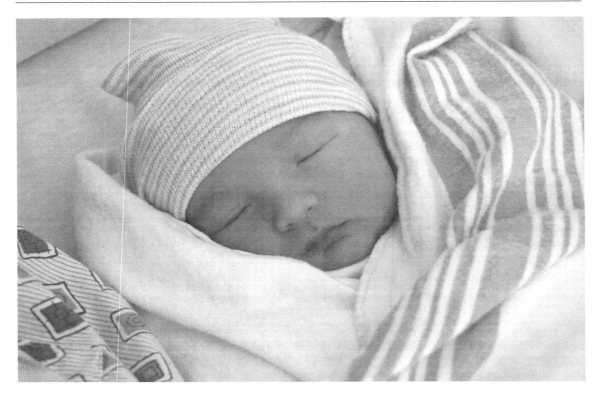

When Scarlett's baby is born, her family and friends come together to make it a happy occasion.
(© Leighton Photography & Imaging | Shutterstock.com)

as the fictional Lakeview suburb. Dessen, like Halley, comes from a privileged middle-class background, going to high school with the like-minded students who became lifelong friends and models for her characters. Though the characters of *Someone Like You* are intelligent students with good grades and are fairly well off, Dessen shows that sex, drugs, parental neglect, teen crime, and teen pregnancy are not just problems for inner-city kids. The culture of Halley's town and suburb are a lot like Chapel Hill's, with friendliness, tolerance, educated parents, neighbors, and support groups for teens offering solutions and possibilities for growth.

American Youth Culture

Historically, all family members lived in the same social culture. Parents taught their children to accept and imitate the behavior of adults so they would be prepared for life. Until the twentieth century, young people of middle and lower classes were considered capable of adult work on farms and in cities at an

early age, and they went from childhood to adulthood without a prolonged period of adolescence. Only the privileged attending college had a period of postponed adulthood.

The feeling of disenchantment after the world wars in the twentieth century led young people to rebel against accepting the values of the previous generation. Youth in the 1920s, for instance, began to cultivate a separate look, lifestyle, and values with free morals. Women smoked, drank, wore short dresses and hair, and went about unchaperoned. As the generation gap between adults and adolescents was noticed more and more, a distinct youth culture arose, with its own values, music, behavior, and dress. This youth culture bridged the gap between childhood and adulthood. It was a time when young people switched their loyalty from parents to peers as they tested their abilities.

In the early twenty-first century, this separate youth culture is found on college campuses and in high schools, as shown in *Someone Like You*, in which the high school students live in their own world, independent of their family lives. Halley suddenly cannot stand any of her mother's values or opinions and wants to be with her peers. She feels that to grow up she has to be different from her parents. This contrasts to the nineteenth-century attitude in *Little Women*, for instance, in which the daughters hold their mother as the ideal they strive for. Rebellion in some form or another is seen as a characteristic of American youth culture, made popular in such films as *Rebel without a Cause*, the 1955 classic starring James Dean and Natalie Wood as confused suburban teens.

CRITICAL OVERVIEW

Dessen's young-adult fiction has been popular with readers and critics since her first book, *That Summer* (1996). *Someone Like You* (1998) is her second novel. Both novels have won awards; their plots are combined in the film *How to Deal* (2003).

In a 1998 review of *Someone Like You* for *Booklist*, Hazel Rochman finds the novel has flaws she did not see in *That Summer*. She remarks, "Dessen has a perfect ear for the immediate daily details of a middle-class teenager's home, school, job, party scene—the elemental push and pull of family and friends." Of *Someone Like You*, however, Rochman writes,

> The metaphors are overstated and contrived, especially the "Grand Canyon" between Halley and her mother. Halley's boyfriend remains vague...all the males in the story...[are] only there as background to the women's conflict.

Rochman praises *Someone Like You* for the friendship between Scarlett and Halley, which she considers the most successful aspect of the book.

A May 1998 review in *Publishers Weekly* lauds the novel as a "realistic portrayal of contemporary teens and their moral challenges" that "breathes fresh life into well-worn themes of rebellion and first love." Nancy Vasilakis, in a 1998 review of *Someone Like You* for *Horn Book*, remarks on another of Dessen's narrative strengths: "The first-person voice is remarkable for its authenticity." She also notes Dessen's fondness for strong family ties and her sense of humor. A review of *Someone Like You* in the *Bookseller* on February 18, 2005, finds that

Dessen tells her story in "a down-to-earth framework free from condescension." In an interview with the teacher Robyn Seglem titled "*Just Listening* to Sarah Dessen" in the *ALAN Review* in 2007, Dessen attributes the popularity of her books to the intensity of her plots, which show how in high school everything is happening to teens for the first time.

CRITICISM

Susan K. Andersen

Andersen is a teacher and writer with a PhD in English. In the following essay, she considers the deeper theme of Someone Like You *as the teen search for an authentic identity.*

Someone Like You is a young-adult novel exploring teen pregnancy. The social context is all important, however, because Dessen's realistic novel about the problem includes the human solution of relationship. A problem can become a means of bonding in a supportive environment. *Someone Like You* contains hope because of the strength of friendship. Halley, the first-person narrator, says that "life is an ugly, awful place to not have a best friend." When Scarlett Thomas moves in across the street, Halley is glad that she makes "a spot for me next to her for the rest of my life." This friendship allows both girls to deal with the problems and sexual pressures teen girls face.

Scarlett becomes pregnant after having sex only once. Halley stands by her as she has to make a difficult decision to be a single mother. Scarlett uses her experience to persuade Halley not to make the same mistake by giving in to Macon. Having an ally one can trust is important. Among all the competing voices trying to influence them, the friends feel they can trust only each other to know their best interests. The deeper message of the novel is about the desperate search of teens for their authentic selves as they negotiate a world that seems uninterested in who they are as individuals. Peer counseling with a trusted friend can help.

Scarlett and Halley's junior year in a nice suburban high school does not go as they imagined it would. It starts with the death of Scarlett's boyfriend and her discovery of her pregnancy. Until then, the red-headed and bold Scarlett, named for one of Dessen's favorite strong female characters, Scarlett O'Hara in *Gone with the*

"

THE DEEPER MESSAGE OF THE NOVEL IS
ABOUT THE DESPERATE SEARCH OF TEENS FOR
THEIR AUTHENTIC SELVES AS THEY NEGOTIATE
A WORLD THAT SEEMS UNINTERESTED IN WHO
THEY ARE AS INDIVIDUALS."

Wind, has been the leader. When she has to start leaning on Halley, Halley, as the less confident girl, has to find her own strength. Halley listens to Scarlett's moral agonizing as the independent-minded teen begins to understand that she does not want an abortion as her mother insists. Halley enlists her boyfriend, Macon, and they rescue Scarlett from the abortion clinic. Halley becomes Scarlett's labor partner, taking Lamaze classes with her and coaching her through the birth. Halley is terrified by this responsibility, but by going through it, she shows love for Scarlett and learns her own strength.

Similarly, Scarlett, who knows both Macon and Halley, stands up to Halley when she wants to give in to Macon's demand for sex. She risks Halley's anger by telling her she had better be sure this is what she wants or she is wasting herself. Halley believes Scarlett is deserting her, but Scarlett is right. The pregnant Scarlett understands that neither her boyfriend, Michael, nor Macon, his friend, are mature or unselfish enough to recognize the gift of love offered them in sex. Halley finds out for herself when she sees that Elizabeth Gunderson has the same pair of earrings that Michael gave Scarlett when he said he loved her. He was sleeping with both girls at the same time.

Tanya Lee Stone, an author of young-adult books, discusses in "Now and Forever: The Power of Sex in Young Adult Literature" the responsibility of authors writing for young-adult audiences in depicting sexual scenes. Since Judy Blume's frank depiction of sex in her novel *Forever* (1975), this has been a controversial issue. Stone argues that although the author has to be careful, sexual issues among teens are more complicated than ever and must be addressed, despite, or maybe because of, the media deluge of sexual images. Dessen's

sensibility is admirable. She may give details such as using condoms and the stages of pregnancy, but she does not describe sexual scenes explicitly. The teen parties include couples tucked away in bedrooms experimenting with sex, so the topic is on the table, but the author respects the innocence of a girl like Halley by putting her in a position of knowing the situation exists but having to make up her own mind about whether it is good for her. Dessen does not make Halley accept a ready-made answer, just as Scarlett does not in her keeping of the baby. The issues are there, says Dessen; now how does a girl decide?

Halley is named for the comet that orbits the sun, but retrograde, that is, in the opposite direction of the planets. This image suggests the character of Halley, who does not want to follow what her parents want her to do. Yet the comet returns, as Halley's comet did in 1986, when Halley's grandmother held her in her lap. Halley does not really want to be a rebel but does want to find out who she is. She does so and returns, fortunately before she ruins her life.

What is important about Dessen's approach is that she trusts her teen characters and their judgment. She shows the teen is more likely to make a right decision by being strong and knowing herself, who she is, and what she wants rather than by following advice. Halley tries to convince herself that Macon loves her and that she wants to have sex, but Scarlett, who knows Halley better, challenges her that she knows it is not right for her. Scarlett does not say it is morally wrong; she says it is wrong for Halley. The situation is not a supportive one for her growth.

Halley finds out for herself what Scarlett means at the New Year's Eve party, where she knows she is out of place. She does not really want to run around with the wild kids, though she was attracted to Macon's rebellious confidence and sense of humor. At first she believes that Macon is taking her in the direction of her real self and that her parents are holding her back. At the party, she understands that the drugs and sex are not about self-esteem or love. She feels betrayed and runs away. When Macon involves her in a drunk driving accident and does not stay at the hospital to see how she is, she knows the relationship is a sham. She finally yields to the rules her parents have made for her safety. Her surrender to her parents is really a surrender to what she wants for herself.

WHAT DO I READ NEXT?

- In *Books That Don't Bore 'Em* (2007), James Blasingame explains how to evaluate the quality of young-adult books, lists recommendations, and provides biographies and interviews with authors of young-adult books.

- Dessen's *Keeping the Moon* (1999) is about a rejected overweight girl who gets a makeover and finds other quirky friends who like her the way she is.

- Charles Dickens's *Bleak House* (1853) features a heroine, Esther Summerson, who is illegitimate, a love child like Scarlett's, and the moral center of the novel. Dickens proves that virtue has nothing to do with the circumstance of birth.

- *The Scarlet Letter* (1850) is Nathaniel Hawthorne's classic story of Hester Prynne and her illegitimate daughter, Pearl, who live as outcasts in Puritan society. Unlike Scarlett, who receives support as an unwed mother in modern society, Hester is shunned.

- Teen friendships can change lives. Cynthia Kadohato's young-adult novel, *Weedflower* (2006), is about the friendship between Sumiko, a Japanese American girl interred in the Poston War Relocation Center during World War II, and Frank, a Mohave boy who lives near the camp on the reservation.

- *Son of the Mob* (2002) by Gordon Korman is a young-adult story about Vince Luca, whose father is a mob boss. He falls in love with the daughter of an FBI agent trying to arrest his father. Vince does not want to follow in his father's footsteps because of his girlfriend.

- Han Nolan's young-adult novel *Pregnant Pause* (2011) details a realistic picture of teen motherhood. Spunky sixteen-year-old Eleanor has to get married when she is seven months pregnant and live with unsympathetic in-laws.

- Tanya Lee Stone's young-adult novel *A Bad Boy Can Be Good for a Girl* (2006) is told in free verse. Three girls in a high school fall for the same bad boy. Two give in to his seduction, but Josie holds out.

- *Heart on My Sleeve* (2004), a young-adult novel by Ellen Wittlinger, tells the love story of Chloe and Julian in e-mails, postcards, and letters during their summer before college.

- *What to Expect When You're Expecting* (4th edition, 2008) by Heidi Murkoff and Sharon Mazel is a classic pregnancy guide like the one Scarlett and Halley read. It details the changes in the body month by month and describes labor and delivery and the days after birth.

The moral is not that mother is always right. Dessen has rounded characters in this realistic coming-of-age story. The adults are not black and white. They are not the enemy, even if they do not always understand how to be a friend. The parents as well as the teens have to grow. Scarlett's mother, Marion, is childish and selfish. She was an unwed pregnant teen like Scarlett, and though she is in her thirties now, she continues to try to recapture her lost teen years by dating and making Scarlett act as the parent and

the manager of the house. She wants Scarlett to have an abortion so she will not repeat her mistake. Scarlett, however, has a different take on her mother's life. She tells Halley that when Marion kept her child, she made the one unselfish decision in her life. Scarlett is inspired by her mother's sacrifice, not put off by it. Eventually, Marion looks forward to her granddaughter's birth.

Halley's mother, Julie, also has to grow. A teen psychologist and expert, she believes she

Halley thinks she is in love with Macon, though he pressures her to move more quickly than she is ready to do. (© Christo / Shutterstock.com)

has all the answers about raising a teen. She is in shock to discover her hitherto perfect daughter suddenly rebels, lies to her, and sneaks out with a wild boy. She does not respect the mother's rules. The mother has to let go of her expertise to deal with real events. It is Julie, however, who uses her professional background to negotiate peace between Scarlett and Marion over the abortion. She also rushes to Halley's aid in the hospital, helps Halley during the birth of Scarlett's child, and finally backs off when Halley explains that she was talking to Macon to tell him in person that she does not want to see him anymore. Julie understands that Halley is gaining her own internal balance and does not need to be nagged or coerced. The job of a good parent, Dessen shows, is ultimately to produce a mature person who can make good decisions for herself.

One of the beauties of *Someone Like You* is that the mother-daughter relationships are given a realistic treatment but shown to be strong enough to survive adolescence intact. Both girls need and want their mothers and are able to

make peace as they mature. Is Dessen just being traditional with her plot outcomes? The positivity of the book is not a liability, as Laureen Tedesco points out in "Sarah Dessen's Cautiously Optimistic Realism: Decades beyond the Teen Problem Novel." Tedesco claims that Dessen revisits the issues of the teen problem novel of the 1970s but without moral observations or tragedy. The best sort of young-adult novel has been shown to be optimistic but not sugary.

Dessen also shows the other teens as rounded characters. The boys, Macon and Michael, are believable in their charming personalities but reckless behavior. They do not seem out to hurt anyone on purpose. Macon has a rich mother who neglects him. Though not needing the money, Macon seems to be involved with other boys or a gang in some kind of crime. Elizabeth Gunderson, the popular cheerleader whom Halley despises, is somewhat sympathetic. She is running with a fast crowd, taking drugs, having sex, being one of Michael's old girlfriends, and eventually becoming Macon's girlfriend. Yet she always seems to be trying to warn Halley, the nice girl, to be careful. She tries to tell Halley about Macon's wildness. Elizabeth is shown in an ordinary situation when Halley sees her on the street babysitting her little sister. All of these touches make her human rather than an archrival.

Scarlett and Halley live in a nice suburb, like the one Dessen grew up in. The neighbors are known, and the other students have been known since childhood. When Scarlett gets into trouble, she receives help from her high school, her employer, and her neighbors. The other students rally around; her friend Cameron takes her to the prom when she is nine months' pregnant. Dessen shows Scarlett receiving support once she decides what she really wants.

Scarlett teaches Halley by example that one must trust oneself. Scarlett had to learn this at an early age when she had to take care of her own mother. "There's only so much faith you can have in people" she says. She listens to the wisdom of her own heart. Halley admires Scarlett's courage and self-confidence. In the beginning, Halley sees Scarlett as a real person but herself is "an outline in a coloring book, with the inside not yet completed." She thinks Macon is helping to fill her in but later understands he is not. She wonders why "you had to fight to be virtuous." After a year of conflict with parents, Scarlett's trouble, and her own car accident, Halley comes back to a settled life with new respect and patience. She knows that her mother and Scarlett are protecting her against Macon because she deserves better. Tedesco praised Dessen for narratives of self-revelation in which the character evaluates her own story, thus proving she has matured.

Source: Susan K. Andersen, Critical Essay on *Someone Like You*, in *Novels for Students*, Gale, Cengage Learning, 2016.

Roger Sutton and Sarah Dessen

In the following interview, Dessen explains that she writes more for female readers than male readers.

As cyclically happens, there's a lot of attention being paid right now to boys reading or, more exactly, boys *not* reading. But what about the girls? In the interests of fair play, following the money, and not ignoring what's already on the radar, I decided it was time for a chat with YA author Sarah Dessen. Having written nine

> WELL-ADJUSTED PEOPLE AREN'T THAT INTERESTING. IT'S A LOT MORE FUN TO WRITE ABOUT THE FRAUGHT STUFF. BUT EVEN WITHIN THE COMPLICATED RELATIONSHIPS IN MY BOOKS, THERE IS LOVE, AND THAT'S WHAT I HOPE TO SHOW."

unabashed—and haunting and literate—"girl books" (including the June release *Along for the Ride*, reviewed in this issue) and having inspired a ferociously loyal readership with fan groups on MySpace, LiveJournal, and Facebook, Dessen says she likes that her book jackets are "pink and cute" and isn't afraid of the term *chick lit*.

ROGER SUTTON: You live in Chapel Hill, North Carolina. Is that where your books are set?

SARAH DESSEN: Actually, I've made an effort to *not* use a specific setting. I wrote a book in college that I did set in Chapel Hill, and I hated that people in my writing workshop were always obsessing about specifics, like how far things were from each other—"It takes longer to get from the airport to the hospital than that!" So I decided that I wouldn't set my books in an actual place anymore; I would create my own little world. It's true that Chapel Hill is where I'm thinking of when I'm writing, but I try to set my books so that they could be anywhere.

RS: In your head, though, do the books feel like they take place in roughly the same area? Sarah Dessenland?

SD: Yes, they do. There are neighborhoods that are mentioned again and again throughout the books—certain landmarks, restaurants. People who have read all the books seem to appreciate that continuity. They like catching all the little details. In the last few books in particular I've been mentioning characters and places from earlier books, kind of an inside joke.

RS: So readers can put it all together into one big meta-narrative.

SD: It's been challenging, because I always think I'm being very clever, sneaking in these mentions. But I guess I'm not nearly as slick as I think I am. With my last few books, practically the day that they're published somebody is on some website saying, "I found them all," and listing them, complete with page numbers.

RS: You have very fervent fans.

SD: They're fantastic—they buy the book the day it comes out and read it incredibly quickly and then immediately e-mail me and ask when the next one is due! It's really the highest compliment. Young adults are an amazing audience to be writing for because you're catching people at their most enthusiastic about reading. Adults are a little more reserved. I still get excited about good books, but I don't get jumping-up-and-down-screaming excited. It's such a passionate time, adolescence. I remember the feeling in high school, and even in middle school, of reading a book and really connecting with it on that elemental level of "somebody understands me." It's so powerful. It's a great market to be writing for because you connect so strongly with your audience.

RS: I think part of that connection is that you create these characters that girls—and I'm assuming that most of your readers are girls—can see themselves in and relate to. Yet they are all individuals. I see a lot of common themes in your books, but each one of those girls is a different person. How do you balance making a character particular with making her universal?

SD: There are certain things about the teenage experience in our culture that are always going to be there: the issues you have with your parents; the boy you have a crush on who doesn't know your name; the friend who isn't nice to you, but for some reason you're friends with her anyway. But then there's room within those experiences to make each character unique.

The thing that all my narrators have in common is that they are girls on the verge of a big change. And how they deal with that change is where the story comes from. When I was in high school, I was never happy with myself and always wanted to believe that there was the potential for a big change to happen in my life. You know—that I was going to meet some amazing guy and come to some stunning realization about myself that was going to make my life better. I think that's very appealing at that age, because it can happen. At that age, a girl can go away for the summer and when she comes back in the fall, she's completely different. She's taller, she's blossomed. There's so much potential.

That's why I like writing about this age, because there's still so much room to come into one's self, so much change happening fast and furious. There's a wealth of material there.

RS: I notice that you often start with a precipitating offstage event. For instance, in The Truth About Forever *the death of the father takes place before the book actually begins, but it sets in motion all the things that happen to the heroine.*

SD: I think that's often how you feel as a teenager, that the world is happening around you, and you're sort of whirling and getting bounced around within it. I remember feeling that way, that I didn't have much control over my own destiny. Everything was *happening* to me, and I was just trying to keep my head above water.

RS: Do you think of yourself as a writer for girls?

SD: I do. I don't kid myself; I don't think a lot of boys are reading my books. My books are so firmly fixed in the girl mindset and the girl point of view. Women tend to want to share our experiences more, to talk about what's going on with us. Especially when things are going badly or you're stressed out, to find some commonality or sense of recognition in a story is very comforting. Boys are different that way. They don't want to talk about everything that's going on with them. One comment I get again and again from girls is, "I read your book and it is my life, it's like it's my school and my teachers."

RS: And that's also the theme of your books. It's not just that you have readers, who, because they are girls, explore their emotions through reading. Your books are about *young women trying to understand themselves and their place in the world.*

SD: My setup, usually, is a character feeling disjointed and out of place, maybe because she once felt more in place and then something happened, as you mentioned in *The Truth About Forever*, that made her lose her footing. Or, she's never felt that she fit anywhere and has been looking for a way to find her place. It's a pretty universal experience: much of adolescence is just trying to figure out where you fit in, where your spot is, who your people are.

RS: Do you think that that's something particular to girls?

SD: No, but I think the willingness to explore it is. Girls are much more willing to face the fact that they're looking for it, and more willing to reach out for it, than boys. People have said to me many times that I should write a book from a boy's point of view. All I can say is that I spent four years of high school sitting around with my friends analyzing what boys were thinking. That's all we did. We would sit at lunch and be like, "He said hi to me in the hall—what did that mean?"

RS: Nothing!

SD: Right, completely cryptic! So I can't even imagine saying what some boy means. Or what he's thinking. I don't know how boys think. I wish I did.

RS: In the 1980s, there was an earlier wave of "let's have more books for boys" going on. A number of women writers tried their hand at a male perspective. But the characters weren't real boys. They were male, but they would talk to each other and to other people as if they were women. It was as if the goal of these books was to take these tough characters and turn them into women. Put 'em in touch with their feelings. Make 'em cry. Make 'em talk about things. And I wasn't convinced.

SD: Teen readers can tell if someone's writing about them and it's not right. One of the most important things in writing for teens is to be genuine, and not to write down to them, not to proselytize or try to force-feed them a message. My books are not about social issues. I'm just telling the kind of story that I want to hear, writing the kind of book I wanted to read when I was in high school.

RS: Do you have an opinion about the term chick lit*?*

SD: I'm not as offended by it as others are. But I also think it's become too wide a term. We sort of throw anything with a pink cover into the category now. It used to be targeted very specifically, and now anything that isn't Literature and has women in it is *chick lit*. It seems like you're one or the other, you're "literary" or you're "chick lit." And that's unfortunate, because there are lots of shades in between. But I'm not offended by it, because I *am* writing books for girls. I *like* that my covers are kind of pink and cute. I'm not gonna lie. In high school that's the kind of cover I wanted to pick up. That's still the kind of cover that I'm drawn to!

RS: I'm looking at Lock and Key *right now with its pink striped cover. Kids who like chick lit are going to pick up this book, even if they don't know your name, simply because of the color and the design.*

SD: My books used to have covers that looked a lot younger. And then Penguin reissued all my books as trade paperbacks and gave them new covers that were much more sophisticated. Now they look more like something a fifteen- or sixteen-year-old wouldn't mind being seen carrying around. I'm grateful for the cover change, because I think it brings my books to a wider audience, which is what I'm always looking for. I'm always hoping that as many people as possible will find something to relate to in the story.

RS: Including a readership beyond YA?

SD: I have quite a few adult readers who started reading my books when they first came out, when they were teenagers, and now it's been ten years and they're still reading my books. And I hear from a lot of moms who read the books because their daughters are reading them. YA is enjoying this big resurgence now anyway, where adults are reading YA and realizing that you don't have to be a teenager now, but if you ever were one, you're going to find something to relate to. People have strong feelings about their high school years. They either *really* liked high school, or *really* hated it. You rarely find people who have no opinion whatsoever.

RS: Where do you fall?

SD: I didn't like it very much at all. I liked my friends and everything, but as far as the whole experience—no. I was not a good student. My brother was this great academic champion, and there was no way to live up to that, so I didn't even try, I just floundered about. And I kind of ran with a bad crowd, whom I'm still with, but now we're all older . . .

RS: Who, like bad girls? Were you smoking dope out in the parking lot? [laughs]

SD: I was definitely hanging out in the parking lot, I'll tell you that. And I was definitely not a stellar student/role model. I wasn't academically driven at all. I didn't really make an impression; I didn't participate in a lot of events; I didn't belong to any clubs—I was just getting through. And then I got to college and cleaned up my act, got very serious about academics, and did very well. But it took me awhile to get it together.

RS: What do you think made you into a writer?

SD: I think the fact that I read so much as a kid, for starters. My parents constantly bought me books and encouraged me to read, and encouraged me to read *up*. Everyone in our household was always reading. And I had a lot of encouragement with my writing. My mom and dad read everything I wrote. And then, after putting my parents through all this stuff in high school and being on the five-and-a-half-year plan in college, I finally graduated. But instead of getting an actual job, I was like, "I think I'm going to write a novel and just keep waiting tables for a while." My poor parents! But they were much more supportive than a lot of people would have been. They paid my health insurance for a while. And they would come to the restaurant where I worked and leave me extravagant tips when they knew I couldn't pay my phone bill.

RS: Speaking of parents, your adolescents have some very fraught relationships with their mothers.

SD: Yeah, definitely. I actually get along very well with my mom, and I always feel bad when people read my books and think she's this overbearing monster. But happy relationships aren't fun to write about. That's the truth. Well-adjusted people aren't that interesting. It's a lot more fun to write about the fraught stuff. But even within the complicated relationships in my books, there is love, and that's what I hope to show. Just because you don't see eye-to-eye with your parents doesn't mean there isn't a connection.

RS: Do you ever wish you could write something completely different?

SD: As far as genre, no, because I can't imagine what else I would write. People ask me if I've ever thought about writing fantasy, and I'm like, "Ugh, no." I'm way too lazy, to be honest. And for the same reason I probably couldn't do historical fiction. I would have to spend a lot of time planning and researching, and I like to sit down and just start writing. I used to be a lot harder on myself about that. I used to worry, "Maybe my books are too similar to each other. They're all using this

same neighborhood in this same little world." But one of my very favorite writers is Anne Tyler. Every single one of her books is set in Baltimore, and they all have certain qualities in common. Yet each novel is unique. So I think it can be done, and that's what I'm endeavoring to do. Eventually I may try something different, but for now, as long as I keep having fresh ideas that I'm excited about, I'll keep on with it.

Source: Roger Sutton and Sarah Dessen, "An Interview with Sarah Dessen," in *Horn Book*, May/June 2009.

Publishers Weekly

In the following review, an anonymous reviewer praises Someone Like You *for giving "fresh life" to often-used young-adult themes.*

Dessen's realistic portrayal of contemporary teens and their moral challenges breathes fresh life into well-worn themes of rebellion and first love. Halley has always been close to her mother, a therapist who publishes books about adolescent behavior. But the summer before her junior year of high school, Halley begins cutting the umbilical cord. She and her best friend, Scarlett, start hanging out with Ginny Tabor ("a cheerleader with a wild streak a mile wide and a reputation among the football team for more than her cheers and famous midair splits"); Halley dumps her nerdy boyfriend (the son of her mother's best friend) and becomes involved with reckless Macon, a boy her parents have forbidden her to see. Then Scarlett discovers she is pregnant two months after her boyfriend Michael is killed in a motorcycle accident. Walking a line between childhood and adulthood, the two girls turn to each other instead of their families for support. Together they explore the meaning of love, sex and responsibility. This romance/coming-of-age story is not as tightly written as Dessen's debut, *That Summer*; it suffers from some scenes reminiscent of soap opera and from flat presentations of almost all the adult characters. But Dessen's fully developed characterizations of charismatic teens, particularly the rebel without-a-cause-type Macon, are sure to attract readers—especially those who, like Halley, have felt the urge to take a walk on the wild side.

Source: Review of *Someone Like You*, in *Publishers Weekly*, Vol. 245, No. 20, May 18, 1998, p. 80.

SOURCES

Cart, Michael, *From Romance to Realism: 50 Years of Growth and Change in Young Adult Literature*, Harper-Collins, 1996, pp. 42–138, 164, 172, 278.

Corbett, Sue, "Welcome to Sarahland: YA Author Sarah Dessen Hits Home with Teens by Bringing Them to Hers," in *Publishers Weekly*, Vol. 255, No. 7, February 18, 2008, p. 26.

Daniels, Cindy Lou, "Literary Theory and Young Adult Literature," in *ALAN Review*, Winter 2006, pp. 78–81.

Dessen, Sarah, *Someone Like You*, Viking, 1998.

Nilsen, Alleen Pace, James Blasingame, Kenneth L. Donelson, and Don L. F. Nilsen, eds., *Literature for Today's Young Adults*, 9th ed., Pearson, 2013, pp. 39–66, 109, 112–20.

Review of *Someone Like You*, in *Bookseller*, Vol. 5166, February 18, 2005, p. 38.

Review of *Someone Like You*, in *Publishers Weekly*, May 18, 1998, Vol. 245, No. 20, p. 80.

Rochman, Hazel, Review of *Someone Like You*, in *Booklist*, Vol. 94, No. 18, May 15, 1998, p. 1622.

Seglem, Robyn, *"Just Listening to Sarah Dessen,"* in *ALAN Review*, Vol. 34, No. 2, 2007, pp. 61–67.

Stone, Tanya Lee, "Now and Forever: The Power of Sex in Young Adult Literature," in *VOYA*, February 2006, pp. 463–65.

Sutton, Roger, "An Interview with Sarah Dessen," in *Horn Book*, May–June 2009, Vol. 85, No. 3, p. 243.

Tedesco, Laureen, "Sarah Dessen's Cautiously Optimistic Realism: Decades beyond the Teen Problem Novel," in *North Carolina Literary Review*, Vol. 15, 2006, pp. 53–63.

Vasilakis, Nancy, Review of *Someone Like You*, in *Horn Book*, July–August 1998, Vol. 74, No. 4, p. 486.

FURTHER READING

Eliot, George, *Adam Bede*, Oxford World's Classics, 2008.
    George Eliot's tragic story, published in 1859, is about Hetty Sorrel, a servant girl who abandons her illegitimate baby and is then tried for murder while the upper-class father gets off free. The book illustrates the traditional social bind for unwed mothers.

Gottfried, Ted, *Teen Fathers Today*, 21st Century, 2001.
    The author looks at common myths and facts about teen fathers in the United States, their economic burdens, and their role in raising a child. The book includes personal stories as examples.

Herz, Sarah K., and Donald R. Gallo, *From Hinton to Hamlet: Building Bridges between YA Literature and the Classics*, Greenwood Press, 2005.
    This practical guide pairs classics such as *The Odyssey* and Shakespeare's plays with young-adult novels that have similar themes.

Hoffman, Saul D., and Rebecca A. Maynard, *Kids Having Kids: Economic Costs and Social Consequences of Teen Pregnancy*, 2nd ed., Urban Institute Press, 2008.
    The United States has higher teen birthrates than other industrialized countries. This book evaluates the consequences to individuals and society with a chapter that looks at intervention programs.

Salzman, Mark, *Lost in Place: Growing Up Absurd in Suburbia*, Vintage, 2011.
    In this amusing 1995 memoir Salzman describes his normal suburban home in Ridgefield, Connecticut, with a social worker father and a music teacher mother. He describes his rebellious teen years, during which he tried to find his own way by smoking marijuana, studying Zen and kung fu, and eventually going to China but settling down to earn a degree from Yale University.

Stringer, Sharon, *Conflict and Connection: The Psychology of Young Adult Literature*, Heinemann, 1997.
    Stringer uses young-adult novels as examples to describe the stages of teen development from a psychological point of view.

SUGGESTED SEARCH TERMS

Sarah Dessen

Someone Like You AND Dessen

young-adult AND fiction

problem novel

bildungsroman

teen pregnancy AND novel

social programs for pregnant teens

suburbs

youth culture

Halley's comet

Unless

CAROL SHIELDS

2002

Written when Carol Shields was battling the breast cancer that would eventually take her life, *Unless* is the final novel of a productive and creative career. Described by critics as variously illuminating and angry, it tracks the emotional journey of Reta Winters, a middle-aged writer and mother trying to make sense of her daughter's withdrawal from the world into a mute campaign of self-declared goodness. As Reta struggles to understand her daughter Norah's decision, she also confronts her own deeply held values, her identity as a writer and mother, and the reality that women are too often confined to secondary positions in society, unseen and unheard in the records of history, politics, and art.

Unless was recognized with a number of prominent nominations, most notably for the Orange Prize for Fiction, the Man Booker Prize, and the Scotiabank Giller Prize, as well as being a finalist for the Governor General's Literary Award.

AUTHOR BIOGRAPHY

Carol Shields was born as Carol Warner on June 2, 1935, in Oak Park, Illinois. She was the youngest of three children of Robert and Inez Warner; her older siblings were twins named Barbara and Robert. Her mother was a schoolteacher, and

Carol Shields (© David Levenson | Hulton Archive | Getty Images)

her father, whom she later described as a remote and quiet man, worked in an office. Following graduation from Oak Park High School, she set off for Hanover College in Indiana, where she studied for two years. Receiving a United Nations Scholarship in 1955, she crossed the Atlantic to study English literature at Exeter University in England for two years. She returned to Hanover College in 1956 to complete her degree in history and education, graduating magna cum laude in 1957. She would later add a master of arts degree in English from the University of Ottawa in 1975.

Upon graduation, she married Don Shields, a Canadian engineer she had met during her stay in Exeter. The couple immediately relocated to Vancouver, British Columbia, where her new husband worked. Although Carol would not take full Canadian citizenship until 1971, the couple stayed in Canada, relocating to Toronto and Ottawa and back to Vancouver before settling in Winnipeg, Manitoba, in 1980. (Their Canadian travels were interrupted briefly by a three-year stay in Manchester, England, in the early 1960s.) The couple lived in Winnipeg for twenty years, before relocating to Victoria,

British Columbia, in 2000. They had five children: John Douglas (born in Toronto in 1958), Anne Elizabeth (Toronto, 1959), Catherine Mary (Manchester, 1962), Margaret Lorin (Toronto, 1964), and Sara Ellisyn (Ottawa, 1968). Shields was both an engaged mother and active academic, teaching English at the University of Manitoba (1982–2000) as well as serving as chancellor of the University of Winnipeg (1996–1999).

To call Shields a prolific writer would be an understatement. Working as a novelist, poet, and playwright, she produced a list of titles that spans decades and includes many literary forms. A list of her best-known titles includes *Small Ceremonies* (1976), *The Box Garden* (1977), *Happenstance* (1980), *A Fairly Conventional Woman* (1982), *Various Miracles* (1985), *Swann: A Mystery* (1987), *The Orange Fish* (1989), *The Republic of Love* (1992), *Coming to Canada* (1992), and *Thirteen Hands* (1993). Two of her most acclaimed books were published within five years of each other: *The Stone Diaries* (1993) and *Larry's Party* (1997). Shields was struggling with breast cancer when her final novel, *Unless*, was published in 2002.

Throughout her career, she won an impressive and eclectic catalogue of awards for her poetry, stories, and plays, including the Arthur Ellis Award for the Best Canadian Mystery of the Year for *Swann: A Mystery* (1988), France's Prix de Lire for *Larry's Party* (1998), and the Charles Taylor Prize for Literary Non-Fiction for *Jane Austen* (2002).

Much loved in her adopted country, Shields was awarded the Officer of the Order of Canada (1998) before being promoted to the Companion of the Order of Canada in 2002. Shields passed away on July 16, 2003, at the age of 68, after an extended battle with breast cancer.

PLOT SUMMARY

Here's

The opening chapter establishes a number of key elements in the novel: that it is a first-person narrative (that is, the narrator is a character in the story, speaking as "I") and that the narrator is "going through a period of great unhappiness and loss." It is June of 2000, in the rolling hills of Orangetown, a small town north of Toronto, Ontario, Canada. Reta, a writer, lists her writing

MEDIA ADAPTATIONS

- A dramatized audio version of *Unless* was produced by BTC Audio Books in 2006, adapted and partially performed by Susan Coyne.

- The novel was adapted for the stage by Shields and Sara Cassidy in 2005. Roy Surette directed the production of the play that ran at Vancouver's Belfry Theatre from October 25 though November 20, 2005.

- Harper Audio released an unabridged audio version of *Unless* in 2002, which was read by Joan Allen. The run time is 450 minutes.

- HarperCollins also released an abridged audio version in 2002, which was read by Lorelei King. The run time is 383 minutes.

successes as a kind of buffer against a still unnamed loss that has set her world reeling.

Reta's loss is gradually revealed in the story of her eldest daughter, Norah, who has suddenly dropped out of university to live in a hostel and spend her days sitting cross-legged on a busy Toronto street corner with a begging bowl and a cardboard sign with a single word printed on it: GOODNESS. She sits in perfect silence every day, collecting money that she, in turn, redistributes to the poor and needy around her. Reta and her family struggle deeply with Norah's withdrawal.

Nearly

It is August, and the family continues to struggle with the loss of Norah to her quest for goodness. Reta and her husband, Tom, enjoy a visit from an old friend, Colin Glass, a physicist whose wife, Marietta, left him only months earlier. He spends the evening trying to explain the theory of relativity to Reta, as though it might explain the loss that both are feeling at the moment, but Reta begins to see such attempts as merely diversions from the deeper and often unanswerable questions they are facing in their lives. Why did

Marietta become so unhappy in the marriage? What happened to Norah to cause such a dramatic life change?

Once

It is early September, and Reta begins a small publicity campaign in support of her most recent translation, this one a memoir of her close friend and mentor, the ardent feminist Danielle Westerman. The specter of Norah travels with Reta throughout each day, as do the comments of a local beautician, who has casually positioned Reta as a woman of early middle age. Reta takes this comment as a mark of her diminishing importance in the world and of her inevitable slide toward invisibility in society.

Meeting a young male journalist for an interview in a trendy cappuccino bar in Toronto, Reta politely endures his self-indulgent pretentiousness and total disregard for her work or, more broadly, for what he brushes aside as light literature.

Wherein

Early October arrives, and Reta begins her research into goodness in an attempt to understand her daughter's decision. In the process, she reconnects with Tessa and Cheryl, who are local librarians, family friends, and ardent book lovers. Tessa has alerted Reta and Tom as to Norah's condition some months earlier when she came across her during a trip to Toronto. It had been a difficult summer in the city, Reta recalls at this point, especially given that a young Muslim woman had set herself on fire in some form of protest. Reta finds herself feeling more isolated within her own town and increasingly dislocated from her sense of who she is and what her life represents.

Nevertheless

This chapter is dedicated to Reta's description of the house in which the family lives. Still known locally as the McGinn house, it was named after the first nonfarming family in the area. It is a house of deep history and rich with discoveries, including letters that Reta still discovers tucked away in various hiding places. Following Norah's dislocation from the family, cleaning the house and all such domestic chores have become a kind of emotional touchstone for Reta, who finds solace and a sense of control in the routine housework that her friend Danielle speaks out against as the bane of female existence.

Reta joins Tom at conference of enthusiasts of trilobites (prehistoric marine animals, now extinct but found as fossils), but she always struggles to engage in any recreation while the questions around Norah continue to swirl through her world.

So

This chapter begins with a flashback to nine-year-old Norah asking Reta why she and Tom have never married, which adds more background to their relationship and family. Part of this history includes Reta's weekly phone calls with her high-school friend Emma Allen, a medical journalist from Newfoundland, Canada, who offers advice on Norah. The chapter also includes a brief section on Tom's history and his fascination with trilobites and one in which Reta and her sixteen-year-old daughter, Christine, discuss the dangers of cigarettes.

Reta meets with several friends at the Orange Blossom Tea Room, and she reflects on how her own family is trying to maintain an appearance of normalcy as they struggle with Norah's situation.

Otherwise

Reta reflects on the surprising success of her light novel, *My Thyme Is Up* and how its success (winner of the Offenden Prize for accessible literature) was a double-edged sword: bringing her much popular attention and a generous sum of prize money, it also pigeonholed her as the writer of light (that is, not serious) literature. She remembers the publicity tour in support of the novel's success, which included some time shopping for the perfect scarf for Norah as well as an uncomfortable lunch with her friend Gwen (who has renamed herself Gwendolyn), who is struggling to find her voice as an aspiring poet.

Instead

Reta thinks about the undervalued role of women in literary history and how such writers as Thomas Hardy and Anton Chekhov are so often cited as influential while female writers such as Virginia Woolf and Iris Murdoch are overlooked. Reta goes on to celebrate the women who have influenced her life and writing: Danielle, Gwendolyn, her mother, and her own daughters. These reflections begin to guide the writing of her next novel, a planned sequel to *My Thyme Is Up* that is taking a much deeper and

darker tone, which reflects Reta's own concerns with Norah.

Thus

The Orange Blossom Tea Room group discusses the concept of goodness in an attempt to better understand Norah and the single-word sign that she wears every day while begging on the streets of Toronto. The conversation is wide ranging and includes consideration of action versus inaction, goodness as distinct from greatness, and, again, the possible connection with the young woman who had self-immolated (set herself on fire) the previous year. As the conversation unfolds, Reta drifts into thinking about her new novel and how it is important that she gives her main characters good friends as part of their stories.

Yet

Reta remembers Norah's first experience at McGill University in 1998 and her decision to transfer to the University of Toronto in order to be near a new boyfriend, Ben Abbot. Norah is unsettled, struggling deeply with her own sense of self and where she might fit into the world.

Insofar As

This chapter takes the form of a letter written by Reta to a company offering an extensive study-at-home program of the great ideas of Western civilization. Her tone is fierce, forward, and focused on one question: why does the faculty of this program include only one woman? Although not spoken directly, Reta is beginning to wonder if Norah's decision to withdraw from the world might not be a pre-emptive response to the invisibility and enforced silences that women are inevitably forced to endure. She signs this letter Reta Winters, The Hermitage, Orangetown.

Thereof

As Reta thinks about the personal history of the characters in her new novel; she also reflects on her own history with Tom, her childhood in a bilingual (French and English) home, and the more specific history of her love of gardening. She drills down even more specifically into the memories of her childhood friendship with Charlotte, who brought to Reta's world new and influential ideas of what constitutes goodness and obedience.

Every

Christine; her younger sister, Natalie; and Reta have a conversation about childbirth and the naming of children. Reta begins to wonder how her daughters will look back on these times and how they will remember their mother as a parent and mentor. She remembers, too, the sisters' account of their first visit to Norah on her street corner.

Regarding

In the form of a letter from Reta to Alexander Valkner from October 2000, this chapter expresses Reta's concern with his exclusion of women writers in his recent article, "The History of Dictionaries." Her letter concludes on a note that is at once political (women are confined to a position of complaint) and personal (her daughters face a future of invisibility). She signs this letter Renata Winters, The Orangery, Wychwood City.

Hence

While Reta continues to struggle with her understanding of Norah, the domestic routine continues with gardening, cooking, and mealtime chatter. One evening, dinner is interrupted by a telephone call from New York to inform Reta that her long-time editor, Mr. Scribano, has died.

Next

Reta recalls the history of her relationship with Mr. Scribano, whom she had met in person only twice. She realizes how little she actually knew about the man who had played such an important role in her professional life: "But I didn't know he was troubled," she admits, "that he lived alone, that he'd ever lectured in Italy, that he had sleep problems; I didn't even know how old he was, but I was told, and later I read it in his obituary." This question about how much she really knows the people around her has become central to Reta's daily routine.

Reta drives to Toronto to see Norah and to touch base with Danielle but finds little changed in either world.

Notwithstanding

It is mid-November, and Reta is surprised that life's routines (including her sex life with Tom) continue despite the fact that Norah is living on the streets of Toronto. She remembers meeting Tom for the first time and their dating stage, and

she debates with herself about her ability to capture the complexities of sex in her own writing.

Thereupon

Reta talks about the Promise Hotel in Toronto, the hostel in which Norah spends her nights now that she spends her days on the street corner. The family visits once, curious and wanting to ensure that Norah is being cared for as best as possible. Although the place is safe, clean, and imbued with a deep sense of peace and balance, the family bursts into tears upon their return to the car.

Despite

Reta continues to work on her next novel and awaits the assignment of her new editor.

Throughout

Reta recalls her visit with Norah's boyfriend, Ben Abbot, as part of her journey toward an understanding of Norah's decision. He is as confused as anyone, and he cries as he tries to share his story with Reta.

Following

Reta works on building the main characters of her new novel, Alicia and Roman, which is an increasingly complicated task as Reta continues to ask herself more and more questions about herself and the people she believes she knows well.

Hardly

Arthur Springer phones to introduce himself as Reta's new editor. He pushes her about her work in progress, while at the same time expressing his passion for her creation of Alicia.

Since

Various people in Reta's life chime in with ideas about how she should deal with Norah, from kidnapping to getting the police involved. Reta continues to explore Norah's life, learning that one of the social workers sees her as determined but sane and that she had argued with an English professor about whether a male author could imagine himself into a woman's life. Danielle is convinced that Norah has simply come to understand the powerlessness of women in contemporary society and does not know how to deal with it.

Only

This chapter takes the form of a letter written to Dennis Ford-Halpren, dated December 2000, in which Reta shares her impressions of his recent book *The Goodness Gap*. She is specifically frustrated at the absence of women in the book's index and in the discussion that is shaped in its pages. At the end of this letter, she signs herself Rita Orange d'Ville.

Unless

The title word for this chapter and novel is discussed in some detail, as is the presence of Danielle in Reta's life. As a mother struggling with the disappearance of the young woman she knew, Reta begins to question Danielle's feminist theories and the ideas that are captured in the books that fill the shelves of her apartment.

Toward

On a December morning, Tom and Reta visit the local cemetery in search of some balanced sense on how lives unfold over time and blend with each other in a kind of cosmic sense of home. Reta reflects on her relationship with Tom's mother, Lois, who likes her well enough but also feels that writing should be a woman's hobby that never intrudes on the role of wife and mother. The Glasses have reconciled after Marietta's fling, and Reta is nearing the end of writing her new novel, *Thyme in Bloom*, which she promises herself will unfold in ways that surprise everyone.

Whatever

It is Christmas week, and Arthur Springer phones Reta, determined to discuss her intentions for the second novel. He urges her to come to New York for a meeting, but when she hesitates, he agrees to fly to Toronto and drive north to spend time with her discussing the book.

Any

This chapter is a letter to Emily Helt, dated December 31, 2000, in which Reta challenges a reviewer of another writer's book (Susan Bright, *An Imperfect Affair*) for his diminishment of women's writing by using the term "miniaturist" and its implications of a lack of range and depth. She closes the letter with a personal commentary on the plight of her daughter before signing off with yet another variation of her name: Xeta d'Orange.

Whether

Reta continues to write the final chapters of her new novel, which has frozen into a pattern of procrastination for the main character, Alicia, whose relationship with Roman has stalled even as their much-anticipated wedding nears.

Ever

Natalie and Christine visit Norah weekly as Christmas approaches, trying to ensure that she has warm clothing and the necessary items for personal hygiene even though they are sure she gives everything to others in need at the first chance. Norah has now manifested a harsh rash on her hands and wrists, which worries her parents more and more. Tom reacts as a doctor might, diving passionately into developing a diagnosis for Norah's condition (eczema for the skin, trauma for the mind), while Reta manages her anxiety through work on the house and novel. Reta is increasingly angered by what she sees as the systemic silencing of women in contemporary culture, which she believes is at the root of Norah's decision to fall into silence voluntarily rather than being forced into silence over time and against her will and intellect.

Whence

In a letter to Peter Harding, dated January 10, 2001, Reta writes not to a man but in response to his obituary, which she read in a national newspaper. She is particular in pointing out how his favorite phrase ("entire universe") was defined by male writers, artists, and musicians. She is, in other words, rallying against the posthumous exclusion of females in any universe, even one imagined by a total stranger. She signs this letter, "I grieve for you too. Rita Hayworth. Orange Blossom City."

Forthwith

Arthur arrives for the promised discussion of the new novel. He is impressed by its size (it is over three hundred pages of manuscript) but is particularly interested in the path that Reta plans to take for the ending. The conversation soon begins to drift away from Reta's plan to some business decisions, including revising the book away from a popular audience to a literary one, changing the characters in order to disconnect it from the previous Offenden Prize–winning novel, and similar changes. Reta resists, determined to keep her book focused on the life and struggles of Alicia rather than making this yet another novel about a heroic male figure.

As

This chapter is the first one to begin where the preceding one left off, with Arthur and Reta still in conversation about the future of her novel. Three things happen simultaneously: Arthur knocks over a bottle of wine, Natalie and Christine arrive home, and Tom calls to inform the family that Norah has been taken to the hospital with pneumonia. While Reta and the girls drive to the hospital, Arthur makes himself comfortable in the Winters's home only to be interrupted by Lois bringing a meal for the family.

Beginning With

Lois and Arthur share dinner and conversation, during which Lois enters into a wandering history of her life, Tom and Reta, and the small town in which all reside.

Already

At the hospital with Norah, Tom points out to Reta that what he thought was a rash on her hands were actually second-degree burns. No one could know how Norah had gotten them, but doctors think that they had occurred at least six months earlier. As Tom, Christine, and Natalie sleep in the family room, Reta sits by Norah's bedside. She is there when Norah awakens.

Hitherto

This chapter is a letter to Russell Sandor, dated February 1, 2001, in which Reta launches a fierce attack on the writer for his depiction of a mastectomy bra in a recent story. She then goes on to tell her own story about Norah, who has not only witnessed the self-immolation of the young Muslim woman but also burnt her hands trying to save her. Her attempts proved futile, and Reta implies strongly that the experience of watching another woman burn to death (plus the reminders on her own hands) triggered her withdrawal into a silenced life of goodness. Reta signs this letter with her true name and address.

Not Yet

The final chapter brings all the threads of *Unless* together, with the story of Norah's attempts to save the woman from flames, to the coincidences that led Tom to discover her in the hospital after being taken from the hostel with pneumonia, to the remarkable literary success of *My Thyme Is Up*, and Reta's preliminary plans for the third book in the trilogy. Norah is recovering quietly at home, resting with the family dog.

CHARACTERS

Ben Abbot

Ben Abbot is Norah's boyfriend and a second-year philosophy student at the University of Toronto. Deeply in love with Norah, he is devastated by her decision, and he never understands, until near the end of the novel, why she made the decision to disappear into silence. His exchange of information with Reta in the chapter "Throughout" reveals the raw emotions associated with her disappearance and makes clear to Reta that she, even as a mother, cannot heal some of the emotional pains her daughter might have endured.

Emma Allen

Emma Allen is Reta's friend since high school, who now lives in Newfoundland. A medical journalist, she calls Reta weekly to talk about Norah.

Sally Bachelli

Sally Bachelli is Reta's friend and a regular member of the Tuesday morning sessions at the Orange Blossom Tea Room. A large woman who wears brightly colored clothes, she is a former actress who runs a local after-school drama group. She is also a mother of a son, the product of artificial insemination.

Charlotte

Charlotte is Reta's childhood friend from a Danish Canadian family who ran a sign-printing business in Toronto. A minor character, she is a symbol to Reta of both the power and plasticity of identity, as well as the struggle for women to find their place in a world dominated by strong and often aggressive men.

Colin Glass

Colin Glass is a physicist friend of Tom's who tries one evening to explain the theory of relativity to Reta. His wife recently left him for another man, claiming that Colin was too wrapped up in his research to engage fully with the real world or, more important, with a committed relationship. The two later reconcile, with

Colin disengaging from his work in order to reengage with his wife.

Marietta Glass
Marietta is Colin Glass's wife, who initially runs off with another man but later reconciles with Colin.

Annette Harris
Annette Harris is Reta's friend and a regular member of the Tuesday morning sessions at the Orange Blossom Tea Room. Jamaica born, she came to Orangetown from Toronto and is, according to Reta, the most beautiful woman in the group. She is a poet and economist, who divorced a violent husband and now works as an outsource employee for a technology company.

Lynn Kelly
Lynn Kelly is Reta's friend and a regular member of the Tuesday morning sessions at the Orange Blossom Tea Room. Originally from North Wales, Lynn is short and wiry, and she has a liking for department-store jewelry and pantsuits. She is a busy lawyer who finds time to balance her business with a family that includes two children.

Cheryl Patterson
Cheryl Patterson is an Orangetown librarian and family friend. She is divorced and in her mid-thirties.

Gwen Reidman
Gwen Reidman is a friend of Reta's. She is the leader of the workshop group known as the Glenmar Collective and of the small publishing venture Stepping Stone Press. She later renames herself Gwendolyn with the intention of marking a turn in her writing from the prosaic to the spiritual.

Tessa Sands
Tessa Sands is an Orangetown librarian and family friend of the Winterses. A woman in her fifties and former biologist before moving to library work, she is married to a classical guitarist and has an adolescent child.

Mr. Scribano
Mr. Scribano is Reta's longtime editor, who dies suddenly after a fall down some stairs. He comes into her life via Danielle, for whom he had been editing for years. Part of the deep linkages between Reta and her feminist mentor, Mr. Scribano also serves as a reminder to Reta that everyone she thinks she knows has some parts of their lives hidden out of view.

Arthur Springer
Arthur Springer is Reta's newly appointed editor following the death of Mr. Scribano. He is nearly a caricature of literary pretension and male manipulation of women's stories that runs as a persistent current throughout the novel. Caught up in his own views to the point of excluding the opinions of even Reta herself, he does, however, guide her second novel to the level of literary success that he promises. Springer is a double-sided character in Reta's life: she resists his overbearing opinions and attitudes, but she recognizes and uses to her benefit his skill as an editor and promoter.

Madame Sylvia
Madame Sylvia is the beautician that Reta visits, who makes comments about Reta's age that have a lingering impact.

Danielle Westerman
Danielle Westerman an eighty-five-year-old woman, a Holocaust survivor and a passionate, uncompromising feminist theorist who is an emotional and intellectual touchstone for Reta. They have been friends since meeting as professor and student at the University of Toronto. Danielle has lived her life with a deep commitment to the ideals that she holds as one of the world's preeminent feminist theorists. As the novel progresses, Danielle and Reta begin to drift apart as the tension between feminist theory (Danielle) and real-world implications for real women (Reta) becomes more and more evident.

Christine Winters
Christine Winters is the sixteen-year-old daughter of Reta and Tom. Intelligent, insightful, and strong-willed, she works to ensure normalcy in her life while remaining connected, spiritually and emotionally, to her sister Norah throughout her ordeal on the street.

Lois Winters
Lois Winters, born Lois Maxwell, is Tom's mother, Reta's mother-in-law. Widowed for twelve years, she spends a good deal of time with Reta's family and serves as part of the

network of women and female stories that interweave as a narrative backdrop to the tragedy that envelopes Norah.

Natalie Winters

Natalie Winters is the fifteen-year-old daughter of Reta and Tom. Athletic, creative, and with a maturity that allows her to recognize and fill awkward family silences, she works to ensure normalcy in her life while dealing with the emotional withdrawal of her sister.

Norah Winters

Norah Winters is the eldest daughter of Reta and Tom. Struggling early in her life with questions about how a woman might embrace and achieve greatness in a world dominated by men, she moves from a world of science (at McGill University) to a world of words (at the University of Toronto). In the process, she moves in with her boyfriend, Ben Abbot. In the wrong place at the wrong time, Norah is forced to bear witness to an act of self-immolation on the streets of Toronto. She reacts powerfully and in an act of great courage leaps to the woman's aid, trying to beat down the flames with her shopping bag. The plastic melts onto her hands, scarring her permanently and leaving her emotionally devastated by the event.

Scarred by her act of greatness, Norah retreats into a world of silence and goodness. Marking herself with a crudely built sign, she is resolutely determined to define her place outside the expectations and pressures of the mainstream world. After being taken to the hospital with pneumonia, she is reunited with her family and begins her return to the world.

Reta Winters

Reta Winters, born Reta Summers, is the middle-aged narrator of the novel and the mother of the lost child Norah. A successful writer, she has an impressive list of translations and original publications to her name but continues to struggle with the preconceptions of her work as being light or popular (as distinct from literary). Reta's anger builds throughout the novel as she comes to realize that Norah is responding, in part, to what Reta herself comes to recognize as the systematic erasure of women from the pages of history, literature, science, and politics.

Reta's struggle to understand Norah's decision is also a journey that tests her own belief about domestic life, feminism, motherhood, and writing. Her anger and her deep desire to save Norah drive Reta to develop a new ferocity in her writing and a new conviction in her voice. Her determination to keep her family together and to elevate her writing according to her vision is interlinked and, ultimately, successful.

Tom Winters

Tom Winters is Reta's common-law husband. Never officially married, they are devoted partners and parents. He is a doctor and a near-obsessive collector of trilobite fossils who displaces his own concern for Norah by understanding it in a diagnostic and scientific way, rather than in a creative and philosophical way.

THEMES

Goodness

From Shields's own perspective, goodness is "the main preoccupation" of *Unless*. "I've been interested in the idea of goodness for a number of years," she comments in the interview with Wachtel. "I certainly believe in it. I'm like those people who talk about modern art, and they say 'I don't understand it but I know it when I see it.'" Reta shows this perspective, suggesting that "goodness is respect that has been rarefied and taken to a higher level. It has emptied itself of vengeance." Reviewing *Unless* for *Quill & Quire*, John Burns points to another important question looming in Shields's novel: "Is there a female goodness, distinct from the male desire for greatness?" Shields's own comments bear out this distinction; she notes in the interview with Wachtel that the "idea of goodness" is often connected in a female world with the idea of

> trying to make people happy, of doing things for people that we love, trying to make them happy. But getting what we want requires being able to articulate that sentence, "I want"— what? Women have not been able to make those kinds of demands on society. What women tend to say is, "This is good for the family," "This is good for all of us."

What Shields set out to explore in *Unless* is a sense of female goodness that is, in many ways, forbidden: "the very idea of the [female] 'I' wanting." Shields reflects,

TOPICS FOR FURTHER STUDY

- *Unless* begins with an epigraph (introductory quotation) from the female British novelist George Eliot: "If we had a keen vision and feeling of all ordinary life, it would be like hearing the grass grow and the squirrel's heart beat, and we should die of that roar which lies on the other side of silence." Shields herself is a fan of epigraphs. In an interview with Eleanor Wachtel quoted in *Random Illuminations: Conversations with Carol Shields*, Shields says: "When I read novels, I always read the epigraphs because I can feel the novelist telling me, This is the way I want to go, so I read them with this idea in mind." Write a thoughtful and well-structured essay in which you unravel the relevance of the epigraph by Eliot to the various stories that weave together throughout this novel.

- Reta is a prolific and, at times, aggressive letter writer. Some letters she actually writes and sends; others she only imagines and keeps to herself. Taking a particularly creative twist on this long tradition of letter writing, fellow Canadian Nick Bantock's *Griffin and Sabine* (1991) imagines a very special correspondence between Griffin Moss, an artist living in London, and Sabine Strohen, a woman he has never met. Create a Bantock-like correspondence (using both art and words) as you might imagine it to unfold between Reta and Norah or between Norah and the unnamed young women who self-immolates in the streets of Toronto. Post your correspondence on a blog and allow your classmates to comment on it.

- Shields, like many writers, sees the process of writing as a process of building or making, as you would a house or do-it-yourself project. Part of the novel-making process is a series of important decisions that a writer has to make about the major characters—imagining their jobs, their names, their ages, where they live, and many other details about their lives. "You'd think this could all be a wonderful fantasy," Shields comments in the interview with Wachtel, "where you're in charge of the world, but in fact some of this is hard work." Options continue to accumulate as a writer delves deeper into building a character. Take on the task of building a character for either a novel or a video game. Put the name of the character in the center of a piece of paper or poster board and create a series of lines radiating out to clusters of information that form the building blocks for this character. One cluster might be about the character's job, for instance, and another about her living arrangement. You might have clusters, too, about family history, dreams and aspirations, wardrobe, or whatever else you feel is important to let a reader or viewer understand the character as completely as possible.

- In the interview with Wachtel, Shields comments: "There is a way in which every novel is about finding this place we call home... the place you've been assigned to but somehow haven't got to." Write a thoughtful and well-structured essay in which you explore this idea of searching for home as it unfolds throughout this novel. Read Julie Berry's *All the Truth That's in Me* (2013), a novel that explores the struggles of another young woman, named Judith, who is forced into isolation and silence by a brutal mutilation. Write a thoughtful and well-structured essay in which you compare or contrast the silences of Judith and Norah. How does each silence relate to a political or social event? Does each silence become a political statement?

I think, sometimes, that we think of goodness as doing nothing. The idea of "do no harm," "make no enemies," "don't defile the planet"—it's become an act of standing still and doing nothing. And this is the path that Norah... takes. She doesn't know how to be great, and she's not allowed to be great, but she can be good; that is, she can do no harm.

In this sense, goodness is clearly distinct from the action-based exercise of greatness, a point that is not lost on Reta as she comes to grips with Norah's decision. One of Reta's letters reads in part:

> Norah took up the banner of goodness—goodness not greatness. Perhaps because there was no other way she could register her existence. In the obscuring distance, melting into sunsets and handsome limestone buildings and asphalt streets and traffic lights, the tiny piping voice of goodness goes almost unheard.

Margaret Steffler, in an article in *Studies in Canadian Literature*, argues that *Unless* "foregrounds 'goodness' over 'greatness' in a desire for a world that is based on connection and community rather than competition and individual heroism." This is an optimistic stance, Steffler suggests; the fact that the "phenomenon of goodness...does not simply disappear in the face of greatness but continues to make its presence known, proves its resilience."

Motherhood

"It's an old truth but a good one," *Chicago Tribune* reviewer Ellen Emery Heltzel notes. "Nothing radicalizes a mother as much as harm to her child. And when the cause of the harm is unknown, the anger and anxiety is free-floating." When Reta's oldest daughter, Norah, drops out of college suddenly in order to spend her days begging silently on a busy Toronto street corner, long-held beliefs in motherhood, domestic stability, and parental responsibilities are brought into a harsh light. As Margaret Gunning (*January Magazine*) notes, *Unless*, at one level, is very much a novel "about a mother's anguish, her concerted attempts to make some kind of sense" of her daughter's sudden and dramatic withdrawal from the world, as well as "the fracturing effect on a whole family as they try to cope, groping towards each other for comfort yet often retreating into numbing distraction."

Reta's reaction is fascinating in its double-sidedness. From one side, the angry Reta emerges to rally passionately against the erasure of women's voices and influence from contemporary society (what she calls often the invisibility of women). Her challenges to male reviewers, authors, and editors are a powerful blend of the academic and the personal, often beginning with classic argumentation before

Reta's daughter, Norah, has decided to leave school and her family and live on the streets.
(© DreamBig | Shutterstock.com)

folding into a personal reflection on the lives (and futures) of her three daughters.

The other side is that of the domestic Reta, the mother who finds spiritual solace in cleaning, organizing, and preparing family meals. While many second-wave feminists saw housework and domestic duties purely as disadvantages for women, Reta marks a new, non-exclusive position that says, effectively, that while women can be imprisoned by domestic expectations forced upon them by a patriarchal structure, women as individuals are also free to engage domesticity on their own terms.

Middle-Class Values

Unless can also be read as a satiric probe of middle-class values and especially of those values that allow those who belong to the middle class to fall into a pattern of complacency and even detachment from the world through a sense of moral, intellectual, and aesthetic distance from the struggles facing millions of people in all corners of the world. The Orange Blossom Tea Room community, for instance, can articulate a certain level of moral indignation at what is happening to women in Nigeria or flood victims in Mozambique, but they remain unable (or unwilling) to understand the differences between a nationality such as Saudi and a religious affiliation such as Muslim or between a chador and a burka, even when a young woman self-immolates in the streets of Toronto. Their indignation is brief and self-rewarding, whereas the truly engaged actions of Norah are seen as foreign to the point of bordering on the pathological.

STYLE

Allusion

Allusion is a figure of speech in which a writer refers directly or indirectly to an object (such as another work of literature or art) or circumstance from an external context—simply put, a reference to something else. It is left to the audience to make the connection and to unfold the echoes of the allusion across a reading of the work itself. Without a reader's recognition of the possible layers of meaning brought to play through an allusion, it becomes merely a decorative device or ornament. When understood more fully, it becomes an effective tool to draw upon a commonly understood catalogue of ideas, cultural layerings, or emotional payload already associated with a topic. Some allusions, especially obscure ones, can also serve as markers of cultural literacy and bring with them a sense of social currency.

Unless abounds with allusions. Some of these connect directly to Shields's themes. Her reference to Arthur Miller's stage play *Death of a Salesman* (1949), for instance, aligns Reta's story with a classic tale of the death of a middle-class dream and the promise that such a dream brings to those who believe in it. Other allusions, such as those to French literary theorist Jacques Derrida, are more indirect and obscure; they serve, at one level, to underscore the gap that Reta comes to recognize between theories of feminism and the real-world events and reactions that

shape the expression of that struggle (from self-immolation to a vow of silence).

First-Person Narration

Unless is a rarity within Shields's body of work as a novelist in that it is written from the first-person point of view. Reta explicitly refers to herself as "I" beginning with the first sentence: "It happens that I am going through a period of great unhappiness and loss." This perspective allows the reader to see her opinions, thoughts, and feelings, but not those of any other characters, including Norah. The novel often tends to present a stream of consciousness in combination with an interior monologue, both of which are classic first-person techniques. Unlike in some novels that use the first-person technique to show an unreliable narrator (forcing the reader to resist entering the narrator's world fully), Reta's reliability is never in question. There is little doubt that the events happened as she describes them or that her sense of loss is as deeply felt as she suggests. In this case, the first-person strategy is used to develop emotional depth and complexity.

Structure and Chapter Titles

Unless is structured around chapter titles that are built from what Reta calls "little chips of grammar (mostly adverbs or prepositions) that are hard to define, since they are abstractions of location or relative position." Each of the book's chapters mimics the themes of the novel itself through the use of words and phrases (like Norah's act of goodness) that are difficult to make sense of when stripped away from the context of a broader narrative. These words effectively force the reader to think beyond the pages of the novel and to reflect upon the social and cultural contexts that come to define goodness or greatness or that place unbearable pressures upon young women. Reta comments:

> Unless you're lucky, unless you're healthy, fertile, unless you're loved and fed, unless you're clear about your sexual direction, unless you're offered what others are offered, you go down in the darkness, down to despair. *Unless* provides you with a trapdoor, a tunnel into the light, the reverse side of not enough. *Unless* keeps you from drowning in the presiding arrangements.

As Shields notes: "I love these words. They're words that grammarians and lexicographers have trouble with, defining exactly these little chips of language that we use, which really situate us in a more-or-less particular position. And I find them resonant, I find them poetic and full of echoes, so I liked using them as chapter heads." According to Shields, such words "situate [readers] in space" and "in a narrative" in complex ways with the worlds inside and outside the novel.

HISTORICAL CONTEXT

Canada in the early years of the twenty-first century was experiencing a marked transition in social and political awareness around issues of race, sexual orientation, and gender politics. Early in 2000, prominent Canadian television journalist Avery Haines had been caught on tape flubbing a line and then joking about it in terms that harkened to an era of much less tolerant social attitudes. Canadian viewers found the comments offensive and made their feelings known loudly. Bookending this event was the death and state burial of former prime minister Pierre Elliott Trudeau in September 2000, which marked the symbolic close of a generation of activism within the country that included an emphasis on multiculturalism, multilingualism, and an openness to progressive economic and cultural ideas.

The events of September 11, 2001, underscored to Canadians, as to citizens of most countries, that chaos, unpredictability, and vulnerability would become commonplace words and feelings as the world spiraled into yet another cycle of violence and terrorism. Any sense that Canadians might have held about being isolated from many world events vanished in the days following the bombing of the New York towers. Whether the result of human error (as in the contamination of water supplies in Walkerton, Ontario, and North Battleford, Saskatchewan) or the horrific realities of human degradation (the arrest of Robert William Pickton, Canada's most notorious serial killer), Canadians were buffeted by example after example of the random forces that might affect lives at any given moment.

The unsettling new reality escalated as Canadian troops joined those of other nations in Afghanistan later in 2001, and anxiety was further deepened by a series of international events that included the much-publicized murder of kidnapped *Wall Street Journal* reporter Daniel Pearl in Karachi, Pakistan; the horrific Godhra train burning, which saw fifty-nine Hindu pilgrims die aboard a train set ablaze by Muslim extremists (another hundred and fifty people would die in subsequent massacres in the region); the terrorist bombing of two nightclubs on the seemingly idyllic island of Bali; and the killing of one hundred in Nigeria during an attack aimed at the Miss World contestants, to name but a few. Seemingly overnight, the world became a place of previously unimagined threats and harsh realities, and Canadians struggled both individually and collectively to adjust.

Reta comes to feel some of the emotional repercussions of this new reality when Norah makes an unpredictable decision in response to witnessing an act of random chaos and violence in the relatively safe streets of Toronto. What she believes to be true about the world begins to fray dramatically as the months pass and Norah seems determined to continue her campaign of goodness. In a world increasingly dominated by stories of violence and destruction, Norah's decision resonates deeply.

The fictional representation of a quiet presence of a young woman sitting silently on a street corner in the largest city in Canada also resonated with advocates of third-wave feminism, who focused, in part, on conscious-raising activism as critical to confront issues that limit or oppress women as well as other marginalized communities. Beginning in the mid-1990s, this third wave was informed by a hybrid of postcolonial and postmodern thought that challenged many traditional notions of female identity, constructions of domesticity, and sexuality. Reta's embracing of housework as spiritually reinvigorating, for instance, would mystify second-wave feminists, who saw housework as a form of oppressive slavery perpetuated by patriarchal cultures. Reta's unspoken response to such assumptions is almost typically third wave. She seems to live by the motto that it is possible to have a clean kitchen, engaged brain, and feminist voice at the same time.

COMPARE & CONTRAST

- **2002:** Given that the mystery behind Norah's decision to withdraw from the world hinges on a security camera videotape that captured Norah's futile and traumatic attempts to extinguish the flames consuming a young woman on the streets of Toronto, technology plays a key role in *Unless*. Although Reta and Tom had heard about the self-immolation on the news, only when they discover the videotape do they realize the connection between that incident and the year that Norah spends on the street. In this sense, Reta's struggle is created by the lapse in technology or in its inability to translate into the world quickly.

  Today: The proliferation of cell phones (augmented with video and photographic technology) makes it likely that Norah's involvement in the traumatic event would have been broadcast immediately and often on both traditional news channels and via social media. It is unlikely, in other words, that Reta and Tom could have remained unaware of the cause of their daughter's trauma, and the story of Reta's struggle would change dramatically.

- **2002:** Every major city has a number of much-loved landmarks, and Honest Ed's discount store is one in the city of Toronto. This store was the last place Norah visited before she came across a young woman self-immolating on a busy street corner. Its proprietor, the flamboyant Ed Mirvish, opened the store in 1948 and oversaw its operations for almost sixty years, until his death in 2007. In 2002, the store is a vibrant business and cultural icon, so it makes perfect sense for Norah to go there for her shopping. As Toronto's prominence as a location for film, television, and music video productions increases, Honest Ed's becomes a familiar shooting location. It can be seen,

  for instance, in the 1996 film *The Long Kiss Goodnight* as well as in the 2010 cult favorite *Scott Pilgrim vs. the World*.

  Today: Many North American cities see large box stores and suburban shopping malls changing the personality of long-established downtown neighborhoods. The property on which Honest Ed's has stood since 1948 is sold in 2013, and the demolition of this iconic city building is under way, with plans for a condominium complex to stand in its place.

- **2002:** This novel, which is set in 2000 but written in 2002, frames the terrorist attacks of September 11, 2001, on New York City and Washington, DC. Shields's decision to have a young woman of Middle Eastern descent self-immolate in the middle of a large North American city is compelling. On the one hand, the decision aligns with Shields's focus in the novel on the fate of women in a world that is increasingly dominated by male politics and acts of aggression. On the other hand, the fact that Reta and her friends are wholly naïve about the differences between the religions, dress, languages, and defining features of people from a very diverse part of the world underscores the pervasive lack of knowledge that many North Americans had of the Middle East at the time.

  Today: Although it is debatable whether the average North American has a clearer understanding of the politics and cultures of the Middle East, the realities of the post-9/11 world have become part of familiar routines. Airport inspections, political debates over the often-named fight on terror, and heightened security around major sporting and cultural events are commonplace.

Through writing, Reta is able to better process her grief. *(© Olesya Feketa | Shutterstock.com)*

CRITICAL OVERVIEW

Heltzel opens her review of *Unless* for the *Chicago Tribune* with a particularly important point: this novel is, on one level, a familiar place for readers of Carol Shields's novels. The protagonist, Reta Winters, is "as familiar as a friend," exemplifying "the type of recognizable female character who Shields has made her specialty." She is a woman still learning to "navigate the choppy waters of marriage, motherhood, and the search for her own identity." Catherine Lockerbie, writing in the *New York Times*, expresses a similar point, calling *Unless* "classic Carol Shields" in its creation of lives that are "lovingly delineated, shot through with recognizable reality." Lockerbie goes on to suggest that the writing in this novel "is perhaps better than ever, pellucid and knowing, as naturally paced as breathing itself, yet with images so apt they pounce off the page." She takes particular notice of the tone of the novel, which she describes as "measured, calm, now wondering and wounded, now overlaid with a light and

exquisite irony. Lives may have been cracked asunder, but wry comedy leavens the tale."

That said, both reviewers also see exquisiteness in the familiar. Heltzel concludes that *Unless* is a rewarding and "an illuminating novel," while Lockerbie concludes that "readers will encounter great poignancy and great wisdom" in the pages of a story that is, in the end, about "hope, grace and redeeming life." Margaret Gunning, writing in *January Magazine*, is equally effusive with her praise, calling it a novel that "brims with all that is human, the hell-bent good intentions, the brokenness, the stumbling imperfection, and the gallant struggle towards anything even resembling the light."

Coral Ann Howell (reviewing *Unless* for *Canadian Literature*) also comments on this sense of the familiar, but she argues that Shields breaks from previous works in that she "dares (for once) to express her anger at women's condition." She does so through developing a narrative that is "strongly retrospective and evaluative, although it is also engaged with the 'precious and precarious' issues of ordinary domestic life and with wider issues of feminist politics." Shields seems pointedly angry, Shelagh Rogers for CBC Radio notes, "that as a woman approaches her fifties she becomes invisible to society." Blake Morrison of the *Guardian* expresses a similar view, labeling *Unless* Shields's "angriest book to date—a study in awakening and the belated loss of innocence."

While appreciating the "assured intelligence and defiant vivacity" of Shields's vision, David Kipen, in a review for *Manoa*, is concerned with the "questionable cohesiveness" of what he sees as three stories running parallel within a relatively short novel. "Its stories and themes cross and recross without ever quite braiding" Kipen notes, "leaving an impression of unforced naturalness that becomes lifelike almost to a fault." Steffler notes that "the emotions conveyed by the novel are controlled and almost detached."

Shelagh Rogers for CBC Radio suggests, though, that "deceptively simple was a Shields trademark. Despite their light touch, her novels are complex, slyly nuanced and far more substantial than they are often given credit for." Lockerbie goes further still, noting:

> All novelists worth their fictional salt can create fine characters; Carol Shields creates lives. Held weightlessly in her quiet, gently ironic words, [readers] gain privileged access not merely to actions and aspirations but to recipes, coiffures, the consolations of cleaning. We are granted knowledge of small habits as well as serious hopes.

Unless was recognized with a number of prominent awards and nominations in the 2002–2003 literary awards seasons, most notably for the Orange Prize for Fiction, the Man Booker Prize, and the Scotiabank Giller Prize, as well as being a finalist for the Governor General's Literary Award. The novel won the BC Book's Ethel Wilson Fiction Prize (2003), and was nominated for the Commonwealth Writers Prize for Best Book.

CRITICISM

Klay Dyer

Dyer is a freelance writer and editor specializing in commentaries on literature, popular culture, and innovation. In the following essay, he examines

> THIS IS A NOVEL, THEN, THAT UNCOVERS LAYER BY LAYER TWO DISTINCT BUT MUTUALLY REFLECTIVE MODELS OF WRITING AND READING STABILITY INTO A WORLD DEFINED BY CHANGE, VULNERABILITY, AND SILENCE."

the protagonist of Unless, *Reta Winters, as a catalyst of change in a world stuck in static, conventional notions of womanhood, domesticity, and creativity.*

As the writer and mother Reta Winters struggles to make sense of a radicalized and changing world in Carol Shields's final novel, *Unless*, she admits that part of what she is doing is learning to read the world again. She is trying, as she notes, to understand both a real world and writing culture that is changing dramatically, punctuated as it is with contradictions, counter-positions, and wholly unexpected (and undefinable) moments of unpredictability. It is an archaeology, too, that poses stubborn challenges for even the most sophisticated reader and, in Reta's case, for a writer seeking to redefine her own voice during a time of personal turmoil.

In "Art Is Making," an onstage interview with Eleanor Wachtel conducted at the Humber School for Writers (Toronto) in 1998, Shields candidly shared her thoughts on a chronic perplexity confronting writers: the nature of creativity and the mystery of capturing it in words or drawings. "I always think that everyone is creative in one way or another," she began, "I've never quite mastered this great dialogue about what is art and what is craft. I honestly think that to make a wonderful meal, for example, or to grow a fine lawn is a creative act that sustains us. Even the ability to tell a good story over the dinner table is a creative act; it gives pleasure to others and to ourselves."

Not surprisingly, *Unless*, which was written as Shields battled cancer, is a novel through which, according to Howell, "runs the energizing narrative self-consciousness of a woman writer for whom writing means survival."

WHAT DO I READ NEXT?

- Gayle Forman's young-adult novel *If I Stay* (2009) follows seventeen-year-old Mia Hall, who finds herself trapped in a coma following a catastrophic car accident involving her family. Experiencing a profound out-of-body experience, Mia watches and listens as friends and family gather at the hospital where she is being treated. She also experiences memories that lead her to understand that she has a decision to make: wake up and lead a life far more difficult than she ever anticipated, or slip away and die.

- Shields's *The Stone Diaries* (1993) was one of her most celebrated works, winning the Pulitzer Prize for Fiction in 1995. The novel also won Canada's Governor General's Literary Award (1993) in Canada, as well as the American Book Critics' Circle Award (1994), the McNally Robinson Award for Manitoba Book of the Year (1995), and the Canadian Booksellers Association Prize (1995). A subtle and multilayered novel, it recounts the life and spiritual growth of its protagonist, Daisy Goodwill Flett, as told from the perspectives of multiple narrators and a variety of letter writers.

- Also by Shields, *Larry's Party* (1997) is probably her most experimental, and in many ways rewarding, novel. Focusing on a character whose life is defined by a growing obsession with mazes, she builds an intricately connected sequence of fifteen chapters, each dedicated to a particular period in Larry's life and each flashing backward and forward in time with dizzying but totally controlled quickness.

- Malala Yousafzai's *I Am Malala: The Girl Who Stood Up for Education and Was Shot by the Taliban* (2013) recounts the true story of a young Pakistani girl who was shot by a Taliban assassin as she fought for her right to go to school and learn.

- Cal Armistead's young-adult novel *Being Henry David* (2014) is a compelling story of seventeen-year-old Hank, who finds himself at Penn Station in New York with no memory of who he is or where he came from. His only possession is a very well-worn copy of Henry David Thoreau's 1845 classic memoir *Walden*. Hank heads out to Thoreau's famous pond, entering into a journey that forces him to face memories of his own past.

- Peter Rossi's *Down and Out in America: The Origins of Homelessness* (1991), while somewhat dated, remains one of the best written and most thoroughly readable histories of homelessness available. Contrasting the homelessness of contemporary times with that of the 1950s and 1960s, it reveals some startling truths about the historical situations facing women, children, and people of various ethnic backgrounds in modern America.

Although Shields admits in a 2002 interview with Wachtel to being somewhat hesitant about the limitations confronting a writer writing about another writer, she was definitely motivated at this point in her life and career to confront the challenge. "When it came right down to it," she states, "I had this novel to write, and I wanted to write about what was terribly interesting to me, and that was writing a novel: how you write a novel, how you *make* a novel."

Just as Reta finds that the writing of *My Thyme Is Up* is crucial to her own understanding of the shifting textures of the archaeology of her own life, Shields finds the related exercises of writing and reading novels to be fundamental to living an engaged and balanced life. In the 2002 interview with Wachtel, Shields offers the rhetorical question "Why do we read novels?" She posits aloud: "What do they do for us?" Her answer is intriguing:

> For me, they allow me into other consciousnesses. I can go where other people think and escape for a minute this voice in my head.... Novels give us access to the thought processes as well as the thoughts of other people, and I think that's a kind of contract that we need and maybe don't have enough of in our regular conversations. We have to have this other layer that connects us more deeply.

For at least one critic, this dual focus on reading and writing (and more specifically on women's reading and writing) is part of the novel's strong feminist politic. Fiona Tolan suggests that Shields's exploration of Reta's struggle "begins to tentatively but cumulatively construct a grand narrative of female displacement, making spiralling connections between housework, women's work, and women's writing." Reta is initially surprised at the questions she faces about being a woman who writes, but soon braces herself to grudgingly answer questions about how she finds the time to write, "what with Tom and the three girls, and the house and garden and meals" to think about.

It is not surprising that one of Reta's own rules of novel making is that her characters work. "I passionately believe a novelist must give her characters work to do," she states. "Fictional men and women tend, in my view, to collapse unless they're observed doing their work, *engaged* with their work, the architect seen in a state of concentration at the drafting table, the dancer thinking each step as it's performed, the computer programmer tracing a path between information and access." And as a writer, wife, and mother, Reta is the first to acknowledge: "I love work."

But even as she comes to find her own balance between the domestic and the creative spheres, Reta is increasingly aware of the inequalities within her own literary workplace. When her first novel is dismissed casually as light, comic writing, Reta begins to draw some deeply felt conclusions linking such criticism with a systemic cultural pressure against female voices and female creativity. Tolan suggests that Reta, "newly cognisant of the enormity of gendered social inequality ... suffers a crisis of confidence in literature." Given that "writing and home represent the good in Reta's life ... this crisis of faith ... replicates in some ways her

fear that the domestic space to which she is committed may be a contributory part of Norah's breakdown."

Archaeological residues begin to overlap and mingle as Reta's anger grows at the symbolic implications of Norah's self-chosen silence. Although Norah's hand-crafted sign and haggard appearance draw attention to her as both part of and removed from the world in which her mother lives and writes, Norah remains silent, announcing through her muteness her sisterhood with the young woman who set herself afire on the same street corner. But, as Reta understands, the layers of silence that have accumulated at this particular corner are much deeper than Norah realizes. Reta realizes that Norah is

> so brimming with goodness that she sits on a Toronto street corner, which has its own textual archaeology.... She sits beneath the lamppost where the poet Ed Lewinski hanged himself in 1955 and where Margherita Tolles burst out of the subway exit into the sunshine of her adopted country and decided to write a great play.

This is a novel, then, that uncovers layer by layer two distinct but mutually reflective models of writing and reading stability into a world defined by change, vulnerability, and silence. At one side of the archaeological site is Reta's friend and mentor, Danielle Westerman, who has passionately rejected domesticity and convention in favor of her theorized resistance, recognition, and life's work. At the other side of the dig is Reta, who blends her imagined version of the homemaker who once lived in the family farmhouse with a fierce feminism that expunges many of artifacts of first- and second-wave feminism that figure prominently in the ideas and politics of her mentor. Reta does not have to be wife *or* feminist; she can be both. She does not have to choose between family meals and first drafts but can embrace the challenges (and celebrate the rewards) of both if she so wishes.

As Margaret Gunning observes "the best novelists don't solve or resolve anything, but force us to sit with the contradictions." Ultimately, one might argue, the force of Reta's writing, and by extension of Shields's writing, lies in her willingness to sit, albeit uneasily, with these contradictions, and to find new ways to bring them together creatively and personally. From the shifting personae of the letters, to her impatience with old friends and static opinions,

Nora's life in Toronto is contrasted with Reta's life in their small hometown an hour outside the city.
(© Domenic Gareri | Shutterstock.com)

to her open challenges to the assumptions of her new editor, Reta emerges from her trials a more passionate mother, a more successful writer, and a more confident woman. (In a turn of playful naming, Springer—his name also referencing a season—seems destined to be positioned between two versions of Reta: Reta Summers, the idealistic young feminist, and Reta Winters, the emerging third-wave feminist and critically acclaimed novelist.)

Stepping back even further, it is this willingness, too, that might provide another answer to the lingering question: why novels in an age when archaeology has gone digital, wireless, and real-time? Shields herself might put it best, in the 2002 interview with Wachtel:

> There's a life outside the novel; there has been all the way through the novel. There's life outside the novel, in the beginning and in the trajectory of the novel, and the novel goes on afterwards. . . . So it's just an arbitrary moment, I think, that the novelist chooses to bring things to a conclusion, and it sounds as though every little strand has been put in this tidy knot. But, in fact, we know better. Anyone who lives an

ordinary life knows better, because those knots aren't going to stay done for more than two minutes, and they're soon changing shape and asking for more attention.

Archaeology, like memory and storytelling, is always a negotiation between stability (the already found and known) and the possibility of disruption (the still to be found). Not only do object and events change over time, but the process of excavation itself inevitably disturbs (and even destroys) the evidence used to build the interpretative text from which stories emerge and form. As Carol Shields shows readers in *Unless*, understanding the work necessary to keep track of the pieces as they are uncovered, recovered, and discovered is all part of a good day's work.

Or as Reta acknowledges, as she plans the third book in her trilogy while monitoring her daughter's recovery, "There you have it: stillness and power, sadness and resignation, contradictions and irrationality. Almost you might say, the materials of a serious book."

> A QUIET REVOLUTION TAKES PLACE IN THE COURSE OF SHIELDS'S OEUVRE AS SHE SUBVERTS TRADITIONAL GENDER DIFFERENCE BY PRESENTING AN EMPHATICALLY MALE-CENTRED DOMESTIC FICTION."

Source: Klay Dyer, Critical Essay on *Unless*, in *Novels for Students*, Gale, Cengage Learning, 2016.

Ellen McWilliams

In the following excerpt, McWilliams ties together the themes of masculinity and domesticity in Shields's work.

In an essay on her own creative process, "Arriving Late: Starting Over," on file in the Carol Shields Archive at the National Library of Canada, Carol Shields makes a lively defence of literary engagements with domesticity and recalls her sense of puzzlement at the sidelining of domestic life in fiction:

> Why had domesticity, the shaggy beast that eats up ninety per cent of our lives, been shoved aside by fiction writers? Because it was too dull? Too insignificant? Too flattened out, too obvious? The inclusion of domestic detail seemed much more to me than just an extra suitcase taken on board to use up my weight allowance. Diurnal surfaces could be observed by a fiction writer with a kind of deliberate squint, a squint that distorts but also sharpens beyond ordinary vision, bringing forward what might be called the subjunctive mode of one's self or others, a world of dreams and possibilities and parallel realities.

The domestic is, then, imbued with visionary potential in Shields's work as her characters, more specifically her male characters, come to identify with an idea of home and domestic endeavour in new and fruitful ways. If, for Virginia Woolf, the Angel in the House needed to be killed off in order for a woman to write, Carol Shields seems more interested in bridging the traditional chasm between domesticity and art for the benefit of the male artist. Her novels develop a paradigm of masculinity that upsets traditional gender boundaries and, in the process, fashions a new model of male artist, one that finds a room of his own within the domestic

sphere. Thus, as a woman writer whose fictional oeuvre shows a distinct commitment to writing masculinity, Shields takes an especially sympathetic view of the male artist at work, and her reconciliation of masculinity and domesticity is a source of enrichment for the men that inhabit her fiction.

Through a renegotiation of the gender discourses that elide or overlook the possibility of positive male engagement with domestic ritual, Shields presents an affirmative view of the possibilities of domestic craft forms for male creativity. Men in Shields's fiction, whether in their working or writing lives, discover that reconnection with the rituals and traditions of the home can be both a source of inspiration and a personal refuge. Whether in sewing, weaving, or gardening, they discover an unexpected talent for, and come to identify with, the art of homemaking in new and unexpected ways. Thus, her novels present the artist as engaged in the tangible world of domestic life and work rather than removed from it. I will focus mainly on two of Shields's novels in which the male artist finds an outlet for his creative endeavours firmly within his domestic environs, *Small Ceremonies* (1976) and *Larry's Party* (1997), but will also consider how Shields's other male characters benefit from a positive reconsideration of the value of domestic work and domestic craft forms, as is the case in *Happenstance* (1991).

Shields's representation of creativity actively destabilizes the artist-as-hero archetype associated with the male tradition of the artist in literature. In her critique of the masculine "portrait of the artist" paradigm in *A Portrait of the Artist as a Young Woman*, Linda Huf asserts that the model of the male artist propounded by critics such as Maurice Beebe in his seminal study, *Ivory Towers and Sacred Founts: The Artist as Hero in Fiction from Goethe to Joyce*, is presented as universal and provides no allowance for female difference. Beebe imagines the artist as necessarily set apart from and defining himself against the society in which he lives and for this reason, according to Beebe, the artist-as-hero inevitably becomes the artist-as-exile. Huf's response calls for a new critical direction in reading the woman artist in literature, one that acknowledges the vastly different coordinates resonant with the experience of the woman writer and artist, and she establishes an argument that, by necessity, directly confronts the male-centred narrative.

Carol Shields's fiction tests the limits of this dialogue as her work poses a challenge to the discourse of the male artist in literature and upsets the oppositionalism evident in such critical debate; there is a deliberate irony in the way that she assigns traditionally female domestic roles to her male artists as they come to place a new value on the private sphere. More than this, they come to conceive of art as inclusive and present in unexpected quarters. She firmly locates artistic inspiration within the domestic sphere and reclaims domesticity as a source and site of creativity for men as well as for women. Men in Shields's novels are most productive and successful in their artistic endeavour when they embark on occupations or projects that have strong links to domesticity and the home. Male characters who seek acclaim through more publicly recognized channels, such as academia or through literary celebrity, are often left disappointed and envious of those who discover inspiration in more private and seemingly unassuming pursuits.

Shields's successful male artists are, then, deliberately modest, hesitant, and reluctant to define themselves as artists and, in a deliberate reversal of gender-based assumptions, they present symptoms similar to the "anxiety of authorship" detected by Gilbert and Gubar as a classic feature of the female artist in *The Madwoman in the Attic*. Looking at the history of the male artist in literature and feminist responses to the tradition, such as Susan Gubar's critique of the valorization of the male artist in a culture immersed in "myths of male primacy in theological, artistic, and scientific creativity," further illuminates the radical nature of Shields's break from this tradition, as Shields's novels refuse to accommodate such myths. Another characteristic of this masculine tradition is what Fiona R. Barnes and Catherine Wiley identify in their introduction to *Homemaking: Women Writers and the Politics and Poetics of Home* as the aggrandizement of exile in the artist-as-hero tradition:

> If exile is to be in flight from, then home is to move towards. In the continuum of home and exile, if exile contains dislocation, isolation, and individualism, then home incorporates connection, relocation, and community. Exile has been the more favored term of the two states in the literary tradition, with many writers and theorists valorizing the tradition that Andrew Gurr terms "creative exile."

Shields's writing works against this trend, as the home and its domestic effects become the more fruitful source of inspiration. Moreover, the male artists in her novels develop an appreciation for the connectedness to the home foregrounded by Wiley and Barnes as a welcome alternative to the artist-as-exile.

In her critical prose, Shields draws attention to the need to test and interrogate received assumptions about literary value, particularly in relation to received wisdom about the literary canon:

> What does a female literary tradition mean and who gets to name it? I see it still growing towards its definition, investigating the question of reclaimed language and redeemed experience. Because I did not have the run of a father's prescribed library, but rather the run of my mother's bookshelf, I am persuaded that the popular tradition must be taken into consideration since it echoes and even interrogates the established tradition, taking liberties, offering models of behaviours, and gesturing— crudely, covertly, often unconsciously— towards the alternate sphere.

This inclusiveness, with its emphasis on placing a new value on popular literary forms, is a recurring feature of Shields's writing. Furthermore, her insistence on the need to address an overlooked "alternate sphere" is mirrored in the way that she reclaims domesticity as a creative sphere for the male characters in her novels.

Although recent studies of the domestic space as a site of cultural production provide a comprehensive survey of women, domesticity, and creativity, they pay very little attention to the meaning or significance of domestic culture for men. This foregrounds the striking and unusual nature of Shields's commitment to writing men into the domestic sphere, a process that is more often than not liberating to both men and women in her novels. A quiet revolution takes place in the course of Shields's oeuvre as she subverts traditional gender difference by presenting an emphatically male-centred domestic fiction. In her study *Masculinity in Male-Authored Fiction 1950–2000*, Alice Ferrebe confronts a seemingly inevitable stumbling block to discussions of literary representations of masculinity: "Attempts to define it as cultural construction still perpetuate a tacit essentialism, and attempts to link it to congenital difference must always acknowledge its public, performative qualities." Shields's characters often have to navigate crude assumptions about gender roles that come to the surface at moments of conflict provoked by an apparent deviation from assumed masculine norms; such norms are contested by Shields as her male characters rise above these prejudices and arrive at a secure understanding of their place in the world by adopting and adapting rituals that are traditionally feminine and domestic....

Source: Ellen McWilliams, "Knitting *Paradise Lost*: Masculinity and Domesticity in the Novels of Carol Shields," in *Women Constructing Men: Female Novelists and Their Male Characters, 1750–2000*, edited by Sarah S. G. Frantz and Katharina Rennhak, Lexington Books, 2010, pp. 171–74.

Caroline Rosenthal

In the following excerpt, Rosenthal explains how Shields contrasts the city and the small town in Unless.

When Carol Shields died in July 2003, she was an internationally acclaimed, award-winning writer, but until the late 1980s her books, which dealt with middle-class families and their quotidian lives, were often described, and in fact belittled, as domestic fiction. With the sweeping success of *The Stone Diaries* Shields's earlier fiction was suddenly also seen in a new, more substantial light. Her last novel, *Unless*, published a year before her death, ironically reflects on both the domestic as a theme in fiction and on the mechanisms of the literary market. Among other things, *Unless* is a novel about a woman writer writing a novel about a woman writer writing. This *mise en abyme* structure serves a metafictional purpose as it makes the readers aware of the processes underlying the making and marketing of fiction. In an interview in 1988, shortly after she had been "discovered" as a "serious" writer, Shields said that all of her novels "have a countertext . . . a kind of mirror commentary" (De Roo 1988, 47). In other words, we have to read her books on two levels at once, because beneath the smooth surface text there is a "mirror commentary" which allows us to read the text against the grain. This "countertext" exposes exactly those ruptures and contradictions which the surface text—out of genre or gender conventions—hides through a coherent narrative. In *Unless*, the inner monologues of the first-person narrator, Reta Winters, produce a smooth surface text which seems to focus on domestic life once more. However, by making

> " AMERICAN LITERATURE USED THE CITY TO GLORIFY THE AMERICAN DREAM BY DEMONIZING THE REALITY OF THE CITY WHILE CANADA POLARIZED ITS WILDERNESS INSTEAD, WHICH HAS ALWAYS BEEN SIMULTANEOUSLY AN ALLURING AND TERRIFYING SPACE, A THREAT AND AN ESCAPE ROUTE."

Reta a believable character but an unreliable narrator, who through her verbal idiosyncrasies provides the reader with indirect information about herself, a mirror commentary underlies *Unless* as well that renders domestic and narrative spaces complex and multi-layered. The objective of this essay is to unravel this metafictional countertext in *Unless*, as well as to show its close connection to urban discourses. *Unless* is not considered here as a domestic fiction but as a contemporary urban novel which uses and rereads the traditional genre of city fiction by ironically reflecting on the prevalent topos of the small town versus the metropolis in Canadian literature.

Unless is set in a small town an hour's drive north of Toronto and in the metropolis itself. Reta lives with her partner, a doctor, and her three daughters in a pretty, old country house in the small community of Orangetown. The Winters are a happy, average Canadian middle-class family when their oldest daughter Norah, a gifted young woman who had just started university, one day, without apparent explanation, starts panhandling on a Toronto street corner, refuses to speak, and puts a sign around her neck demanding "goodness." This event completely throws the first-person narrator off balance, not only because she is afraid of losing her daughter, but also because her daughter's act is so inexplicable that it entirely challenges Reta's rational, humanistic worldview. Norah's act is the "unless," the unexpected event which can shatter one's life and disrupt one's life story. At the very end of the novel, a logical explanation is offered for why Norah starts panhandling on one of the busiest corners of downtown Toronto—at the intersection of Bloor and Bathurst across from the bargain store Honest Ed's.

As her parents find out later, Norah witnessed how a Muslim woman set herself on fire in downtown Toronto, and after this traumatizing event stops talking and commences sitting on the corner where the tragedy had happened. For a long time, however, Norah's family does not have a clue about her behavior, and the sign "goodness," which she wears around her neck, remains an enigma around which the narrative constitutes itself. Reta projects her own fears, worries, and rage onto her daughter's demand for goodness. She believes that with respect to gender goodness is a binary opposition to greatness, as women are allowed to occupy the space of goodness but not greatness in either society or the literary canon. The plot of *Unless* seems simple, but Shields masterfully creates a first-person narrator who in her peculiar speech and demeanor sarcastically comments on the interrelation of gender, genre, and national canons— and for these aspects the novel's setting is crucial.

The setting of *Unless* is vital, first, because Norah holds up her sign in a city that has been apostrophized as "Toronto, the Good," and secondly because the small town versus metropolis paradigm illustrates the mother-daughter conflict at the heart of the story. Although it is never mentioned explicitly, *Unless* draws heavily on the urban myth of Toronto's goodness—after all Norah is sitting across from the bargain store *Honest Ed's*, which of all landmarks is the one which in its very name most vividly recalls the philanthropic mission of early Toronto. The label "Toronto, the Good" reaches back to Toronto's early history as a predominantly British city, which had a high density of Anglican churches and charity and which, in contrast to many American cities, was ruled by municipal law and civic order. The rhetoric of "Toronto, the Good" hence evokes a distinctly WASP context of the city. Since the 1950s, of course, Toronto's distribution of ethnic groups has changed as much as its image so that present-day Toronto is regarded as one of the most multicultural cities in the world. However, it is still an essential part of the city's self-image to be a cleaner and safer version of The Big Apple. Torontonians take pride in having outnumbered New York City for once in its foreign born population, and for having allegedly mastered the challenges of globalization and multiculturalism far more gracefully (Kröller 2001). Both Norah's demand for goodness and the story of the Muslim woman

who ignites herself in the center of downtown challenge these myths of the city by insinuating that integration is not at its best and that "goodness" has become an empty phrase, a signifier without a signified.

Norah's act, however, is not only a silent political protest but can be read as a teenager's rebellion against her mother's suburban middle-class values. When Norah leaves home for Toronto she is confronted with the complexity of an urban experience that her mother had always tried to suppress in their small-town life. Here Shields deliberately and ironically brings to mind the myth of the small town so vital in English-Canadian literature. Orangetown, where the Winters' are living, resonates with the garrison mentality; it is not only, as the narrator wants us to believe, a protected and harmonic space, but a suburban *Ersatzgemeinschaft* that Richard Sennett has defined as "a society that in its anxiety to control or repress perceived threats, has locked itself into an anti-metropolitan identity of an *ersatz* and consequently dysfunctional *Gemeinschaft*" (Sennett in Parker 2004, 143). Orangetown serves as an idyllic anti-metropolitan community for ex-Torontonians who seek a cleaner, safer, and decidedly "waspisher" rendition of the metropolis as well as an escape route from the complexity, multiculturalism, and new urban life-styles of the city. The fictional Orangetown in *Unless* is probably modeled on the really existent Orangeville: a stronghold of protestant values, as the color orange—which throughout the book is associated with Reta—signifies. Reta prefers the wasp suburban order—where she can leave her house unlocked and ride her bicycle without fear of road rage—to the complexities of the metropolis, but Shields, the author, also mocks these attitudes of her protagonist. Reta is brimming with female, Canadian, and suburban goodness: She listens to "the white-throated sparrows in the woods behind our house; their song resembles the Canadian national anthem, at least the opening bars." The "white-throated" sparrows call up associations of innocence, the "woods" evoke the wilderness bordering on the small town; and by having her first-person narrator imagine the birds to whistle the opening bars of the national anthem they come to stand for a Canadian spirit as a whole. The quote expresses Reta's idiosyncratic need for idyllic domestic, natural, and national spaces. Orangetown, however, offers not only protection but also surveillance: Reta tells us that she does not dare include sex scenes in her novels because people in Orangetown would frown at her and because her doctor husband would run the risk of losing his patients.

Yet, *Unless* not only ridicules prudish small-town values but makes a statement on the genre of city fiction within a Canadian cultural context in general. The city has been largely absent from English-Canadian fiction, as critics like Heinz Ickstadt, Walter Pache, and Nancy Burke have pointed out. It is indeed a truism by now that, in contrast to French-Canadian fiction, the English-Canadian imagination has been captured by the small town and the wilderness rather than the metropolis. Nonetheless, the assumption that there is no city fiction in English-Canadian literature can be challenged in a two-fold way. Firstly, the definition of what is city fiction has been so narrow and so much centered on the US in the past that it has in fact eclipsed Canadian city fiction in a North American context. One central criterion for city fiction according to Gelfant or Levy is that the city attains the status of a protagonist, another that the urban experience is reflected in the artistic means of representation. Novels that deal with the city and with a distinctly urban experience but that veered from this definition are less easily recognized as city fiction. As Dallmann has recently shown, this narrow definition has produced a fairly limited corpus of prototypical city novels in national contexts— Dos Passos's *Manhattan Transfer* for the US and Joyce's *Ulysses* for Ireland—while obscuring other urban fictions, especially those by women writers (Dallmann 2003). In a North American context, Anglo-Canadian city fiction is also often not recognized because the genre is marked by characteristics that apply far more easily to American cities and American founding myths than to real or metaphorical Canadian cities. American literature used the city to glorify the American dream by demonizing the reality of the city while Canada polarized its wilderness instead, which has always been simultaneously an alluring and terrifying space, a threat and an escape route. In order to understand differences in the representation of the city in American and English-Canadian fiction one has to closely look at the counter-space of the city, at nature, and at how pastoral traditions significantly differ in both nations. Furthermore, when in the 1970s a

Canadian literary canon was established for the first time it was done under the premise of discovering an authentic voice, one that distinctively had to differ from that of the southern neighbor, so that English-Canadian fiction turned naturally to the wilderness and the small town and not the metropolis. All this, however, neither indicates that there has been no city fiction in English-Canadian literature nor that there have been no distinctive Canadian cities but rather that we have to rethink our terminology and our understanding of what a city and city fiction are. . . .

Source: Caroline Rosenthal, "Textual and Urban Spaces in Carol Shields's *Unless*," in *Reading(s) from a Distance: European Perspectives on Canadian Women's Writing*, edited by Charlotte Sturgess and Martin Kuester, Wissner, 2008, pp. 175–79.

SOURCES

Burns, John, Review of *Unless*, in *Quill & Quire*, 2002, http://www.quillandquire.com/review/unless/ (accessed December 7, 2014).

Gunning, Margaret, "Bold Creative Risks," in *January Magazine*, May 2002, http://www.januarymagazine.com/fiction/02unless.html (accessed December 7, 2014).

Heltzel, Ellen Emery, "Carol Shields Again Gives Voice to Women's Concerns," in *Chicago Tribune*, May 12, 2002, http://articles.chicagotribune.com/2002-05-12/entertainment/0205110010_1_carol-shields-reta-bookish-people (accessed December 7, 2014).

Howell, Coral Ann, "Regulated Anger," in *Canadian Literature*, No. 179, Winter 2003, pp. 107–109.

Kipen, David, Review of *Unless*, in *Manoa*, Vol. 15, No. 1, 2003, pp. 185–86.

Lockerbie, Catherine, "For Goodness' Sake," in *New York Times*, May 12, 2002, http://www.nytimes.com/2002/05/12/books/for-goodness-sake.html (accessed December 7, 2014).

Morrison, Blake, "Hell Hath No Fury," in *Guardian*, April 27, 2002, http://www.theguardian.com/books/2002/apr/27/fiction.carolshields (accessed December 7, 2014).

Rogers, Shelagh, "From the Archives: Carol Shields Talks about *Unless* with Shelagh," CBC website, December 28, 2010, http://www.cbc.ca/books/2010/12/from-the-archives-carol-shields-talks-about-unless-with-shelagh-rogers.html (accessed December 7, 2014).

Shields, Carol, *Unless*, Random House Canada, 2002.

Steffler, Margaret, "A Human Conversation about Goodness: Carol Shields's *Unless*," in *Studies in Canadian Literature*, Vol. 34. No. 2, 2009, pp. 223–44.

Stovel, Nora Foster, "'Because She's a Woman': Myth and Metafiction in Carol Shields's *Unless*," in *English Studies in Canada*, Vol. 32, No. 4, December 2006, pp. 51–73.

Tolan, Fiona, "'Cleaning Gives Me Pleasure': Housework and Feminism in Carol Shields's *Unless*," in *Australasian Canadian Studies*, Vol. 28, No. 1, 2010, pp. 1–15.

Wachtel, Eleanor, *Random Illuminations: Conversations with Carol Shields*, Goose Lane Editions, 2007.

FURTHER READING

Besner, Neil K., *Carol Shields: The Arts of a Writing Life*, Prairie Fire Press, 2003.

> A diverse and deeply moving collection of essays, memoirs, and interviews written by critics from around the world as well as by friends and family, this book includes a contribution by Shields's daughter Anne. It also includes an original essay by Shields herself titled "About Writing," in which she adds substance to a subset of work within her broader body of work: meditative and critical reflections on the challenges and rewards of leading a life dedicated to (and defined) by writing.

Goertz, Dee, and Edward Eden, *Carol Shields: Narrative Hunger, and the Possibilities of Fiction*, University of Toronto Press, 2003.

> Although focused primarily on Shields's longer fiction, this collection of well-written though at times difficult essays sheds light on many of the themes and techniques that she carries over to her short stories as well. Collectively, they raise some interesting questions about Shields's interest in the dynamics of fictional autobiography and disrupted or ruptured narratives and about her use of allusions to other works of literature and film in her writing.

Ramon, Alex, *Liminal Spaces: The Double Art of Carol Shields*, Cambridge Scholars, 2009.

> Focusing on Shields's powerful but subtle manipulation of liminal spaces (thresholds between two places, conditions, or states of mind), Ramon presents a provocative rereading of Shields's works as a determined questioning of such topics as change, memory, and creativity.

Shields, Carol, "The Same Ticking Clock" and "Arriving Late, Starting Over," in *How Stories Mean*, edited by John Metcalf and J. R. (Tim) Struthers, Porcupine's Quill, 1993, pp. 88–89, 244–51.

> A lifelong teacher as well as writer, Shields was adept at writing reflectively about the creative process and the discipline of writing. These two short essays are among her most insightful articulations of the complexities of the creative process.

van Herk, Aritha, and Conny Steenman-Marcusse, *Carol Shields: Evocation and Echo*, Barkhuis, 2009.

> This collection of international responses from critics and fellow writers reflects the deep and lasting influence that Shields's writing has had on both her contemporaries and writers of a later generation.

SUGGESTED SEARCH TERMS

Carol Shields

Unless AND Carol Shields

Shields AND novel

Shields AND goodness

Shields AND feminism

Shields AND writing

goodness AND fiction

domestic AND fiction

Yonnondio: From the Thirties

TILLIE OLSEN

1974

Tillie Olsen's novel *Yonnondio* was titled after a poem by the same name by Walt Whitman. Its subtitle is "From the Thirties," yet Olsen indicates just before the first chapter that the novel takes place in the early 1920s. This has led to confusion as to when the novel actually takes place. In fact, Olsen draws from both the 1920s and the 1930s throughout the course of the work. The novel is concerned with poverty both in the 1920s—the time frame of the novel—and during the Great Depression of the 1930s—the time during which Olsen wrote the draft. The work is focused in particular on the struggles of the Holbrook family. Based loosely on Olsen's own life of poverty and struggle, the novel unrelentingly depicts the loss of hope, innocence, and potential experienced by all members of the Holbrook family.

Olsen began writing the novel in the early 1930s, when she was nineteen. Later in life, when she rediscovered the manuscript, she edited her early drafts but did not rewrite the work, and it was finally published in 1974. Much of the story is told from the point of view of the young Mazie Holbrook, just six years old when the novel opens. As the work progresses, the family moves from a mining town in Wyoming to a tenant farm in Nebraska and then to Omaha, Nebraska, where Jim Holbrook secures a position at a slaughterhouse. The work focuses not only on the effects of poverty but on the terrible conditions endured by the workers in the mining

Tillie Olsen *(© Chris Felver | Archive Photos | Getty Images)*

and meat-packing industries. In the novel, Olsen takes a firm political stance against the oppression of the workers inflicted by capitalist factory owners; Olsen would later align herself with the Communist Party, which she saw as working against this abuse. The novel is both an intimate portrait of the way oppression and poverty affect a family and a political condemnation of the social structures that allow the existence of the horrendous conditions endured by the Holbrooks.

AUTHOR BIOGRAPHY

Tillie Olsen was born Tillie Lerner, to parents Samuel and Ida Lerner. She was born on January 14 of 1912 or 1913 (no birth certificate exists, and the date is based on scholarly speculation). She was the second of six children. Her parents were Socialist Jews who left Russia in the aftermath of the failed 1905 revolution. Olsen was born on a farm outside Omaha, where she and her family lived until 1917. The Lerners then moved to Omaha, where Samuel first worked as a peddler and, later, at a candy company. Her parents were active in the Socialist Party

and founded a social and political organization for working-class Jews. Lerner attended Central High School in Omaha but dropped out before graduating. She then joined the Young Communist League and in 1931, at the age of eighteen, moved to Kansas City.

After being jailed for handing out Communist leaflets to packinghouse workers, she returned to her family in Omaha. In 1932, she moved again, to Faribault, Minnesota. She penned the first draft of *Yonnondio* there, while she was ill during her pregnancy with her first child. The following year, she moved to San Francisco, California, where she married Jack Olsen in 1944. He was a printer and a fellow Communist, and the two were active within the Communist Party for many years. Olsen worked odd jobs in the 1940s and 1950s and raised four daughters. In 1953, when her youngest daughter was in school, Olsen took a creative writing course at San Francisco State University.

As Olsen pursued her writing career, she won a Wallace Stegner Fellowship to attend Stanford University. Later, in 1959, she won a Ford Foundation grant. Her most famous work, *Tell Me a Riddle*, was published in 1961. It contains a novella by the same name and several short stories, including the well-known story "I Stand Here Ironing." In 1980, *Tell Me a Riddle* was adapted as an Oscar-winning film by the same name. Over the decades, her short fiction and novellas have frequently been anthologized. *Yonnondio* was published in 1974, after Olsen reconstructed the manuscript from drafts she had written years before. She continued to work as a writer and as a visiting professor at a number of institutions, including the University of Minnesota and Kenyon College in Ohio. She died on January 1, 2007.

PLOT SUMMARY

Chapter 1

This opening chapter of *Yonnondio* introduces us to one of the work's narrators, young Mazie Holbrook, after providing a brief note that the setting of the book's opening is the early 1920s in a Wyoming mining town. Mazie awakens listening to the sound of whistles coming from the mine. She reflects that when they sound during the day, it is to alert the town to the death of a miner. Mazie's parents are discussing the child of a friend; the teenage Andy Kvaternick is about to start work in the mine. Andy is the son of Chris Kvaternick, who died in the mine, and Marie Kvaternick. Anna Holbrook sees her husband, Jim, off to work and then returns to bed, after which Mazie falls back asleep. The narration switches to Anna Holbrook's perspective. She thinks about the children in the mining town—her own children and those of her friends—and considers how living in poverty, with the threat of death hanging over them, makes children like Mazie old before their time. When Mazie and her mother wake up, they discuss the concept of education. Anna insists that "edjication" is the means by which the children will escape their present life of poverty. As the chapter progresses, the reader is provided intimate glimpses into the minds of Mazie, Anna, and Jim, as well as more minor characters. This stream-of-consciousness section conveys the horror that poverty has meant for the characters. The terror of the mine is depicted, as well as the physical violence that Jim inflicts upon his wife and children.

One night, Mazie follows her father when he heads out for a drink. She pleads with him to explain the fear and sadness she sees in those around her. He tries to comfort her and tells her not to worry, but she continues her questioning. She asks whether it is true that the boss of the mine has indoor plumbing and a bathtub in his house—luxuries almost beyond belief to Mazie. As Jim tries to make sense of these inequalities for her, he falters, and Mazie clings to the notion that at least her father could beat up the boss if he wanted to. He proceeds on his way, and she wanders off. She is stopped by the crazed Sheen McEvoy, who was injured and burned in a mining explosion. McEvoy becomes possessed by the notion that if he sacrifices Mazie to the mine, the deaths will stop. He picks her up and is about to throw her down the mine shaft, but he is interrupted by the night watchman. The watchman fights with and eventually shoots McEvoy, who falls down the mineshaft. That night, after taking Mazie home, Jim tells Anna they are moving away from the mining town in the spring. Mazie's siblings are referred to only in general terms, such as "the children" or "the baby," in the opening chapter, but they are treated more individually as the novel continues. The Holbrook children include Mazie, Will, Ben, and the baby, Jimmie. Later, Anna will have another baby, Bess.

Chapter 2

As the chapter opens, Anna looks forward to the new life that Jim has promised, even while the family endures a brutal autumn and winter with almost nothing to eat and few clothes to keep them warm. The children are fearful, seeing their father behave so differently in the aftermath of the attack on Mazie. He is at home most nights, and he is "awkwardly gentle" and peaceful. The children attempt to comfort themselves; they sense the fear in their household and in the town in general. Mazie and Will talk about the way people seem to be crying all the time. They discuss death and what it means. For a moment, after hearing the mine whistle, they consider running away, but instead they run back to town and to the mine, where they learn that an explosion has occurred.

Finally, in April, the Holbrooks are prepared to leave the mining town. Jim plans to move the family to the country, where he will become a tenant farmer. He has already made the arrangements to move to the tenant farm, and the family only awaits better traveling weather. The whole family is eager and hopeful.

Chapter 3

Although the Holbrooks face weather-related challenges on their journey, the move to the farm initiates a new and more positive change in their daily lives. "Laughter came from the skies, blowing something that was more than coal dust out of their hearts," Olsen writes.

Chapter 4

This chapter depicts life on the farm in glowing terms, in sharp contrast to the misery of the mining town. The Holbrooks are tentatively happy, despite the warning from a neighbor, Benson, that tenant farming (that is, renting the land that they work) will never be profitable. Through spring and summer, the family knows both hard work and bounty. They experience satisfaction, nourishment, and peace. Mazie strikes up a friendship with a neighbor, Old Man Caldwell, and she looks up to him as a source of wisdom and knowledge. In the fall, Mazie and Will attend school, where they are teased for their inability to read. Mazie is aware of her poverty and her tattered clothing.

One evening, Mazie overhears her parents; her father is angry, her mother afraid. Mazie flees the house and makes her way to the Caldwell home. She is greeted by Bess Ellis, Old Man Caldwell's daughter, who tells her that Old Man Caldwell is sick. Mazie visits with him for a moment. Once home, Mazie hears her father talking about owing "them" (the bank) money even after slaving all year on the farm. Benson's prediction has come true: the farm is not profitable.

Old Man Caldwell dies not long after this. The weather grows very cold, and the family clusters around the stove in the kitchen day and night to keep warm. Will gets sick, and Anna is pregnant, ill, and exhausted. Jim is frustrated with her inability to do the household chores, and tension returns to the home. One morning, Jim retrieves some half-frozen baby chicks from a drift of snow. He brings them into the house and puts them in the oven to get warm; he then leaves to visit a neighbor. That afternoon, neither Anna nor the children notice the peeping of the chicks. When Jim returns that evening, they all realize that the chicks have burned to death. Jim is livid, and he and Anna argue violently. Jim hits her and then leaves the house. A terrible snowstorm strikes. Anna and the children try to tend to the animals themselves, as Jim has disappeared. He is gone for ten days.

The narration resumes in March. Anna is about to have the baby, and Jim wakens Mazie and tells her to help with the birth. He says that he is taking the older boys, Will and Ben, with him to visit his friend, Mr. Ellis, whose daughter, Bess, comes to the farm to help Anna with the birth. Mazie is terrified of seeing her mother in so much pain. Anna tells Mazie that she asked Jim not to leave Mazie with her. Mazie helps as best she can until neighbor women come to assist Anna. Mazie hides in the barn. She wakes to find her father carrying her back into the house. Bess Ellis comforts Mazie while asking Jim if he is really planning on leaving. He insists that moving to the city to find a job at the slaughterhouse is the best thing for the family. Not long after this, the Holbrooks leave the farm.

Chapter 5

This chapter opens with a description of the city, primarily characterized by the stench of the slaughterhouse. The children begin school and are teased once again for their ignorance and poverty. Anna and Jim reconnect with friends from their youth, Alex and Else Bedner. They are well off compared with the Holbrooks. They live far enough away from the slaughterhouse

that the stench can barely be detected. The house is clean and large, and they have a piano. Alex is employed as a tool and die maker. The visit is strained, as the economic and social gap between the two families is readily apparent. As their days press on, Anna becomes increasingly ill, faint, nauseated, and exhausted. She attempts to nurse the baby, Bess, while her family struggles on around her. Jim is working in the sewers while he waits for the slaughterhouse to start hiring. The children struggle. Ben is asthmatic and has difficulty breathing, and Mazie feels assaulted by the sights and sounds of the city. She wills herself to mentally remain on the farm, even as she wanders, dazed, through the city. Will turns to the city for excitement, finding others with whom to run wild through the streets and around the nearby cliffs.

As this chapter unfolds, Olsen weaves together specific events and references to the general hopelessness under which the entire family exists. The effect is that the storytelling does not seem linear. There are a few plot points, but more than anything Olsen attempts to convey despair. Anna exists in an almost permanent stupor and has become almost completely unable to care for the children. The children largely fend for themselves. In one scene, the young Ben watches over Jimmie, who is little more than a toddler. Jimmie is sitting in the dirt at the dump, playing with a stick and ashes, when Ben retrieves his brother and takes him with him to attempt to save a dog from being tortured by a group of men. Daily, Anna attempts to find enough strength to have dinner on the table, with the help of the children, before Jim arrives home from work. Olsen conveys Anna's general efforts at dinner-making, as well as specific incidents of failure where she is beaten or verbally abused by Jim in retaliation. Just as Anna is shown to be in a stupor of pain and exhaustion and despair, Olsen captures a similarly fog-like state with Mazie, who attempts to cling to her imaginary vision of the farm as a mental escape from the city. On one occasion, she is pushed to the street in a throng of people and falls to the pavement. Terrified, she runs home. One evening, during a dinner that Anna and the children have managed to scrape together, Jim grows irate at Anna when he sees that Ben has an infected finger that Anna has failed to take care of. As that night wears on, Anna manages to nurse the baby and comfort Ben before she faints. Ben runs for the neighbor,

Mrs. Kryckszi, to help. She revives Anna and helps her through the rest of the evening.

When the drunken Jim returns home after hours out at the tavern, he forces himself on Anna, though she cries out and tells him how much pain she is in. Afterward, she faints again, and Mazie sees her bleeding on the floor. Mazie alerts her father. Jim leaves and returns with the doctor, who informs Jim that Anna has had a miscarriage. Panicked, Mazie flees the house; Jim comes to look for her, finds her, and carries her home. He explains that Anna is sick.

Chapter 6

Anna rests and tries to recuperate. It is now summer, and the older children are home from school. Neighbors come to help Anna care for the children and do household chores: Else comes in the mornings and Mrs. Kryckszi in the evenings. Anna, still weak and mostly bed-ridden, is frustrated that she cannot do more. She worries about how her children are playing in the filthy streets, and she grows increasingly anxious that they will become ill. She tries to do more but is easily overwhelmed, and her despair becomes an intense wave that washes over her. Anna feels helpless to make a better life for her children, and she has become exhausted by the futile prospect of continuing to try. When Jim tries to comfort her, she grows angry. She shares her desperation with him: "The children. What's going to happen with them? How we going to look out for them in this damn world? Oh Jim, the children. Seems like we cant do nothing for them."

Chapter 7

Anna improves slowly and is emotionally tormented by her inability to make her children's lives better. But she tries: she takes on a laundering job, long before she is back to her former strength. She eagerly tells Jim about the dollar a month she will earn, but Jim is angry, feeling that she is not well enough to take care of her own family's laundry, let alone someone else's. Anna has told him that she wants to use it to invest in Will's future, to save for his education. Jim mocks the plan and tells her to forget about it.

With the rent due and not much left to eat, Anna takes Mazie, Ben, and Jimmie out with her to empty lots to find dandelion greens to eat. She leaves the baby with Mrs. Kryckszi. They wander from lot to lot, Anna in a dreamy state that

Mazie cannot understand. Mazie grows increasingly irritated with her mother and her little brothers. They find a vacant lot that Anna realizes was someone's home once. Anna talks to Mazie about when she was a little girl. Mazie notices the distant look on her mother's face and senses that her mother has forgotten them, has become another person, happy and distant. For a moment, Mazie loses herself as well, feeling peaceful and remembering the farm, but she snaps herself out of it and calls out angrily to her mother. Anna beckons her children to sit with her under a tree, where she sings to them and strokes their hair. Mazie feels her mother's happiness, which has nothing to do with the children; Anna is far away. Still, Mazie feels surrounded by this sense of joy and wholeness, and for a moment she feels her own "happiness and intactness and selfness." The spell is broken, though, when Ben announces that he's hungry and the boys begin to fidget.

Chapter 8

As this chapter opens, the heat of the summer oppresses the city. Jim, who has been working in the sewers until this point, has just secured a job at the slaughterhouse. The pay is better than the sewer work; he will be earning forty-five cents an hour. It is the Fourth of July, and Jim buys fireworks to celebrate. Mazie is angry because only the boys are allowed to handle the fireworks, so she and her friend Annamae separate themselves from the group and go to the roof. Anna is tense, fearing that the boys will get hurt, and she is anxious about Alex and Else coming over to celebrate with them. She is worried about Mazie and her hurt feelings as well, but allows herself a moment to sit and enjoy the spectacle of the fireworks.

As the summer wears on, Anna recovers her strength. She feels in charge of her household once again, and secretly puts away money for Will. Jim has his own secret, trying to find a second-hand sewing machine for Anna. The garden that Anna has planted begins to flourish and provide some food for their meals. One day, Anna takes her children to the library, but Mazie and Will are uninterested in the books that they bring home. They have been told at school that they are too stupid to read or understand books. Mazie and Will roam the city instead, seeking excitement. They find treasures at the dump—cracked dishes, broken chairs— that they bring home for their mother. Also at the dump is a tent set up by a girl named Ginella, who is twelve years old. Here, Ginella has collected anything she finds that shines or shimmers, anything lacy and feminine, feathers and high-heeled shoes. She has scraps of magazines and movie posters featuring glamorous celebrities.

The heat of the summer intensifies. Will takes his mattress out into the yard to sleep there, and Mazie follows him. They endure the mosquitoes and find only slight relief from the stifling air inside the house. Most nights, Anna sits up with most of the children at one point or another. Ben is ill.

At the slaughterhouse, the heat is nightmarish. "A hundred and ten in the kill room," Mr. Kryckszi informs Jim. The description of the slaughterhouse in the heat is hellish; everything is bloody and slippery.

Will and his friend do not want girls to come along with them as they play, but Mazie tries to follow them anyway; she falls in the gravel while trying to chase them. She then returns to the girls gathered in Ginella's tent, where Ginella tells her she is ugly. The group is approached by Erina, who has a deformed arm; they are frightened of her. She bullies others to protect herself. Erina has been told by her family that God punishes sinners, that God made her this way, and Mazie is afraid yet compassionate. Erina, with pus oozing from her eyes and sores on her body, tells Mazie that her father hit her and told her that she sinned too much for God to make her better. Mazie's pity grows as she senses how sick Erina is and when she realizes that what seemed like dirt on her cheek is a bad bruise. When Mazie returns home, she bullies her brothers Ben and Jimmie, stealing the doll they are playing with and throwing it across the yard. Mazie feels confused, sad and mean and angry. Her fury increases when her mother makes her help with chores and tells her that Will does not have to because he is a boy. After fighting with her mother, Mazie runs off.

Back at the slaughterhouse, the heat is intolerable, the sights and smells horrific. At home, Anna is trying to finish making jelly, her work heating up the house even further. Time seems to slow as everyone tries to work through the heat and survive. Will returns home with a radio set borrowed from the Metzes, and the family listens "for the first time" to the static-filled yet wondrous sound. As the novel closes, Anna tells Jim, "The air's changin', Jim. I see for it to end tomorrow, at least get tolerable."

CHARACTERS

Alex Bedner

Alex Bedner and his wife, Else, are former friends of the Holbrooks. When Jim Holbrook moves his family to the city, he and Anna attempt to reconnect with the friends they once knew. Alex and his wife can now afford a much higher standard of living than the Holbrooks have ever known, and this inequality strains their renewed friendship.

Else Bedner

Else Bedner is Alex's wife. She is shocked to see how life has changed her onetime friend so drastically. While Anna has had five children and attempts to raise them on almost no income, Else is the wife of a tool and die maker with a comfortable income. The couple has no children, though Else has indicated that they wanted to have a family but were unable to. When Anna is ill after her miscarriage, Else is one of the women who come to her aid.

Fred Benson

Fred Benson is the Holbrooks' neighbor during their farming days. He warns Jim that the only thing worse than farming for oneself is being a tenant farmer, and that the bank will take everything he earns and then some. He accurately predicts the Holbrooks' fate.

Elias "Old Man" Caldwell

Old Man Caldwell is one of the Holbrooks' farming neighbors. He strikes up a friendship with Mazie, who seems thirsty for the knowledge he possesses. He has been well educated, and he shares what he knows with Mazie about the natural world, astronomy, and books, among other topics. Mazie is able to see him shortly before he dies.

Bess Ellis

Bess Ellis is Old Man Caldwell's daughter. She is kind to Mazie when she visits Old Man Caldwell, and, as a midwife, she helps Anna Holbrook when she gives birth to Bess in the farmhouse.

Mr. Ellis

Mr. Ellis is Bess Ellis's husband and Jim Holbrook's friend.

Erina

Erina is a girl Mazie encounters at the dump after the Holbrooks move to the city. She has a deformed arm, and she has been told by her family that her suffering is a result of her sin. A pitiable child—epileptic, ill, impoverished, and abused by her family—she alternately bullies others and cowers away from them. Mazie, like the other children, is afraid of Erina, but she nonetheless feels a sense of compassion toward the girl.

Ginella

Ginella is the daughter of Polish immigrants. A few years older than Mazie, she sets up a tent near the dump and embellishes it with the treasures she finds there, usually anything involving femininity or sexuality. She longs for the glamorous world she sees depicted in scraps of magazines.

Anna Holbrook

Anna Holbrook is Jim's wife and the mother of Mazie, Will, Ben, Jimmie, and Bess. She endures the miscarriage of a sixth child late in the novel. Anna, perhaps more than any other character in the novel, demonstrates the way poverty oppresses people. Unlike her children, who cannot understand what a better life would have been like or how education could have helped them, Anna comprehends the pain of lost potential—her own and that of her children. She thinks about the hopes she once had for her future, and she sees what her children ought to have in life and probably never will. Anna laments how little she and Jim are able to provide, how much they cannot protect or save the children from. Through pain, exhaustion, and loss, Anna begins to lose her ability to connect with her children; she detaches from them and finds happiness only when she loses herself in memories of her own youth. Mazie seems acutely aware of this, and it both angers and grieves her.

Ben Holbrook

Ben is the middle child in the Holbrook family, situated between his older siblings Will and Mazie and the younger Jimmie and Bess. He is characterized as inquisitive and sensitive. Of all the children, he seems to need the reassurance and comfort of his mother the most. He often annoys his father with his constant questioning. He is often sick and appears to suffer from asthma, as he has difficulty breathing.

Bess Holbrook

Bess Holbrook is the baby of the Holbrook family. She is born on the farm with the help of Bess Ellis. Sometimes she is a source of comfort to Anna; at other times, she primarily serves as a symbol of hunger, depicted as little more than a mouth to feed.

Jim Holbrook

Jim Holbrook, Anna's husband, is the father of Mazie, Will, Ben, Jimmie, and Bess. When the book opens, he is employed as a miner. Eager to escape the dangers of the mine itself and the fearful and impoverished community that surrounds it, Jim takes up tenant farming. On the farm, his family enjoys a brief respite from hunger and deprivation, although they are still poor. When he learns how much he owes the bank after harvesting his crop, Jim despairs; he has earned nothing for his family at the end of the season. They endure a bitter winter, during which Anna gives birth to Bess. Jim then moves the family to the city, where he is first employed in the sewers but where he hopes to find a position in the slaughterhouse. He finally does, and the work is revealed to be more nightmarish than anything he has endured. His constant need to provide for his hungry family and his inability to do so because of his low-paying jobs generate in Jim a fierce fury that he often unleashes on his family. At the same time, he periodically displays great tenderness for them and a continued desire to protect and provide. He forces himself on Anna. Later, he is caring in the aftermath of her miscarriage.

Jimmie Holbrook

Jimmie Holbrook is baby of the Holbrook family when the novel opens, but he is soon displaced from this position by the birth of Bess. Mazie often has to look after Will, Jimmie, and Ben, and when the children are a little older near the end of the novel, it is Ben who is attempting to look after his little brother Jimmie.

Mazie Holbrook

Mazie Holbrook is the protagonist of the novel, and her experiences are loosely based on Olsen's own life. She is an intelligent and empathetic child, loving toward her family and fearful of the brutal world around her. She often retreats to an inner fantasy world as a means of coping with the horrors of the poverty and hunger she endures. Mazie blossoms when the family moves to the farm. Away from the oppression of the mine, out in the open, Mazie thrives, and she finds, along with her family, a tentative happiness that is shattered when her father discovers how much he owes the bank after a season of toil. Repeatedly forced to take up the chores of housework and caring for her siblings, Mazie is told that these are her duties as a girl. Will, on the other hand, is often left free to roam, particularly in the city when the children are older. Mazie attempts to insulate herself from the horrific smells generated by the slaughterhouse, and she pretends she is back on the farm, but she cannot live in this world of imagination for long. She grows increasingly angry and often confused by her own mixture of rage, fear, anger, and bitterness. By the end of the novel, she seems isolated from family and friends.

Will Holbrook

Will is the second oldest of the Holbrook children. He and Mazie are companions in the first half of the novel, but after the children get a little older, he appears to be uninterested in spending time with her because she is a girl.

Mr. Kryckszi

Mr. Kryckski is the husband of Mrs. Kryckszi. He works with Jim at the slaughterhouse.

Mrs. Kryckszi

Mrs. Kryckszi is a neighbor who assists Anna with child care and household chores after Anna suffers a miscarriage.

Andy Kvaternick

Andy Kvaternick is the son of Marie Kvaternick and her deceased husband, Chris. He is a young boy of thirteen, but he is already beginning work in the mine. The brief section of the novel told from his perspective reveals his fears.

Chris Kvaternick

Chris Kvaternick, a former coworker of Jim Holbrook's, dies in a mining accident.

Marie Kvaternick

Marie Kvaternick is the widow of Chris Kvaternick and mother of Andy.

Sheen McEvoy

McEvoy is a former miner who has been injured and disfigured in a mining accident. Driven mad by this incident, he sees the mine as a living thing,

a god of death that needs to be appeased with sacrifices. He presumes this is why so many men die in the mine. When he sees Mazie wandering the town at night, he seizes on the idea that if he sacrificed someone pure of heart to the mine, it would be appeased and the men would stop dying. This belief motivates his ultimately unsuccessful attempt to throw Mazie down the mine shaft.

THEMES

Poverty

In *Yonnondio*, poverty is among the overriding themes of the Holbrook family's daily life. Their poverty dictates every aspect of every day. They wake every day to empty bellies, and they sleep every night in substandard conditions, with the children crowded together in one room. This poverty is shared by others where the Holbrooks live, and an overwhelming atmosphere of desperation and violence haunts the family. Jim Holbrook attempts to keep providing for his family, and despite his lack of education, he repeatedly attempts to improve the lives of his wife and children. He makes two major decisions that he hopes will change things for the people in his life. In the beginning of the novel, he works in a small community for a mining company. The mine is unsafe, and the men who work there are in constant danger. Olsen's opening words indicate this. Mazie hears the whistle upon waking. It either alerts the men that the workday is beginning or, when heard during the course of the day, indicates that an accident has led to the death of a worker. It is a dreaded sound in the community, the tolling of a death knell. Through the sound of the bell, Olsen yokes the notions of poverty and death. In an attempt to stay one step ahead of poverty, desperate men risk death by continuing to work at the mine.

After Sheen McEvoy attempts to appease the mine by sacrificing Mazie to it, Jim grows fearful about the safety of his family. He makes the first major decision to try and make their lives better and takes up tenant farming. For a while, his family knows peace, though they remain poor. The small satisfaction they achieve during this phase of their life is quickly undone when the reality of tenant farming is made plain after harvest: the bank takes all their profit and then some. Jim is disillusioned and angry. Anna

TOPICS FOR FURTHER STUDY

- Olsen's novel takes its name from a Walt Whitman poem with the same title. Read Whitman's poem and consider why Olsen chose this title. What are the themes of the poem? In what ways do you think the novel is related to the poem? Write an essay in which you compare the two works. Consider the time periods in which each author was writing and the historical context that shaped each work.

- David Treuer is a Native American author whose novel *Little* was published in 1996. It tells of life on a reservation called Poverty. The narrative traces the history of the reservation and its inhabitants since the turn of the twentieth century and explores the impact of poverty, alcoholism, and war on the community. Read Treuer's novel and examine how the author analyzes the issue of rural poverty. How does he show its causes and its effects? How are its effects upon the people and the community shown? Write an essay in which you provide a thematic analysis of the work.

- The young-adult novel *Whistle in the Dark*, by Susan Hill Long, was published in 2013.

It centers on a thirteen-year-old boy who is forced by his family's circumstances to go to work in a lead mine in rural Missouri. With a small group, read *Whistle in the Dark*. Consider the ways in which the novel's protagonist, Clem, is similar to the Holbrook children in *Yonnondio*. Are there similarities in how the authors depict life in an impoverished mining town? How are Clem's experiences like or different from Mazie's? Create an online blog that you use as a forum to discuss these and other ideas about the novel.

- Olsen focuses some attention on working conditions endured by laborers in her novel, and she worked for the Communist Party during her lifetime. Research the history of the Communist Party in America during the 1920s and 1930s. Discuss the impact the party had on the rise of labor unions in America. Consider the ways in which those working for the Communist Party were treated by their communities and by the government. Prepare a visual report such as a time line or an interactive website and discuss your findings.

---

has insisted throughout the novel that an education is the means by which her children could escape poverty, and she encourages them in their efforts at school. Jim's dim understanding of the economics of tenant farming suggests that his own lack of education has been a handicap in his life: he might not have taken this route if he had understood the costs. At the same time, though, his lack of education means that there are very few doors open to him, and even if he had fully understood the financial risk, he might have still accepted the venture.

The threat of continued poverty forces Jim to make the second major decision he hopes will change their fate. He moves the family to the

city, where he hopes to get a job at a slaughterhouse. First, he works in the sewers. In Omaha, the stench of the slaughterhouse serves the same function that the sound of the whistle in the mining town did. It is a persistent reminder of how bad things are; the community is surrounded by death, thrives on it, in fact. Anna continues to believe in the power of education, taking out library cards for her children and secretly saving for Will's educational future. At the same time, Jim continues to pursue what upward mobility is available to him, finally making the move from the sewer to the slaughterhouse. He is elated at the opportunity to make forty-five cents an hour.

The family's poverty, which persists despite Jim's efforts and Anna's dreams, is emphasized in other ways throughout the work. Because Olsen privileges Mazie's perspective over that of the other children, the reader is more intimately acquainted with the way Mazie experiences and copes with her hunger, although the other children are seen expressing to their mother how hungry they are at many points in the novel. Mazie, though, becomes almost delusional in the way she retreats into her imagination to escape the horror of her life. Olsen highlights other aspects of deprivation through Ginella, who attempts to create a glamorous escape from poverty by living in a tent decorated with objects from the dump, and Erina, whose deformed and sick presence fills Mazie with terror and pity. Erina's family, notably, attempts to understand their suffering through a fundamentalist religious perspective.

Social Class

While the poverty the Holbrooks endure is a pervasive reminder of their low social class, Olsen takes pains to contrast their situation with that of other characters. Olsen shows that while an overwhelming number of people work in horrendous conditions just to earn enough to barely survive, a select few live in another world entirely and are barely aware of the suffering of others. In both the mining community and in the city where Jim is employed first in the sewers and then in the slaughterhouse, Olsen makes reference to the people who own the industries and the luxury in which they live. Mazie asks her father about the boss of the mine: "Pop, does the boss man honest have a white shiny tub bigger than you and he turns somethin and the water comes out? Or is it a story? And does he honest have a toilet right inside the house? And silks on the floor?" Jim answers affirmatively. "How come he aint livin like we do? How come we aint livin like him, Pop?" The question is hard for her father to answer. "Why indeed? For a moment Jim was puzzled. ''Cause he's a coal operator, that's why,'" he answers. The disparity, as Olsen points out, stems from their relative positions—Jim is a worker, a drone, and the boss is manager. Mazie does not understand, and to Jim it does not make sense either; it is simply the way his world works, the way it always has worked.

Jim does not earn enough to support his family working at the coal mine, which drives him to drink and to beat his wife and children.
(© Sopotnicki | Shutterstock.com)

The Bedners represent another social class. Though not the wealthiest members of society, not like those who own the mines and the slaughterhouses, they have found a way to do better than Anna and Jim, their childhood friends. The couples have not seen each other for seven years. Alex Bedner, a tool and die maker, lives "in a five-room house with a piano and a stained-glass window, and it didn't smell around there, except when the wind blew strong from the south." Although Olsen does not make it clear what Anna's life was like before she met Jim—though there are memories of a peaceful childhood—nor of Jim's and Anna's prior to their life in the mining town, it seems reasonable to assume that if they were once friends of the Bedners, they once existed in a similar social and economic class. The tidy and comfortable life the Bedners now have is a reminder to Anna and Jim of how far they have fallen.

STYLE

Third-Person and Stream-of-Consciousness Narration

Olsen uses several experimental narrative techniques in *Yonnondio*. She combines the use of third-person narration—both close and omniscient—with the use of stream-of-consciousness narration. In stories told in the third person, the narrator refers to the point-of-view character—the person from whose perspective the story is being told—as "he" or "she." This is in contrast to stories told from a first-person perspective, in which the point-of-view character refers to himself or herself as "I." There are different types of third-person narration. In the kind of storytelling called close, intimate, or limited third-person narration, the author limits the narration to the perspectives of certain characters, usually only one or two. The author gives the reader access to the thoughts, feelings, and knowledge of these characters. In omniscient third-person narration, on the other hand, an omniscient (all-knowing) narrator relates the events of the story, moves among the perspectives of many characters, and may make observations about events or society as a whole. Stream-of-consciousness narration is a technique in which the author presents the interior world of a character, conveying thoughts as they unfold without summary or interpretation. Olsen uses all of these techniques in her novel. She provides commentary on the communities in which the Holbrooks live, she narrates primarily from the perspective of Mazie and Anna (and occasionally Jim or other minor characters), and she sometimes takes readers deep into the thoughts of some characters.

Throughout much of the novel, Olsen moves between close and omniscient third-person narration. She focuses on a particular character, pulls away from that character's thoughts and views to provide a broader perspective, and then narrows back in on either the first character or another one. In one instance, Olsen centers on the experiences and thoughts of a more minor character, Andy Kvaternick, using close third-person narration, staying within Andy's viewpoint for a few paragraphs. She then shifts to an omniscient summarizing tone, describing Jim Holbrook's mood and the way it hangs over the household for a period of several weeks. The omniscient narrator then describes how Anna is affected by Jim's mood and begins to behave brutally toward the children herself. The narrator then characterizes Jim's violent interaction with his children before moving to an even broader perspective: "Outside the wind gibbered and moaned. The room was suddenly chill. Some horror, some sense of evil seemed on everything." In the next paragraph, Olsen returns once again to a close third-person narration, focusing on Mazie and her sense of fear.

Although stream-of-consciousness narration is not a regular feature of the novel and occurs only a few times, when Olsen does use it, she does so for an extended period, not just one or two sentences. Mazie is both the primary point-of-view character in the novel and a child with a vivid interior world. These qualities give Olsen ample opportunity to use the stream-of-consciousness technique. Mazie's understanding of her world is colored by pain and suffering and by her attempts to understand her circumstances. When she is thinking about the mining community and her family's place in it, she reminds herself, as she struggles to comprehend her own identity, "I am Mazie Holbrook....I am a-knowen things....I know words and words." As she considers the mine, she thinks,

> Bowels of earth. It means the mine. Bowels is the stummy. Earth is a stummy and mebbe she ets the men that come down. Men and daddy goin' in like the day and comin out black. Earth black and pop's face and hands black and he spits from his mouth black....The sun is makin a fire on me, but it is not black.

The tidal shifts of thought and feeling are represented as if these ideas are ebbing and flowing in Mazie's mind in the moment. Although the instances of this technique, combined with the quick movements between close and omniscient narration, sometimes seem chaotic, they in fact reflect Olsen's theme of poverty and the way poverty makes chaos of the lives of individuals.

Mixed Tense

Just as Olsen experiments with different perspectives in her narrative, she also shifts verb tense in various sections of the novel. Most of the novel is narrated in the past tense, but portions of it switch to present tense, emphasizing the immediacy and intensity of a particular character's experience. In one section of the novel, directly following a long stretch of stream-of-consciousness narration from Mazie's point of view, Olsen switches from the third-person past tense narration, in which Mazie's thoughts were introduced, to third-person present tense, from Andy Kvaternick's perspective. The section begins, "Andy Kvaternick stumbles through the night. The late September wind fills the night with lost and crying voices and drowns all but the largest stars. Chop, chop goes the black sea of his mind." As this section continues, the narration turns from third-person narration to second-person, with the narrator apparently addressing not just Andy, but others like him who work in the mine. "And no more can you stand erect. You lose that heritage of man, too." In switching so rapidly between modes, Olsen creates an effect that sometimes seems disjointed, but intentionally so; this movement between multiple narrative modes underscores the sense of fragmentation and isolation experienced by the characters.

HISTORICAL CONTEXT

Poverty in the 1920s and 1930s

As Linda Ray Pratt indicates in the introduction to *Yonnondio*, "Olsen was Mazie's age of nine or ten in the early 1920s and this novel 'from the thirties' mixes the two decades." Pratt notes that the movies referenced in the book date from 1919 through 1931, and workplace conditions at the slaughterhouse "reflect Olsen's early political activism in 1931–32." Further, Olsen references Depression-era "Hoovervilles," the shantytown communities that were named after President Herbert Hoover (whom many people blamed for the poor economy). In short, Olsen draws on issues of class and wealth that pervaded American society for two decades and encapsulates them into roughly a few years. The 1920s is often associated with great prosperity in American history; the era has been called the Roaring Twenties due to the wealth and excess enjoyed by many Americans. Yet some segments of the population did not partake of this financial success. As Brian Payne explains in an article for the *Bridgewater Review*, the United States experienced an economic recession in 1920 and 1921. Although the nation in general rebounded in the aftermath of this recession and enjoyed an economic boom, "good years were often as difficult as bad years for the working poor. Take, for example, the supposed 'roaring' decade of the 1920s, which historians now see as an awfully problematic decade that played a

considerable part in shaping the tragedy of the 1930s." Payne goes on to state that during that decade "long periods of unemployment and underemployment combined with increasing control of large corporations in shaping the nature of work left many working Americans totally unprepared for the 1930s." In assessing the Great Depression for the Social Welfare History Project, Jerry D. Marx asserts,

> The overall prosperity of the United States in the 1920s overshadowed the chronic poverty of certain vulnerable populations. These were the same populations that had always been at risk in American history: children, older Americans, minorities, female-headed families, people with disabilities, and workers with unstable or low-paying jobs.

The event that triggered the Great Depression was the stock market crash in 1929. The crash caused bank failures and, in a domino effect, unemployment and poverty. Marx observes, "Between 1929 and 1933, unemployment in the United States jumped from 3.2 percent to 24.9 percent, almost a quarter of the official labor force." In some cities it was as high as 80 percent. Consumer spending, manufacturing, and construction plummeted. Politicians feared massive rebellion by unemployed workers who were unable to feed their starving families. Looting and protests were prevalent. These trends directly corresponded with the presidency of Herbert Hoover, and his years in office are judged on his handling, or mishandling, of the economic and social issues of the Depression. Franklin Roosevelt was elected in 1932; after he took office in 1933, he began to implement measures to relieve the hardships suffered by the majority of the American population. Roosevelt established a number of new federal agencies and programs during his unprecedented four terms in office. The first was the Federal Emergency Relief Act of 1932, which in turn created the Federal Emergency Relief Administration. Marx writes, "FERA was given primary responsibility for managing the effort to distribute relief funds to individual states." Other job-creating organizations were created during this time, including the Civilian Works Administration, the Public Works Administration, and the Civilian Conservation Corps. However, it was the onset of World War II in 1939, and America's entry into the war in 1941, that ultimately did the most to alleviate

COMPARE & CONTRAST

- **1920s and 1930s:** Unemployment skyrockets to nearly a quarter of the workforce by 1933, as the effects of the stock market crash of 1929 seep into virtually every aspect of the American economy.

  1970s: During the 1970s, the United States undergoes a period of economic recession. The rate of unemployment increases from 4.5 percent in 1970 to a peak of 8.5 percent in 1975, before gradually decreasing to 5.8 percent in 1979.

  Today: The global economic crisis that began in 2008 is linked to a high unemployment rate in the United States. The rate of unemployment grows from 5.8 percent in 2008 to a high of 9.6 percent in 2010. By 2014, it has dropped to 6.2 percent.

- **1920s and 1930s:** The meatpacking industry is a vital part of the American economy. Midwestern cities such as Chicago, Kansas City, and Omaha are the largest meatpacking cities in the nation. Terrible working conditions result in the growth of labor unions in this industry.

  1970s: Drastic changes occur in the meatpacking industry in the 1960s and 1970s. After the growth of labor unions in the first decades of the twentieth century, meatpacking had become one of the highest-paying industries in the United States and had relatively low turnover rates. In the 1960s, the Iowa Beef Packers (IBP) company begins opening plants in rural areas where there is no union presence and begins hiring a large number of immigrant workers. By the 1970s, wages in the industry are falling rapidly as competitors struggled to keep pace with IBP.

  Today: The meatpacking industry in the twenty-first century has one of the highest turnover rates in the United States and is among the lowest-paying industries.

- **1920s and 1930s:** Official records of poverty rates during this time period are unavailable. During the 1920s, despite booming economic times for middle-class and upper-class Americans, the working-class poor suffer. As unemployment rates grow during the Great Depression, the ranks of Americans living in poverty swell. Many lose their homes and are forced to live on the streets in tents and shacks.

  1970s: The poverty rate is 11.2 percent in 1974. It is a year plagued by an economic recession.

  Today: The poverty rate in the United States falls to 14.5 percent in 2013, dropping from 15 percent in 2012.

---

the unemployment crisis in America. In the postwar years, America experienced another period of economic expansion.

The Midwest Meatpacking Industry in the 1920s and 1930s

The meatpacking industry played a large role in the nation's economy during the 1920s. As Linda Ray Pratt writes in the introduction to *Yonnondio*, "In the 1920s and 1930s Omaha was the third largest meatpacking city in the United States behind Chicago and Kansas City." It was fueled by largely by the efforts of ethnic (Czech and Polish) and racial (Mexican and African American) minorities. Olsen makes some references to the various ethnic groups vying for jobs in the slaughterhouse in her work. Pratt explains that between 1921 and 1922, large meatpacking companies—Armours, Swift, and Cudahy—succeeded in diminishing the influence of labor unions in the industry following a nationwide strike. Omaha, where part of Olsen's novel takes place, continued to be an integral part of the meatpacking industry

Although Jim disapproves, Anna takes in laundry to help make ends meet. *(© leonardo_da_gressignano /*
Shutterstock.com)

throughout these decades. Yet some meatpacking plants reestablished a union presence in the years that followed the nationwide strike. As Olsen indicates in the novel, Omaha was home to an Armours plant. The company also had plants in other Midwestern cities, including Kansas City. By the 1930s, that plant was among the largest in Kansas City and was home to Packing House Workers Industrial Union No. 232, according to David Fairris in *Shopfloor Matters: Labor–Management Relations in Twentieth-Century American Manufacturing*. In 1938, the plant managers at the Amours plant announced a mandated increase in one of their production standards, the "kill rate." Fairris writes:

> After a week of struggling under the new production standards, six workers in the hide cellar requested extra help, complaining that the work was too much for them. When the company refused to comply with the workers' request, the men sat down.

A struggle between labor and management ensued and resulted in a sit-down strike of seventeen hundred workers. The union ultimately prevailed, and the management gave in to their demands, not only in hiring the extra workers needed to increase the pace of work but also in paying for the time of the workers who testified in the original proceeding. In *Yonnondio*, Olsen provides a glimpse into the horrific working conditions endured by workers in the meatpacking industry, such as when she takes the reader into the slaughterhouse on a brutally hot summer day. What she depicts in the novel was inspired by what she witnessed in her own life. As a member of the Young Communist League, she distributed Communist leaflets outside a meatpacking house and was subsequently jailed for this effort to urge meatpacking workers to unite and fight for their rights.

CRITICAL OVERVIEW

Yonnondio is often discussed in light of its unconventional compilation and its publication history. The work was assembled in the early 1970s after fragments, some previously published and some not, were rediscovered by Olsen decades after she wrote them. Many critics have examined the novel within this context. Lisa Fry Dresdner, writing for the *Dictionary of Literary Biography*, traces some of this history, noting that Olsen rewrote none of the novel and pieced together the fragments. Dresdner goes on to characterize the novel as "a scathing indictment of the political and economic system that oppressed so many people," but she notes as well that "its humanistic themes suggest that the power to change comes from love." Other critics have examined the structure of the novel, which includes what Constance Coiner, in *Better Red: The Writing and Resistance of Tillie Olsen and Meridel Le Sueur*, describes as "narrative intrusions." These are instances where Olsen interrupts the narrative flow of the novel to include perspectives and tense shifts that are notable outliers, such as the Andy Kvaternick narration. Coiner studies the way these narrative shifts "challenge the reader in several ways." She states: "In each of the interpolations the changeling narrator assumes different stances and voices." Other critics investigate the tensions between the individual and the working class in particular or society in general. Lisa Orr, in an essay collected in *What We Hold in Common: An Introduction to Working-Class Studies*, explores themes of fragmentation and the notion of the "divided self" in the novel and observes that Olsen is "also obviously advocating a communist revolution." Orr argues that Old Man Caldwell pushes Mazie to understand her connection to her class. Orr finds an expression of hope in Mazie's downtrodden state, saying, "The conditions that make her life too horrible to escape even in dreams are the very conditions that make her a potential agent for revolutionary change."

CRITICISM

Catherine Dominic

Dominic is a novelist and freelance writer and editor. In the following essay, she studies the way Olsen explores the relationship between female

WHAT DO I READ NEXT?

- Olsen's famous novella *Tell Me a Riddle* is collected with other short works in *Tell Me a Riddle, Requa I, and Other Works*. The collection was published in 2013.

- Walt Whitman's poetry collection *Leaves of Grass* was original published in 1855. He subsequently published later editions of the collection with additions of other sections of poems. The 1891/1892 edition included a section called "Sands at Seventy," which includes the poem "Yonnondio." The collection that contains all of Whitman's revisions and additions is often referred to as the "Deathbed Edition."

- John Steinbeck's *The Grapes of Wrath*, like *Yonnondio*, focuses on the plight of an impoverished family. Steinbeck's novel takes place during the Great Depression and was published in 1939, during the same period when Olsen was writing the first draft of her novel. It is available in a modern reprint published by Penguin Books in 2002.

- Theodore Draper's 1957 *Roots of American Communism* provides a comprehensive history of the Communist Party in America from the early to mid-twentieth century.

- In 1971, Mexican-born author, poet, and labor activist Ernesto Galarza published a fictionalized memoir roughly based on his family's journey from a Mexican village to Sacramento, California. Like Olsen's work, it was written decades after the events took place, and both Olsen and Galarza look back on a life of poverty and struggle in the 1920s. *Barrio Boy*, which is targeted at a young-adult audience, was reissued in 1991 by the University of Notre Dame Press.

- David E. Kyvig's *Daily Life in the United States, 1920–1940: How Americans Lived through the Roaring Twenties and the Great Depression*, published in 2004, is a young-adult resource that provides students with historical, cultural, and political information on the 1920s and 1930s.

AT THE SAME TIME, ANNA IS A LIVING
EXAMPLE OF THE RELATIONSHIP BETWEEN FEMALE
SEXUALITY, MOTHERHOOD, AND POVERTY.
MAZIE WITNESSES ANNA'S SUFFERING AS A WOMAN
AND AS A MOTHER THROUGHOUT THE NOVEL."

sexuality, motherhood, and poverty in the novel
Yonnondio.

In *Yonnondio*, Olsen explores, among other
themes, the particular way poverty affects
women. Although she paints a full portrait of
the Holbrook family and allows the reader
access to the experiences of men, women, and
children, the central roles of Mazie and Anna in
the novel direct the reader's attention to issues of
poverty and early-twentieth-century notions of
gender and gender roles. Olsen's depiction of
Anna as wife and mother, and later of Mazie as
an adolescent, demonstrate the way in which a
woman's sexuality is a source of danger in the
world of the working-class poor depicted in the
novel.

Linda Ray Pratt touches on these ideas in
her introduction to the novel. She writes,

> The terrible life poverty imposes on Jim and
> Anna acts out its psychic consequences in the
> violence between them. . . . [Anna] taunts [Jim]
> with his failure to provide for the family and he
> exercises in physical and sexual force the power
> he lacks in any other space of his life.

While this exercising of male power and the
victimization of women are not troubles unique
to those suffering from poverty, the experience
of poverty, as Pratt suggests, heightens Jim's
sense of powerlessness and consequently his
need to wield power over his wife. Anna is then
victimized and subject to numerous pregnancies,
one of which ends in miscarriage after Jim rapes
her. She has no choice over what happens to her
body or over the number of children she brings
into the world, and she suffers the excruciating
pain of a mother unable to properly care for her
children. Her emotional though often-unspoken
refrain throughout the novel is finally verbalized
late in the book when she pleads to Jim, "The
children. What's going to happen with them?

How we going to look out for them in this
damn world? Oh Jim, the children. Seems like
we cant do nothing for them." Jim does not
reply.

Anna is introduced to the reader through a
conversation with Jim, which Mazie overhears.
They are discussing the death of a fellow miner,
Chris, and the concerns of his widow, Marie,
about their child beginning work in the mine at
age thirteen. Anna tells Jim how much Chris
wanted his son to be educated so he would not
have to work in the mine. When Jim comments,
"Them foreigners do have funny ideas," Anna
gently contradicts her husband. "Oh, I dunno,"
she begins. She then tells Jim how Marie wanted
her daughters to become nuns, so they would not
go hungry "or have to have kids." Jim responds,
"Well, what other earthly use can a woman have,
I'd like to know?" This exchange establishes the
foundation for the gender issues Olsen explores
in the novel and in particular the way a woman's
sexuality and childbearing potential intersects
with poverty. Anna's comment, "Oh, I dunno,"
provides significant insight into her character.
She has a difficult time directly contradicting
her husband—as the novel progresses, his physical abuse of her makes this reluctance more
understandable—but here, she gently questions
his dismissive comment about Marie's "funny
ideas" and her otherness, as a "foreigner." To
Jim, the idea that a woman could or should have
any other function besides childbearing is outlandish; it is, in fact, foreign to his way of thinking. But Anna clearly sympathizes with Marie's
desire to have her children avoid the pain of both
hunger and childbirth. Both Marie and Anna
understand what it is like to mother a child in
the brutal, deprived conditions in which both
families exist, and they want better for their
daughters. Marie actively and vocally wishes
that her daughters would renounce their sexuality, and she regards this as their path out of
poverty.

Within a few paragraphs, Anna's own
thinking about providing a path out of poverty
for her children is revealed. Mazie, having overheard her parents speaking about Marie's wish
for her son to receive an education, asks her
mother what, exactly, "edication" is. Anna
replies, "An edjication is what you kids are
going to get. It means your hands stay white
and you read books and work in an office."
Throughout the novel, Anna clings to the idea

of educating her children. Unlike Marie, she never voices a wish that her daughter turn away from her sexuality and avoid motherhood. At the same time, Anna is a living example of the relationship between female sexuality, motherhood, and poverty. Mazie witnesses Anna's suffering as a woman and as a mother throughout the novel.

Once the Holbrooks have moved to the farm and Jim has learned that all of his hard work rewards the bank and not his own family, the brief period of happiness the family enjoyed disappears. One winter night, when Jim reaches out to strike Anna, she yells at him not to touch her. He responds, "Don't touch ya, huh. You don't always talk like that. No wonder I never got anywhere. No wonder nothing ever comes right. Lots of help I get from my woman." Jim seems to be suggesting that Anna sometimes does want to be "touched." The implication is that she seeks out sexual interaction with him, and here he mocks her desire. His next words seem ambiguous—the "no wonder" comments about how he has never been successful and how he seems to blame Anna. When she tells him all the ways she does help, with housework and mothering, Jim responds, "Who asked for your goddam brats?" Now, his early hints are further elaborated on. He seems to be indicating that because Anna has sought a sexual relationship with him, he fathered children he never wanted and that this has led to his personal lack of success (and consequently the family's poverty). He places the burden of desire on Anna and sees the resulting offspring as somehow her fault. In this exchange, Olsen once again links female sexuality, motherhood, and poverty by having Jim link sex with parenthood and the resulting offspring with poverty. Yet Jim places the burden of blame—for desire, for unwanted children, for lack of financial success—all on Anna. The children are witness to this argument. Not long after, Anna gives birth to a baby girl, and the theme of the argument between Anna and Jim is given a bodily presence in the story.

After the family moves to Omaha, Anna becomes ill. She can barely function as a mother and homemaker; she is frequently on the verge of fainting and is in constant pain. In this state, Jim rapes her when he comes home drunk one night. Mazie overhears, though she does not completely understand what she is hearing. His words to her suggest it is her duty to "hold still" for him so that he does not have to seek sexual satisfaction elsewhere. Mazie later finds her mother in a pool of blood. After Jim fetches a doctor, it is revealed that Anna was pregnant again and has suffered a miscarriage as a result of Jim's attack. Anna's care afterward is ensured by women in the community who step in to help her. Mazie, too, is required to become a caretaker for baby Bess and to help with household chores. The boys pitch in as well, but the burden is primarily on Mazie because she is a girl.

Anna's recovery is hampered by her sense of duty to take care of the home and the children, and she remains constantly plagued by the poverty in which they live. She becomes obsessed with cleaning after a trip to the clinic, where she sees a poster urging mothers to keep households clean to prevent disease in children. Over and over, Anna receives the same messages about her duty to her children, about her role in bringing them into the world, and daily she is aware of her failure to care for them properly. A sense of futility overwhelms her. She thinks,

> It was that she felt so worn, so helpless; that it loomed gigantic beyond her, impossible ever to achieve, beyond any effort or doing of hers: that task of making a better life for her children to which her being was bound.

As Jim suggested, the children are, in part, the reason for Jim's and Anna's poverty. They need food, clothes, and shelter, and the cost of these needs outweighs what the uneducated Jim is able to earn. Further, Jim seeks relief in both alcohol and intercourse. Access to birth control was limited during the 1920s, and Anna does not have the option of abstinence, since Jim takes her by force, despite the fact that he has suggested it is her desire that has yielded unwanted offspring. Jim's behavior and the couple's lack of education perpetuate a cycle through which Anna's body is used and more children they cannot afford are brought into their lives.

Olsen refers to this connection between poverty and sexuality and gender again and again. Toward the end of the novel, it is underscored once more, through the now-adolescent Mazie. Mazie has been trying to continue her close relationship with her brother Will, though he no longer wishes to spend time with her because she is a girl. She begins to grow resentful that Will is excused from chores because he is a boy and that she cannot shoot off fireworks because she is a girl. She and Will used to follow the ice

The story ends with the family listening to the radio for the first time. (© Pyast | Shutterstock.com)

trucks in the heat of the summer (ice blocks were used for food storage in the days before mechanical refrigerators were common), waiting for ice that the deliveryman dropped. They would hitch a ride on the trucks as they moved through the streets. But Mazie stops following Will and his friends once they begin to raise a rowdy chant about everyone being able to see her underwear, her "pie," a euphemism for her genitalia. After the chant begins, "shame and self consciousness make her body awkward. . . . No more for her that lithe joy, that sense of power." Mazie loses the freedom and power she enjoyed when she went running after the ice trucks with the boys, once they notice that she is a girl, once they reference her sexuality. After this incident, Mazie is confined to the feminine sphere, to the tent that Ginella has erected near the dump. Here, everything feminine is idealized, and Mazie feels out of place. Here she is subjected once again to a reminder of her sexuality, when Ginella wraps "her arms tight around Mazie" and whispers passionately to her a line from a movie. Unready to accept her own sexual identity, Mazie remains isolated. Her feelings are

symbolized in her actions—when she finds a picture in a magazine at the dump, Mazie destroys an image of girlhood: "Mazie tore the little girl and the scary lines into teeny kite bits but didn't have any breath to blow them." In this image Olsen emphasizes Mazie's frustration with her feminine identity as well as her sense of futility about her fate as a woman in the society she inhabits. This futility mirrors Anna's experience, and it is the overriding idea that Olsen links with poverty and female sexuality throughout the novel.

Source: Catherine Dominic, Critical Essay on *Yonnondio: From the Thirties*, in *Novels for Students*, Gale, Cengage Learning, 2016.

Lisa Orr

In the following excerpt, Orr discusses the idea of a divided self in Yonnondio.

Reading Tillie Olsen's *Yonnondio* makes me tired and unhappy. In my mind, I am back in the neighborhood where I grew up. Surrounded by corner bars and turn-of-the-century factories, we lived our lives by the rhythms of the unemployment rate. When times were good, we tried

> IN PORTRAYING INDIVIDUALS IN MOMENTS
> WHEN THEY ARE SOMETHING MORE THAN PRODUCTS
> OF THE SYSTEM, SOMETHING MORE THAN VICTIMS,
> OLSEN CAN ALSO BE WRITING SUBVERSIVE PROSE."

to pay off our bills: five dollars a month to the dentist, more money down on the credit cards. When times were bad, we juggled who got paid that month by how nasty their demands for payment sounded: who would turn off service first, the phone company or the gas and electric? With each layoff we sank deeper into debt. With each plant closing my parents found fewer jobs that paid more than minimum wage. There was no money to move, and there certainly wasn't enough to stay. For us, living constantly in the red, escape seemed impossible.

I got out on other people's money—economic opportunity grants and scholarships. Reading *Yonnondio* renewed the guilt I feel about the others left behind, because *Yonnondio* is stunningly accurate in the oppressive, hopeless feelings it reproduces. The sense of "horror . . . on everything," which critic Annie Gottlieb unfortunately characterizes as melodramatic, is actually one of the most authentically reproduced aspects of working-class life in the book.

I have spent years hiding that part of my life. Finding a book that proved that literature could include the lives of working-class people was wonderful. But the fact remains that reading this book does not feel empowering to me. If anything, it makes me want to start taking the rungs two at a time on my way to the bourgeoisie. I don't want to identify with the working class in this book—it is just too painful.

The reader experiences what the characters feel: hopes collapse with the knowledge that life will continually beat one down. I have watched this sense that nothing can change prevent fellow workers from voting, participating in a union, turning in companies that violate safety codes—in short, from attempting anything that might improve their living conditions. The possibility of a person's having any effect on the system appears nil.

Disturbed by this hopelessness reflected in *Yonnondio* and in my own experience, I turned to Ernesto Laclau's *New Reflections on the Revolution of Our Time* to examine the question of agency. Writing in the late 1980s, in the midst of the transformations of various "socialist" countries into free-market economies, Laclau observes that classical Marxism cannot account for the survival of capitalist states. This leads him to reexamine Marx's argument that the proletariat will inevitably overthrow capitalism.

What Marx could not foresee was the extent to which capitalism could create an efficient, nondisruptive worker who would readily produce and consume products. Capitalism's longevity has led neo-Marxists such as Louis Althusser to posit that ideology creates the subjects necessary to perpetuate capitalism. But if workers are entirely determined by outside forces, they will, according to Laclau, be incapable of overthrowing capitalism.

Rather than accept this conclusion, Laclau notes that the belief that the worker is constructed by the system does not account for all the historical effects of capitalism. As he points out, capitalism has disrupted the lives of workers, but it has also generated unions and strikes, as well as worker-organized destruction of machinery. The system has defined groups of people who are linked by economic circumstances. Eventually this group will disband; the individual members dispersing to join other groups defined by different circumstances, such as race or gender. In this way, Laclau believes, the voices of opposition become stronger, as they can rally against numerous points.

Thus, for Laclau, the distinction between subjects who are completely inscribed by social forces and free agents who create their own society is an artificial one. The reality is constantly sliding between these two extremes. It is in this sense that Laclau sees a possibility of agency.

Olsen too sees capitalism as damaging people, who nonetheless retain some sense of human agency. Olsen, however, does not pass over the "ravages of circumstance" inflicted on workers by capitalism as easily as Laclau does. Her novel shows us the human cost of the system Laclau so optimistically views as generating its own downfall. For example, *Yonnondio* demonstrates how economic status has a direct effect on behavior. When times are good—such as when the Holbrooks begin their life on the farm—Jim and

Anna are happier together and kinder to their children. When money is tight, Jim cuffs them all around, and Anna strikes the children. She realizes, "'Twasn't them I was beatin up on. Somethin just seems to get into me when I have something to hit." The text takes a forgiving attitude toward Jim and Anna. The constant money worries, Jim's crippling, dangerous work, and Anna's struggle to care for her children without even the basics create tension and anger that cannot always be contained.

Significantly, we don't learn what Jim and Anna look like until they leave the mining town. Jim, on the way to the farm, wears "a look of being intoxicated, his heavy brown hair blowing back, his blue eyes glittering." Later, at the barn dance, we see Anna with her "black eyes laughing, her black hair smooth and shiny to purple." This is the most personal description the two receive in the novel. By the time they are described again, in Omaha, their personal traits are subsumed by the suffering or sullen appearance of most of their class. Anna's "great dark eyes" are lost "down a terrace of sunken flesh," and all that remains familiar of Jim is the strange blue of his eyes. In this sense capitalism does appear to be turning human beings into anonymous, identity-less workers.

The belief that the system cannot be changed is, as Laclau points out, paralyzing. Even the reader is conditioned to feel hopeless in this novel: we learn from experience to dread the bad times sure to follow any respite. Thus, when Olsen writes "in everyone's heart coiled the fear of a blowup," describing the family's final days at the mining town, she does more than create suspense. Suspense is only possible when there is a possibility that an incident may be averted. But Olsen's reference to a facile company statement on the "unavoidable catastrophe" indicates that this is an oft-repeated tragedy. The incompetence of the bosses, the gas-filled caves, the untimbered roofs make an "accident" not only difficult to avoid, but inevitable.

Outside forces collude to keep the Holbrooks down. Once at the farm, their neighbor Benson warns them, "You can't make a go of it . . . bad or good year, the bank swallows everything up and keeps you owin 'em." Anna's "cumulating vision of hostile, overwhelming forces" is based on fact: the banks, the bosses, and the landlords all have a stake in extracting

profit from the Holbrooks. No wonder Mazie cannot enjoy her family's fireworks. "O it's us again," she rejoices for a moment, but then realizes, "Now something bad's going to have to happen. Again."

Jim's misguided optimism at getting work at the packinghouse—"Didn't I tell you we'd manage? Good times comin, honey, good times"—is no antidote. His failure to analyze the forces that shape his life leads him to believe that a few more pennies a day will make a difference. The reader, like Jim's friend Kryckszi, knows better.

These ominous passages must not be read simply as foreshadowing. Olsen clearly is not interested in aesthetic effects alone, as her comments during the blowup scene at the mine illustrate: "And could you not make a cameo of this and pin it onto your aesthetic hearts? . . . Surely it is classical enough for you—the Greek marble of the women, the simple, flowing lines of sorrow." Olsen's foreshadowing carries a political message: "hostile forces" attempt to convince working people that they are helpless, that nothing will ever get better, that resistance is useless.

With this knowledge, we can understand why Mazie is afraid to hope any longer. At one point she allows herself to pretend she is back on the farm, but then harshly chastises herself: the grief, the mourning is too hard to bear. This is how a working-class child is forced to cripple her own imagination. With even imaginative escape a cause of pain, the future for Mazie appears unalterably bleak.

According to many critics, what *Yonnondio* offers as a source of hope is the transcendence of the individual, such as the survival of "Anna's remarkable character." The final scene, in which baby Bess discovers her ability to affect the world around her, has also been read as an illustration of that fundamental optimism. But to read this novel as only a story of the "rebirth of the spirit," as a *Village Voice* critic rhapsodizes on my edition's back cover, is to gloss over what it has to tell us about the destruction that capitalism causes, the destruction that Laclau so easily passes over. These critics are ignoring what actually occurs in the novel: while Olsen imagines children born with a self intact, their circumstances crush it out of them. No workers survive undamaged. At best they manage to retain something of their identity. This is why Olsen's novel focuses on retaining a sense of self, while at the same time she has been quoted as saying, "It is irrelevant to even talk of a core of Self when circumstances do not sustain its expression or development, when life has tampered with it and harmed it." Worrying about having a self, she suggests, is a luxury. But it is also a form of resistance.

Anna knows the value of keeping one's inner self alive, and tries to pass this knowledge on to her children. On the one day when Anna is free of her daily routine—the day she and the children pick dandelion greens—Anna repieces the parts of herself that have been scattered by the various demands on her.

At first it seems that Anna's escape comes at the expense of her children. She wears a "remote, shining look . . . on her face, as if she had forgotten them, as if she . . . was not their mother any more." Later, "Mazie felt the strange happiness in her mother's body, happiness that had nothing to do with them, with her; happiness and farness and selfness." Her mother's distance is profoundly disturbing to Mazie, who longs to snap her fingers under her mother's nose.

But having momentarily recovered a selfhood, Anna can offer her children the kind of mothering that gets lost in caring for everyday needs. Her fingers stroke Mazie "into happiness and intactness and selfness." In this mood Anna can heal the "hurt and fear and want and shame" that she ordinarily cannot redress.

The interlude does not last long. A whiff of the packinghouse brings back "the mother alertness, attunement, in her bounded body." But even after her return to boundedness, she uses a phrase the children have never heard her say before: "Holy Meroly." Something of the Anna who is more than clothes-washer, cook, or cleaning lady survives.

In interviews, Olsen insists that "her involvement in a 'full extended family life' did not fracture her selfhood." Anna cannot be conflated with Olsen, but Olsen's insistence suggests we should read this scene carefully. The fact that the packinghouse smell brings Anna back to motherhood is significant. It is not motherhood that limits women, it is motherhood in these economic circumstances. While Anna has been ill, "a separation, a distance—something broken and new and tremulous—ha[s] been born in her." It is free to develop because the house is neglected, a neighbor tends the baby, someone else prepares the meals—for a while she is free of her deadening routine.

In Laclau's terms, the Anna who sits under a tree stroking Mazie's hair is not the same Anna who hits her children. Olsen optimistically sees the Anna who sings to her children as Anna's "real self" who can bring out the "selves" within her children; to Laclau this very fragmentation precludes any essential self, which, to use his terms, is both "blocked" and "affirmed" by the forces arrayed against it. But Laclau would agree that Anna is not reducible to the sum of capitalism's effects on a working-class wife. The Anna who stubbornly insists "Better . . . to be a cripple and alive than dead, not able to feel anything" is a source of resistance in the novel.

Mazie, too, resists the "inevitable . . . reduction of iron-willed humans to scrap." Repeatedly she seeks confirmation from those around her that she is a human being. In the first chapter she seeks out her father in order "to force him into some recognition of her existence, her desire, her emotions." When the family moves to Omaha, Mazie feels most threatened by the anonymous faces passing her on the street, "faces that knew her not, that saw her not."

Yonnondio demonstrates repeatedly how ugliness can crush the spirit. For Mazie the shock of the city is so great that she wanders in a dream until a drunken passerby knocks her down. Later, she suddenly notices the morbid, depressing stories Ben has been telling Jimmie, and realizes they are destructive. As the narrator explains, "The conjurer is working spells on Anna's children. Subtly into waking and dreaming, into imagination and everyday doings and play, shaping, altering them." The poems Ben recites are part of the spell, hardening them, numbing their senses. Mazie seeks out happier children's stories from her parents, but her father can no longer tell them: "The day at Cudahy's has thieved Pop's text." Anna might remember some, but by the time she finishes her household chores, "it is too late for texts."

Thus Anna, dreaming of a future on the farm and beautiful things to keep, is not succumbing to bourgeois brainwashing. She is not a materialist dreaming of acquiring objects for the sake of status. She simply knows the price of raising children in such surroundings. An ugly world is as deadening to the senses as meaningless, monotonous work. Locating beauty is not an empty aesthetic exercise but a tool for survival.

In the struggle to maintain selfhood, Mazie has an advantage that Anna and perhaps Ben share. She has a gift for finding beauty in surprising places, and she uses this gift to resist the numbing effects of her circumstances.

... Mazie, if a self-absorbed artist, would not be a voice for her silenced class. The fact that Mazie has been damaged, that even the "terrible lands of dream" offer no escape to her, makes her the better activist. When Caldwell tells Mazie "Whatever happens, remember, everything, the nourishment, the roots you need, are where you are now," he is pushing her to remain loyal to her class. But he is also reminding her of the source of her political usefulness. The conditions that make her life too horrible to escape even in dreams are the very conditions that make her a potential agent for revolutionary change.

Mazie can interact with and change the structure because the structure has partially created in her a person capable of undermining it. As Laclau explains, human beings create their own identities in the decisions they make, decisions that are made possible by the gaps in the structure. Thus "the constitution of a social identity is an act of power and ... identity as such is power."

As we have seen, this leaves us with a subject who is divided and unpredictable. But Laclau sees this fragmented subject as a source of optimism. In his words, "One of the consequences of fragmentation is that the issues, which are the rallying point for the various social struggles, acquire greater autonomy and face the political system with growing demands. They thus become more difficult to manipulate and disregard."

Tillie Olsen's work demonstrates the importance of this divided self, even though she is also obviously advocating a communist revolution. Rosenfelt has written that Olsen "found herself unable to document the political vision of social revolution as authentically and nonrhetorically as she was able to portray the ravages of circumstance on families and individuals and the redeeming moments between them." But the two subjects are not necessarily exclusive. In portraying individuals in moments when they are something more than products of the system, something more than victims, Olsen can also be writing subversive prose. In doing so, she prefigures Laclau by almost sixty years.

Laclau's optimism about the fragmented self is then justified. As he predicted, the system has produced an individual who has the potential to overthrow it. Rereading *Yonnondio* with Laclau in mind helps me see room for hope in it. *Yonnondio* does not merely reproduce that despair which can be so crippling and antirevolutionary. Ultimately, Laclau helped me understand what originally seemed like a contradiction in Olsen. Olsen can say in the same interview, "I am a destroyed person" and "I am a survivor," because they are both true at once.

Source: Lisa Orr, "'People Who Might Have Been You': Agency and the Damaged Self in Tillie Olsen's *Yonnondio*," in *What We Hold in Common: An Introduction to Working-Class Studies*, edited by Janet Zandy, The Feminist Press at the City University of New York, 2001, pp. 199–203, 205–206.

SOURCES

Coiner, Constance, "Olsen's *Yonnondio: From the Thirties*," in *Better Red: The Writing and Resistance of Tillie Olsen and Meridel Le Sueur*, Oxford University Press, 1995, pp. 174–91.

Dresdner, Lisa Fry, "Tillie Olsen," in *Dictionary of Literary Biography*, Vol. 206, *Twentieth-Century American Western Writers, First Series*, edited by Richard H. Cracroft, The Gale Group, 1999, pp. 234–42.

Fairris, David, *Shopfloor Matters: Labor–Management Relations in Twentieth-Century American Manufacturing*, Routledge, 1997, pp. 89–98.

"Labor Force Statistics from the Current Population Survey," in *Databases, Tables & Calculators by Subject*, US Bureau of Labor Statistics, http://data.bls.gov/time series/LNU04000000?years_option = all_years&periods_ option = specific_periods&periods = Annual + Data (accessed January 17, 2015).

Luhby, Tami, "U.S. Poverty Rate Drops for First Time since 2006," CNN, September 16, 2014, http://money .cnn.com/2014/09/16/news/economy/median-income- poverty-rate-down-census/ (accessed January 17, 2015).

Marx, Jerry D., "American Social Policy in the Great Depression and World War II," Social Welfare History Project, http://www.socialwelfarehistory.com/eras/ american-social-policy-in-the-great-depression-and-wwii/ (accessed January 17, 2015).

Olsen, Tillie, *Yonnondio*, University of Nebraska Press, 2004.

Orr, Lisa, "'People Who Might Have Been You': Agency and the Damaged Self in Tillie Olsen's *Yonnondio*," in *What We Hold in Common: An Introduction to Working-Class Studies*, edited by Janet Zandy, The

Feminist Press at the City University of New York, 2001, pp. 199–206.

Payne, Brian, "Poverty in the Prosperous Years: The Working Poor of the 1920s and Today," in *Bridgewater Review*, November 2013, Vol. 32, No. 2, pp. 11–15, http://vc.bridgew.edu/br_rev/vol32/iss2/6 (accessed January 17, 2015).

Pratt, Linda Ray, Introduction to *Yonnondio*, in *Yonnondio*, by Tillie Olsen, University of Nebraska Press, 2004, pp. v–xvi.

Schlosser, Eric, "The Chain Never Stops," in *Mother Jones*, July/August 2001, http://www.motherjones.com/politics/2001/07/dangerous-meatpacking-jobs-eric-schlosser (accessed January 17, 2015).

Warren, Wilson J., *Tied to the Great Packing Machine: The Midwest and Meatpacking*, University of Iowa Press, 2007, pp. 49–72.

Amendment, which gave women the right to vote. He explores women's inequality in terms of sexual division of labor and studies the changing face of feminism in America.

Olsen, Tillie, *Silences*, The Feminist Press at CUNY, 2003.
> Originally published in 1978, *Silences* is a collection of essays that explores women's writing and the writing of working-class individuals. Olsen focuses on the ways in which gender, race, and class can silence the creative process.

Ottanelli, Fraser, *The Communist Party of the United States from the Depression to World War II*, Rutgers University Press, 1991.
> Ottanelli's work offers an accessible overview of the Communist Party and its impact on American politics and the labor movement.

FURTHER READING

Brown, Jonathan, *Farming in the 1920s and '30s*, Shire Library, 2012.
> Brown's volume explores the way that, in the aftermath of World War I, farmers in the 1920s were forced to adapt to the low crop prices of peacetime. They had to earn a living by farming during a recession and later during the Great Depression.

Chafe, William H., *The American Woman: Her Changing Social, Economic, and Political Roles, 1920–1970*, Oxford University Press, 1972.
> Chafe focuses his examination on the status of women in American society in the decades following the passage of the Nineteenth

SUGGESTED SEARCH TERMS

Tillie Olsen AND Yonnondio

Tillie Olsen AND feminism

Tillie Olsen AND Communism

Tillie Olsen AND labor movement

Roaring Twenties AND poverty

Great Depression AND farming

1920s AND mining communities

1920s AND meatpacking industry

meatpacking industry AND labor unions

labor unions AND Communism AND 1920s

Glossary of Literary Terms

A

Abstract: As an adjective applied to writing or literary works, abstract refers to words or phrases that name things not knowable through the five senses.

Aestheticism: A literary and artistic movement of the nineteenth century. Followers of the movement believed that art should not be mixed with social, political, or moral teaching. The statement "art for art's sake" is a good summary of aestheticism. The movement had its roots in France, but it gained widespread importance in England in the last half of the nineteenth century, where it helped change the Victorian practice of including moral lessons in literature.

Allegory: A narrative technique in which characters representing things or abstract ideas are used to convey a message or teach a lesson. Allegory is typically used to teach moral, ethical, or religious lessons but is sometimes used for satiric or political purposes.

Allusion: A reference to a familiar literary or historical person or event, used to make an idea more easily understood.

Analogy: A comparison of two things made to explain something unfamiliar through its similarities to something familiar, or to prove one point based on the acceptedness of another. Similes and metaphors are types of analogies.

Antagonist: The major character in a narrative or drama who works against the hero or protagonist.

Anthropomorphism: The presentation of animals or objects in human shape or with human characteristics. The term is derived from the Greek word for "human form."

Anti-hero: A central character in a work of literature who lacks traditional heroic qualities such as courage, physical prowess, and fortitude. Anti-heroes typically distrust conventional values and are unable to commit themselves to any ideals. They generally feel helpless in a world over which they have no control. Anti-heroes usually accept, and often celebrate, their positions as social outcasts.

Apprenticeship Novel: See *Bildungsroman*

Archetype: The word archetype is commonly used to describe an original pattern or model from which all other things of the same kind are made. This term was introduced to literary criticism from the psychology of Carl Jung. It expresses Jung's theory that behind every person's "unconscious," or repressed memories of the past, lies the "collective unconscious" of the human race: memories of the countless typical experiences of our ancestors. These memories are said to prompt illogical associations that trigger powerful emotions in the reader. Often, the emotional process is primitive, even primordial. Archetypes are the literary images that grow out of the "collective unconscious." They appear in literature as incidents and plots that repeat basic patterns of life. They may also appear as stereotyped characters.

Avant-garde: French term meaning "vanguard." It is used in literary criticism to describe new writing that rejects traditional approaches to literature in favor of innovations in style or content.

B

Beat Movement: A period featuring a group of American poets and novelists of the 1950s and 1960s—including Jack Kerouac, Allen Ginsberg, Gregory Corso, William S. Burroughs, and Lawrence Ferlinghetti—who rejected established social and literary values. Using such techniques as stream of consciousness writing and jazz-influenced free verse and focusing on unusual or abnormal states of mind—generated by religious ecstasy or the use of drugs—the Beat writers aimed to create works that were unconventional in both form and subject matter.

Bildungsroman: A German word meaning "novel of development." The *bildungsroman* is a study of the maturation of a youthful character, typically brought about through a series of social or sexual encounters that lead to self-awareness. *Bildungsroman* is used interchangeably with *erziehungsroman,* a novel of initiation and education. When a *bildungsroman* is concerned with the development of an artist (as in James Joyce's *A Portrait of the Artist as a Young Man*), it is often termed a *kunstlerroman.*

Black Aesthetic Movement: A period of artistic and literary development among African Americans in the 1960s and early 1970s. This was the first major African-American artistic movement since the Harlem Renaissance and was closely paralleled by the civil rights and black power movements. The black aesthetic writers attempted to produce works of art that would be meaningful to the black masses. Key figures in black aesthetics included one of its founders, poet and playwright Amiri Baraka, formerly known as LeRoi Jones; poet and essayist Haki R. Madhubuti, formerly Don L. Lee; poet and playwright Sonia Sanchez; and dramatist Ed Bullins.

Black Humor: Writing that places grotesque elements side by side with humorous ones in an attempt to shock the reader, forcing him or her to laugh at the horrifying reality of a disordered world.

Burlesque: Any literary work that uses exaggeration to make its subject appear ridiculous, either by treating a trivial subject with profound seriousness or by treating a dignified subject frivolously. The word "burlesque" may also be used as an adjective, as in "burlesque show," to mean "striptease act."

C

Character: Broadly speaking, a person in a literary work. The actions of characters are what constitute the plot of a story, novel, or poem. There are numerous types of characters, ranging from simple, stereotypical figures to intricate, multifaceted ones. In the techniques of anthropomorphism and personification, animals—and even places or things—can assume aspects of character. "Characterization" is the process by which an author creates vivid, believable characters in a work of art. This may be done in a variety of ways, including (1) direct description of the character by the narrator; (2) the direct presentation of the speech, thoughts, or actions of the character; and (3) the responses of other characters to the character. The term "character" also refers to a form originated by the ancient Greek writer Theophrastus that later became popular in the seventeenth and eighteenth centuries. It is a short essay or sketch of a person who prominently displays a specific attribute or quality, such as miserliness or ambition.

Climax: The turning point in a narrative, the moment when the conflict is at its most intense. Typically, the structure of stories, novels, and plays is one of rising action, in which tension builds to the climax, followed by falling action, in which tension lessens as the story moves to its conclusion.

Colloquialism: A word, phrase, or form of pronunciation that is acceptable in casual conversation but not in formal, written communication. It is considered more acceptable than slang.

Coming of Age Novel: See *Bildungsroman*

Concrete: Concrete is the opposite of abstract, and refers to a thing that actually exists or a description that allows the reader to experience an object or concept with the senses.

Connotation: The impression that a word gives beyond its defined meaning. Connotations may be universally understood or may be significant only to a certain group.

Convention: Any widely accepted literary device, style, or form.

D

Denotation: The definition of a word, apart from the impressions or feelings it creates (connotations) in the reader.

Denouement: A French word meaning "the unknotting." In literary criticism, it denotes the resolution of conflict in fiction or drama. The *denouement* follows the climax and provides an outcome to the primary plot situation as well as an explanation of secondary plot complications. The *denouement* often involves a character's recognition of his or her state of mind or moral condition.

Description: Descriptive writing is intended to allow a reader to picture the scene or setting in which the action of a story takes place. The form this description takes often evokes an intended emotional response—a dark, spooky graveyard will evoke fear, and a peaceful, sunny meadow will evoke calmness.

Dialogue: In its widest sense, dialogue is simply conversation between people in a literary work; in its most restricted sense, it refers specifically to the speech of characters in a drama. As a specific literary genre, a "dialogue" is a composition in which characters debate an issue or idea.

Diction: The selection and arrangement of words in a literary work. Either or both may vary depending on the desired effect. There are four general types of diction: "formal," used in scholarly or lofty writing; "informal," used in relaxed but educated conversation; "colloquial," used in everyday speech; and "slang," containing newly coined words and other terms not accepted in formal usage.

Didactic: A term used to describe works of literature that aim to teach some moral, religious, political, or practical lesson. Although didactic elements are often found in artistically pleasing works, the term "didactic" usually refers to literature in which the message is more important than the form. The term may also be used to criticize a work that the critic finds "overly didactic," that is, heavy-handed in its delivery of a lesson.

Doppelganger: A literary technique by which a character is duplicated (usually in the form of an alter ego, though sometimes as a ghostly counterpart) or divided into two distinct, usually opposite personalities. The use of this character device is widespread in nineteenth- and twentieth-century literature, and indicates a growing awareness among authors that the "self" is really a composite of many "selves."

Double Entendre: A corruption of a French phrase meaning "double meaning." The term is used to indicate a word or phrase that is deliberately ambiguous, especially when one of the meanings is risqué or improper.

Dramatic Irony: Occurs when the audience of a play or the reader of a work of literature knows something that a character in the work itself does not know. The irony is in the contrast between the intended meaning of the statements or actions of a character and the additional information understood by the audience.

Dystopia: An imaginary place in a work of fiction where the characters lead dehumanized, fearful lives.

E

Edwardian: Describes cultural conventions identified with the period of the reign of Edward VII of England (1901-1910). Writers of the Edwardian Age typically displayed a strong reaction against the propriety and conservatism of the Victorian Age. Their work often exhibits distrust of authority in religion, politics, and art and expresses strong doubts about the soundness of conventional values.

Empathy: A sense of shared experience, including emotional and physical feelings, with someone or something other than oneself. Empathy is often used to describe the response of a reader to a literary character.

Enlightenment, The: An eighteenth-century philosophical movement. It began in France but had a wide impact throughout Europe and America. Thinkers of the Enlightenment valued reason and believed that both the individual and society could achieve a state of perfection. Corresponding to this essentially humanist vision was a resistance to religious authority.

Epigram: A saying that makes the speaker's point quickly and concisely. Often used to preface a novel.

Epilogue: A concluding statement or section of a literary work. In dramas, particularly those of the seventeenth and eighteenth centuries, the epilogue is a closing speech, often in verse, delivered by an actor at the end of a play and spoken directly to the audience.

Epiphany: A sudden revelation of truth inspired by a seemingly trivial incident.

Episode: An incident that forms part of a story and is significantly related to it. Episodes may be either self-contained narratives or events that depend on a larger context for their sense and importance.

Epistolary Novel: A novel in the form of letters. The form was particularly popular in the eighteenth century.

Epithet: A word or phrase, often disparaging or abusive, that expresses a character trait of someone or something.

Existentialism: A predominantly twentieth-century philosophy concerned with the nature and perception of human existence. There are two major strains of existentialist thought: atheistic and Christian. Followers of atheistic existentialism believe that the individual is alone in a godless universe and that the basic human condition is one of suffering and loneliness. Nevertheless, because there are no fixed values, individuals can create their own characters—indeed, they can shape themselves—through the exercise of free will. The atheistic strain culminates in and is popularly associated with the works of Jean-Paul Sartre. The Christian existentialists, on the other hand, believe that only in God may people find freedom from life's anguish. The two strains hold certain beliefs in common: that existence cannot be fully understood or described through empirical effort; that anguish is a universal element of life; that individuals must bear responsibility for their actions; and that there is no common standard of

behavior or perception for religious and ethical matters.

Expatriates: See *Expatriatism*

Expatriatism: The practice of leaving one's country to live for an extended period in another country.

Exposition: Writing intended to explain the nature of an idea, thing, or theme. Expository writing is often combined with description, narration, or argument. In dramatic writing, the exposition is the introductory material which presents the characters, setting, and tone of the play.

Expressionism: An indistinct literary term, originally used to describe an early twentieth-century school of German painting. The term applies to almost any mode of unconventional, highly subjective writing that distorts reality in some way.

F

Fable: A prose or verse narrative intended to convey a moral. Animals or inanimate objects with human characteristics often serve as characters in fables.

Falling Action: See *Denouement*

Fantasy: A literary form related to mythology and folklore. Fantasy literature is typically set in non-existent realms and features supernatural beings.

Farce: A type of comedy characterized by broad humor, outlandish incidents, and often vulgar subject matter.

Femme fatale: A French phrase with the literal translation "fatal woman." A *femme fatale* is a sensuous, alluring woman who often leads men into danger or trouble.

Fiction: Any story that is the product of imagination rather than a documentation of fact. Characters and events in such narratives may be based in real life but their ultimate form and configuration is a creation of the author.

Figurative Language: A technique in writing in which the author temporarily interrupts the order, construction, or meaning of the writing for a particular effect. This interruption takes the form of one or more figures of speech such as hyperbole, irony, or simile. Figurative language is the opposite of literal language, in which every word is truthful, accurate, and free of exaggeration or embellishment.

Figures of Speech: Writing that differs from customary conventions for construction, meaning, order, or significance for the purpose of a special meaning or effect. There are two major types of figures of speech: rhetorical figures, which do not make changes in the meaning of the words, and tropes, which do.

Fin de siecle: A French term meaning "end of the century." The term is used to denote the last decade of the nineteenth century, a transition period when writers and other artists abandoned old conventions and looked for new techniques and objectives.

First Person: See *Point of View*

Flashback: A device used in literature to present action that occurred before the beginning of the story. Flashbacks are often introduced as the dreams or recollections of one or more characters.

Foil: A character in a work of literature whose physical or psychological qualities contrast strongly with, and therefore highlight, the corresponding qualities of another character.

Folklore: Traditions and myths preserved in a culture or group of people. Typically, these are passed on by word of mouth in various forms—such as legends, songs, and proverbs—or preserved in customs and ceremonies. This term was first used by W. J. Thoms in 1846.

Folktale: A story originating in oral tradition. Folktales fall into a variety of categories, including legends, ghost stories, fairy tales, fables, and anecdotes based on historical figures and events.

Foreshadowing: A device used in literature to create expectation or to set up an explanation of later developments.

Form: The pattern or construction of a work which identifies its genre and distinguishes it from other genres.

G

Genre: A category of literary work. In critical theory, genre may refer to both the content of a given work—tragedy, comedy, pastoral—and to its form, such as poetry, novel, or drama.

Gilded Age: A period in American history during the 1870s characterized by political corruption and materialism. A number of important novels of social and political criticism were written during this time.

Gothicism: In literary criticism, works characterized by a taste for the medieval or morbidly attractive. A gothic novel prominently features elements of horror, the supernatural, gloom, and violence: clanking chains, terror, charnel houses, ghosts, medieval castles, and mysteriously slamming doors. The term "gothic novel" is also applied to novels that lack elements of the traditional Gothic setting but that create a similar atmosphere of terror or dread.

Grotesque: In literary criticism, the subject matter of a work or a style of expression characterized by exaggeration, deformity, freakishness, and disorder. The grotesque often includes an element of comic absurdity.

H

Harlem Renaissance: The Harlem Renaissance of the 1920s is generally considered the first significant movement of black writers and artists in the United States. During this period, new and established black writers published more fiction and poetry than ever before, the first influential black literary journals were established, and black authors and artists received their first widespread recognition and serious critical appraisal. Among the major writers associated with this period are Claude McKay, Jean Toomer, Countee Cullen, Langston Hughes, Arna Bontemps, Nella Larsen, and Zora Neale Hurston.

Hero/Heroine: The principal sympathetic character (male or female) in a literary work. Heroes and heroines typically exhibit admirable traits: idealism, courage, and integrity, for example.

Holocaust Literature: Literature influenced by or written about the Holocaust of World War II. Such literature includes true stories of survival in concentration camps, escape, and life after the war, as well as fictional works and poetry.

Humanism: A philosophy that places faith in the dignity of humankind and rejects the medieval perception of the individual as a weak, fallen creature. "Humanists" typically believe in the perfectibility of human nature and view reason and education as the means to that end.

Hyperbole: In literary criticism, deliberate exaggeration used to achieve an effect.

I

Idiom: A word construction or verbal expression closely associated with a given language.

Image: A concrete representation of an object or sensory experience. Typically, such a representation helps evoke the feelings associated with the object or experience itself. Images are either "literal" or "figurative." Literal images are especially concrete and involve little or no extension of the obvious meaning of the words used to express them. Figurative images do not follow the literal meaning of the words exactly. Images in literature are usually visual, but the term "image" can also refer to the representation of any sensory experience.

Imagery: The array of images in a literary work. Also, figurative language.

In medias res: A Latin term meaning "in the middle of things." It refers to the technique of beginning a story at its midpoint and then using various flashback devices to reveal previous action.

Interior Monologue: A narrative technique in which characters' thoughts are revealed in a way that appears to be uncontrolled by the author. The interior monologue typically aims to reveal the inner self of a character. It portrays emotional experiences as they occur at both a conscious and unconscious level. images are often used to represent sensations or emotions.

Irony: In literary criticism, the effect of language in which the intended meaning is the opposite of what is stated.

J

Jargon: Language that is used or understood only by a select group of people. Jargon may refer to terminology used in a certain profession, such as computer jargon, or it may refer to any nonsensical language that is not understood by most people.

L

Leitmotiv: See *Motif*

Literal Language: An author uses literal language when he or she writes without exaggerating or embellishing the subject matter and without any tools of figurative language.

Lost Generation: A term first used by Gertrude Stein to describe the post-World War I generation of American writers: men and women haunted by a sense of betrayal and emptiness brought about by the destructiveness of the war.

M

Mannerism: Exaggerated, artificial adherence to a literary manner or style. Also, a popular style of the visual arts of late sixteenth-century Europe that was marked by elongation of the human form and by intentional spatial distortion. Literary works that are self-consciously high-toned and artistic are often said to be "mannered."

Metaphor: A figure of speech that expresses an idea through the image of another object. Metaphors suggest the essence of the first object by identifying it with certain qualities of the second object.

Modernism: Modern literary practices. Also, the principles of a literary school that lasted from roughly the beginning of the twentieth century until the end of World War II. Modernism is defined by its rejection of the literary conventions of the nineteenth century and by its opposition to conventional morality, taste, traditions, and economic values.

Mood: The prevailing emotions of a work or of the author in his or her creation of the work. The mood of a work is not always what might be expected based on its subject matter.

Motif: A theme, character type, image, metaphor, or other verbal element that recurs throughout a single work of literature or occurs in a number of different works over a period of time.

Myth: An anonymous tale emerging from the traditional beliefs of a culture or social unit. Myths use supernatural explanations for natural phenomena. They may also explain cosmic issues like creation and death. Collections of myths, known as mythologies, are common to all cultures and nations, but the best-known myths belong to the Norse, Roman, and Greek mythologies.

N

Narration: The telling of a series of events, real or invented. A narration may be either a simple narrative, in which the events are recounted chronologically, or a narrative with a plot, in which the account is given in a style reflecting the author's artistic concept of the story. Narration is sometimes used as a synonym for "storyline."

Narrative: A verse or prose accounting of an event or sequence of events, real or invented. The term is also used as an adjective in the sense "method of narration." For example, in literary criticism, the expression "narrative technique" usually refers to the way the author structures and presents his or her story.

Narrator: The teller of a story. The narrator may be the author or a character in the story through whom the author speaks.

Naturalism: A literary movement of the late nineteenth and early twentieth centuries. The movement's major theorist, French novelist Emile Zola, envisioned a type of fiction that would examine human life with the objectivity of scientific inquiry. The Naturalists typically viewed human beings as either the products of "biological determinism," ruled by hereditary instincts and engaged in an endless struggle for survival, or as the products of "socioeconomic determinism," ruled by social and economic forces beyond their control. In their works, the Naturalists generally ignored the highest levels of society and focused on degradation: poverty, alcoholism, prostitution, insanity, and disease.

Noble Savage: The idea that primitive man is noble and good but becomes evil and corrupted as he becomes civilized. The concept of the noble savage originated in the Renaissance period but is more closely identified with such later writers as Jean-Jacques Rousseau and Aphra Behn.

Novel: A long fictional narrative written in prose, which developed from the novella and other early forms of narrative. A novel is usually organized under a plot or theme with a focus on character development and action.

Novel of Ideas: A novel in which the examination of intellectual issues and concepts takes precedence over characterization or a traditional storyline.

Novel of Manners: A novel that examines the customs and mores of a cultural group.

Novella: An Italian term meaning "story." This term has been especially used to describe fourteenth-century Italian tales, but it also refers to modern short novels.

O

Objective Correlative: An outward set of objects, a situation, or a chain of events corresponding to an inward experience and evoking this experience in the reader. The term frequently appears in modern criticism in discussions of authors' intended effects on the emotional responses of readers.

Objectivity: A quality in writing characterized by the absence of the author's opinion or feeling about the subject matter. Objectivity is an important factor in criticism.

Oedipus Complex: A son's amorous obsession with his mother. The phrase is derived from the story of the ancient Theban hero Oedipus, who unknowingly killed his father and married his mother.

Omniscience: See *Point of View*

Onomatopoeia: The use of words whose sounds express or suggest their meaning. In its simplest sense, onomatopoeia may be represented by words that mimic the sounds they denote such as "hiss" or "meow." At a more subtle level, the pattern and rhythm of sounds and rhymes of a line or poem may be onomatopoeic.

Oxymoron: A phrase combining two contradictory terms. Oxymorons may be intentional or unintentional.

P

Parable: A story intended to teach a moral lesson or answer an ethical question.

Paradox: A statement that appears illogical or contradictory at first, but may actually point to an underlying truth.

Parallelism: A method of comparison of two ideas in which each is developed in the same grammatical structure.

Parody: In literary criticism, this term refers to an imitation of a serious literary work or the signature style of a particular author in a ridiculous manner. A typical parody adopts the style of the original and applies it to an inappropriate subject for humorous effect. Parody is a form of satire and could be considered the literary equivalent of a caricature or cartoon.

Pastoral: A term derived from the Latin word "pastor," meaning shepherd. A pastoral is a literary composition on a rural theme. The conventions of the pastoral were originated by the third-century Greek poet Theocritus, who wrote about the experiences, love affairs, and pastimes of Sicilian shepherds. In a pastoral, characters and language of a courtly nature are often placed in a simple setting. The term pastoral is also used to classify dramas, elegies, and lyrics that exhibit the use of country settings and shepherd characters.

Pen Name: See *Pseudonym*

Persona: A Latin term meaning "mask." *Personae* are the characters in a fictional work of literature. The *persona* generally functions as a mask through which the author tells a story in a voice other than his or her own. A *persona* is usually either a character in a story who acts as a narrator or an "implied author," a voice created by the author to act as the narrator for himself or herself.

Personification: A figure of speech that gives human qualities to abstract ideas, animals, and inanimate objects.

Picaresque Novel: Episodic fiction depicting the adventures of a roguish central character ("picaro" is Spanish for "rogue"). The picaresque hero is commonly a low-born but clever individual who wanders into and out of various affairs of love, danger, and farcical intrigue. These involvements may take place at all social levels and typically present a humorous and wide-ranging satire of a given society.

Plagiarism: Claiming another person's written material as one's own. Plagiarism can take the form of direct, word-for-word copying or the theft of the substance or idea of the work.

Plot: In literary criticism, this term refers to the pattern of events in a narrative or drama. In its simplest sense, the plot guides the author in composing the work and helps the reader follow the work. Typically, plots exhibit causality and unity and have a beginning, a middle, and an end. Sometimes, however, a plot may consist of a series of disconnected events, in which case it is known as an "episodic plot."

Poetic Justice: An outcome in a literary work, not necessarily a poem, in which the good are rewarded and the evil are punished, especially in ways that particularly fit their virtues or crimes.

Poetic License: Distortions of fact and literary convention made by a writer—not always a poet—for the sake of the effect gained. Poetic license is closely related to the concept of "artistic freedom."

Poetics: This term has two closely related meanings. It denotes (1) an aesthetic theory in literary criticism about the essence of poetry or (2) rules prescribing the proper methods, content, style, or diction of poetry. The term poetics may also refer to theories about literature in general, not just poetry.

Point of View: The narrative perspective from which a literary work is presented to the reader. There are four traditional points of view. The "third person omniscient" gives the reader a "godlike" perspective, unrestricted by time or place, from which to see actions and look into the minds of characters. This allows the author to comment openly on characters and events in the work. The "third person" point of view presents the events of the story from outside of any single character's perception, much like the omniscient point of view, but the reader must understand the action as it takes place and without any special insight into characters' minds or motivations. The "first person" or "personal" point of view relates events as they are perceived by a single character. The main character "tells" the story and may offer opinions about the action and characters which differ from those of the author. Much less common than omniscient, third person, and first person is the "second person" point of view, wherein the author tells the story as if it is happening to the reader.

Polemic: A work in which the author takes a stand on a controversial subject, such as abortion or religion. Such works are often extremely argumentative or provocative.

Pornography: Writing intended to provoke feelings of lust in the reader. Such works are often condemned by critics and teachers, but those which can be shown to have literary value are viewed less harshly.

Post-Aesthetic Movement: An artistic response made by African Americans to the black aesthetic movement of the 1960s and early '70s. Writers since that time have adopted a somewhat different tone in their work, with less emphasis placed on the disparity between black and white in the United States. In the words of post-aesthetic authors such as Toni Morrison, John Edgar Wideman, and Kristin Hunter, African Americans are portrayed as looking inward for answers to their own questions, rather than always looking to the outside world.

Postmodernism: Writing from the 1960s forward characterized by experimentation and continuing to apply some of the fundamentals of modernism, which included existentialism and alienation. Postmodernists have gone a step further in the rejection of tradition begun with the modernists by also rejecting traditional forms, preferring the anti-novel over the novel and the anti-hero over the hero.

Primitivism: The belief that primitive peoples were nobler and less flawed than civilized peoples because they had not been subjected to the tainting influence of society.

Prologue: An introductory section of a literary work. It often contains information establishing the situation of the characters or presents information about the setting, time period, or action. In drama, the prologue is spoken by a chorus or by one of the principal characters.

Prose: A literary medium that attempts to mirror the language of everyday speech. It is distinguished from poetry by its use of unmetered, unrhymed language consisting of logically related sentences. Prose is usually grouped into paragraphs that form a cohesive whole such as an essay or a novel.

Prosopopoeia: See *Personification*

Protagonist: The central character of a story who serves as a focus for its themes and incidents and as the principal rationale for its development. The protagonist is sometimes referred to in discussions of modern literature as the hero or anti-hero.

Protest Fiction: Protest fiction has as its primary purpose the protesting of some social injustice, such as racism or discrimination.

Proverb: A brief, sage saying that expresses a truth about life in a striking manner.

Pseudonym: A name assumed by a writer, most often intended to prevent his or her identification as the author of a work. Two or more authors may work together under one pseudonym, or an author may use a different name for each genre he or she publishes in. Some publishing companies maintain "house pseudonyms," under which any number of authors may write installations in a series. Some authors also choose a pseudonym over their real names the way an actor may use a stage name.

Pun: A play on words that have similar sounds but different meanings.

R

Realism: A nineteenth-century European literary movement that sought to portray familiar characters, situations, and settings in a realistic manner. This was done primarily by using an objective narrative point of view and through the buildup of accurate detail. The standard for success of any realistic work depends on how faithfully it transfers common experience into fictional forms. The realistic method may be altered or extended, as in stream of consciousness writing, to record highly subjective experience.

Repartee: Conversation featuring snappy retorts and witticisms.

Resolution: The portion of a story following the climax, in which the conflict is resolved.

Rhetoric: In literary criticism, this term denotes the art of ethical persuasion. In its strictest sense, rhetoric adheres to various principles developed since classical times for arranging facts and ideas in a clear, persuasive, appealing manner. The term is also used to refer to effective prose in general and theories of or methods for composing effective prose.

Rhetorical Question: A question intended to provoke thought, but not an expressed answer, in the reader. It is most commonly used in oratory and other persuasive genres.

Rising Action: The part of a drama where the plot becomes increasingly complicated. Rising action leads up to the climax, or turning point, of a drama.

Roman à clef: A French phrase meaning "novel with a key." It refers to a narrative in which real persons are portrayed under fictitious names.

Romance: A broad term, usually denoting a narrative with exotic, exaggerated, often idealized characters, scenes, and themes.

Romanticism: This term has two widely accepted meanings. In historical criticism, it refers to a European intellectual and artistic movement of the late eighteenth and early nineteenth centuries that sought greater freedom of personal expression than that allowed by the strict rules of literary form and logic of the eighteenth-century neoclassicists. The Romantics preferred emotional and imaginative expression to rational analysis. They considered the individual to be at the center of all experience and so placed him or her at the center of their art. The Romantics believed that the creative imagination reveals nobler truths—unique feelings and attitudes—than those that could be discovered by logic or by scientific examination. Both the natural world and the state of childhood were important sources for revelations of "eternal truths." "Romanticism" is also used as a general term to refer to a type of sensibility found in all periods of literary history and usually considered to be in opposition to the principles of classicism. In this sense, Romanticism signifies any work or philosophy in which the exotic or dreamlike figure strongly, or that is devoted to individualistic expression, self-analysis, or a pursuit of a higher realm of knowledge than can be discovered by human reason.

Romantics: See *Romanticism*

S

Satire: A work that uses ridicule, humor, and wit to criticize and provoke change in human nature and institutions. There are two major types of satire: "formal" or "direct" satire speaks directly to the reader or to a character in the work; "indirect" satire relies upon the ridiculous behavior of its characters to make its point. Formal satire is

further divided into two manners: the "Horatian," which ridicules gently, and the "Juvenalian," which derides its subjects harshly and bitterly.

Science Fiction: A type of narrative about or based upon real or imagined scientific theories and technology. Science fiction is often peopled with alien creatures and set on other planets or in different dimensions.

Second Person: See *Point of View*

Setting: The time, place, and culture in which the action of a narrative takes place. The elements of setting may include geographic location, characters' physical and mental environments, prevailing cultural attitudes, or the historical time in which the action takes place.

Simile: A comparison, usually using "like" or "as," of two essentially dissimilar things, as in "coffee as cold as ice" or "He sounded like a broken record."

Slang: A type of informal verbal communication that is generally unacceptable for formal writing. Slang words and phrases are often colorful exaggerations used to emphasize the speaker's point; they may also be shortened versions of an often-used word or phrase.

Slave Narrative: Autobiographical accounts of American slave life as told by escaped slaves. These works first appeared during the abolition movement of the 1830s through the 1850s.

Socialist Realism: The Socialist Realism school of literary theory was proposed by Maxim Gorky and established as a dogma by the first Soviet Congress of Writers. It demanded adherence to a communist worldview in works of literature. Its doctrines required an objective viewpoint comprehensible to the working classes and themes of social struggle featuring strong proletarian heroes.

Stereotype: A stereotype was originally the name for a duplication made during the printing process; this led to its modern definition as a person or thing that is (or is assumed to be) the same as all others of its type.

Stream of Consciousness: A narrative technique for rendering the inward experience of a character. This technique is designed to give the impression of an ever-changing series of thoughts, emotions, images, and memories in the spontaneous and seemingly illogical order that they occur in life.

Structure: The form taken by a piece of literature. The structure may be made obvious for ease of understanding, as in nonfiction works, or may obscured for artistic purposes, as in some poetry or seemingly "unstructured" prose.

Sturm und Drang: A German term meaning "storm and stress." It refers to a German literary movement of the 1770s and 1780s that reacted against the order and rationalism of the enlightenment, focusing instead on the intense experience of extraordinary individuals.

Style: A writer's distinctive manner of arranging words to suit his or her ideas and purpose in writing. The unique imprint of the author's personality upon his or her writing, style is the product of an author's way of arranging ideas and his or her use of diction, different sentence structures, rhythm, figures of speech, rhetorical principles, and other elements of composition.

Subjectivity: Writing that expresses the author's personal feelings about his subject, and which may or may not include factual information about the subject.

Subplot: A secondary story in a narrative. A subplot may serve as a motivating or complicating force for the main plot of the work, or it may provide emphasis for, or relief from, the main plot.

Surrealism: A term introduced to criticism by Guillaume Apollinaire and later adopted by Andre Breton. It refers to a French literary and artistic movement founded in the 1920s. The Surrealists sought to express unconscious thoughts and feelings in their works. The best-known technique used for achieving this aim was automatic writing— transcriptions of spontaneous outpourings from the unconscious. The Surrealists proposed to unify the contrary levels of conscious and unconscious, dream and reality, objectivity and subjectivity into a new level of "super-realism."

Suspense: A literary device in which the author maintains the audience's attention through the buildup of events, the outcome of which will soon be revealed.

Symbol: Something that suggests or stands for something else without losing its original identity. In literature, symbols combine their literal meaning with the suggestion of an abstract concept. Literary symbols are of two types: those that carry complex associations of meaning no matter what their contexts, and those that derive their suggestive meaning from their functions in specific literary works.

Symbolism: This term has two widely accepted meanings. In historical criticism, it denotes an early modernist literary movement initiated in France during the nineteenth century that reacted against the prevailing standards of realism. Writers in this movement aimed to evoke, indirectly and symbolically, an order of being beyond the material world of the five senses. Poetic expression of personal emotion figured strongly in the movement, typically by means of a private set of symbols uniquely identifiable with the individual poet. The principal aim of the Symbolists was to express in words the highly complex feelings that grew out of everyday contact with the world. In a broader sense, the term "symbolism" refers to the use of one object to represent another.

T

Tall Tale: A humorous tale told in a straightforward, credible tone but relating absolutely impossible events or feats of the characters. Such tales were commonly told of frontier adventures during the settlement of the west in the United States.

Theme: The main point of a work of literature. The term is used interchangeably with thesis.

Thesis: A thesis is both an essay and the point argued in the essay. Thesis novels and thesis plays share the quality of containing a thesis which is supported through the action of the story.

Third Person: See *Point of View*

Tone: The author's attitude toward his or her audience may be deduced from the tone of the work. A formal tone may create distance or convey politeness, while an informal tone may encourage a friendly, intimate, or intrusive feeling in the reader. The author's attitude toward his or her subject matter may also be deduced from the tone of the words he or she uses in discussing it.

Transcendentalism: An American philosophical and religious movement, based in New England from around 1835 until the Civil War. Transcendentalism was a form of American romanticism that had its roots abroad in the works of Thomas Carlyle, Samuel Coleridge, and Johann Wolfgang von Goethe. The Transcendentalists stressed the importance of intuition and subjective experience in communication with God. They rejected religious dogma and texts in favor of mysticism and scientific naturalism. They pursued truths that lie beyond the "colorless" realms perceived by reason and the senses and were active social reformers in public education, women's rights, and the abolition of slavery.

U

Urban Realism: A branch of realist writing that attempts to accurately reflect the often harsh facts of modern urban existence.

Utopia: A fictional perfect place, such as "paradise" or "heaven."

V

Verisimilitude: Literally, the appearance of truth. In literary criticism, the term refers to aspects of a work of literature that seem true to the reader.

Victorian: Refers broadly to the reign of Queen Victoria of England (1837-1901) and to anything with qualities typical of that era. For example, the qualities of smug narrow-mindedness, bourgeois materialism, faith in social progress, and priggish morality are often considered Victorian. This stereotype is contradicted by such dramatic intellectual developments as the theories of Charles Darwin, Karl Marx, and Sigmund Freud (which stirred strong debates in England) and the critical attitudes of serious Victorian writers like Charles Dickens and George Eliot. In literature, the Victorian Period was the great age of the English novel, and the latter part of the era saw the rise of movements such as decadence and symbolism.

W

Weltanschauung: A German term referring to a person's worldview or philosophy.

Weltschmerz: A German term meaning "world pain." It describes a sense of anguish about the nature of existence, usually associated with a melancholy, pessimistic attitude.

Z

Zeitgeist: A German term meaning "spirit of the time." It refers to the moral and intellectual trends of a given era.

Cumulative Author/Title Index

Cumulative
Nationality/Ethnicity Index

Cumulative Nationality/Ethnicity Index

Subject/Theme Index

Rescue
  Code Name Verity: 26, 29
  O Brother, Where Art Thou?: 146,
    159
Resentment
  The Guide: 55
  Lie Down in Darkness: 82
Resistance
  Burger's Daughter: 1
  Unless: 289
Respect
  Code Name Verity: 28, 30
Responsibility
  Lie Down in Darkness: 83, 86
  Someone Like You: 259, 264
Revelation
  Lie Down in Darkness: 85
Revenge
  Lie Down in Darkness: 73, 75
  O Brother, Where Art Thou?: 146
  Rebecca: 179, 180
Revolutions. *See* Rebellion
Rituals
  The Guide: 55
Romantic love
  Rebecca: 164, 179
  Unless: 278

S

Sacrifice
  The Guide: 50, 51, 62
  Rickshaw Boy: 202
Sadness
  The Magicians: 134
  Rickshaw Boy: 205
  Yonnondio: From the Thirties: 299
Sainthood
  The Guide: 45, 48, 54, 55, 61
Salvation
  Lie Down in Darkness: 85–87
  The Loved One: 99
Sarcasm
  Someone Like You: 256
Satire
  The Loved One: 94, 99, 101, 102,
    105–107
  O Brother, Where Art Thou?: 158,
    159
  Rickshaw Boy: 203, 204
  Unless: 282–283
Seduction
  The Sheltering Sky: 237
Self
  The Guide: 61
  Yonnondio: From the Thirties:
    316–317
Self confidence
  Rebecca: 177
  Someone Like You: 257
  Unless: 290
Self consciousness
  Rebecca: 172

Self control
  Lie Down in Darkness: 80
Self deception
  The Guide: 54
Self destruction
  Rickshaw Boy: 195
Self identity
  Burger's Daughter: 6, 18–21
  The Magicians: 126
  Someone Like You: 263
  Unless: 286
  Yonnondio: From the Thirties:
    316–317
Self indulgence
  Lie Down in Darkness: 89
Self knowledge
  Code Name Verity: 34–36
  Someone Like You: 260
Self-pity
  The Guide: 47
Self-righteousness
  Code Name Verity: 36
  Lie Down in Darkness: 90
Self sacrifice. *See* Sacrifice
Self worth
  Someone Like You: 251, 255
Selfishness
  The Guide: 61
  The Loved One: 113
  Rickshaw Boy: 188
  Someone Like You: 256
Selflessness
  The Guide: 55, 62
Sentimentality
  The Loved One: 102
Setting (Literature)
  The Guide: 57
  Lie Down in Darkness: 87–88
  The Magicians: 131
  The Sheltering Sky: 239
  Someone Like You: 267
  Unless: 293–295
Sexuality
  The Guide: 58
  Rebecca: 184, 185
  The Sheltering Sky: 237
  Someone Like You: 264
  Yonnondio: From the Thirties: 313,
    314
Shame
  The Magicians: 134
Shyness
  Rebecca: 170, 183
Silence
  Unless: 278, 280, 289
Sin
  Lie Down in Darkness: 86
Small town life
  Someone Like You: 261–262
  Unless: 293–295
Snobbery
  Someone Like You: 256

Social change
  Yonnondio: From the Thirties: 311
Social class
  The Guide: 59
  The Loved One: 101
  Rebecca: 172–173, 178–179
  Yonnondio: From the Thirties: 306,
    316
Social commentary
  Rickshaw Boy: 203
  Yonnondio: From the Thirties: 298
Social convention
  Rebecca: 178
Social decay
  Rickshaw Boy: 202
Social roles
  Rebecca: 164
Social satire
  O Brother, Where Art Thou?: 156
  The Secret History: 227
South African history
  Burger's Daughter: 1, 11–13,
    17–19
Southern United States
  Lie Down in Darkness: 77–79, 89
  O Brother, Where Art Thou?: 149,
    152, 158
  Someone Like You: 261–262
Spirituality
  The Guide: 54
  Lie Down in Darkness: 85–87
Spouse abuse. *See* Domestic violence
Stereotypes (Psychology)
  The Magicians: 131
Stoicism
  Lie Down in Darkness: 72
Storytelling
  Code Name Verity: 36, 37
  Rickshaw Boy: 203
Stream of consciousness
  Yonnondio: From the Thirties: 307
Strength
  Code Name Verity: 28–29
  Someone Like You: 259, 260, 264
Structure (Literature)
  Lie Down in Darkness: 64
  Unless: 283–284
Struggle
  Rickshaw Boy: 198, 200
  Unless: 289
  Yonnondio: From the Thirties: 316
Suburban life
  Someone Like You: 260–261, 267
  Unless: 294
Success
  The Guide: 47, 49
Suffering
  Rickshaw Boy: 201
  Yonnondio: From the Thirties:
    313